NATURALIZING PHENOMENOLOGY

WRITING SCIENCE

EDITORS Timothy Lenoir and Hans Ulrich Gumbrecht

Contributors

Renaud Barbaras

Juan-José Botero

Roberto Casati

Natalie Depraz

Jean-Pierre Dupuy

Dagfinn Føllesdal

Giuseppe Longo

Ronald McIntyre

Alva Noë

Elisabeth Pacherie

Bernard Pachoud

Luiz Pessoa

Jean-Luc Petit

Jean Petitot

Jean-Michel Roy

Jean-Michel Salanskis

Barry Smith

David Woodruff Smith

Evan Thompson

Tim van Gelder

Francisco J. Varela

Maria Villela-Petit

NATURALIZING PHENOMENOLOGY

ISSUES IN CONTEMPORARY PHENOMENOLOGY
AND COGNITIVE SCIENCE

EDITED BY

Jean Petitot
Francisco J. Varela
Bernard Pachoud
Jean-Michel Roy

STANFORD UNIVERSITY PRESS
STANFORD, CALIFORNIA

Stanford University Press
Stanford, California
© 1999 by the Board of Trustees of the
Leland Stanford Junior University

Printed in the United States of America
CIP data appear at the end of the book

ACKNOWLEDGMENTS

We would like to thank the Centre de Recherches en Epistémologie Appliquée and the Ecole Normale Supérieure for hosting the regular meetings of the Phénoménologie et Cognition Research Group, as well as Professor Jean François Courtine, director of the Paris Husserl Archives, for his generous help on numerous occasions.

This book is mostly the result of the various activities carried out by the Phénoménologie et Cognition Research Group. The conference "Actualité cognitive de la phénoménologie: Les Défis de la naturalisation," in particular, played a key role in its realization. We are deeply grateful to the various French institutions that made that conference possible: the Musée d'Art Contemporain of the city of Bordeaux, where it took place; the Cognitive Science Program of the Ministère de l'Enseignement Supérieur et de la Recherche; the Direction Générale du Centre National de la Recherche Scientifique; the Ministère des Affaires Etrangères; the Conseil Régional de la Région Aquitaine; the Réseau Cogniseine; and the Ecole Normale Supérieure.

At different stages of the organization of this conference, we also received invaluable assistance from Anne-Marie Cocula, Catherine Larrère, Elizabeth Rigal, Daniel Andler, Alain Berthoz, Bernard Claverie, Jean-Marc Deshouillers, Etienne Guillon, Marc Jeannerod, and Jean Mondot.

To these institutions and individuals, the very existence of this book is perhaps the most eloquent token of our gratitude.

Stanford University Press made the arduous task of transforming into a book the work accomplished in the conference, and the seminars antecedent to it, almost an easy experience, and certainly always a pleasant and enriching one. Professors Tim Lenoir and Hans Ulrich Gumbrecht welcomed our voluminous, demanding, and unconventional project in their Writing Science Series with great enthusiasm and openness of mind. Helen Tartar helped us bring the volume to life with a sure hand, and an unfailing patience for our Latin idiosyncrasies. Nathan MacBrien and Andrew Lewis did a remarkable job of surmounting countless difficulties of language, style, and presentation. Although inherent to any book, these difficulties were dramatically increased in number and intensity by the variety of disciplines, intellectual traditions, and cultural identities included in this one. To all of them we are deeply and truly thankful.

CONTENTS

FOREWORD ... xiii
CONTRIBUTORS ... xvii

1. Beyond the Gap: An Introduction to Naturalizing Phenomenology ... 1
   JEAN-MICHEL ROY, JEAN PETITOT, BERNARD PACHOUD, AND FRANCISCO J. VARELA

Part One Intentionality, Movement, and Temporality

Intentionality

2. Intentionality Naturalized? ... 83
   DAVID WOODRUFF SMITH

3. Saving Intentional Phenomena: Intentionality, Representation, and Symbol ... 111
   JEAN-MICHEL ROY

4. *Leibhaftigkeit* and Representational Theories of Perception ... 148
   ELISABETH PACHERIE

Movement

5. Perceptual Completion: A Case Study in Phenomenology and Cognitive Science ... 161
   EVAN THOMPSON, ALVA NOË, AND LUIZ PESSOA

6. The Teleological Dimension of Perceptual and Motor Intentionality ... 196
   BERNARD PACHOUD

7. Constitution by Movement: Husserl in Light of Recent
   Neurobiological Findings   220
   JEAN-LUC PETIT

   Temporality

8. Wooden Iron? Husserlian Phenomenology Meets
   Cognitive Science   245
   TIM VAN GELDER

9. The Specious Present: A Neurophenomenology
   of Time Consciousness   266
   FRANCISCO J. VARELA

Part Two   Mathematics in Phenomenology

   Formal Models

10. Truth and the Visual Field   317
    BARRY SMITH

11. Morphological Eidetics for a Phenomenology of Perception   330
    JEAN PETITOT

12. Formal Structures in the Phenomenology of Motion   372
    ROBERTO CASATI

   Phenomenology and Mathematics

13. Gödel and Husserl   385
    DAGFINN FØLLESDAL

14. The Mathematical Continuum: From Intuition to Logic   401
    GIUSEPPE LONGO

Part Three   The Nature and Limits of Naturalization

　Philosophical Strategies of Naturalization

15. Naturalizing Phenomenology? Dretske on Qualia   429
    RONALD MCINTYRE

16. The Immediately Given as Ground and Background   440
    JUAN-JOSÉ BOTERO

17. When Transcendental Genesis Encounters the
    Naturalization Project   464
    NATALIE DEPRAZ

　Skeptical Attitudes

18. Sense and Continuum in Husserl   490
    JEAN-MICHEL SALANSKIS

19. Cognitive Psychology and the Transcendental Theory
    of Knowledge   508
    MARIA VILLELA-PETIT

20. The Movement of the Living as the Originary
    Foundation of Perceptual Intentionality   525
    RENAUD BARBARAS

　Historical Perspectives

21. Philosophy and Cognition: Historical Roots   539
    JEAN-PIERRE DUPUY

    NOTES   561
    BIBLIOGRAPHY   597
    INDEX OF PERSONS   631
    INDEX OF TOPICS   635

FOREWORD

The ambition of this book is to shed new light on the relations between phenomenology of a Husserlian kind or origin and the contemporary efforts toward a scientific theory of cognition, with its complex structure comprising various disciplines, different levels of explanation, and conflicting hypotheses.

The project of a science of cognitive phenomena did not reach full maturity until the middle of the twentieth century, even though its roots go as far back as the emergence of rational knowledge, and several of its component disciplines severed their ties with philosophy or embraced the experimental method at the dawn of the nineteenth century (or even at the end of the eighteenth). It has become commonplace to refer to this shift as the emergence of a Cognitive Revolution[1] that has also revived many fundamental issues of Husserlian phenomenology.[2] The contributions in this volume should first and foremost be understood as attempts to contribute further to these developments.

Accordingly, the book's primary goal is not to engage in a new exegesis of Husserl's writings, although it certainly does not dismiss the importance of interpretive and critical work. It is rather to assess the extent to which the sort of phenomenological investigation he initiated can favor the construction of a scientific theory of cognition and, more particularly, contribute to progress in specific contemporary theories, by complementing them in some crucial aspects and calling them into question in others.

It is clear, however, that Husserlian phenomenology cannot become instrumental for the development of contemporary cognitive science without undergoing substantial transformations itself. Therefore, this book will also be centrally concerned with the reorientation of Husserlian phenomenology. To what extent, for instance, do recent contributions in cognitive neuroscience, as well as in physico-mathematical and computational modeling of perception, throw new light on the most general assumptions underlying this phenomenology and possibly modify them in a radical way?

There is an unavoidable *reciprocal movement* between the attempt to reinforce cognitive research with the help of Husserlian phenomenology and the need to transform that phenomenology itself. Even more, this reciprocal movement naturally suggests a further conjoint issue: is there something fundamentally complementary about these two lines of research that makes a unified cross-fertilization the most productive direction for both of them?

No single volume could satisfactorily apprehend the numerous facets of this wide-ranging interrogation of the relevance of Husserlian phenomenology to contemporary cognitive research and the relevance of contemporary cognitive research to Husserlian phenomenology. This is why the articles collected here take as their focus the issue of naturalization. Nevertheless, this perspective remains far-reaching enough to let them cover a great variety of problems, ranging from the general structures of intentionality to the nature of the founding principles of cognitive science and the analysis of temporality or perception.

The justification for choosing such a perspective is clear. One of the major concerns behind the investigation of cognitive phenomena today is the construction of a science of cognition that is continuous with the most basic sciences of nature and, accordingly, to understand how a *res extensa* could become complex enough through evolution to possess the various attributes of a *res cogitans*. Even though this concern for naturalization is not unanimous, and is actually even dismissed by a minority, it can hardly be denied that it lies at the core of current research in the field. Suffice it here to mention the classical computational theory of cognition, which played a key role in the revival of the study of cognition in the early 1960s, and whose power of attraction largely rested, both among those who contributed to its scientific elaboration and among those who analyzed it from a philosophical angle, on its seeming ability to offer at long last a viable materialist solution to the mind-body problem—at least as far as cognitive abilities are concerned.

This is why the two-part question at the core of this work can be more specifically reformulated in the following terms: how can Husserlian phenomenology contribute to the naturalizing aspect of the contemporary search for a scientific theory of cognition, and how far can a successful naturalization of the theory of cognition, in turn, transform Husserlian phenomenology, and in particular confer upon it an uncontroversial scientific dimension?

It is important to underline that the issues involved are as much scientific as they are methodological and philosophical. This renewed examination of Husserlian phenomenology is also meant as a tribute to Husserl's unwavering commitment to rationality and rigor. As such it departs in a substantial way from a variety of other continuations of his work, such as existential analysis or the metaphysics of phenomenality.

This book is largely the direct outcome of the activities of the Phénoménologie et Cognition Research Group we created in Paris in October 1993. These activities included a series of seminars, held at the Centre de Recherche en Epistémologie Appliquée of the Ecole Polytechnique and at the Paris Husserl Archives of the Ecole Normale Supérieure, as well as the conference "Actualité cognitive de la phénomenologie: Les Défis de la naturalisation" organized by Jean-Michel Roy in October 1995 in the city of Bordeaux, in collaboration with the Pierre Duhem Research Group of the Department of Philosophy of Michel de Montaigne University. Most of the contributions to this volume have their origins in these various meetings.

The creation of the Phénoménologie et Cognition Research Group was intended as an answer to the recent revival of interest in France in the study of the relations between Husserlian phenomenology and contemporary scientific research. Four main trends can be distinguished in this revival:

1. A number of Husserl specialists, especially among the members of the Paris Husserl Archives, were working on a reassessment of the conflicts between his phenomenology and the sciences of his time, with a view to show that many of these conflicts were made largely obsolete by scientific progress, in particular in the areas of cognitive psychology and cognitive neurosciences as well of physico-mathematical modeling of cognition.

2. As early as the mid-1970s various authors were emphasizing the strong parallels existing between contemporary morphological theories on the one hand, and the main aspects of Husserlian theory of perception, gestalt theory, and Gibsonian perceptive ecology on the other hand. The results of these endeavors were a series of attempts at a topological, geometrical, and dynamic modeling of a phenomenology of perception. In the course of the 1980s this line of investigation was pushed further by the search for new relations between such modeling and the neurosciences of vision as well as by recent work in computational vision.

3. At the same time various parts of the philosophical community became newly interested in studying how contemporary philosophy of logic, language, and mind as well as classical cognitivism were readdressing many of Husserl's central issues. These investigations received a strong impulse from different sources, and mostly from the work of D. Føllesdal and J. Hintikka, and their former students; the collection Husserl, *Phenomenology and Cognitive Science*, edited by Hubert Dreyfus (MIT Press, 1992); and the his-

torical investigations of Kevin Mulligan, Peter Simons, and Barry Smith into the development of ontological theory and mereology.

4. Finally, there was also a growing interest in developing an interface between the phenomenology of embodiment and action in the later work of Husserl and Merleau-Ponty and contemporary research in neurosciences, artificial life, and evolution theory, especially research conducted from a situated, embodied, or enactive perspective—a trend progressively more visible in the contemporary debate within cognitive science.

This book finds its unity in the cross-linking of these various motivations and is accordingly directed at an unusual variety of audiences ranging from cognitive scientists to philosophers of supposedly opposite persuasions. We hope through this book the research programs of Husserlian phenomenology and of the cognitive sciences will be brought closer and mutually enriched. We also hope thereby to throw further light on the conditions to be fulfilled by a science of cognition both naturalist and adequate to "the things themselves."

Finally, a word about the conventions we have used in the text. In citing the works of Husserl, whenever possible we have referred to the Husserliana edition, by paragraph and page number(s). Where an English-language translation of Husserl has been given, it is cited by the translator's name, followed by paragraph and page number(s). For the abbreviations used in the text for works by Husserl, see the Bibliography, pp. 600–602.

CONTRIBUTORS

Renaud Barbaras is an associate professor at the University of Paris—Sorbonne and a member of the Institut Universitaire de France. A Merleau-Ponty scholar, he is the author of *De l'être du phénomène: Sur l'ontologie de Merleau-Ponty* (Grenoble: Millon, 1991) and *Le Tournant de l'expérience: Recherches sur la philosophie de Merleau-Ponty* (Paris: Vrin, 1998).
Université de Paris IV, Département de Philosophie, 17 rue Victor Cousin, 75005, Paris, France

Juan-José Botero is the director of the Department of Philosophy of the Universidad Nacional de Colombia (Bogotá) and a former editor of the philosophical journal *Ideas y valores* (Bogotá). He is the author of several articles in the philosophy of science and the philosophy of mind.
jjbo5001@inter.net.co

Roberto Casati is a researcher at CNRS (CEPERC, Aix-en-Provence, and CREA, Paris). He is the coauthor, with A. Varzi, of *Holes and Other Superficialities* (Cambridge: MIT Press, 1994) and the author of *Parts and Places* (Cambridge: MIT Press, 1999), as well as numerous papers in the philosophy of cognitive science.
Casati@poly.polytechnique.fr

Natalie Depraz is an affiliate of the Paris Husserl Archives (CNRS). A founding editor of *Alter: Revue de phénoménologie* (Editions Alter, Paris), she is the author of *Transcendance et incarnation: Le Statut de l'intersubjectivité comme altérité à soi chez Husserl* (Paris: Vrin, 1995) and of several papers on Husserlian phenomenology.
frj@ccr.jussieu.fr

Jean-Pierre Dupuy is professor of social and political philosophy at the Ecole Polytechnique (Paris) and the founding director of the CREA. He has published extensively on self-organization theory. His publications include

L'Auto-organisation: De la physique au politique (Paris: Le Seuil, 1983), *Aux origines des sciences cognitives* (La Découverte, 1994), *Self-Deception and Paradoxes of Rationality* (Stanford, Calif.: CSLI, 1998).

jpdupuy@poly.polytechnique.fr

Dagfinn Føllesdal is the C. I. Lewis Professor of Philosophy at Stanford University and a professor of philosophy at the University of Oslo. He has written and edited numerous volumes, including *Husserl und Frege* (Oslo: Norwegian Academy of Science, 1958) and *Rationale Argumentation* (Berlin: De Gruyter, 1986). He also served as an editor of the *Journal of Symbolic Logic* from 1970 to 1982.

dagfinn@csli.stanford.edu

Giuseppe Longo is a CNRS Director of Research at the Ecole Normale Supérieure (Paris). He coauthored *Categories, Types, and Structures* (Cambridge: MIT Press, 1991) and has written extensively in the area of mathematical logic and its applications to computer science. He is the editor-in-chief of *Mathematical Structures for Computer Science* (Cambridge University Press).

longo@dmi.ens.fr; http://www.dmi.ens.fr/users/longo

Ronald McIntyre is a professor of philosophy at California State University, Northridge. He is the author (in collaboration with David W. Smith) of *Husserl and Intentionality: A Study of Mind, Meaning, and Language* (D. Reidel, 1982) and of several studies in the philosophy of mind and language.

vcoa0087@huey.csun.edu

Alva Noë is an assistant professor of philosophy at the University of California, Santa Cruz. He received his doctorate from Harvard University and works on topics in the philosophy of perception and the philosophy of mind and contributed several articles in these areas.

Board of Studies in Philosophy, University of California, Santa Cruz,
Santa Cruz, CA, 95064

Elisabeth Pacherie is a researcher at CNRS (CEPERC, Aix-en-Provence, and CREA, Paris). She is the author of *Naturaliser l'intentionnalité* (Paris: PUF, 1993) and of several papers in the theory of action and the philosophy of mind.

Pacherie@poly.polytechnique.fr

Bernard Pachoud teaches psychology at the University of Picardie, Amiens, and is a research affiliate of CREA (Paris). He has published on the pragmatic approach to thought and language disorders in schizophrenia. He is currently researching the psychology and philosophy of consciousness.

    Pachoud@ext.jussieu.fr

Luiz Pessoa is an assistant professor of computer and systems engineering at the Federal University of Rio de Janeiro, Brazil. He received his doctorate in cognitive and neural systems from Boston University and has contributed articles on computational modeling of vision, visual psychophysics, and neural network models.

    Department of Computer and Systems Engineering, Federal University of Rio de Janeiro, Centro de Tecnologia, Bloco H, Sala H-319, Ilha do Fundao, Rio de Janeiro, RJ, Brazil

Jean-Luc Petit is a professor of philosophy at the University of Strasbourg II. A former director of the Centre d'Analyse des Savoirs Contemporains (Strasbourg), he has published extensively on the relations between analytical philosophy of action and Husserl's phenomenology. His most recent publication is *Les Neurosciences et la philosophie de l'action* (Paris: Vrin, 1997).

    petit@monza.u-strasbg.fr

Jean Petitot is a professor at the Ecole des Hautes Etudes en Sciences Sociales in Paris and a research associate at Ecole Polytechnique (CREA). His publications include *Morphogenèse du Sens* (Paris: PUF, 1985), *Les Catastrophes de la parole: De Roman Jakobson à René Thom* (Paris: Maloine, 1985), *Physique du sens* (Paris: CNRS, 1992), and numerous papers on the relations between Husserlian phenomenology and cognitive science.

    petitot@poly.polytechnique.fr;
    http://www.polytechnique.fr/laboratoires/crea/JeanPetitot/home.html

Jean-Michel Roy teaches philosophy in the departments of Philosophy and Cognitive Science of the University of Bordeaux. He is also a research affiliate of the Paris Husserl Archives and the Laboratoire Physiologie de l'Action et de la Perception (CNRS). His publications include the editing of *La Théorie computationnelle de l'esprit* (Paris: PUF, 1992) and of "Signification, phénoménologie et philosophie analytique" (Paris: PUF, 1995).

    roy@heraclite.ens.fr

Jean-Michel Salanskis is a professor in the Department of Philosophy at the University of Lille III. His main publications are in the philosophy of mathematics and the field of hermeneutics. They include *L'Herméneutique formelle* (Paris: Editions du CNRS, 1991), *Le Labyrinthe du continu* (Berlin: Springer Verlag, 1992), and *Husserl* (Paris: Belles Lettres, 1997).

    salanskis@univ-lille3.fr (Lille)

Barry Smith is a professor of philosophy and a member of the Center for Cognitive Science at SUNY Buffalo. Editor of *The Monist*, he has published on the history of Austrian philosophy (*Austrian Philosophy*, Open Court, 1994) and the development of formal ontology (*Parts and Moments*, Philosophia Verlag, 1985). He is also a coeditor of *The Cambridge Companion to Husserl* (Cambridge: Cambridge University Press, 1995).

    phismith@ubvms.cc.buffalo.edu; http://wings.buffalo.edu/philosophy/faculty/smith

David Woodruff Smith is a professor in the Department of Philosophy at the University of California, Irvine, and a researcher at Ontek Corporation. A coeditor of *The Cambridge Companion to Husserl* (Cambridge University Press, 1995) and of *Husserl and Intentionality* (with Ronald McIntyre, Kluwer Academic Publishers, 1982), he has also published *The Circle of Acquaintance* (Kluwer Academic Publishers, 1989).

    dsmith@ontek.com

Evan Thompson is an associate professor in the Department of Philosophy and a member of the Centre for Vision Research at York University, Toronto, Canada. He is the author of *Colour Vision: A Study in Cognitive Science and the Philosophy of Perception* (London: Routledge Press, 1995) and coauthor, with Francisco J. Varela and Eleanor Rosch, of *The Embodied Mind: Cognitive Science and Human Experience* (Cambridge: MIT Press, 1991).

    evant@yorku.ca

Tim van Gelder is an associate professor (Principal Fellow) in the Department of Philosophy, University of Melbourne. He received his doctorate from the University of Pittsburgh. His work in the foundations of cognitive science includes coediting the volume *Mind as Motion: Explorations in the Dynamics of Cognition* (Cambridge: MIT Press, 1995) and several contributions.

    tgelder@ariel.ucs.unimelb.edu.au

Francisco J. Varela is the director of research at CNRS (LENA and CREA, Paris). A neurobiologist, he has written and edited numerous volumes on the autonomy approach to biological systems. His main publications include *Principles of Biological Autonomy* (Amsterdam: North Holland, 1979), *Au-*

topoiesis and Cognition (with Humberto Maturana; Reidel, 1980), and *The Embodied Mind* (Cambridge: MIT Press, 1992).
    fv@ccr.jussieu.fr; http://www.ccr.jussieu.fr/varela/welcome.html

Maria Villela-Petit is a researcher at CNRS (Paris Husserl Archives). A Husserl scholar, she has written on the interpretation of Husserlian phenomenology and its development in the works of Heidegger, Merleau-Ponty, and Paul Ricoeur. She is also the author of essays on ancient philosophy and aesthetics.
    Villela@heraclite.ens.fr

NATURALIZING PHENOMENOLOGY

CHAPTER ONE

Beyond the Gap: An Introduction to Naturalizing Phenomenology

JEAN-MICHEL ROY, JEAN PETITOT, BERNARD
PACHOUD, AND FRANCISCO J. VARELA

> We are fighting against the naturalization of consciousness.
> —Edmund Husserl, "Philosophie als strenge Wissenschaft"

The purpose of this introductory essay is to make explicit the general intellectual project behind the book. It should be clear that it expresses the opinion of the editors; none of the contributors has been invited to discuss or modify it. In fact this essay does not even fully reflect the opinions of the editors, because it gives no room to the differences existing in their concerns and philosophical orientations. A more adequate statement of their respective positions is to be found in their individual contributions.

1. THE PROBLEM OF PHENOMENOLOGICAL DATA

Researchers in the contemporary sciences of cognition have begun to approach many of the central problems of Husserlian phenomenology with new perspectives and new tools. Some of these problems, such as the necessity of "going back to the phenomena," the nature of consciousness, and the importance of intentionality as the hallmark of mental states or the embodiment of cognitive structures, are of special importance. Accordingly, each of them offers a possible way of introducing the general project of integrating Husserlian phenomenology into contemporary cognitive sciences. We have chosen to take as a guideline the idea, currently growing in importance within the cognitive science community, that a successful scientific theory of cognition must account for *phenomenality*, that is—to put it in quite general terms—for the fact that for a whole set of cognitive systems, and for the human one in particular, things have appearances. We will argue that on the basis of its past achievements in describing such phenomenality, Husserlian phenomenology can play a key role in helping to meet this requirement, provided that it can be naturalized, and even though Husserl himself strongly opposed naturalism. By "naturalized" we mean integrated into an explanatory framework where every acceptable property is made continuous with the properties admitted by the natural sciences.

After examining the content and legitimacy of this naturalizing claim, we will recall the most fundamental tenets of Husserlian phenomenology with an emphasis on their antinaturalist orientation (2). We will then review the main motives for considering that this antinaturalist commitment can be today abandoned to the benefit of a naturalist perspective (3). After placing this naturalist project within the more general context of the contemporary revival of Husserlian phenomenology (4), we will discuss its conditions of realization (5) and briefly review the main foundational issues it raises (6).

1.1. THE EXPLANATORY GAP ARGUMENT

The deep break with metaphysical traditions (especially the Aristotelian) introduced by the emergence of the Galilean sciences gave rise to a fundamental conflict in the strategies of explanation of phenomena, as many domains—most important, the biological and the mental—resisted the underlying mechanistic reductionism of these sciences. Consider Leibniz, who was deeply concerned by the conflict between a mechanistic ontology and the ontological status of the intelligible, or Kant, who had to write a third *Kritik* in order to account for the organization of living organisms and for the phenomena of signification.

Since that time it has become a leitmotiv in the philosophical and psychological literature to complain about the widening gap between the sciences of nature and the science of mind, understood as the main element in a scientific investigation of human affairs. Philosopher after philosopher, psychologist after psychologist, has lamented the lack of progress in and the extreme paucity of valuable results produced by the human sciences in general, and of mental phenomena in particular, and contrasted this state of affairs with the breathtaking achievements of the various branches of the natural sciences. David Hume is certainly to be credited with the most famous of the early voicings of such a complaint about the discrepancy between moral and natural philosophy, as it was customary to label them in those days. And his explicit ambition was to remedy the situation by being the Newton of mental phenomena.

Indeed the most widespread result of this critical attitude has been, not skepticism about the possibility of turning the mind into a scientific object, but a renewed ambition to lay at long last the foundations of a truly scientific investigation of it. Franz Brentano's attempt at redefining psychology in his *Psychology from an Empirical Point of View* (1874) is a perfect case in point. Many other examples could be cited, since the same move can be found at the root of almost every major transformation of the field, including the most recent one, namely the advent of Cognitive Science in the early 1960s.[1]

The general feeling, however, is that there is something different about this new form of theorizing about the mind, a feeling reflected in the very name given to it: Cognitive Science is, after all, a specific hypothesis about the mind which has appropriated the generic name of a discipline.[2] Indeed it is widely held that to the extent that the theory of mind is concerned with cognitive phenomena—which by no means exhaust the mental field—it has finally entered with Cognitive Science, after so much wandering, a truly scientific era. More than just a new theory, it is taken to be the first truly scientific theory of mind ever devised. It is generally considered, for instance, that some mechanisms of information processing or dynamical emergence in complex systems have found the appropriate level of explanation, similar to that of forces for motion, or cellular processes for life. As such, Cognitive Science remains, of course, a hypothesis. However, it is believed to have achieved for the mind what Galileo achieved for movement: putting the investigation on the right foundations, and thus on the right track, the track leading through the well-known game of conjecture and refutation, trial and error, to an increasingly better understanding of the cognitive dimension of the mind.

Many advocates of this general analysis of the current state of cognitive research would nevertheless agree that some foundational issues still stand in need of further clarification. Chief among them is the problem of the relation of Cognitive Science to phenomenological data, which has over the last few years generated a growing number of publications. At the core of the problem is the concern that Cognitive Science fails to account for such data. In other words, the argument is that Cognitive Science does not constitute a full theory of cognition, in the sense that its most general tenets do not apply to a certain range of mental phenomena. In the felicitous wording of Joseph Levine (1983), the worry is that Cognitive Science suffers from an "explanatory gap."

One of the main ideas behind the project discussed in this volume is that many descriptions of cognitive phenomena belonging to the Husserlian tradition make possible a better understanding of the relation between cognitive processes and their phenomenal manifestations. Accordingly, the attempt to naturalize Husserlian phenomenology might usefully be seen as an attempt to close this explanatory gap, although its ambition looms larger and its intellectual origins are far more complex.

The explanatory gap argument is by no means new and has been raised under various guises from very different parts of the cognitive community. Within contemporary Anglo-Saxon philosophy of cognitive science, it can be traced back at least to Thomas Nagel's celebrated 1970 article "What

Is It Like to Be a Bat?" which was followed by numerous studies on qualia, consciousness, and experience addressing the same issue more or less directly.[3] Since the late 1980s and early 1990s it has received a more articulated formulation as well as a more systematic treatment in a series of book-long analyses devoted to consciousness, such as Ray Jackendoff's *Consciousness and the Computational Mind* (1987), Daniel Dennett's *Consciousness Explained* (1991), John Searle's *Rediscovery of the Mind* (1992), Owen Flanagan's *Consciousness Reconsidered* (1992), and David Chalmers's *Conscious Mind* (1996), to name just a few.

But the argument has also played an important although frequently less explicit part in recent work carried out by cognitive scientists belonging to different disciplines.[4] In fact it seems to have had two apparently contradictory effects. On the one hand, it has elicited new efforts, especially on the part of neuroscientists, to show that Cognitive Science can indeed account for phenomenological data. On the other hand, it has nourished a more or less radical criticism of the general picture of the cognitive mind which emerged from the Cognitive Revolution. It will be sufficient to present here the explanatory gap argument in a very schematic form.

However, it is first necessary to further specify the content of the general picture of the cognitive mind brought about by the Cognitive Revolution. Our goal is not to offer here an original and fine-grained analysis of this scientific transformation, which is a very complex event like any other major transformation of its kind; nor is it to challenge the value of its dominant interpretation, although a great deal of historical and critical work still is clearly in order. We need only lay out the most fundamental principles of the received interpretation commonly presupposed by the explanatory gap argument. They can be summarized as follows:

1. In sharp opposition to behaviorism, Cognitive Science offers a theory of what goes on inside an organism with cognitive capacities when it engages in cognitive behavior. In other words, Cognitive Science retains behavior as its specific object of investigation but opens the "black box" that behaviorism kept closed.

2. Cognitive Science makes the basic assumption that what goes on inside the black box is some kind of explicit process, usually referred to as "information processing." This "information processing" activity is anything but uniquely defined; indeed, the various ways in which it may be given content are tantamount to different overall approaches to cognition. The main division so far has been between "symbolic" and "connectionist" approaches, but we will return later to the diversity of trends within Cognitive Science.

3. Cognitive Science makes the crucial assumption that the processes sustaining cognitive behavior can be explained at different levels and varying degrees of abstraction, each one corresponding to a specific discipline or set of disciplines. At the most concrete level the explanation is biological, whereas at the most abstract level, the explanation is only functional in the sense that "information" processes are characterized in terms of abstract entities, functionally defined. A definition is functional when it says no more about the *definiendum* than what it does, and consequently says nothing about its composition.[5] In this sense, Cognitive Science differs from strict eliminativism, which recognizes only the basic biophysical level as objectively real and banishes all others.

4. This functional level of explanation is further assimilated with a psychological and mental one. In other words, Cognitive Science maintains that there is no substantial difference between giving a functional explanation of the information-processing activity responsible for the cognitive behavior of an organism and explaining this behavior in mental terms. It is only through this supplementary hypothesis that Cognitive Science becomes sensu stricto a new form of the theory of mind.

5. Finally, by interpreting cognitive mental concepts functionally, Cognitive Science claims to have discovered a noncontroversial materialist solution to the mind-body problem. Because they are purely functional in character, mental entities postulated at the upper level of explanation do not have to be seen as ontologically different from the biological ones postulated at the lower level. They are exactly the same although characterized in terms of the role they play in cognitive processing. A cognitive mind is what an embodied brain looks like when contemplated through a functional window.

Within Cognitive Science so defined, it seems useful to distinguish at least three major approaches: (1) the computationalist-symbolic, (2) the connectionist-dynamic, and (3) the embodied-enactive (see Varela 1989). These trends have all been present from the inception of Cognitive Science, but over time the once-predominant computationalist view has given way to the other two, to the point that now the three coexist in contemporary research. They can be distinguished roughly as follows.

As has been often stated, the fertile postulate of the symbolic-computationalist view, which gave it its visibility, is that cognitive processes are of the kind involved in a general theory of computation derived from the early work of Turing and von Neumann. The mind literally processes information in the sense that it manipulates discrete symbols according to sets of rules. In a radical form, this gives rise to a functionalism in which the biological substrate is entirely irrelevant: it is the software, not the hardware, that matters for the mind.

In the late 1970s, connectionism introduced a novelty by proposing that the cognitive machinery is not a system of rules for the manipulation of symbols, but a system of networks that give rise to typical and regular dynamical behavior that can be interpreted as rules at higher levels of description. Connectionism thus challenged the traditional computationalist orthodoxy by putting into question the discrete nature of symbols and the appropriateness of rule manipulation as an object of research. Instead it posited the search for mechanisms formulated in the language of an entirely different formal discipline, that of nonlinear dynamical systems (cf. Port and van Gelder 1995). In this sense connectionism ceased to be "information processing" in the strictest sense. Furthermore, it introduced to cognitive science a radically new and important idea: the *emergence* of high-level structures or entities from the interaction of lower-level terms. The notion of emergence, which is intrinsic to a dynamical formulation, is derived from the idea of self-organization and has recently received renewed attention from the so-called sciences of complexity. As we will discuss in greater depth later (3.2), connectionism thus introduced a new style for research by exploiting a deep property of nature and playing it into the basic assumptions of Cognitive Science. The debates sparked by this move figure prominently in several of the contributions to this book.

However, connectionism (in its dominant form at least) shares with computationalism (in its dominant form) an unquestioned *representationalism*, according to which internal entities stand for or correspond to world properties and events. And it is this semantic-like correspondence that gives internal processes their behavioral efficacy. The embodied-enactive view, on the other hand, although it shares with connectionism a belief in the importance of dynamical mechanisms and emergence, questions the relevance of representations as the explanatory device for cognition. Instead, according to this third approach, cognitive processes are seen as emerging or enacted by situated agents. It is the actions of these agents that drive the establishment of meaningful couplings (in ontogeny and phylogeny) of regular interdependencies with their surroundings from which meaning becomes inseparable. As was the case for connectionism, these ideas have their roots in the early days of Cognitive Science (such as the work of J. J. Gibson), but it has been taken up with vigor in the last five years in various areas such as robotics and artificial intelligence, neuroscience, and linguistics, and has generated lively philosophical debates (see, for example, Clark 1997). This trend to underline the embodied, situated nature of cognition is an important underpinning of several contributions in this volume.

In all three basic approaches and the various combinations thereof, Cognitive Science can claim that the traditional philosophical mind-body problem has become a scientific problem that can be solved scientifically: the link is provided precisely by the processes that give rise to the mental, however one prefers to couch them.

According to the explanatory gap argument, however successful any of these proposed approaches can be estimated when measured in terms of explanation and prediction of cognitive behavioral data, the naturalized mentalism that is thus part and parcel of Cognitive Science as a whole fails to fully account for the mental as it looks to us subjectively; that is, it fails to account for mental *phenomena* properly speaking.

Indeed Cognitive Science remains faithful to behaviorism not only by focusing on behavior but also by rejecting any evidence of a nonbehavioral kind. Consequently, it only apprehends the mental through behavioral data, treating mental entities as theoretical ones. Yet the mental is something we do seem to have an immediate experience of. The notion of consciousness has been used to mainly designate such an experience, although it can be argued that the two notions do not coincide. We will prefer here the more neutral and general term *phenomenological data* to refer to the contents of consciousness and experience. By itself this term does not carry any Husserlian connotation and is of current use in the literature, including the materialist tradition. Although prime examples of phenomenological data are more emotional or sensitive than cognitive, it is clear that if we are conscious at all in the sense of experiencing something, we are also conscious of the cognitive part of the mental. Perception, memory, and judgment are not only processes sustaining forms of behavior but also processes we are conscious of. Which is not to say that we are conscious of the totality of the mental, nor that we are conscious of the mental as it really is.

But if Cognitive Science entirely disregards phenomenological data as they have been defined because of its methodological commitments, then it leaves out a substantial aspect of mental phenomena. In short, it is a theory of the mind without being a theory of consciousness. It is a theory of what goes on in our minds when they are cognizing without being a theory of what is it like to be a cognizing mind. And in its stronger form, this is precisely what the explanatory gap argument denounces. For its partisans, there can be no satisfactory theory of cognition that does not tackle the phenomenological data of cognition. As Flanagan puts it in *Consciousness Reconsidered*: "The irony is that the return of the mind to psychology attending the demise of behaviorism and the rise of cognitivism did not mark the return of consciousness to the science of mind. Mind without consciousness. How is that possible?"

There is, however, a weaker form of the explanatory gap argument. Under this second form, the problem is not that Cognitive Science has refused to account for phenomenological data (although it is far from clear how it can really do so without seriously relaxing its common methodological commitments) but that it has failed to account for them properly. The theories that Cognitive Science has elaborated to explain mental phenomena are inadequate: there is a gap between the mental as evidenced by behavioral data and the mental as evidenced by phenomenological data. Consequently, it leaves these out also, although in a different sense of the word.

It should be underlined that in both cases leaving phenomenological data out means not only leaving them unexplained but also leaving them unnaturalized. The relation of the mental as we experience it to the brain remains mysterious. Although these two points are sometimes argued independently, it is clear that if the mentalism of Cognitive Science is intrinsically linked with a naturalist solution to the mind-body problem, denouncing the inadequacy of its mentalism is also denouncing the inadequacy of its naturalism.

In *Consciousness and the Computational Mind*, Jackendoff has nicely summarized the explanatory gap argument and its consequences with Figure 1.1. According to Jackendoff, the current state of cognitive theory is like a drama with three characters: the brain, the cognitive mind as conceived by Cognitive Science (the computational mind in Jackendoff's terminology, but the connectionist or embodied mind could be used just as well), and the cognitive mind as subjectively apprehended. And the explanatory gap argument claims that even if it is *ex hypothesi* granted that Cognitive Science has satisfactorily solved the mind-body problem in the domain of cognition, it has

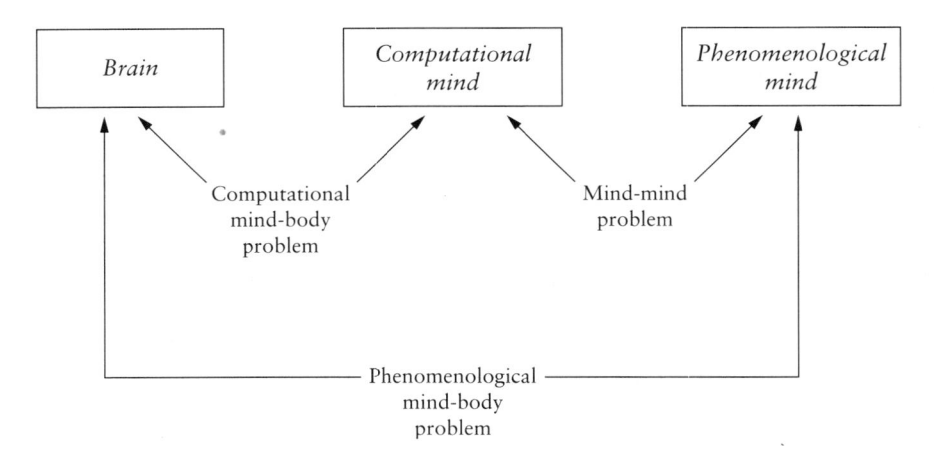

FIGURE 1.1. Jackendoff's view of the explanatory gap.

done so at the cost of creating a conflict with the phenomenological mind, thereby raising a mind-mind problem: how does the cognitive mind we experience relate to the cognitive mind as seen by Cognitive Science? But the emergence of this mind-mind problem necessarily implies that the mind-body problem has not in fact been entirely solved. What has been solved is the problem of the relation between the brain and the cognitive mind as Cognitive Science sees it, not as we *experience* it.

Understood in this way, the explanatory gap argument naturally raises two main problems: (1) is the point it makes true, and (2) if so, how can it be solved? The following two sections will briefly address these issues.

1.2. THEORY OF COGNITION AND PHENOMENOLOGICAL DATA

Assessing the truth of the explanatory gap argument first requires that we examine the extent to which Cognitive Science can be fairly accused of not accounting for phenomenological data (1.2.2). But there is no point of making such an accusation without establishing that a scientific theory of cognition should and can in principle account for these data (1.2.3).

1.2.1. The Notion of Phenomenological Data

Some preliminary clarification of the notion of phenomenological data itself is clearly needed. As already mentioned, the explanatory gap argument is variously put in the relevant literature in terms of subjectivity, consciousness, qualia, or experience. It is important to disentangle these different concepts and see how they are related to the concept of phenomenological data offered here as a substitute.

In spite of the variety of the terminology being used, a sort of consensus seems to have emerged around the idea that Nagel's expression "what it is like to be" succeeds in capturing what is essentially at stake, although the adequacy of this expression might be differently appreciated. It seems therefore appropriate to start with an elucidation of what it is meant to designate.

Clearly "what it is like to be" a bat or a human being refers to how things (everything) look to a bat or a human being. In other words it is just a more casual way of talking about what philosophers have technically and more accurately called *phenomenality* since the pre-Socratics. A phenomenon, in the most original sense of the word, is an appearance and therefore something intrinsically relative. By its very definition an appearance is indeed what something is for something else; it is a being *for* as opposed to a being *in* itself, something as apprehended by another entity rather than something as it is independent of its apprehension by another entity.

Phenomenality certainly is a crucial fact for two main reasons. First, only a few natural beings have an obvious capacity for phenomenality: it would be quite surprising if there were such a thing as "what it is like to be a stone." In the second place, phenomenality is arguably extremely variable. It is for instance very likely, as Nagel has argued, that an organism with a sonar system (like the bat) does not experience what an organism equipped with a visual system (like a human being) can experience: at least the external world looks different to each. It is also very likely, although to a much lesser extent, that the external world looks quite different to two individuals belonging to the same species.

It is important to underline that phenomena fall into two main categories: internal and external. Broadly speaking, the notion of internal phenomena refers to how things happening in a subject look to that subject itself: it is clear for instance that feelings or judgments are not apprehended as located in the perceptual space where we locate our immediate environment. External phenomena, on the other hand, do have such a localization: when I see a house I see it outside "myself." But according to the previous definition, these still count as relative in the sense that they are what external things look like to a subject. As a matter of fact, external phenomena are usually the prime examples mentioned when denouncing the insufficiencies of Cognitive Science's explanation of "what it is like to be" properties.

Finally, when it is defined in this way, phenomenality does not differ in any substantial way from subjectivity, if by subjectivity we mean the subjective side of things, the way things are from a subject's point of view. Accordingly, it also sounds fair to say that what advocates of the explanatory gap argument complain about is that Cognitive Science is a theory of the cognitive mind that leaves out phenomenality or subjectivity, either because it does not attempt to account for it or because its efforts to do so have failed.

It might be tempting to assimilate the notion of phenomenological data so understood to that of content of consciousness. However, the progress of psychology as well as the development of psychoanalysis have made familiar the idea that something might happen for a subject, but nevertheless not be accessible to this subject. We naturally describe such cases by saying that the subject is not conscious of the phenomenon in question: there are, for instance, numerous aspects of external things which we perceive without being conscious of them. The notion of consciousness is here clearly meant to designate first and foremost the fact that the subject knows about, is informed about, or in other words is aware of, the phenomenon. This definition of consciousness as awareness accommodates perfectly well with the distinction between external and internal phenomena: the division between internal and external consciousness, or between object-consciousness and self-consciousness, is indeed one of the oldest in the philosophy of mind. It can be further argued that awareness, in both its internal and its external forms, is analyzable in terms of reflexivity, although this is a point of controversy. The notion of phenomenological data will designate here both the conscious and the nonconscious phenomena, although the explanatory gap argument has been mainly concerned with the first category, which will accordingly receive special emphasis in the following developments.

Finally, it should be emphasized that if this notion of phenomenological data seems pretty close to that of experience, it is somewhat different from the concept of qualia as it is mainly used in the relevant literature, although the two terms are often used interchangeably (see, for instance, Shoemaker 1984). By a *quale* or qualitative aspect of a mental event, philosophers and psychologists primarily mean a feature of the mental that is both phenomenal and intrinsically conscious in the sense just given to these two notions. Pain is the most familiar example: a pain with no phenomenality and no awareness sounds like a painless pain. In addition most of them also see in a quale something which is necessarily subjective to the point of being absolutely unique, as well as ineffable and incommunicable. In his well-known attack on the admission of qualia, Dennett (1988) aptly summarizes the resulting concept when he writes: "So, to summarize the tradition, qualia are supposed to be properties of a subject's mental states that are (1) ineffable, (2) intrinsic, (3) private, (4) directly or immediately apprehensible in consciousness." Some authors actually find qualia so ineffable that they consider the very concept clarifiable only by means of some sort of ostensive definition.[6] Even if one agrees that there are qualia so defined, it is clear that they hardly exhaust the range of phenomenological data and that the two concepts—phenomenological data and qualia—can be considered as synonymous only under the condition that qualia be extended to cover the full range of subjective data.[7]

It is of a particular importance to take into account this difference between phenomenological data and qualia as commonly conceived when adopting a naturalist perspective. If phenomenal appearance is too quickly reduced to something wholly ineffable and incommunicable, the very project of a naturalization of phenomenological descriptions becomes a contradiction in terms. How can something ineffable be scientifically explained? If, however, the two notions are clearly distinguished, the meaning of a naturalist approach becomes clear: what is at stake is *a scientific study of the processes of the phenomenalization of reality*.

1.2.2. Assessing the Reality of the Explanatory Gap

In view of this clarification of the nature of phenomenological data, to what extent can it be legitimately claimed that Cognitive Science leaves them out?

It is first undeniable that Cognitive Science pretends to be a theory about what is happening inside the "black box," given that its main goal is to explain cognitive behavior by devising hypotheses about the internal mechanisms responsible for behavioral data and eventually by seeking lawful correlations between these data and elements of the environment. But explaining what is happening inside the black box is not explaining what is happening *for* the black box, so to speak. It is one thing to try to account for what is going on in the brain—at whatever level of explanation—when, for instance, we memorize something, and another one to try to account for what we feel or think is going on when memorizing. Undoubtedly, the real concern of theories of memory elaborated within the framework of Cognitive Science is with the former. The point can be easily generalized to other areas of investigation. To put it in a nutshell, Cognitive Science purports to say how the cognitive mind/brain works *in* itself and not how it comes to seem to be working *for* itself the way it does.

However, adopting such a perspective on the problem of cognition does not suffice to make phenomenological data *ipso facto* irrelevant. It could very well be after all that the best way to know what is happening in the black box at the mental level is *also* to investigate what seems to be happening in it according to the subject.[8] In such a case it would be necessary to take phenomenological data as a basis for theory construction as well as for theory confirmation. Accordingly, accounting for the cognitive workings of the mind would also be accounting for these data themselves, although not yet for our very ability to access them. But it is correct to say that Cognitive Science almost universally makes the additional methodological assumption, inherited from the earlier rejection of introspection as a method of psychological inquiry, that consciousness is too limited and too unreliable to provide valuable information about the workings of cognition. As a result it feels entitled to largely disregard phenomenological data and to consider them as excluded from its proper field of investigation not only for theoretical reasons but also for methodological ones.

Although it certainly fits the official doctrine, this conclusion calls for qualifications. The real attitude of Cognitive Science vis-à-vis phenomenological data is more complex. From a purely methodological point of view self-report is for instance a current psychological practice in cases where the focus is on what the subject really perceives as opposed to what she thinks she is perceiving. Furthermore, some phenomena falling into the field of investigation of Cognitive Science obviously have a conscious dimension that has to be accounted for, such as, for instance, attention. Even a theory of visual perception has to be a theory of what we are visually aware of as well as a theory of what is manifested to us even unconsciously. Neuropsychological observations such as hemilateral neglect or blindsight have made phenomenological data impossible to eliminate. Finally, it is arguable that even the biological level of explanation is not in fact perfectly independent, not only from a mental one, but also from a phenomenological one. Neurobiologists have to interpret some of their results in mental terms, and in doing so they frequently allude to mental data of a phenomenological kind. It sounds on the whole more appropriate to conclude that Cognitive Science does not strictly repudiate phenomenological data either from its explananda or from its sources of information about cognitive processes, especially at the mental level. Nonetheless, given the definition of its object of investigation as well as its methodological commitments, it cannot be considered as a theory of phenomenological data either in the sense of including a general and systematic theory of how we are aware of what we are aware of, or in the sense of a theory systematically relying on such data to explain the cognitive mind.

It is undeniable that in certain areas of Cognitive Science serious efforts have recently been undertaken to overcome this limitation, and that the recent outburst of consciousness studies (the "Consciousness Boom") can be read in part as an attempt to demonstrate that the principles on which the Cognitive Revolution was based do not rule out a systematic investigation of phenomenological data. Here again Jackendoff's attempt at reconciling the computational mind with the phenomenological mind serves as a perfect illustration. The limits of this introductory essay do not permit us to evaluate these efforts properly and, therefore, to assess fully the soundness of the weak form of the explanatory gap argument (however, see 1.3.2). A few general remarks can, nevertheless, reasonably be made in this regard:

1. These various attempts unquestionably represent a substantial departure from the early determination of the domain, the problematic and the methodology of Cognitive Science in all of its variants.
2. They all share to some degree the conviction that accounting for phenomenological data is more than just an additional problem. It is a challenge in the sense that it is a particularly difficult issue, or at least a very particular one.
3. They widely agree that the difficulty of the problem derives from the necessity to establish between the biological level and the phenomenological one an explanatory link and not a mere correlation.
4. They are confronted with serious criticism of the very idea they are trying to defend. An important aspect of the Consciousness Boom has been indeed to question the most fundamental tenets of Cognitive Science, thereby echoing previous and differently motivated attacks launched either by philosophers such as Herbert Dreyfus or John Searle, or by cognitive scientists trying to elaborate what George Lakoff has called an "alternative paradigm."[9]
5. Finally, with a few exceptions such as Dennett, there is a large consensus among consciousness theorists, including those who believe in the possi-

bility of extending the power of the explanatory principles of Cognitive Science beyond their original range of application, that the integration of phenomenological data into a full-fledged naturalistic theory of cognition still remains quite preliminary. In short, the problem stands pretty much ahead of us.

These various remarks converge on the conclusion that it is definitely premature to consider the weak form of the explanatory gap argument as having been conclusively refuted.

1.2.3. Should Cognitive Science Fill the Gap?

At this point it is wise to ask whether Cognitive Science is not after all wasting energy in trying to explain something it does not have to explain qua theory of cognition. It is probably true that the problem of consciousness is particularly resistant, but it may be a resistance that cognitive scientists do not have to overcome.

As a matter of fact, the belief that they do not is perhaps one of the main reasons for the lack of real interest in consciousness shown by the Cognitive Science community prior to the Consciousness Boom. The underlying hypothesis is that the conscious dimension of cognition does not play any essential cognitive role, and that although human cognition eventuates in subjective manifestations, it could very well be realized without them. If this is the case, the essential goal of Cognitive Science of explaining the cognitive mind can be fulfilled without addressing the problem of how and why we experience the phenomenological data we do in fact experience. The traditional conception that consciousness is epiphenomenal, or causally impotent, is clearly one aspect of this belief.

A growing number of objections have been posed to this "consciousness inessentialism,"[10] which is of course more an implicit assumption than an explicit doctrine, on the basis of the very simple observation that what we are conscious of clearly seems to be an obvious determinant of our cognitive behavior. If movements based on perceptions can count as cognitive behavior at all, it is hard to deny that this sort of behavior is highly dependent on phenomenological data and therefore cannot be fully explained without a serious account of these data themselves. Similarly, the coming into awareness of a mental content, say, when willingly seeking new interpretations during a cognitive task, can substantially modify the nature of this content.

The methodological assumption that consciousness is limited and unreliable is of course a further reason for claiming that a theory of cognition does not have to be a theory of phenomenological data. If a theory of cognition deals with the real workings of the mind and if phenomenological data are not valuable data about how the mind works, there is indeed no good reason for caring about them. But it looks more and more arguable that this methodological assumption needs serious qualifications. There is an increasing feeling that cognitive theory might be overreacting to the excessive introspectionism that marked early psychological theories by retreating into excesses of experimentalism. Various articles in this volume, for example, speak to surprising similarities between results obtained at the biological level of inquiry and results obtained by phenomenological inquiry. In view of such correlations it does not sound foolish to suppose that the functioning of the brain, at the different levels where it is being investigated, might be closer to what we are aware of than has been traditionally accepted.

Finally, as it has in fact been recently argued by various authors, even if consciousness is an inessential feature of many human cognitive processes, a theory of human cognition cannot be complete unless it accounts for the phenomenological data related to these cognitive processes.

1.2.4. Phenomenological Data and Scientific Skepticism

Despite the foregoing, it is not sufficient to build a reasonable case in favor of the indispensability of a theory of phenomenological data within a theory of cognition. It might still very well be that, in spite of all its desirability, the goal of elaborating such a theory cannot be achieved and that the modesty of early Cognitive Science in this regard is to be preserved. Every new attempt to push back the frontiers of scientific knowledge elicits skeptical reactions, and the attempt to construct a theory of phenomenological data is no exception. Skepticism has been advocated along two main lines of argument. The first one maintains that phenomenological data probably lie beyond the limits of science by their very nature. They are just not the sort of thing there can be a science of. The second maintains that although a science of phenomenological data is possible, a *naturalized* one is not.

Although these two arguments can be developed rather independently, it is clear that they also have close connections. As a matter of fact they are frequently intertwined in the literature, and the seminal article by Nagel already mentioned is a perfect illustration of this. Nagel's fundamental concern is that consciousness makes a naturalist or materialist approach to the mind/body problem "intractable" and "hopeless." But the source of his worry lies in the possibility of reconciling the commitment for objectivity of scientific knowledge and the irreducible subjective nature of phenomenological data:

> "If the facts of experience—facts about what it is like for the experiencing organism—are accessible only from one point of view . . . , then it is a mystery

how the true character of experiences could be revealed in the physical operation of the organism. The latter is a domain of objective facts *par excellence*—the kind that can be observed and understood from many points of view and by individuals with differing perceptual systems."[11]

The point made here can be fairly summarized with the three following propositions:

1. If a phenomenological datum is what there is *from the point of view of* an individual organism O_1, then it can be apprehended only *from the point of view of* O_1 or from the point of view of an organism O_x sufficiently similar to O_1 (otherwise it could not be properly considered as something *for* O_1, i.e., as something intrinsically relative to O_1).

2. Scientific characterizations, especially physical ones, are objective in the sense of including no intrinsic reference to any special kind of organism, and therefore of requiring no specific point of view in order to be apprehended.

3. Consequently, phenomenological data cannot be naturalized without loosing their very phenomenological character.

This argument requires a more detailed critical analysis than can be given here. Its first premise is nevertheless clearly disputable. It is far from obvious that what is relative to the point of view of an apprehending organism O is logically not recoverable to a large extent in terms not referring to this point of view. Various attempts at establishing de facto the second point will be found in the contributions collected here.

In addition, Nagel's argument arguably embodies two disputable assumptions of a more general nature which are typical of most forms of scientific skepticism.

Phenomenality, physical objectivity, and realism. It is first arguable that it contains an implicit assimilation of the notion of objectivity with that of a reality ontologically independent of any observer and free of any specific perspective, and that such an assimilation is equivocated. Many epistemologists from Kant to the members of the Vienna Circle and more contemporary ones such as Bas C. van Fraassen and Bernard d'Espagnat have insisted that physical knowledge deals only with physical *phenomena*. In classical mechanics the essential feature of physical phenomena is their spatiotemporality, that is to say, the fact they are perceptually given or *measured* by the system perceiving them. However, space and time are not ontologically independent. They are relative to an observer, and it is well established that relativity groups—the groups of changing observers—play a constitutive role in physical theories.

In the same manner, in quantum mechanics, a physical phenomenon owes its existence to measuring instruments. Physical theories can only be about observables, not about independent entities. This purely relational status of physical objects (resulting in the integration of the conditions of observation of the object into the object itself) has often been emphasized (by Niels Bohr in particular). Epistemologists of quantum physics have even coined the term "weak objectivity" to designate it. Indeed, the main problem of physical theories is to attain objectivity in spite of the unavoidable interaction of their objects with the instruments of measurement.

Their main achievement certainly is to have solved this paradoxical situation by taking into account the relational nature of phenomena, conceived as the result of the action of an "emitting source" (external nature) on a "receptor" (the perceiving subject and the instruments of measurement) and by eliminating at the same time all reference to the specific nature of this receptor. In classical mechanics as well as in relativity theory, the application of this strategy consists in eliminating the subjective aspects of space and time (eliminating any reference to the internal structure of the perceiving system) through their geometrization and the transformation of observers into reference points (observers in the Einsteinian sense of the term), thus reducing objectivity to a "covariance," that is, an invariance with respect to the influences of the relativity groups. Objectivity is transformed into a form of "intersubjectivity" and loses any nonphenomenal dimension. This definition implies that the mathematical entities used for describing the physical ones must have an intrinsic geometrical meaning independent of the frame of reference.

Similarly, in quantum mechanics, constraints on observability (such as the Heisenberg uncertainty principle) are introduced without having the quantum theory refer to the specific nature of the instruments used. The axioms of quantum mechanics about the amplitudes of probability are an expression of the various ways micro-objects can interact with different sorts of instruments.

Given this fundamental restriction of the object of the physical sciences to phenomena or observables, it is clearly disputable to assimilate physical objectivity to an ontologically independent reality and to contrast its study with that of phenomena. The difference between physics and phenomenology is better seen in the following way: physics "purifies" the phenomena by eliminating all reference to the internal dimension of the receptors as well as (as Husserl clearly noted, see 2.2.2) to their qualitative and morphological aspects.

The impossibility of anticipating the limits of science. In addition, to assert that certain kinds of phenomena are in *principle* beyond the limits of science is not scientifically legitimate. The limits of science are unknown and cannot be anticipated except when a limitation theorem can be found that shows the impossibility of a definite project (for example, the squaring of the circle because π is an irrational transcendental number, the equivalence between syntactic demonstrability and semantic truth because of Gödel's results, the existence of a perpetual motion because of the second principle of thermodynamics, and so on). Such cases are rare, and so far no such principle has been found in the issue under discussion.

In fact, the situation is almost the opposite: it is very difficult to anticipate what can be scientifically known. It is, for example, almost impossible to know what is implicitly contained in the equations of physics. It is not by contemplating Newton's equations that we can anticipate the rings of Saturn (this is an N-bodies hypercomplex problem), or Navier-Stokes's equations that we can anticipate turbulence, or Schrödinger's equations that we can anticipate superconductivity, or Dirac's equations that we can anticipate antimatter. Every one of these deep and subtle phenomena is nevertheless somehow encoded in these equations. Once more, who could have anticipated that the equations of magnetic spin glasses once reinterpreted by John Hopfield in terms of formal neurons could contain a theory of categorization, of rule extraction, or of inference?

One of the major contributions of contemporary science is on the contrary to have demonstrated that entire classes of phenomena, the self-organization of complex systems in particular, which had been a priori excluded from the field of natural sciences for centuries, are nevertheless part of them.

1.3. THE CLAIM FOR A NATURALIZED PHENOMENOLOGY

1.3.1. A Place for Phenomenology

In light of the preceding analyses, it sounds fair to conclude that the relation of phenomenological data to Cognitive Science, and to scientific theories of cognition in general, remains very much an open problem: so far it has not conclusively been shown to be either illegitimate, or impossible to solve in principle, or satisfactorily settled. Accordingly, the main difficulty is to find the right way to close the explanatory gap.

It is no less reasonable to suppose that it probably cannot be closed without appealing to some sort of phenomenology. This appeal remains nevertheless perfectly vacuous until the notion of phenomenology has been specified, since the word by itself designates nothing else than a theory of phenomenological data. But in the philosophical tradition it has also been used in a more specific way to designate an enterprise primarily dedicated to the careful establishment, through first-person description and analysis, of phenomenological data understood as what we are really aware of, as opposed to what we believe we are aware of.

As a matter of fact the necessity for such a phenomenology has been felt and explicitly acknowledged by a growing number of the people concerned with the explanatory gap. Nagel himself ended the skeptical developments of his 1970 article on a more promising note by calling for what he labeled an "objective phenomenology." By objective phenomenology he meant an attempt to characterize phenomenological data at a level sufficiently abstract from the singularity of individual viewpoints to make these data conveyable to individuals with widely diverging perspectives. In short, he thought of it as a "speculative proposal" designed to start bridging the gap between the subjective and the objective. As he put it, "Though presumably it would not capture everything, its goal would be to describe, at least in part, the subjective character of experiences in a form comprehensible to beings capable of having those experiences."[12] But narrowing the distance separating the subjective and the objective was evidently for him also a way of narrowing the gap between the mental and the physical. He added that "apart from its own interest, a phenomenology that is in this sense objective may permit questions about the physical basis of experience to assume a more intelligible form. Aspects of subjective experience that admitted this kind of objective description might be better candidates for objective explanations of a more familiar sort."

This further specification throws light on an additional feature of the sort of phenomenology needed to close the gap: it should be a naturalized or naturalistic one in the minimal sense of not being committed to a dualistic kind of ontology. In other words, it is not enough that such a phenomenology be descriptive and analytical; it should also be explanatory, and the explanations it gives should make clear how phenomenological data can be properties of the brain and the body without the help of any spiritual substance. It is clear that this additional feature has been less traditionally attached to the notion of phenomenology than the previous one. As a matter of fact it is fair to say that up to now most phenomenological attempts have been non-naturalistic.

It is only recently that, in parallel to the scientific breakthrough emphasized above, this claim for a naturalistic phenomenology has found an echo in a series of individual investigations.

1.3.2. Recent Developments Toward a Naturalized Phenomenology

A brief review of some recent developments toward a naturalized phenomenology will suffice, however, to indicate the extent to which the general project of introducing a phenomenological level of investigation into the naturalist framework of the sciences of cognition could greatly benefit from the richness and the rigor of the Husserlian phenomenological tradition.

Jackendoff's *Consciousness and the Computational Mind* (1987) is in many ways a direct antecedent and pioneer of the search for a naturalized phenomenology. His explicit purpose is to bring into cognitive science what he himself calls the phenomenological mind. His previous *Semantics and Cognition* (1983) can actually be seen as a first step in this direction. One of Jackendoff's major concerns in this book is the analysis of the relation between the perceptual world and language. The world we are talking about is indeed first and foremost the world immediately apprehended in sense perception. Jackendoff suggests that the articulation between language and phenomena is made possible by a cognitive architecture that includes a central representational level of information processing (the level of conceptual structure) where perceptual, linguistic, and perceptual information are made compatible.

His 1987 general theory is more directly based on a Fodorian modularist conception of cognitive architecture and on David Marr's idea of a hierarchical organization of representational levels corresponding to increasingly complex and centralized stages of information integration. In his opinion cognitive processing is primarily a matter of transforming representations from a lower level to a more integrated as well as more central one. From this perspective, visual perception, for instance, is a process of transformation of low-level representations derived from visual input into high-level integrative and centralized ones. Jackendoff's interesting suggestion about consciousness is to argue that phenomenality is not connected with the highest levels of representation, because their main function is to give meaning, and meaning often goes beyond what we are really conscious of. In language perception, for instance, what we are conscious of is the phonological dimension of language, which corresponds to an intermediate level of representation requiring further treatment in order to reach understanding.

Similarly, Jackendoff offers an interesting reading of Marr's theory of visual perception. The main problem confronting vision theory according to Marr is to explain the reconstruction by the brain of the properties of three-dimensional objects from the two-dimensional image on the retina. To this effect Marr introduces a series of intermediate levels of representation, most important the two-and-a-half-dimensional level responsible for the emergence of object shapes. And it is only at the most central level that the tridimensionality of objects is obtained. Jackendoff's argument is that this two-and-a-half-dimensional level is closer to the actual content of visual consciousness, "to the way things are perceived," while the three-dimensional level corresponds in his opinion to the way visual phenomena are understood. Although Jackendoff makes no reference to Husserlian phenomenology, it is quite surprising to see how closely his analysis parallels those of Husserl, who emphasized that what we actually perceive is no more than a series of profiles (see 2.1.1) serving as a basis for the construction of the so-called perceived object.

But in spite of these interesting phenomenological openings, Jackendoff leaves the characterization of the notion of phenomenological mind rather vague, as something that is pertinent to the personal, to the mind as "mine." Nowhere in his remarkably pioneering book is there a reference to the technical developments of Husserlian phenomenology. Nevertheless, that does not stop him from claiming that insights into experience act as constraints for a computational theory of mind, although he follows that claim with no methodological recommendations except "the hope that the disagreements about phenomenology can be settled in an atmosphere of mutual trust" (1987: 275).

Jackendoff is not alone in resorting to the term "phenomenology" but making it mean nothing more than firsthand analysis. A number of other authors mention phenomenology without ever actually mobilizing its sources and resources, thereby ignoring the substantial contribution of the Husserlian tradition. The group gathered here is a varied one, with contributions such as George Lakoff and Mark Johnson's approach to cognitive semantics, Searle's ideas on ontological irreducibility, and Chalmers's definition of a "hard problem" of consciousness.

The same ignorance of the achievements of Husserlian phenomenology can be detected in the more explicitly dismissive attitude adopted by Dennett in his *Consciousness Explained*, in which he swiftly concludes that Husserl's phenomenology has failed. He remarks: "Like other attempts to strip away interpretation and reveal the basic facts of consciousness to rigorous observation, such as the Impressionistic movements in the arts and the Introspectionist psychologists of Wundt, Titchener, and others, Phenomenology has failed to find a single settled method that everyone could agree upon" (1991: 44). This paragraph goes a long way to reveal to what extent Dennett's rejection of Husserlian phenomenology rests on serious misunderstandings. There is no better way of clarifying these misunderstandings than by reviewing his own conception of the nature of phenomenological investigation and of the role it can play in the study of cognition.

1. Rejection of qualia. According to Dennett, phenomenality (which comes under three main forms, external, internal, and affective) has been wrongly associated with a special sort of mental entity of a purely qualita-

tive nature (the quale) because there is no such thing as a phenomenon dissociated from an interpretation. Accordingly, what philosophers distinguish as qualia are just propositional attitudes and can be adequately expressed in the usual form "I believe that p . . ." or "I judge that p . . ." In the sense in which a phenomenology is an investigation of qualia, there is therefore "no such thing as phenomenology."

2. Rejection of the privileges of first-person access. This rejection of the specificity of qualia is complemented by his rejection of the possibility of a phenomenological investigation conceived as a first-person descriptive theory of what a subject has privileged access to. Dennett disputes the well-entrenched idea that first-person access is the best way to capture phenomenality, insisting on the contrary on how mistaken we can be when we attempt to describe what we are conscious of.

3. Heterophenomenology. Consequently, he finds it necessary to restrict the study of phenomenality (the "phenom" as he likes to put it) to a regular third-person kind of scientific study. Hence the notion of heterophenomenology: consciousness can only be investigated as the consciousness of the other. The paradox of this third-person approach to phenomenality is that it does not face any of the phenomena under study: the data of heterophenomenology are of a behavioral nature, and heterophenomenology itself is no more than a way of interpreting them. In Dennett's favored terminology it is nothing else than a heterophenomenological stance toward the explanation of behavior. Furthermore, in his eyes nothing seems to distinguish this stance from the intentional one. Making sense of an organism's behavior in terms of beliefs and desires is making sense of this behavior in terms of what these beliefs and these desires are for the subject who has them. Finally, assimilating the study of consciousness with the intentional stance is fruitful from the point of view of naturalization: it is made ontologically neutral and therefore compatible with the naturalist perspective (for more detail on this point, see 5.2).

This conception of the study of consciousness is disputable on many grounds. It could be argued, for instance, that it rests on an insufficient discrimination between the notion of mental state and the notion of state of consciousness. In spite of the fact that a mental state can be conscious and that both kinds of states can also be intentional, the two notions seem to differ substantially. The concept of a mental state is intrinsically linked with the problem of explaining behavior. We explain and predict the behavior of others by attributing to them mental states we characterize as beliefs and desires and making these mental states responsible for their behavior. But self-attribution of states of consciousness does not primarily answer an explanatory concern. It is only by ignoring this fundamental difference that Dennett can transform conscious states into propositional attitudes and apply to them his well-known instrumentalist interpretation. It seems likely, however, that in this move he misses something important.

Furthermore, it is hard to see how phenomenality can be studied satisfactorily without ever accessing it directly, that is, by treating it as a mere theoretical posit. Dennett seems in particular to be oblivious to the fact that commonsense attributions of phenomenality (what it looks like for X) have a strong projective element in them, and that any such attribution is probably ultimately to be referred to a first-person experience. This is of course not to deny that interesting generalizations about consciousness can be reached on the basis of behavioral data. But the whole point and difficulty is that we need more than behavioral data: we need phenomenological data. And this is why, in an important and long-standing sense of the very term of phenomenology, heterophenomenology is not phenomenological: it is a nonphenomenological approach to the "phenom." Dennett claims that heterophenomenology offers a solution to the problem raised by Nagel of making subjective facts amenable to the third-person objective viewpoint required by science. But it seems more likely that the solution, as Nagel himself acknowledges, is to be found in the intersubjective dimension of conscious experiences.

Whatever the real value of his heterophenomenology, it is clear that Dennett's unduly quick dismissal of Husserlian phenomenology is a consequence of his assimilating it with something it is not; namely, a study of qualia in the sense of purely individual data, and a study conducted in a nonrigorous and impressionistic way. But as the following section will hopefully make it clear, Husserl's phenomenology is an attempt at devising a rigorous characterization of phenomena with an intersubjective value, and as such it requires a more carefully argued refutation.

Flanagan is certainly a stronger advocate of a truly naturalized phenomenology than either Dennett or Jackendoff. In his previously mentioned *Consciousness Reconsidered*, he explicitly calls for the full inclusion of a phenomenological level of investigation into the cognitive sciences. Far from seeing such an inclusion as a departure from the naturalistic point of view, he recommends putting phenomenological descriptions on an equal footing with the hypotheses of experimental psychology and neuroscience in the investigation of any cognitive phenomenon. What he calls the "natural method" (see Flanagan 1992, chap. 1) consists in treating phenomenology, psychology, and neuroscience as three mutually constraining approaches to cognitive phenomena. This natural method remains, however, largely programmatic at this point. In particular, Flanagan has not yet provided detailed phenomenological descriptions of any aspect of cognition. In his few attempts to do so, his reliance on William James's descriptive work seems too narrow and his resolute ignorance of the Husserlian tradition unwarranted. Finally, it is arguable that there is much more to do, in order to naturalize a phenomenology of cognition, than putting it in a mutually constraining relation with cognitive psychology and neurosciences.

2. HUSSERL'S PHENOMENOLOGY AND THE CRITIQUE OF NATURALISM

Analyzing the possibility, the methods, and the implications of such a naturalized phenomenology is precisely the main concern of this book. More specifically, its central ambition is to assess the extent to which the phenomenological enterprise initiated by Husserl could be instrumental for this project.

As indicated by our critical remarks, it is indeed our contention that the various attempts mentioned in the previous section have failed to give enough substance to a naturalized phenomenology, and that a line of research based on Husserl's seminal ideas can lead to much more promising results.

There are two main motives for directing one's attention to Husserl. The first one is that Husserlian phenomenology is by and large the most thorough of modern times, if not of the whole history of thought. And the second is that, as we shall see on many occasions in this volume, a surprising convergence can be established between some Husserlian descriptions of phenomenological data and recent results obtained in the cognitive sciences, especially in the domain of biology and mathematical modeling.

It seems, therefore, indispensable to start with a review of the most fundamental tenets of Husserlian phenomenology. Even modestly conceived, the task nevertheless clearly goes beyond the scope of this introduction. Husserl's own theories have given rise to a number of seriously conflicting interpretations (as the contributions to this volume themselves testify), and his descendants are too numerous and heterogeneous to be encompassed in a matter of a few paragraphs. Accordingly, the following presentation will be limited to an overview of Husserl's most essential theses, formulated as uncontroversially as possible, but without compromise on decisive points of interpretation.[13]

2.1. HUSSERL'S DEFINITION OF PHENOMENOLOGY

Husserl's ideas evolved substantially from the publication of his *Philosophie der Arithmetik* in 1891 to that of *Die Krisis der europäischen Wissenschaften und die transzendentale Phänomenologie* in 1936. Moreover, he left an amazing number of manuscripts still in the process of being deciphered and published in Louvain, in which he constantly explores new directions of thought, so that his widely read publications are more the tip of an iceberg than the full body of a doctrine. It seems, nevertheless, legitimate to focus on the classical doctrine expounded in the first volume of the *Ideen zu einer reinen Phänomenologie und phänomenologischen Philosophie* (hereafter *Ideen* I) and then to provide some information about the later developments of the Husserlian project. To define the scientific part of Husserl's phenomenology as briefly as possible, it is undoubtedly fair to say that, in spite of its other irreducible philosophical pretensions, it is a theory of mind in the broad sense of the term, although one encompassing a general ontology as well as a theory of knowledge. As a matter of fact, because of the widespread belief in a sharp division between Continental philosophy and analytical philosophy, it is frequently forgotten that Husserl's enterprise took its point of departure in the very same problem Frege's and Russell's did, namely securing the foundations of mathematical knowledge.

Ideen I contains (in §75) one of the more concise and precise definitions of phenomenology published by Husserl himself, according to which phenomenology is to be technically understood as a "descriptive theory of the essence of pure lived experiences [*reine Erlebnisse*]" ("pure" meaning, as we shall see presently, that the lived experience is abstracted from its connections with natural reality). In other words, it is nothing other than a certain kind of theoretical knowledge with a specific domain of investigation as well as a specific epistemological form.

2.1.1. The Domain of Phenomenology

The nature of this domain can be clarified only by unfolding some of the main principles of Husserl's theory of cognition and knowledge. The most fundamental one, as made clear in §24 of *Ideen* I, where it is labeled "the principle of all principles," is a form of "intuitionism." It asserts not only that the human mind can have a special cognitive relation with objects in which these are apprehended directly, but also that the purest form of intuition, called "originary intuition" and characterized by the effective presence (and therefore the reality) of what is intuited (see *Ideen* I, §1), is "the source and *de jure* foundation" of all knowledge. Originary intuition is itself of three main kinds: transcendent, eidetic, and immanent.

Consequently, there are as many types of scientific knowledge as there are types of originary intuition; and there are as many types of originary intuition as there are types of objects or, in Husserl's terminology, "ontological regions." The notion of the object is to be taken here in its most general sense: in fact, Husserl usually prefers to use the word *Gegenständlichkeit*, to be rendered by the neologism "objectity."

Pure lived experiences represent just one such type of ontological region, and phenomenology is the theoretical knowledge based on the originary intuition revealing them, namely immanent intuition. The necessary basis for accessing this form of originary intuition is the suspension of habitual beliefs or *epochē*, also called *phenomenological reduction*, a methodological bracketing that underlies the entire edifice of Husserlian analysis, and which includes many variants and modes, as we shall presently see.

The specificity of this immanent intuition is best grasped against the background of the two other kinds of originary intuition already mentioned: transcendent and eidetic.

Transcendent intuition. Transcendent intuition is the most natural of the three, since it is mainly illustrated by sense perception. Through transcendental intuition we are directly acquainted with individual contingent objects endowed with sensible properties and inseparable from a network of causal relations with other objects of the same kind (*Ideen zu einer reinen Phänomenologie und phänomenologischen Philosophie*, vol. 2, §31; hereafter, *Ideen* II). But its main feature is that objects are apprehended as spatiotemporal entities: no object can be given in a transcendent intuition without a specific localization in space and time. Accordingly, transcendent intuition puts us in immediate contact with an infinite set of causally interconnected individuals existing in space and time which, all together, constitute the domain of natural realities. In other words it is the source and foundation of our belief in the world or nature. Such a belief is itself natural in the sense of being spontaneous: it is the core of what Husserl calls our *natural attitude* in life. Finally, natural objects also constitute the scientific domain of natural sciences. Natural sciences are empirical disciplines establishing by experimental methods laws understood as general synthetic and contingent propositions: they are what Husserl calls sciences of facts.

Transcendent intuition can be internal or external, an important subdivision, corresponding to the traditional distinction between internal and external perception.[14] Through internal transcendent intuition, we come to grips with natural entities of the psychological type or "lived experiences" (*Erlebnisse*), through external transcendent intuition we come to grips with natural entities of the physical type or "things." Following Descartes, Husserl sees in spatial extension the most essential and therefore distinctive attribute of things (*Ideen* I, §40, p. 4: "Extension is the eidetic nucleus of corporal nature"),[15] although these are also of a temporal nature. This intrinsic spatiality has dramatic implications for the nature of external intuition: it can never be adequate in the sense of delivering at the same time all the determinations of the object perceived. External intuition is therefore an endless fragmentary process through which the subject gets successively acquainted with the different "faces" of an object one after the other, adumbration (*Abschattung*) by adumbration, as Husserl likes to put it, but without ever capturing them all in a single isolated act of perception: "It is evident and drawn from the essence of spatial things . . . that necessarily a being of that kind can be given only through an adumbration" (*Ideen* I, §42, trans. F. Kersten, p. 91).

As a result, a thing is always intuited as something exceeding that aspect of itself which is actually perceived; the thing, so to speak, is always beyond the perception of the thing. For that reason it is labeled a *transcendent* entity, and the intuition that apprehends it is labeled a *transcendent* intuition. A transcendent intuition is thus always intertwined with a set of nonintuitive lived experiences anticipating some of the determinations of the object not actually intuited or "given" and constituting what Husserl calls its "horizon of co-donation."

As for internal intuition, its definition faces the following dilemma: how can it be reasonably considered as a kind of transcendent intuition if all natural things are by definition spatial ones? How can psychological realities be extended if not by sheer metaphor? As a matter of fact, Husserl acknowledges that a psychological lived experience "does not appear by adumbrations" (*Ideen* I, §53), and therefore is not extended. However, he no less explicitly states that it "takes place in the space and time of nature" (*Ideen* I, §53). This apparent contradiction is eliminated through the idea that things are transcendent entities in the "prime and original sense of the term" (§53), and that the psychological lived experience is indissociable from such entities because it is necessarily apprehended as belonging to a human body. In other words, a psychological lived experience is only indirectly spatial by virtue of an intrinsic reference to a privileged bona fide natural entity, and as such it constitutes an "original transcendence" (§38). In *Ideen* II, Husserl writes that the psychological properties "are given as belonging to the body . . . and it is precisely because of them that it is called a body or organism, that is, an 'organ for a soul,' or 'for a spirit'" (§14, p. 36; Kersten trans., modified).

However, the truly distinctive feature of the psychological lived experience in the realm of natural entities is to be found in the property of intentionality. Although Husserl criticized Brentano's thesis to the effect that intentionality is the mark of the mental as early as 1900 (see *Logische Untersuchungen*), he maintained that intentionality is the central feature of the psychological lived experience. By intentionality he meant that same property of aboutness which is at the center of so many discussions in the philosophy of mind nowadays, but he gave a fairly distinct analysis of it. Since they are highly dependent on his notion of immanent intuition, the main elements of this analysis will be presented later.

Finally, the distinction between the physical and the psychological within the region of natural being also delineates two different domains for scientific investigation, namely those of physics (broadly construed) and psychology, which are the two main branches of natural science and admit further subdivisions.

Eidetic intuition. One of Husserl's strongest epistemological credos is that the empirical inquiry of natural reality does not exhaust the science of nature. Indeed he was one of the most committed twentieth-century advocates of the possibility of establishing a priori synthetic and necessary laws about physical things and psychological lived experiences. Such a possibility is grounded in his eyes in our capacity for originary eidetic intuition. Eidetic intuition is a vision of essence (*Wesens-Schauung*), an acquaintance with a nontemporal and nonspatial general object corresponding to a set of individual natural entities and containing their essential properties. An essence amounts to a set of rules that a priori prescribe what must belong generically to empirical data. That we are endowed with such a capacity is according to Husserl an obvious cognitive fact, and he heavily criticized the empiricist tradition for ignoring it (see *Logische Untersuchungen*, II/1, Second Investigation). Technically speaking, he saw an eidetic intuition as the result of a process of "eidetic reduction" by which an individual object given in an intuition is progressively stripped of all its particular features through a series of imaginary variations ("eidetic variations"). These essences are hierarchized according to their degree of generality. At the upper levels of this hierarchical structure are the most generic ones, which are the "regional essences."

Chief among them is the regional essence of nature and its immediate subdivision between the regional essences of a thing and of a psychological lived experience. And each of these regional essences "determines 'synthetic' eidetic truths, that is to say, truths that are grounded in it as this generic essence, but are not mere particularizations of truths included in formal ontology" (*Ideen* I, §16, p. 37).

Accordingly, the empirical science of nature is to be completed by what Husserl calls an eidetic science of nature or an ontology of nature, including both an eidetic physics and an eidetic psychology. Although it benefits from a certain degree of independence in the *ordo investigandi* because it is based on a separate intuitive source, an empirical science is for Husserl to be founded on, and therefore logically dependent upon, a corresponding a priori eidetic science. Empirical psychology is for instance dependent upon eidetic psychology.

In addition, Husserl includes this ontology of nature in the more general category of material ontology, which is itself contrasted with formal ontology. Formal ontology designates the eidetic investigation of the most general properties of any kind of entity that can be given in an originary intuition. It is concerned with a formal analytic theory of general objects and axiomatizes formal categories and concepts such as object, quality, relation, identity, equality, plurality, number, magnitude, whole, part, genus, species, state of affairs, and so on. Its results are applicable both to material eidetic entities and to empirical ones, as well as to its own domain. Like the early Russell, Husserl conceives of the forms of objects as objects themselves, that is, as formal objects.

Immanent intuition. The admission of eidetic intuition represents a first extension of the natural domain of being that has traditionally raised animated controversies in philosophy, especially in modern times where nominalism has prevailed. Immanent intuition is an even more radical departure from commonsense ontology. In its most basic form, immanent intuition is an internal originary intuition through which the mind gets acquainted with non-natural individual objects. These nonspatial and nontemporal objects are the pure lived experiences (*reine Erlebnisse*), also called the immanent lived experiences (because they are given by immanent intuition). In other words, immanent intuition lays bare a new and nonpsychological dimension of the mental. Husserl's most fundamental claim is indeed to have discovered for the first time in the history of thought, and in spite of close anticipations by some philosophers, the existence of such an intuition, which, like any other basic type of intuition, reveals a new field of investigation. This is the field of phenomenology.

As a first approximation, this discovery can be seen as the result of a new interpretation of the outcome of Descartes's radical doubt. Husserl agrees with Descartes that every belief based on transcendent intuition is "revocable," in the sense that there is a rational possibility that it might be false. But he disagrees with him in claiming that when every such belief has been suspended and no more credit is granted to the sort of intuition on which they are grounded, there still is a zone of intuition left untouched and giving access to "a new region of being never before delimited in its own peculiarity—a region which, like any other region, is a region of individual being" (*Ideen* I, §33, p. 70). The reason why it is left untouched is simply that it makes Cartesian hyperbolic doubt useless. Indeed, the main epistemological characteristic of immanent intuition in Husserl's eyes is its adequacy: the objects given in it are given with the totality of their determinations and as they are in themselves. This adequacy is a consequence of the absence of any intrinsic connection between these objects and spatiality. By contrast, the fallibility of transcendent intuition is a corollary of its inadequacy, which itself results from the impossibility for an extended entity, even an indirectly extended one such as a psychological lived experience, to ever be given with the totality of its determinations in a single intuitive act. In short, Husserl's deep conviction is that immanent intuition opens up the doors of apodictic knowledge and apodictic knowledge makes doubt useless and nonrational.

In fact, the nature of the intellectual operation revealing immanent intuition, which Husserl famously called *transcendental reduction*, differs from Cartesian doubt on a crucial point: it does not amount to considering all knowledge based on transcendent intuition as false because of its uncertainty, but simply to refusing to grant it any truth-value. In Husserl's phraseology it is a mere suspension of belief or *ēpochē*.

It would, however, be inaccurate to reduce the specificity of pure lived experiences to their lack of spatiotemporality as well as to their capacity for being the object of absolute knowledge. The entities laid bare by transcendental reduction are more than just another ontological region: they constitute the most fundamental one of all, in the sense that all other types of beings, be they natural or eidetic ones, are relative to it. Although Husserl's idealism probably is the most debated of all the issues raised by the interpretation of the transcendental turn taken in *Ideen* I, this phase of his philosophical itinerary clearly represents an idealistic bent. *Ideen* I contains very sharp statements to the effect that there is no such thing, for instance, as a natural object in itself, but only *for* a pure subject. This ontological dependence extends to psychological lived experiences themselves and is rooted in the constitutional power of the intentionality of pure lived experiences. Pure lived experiences have for Husserl the property of intentionality, but what they are about is not to be understood as a term preexisting the intentional relation. It is constituted by this relation. To put it in a nutshell, beings other than pure lived experiences are only beings *for* the pure lived experiences (more accurately, for the pure subject or transcendental ego), and they are such because they are beings *only* by virtue of the pure lived experiences. Husserl writes in §49 of the same book that

> the whole spatiotemporal world, which includes human being and the human Ego as subordinate single realities is, according to its sense, a merely intentional being, thus one which has the merely secondary sense of a being for a consciousness. It is a being posited by consciousness in its lived experiences which, of essential necessity, can be determined and intuited only as something

identical belonging to motivated multiplicities of appearances: beyond that it is nothing. (Kersten trans., p. 112)

If phenomenology can ultimately be defined as the science which takes immanent intuition as its source and foundation, it also relies on eidetic intuition, since its proper field of investigation is not constituted by pure lived experiences themselves, which are individual entities, but by their corresponding essences. Phenomenology is the eidetic science or ontology of pure consciousness, just as pure physics is for Husserl the science of the essential features of natural things. And as such it is a *scientia* both *prima* and *absoluta*: *prima* because it studies the essence of ontologically primary entities, and *absoluta* because this essence can be adequately intuited. For these reasons Husserl saw in phenomenology the late realization of an epistemological ideal defined by Plato at the very beginnings of philosophy and guiding the philosophical tradition throughout the ages.

2.1.2. The Epistemological Status of Phenomenology

This traditional aspect of phenomenology is moderated by its willingness to incarnate a radically new type of eidetic science, namely, a descriptive one. Descriptive eidetics is contrasted by Husserl with the axiomatic eidetics best illustrated by mathematics and more generally by all mathematized natural sciences. An axiomatic (Husserl also says mathematical) eidetics, in Husserl's analysis, is a discipline proceeding through the construction of new concepts out of a restricted conceptual basis as well as through the deductive demonstration of theorems from a selection of axioms. Only the knowledge of the primitive elements of such a science is of an immediately intuitive nature; the concepts and the theorems derived from these primitive elements do not receive an immediately intuitive justification themselves, but are only indirectly grounded in intuition. On the contrary, a descriptive eidetic barely uses any procedure of indirect justification, such as rules of definition or rules of deduction. Every element is directly grounded on intuition, and for this reason its methodology is descriptive: it tries to express as accurately as possible what is actually given in immanent intuition and not to anticipate, with the help of reason and on the basis of a limited primitive intuition, what will be given in it.

The choice between an axiomatic and a descriptive eidetics is not an arbitrary one: it is determined by the essences under investigation. According to Husserl, essences can be not only material or formal but also exact or non-exact ones. Non-exact or vague essences, unlike exact ones, are not fully determined. In other words, they do not have accurately statable conditions of individuation and they are therefore fundamentally inappropriate for the application of the axiomatic approach, which requires a high level of exactitude. Consequently, they can only be investigated in a descriptive way. This point is crucial in Husserl's argumentation. We will return to it in 2.2.2 and later argue that in fact the development of mathematics has made the opposition between mathematical eidetics and inexact idealities disputable.

Essences of pure lived experiences fall into the category of vague essences. Their inexactitude is the correlate, at the eidetic level, of what Husserl calls the "flowing" character of individual pure lived experiences. At its most concrete level, the given of the immanent intuition is not a succession of clearcut discrete elements, but a continuum where separate entities cannot be really distinguished. Phenomenology is, therefore, conceived of as a descriptive and nonmathematical eidetic science. And as such it represents in Husserl's eyes a major epistemological innovation. For all eidetic sciences have so far been axiomatic, even in domains where the requirements of exactitude could not apparently be met. In such cases, for instance in mathematical physics, exact essences have been substituted for non-exact ones: perfect geometrical figures have, for example, replaced the actual and imperfect shapes of physical bodies. According to Husserl, exact essences are also ideal, in the sense that all individuals which can be subsumed under these essences only approximately possess the properties which they contain: no individual shape will ever fully satisfy, for example, the essence of the circle.

These different types of intuitions and of corresponding objects may now be summarized for the sake of clarity with Figure 1.2.

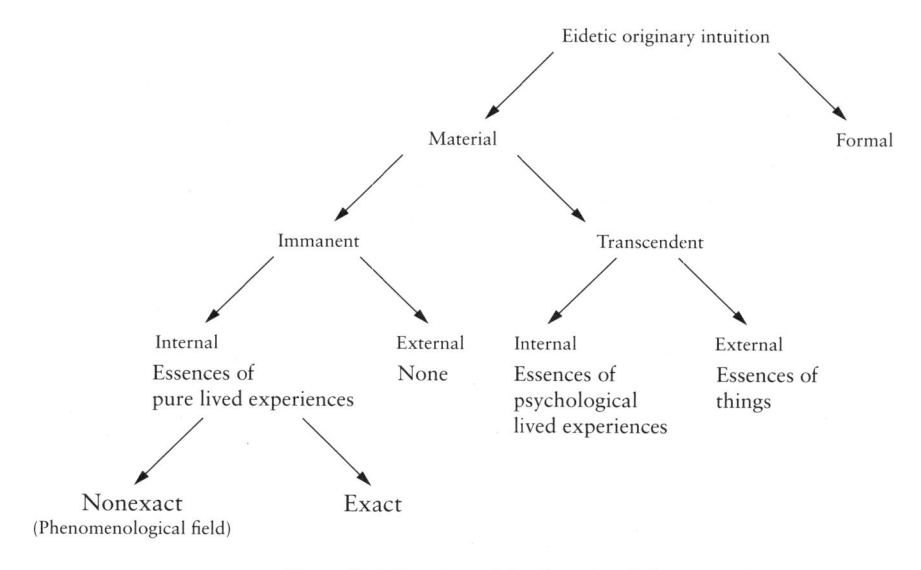

```
                          Eidetic originary intuition
                            /                    \
                      Material                    Formal
                      /      \
                Immanent    Transcendent
                /   \          /      \
         Internal  External  Internal  External
         Essences   None     Essences  Essences
         of pure             of psych- of things
         lived                ological
         experiences          lived
         /      \             experiences
    Nonexact   Exact
 (Phenomenological field)
```

FIGURE 1.2. Husserl's delineation of the domain of phenomenology.

2.1.3. The Main Areas of Phenomenological Investigation

Intentionality and noematics. Given on the one hand that intentionality is the central feature of the pure lived experiences revealed by immanent intuition, and on the other hand that the domain of pure lived experiences is a transcendental one in the sense previously explained, the central problem of Husserlian phenomenology is thus that of describing the constitution of the various domains of objects by the flow of pure lived experience, also designated by Husserl as the pure consciousness. Phenomenology is thus fundamentally a theory of intentionality of a constitutive or transcendental kind. Indeed Husserl writes in *Ideen* I that "intentionality is the name of the problem encompassed by the whole of phenomenology. The name precisely expresses the fundamental property of consciousness; all phenomenological problems, even the hyletic ones, find a place within it" (§146, p. 357). This central task makes it necessary to first lay bare a fundamental structure in the phenomenological data given by immanent intuition. The classification introduced in *Ideen* I, representing no more than a certain level of description calling for further analysis, is summarized in Figure 1.3.[16]

It is important to note that noetic elements (or "acts" in the terminology of *Logische Untersuchungen*) are the core of the intentional relation: through continuous rule-governed synthetic activity they constitute noemas on the basis of hyletic data. A noema is to be sharply distinguished from the corresponding transcendent object. While a noema belongs to the domain of pure lived experiences, the transcendent object does not. The noema is both the correlate of the constitutive activity of noesis applied to hyletic data and a necessary intermediary structure making the intentional relation between a transcendental Ego and the transcendent object possible. It is revealed by the reduction of a transcendent intuition, which "puts into brackets" the belief in the reality of this object.

The admission of noemas has far-reaching implications for the delimitation of the field of pure lived experiences: indeed all nonimmanent objects, which are neutralized by the transcendental reduction, end up being somehow reintroduced into the domain of phenomenology under the guise of noematic elements—of phenomenological data. In §76 of *Ideen* I, Husserl writes: "This is why physical Nature is put into brackets, while at the same

Pure lived experience (Immanent Being)				Transcendent Being
[*Reel*]		[Not *reel*]		[*Real*]
Transcendental I	Noesis	Hyle	Noema	Transcendent Object

FIGURE 1.3. Basic structures of pure consciousness in *Ideen* I.

time there is not only a phenomenology of scientific consciousness ... but also a phenomenology of nature itself as the correlate of scientific consciousness" (p. 174).

Similarly, although psychological experiences are excluded from the domain of phenomenology, their noemas belong to it, and it is one of the tasks of phenomenology to describe how psychological experiences are constituted by pure consciousness.[17]

The investigation of such general structures of pure experience is of course supplemented by descriptions of more specific phenomena organized along different lines. The most important thematic orientation of Husserl's descriptive analysis in *Ideen* I is undoubtedly transcendent perception. However, there are many other themes that Husserl only addresses in a superficial way, even though he had investigated them in great detail in his previous works. These issues, such as time consciousness, lived body consciousness, and the perception of the other, are important for Husserlian phenomenology, and they played a major role in the investigations subsequent to those of *Ideen* I. In fact they are often seen as what Husserlian phenomenology is mainly, if not all, about, and for this reason they should be granted special attention here.

Time consciousness. If Husserl only briefly alluded to the problem of time in *Ideen* I, because he considered "the enigma of time consciousness"—to which he had previously devoted his *Vorlesungen zur Phänomenologie des inneren Zeitbewußtseins* (hereafter cited as *PZB*)—out of place in an introductory book, he nevertheless insists that the temporal dimension of pure experiences is the "absolute" foundation of all forms of object consciousness (§81).

The phenomenological analysis of time[18] is a clear illustration of the Husserlian project: it is an analysis of the temporality of pure consciousness as revealed by the bracketing of objective time, that is, by the time of natural objects, which Husserl also called mundane time. And the main goal of this analysis is to understand how this objective time, thus reduced to a mere phenomenon, is constituted by pure consciousness on the basis of its own specific temporality. Husserl focuses his investigation on the constitution of the phenomenon of duration of an object, such as an extended sound or a melody. In his eyes the main problem raised by the constitution of duration is that it cannot be understood if the time of pure consciousness itself is interpreted on the commonsensical model of a succession of discrete instants. He is thus led to his famous assertion that every present pure lived experience is also a retention of a past one and a protention toward a future one. In other words, there is no such thing as a pure instantaneous present in the temporality of pure consciousness.

This specific temporal structure is also what makes the self-constitution of the flux of pure lived experiences possible. In his 1905 lectures Husserl introduced the concept of "longitudinal intentionality" to designate this auto-constitutive activity by means of retentions and protentions, relabeling the intentional relation with transcendent objects "transversal intentionality." Indeed this temporal dimension lies primarily in the fact that pure experiences are integrated into a single continuous flux. And this continuous flux is, on the one hand, what serves as the ultimate basis of the constitution of transcendent objects, and on the other, not constituted by anything but itself. Therefore, it is not relative to anything. Being self-constituted, it is also absolute.

Lived body consciousness. In *Ideen* I Husserl does not elaborate either on the problem of the lived body (*Leib*) in spite of the substantial developments on the matter contained in his 1907 lectures (*Ding und Raum: Vorlesungen* [hereafter cited as *DR*]). Only in the second volume of the book, which was written later and posthumously published, does he come back to it. The main point of his analysis is to describe the constitution of the body and the key role played by body consciousness in the constitution of other spatiotemporal objects. Because of the emphasis put on visual perception in *Ideen* I, Husserl's theory conveys the impression of ignoring this role. In *Ideen* II, however, he gives full recognition to the general importance of movement in perception, and in particular to the movements of the body of the perceiving subject. These movements are the source of *kinesthesia*, a special kind of hyletic data, which are according to Husserl a basic element in the constitution both of the body of the perceiver and of the objects perceived. Consequently, in his analysis the perceptive consciousness of external objects is not separable from the consciousness of the body as a moving element. In this sense, perception cannot be assimilated to a form of mere contemplation: it is both incarnated and practically oriented.

However, Husserl also insists that the consciousness of the body involved in external perception cannot be simply equated with the perception of a privileged object. In his eyes it is of a different nature: it is a non-objective form of external consciousness. We do not apprehend our body as an external reality among others, but as something we are and live, as what Husserl terms with the appropriate German word *Leib*. He of course does not deny that we can also apprehend our body as a mere object, such as, for instance, when we see our hand as lying on a table instead of seeing it as a moving part of ourselves. In such a case our body is not apprehended as a *Leib* anymore but as a mere *Körper*.

Alterity and intersubjectivity. Husserlian transcendentalism is obviously vulnerable to the charge of solipsism in the sense in which I am the only consciousness and the world I constitute is my own world. In order to escape these problems made familiar by Descartes, Husserl was first led to admit the existence of other consciousnesses. To this end he devoted important analyses to the constitution of the consciousness of the other, most important, in his fifth *Cartesianische Meditationen*.[19] There he puts a strong emphasis on the role played in this process by the consciousness of the body of the other and the analogy we establish with the consciousness of our own. I get access to the other by perceiving her body (*Körper*), but her body, just like mine, is at the same time also apprehended as a *Leib*, that is, as the basis of an experience or a subjectivity. The duality of our body as *Leib* and *Körper* is somehow extended to the other and plays a key role in the constitution of the other as an *alter ego*.

It is nevertheless not enough to have the existence of other consciousnesses recognized, because this recognition immediately leads to the further problem of the plurality of worlds. Each one of these consciousnesses can constitute a world of its own. However, the idea of a plurality of worlds correlating to the plurality of consciousnesses contradicts our immediate experience of a common world. But constituting a common world, in the sense of a world which another consciousness can recognize as its own constituted world, is necessarily co-constituting this world. In other words, the notion of a common constituted world directly leads to the notion of a commonly constituted world, and therefore to that of a constitutive intersubjectivity.[20]

This difficulty is clearly connected with what Husserl calls the Cartesian approach to the reduction, namely, the idea that the reduction is a suspension of the belief in transcendent objects. This is why Husserl started exploring new ways of conceiving the transcendental reduction, and in particular to develop a notion of intersubjective reduction in his late manuscripts and in his 1936 *Die Krisis der europäischen Wissenschaften und die transzendentale Phänomenologie* (hereafter cited as *Krisis*). This hidden iceberg of Husserl's later works is slowly emerging thanks to the publication of his massive studies on constitution[21] and intersubjectivity.[22]

2.1.4. The Evolution of Husserl's Investigations

The sort of phenomenological analysis conducted in *Ideen* I typically takes as a starting point as well as a guideline a well-defined object, and then tries to understand how this object is constituted by the flux of pure experiences. It therefore assumes the previous constitution of this flux as well as that of a correlative ego and does not examine how they are themselves constituted. This is why Husserl came to call this form of phenomenological investigation a "static" phenomenology.

Although he realized its importance as early as 1905 in the course of his inquiry on temporality, it is only later, in the years 1917–21, that he attempted to complement this static phenomenology with a "genetic" one. The basic idea of genetic phenomenology is to push constitutional analysis further and to investigate the processes of auto-constitution of the ego and of the flux of pure experiences. In Husserl's eyes the ego is not a mere egological pole of intentional experiences, as the noetico-noematic framework of static intentionality implies. It also has a historical dimension in the sense that, through its continuous constitutional activity, it is progressively building up habits and properties, thereby making the present constitutions dependent upon the past ones. In his *Cartesianische Meditationen* Husserl writes: "But it is noted that this centering Ego is not an empty pole of identity, any more than any object is such. Rather, according to the law of 'transcendental generation,' with every act emanating from him and having a new objective sense, he acquires a new abiding property" (§32, trans. D. Cairns, p. 66). This process of enrichment of the ego drives Husserl to assert that "the ego constitutes himself for himself so to speak in the unity of a 'history'" (§37, Cairns trans., p. 75). Further, Anthony Steinbock (1995) has brought to light the need for a distinction within genetic constitution between genesis (*Genesis*) and generativity (*Generativität*). In the latter, the constitutional analysis is directed, not to the sphere of the subject-ego, but to the transcendent sphere of the intersubjective life-world. Roughly stated, by generativity Husserl means the process of becoming (whence generation) as well as that of articulation across time (whence the link to generations).[23]

2.2. HUSSERL'S ANTINATURALISM

2.2.1. Husserl's Fight Against Philosophical Naturalism

From this review of its essential tenets, it is immediately clear that one of the most salient features of phenomenology is its divergence from the natural sciences. As a matter of fact, phenomenology investigates a region of being that is not natural, first, because it is composed of essences, and second, because these essences are essences of pure lived experience. In addition, its descriptive form differs from the axiomatic one of the eidetic sciences of natural objects. In fact the whole point of Husserl's enterprise is to claim that there is a dimension of the mental that escapes the natural sciences and requires a specific kind of scientific investigation. And this dimension is all the more crucial because it is ontologically anterior to natural being, both psychological and physical. He writes for instance in §51 of *Ideen* I: ". . . there is such a thing as the field of pure consciousness, indeed, there is such a thing which is not a component part of Nature, and is so far from being one that Nature is possible only as an intentional unity motivated in transcendentally pure consciousness by immanent connections" (Kersten trans., p. 114)

It is actually possible to go one step further and say that as a science of the mind, Husserl's phenomenology is not only non-naturalist, it is antinaturalist. Indeed, in "Philosophie als strenge Wissenschaft" Husserl goes as far as writing, "We are fighting against the naturalization of consciousness" (our translation) and launches a more global attack on what he labels "philosophical naturalism." This philosophical naturalism can be defined in Husserlian terms as a general ontology and epistemology grounded in the conviction that transcendent intuition is the only kind of intuition we have, thereby refusing the admission of any non-spatiotemporal individual entity as well as any non-individual entity altogether. Against such a philosophical position, which Husserl correctly saw as dominant at the time when he wrote, phenomenology was to defend the natural rights of a more generous ontology, which permits the admission of both idealities and pure lived experiences. In other words, phenomenology is antinaturalist in the sense that its own fundamental theses stand in direct opposition to those of philosophical naturalism.

The belief in the possibility of a descriptive eidetics of pure lived experiences is not the only form taken by Husserl's antinaturalism. There are two other important ones that should at least be mentioned. On the one hand, Husserl was also one of the sharpest critics, at the turn of the century, of the idea that the only way for empirical psychology to be truly scientific is by being "an extrinsic model of natural science" (see his "Philosophie als strenge Wissenschaft"). On the other hand, under the impulse of Frege's criticism of his *Philosophie der Arithmetik*, he became the best advocate of logical antipsychologism (see the first volume of his *Logische Untersuchungen*) at a time when he had not yet clearly formulated his phenomenological project. The psychological interpretation of logic rested in his eyes on a fundamental confusion between judgment as a psychological event and judgment as a propositional content, thereby reducing logical laws to psychological laws, and therefore to a species of natural law. In stark opposition to this assimilation, which he saw as grounded upon the misguided refusal to acknowledge our capacity for eidetic intuition characteristic of philosophical naturalism, he claimed that propositional contents are ideal entities.

It should be underlined that in Husserl's eyes philosophical naturalism derives its strength from its continuity with common sense. In other words, it is natural attitude turned into a dogma. Nowhere more than in the theory of transcendental reduction is this continuity between naturalism and natural attitude better seen at work. Indeed transcendental reduction is nothing more than an artificial operation of denaturalization of the pure lived experience which is spontaneously naturalized in so-called natural attitude. We naturally apprehend the mental as something psychological. But a psychological lived experience is not radically different from a pure lived experience; on the contrary, it is a pure lived experience considered as belonging to a physical body. Husserl writes: "The pure 'mental process' lies, in a certain sense, within what is psychologically apprehended . . . ; while preserving its own essence, it takes on the form of a state of consciousness" (*Ideen* I, §53; Kersten trans., p. 126, adapted). Nevertheless, because of the relation established with the physical body the pure lived experience is transformed into something natural. In the same paragraph of *Ideen* I, Husserl also says: "[Pure consciousness] has become something other, a component part of Nature. In itself, it is what it is by its absolute essence. But it is not seized upon in this flowing thisness; it is instead apprehended as 'something'; and in this specifically peculiar apprehending a transcendence of a peculiar kind becomes constituted" (Kersten trans., p. 125). Accordingly, by neutralizing this natural tendency to apprehend the pure lived experience in relation with a physical body, transcendental reduction is a way of extracting it from its psychological envelope and therefore of denaturalizing it. In Husserl's words psychological lived experience "becomes a pure consciousness, it . . . no longer has the sense of an event in Nature" (ibid.). However, given that psychological lived experience is noematically constituted (cf. 2.1.3), phenomenology also contains a descriptive study of the embodiment of the mental, a theme of utmost importance in Husserl's later works. As we shall see, this theme provides one major avenue for the naturalization of the mental that will be explored in several contributions to this volume.

2.2.2. The Scientific Motives of Husserl's Antinaturalism

This brief review of the main forms assumed by Husserl's antinaturalism does not shed sufficient light on the motivations supporting it. Those motivations just mentioned can be considered philosophical, inasmuch as they appeal to considerations of a cognitive, epistemological, ontological, or methodological kind. However, Husserl's position also rests on more scientific grounds, a lesser-known aspect of his critical attitude vis-à-vis naturalism.

Indeed this attitude is also the result of the limitations of the scientific notions of his day, limitations Husserl thought impossible to overcome, making it thereby also impossible for the physico-mathematical sciences to offer a scientific reconstruction of the phenomenality of the surrounding world.

The impossibility of a physics of phenomenality. Everyone admitting the possibility of the mathematical physics of pure lived experience that would result from a naturalization of Husserl's phenomenological descriptions would certainly not dispute that formidable difficulties stand in the way of its realization. It would just as readily be admitted that, at the very least, such a mathematical physics would have to account for the noematic correlates of external perception and, as a consequence, for the corresponding forms and qualities of the sensible world that are perceptually apprehended and linguistically described in the natural attitude. In other words, the possibility of a mathematical physics of pure lived experience as described by Husserl presupposes, at a minimum, that of a mathematical physics of the qualitative manifestation of the world. However, Husserl was convinced that on this point mathematics and the sort of theoretical physics originating with Galileo were not up to the task, and for essential reasons having to do with the nature of axiomatization.

Indeed, as briefly explained in 2.1.2, in Husserl's eyes the fundamental characteristic of an axiomatics is to enable us to anticipate in a systematic way the eidetic intuition of the properties of the essences belonging to a certain region (see *Krisis*). And according to him this "unbelievable" possibility is rooted in the substitution of exact and consequently ideal essences for inexact and abstract ones.

However, this theoretical advantage is purchased at a high price in two of the domains where it is applied, namely, geometry as a science of forms and physics as a science of qualitatively filled forms. Indeed geometry could only become what it is because it has been "torn out" of the Heraclitean flux of sensible morphologies, because it has excluded the universe of "vague morphological essences" and inexact proto-geometrical forms akin to perception and natural language. Similarly, in Husserl's opinion, starting with Galileo, physics attempted for nature what mathematics had already achieved with geometry. It tried to axiomatize the sciences of material reality. But here again there is a reverse side to this ideal. Just as with geometry, first the Heraclitean flux of sensible morphologies, and then the sensible qualities across which phenomena are concretely given, had to be excluded. These proto-geometrical morphologies and these secondary qualities were considered impossible to mathematize. And Husserl thought that this limitation of the Galilean sciences was an insuperable one.

He did not, however, share the philosophical conclusion traditionally drawn from the recognition of such limitations with respect to the ontological status of sensible properties. Indeed, as a consequence of their falling out of reach of the mathematical tools used in the investigation of nature, they have usually been reduced to mere "subjective-relative" elements of a *psychological* kind, sheer appearances *in* the mind of the subject indicative of an underlying objectivity. Whence a "fundamental gap" between the physical being and its manifestation, as well as the substitution, for the prescientific world given in intuition, of a formal reconstruction of it; whence also the substitution, for the "concrete universal lawfulness" of nature, of a purely mathematical lawfulness.

However, Husserl saw that conclusion as self-contradictory. He claimed that it was inconsistent first to constitute scientific objectivity at the expense of manifestation, and then to take it as the cause of the morphologies and qualities that appear in manifestation. On the contrary, he claimed that:

> The physical thing is not alien to that which appears physically to the senses; it is announced in and through this appearance and indeed a priori (for unimpeachably eidetic reasons) cannot make itself known in a genuinely original way save in and through the latter. Henceforward, the sensible status of any determination of that X whose function is to uphold physical determinations can no longer be regarded as something alien to these same determinations and which hides them from view; on the contrary, it is only to the extent that this X is the subject of sensible determinations that it is also the subject of physical determinations, which, for their part, make themselves known in sensible determinations. (*Ideen* I, §52, Kersten trans., p. 125)

In short, according to Husserl, because of the intrinsic limitations of their axiomatic approach, the physical sciences do not and cannot do justice to the link between physical reality and phenomenal properties. A fortiori, they clearly could not in his mind be extended in such a way as to account for pure lived experience in both its noematic and noetic dimensions.

The impossibility of a geometrical descriptive eidetics. Husserl's rejection of a phenomenal physics is thus intrinsically connected with his opinion that geometry cannot be an axiomatic discipline and at the same time account for the forms and shapes actually encountered in immediate experience. In other words, it is indissociable from his idea that something like a geometrical descriptive eidetics, and more generally a mathematical or axiomatic eidetics of non-ideal and inexact essences, is impossible.

Nowhere more clearly perhaps than in the well-known contrast of phenomenology with geometry understood as the paradigm of all axiomatic eidetics, set out in §§71–75 of *Ideen* I, did Husserl make his opposition to such a science explicit. There he asks the following question: "Should one, or even can one, constitute phenomenology as a geometry of pure lived experience?" (*Ideen* I, §72, p. 165). And he gives it a sharply negative answer, arguing that "conceived as the descriptive science of essences, [phenomenology] belongs to a fundamental class of eidetic sciences, one which differs totally from the mathematical sciences" (ibid.). A scientific investigation of the essences of pure lived experiences cannot take the mathematical or axiomatic form best exemplified by geometry. Once again (cf. 2.1.2), this impossibility is in his eyes the result of a radical difference separating the exact essences and the ideal concepts of mathematics from the inexact and vague morphological essences involved in what we experience immediately, together with the descriptive concepts associated with them. Geometry could only be axiomatized at the cost of substituting ideal and fully determinable forms for the ones offered in sense perception. Hence this extraordinary opposition between the approach of geometry and the purely descriptive approach to be found at a certain stage of the investigation of nature: "The geometer is not interested in factual sensible intuitive shapes, as the descriptive natural scientist is. He does not, like the latter, fashion *morphological concepts* of vague configurational types which are directly seized upon on the basis of sensible intuition and which, in their vagueness, become conceptually and terminologically fixed" (*Ideen* I, §74, Kersten trans., p. 166, adapted).

Husserl was thus deeply convinced of a necessary incompatibility between the general nature of phenomenological data (in both their loose and technically Husserlian senses) and the basic requirements of mathematization, thereby introducing a sharp contrast between phenomenology and the Galilean sciences of nature.

This point is of crucial importance for any naturalizing program of Husserlian phenomenology. It is our general contention indeed (see section 3) that phenomenological descriptions of any kind can only be naturalized, in the sense of being integrated into the general framework of natural sciences, if they can be mathematized. We see mathematization as a key instrument for naturalization, being in fact consonant on this point with Husserl himself although drawing opposite conclusions from it. Accordingly, if the opposition he introduced between mathematics and his phenomenological investigations cannot be overcome, naturalizing Husserlian phenomenology is bound to be a desperate research program from the start.

However, we believe (see 3.3) that Husserl's position is the result of having mistaken certain contingent limitations of the mathematical and material sciences of his time for absolute ones. In our opinion it is indeed arguable that scientific progress has made Husserl's position on this point largely obsolete and that this *factum rationis* puts into question the properly scientific foundations of his antinaturalism.

3. THE NATURALIST REVERSAL OF HUSSERLIAN PHENOMENOLOGY

The project of integrating a phenomenological investigation of a Husserlian kind into the contemporary sciences of cognition therefore leads to an obvious paradox. On the one hand, this investigation should be not only descriptive but also explanatory and naturalist in the sense of accounting for the existence and nature of phenomenological data on the basis of lower levels of explanation, and in particular of the mathematical models of the neurobiological level of explanation. On the other hand, Husserlian phenomenology is intrinsically rooted in a perspective quite at variance with that of naturalist explanation, and in fact quite opposed to it. Once again, far from being a new branch of the natural sciences, Husserlian phenomenology claims to incarnate a new sort of knowledge epistemologically and ontologically different from them, and furthermore capable of founding them all.

Linking Husserlian descriptions of cognitive phenomena and the contemporary sciences of cognition thus seems to require cutting Husserlian phenomenology from its antinaturalist roots, that is to say, naturalizing it. Is this possible? And if so, how? We will now give an overview of the main motives for favoring a positive answer to the first of these two questions, and then turn to an examination of the second in sections 4 and 5.

3.1. THE PROBLEM OF NATURALIZATION

It is first necessary to delineate further the notion of naturalization as it is used today in the context of the sciences of cognition. The expression is sometimes made so vague that one could doubt it designates a well enough articulated project. But while there certainly are different ways of naturalizing a science of cognition, the problem of naturalization itself is something quite definite.

In the first place it is a problem with a history, and a glimpse at this history is enough to get an understanding of its most essential elements. The origins of the difficulty can be legitimately traced back to the first philosophical meditations on the question of the unity of scientific knowledge, but it owes its modern formulation mainly to the invention of mechanics in the seventeenth century. The scientific achievement represented by the invention of a mathematical theory of movement raised it again with special acuteness in the following new form:

1. Wherein lies the specificity of the sort of scientific knowledge illustrated by mechanics, and to what extent can it be extended to phenomena other than movement?
2. Is it necessary, in order to possibly extend it to other domains of investigation, to ontologically unify these domains and consider them as constituted of entities of the same sort as moving bodies?

At the end of the nineteenth century these two questions gave rise to an important debate about the relationships between the sciences of nature and the sciences of mind, which was largely initiated by W. Dilthey and which can be legitimately seen as the direct antecedent of the current discussions about naturalizing the sciences of cognition.[24] Opposing the ideas expressed by John Stewart Mill in 1843, Dilthey defended the thesis that the *Geisteswissenschaften* (in the general sense of the science of cultural formations) are concerned with a domain heterogeneous to that of the *Naturwissenschaften*, and accordingly require both a different problematic and a different methodology. While the *Naturwissenschaften* explain material entities, the *Geisteswissenschaften* provide an understanding of nonmaterial ones having the special property of being endowed with meaning. The contemporary project of elaborating a naturalist theory of cognitive phenomena can therefore be construed as a direct attempt at refuting the cleavage introduced by Dilthey and his various followers, including Husserl.[25]

As such, this project is thus centered around two main issues. The first one is epistemological: can we adequately account for the mental dimension of cognitive phenomena by adopting the explanatory form of questioning and the experimental methodology used in the investigation of natural phenomena? The second one is ontological: is it possible to transform mental cognitive properties into natural ones? And if so, how? In this context the notion of natural property refers first to neurobiological properties, but it should be taken in a broader way as designating the whole set of properties postulated by the most fundamental sciences of nature, however abstract these properties might actually be and whatever their philosophical interpretation.

The problem of the logical priority between the epistemological and the ontological sides of the naturalization problem has been at the center of many discussions in the development of the *Geisteswissenschaften* and *Naturwissenschaften* debate. In the contemporary context of the sciences of cognition, it is fairly straightforward to say that the ontological aspect of the naturalization problem is seen as by far the more important as well as the more difficult of the two. It is therefore necessary to understand quite clearly what is involved in it.

The definition of the ontological problem of naturalization just given could indeed look insufficient. Can't it after all be said that a dualist theory such as Descartes's also intends to show how mental properties can belong to a material entity and thus to transform them into natural ones? The problem is that dualism resorts to a specific substance in its demonstration and consequently does not treat mental properties as authentically natural. Mental properties belong only indirectly to the body. The distinctive feature of the naturalist perspective is, on the contrary, to try to transform these properties into properties sensu stricto of the body, or more generally of natural entities as characterized by the physical sciences.

It should thus be clear that eliminativism, that is, the elimination of all mental levels of explanation, cannot fulfill this requirement. It certainly represents a naturalist form of the investigation of cognitive phenomena, but not a naturalizing one. Mental properties are a priori eliminated and not transformed into natural equivalents.

In a similar fashion, a naturalist transformation of mental properties cannot be achieved through the mere elaboration of a neurobiological counterpart, in the sense of a neurobiological explanation parallel to the mentalist one. And the reason is, once again, that the real difficulty is to make understandable the very fact that what is amenable to a neurobiological explanation is also amenable to a mental explanation. It is consequently not enough to pile up levels of explanation; they have to be integrated into a single hierarchized explanatory framework that demonstrates their mutual compatibility.

This is also why it is not sufficient simply to assert the naturalist character of the mental level of explanation by treating de facto mental properties as properties of a natural entity such as the central nervous system and the body at large. This attitude amounts to no more than a form of naturalist dogmatism, leaving perfectly unanswered the problem of naturalizing mental properties and reproducing the error of vitalism. As a matter of fact, vitalism accepted that biological phenomena cannot be accounted for without resorting to specific properties heterogeneous with the properties introduced by the physical sciences. However, it certainly did not reject the idea that a living organism is a natural entity in a physico-chemical sense. It only rejected the idea that it is no more than that. However, vitalism offered no satisfactory explanation for the possession of nonchemical and nonphysical properties by a physico-chemical entity.

In the same manner, merely postulating that mental properties sensu stricto belong to an entity endowed with neurobiological properties is a way of treating them as natural properties, and accordingly of naturalizing them, but without giving any justification for doing so. On the contrary, the heart of the problem of naturalization is to make intelligible the fact that one entity can have both the properties characteristic of matter and those characteristic of mentality in spite of an apparent heterogeneity between them. This problem can only be answered by making this heterogeneity vanish, and thus transforming in one way or another the characterization of the mental properties.

Finally, it is important to emphasize that this definition of the ontological problem remains a preliminary one. Its only ambition is to provide a clearer picture of an intellectual operation whose specific nature can come fully to light only in the course of its very realization. As a matter of fact, one of our main concerns is to reexamine the usual concept of naturalization in order to lay bare its possible limitations and insufficiencies. In other words, the question we want to ask is not just how Husserlian phenomenology can be naturalized, but what is really involved in the process of naturalizing a scientific theory if it turns out to be possible to naturalize Husserlian phenomenological descriptions in order to reach an adequate science of cognition?

3.2. NATURALIZATION AS A RECATEGORIZATION OF ONTOLOGIES

One point in this regard deserves special emphasis. According to the definition just offered, the problem of naturalization can be considered as a special case of a more general process of recategorization of the ontological divisions of reality recurrent in the development of scientific ideas. Indeed it has been characterized as the problem of understanding how the essential properties of objects classified in a certain ontological division (the mental one) can be made to belong to objects classified in a separate and different one (matter, to put it briefly), thereby transforming the ontological categorization of the former and doing away with a time-honored opposition. Now all such transformations previously realized in the course of history seem to share an important number of basic features.

The paradigmatic example is of course the emergence of classical mechanics, which can be said to result from the *neutralization* of a conflict between the "sublunar" and the "supralunar" worlds through the establishment of a *new* division of scientific objectivity. This ontological recategorization was of a "revolutionary" nature and stemmed in part from an entirely new technological practice (that of the engineers). Four of its main characteristics should be stressed:

1. At the time of Galileo and Newton the ontological opposition between the supralunar and sublunar worlds was drawn from common sense and regarded as irreducible. Also considered as the foundation of a methodologi-

cal and epistemological division, it was linked with numerous other oppositions, such as those between the necessary and the contingent, the divine and the human, the eternal and the corruptible, and it had been the subject of metaphysical discussion for centuries. Classical mechanics overcame that fundamental ontological disjunction through the recognition of new common properties in the sublunar and supralunar phenomena of movement, including universal gravitation.

2. An essential condition for such a destruction of the sublunar/supralunar ontological scheme was that movement was characterized by classical mechanics in terms sufficiently abstract to make it independent from the specific ontological composition of the moving entities. As soon as inertial mass has been ascribed to such entities, they become susceptible to movement. The explanation of gravitational phenomena only brings to bear relations of distance, forces and fields, that is, entities and spatiotemporal processes of propagation that are themselves indifferent to the traditional ontological divisions. Accordingly, classical mechanics represents an abstract level of explanation.

3. Most important, classical mechanics opened the road to the mathematical reconstruction of the entire diversity of the phenomena of movement. By means of equations expressing general physical principles, a "computational synthesis" of these phenomena can be carried out with remarkable precision. Thanks to an appropriate mathematical interpretation (requiring in fact the highly sophisticated techniques of integral and differential calculus, of Poincaré's qualitative dynamics, of complex dynamical systems theory, and of symplectic geometry) concepts can be transformed into algorithms capable of generating a diversity of constructed (computed) phenomena that can then be placed in relation (right up to complete coincidence) with the data of observation.

4. Finally, this abstract level of mechanical explanation was later progressively integrated into the subsequent developments of lower-level physical and chemical explanations, in particular with the atomic theory of matter, and thereby naturalized.

The evolution of several of the physical sciences has been dominated by transformations of this kind, that is, by the destruction of an ontological division through the discovery of a new set of properties opening the doors of a unifying level of investigation with a sufficient degree of abstraction and mathematization to be later articulated with lower-level disciplines. They make it possible to reconstruct within a new single framework phenomena previously seen as belonging to very different regions of reality, and then to proceed to their naturalization.

This general schema looks equally appropriate for the analysis of the current efforts to achieve a naturalization of the mental. A key element to the transformation of mental properties into natural ones has indeed been provided by two "scientific revolutions," namely, the emergence of a theory of computational processes as well as of a theory of the self-organization of complex systems. We already made reference (see 1.1) to these two major scientific achievements when discussing the different trends within modern Cognitive Science: a sophisticated theory of computation lies at the root of the classical symbolic approach, and theories of complexity were at the basis of the shift to connectionism and to its further elaboration as embodied Cognitive Science. After leading to the collapse of the classical ontological opposition between the physical and the vital, thereby paving the way for modern biological theories, the emergence of this general science of the computational and organizational features of complex systems is now promoting the collapse of the ontological opposition between body and mind, in much the same way as the emergence of classical mechanics ruined the division between the sub- and the supra-lunar. Although not perfect, the parallel is quite remarkable indeed.

1. The point of departure is an ontological distinction drawn from common sense, considered as irreducible and debated metaphysically for centuries, namely, that between the physical and the mental realms.
2. As a result of the development of computer and information theory as well as of mathematical theories of (self-) organization, new elements are being disclosed which cut across these two ontological categories and are consequently independent of them.
3. A reconstruction (in the sense of an effective mathematical synthesis) of the diversity of mental phenomena by means of algorithms derived from computational and organizational theories is thereby made possible.
4. Finally, the problem of naturalization also receives a well-defined formulation: namely, integrating this mathematical reconstruction of mental phenomena into the lower-level sciences of natural phenomena.

Now, the main idea in this essay is that this general process of recategorization of the mental can be extended to phenomenological data themselves. In other words, its general hypothesis is that, when provided with adequate characterizations such as those conducted along the lines of Husserlian phenomenology, phenomenological data can be adequately reconstructed on the basis of the main tenets of Cognitive Science, and then integrated into the natural sciences. Naturalization is thus seen as including the three following stages:

(1) Phenomenological data ⟶ Husserlian description ⟶
(2) mathematization ⟶ algorithms ⟶
(3) naturalistic account

More detailed formulations of this hypothesis, as well as attempts at giving it concrete illustration, are to be found in some of the following contributions (see Petitot and Varela). Suffice it to add here that in this perspective a key role is granted to mathematics because it alone is seen as capable of generating naturalistically implementable reconstructions of phenomenological data.

3.3. THE OPENNESS TO NATURALIZATION OF HUSSERL'S THOUGHT

On the basis of this clarification of how we understand the general project of naturalizing Husserlian phenomenology, it is important to indicate that despite his own strongly antinaturalist statements, Husserl himself clearly admitted a certain form of naturalization of his phenomenological descriptions. And it is arguable that, by doing so, he paved the way for the more radical transformation we advocate. This point is a fairly technical as well as delicate one, and it cannot be dealt with in sufficient detail here. We will only substantiate this claim with three general remarks.

First, Husserl explicitly acknowledges the possibility that the proper domain of phenomenology might one day become the object of an eidetic investigation that is no longer simply descriptive but rather axiomatic, thereby providing a sort of mathematical counterpart to the descriptive theory of pure lived experiences (cf. 3.3.1). Second, he readily admits that his transcendentalist conception of the constitution of natural objects is logically compatible with a realist and causal theory of perception in the sphere of the natural attitude (cf. 3.3.2). Finally, by maintaining the necessity for a psychology understood as an empirical investigation of embodied pure lived experiences and at the same time requiring that psychological theories be founded upon and consonant with phenomenological descriptions of pure lived experiences, he accepts the idea that descriptions with an identical content but a different epistemological value can be achieved within the natural attitude.

3.3.1. The "Scientific Counterpart" of Descriptive Phenomenology

We have seen how forcefully Husserl argues in §§71–75 of *Ideen* I for the impossibility of a mathematics of pure lived experiences. However, with his familiar lack of dogmatism as well as impressive intellectual acuteness, he concludes his development on an open note:

> True, we have not attempted to respond to one urgent question: looking at the entire eidetic domain of phenomena subjected to the reduction . . . , can

we find room, within this domain and alongside our descriptive procedures, for an idealizing procedure that would replace what is intuitively given with pure and rigorously defined objects? If so, the latter could then serve as a basic instrument for a mathematics of lived experience and would feature as the counterpart to any *descriptive* phenomenology. (*Ideen* I, §75, p. 173)

Such recognition of the possibility of a mathematical "counterpart" to phenomenological description is of fundamental importance. It reveals that Husserl's opposition is directed less at the notion of a mathematics of pure lived experience than at the idea that such a mathematized discipline could fulfill the same function as a descriptive one. Indeed his opinion is that even if new mathematical tools more appropriate to phenomenological data than the mathematics of his time could be invented, they would still result in a discipline unraveling the eidetic properties of an idealized form of such data, and not of the data "themselves."

However, if today such a mathematical counterpart can be shown to be not only a reality but in fact also able to characterize phenomenological data just as they are given (thereby overcoming the opposition between the ideal and the real), it is then arguable that his theory came very close to acknowledging the possibility of a naturalist reversal in the sense intended here.

3.3.2. Reciprocity Between Phenomenological Constitution and Natural Causality

Another way to naturalization left open by Husserl is the reciprocity that, according to him, operates between the transcendental constitution of natural realities on the basis of pure lived experiences and the causal explanation of the associated psychological lived experiences on the basis of these same natural realities. The point is best illustrated by three-dimensional external objects. In *Ding und Raum*, Husserl goes to great lengths to analyze the constitution of three-dimensional objects on the basis of the flux of their two-dimensional adumbrations in the visual field, and then explains how an *inversion* of attitude is possible. Starting out from externally objective constituted space and from the "I-pole" (the origin of a system of coordinates adapted to our own body) rather than from the constitutive processes themselves, that is, by adopting the natural rather than the phenomenological attitude, a flux of empirical two-dimensional images can be interpreted *as if* our body were embedded in three-dimensional objective space, as if the ocular-motor field were a surface fragment defined by the position of this body and three-dimensional external objects were projected upon it. As he puts it: "From a formal point of view therefore, the manifold of these [adumbrations] can be treated in exactly the same way as the projections of a geometrical body upon a plane surface" (*DR*, §69, p. 241). This is all-important, since it means that "from a formal point of view," which is precisely that of an appropriate mathematical reconstruction, an *equivalence* can be found between the phenomenological constitutive approach and the objective causalist one.

3.3.3. Pure and Embodied Lived Experiences

Finally, Husserl himself insisted on numerous occasions on the fact that the foundational position of phenomenology with regard to psychology makes it possible to preserve the content of phenomenological descriptions within the natural attitude, at least at the level of what he calls, in *Cartesianische Meditationen*, a pure eidetic psychology. At §76 of *Ideen* I (p. 176) he writes: "Any phenomenological affirmation bearing upon absolute consciousness can be interpreted in terms of eidetic psychology (the latter, upon close inspection, is to be sharply distinguished from phenomenology)." Husserl was never sufficiently specific about the nature of the relations obtaining between the different levels he distinguished in the investigation of lived experience; constantly postponing their full clarification, he regarded them as a matter of great complexity. It is nevertheless clear enough that pure eidetic psychology is for him unlike experimental psychology in that it investigates the essence of psychological facts (this what makes it eidetic) and disregards the natural dimension that lived experience acquires by virtue of being connected with a body (this is what makes it pure), but without for all that leaving the field of the natural attitude, that is to say, without first going through a transcendental reduction. As a result, Husserl clearly introduced the possibility of preserving the substance of the descriptive discoveries of phenomenology while still refusing to acknowledge the existence of the ontological region of pure lived experience. Thus we find him writing at §35 of his *Cartesianische Meditationen* (p. 107): "When, on the basis of the natural attitude, we strive for a psychology, as a positive science and, first of all, for that pure intentional psychology that this positive science demands . . . we can make use of all of the fundamental analyses which we have just carried out, by simply subjecting them to a few small modifications." And again at §57: "Every analysis and every theory of transcendental phenomenology—including the theory of the transcendental constitution of the objective world—can be developed at the natural level, by simply abandoning the transcendental attitude" (p. 159).

As minor as these difference might be in terms of descriptive content, they nevertheless remain, in Husserl's eyes, major ones from a philosophical point of view. They include nothing less than what separates a naturalistic realism from a transcendental idealism. And indeed Husserl is careful to note that they "obviously nullify the transcendental status" of phenomenological descriptions. However, by acknowledging such a close parallelism between the content of phenomenological descriptions and the results obtained at a certain level of psychological investigation, he implicitly admitted the possibility of dissociating the specific philosophical interpretation he hoped to confer upon his descriptions from what one is tempted to call their scientific content. Further, this dissociation is inseparable from a certain form of naturalization, since eidetic psychology is, in his eyes, a discipline that belongs within the fold of the natural sciences in the same way that eidetic physics does.

3.4. ANTECEDENTS FOR A NATURALIST REORIENTATION OF HUSSERLIAN PHENOMENOLOGY

Another indication in favor of the possibility of the sort of naturalist reversal of Husserlian phenomenology proposed here is to be derived from Husserl's descent. Indeed a number of his followers reoriented his phenomenolgical perspective into a new direction which on many counts can be considered as a naturalist one.

Thanks to the research carried out by Karl Schuhmann, the important role played by the work of Johannes Daubert (1877–1947)[26] in the development of the phenomenological movement is now well established. A very influential philosopher from Munich and one of the first defenders of the *Logische Untersuchungen*, Daubert was, according to Karl Schuhmann and Barry Smith, "the true architect of the phenomenological movement." His main concern was with "the subject's cognitive relation to the world, mainly to the world of nature," and he developed a naturalist alternative to Husserl's notion of a transcendentally constituting consciousness.

Daubert granted absolute primacy to perception as a way of relating to the world and described it as a "direct awareness." This "direct awareness" (*Innesein*) he understood as an immediate and certain type of evidence, as well as a pre-predicative mode of experience arising out of the active engagement of a living being with its environment. On this basis he set about criticizing Husserl's idealism, rejecting in particular his distinction between noema and transcendent object. As a consequence, Daubert also rejected the independence of consciousness, the most crucial step of his critique of Husserlianism. He conceived of consciousness as something that can only exist in connection with the world and simply acquires autonomy through an act of reflection, thereby dismissing the idea of its ontological specificity as groundless. Consciousness was for him no more than a *function* that cannot be isolated by neutralization, *ēpochē*, or reduction.

Among the second wave of thinkers that picked up the lines opened by Husserl, Maurice Merleau-Ponty has had a durable influence on a certain opening to the naturalization enterprise. His philosophical perspective is complex and multifarious. Nevertheless, there are two main axes of his work that bear directly upon our concerns.

The first and foremost is his analysis of the primacy of perception and the body, a concern that appears throughout his thinking in his early writings, *La Structure du comportment* (1942) and *Phénoménologie de la perception* (1945), until his unfinished opus *Le Visible et l'invisible* (1964). His early books are marked by an abundance of explicit references to the neurosciences and psychology of his time. He does not hesitate to draw from basic and clinical material. In this he was particularly influenced by Kurt Goldstein's theories of the organism and the Gestalt psychologists Kurt Koffka and Wolfgang Köhler. For instance, in discussing the body as it appears in intero- and exteroception he introduces quite forcefully the evidence stemming from the phenomenon of a phantom limb.[27] Merleau-Ponty's interest in perception is not about the act of perception but about the way the perceived world *appears*, and in this he systematically gave the "mechanistic physiology" short shrift. His move was to turn to the body as the locus of the experiencing subject. This represented a daring departure from Husserl's transcendental leaning most in view during Merleau-Ponty's time, although, as we have seen, this concern is hardly absent from Husserl's own writings (cf. 2.1.3). It emphasizes the importance of grounding phenomenological analysis in the dimension of embodiment that entails an openness to the world, where perception is not understood just as a mediator between world and consciousness. This dimension of embodiment will reappear in later phenomenologists, and is represented also in this volume as it links with the current for an embodied cognitive science (see 4.2).

The second axis can be found in his lesser known views about *Naturphilosophie*, reframed in phenomenological terms. In some of his last lectures at the Collège de France (collected in Merleau-Ponty 1968 and 1996) he sought to understand the relationship between natural organizations, phenomenological appearing, lived experience, and meaning. In order to do this, he showed that, in addition to an eidetic description, one needs *a dynamic theory of forms and structures* to explain the "flux of determination," the "morphogenetic gradients" of natural morphologies, that is, to account for the manner in which "the organization invests physical space" on a physical, biochemical, thermodynamic, and even "cybernetic" basis. One needs a "phenomenal topology" (an admirable expression) and a "phenomenological *phusis*" to understand "the emergence of original macrophenomena, which are singular spatial loci, from between microphenomena."

Aron Gurwitsch and Ervin Strauss could be cited as two further examples of a naturalist reorientation of Husserlian phenomenology. But in his key although still little known book *Le Monde comme realité et répresentation* (1974) Roger Chambon probably was the most successful of all in posing the problem of the ontological and epistemological status of a transcendent objective being possessing within itself the conditions of possibility of its own phenomenalization.

Adopting at the outset the perspective of naturalistic monism, Chambon's central concern is indeed with understanding how natural entities can manifest themselves to the human perceiving organism. And his main thesis is that the traditional understanding of perception as a cognitive act built up on the basis of sensorial receptivity does not exhaust the problem of perceptibility. In his opinion, perceptibility is rooted in the very nature of the things perceived, which raises the following problem: "How does a world have to be if it is to bear within itself the potentiality for its own appearing?" (Chambon 1974: 17). In order to answer this question, it proves necessary to recast the very idea of nature and modify accordingly our modern conceptions of objectivity, subjectivity, and knowledge. And Chambon's strategy in trying to carry out this philosophical task is to use the findings of phenomenology as *constraints* upon the development of the notion of nature. Finally, in this perspective consciousness itself is seen as stemming from the phenomenalization of the natural world and is deprived of any ontological autonomy.

3.5. CRITICISM OF THE SCIENTIFIC MOTIVES OF HUSSERL'S ANTINATURALISM

Finally, it can be argued that most of the genuinely scientific reasons that Husserl might have had for refusing to allow his phenomenology to be integrated into the field of the natural sciences, and that were rapidly presented in 2.2.2, have been invalidated by progress in the sciences and can now be regarded as false. One can even say that their invalidation provided the deeper philosophical significance of certain major contemporary scientific innovations. In a certain sense, Husserl focused his attention on scientific "holes" destined to be filled by phenomenology as an *alternative* to the sciences of his time. But these holes have in fact been filled by crucial advances in the natural and mathematical sciences. By transforming the historical situation of Husserlian phenomenology with regard to scientific knowledge, these very advances have removed the main obstacle standing in the way of its naturalization.

3.5.1. Elements of a Physics of Phenomenality

With respect to natural morphologies, we already noted at 3.2 that there do now exist *physical* theories of qualitative manifestation. These are physico-mathematical theories (such as those dealing with catastrophes, attractors and bifurcations of nonlinear dynamical systems, critical phenomena and symmetry breakings, self-organization and critical self-organizing states, nonlinear thermodynamics and dissipative structures, and so on) which make it possible to explain how small-scale ("microscopic") units can get organized into large scale ("macroscopic") emergent structures on the basis of coordinated (cooperative and conflictual) collective behavior situated at an intermediary ("mesoscopic") level.[28]

Such theories represent the first steps of a qualitative physics of phenomenal morphologies, of what could be termed a "pheno-physics." They show how the morphologically emergent "macro" level gets organized essentially around the singularities—qualitative discontinuities—of the underlying "micro" processes, singularities which are phenomenologically dominant and structure the appearing. They therefore demonstrate that what Husserl called "inexact morphological essences," essences foreign to fundamental classical physics, are indeed amenable to a physical account, provided that we rely upon the qualitative macrophysics of complex systems (and no longer upon the microphysics of elementary systems). Our understanding of the phenomenalization of physical objectivity in terms of macro qualitative structures is constantly improving, thereby making obsolete the difficulties on which Husserl grounded his claim of the impossibility of a physics of phenomenality.

3.5.2. Elements of a Morphological Descriptive Eidetics

The same can be said of the idea of a morphological descriptive geometry. To be sure, it is not easy to see how one could directly "axiomatize" the diversity of natural forms to make of them a "definite manifold" (*Mannigfaltigkeit*). But what Husserl could not have foreseen is that they can be modeled by means of tools taken from differential geometry and topology. This is indeed precisely what has happened with the morphodynamical models mentioned earlier. To this extent the latter can be seen as the first example of a geometrical descriptive eidetics designed for inexact morphological essences.[29] They do indeed meet at least two of the distinguishing criteria of descriptive eidetics according to Husserl:

1. They operate in a descriptive fashion in the sense of proceeding by abstraction and categorization (versus idealization), thereby providing a qualitative classification of the individuated spatial forms we actually experience as well as of their singularities.
2. They allow us to construct morphological concepts bearing on inexact types of forms. Indeed, they have been frequently accused of sharing this characteristic with the descriptive concepts of natural languages.

It is thus arguable that such models amount to more than just a simple "scientific counterpart" to phenomenology in the sense given at 3.3.1. They represent a genuine mathematical descriptive eidetics (a *contradictio in terminis* for Husserl) to the extent that, in spite of being mathematical, its concepts are not ideal but adequate to the determinations of the phenomenological data. By contrast, the counterpart Husserl contemplated as a possibility remained a science of ideal essences. Given the pivotal role of mathematization in naturalization, the emergence of this new kind of mathematical theory is an additional argument in favor of the possibility of achieving a naturalization of Husserlian phenomenology.

4. THE RENEWAL OF HUSSERLIAN PHENOMENOLOGY

In addition to finding support in Husserl himself, in the orientation given to his work by some of his followers, and in the evolution of scientific knowledge, it can be argued that the project presented here receives precious help from a recent renewal of Husserlian phenomenology, either by being provided with immediate bases for further investigation or through the demonstration that certain lines of inquiry should be put aside. The various investigations responsible for this renewal of Husserlian phenomenology can be organized in two different categories, although some of them clearly belong to both. On the one hand is a series of works of a purely critical nature, dealing exclusively with the interpretation and assessment of Husserlian phenomenology—and that of Husserl himself in particular—and on the other hand is a number of proposals oriented more toward theory-construction which share the concern of integrating phenomenology into the contemporary sciences of cognition.

We will offer here a short presentation of a few of them in order to shed some light on what we actually see as decisive contributions to our project, and also to make its specificity more apparent in the context of this Husserlian renewal.

4.1. THE ANALYTICAL AND THE COGNITIVIST READINGS OF HUSSERL

Priority should be given to what is frequently called the analytical and the cognitivist readings of Husserl, many protagonists of which also are contributors to this volume. These two interpretations of Husserl have played a major role: the first one in renewing the interpretation of the relationships between Husserl and the founding fathers of analytical philosophy, and the second one in opening the confrontation of Husserlian phenomenology with contemporary sciences of cognition. They are closely connected with each other, as the collection edited by Hubert Dreyfus and H. Hall shows; this book marks an important stage in the process of a cognitive reorientation of Husserlian phenomenology, although its limitations have grown clearer over time.[30]

4.1.1. Two Analytical Readings: Dagfinn Føllesdal and J. Hintikka

The expression "analytical reading of Husserl" refers primarily to Føllesdal's 1969 article, "Husserl's Notion of Noema," in which Føllesdal claims that Husserl's analysis of intentionality is parallel to Frege's analysis of sign. Yet to call this an analytical reading is somewhat misleading, for doing so might suggest that Føllesdal performs a Fregeanization of the Husserlian theory of intentionality, while in fact Føllesdal's main point, developed in a series of eleven clearly stated theses for the most part quite uncontroversial, is simply that Husserl's concept of noema offers substantial analogies with the concept of linguistic meaning as defined in the first of his own logical investigations. And it is only because of the resemblance between this concept of meaning and the one forged by Frege that Føllesdal further introduces the idea that the Husserlian theory of intentionality includes in every intentional content an element playing the same role as the *Sinn* does in every semantic content according to Frege's analysis. The real question raised by Føllesdal's contribution is therefore the following one: does Husserl assimilate the general structure of the intentional state to that of a linguistic symbol (and incidentally of a linguistic symbol conceived in Fregean terms)? Føllesdal's article does not say anything that explicit, although it sounds like a natural conclusion to draw from his remarks.[31]

Hintikka is probably to be credited with the most explicit and concise statement of such a thesis in his article "The Phenomenological Dimension" (1995), where he radicalizes Føllesdal's analysis by asserting the equivalence of the following terms:

$$\frac{\text{Husserl:}\quad \text{act}}{\text{Frege:}\quad \text{expression}} = \frac{\text{noema}}{Sinn} = \frac{\text{object}}{Bedeutung}$$

According to Hintikka, the Husserlian noema is to the intentional object and the intentional part of the pure lived experience as the Fregean *Sinn* is to the referent and the expression. This interpretation unequivocally assimilates the Husserlian general structure of the intentional state to the general structure of a symbol as seen by Frege.

4.1.2. A Cognitivist Reading: Dreyfus

The expression "cognitivist reading of Husserl" applies in the first place to the interpretation of Husserlian phenomenology defended by H. Dreyfus in the introduction to *Husserl, Intentionality, and Cognitive Science* (Dreyfus and Hall 1982). In this pioneering work, Dreyfus wants to show that Husserl can be considered the founding father of classical Cognitive Science. His attitude toward Husserl is in fact an ambivalent one. On the one hand, he seems to see in Husserl's noematic analysis a more convincing version of computational representationalism than can be found in many of its contemporary heirs: the very notion of noema offers in his eyes a better understanding of the intentional dimension of consciousness. But on the other hand, although he welcomes the break with the "linguistic turn" represented by the return of the theory of mind to the foreground of the philosophical scene, Dreyfus is a well-known opponent of the idea that cognitive processes are no more than computational ones. Accordingly, he thinks that Husserl's phenomenology is fundamentally mistaken as a theory of cognition and is of limited help to contemporary cognitive science. A closer look at this criticism is clearly in order because of its widespread implications for the image of Husserlian phenomenology within the Cognitive Science community.

According to Dreyfus, Husserl's phenomenology converted into a form of Fodorian computational theory of cognition through the famous transcendental turn taken at the time of the first volume of his *Ideas*. Dreyfus substantiates his claim with three main arguments:

1. Ontological neutrality: The transcendental reduction opens the doors of an ontological neutrality similar to the one resulting from the adoption of methodological solipsism by Fodor.

2. Rule-governed processes: The emergence of the noematic level of description, which is part and parcel of the transcendental turn, amounts to a substantial transformation of the role played by intentional content. Its function is no longer simply to determine the nature of the intentional object in the same way as the sense of an expression determines its extension, but also to make the intentional relation with that object possible. Indeed Dreyfus sees the Husserlian noema as playing three main roles: referring to an object and thereby making consciousness intentional, describing the various properties of that object by means of predicates, and finally synthesizing these properties in such a way that they are apprehended as the properties of one and the same object. Husserl's phenomenology thus becomes a theory of the mental conditions of possibility of the intentional relation, that is to say, a transcendental theory. But as such it is intrinsically connected with a conception of cognition as a rule-governed activity. And this is the reason why the transcendental turn can be assimilated to a transfomation from a purely representationalist conception of intentionality (à la Searle) to a Fodorian one, where priority is given to the discovery of the rules governing the synthetic activity of the mind.

3. Formality: Dreyfus pushes his assimilation one step further by considering that the rules governing the processes of transcendental constitution are formal ones. Indeed he conceives the constitutional process as an application to primitive elements labeled "sense-predicates" of two sorts of rules, rules of combination and rules of synthesis, and he assimilates these predicates with symbolic forms that differ in no way from the syntactic forms of linguistic symbols (Dreyfus and Hall 1982: 10). As a consequence, Dreyfus's interpretation is compatible with the idea that a Husserlian intentional state is a sort of mental linguistic symbol, or at least is crucially related to such a symbol. This cognitivist reading differs substantially from the analytical one, despite Dreyfus's claim that his analysis derives from Føllesdal's. Indeed, although he lacks clarity on this point, Dreyfus seems to understand these symbolic elements as the primitive constituents of noemas ("the sense-predicates"); on the contrary, in Føllesdal's and Hintikka's versions, the noema itself is a sense and not a symbol. This symbolic aspect of his interpretation plays a major role in his rejection of Husserl's phenomenology in favor of the work of Merleau-Ponty and Heidegger. He believes that Husserl's phenomenology cannot be accommodated with an adequate description of the qualitative structuration of the world considered as an antepredicative datum of lived experience.

As a result of the criticism offered by Ronald McIntyre, Dreyfus later abandoned this interpretation (see Dreyfus 1988). His new reading maintains the idea that Husserl's phenomenology is a form of cognitivism close to Fodorism although not sensu stricto a computational and therefore symbolic one. McIntyre, from whom this modified interpretation is borrowed, makes this point clear in his 1986 article, "Husserl and the Representational Theory of Mind."

Given that McIntyre is also an advocate of Føllesdal's analytical reading—to the point that in the 1982 article "Husserl's Identification of Meaning and Noema," which he coauthored with D. W. Smith, he offers a radicalized version of it defending the idea that the noema of an expressive act is for Husserl nothing else than the noematic sense of the act expressed—this new reading clearly amounts to an attempt at dissociating Føllesdal's original idea that a noema is like a linguistic *Sinn* from the conclusion that the structure of an intentional state is to be assimilated with a symbolic structure. However, McIntyre seems paradoxically to persist in attributing syntactic and semantic properties to noemas.

Two general conclusions can be drawn from this critical overview.[32] First, it is necessary to distinguish at least two different versions of both the analytical reading (Føllesdal's and Hintikka's rendering of Føllesdal's) and the cognitivist reading (that found in Dreyfus 1982 and that found in McIntyre 1986 and Dreyfus 1991) of Husserlian phenomenology. Second, these four interpretations all seem to be committed, although to different degrees, to the idea that the general structure of a Husserlian intentional state is symbolic. Such a symbolic or semantic approach to Husserl's conception of intentionality nevertheless raises important difficulties which are partly dealt with in the first part of the book (see the contributions by Elisabeth Pacherie and J.-M. Roy).

It seems today important to more sharply dissociate Husserlian phenomenology from the kind of theory of cognition represented by the computational-symbolic trend within Cognitive Science. This is all the more so that the pioneering work of Dreyfus has also had a perverse effect: for practicing cognitive scientists it became *the* interpretation. On the strength of it they came to regard Husserl as some sort of proto-computationalist and to assume that this is all there is to know about phenomenology.[33]

4.2. THE THEME OF EMBODIMENT IN RECENT PHENOMENOLOGY AND COGNITIVE SCIENCE

Among the intrinsic tensions that counterbalance the antinaturalistic discourse of Husserl's phenomenology is what Husserl calls the "incestuous" relation between transcendental analysis and the fact that, once constituted, pure lived experiences also appear as psychological, internal states, which are in the eyes of modern cognitive scientists de facto relatable to accounts rooted in neuroscience, biology, and evolution (see 3.3.3). This sort of permeability between the constitutional analysis of transcendental phenomenology and the natural world is at the base of a long lineage of studies.

As mentioned already, for Husserl and Merleau-Ponty, the body is not only an object in the world (a *Körper*) but also a medium whereby the world comes into being, an experiencer (a *Leib*) (see 2.1.3). Intrinsic to the phenomenological analysis is the realization that, contrary to the Cartesian interpretation, this twofold character of the experienced body is not a duality: embodiment is where both subjectivity and objective givens appear side by side. It is the specific property of our own body to be both sensible and sensitive. The same hand can touch and be touched; these are not different bodies. The *Leib* is one manner in which the lived body shows itself, and thus the locus where a *transcendental analysis and a natural account are intrinsically joined*. In turn, the theme of embodiment cannot be separated from the analysis of an expanded horizon where *Leib* finds itself, and which was developed by the later Husserl under the general topic of the life-world (*Lebenswelt*), where empathy, affect, and intersubjectivity are dominant.[34]

The concern for the theme of embodiment within phenomenology finds a strong resonance in the trend we have before only briefly referred to as embodied or enactive Cognitive Science (1.1), a revival of notions dating back to the origins of Cognitive Science but nearly dormant during the strong dominance of the computationalist viewpoint. This new synthesis seeks a close and explicit relationship between brain mechanisms, their existence within an organism, and a surrounding world within which there is an unceasing coupling. Hence this view highlights the role of the agent's actions and interests, the way the organism enacts its being, adapting with plasticity to the environment over time. The centrality of these ideas, together with a view of the environment as a rich source of fluctuating raw encounters, was also a motivation for Gibson's ecological and J. Piaget's epigenetic views.

More specifically, this view is based on situated, embodied agents which have two complementary aspects.

1. On the one hand, the ongoing coupling of the cognitive agent, a permanent coping that is fundamentally mediated by sensori-motor activities.
2. On the other hand, the autonomous activities of the agent whose identity is based on emerging, endogenous configurations (or self-organizing patterns) of neuronal activity.

Embodiment, thus, implies that sensori-motor coupling modulates (but does not determine) an ongoing endogenous activity that it configures into meaningful world items in an unceasing flow. This makes it naturally framed in the tools derived from dynamical systems, which it shares with connectionism.

Such views have been developed with vigor in the last five years in various areas such as robotics and artificial intelligence, linguistics, neuroscience, developmental cognition, and medicine.[35] For example, research has shown that the process of vision in primates is not a reconstruction of the image on the retina inside the brain by some inverse optics. Instead, eye movements actively select an object following points of interest for the organism. What counts as an object is also dependent on the segments the organism actively provides, and movements of head and body provide such key information about depth that space cannot be seen as some neutral locus decoupled from bodily placement. Not only are these ideas important for the understanding of natural cognition, but because they can be implemented, they provide the key to far more effective designs in robotics.

Further, from an enactive viewpoint, any mental act is characterized by the concurrent participation of several functionally distinct and topographically distributed regions of the brain and their sensori-motor embodiment. It is the complex task of relating and integrating these different components that is the root of the temporality as seen from the perspective of the neuroscientist. This topic will be the focus of the contributions to this book by Tim van Gelder and Francisco J. Varela. A central idea pursued there is that these various components require a frame or window of simultaneity which corresponds to the duration of lived present. The constant stream of sensory activation and motor consequences is incorporated on an endogenous dynamics framework which is the basis for its depth or incompressibility.

What is interesting about this recent work in cognitive science discussed here is that although motivated, argued, and published within the framework of Cognitive Science, it all makes explicit reference to phenomenology. And the recurrent entry point for this cross-reference is, precisely, a bodily process that can also be thematized as a lived body (as the famous example of phantom limbs in *Phenomenology of Perception* illustrated). The status of this mutual interface between bodily accounts and the lived body is the heart of one important mode of naturalization (see 5.2).

4.3. FORMAL ONTOLOGY, MEREOLOGY, AND GESTALT THEORY

Finally, a third important aspect of the scientific renewal of phenomenology concerns Husserl's reflections on formal ontology (see 2.1.1) and his attempt at pushing it beyond standard set theory. Chief among these reflections are his investigations of mereological whole-part relations and dependence relations in general, as well as of their links with Gestalt theory, which later provided a foundation for several schools of Polish logic (Lukasiewicz, Lesniewski, Ajdukiewicz) and even of structuralism.[36]

In an impressive attempt to rehabilitate the *Logische Untersuchungen* (in particular, the third investigation) and Gestalt theory, Kevin Mulligan, Barry Smith, Peter Simons, and their colleagues from the Seminar for Austro-German Philosophy have devoted over the past fifteen years numerous studies to this aspect of Husserlian phenomenology.[37] In addition to the considerable contribution they have made to historical analysis, they have analyzed in detail the possibilities of axiomatizing the relations of dependence. Of a basically realist persuasion, their pioneer work has been one of the principal sources of the revival of scientific phenomenology in Europe, as witness, for example, the work of Roberto Casati, Roberto Poli, Liliana Albertazzi, and Claire Hill.

The relevance of this aspect of the renewal of Husserlian phenomenology to the contemporary study of cognition is immediate, for it offers new tools for the investigation of various cognitive areas, most important in the study of the relationship between language and perception.

5. WAYS OF NATURALIZING: AN OVERVIEW

In view of these various considerations, which all converge on making the naturalization of Husserlian phenomenological descriptions a reasonable and scientifically interesting challenge in spite of its paradoxical outlook, the main issue clearly is the following: how can such a project be carried out?

Earlier in this essay (see 3.2) we sketched out a hypothesis about the general meaning of naturalization which carries substantial implications for an answer to this question. Indeed, this hypothesis assumes that sensu stricto the problem of naturalizing a Husserlian description amounts to articulating its mathematical reconstruction with relevant lower-level natural sciences, neurobiological disciplines being of course of primary importance. At that point we said nothing further about how this articulation was to be realized.

The truth is that different strategies can be adopted, and in this essay we do not wish to defend any specific view in this respect. In fact, neither does the book taken as a whole advocate a single approach to the problem. The idea itself that a mathematical reconstruction is a possible and necessary step in the process is solely the opinion of the editors, although it is echoed in a number of contributions throughout the volume. Even more, the very possibility of carrying out such a naturalization project is disputed from different angles in Part III. Our ambition has been to discuss in a fully critical spirit an issue we consider to be of high importance for the development of contemporary cognitive sciences, not to offer the first elements of a unified theory. Accordingly, the reader is referred to the numerous contributions directly addressing the issue of the naturalization strategy, although not always in a perfectly explicit manner. Some contributors have chosen to indicate their way through the problem by means of case studies rather than theoretical considerations.

With a view to supplementing this series of disconnected individual analyses we wish, however, to offer in the following paragraphs a quick overview of what can be seen as the main possible options to be taken on the problem as well as of the main difficulties with each. This presentation has no ambition to be either exhaustive or systematic. And because our only goal is to provide the reader with a general framework for the discussions to follow, we will not build directly on the hypothesis previously sketched. For an analysis of how some of these options can be conjoined with the idea of a mathematical reconstruction of Husserlian descriptions, the reader is once again primarily referred to Petitot's and Varela's contributions.

5.1. NATURALIZATION AS REDUCTIONISM

The classical approach to naturalizing Husserlian phenomenology is reductionism, in the traditional sense of the logical integration of two scientific theories into a unitary deductive construction through the derivation of the concepts and propositions of one of them on the basis of the concepts and propositions of the other. This reductionist technique is as old as the invention of the notion of a deductive system through the constitution of Euclidean geometry. Although it has played an important part in the field of formal and natural sciences (in particular for elucidating the relations between microscopic statistical physics with macroscopic thermodynamical physics), it is only with the progress of logic and the revival of the notion of an axiomatic system at the end of the nineteenth century that it became possible to apply it to the relations between the sciences of the mind and the sciences of nature. It was the backbone of the two main programs of naturalization in the period preceding the Cognitive Revolution, namely logical behaviorism[38] and central identity theory.[39] In spite of the differences separating them, both in terms of methodological details and in terms of the choice of the basis for the reduction, the common idea of these two programs was to reduce every mental property to a natural one by means of a conceptual substitution warranted by coextensionality.

Furthermore, both of them manifested a real concern with avoiding any gap with phenomenological data. As clearly illustrated by J.-J.-C. Smart's famous article "Sensation and Brain Processes" (in Borst 1970), the theory of central identity springs from the denunciation of the inability of logical behaviorism to account for phenomenological properties, although this notion is understood in the restricted sense of qualia (Borst 1970: 48). It is also often ignored that the autopsychological level that Carnap chooses as a basis for his constructional system of 1929 is explicitly assimilated with a phenomenological level of pure lived experiences in the technical sense of Husserl. Indeed Carnap writes in §64 of *The Logical Structure of the World* (1969): "At the beginning of the system, the experiences must simply be taken as they occur. We shall not claim reality or nonreality in connection with these experiences; rather, these claims will be bracketed (i.e. we will exercise the phenomenological 'withholding of judgment,' *epochē*, in Husserl's sense)."

It is therefore natural to ask whether the techniques of naturalization elaborated by these reductionist programs could be put to use in naturalizing Husserlian-style descriptions of phenomenological data.

Although such a line of inquiry deserves a closer examination, it can be a priori feared that the difficulties standing on its way are too great to be overcome. Nothing in particular makes it reasonable to hope that the well-known objections opposed by functionalists to the search for coextensionality between behavioral or neurobiological properties on the one hand and mental properties on the other would become pointless because of a mere change in the phenomenological properties taken into consideration.

5.2. NATURALIZATION AS AN "AS IF" STRATEGY

Another naturalizing strategy is to consider that, although they might have no genuinely objective content, phenomenological descriptions are nevertheless necessary instruments for the prediction of behavior. This strategy is best exemplified by Dennett's view of intentional explanation or "heterophenomenology." According to Dennett, the very complexity of cognitive systems rules reductionism out de facto and makes it necessary to introduce two levels of prediction different from, and more abstract than, the biophysical level of explanation. One of them is to be formulated in terms of the functional organization of the system under consideration and the other one corresponds to the intentional apparatus of so-called folk psychology. In this perspective a mental process is not an empirical reality but only the result of a predictive strategy resting on the attribution of states, acts, contents, and so on, which are not to be considered as objective. Intentional concepts are a heuristic tool in a very strong sense of the term: everything happens *as if* they possessed an objective value.

This strategy is surprisingly reminiscent of the attitude adopted by Kant in the second part of his *Critique of Judgment* on the old issue of vitalism in the explanation of biological organisms. Although he sees mechanism as the only proper sort of genuine explanation for natural entities, Kant considers that both the limitations of our understanding and the complexity of living organisms make it necessary to resort in biology to an additional set of specific concepts, such as that of "internal finality." Hence a duality of *maxims of judgment*, the "mechanistic" one and the "teleological" one. The second one however should be considered as having no objective value, strictly speaking, beyond the descriptive. Although no more than a heuristic tool, it is nevertheless employed *as if—als ob*—it had objective validity.

Similarly, one could say that the three "stances" distinguished by Dennett, the "physical stance," the "design stance," and the "intentional stance," function as three maxims of judgment. Even though the physical maxim is the only one with a truly objective value, both the functional and the intentional ones are made necessary by our intellectual limitations and the complexity of the phenomena under consideration.

One of the main possible lines of criticism against such an instrumentalist approach is simply that it offers too easy a way out of the central difficulty of naturalization. Indeed the mental and phenomenological stances can be considered as ontologically neutral levels of investigation merely *juxtaposed* to the physical one, thereby saving the trouble of showing *how* what is amenable to physical explanation can also described in phenomenological terms.

5.3. NATURALIZATION AS MUTUAL CONSTRAINING

The theme of embodiment in both phenomenology and Cognitive Science discussed in 4.2 opens up a different approach to naturalization. Broadly conceived, the idea is to explore seriously the close "relationship" between the subject and its body (both as *Leib* and *Körper*), for it is there that one has direct access to both the constitutive natural elements familiar to Cognitive Science and the phenomenological data required. Depending on specific cases, various kind of neuroscientific, psychological, evolutionary, and anthropological evidence can be brought to bear.

At the Bordeaux conference out of which this book grew, the discussion focused substantially on what became referred to as the "the wavy line" problem. This was a code name to designate the problematic nature of the exercise of investigating such counterparts, putting on one side a list of (in these cases) neurobiological items or processes, and on the other seeming equivalencies as phenomenological data, and separating the two sides by a wavy line. Figure 1.4 underscores the unresolved nature of the "wavy" middle line, and the circulation between the terms which this approach to

Neurobiological data ⦃ *Phenomenological data*
mirror cortical neurons   intersubjective constitution
efference copy   voluntary action
resonant cell assemblies   cognitive states

FIGURE 1.4. The wavy line problem.

naturalization must necessarily resolve, as several essays in this volume attest (Petit, van Gelder, Thompson, Varela, Pachoud). The challenge is not simply to draw the parallel and then leave it unexamined: phenomenological analysis becomes an aside or adornment to the neurobiological account, a sort of extra validation.

On the one hand, we are concerned with a process of external emergence with well-defined neurobiological attributes. On the other, with a phenomenological description that stays close to our lived experience. The nature of the circulation one seeks is no less than one of mutual *constraints* between both accounts, including the potential bridges and contradictions between them.[40] Accordingly, this research program has been recently summarized as follows: "*Working Hypothesis of Neurophenomenology*: Phenomenological accounts of the structure of experience and their counterparts in cognitive science relate to each other through reciprocal constraints" (Varela 1989).

The nature of this double circulation can be identified as being one of three distinct possibilities:

Bridge locus. A number of authors have taken very specific neural responses or structures and proposed that they constitute the *bridge locus* between the percept and the neural substrate. This take is very common with the advent of the techniques for brain imaging where "hot" regions light up during a cognitive performance. Or at the cellular level, for instance, illusory contours (edges that are clearly perceived, but that do not correspond to any physical edges) activate specific neurons in the visual cortex that respond to these illusory contours. In both cases the thesis works on the form of a reasoning that Davida Teller calls linking propositions. These are propositions of the form

$$\Phi \text{ "looks like" } \Psi \rightarrow \Phi \text{ "explains" } \Psi$$

where Φ are neural-psychological terms and Ψ are phenomenal terms, and the implication operator has a conditional sense: if the empirical events "look like" the phenomenal events, then they explain these phenomenal events. But are these kinds of *linking propositions* really anything but the traditional eliminativist approach under a phenomenological guise?

Isomorphism. Another interpretation of the wavy line represented in this volume is that this link is an isomorphic one: the cognitive neuroscientist needs to take into account the phenomenological evidence in order to properly identify the correct explanatory mechanisms on the neural and subpersonal levels. For example, the static constitution of time excludes a cognitive view of temporal mechanism based on computational ideas. This is a reasonable and productive option and one that has several variants depending on the degree or force of constraint that one allows phenomenology to have. In the reverse direction, phenomenology is rendered more intelligible because it receives a causal explanation underlying the appearances analyzed and a natural link to the bodily phenomena. For instance, the paradoxical nature of retention is rendered intelligible by a dynamical reformulation.

But this isomorphic option makes the implicit assumption of keeping disciplinary boundaries: the job of phenomenology is to provide descriptions relevant to first-person phenomena. The job of natural science is to provide explanatory accounts in the third person. Both approaches are joined by a shared logical and epistemic accountability. But is this really possible or even productive? Is this not another form of psycho-neural identity theory?

Generative passages. A more demanding approach will require that the isomorphic idea be taken one step forward to provide the passage where the mutual constraints not only share logical and epistemic accountability, but are further required to be operationally *generative*, that is to say, to be in a position to generate in a principled manner eidetic descriptions that can directly link to explicit processes of biological emergence. For this to happen at least both sides of the wavy line must be joined at a level of description sufficiently abstract that it rightly belongs to both sides at the same time. In other words, the neurobiological and the phenomenological accounts have to achieve a level of formal and mathematical precision to make this passage possible. In the case of bodily schemes and the constitution of temporality, the growing importance of dynamical tools makes this seem like a viable possibility. But is this level of rigor perhaps not too high for many or most topics central to cognitive science?

5.4. NATURALIZATION AS ENLARGEMENT OF THE CONCEPT OF NATURE

A fourth strategy for naturalization consists in generalizing the concept of nature in such a way as to include processes involving a phenomenalization of physical objectivity. We already came across an example of this kind with Chambon's naturalism (§3.4). Gibson's perceptual ecologism may also be cited.

Positions of this kind are defended in this book by Barry Smith, David Woodruff Smith, and Jean Petitot. With his theory of "unionism," D. W. Smith develops the idea that it is possible to extend the concept of the natural world to include mental intentionality, under the condition that the unity of the mental and the physical be understood as the product of a categorial constitution and not as a factual reality. His basic idea is that by appealing to formal categories of a Husserlian kind, an ontology can make several opposing material categories homogeneous (cf. the Husserlian concept of regional ontologies evoked at 2.1.1).

As for Barry Smith, he shows how Gibsonian ecologism makes it possible to develop a realist interpretation of Husserlian transcendentalism. As a result of evolutionary adaptation, the perception and action of a living organism are pretuned to the qualitative structure of its *Umwelt*: forms, qualities (colors, textures), and so on. These have become for it intrinsically significant. To be sure, the world can be considered as the product of a constitutive process undertaken by transcendental consciousness, but to take up again the categories of evolutionary theory, it is so only at the "ontogenetic" level. At the "phylogenetic" level, on the contrary, it is consciousness that has to be adapted to the world (as was acknowledged a long time ago by realists such as Daubert, Merleau-Ponty, and Chambon; see 3.4). By virtue of the general principle that what is ontogenetically a priori is phylogenetically a posteriori, a neo-Gibsonian realist conception can perfectly well be developed from an evolutionary standpoint.

The morphodynamical approach emphasizes that such a perspective presupposes the possibility of describing in a physical way the morphological and qualitative structures of the *Umwelten* as emergent macroscopic organizations. And also that, to this end, the physico-mathematical theories of complex systems mentioned at 3.5 are of critical importance.

In fact, in the absence of such theories, ecological approaches are open to the well-known criticism brought against Gibson by Jerry Fodor and Zenon Pylyshyn. Gibson's basic thesis is that perception is capable of extracting from the environment invariants possessing both an objective content and a perceptual meaning. Fodor and Pylyshyn have tried to destroy this theory on the basis of the classical hypothesis that, in order to be a cognitive process, perception must necessarily be an inferential and symbolic computational one (Fodor and Pylyshyn 1981: 139–96). With remarkable acuteness, they bring out an inconsistency in Gibson's ecological theory. According to them, its main defect is to postulate the existence of objective information that although not physical is nevertheless supposed to be present in the luminous medium (for example, discontinuities, forms, deformations, reflectance, and so on of visible surfaces). But they consider such an "information in the light" to be quite enigmatic. In their opinion, because of the dualism of the physical and the symbolic, information has to be either physical or symbolic. Consequently, if it is not really physical but "ecological," it must necessarily be symbolic. In short, Gibson appeals to ecological information that is nowhere to be found. He criticizes both physical reductionism and psychological mentalism but provides no alternative, thereby leading to a vicious circle. Hence Fodor and Pylyshyn's conclusion: "What we need, of course, is some criterion for being ecological *other than perceptibility*. This, however, Gibson fails to provide."

Fodor and Pylyshn's entire argument comes down to the following. The only possible direct extraction of invariants is the one accomplished by sensorial transduction. Transducers can only be sensitive to the physical properties of the light signal, for their functioning is ruled by laws (it is nomological) and the only available laws are physical ones. Transducers (even compiled transducers, i.e., those operating right up to post-retinal levels) supposedly extracting from the signal ecological properties of a nonphysical nature cannot, therefore, exist. According to Fodor and Pylyshyn, Gibson is making a category mistake. For Gibson, information is contained *in* light. But for them the concept of information is a *relational* one. Light contains information about the environment and "containing information about" means "being correlated with." Properties of the environment are then inferred from the structure of the light signal on the basis of prior knowledge about these correlations. By replacing "containing information about" with "information contained in," Gibson surreptitiously reifies the relational concept of information. He treats it "as a thing rather than a relation."

It can nevertheless be objected that this interesting criticism rests on a double prejudice: namely, that physical reality possesses no macroscopic emergent properties and that what is significant must necessarily be symbolic. And as a consequence, that the environment cannot contain intrinsically significant structures encoded in a light signal. From the morphodynamical standpoint, however, the existence of objective morphological information undermines this prejudice and makes a morphodynamical ecologism possible. Gibson was indeed on the right track with his notion of extraction of invariants. Fodor and Pylyshyn are equally correct in identifying a vicious circle in his thinking. In other words, it is indeed true that "what we need is some criterion for being ecological other than perceptibility." But this criterion cannot be rigorously defined save by resorting to sophisticated, contemporary physico-mathematical and biological theories. One is brought to see to what a degree the philosophical debate about the naturalization of phenomenology depends, here and now, on contemporary scientific breakthroughs.

5.5. FUNCTIONALIST NATURALIZATION

The notion of functionalism designates a general form of explanation which should not be identified with its computational (classical or connectionist/dynamical) and causal versions, although these were of particular importance in the development of contemporary cognitive science (cf. Pacherie 1995b). As Hilary Putnam had rightly emphasized as early as 1963, functionalism should not be considered naturalist per se. But if it is logically compatible with a dualist attitude, it has mostly been put at the service of the naturalization of mental explanation.

Indeed, the main objective of contemporary functionalism, which was essentially developed as a reaction against logical behaviorism and identity theory, is to transform mental properties into natural properties of a functional kind. As such these properties are to be distinguished from natural properties of a substantial kind, because they do not specify what an entity is made of but what it does, the function it fulfills. In fact they are conceived as properties of substantial natural properties, and consequently as more abstract as well as of a higher logical type. Considering that a functional property can be shared by different substantial properties, functionalism claims to provide a solution for the multiple realizability problem confronting reductionist theories. The naturalist strategy adopted is of a logical nature similar to the one adopted by classical reductionism. It first and foremost consists in introducing a relation of coextensionality between a mental property and a natural one. The difference lies in the type of the natural property retained to this effect.

The validity of functionalism as a naturalizing strategy is a much debated issue and should not be taken for granted. It is in particular disputable that both forms of computational functionalism are of similar value in this regard. Classical computationalism has even been accused of dissimulated dualism because of the sharp discontinuity separating classical computational properties and the ones serving for their implementation at the physical level. On the contrary, dynamical properties directly emerge from the nature of the biological or artificial substrate to which they belong. Using a somewhat provocative terminology, these two sorts of computational functionalisms could be opposed as extraphysical and intraphysical.

There are in any case two main ways of extending a functionalist strategy of naturalization to Husserlian descriptions.

The first is to try to assimilate these descriptions to functional statements in one of the prevailing computational senses of the term, that is either in the sense of classical automata theory or in a topological and dynamical sense. If, following the line of interpretation opened by the cognitivist reading of Dreyfus, the Husserlian transcendental reduction is seen as a way of adopting a form of ontological neutrality, it can even be argued that Husserl's phenomenology is per se a form of functionalist computationalism. Furthermore, his descriptions of certain cognitive phenomena, such as perception, can be interpreted as involving elements of both kinds of computationalism with a foundational priority given to dynamical processes over classical ones.

The second way is also based on the idea that Husserlian phenomenological descriptions have an intrinsically functional dimension, although not of a computational and causal nature. As a matter of fact, Husserl himself, if not any of his followers, repeatedly couched crucial aspects of his theory in functional terms. In §86 of *Ideen* I, he writes for instance that the problem of transcendental constitution is the central problem of phenomenology as well as a functional problem: "The functional point of view is central to phenomenology: the rays that issue from this center encompass gradually the entire sphere of phenomenology. In the end all phenomenological analysis enters one way or the other into its service as constitutive elements or infrastructures" (p. 213). But he also makes it quite clear that the concept of function involved is not logico-mathematical: "Function in this sense is entirely different from its mathematical sense." This constitutional functionalism is not causal either: according to Husserl, the category of causality is not adequate to the realm of pure lived experiences, where it should be replaced by the category of motivation.

The problem is, therefore, to estimate to what extent such a functional dimension of phenomenology can really open the doors to an integration of phenomenological descriptions into a naturalist framework. The Husserlian concept of function raises problems of compatibility with the notion of first-order natural property that the causal and the computational ones seem to avoid. In addition the Husserlian concept also has to be made compatible with the computational notion of function in order to ensure the possibility of an articulation of these descriptions with contemporary theories of cognitive phenomena, most of which are intrinsically linked with a computational perspective.

6. FOUNDATIONAL DIFFICULTIES

In addition to the technical problems just reviewed surrounding the naturalist transformation of Husserlian phenomenology, several difficulties of a more foundational nature should finally be mentioned. Of special importance are those regarding (1) the methodological implications of the naturalist reversal, (2) the myth of phenomenological data and other philosophical myths, and (3) the limits of the naturalist reversal. Although they are certainly not ignored in this book, they do not receive the full treatment they deserve and which should be given to them in a systematic analysis of the problem of naturalizing Husserlian phenomenology. This amounts to making a clear distinction between the overall project of naturalization argued for in this essay and the inherent limitations of this particular volume.

6.1. METHODOLOGICAL BASIS FOR A NATURALIZED HUSSERLIAN PHENOMENOLOGY

It is clearly not sufficient to search for a way of naturalizing phenomenological descriptions provided by Husserl or by one of his followers. In order for the naturalization of Husserlian phenomenology to correspond to a truly scientific project, it is necessary that the phenomenological level of investigation be further developed. To this end the implications of the adoption of a naturalist perspective on the phenomenological methodology should be clarified, thereby also throwing further light on the relation between phenomenology and psychology.

In this regard, as we have already mentioned, every phenomenological study proper must begin with an explicit gesture of reduction, leading to descriptive invariants. Husserl makes no exception to this rule. Roughly stated, reduction starts by a disciplined suspension of the habitual attitudes we hold on a subject, a bracketing of what it seems we know, to open a fresh look into the phenomena as they appear directly to us, in flesh and bone. Whence Husserl's famous dictum: "Back to the things themselves!"[41] by which he meant not a third-person objectification but a return to the world as it is experienced in its immediacy. Reduction can also be described as a special type of reflection; reduction does not mean to consider a different world but rather to consider the present one otherwise. As any reflection, it opens up for investigation new varieties of mental contents.

This concern about reduction as a task or an aptitude contrasts with current usage both among those interested in a naturalized phenomenology as well as those concerned with Husserlian phenomenology itself, both of whom remain silent about reduction. This is clearly true of those coming from the tradition of Anglo-American philosophy of mind (such as Jackendoff; see 1.3). But it is no less valid for those with roots in phenomenology itself. For instance, in his lucid treatment of generative constitution, Steinbock does not even list reduction as a topic, although it is clear that only through reduction can such genetic analysis be carried out.

Neither attitude will do. At least for some of the editors of this volume, what is sorely needed is a method that receives both (1) a sustained effort to theorize it and (2) an explicit prescription for its cultivation and training over time. This is the center of the Seminar Psychologie et Phénoménologie,[42] a parallel research group in Paris that has been an integral part of the context for this book. In one recent formulation, all forms of reduction can be analyzed into four intertwined moments or aspects: (1) inducing the attitude of suspension, (2) gaining intuitive evidence concerning a domain, (3) providing descriptive invariants, and (4) long-term training to acquire expertise in 1–3 (cf. Varela 1996). A first challenge is to lay bare each one of these aspects of reduction, to transform them into a phenomenological pragmatics beyond vague usage (see Depraz, Varela, and Vermersch, forthcoming). The failure to make reduction into a concrete method through these steps is arguably the most salient weakness of current appeals to Husserlian phenomenology. As a result, a substantial amount of phenomenological literature has strayed into textual analysis and repetition of descriptions from Husserl or others, without the disciplined engagement to redo such descriptions afresh. A second challenge is that of a call for transforming the style and values of the research community itself. Unless we accept that at this point in intellectual and scientific history some radical relearning is necessary, it will be hard to move forward into a productive interface with Cognitive Science. But this can only happen when the entire community adjusts itself to the corresponding acceptance of arguments, standards, and editorial policies in major scientific journals that can make this added competence a benefit for young researchers. It requires us to leave behind a certain image of how science is done, and to question a style of training in science which is part of the very fabric of our cultural identity.

6.2. PHENOMENOLOGY AND PHILOSOPHICAL MYTHS

Since the end of the nineteenth century, the evolution of philosophical reflection has frequently taken the form of a denunciation of myths, at least as far as its pivotal transformations are concerned. One after another, modern and then postmodern philosophers have endeavored to show how their predecessors did not simply make mistakes but were victims of illusions, how they held mythical beliefs and not only erroneous rational ones.

A familiar criticism is that Husserlian phenomenology shares most of these myths patiently unveiled over a century of philosophical criticism. The truth is that Husserlian phenomenology might be in serious jeopardy indeed if this view is correct, for the list of myths it might apparently be accused of subscribing to is frighteningly long: the myth of signification, the myth of foundationalism, the myth of the determination of extension by intension, the myth of immediate knowledge, the myth of the a priori, the myth of qualia ...

An important and deep issue is thereby raised: even if it can be naturalized, is not Husserlian phenomenology after all resting on philosophical foundations too obsolete to have any real scientific relevance for contemporary sciences of cognition? There is no other way of answering this problem in a convincing way than by confronting phenomenology with the various criticisms offered by modern philosophy of the positions it takes on all foundational issues, and not only those sustaining its committed antinaturalism. The naturalization of Husserlian descriptions of cognitive phenomena cannot, therefore, be dissociated from an investigation of their overall philosophical underpinnings, as well as of the various ways these can possibly be reconciled with some of the innovations of modern philosophical research. In other words, an articulation of Husserlian phenomenology with contemporary scientific knowledge of cognition cannot reasonably be undertaken without also developing a critical examination of the impact of the recent transformations of philosophical thought.

This additional requirement elicits a whole set of questions that are for the most part left untouched in this volume, although we certainly do not see them as illegitimate or uninteresting. Our priorities have been different. One of the most fundamental of them is nevertheless at the center of J.-J. Botero's contribution: to what extent is Husserlian phenomenology a victim of the "myth of the given"? The important point is that crucial questions such as this one should be answered in a nondogmatic way. If the numerous "myth-reversals" of contemporary philosophy cannot be ignored, the soundness of their conclusions should certainly not be taken for granted.

6.3. THE LIMITS OF A NATURALIST REVERSAL OF HUSSERLIAN PHENOMENOLOGY

Once again, the general project defended in this introductory essay is based on the fundamental hypothesis that today the progress of the sciences of cognition make it possible to unify the investigation of phenomenological data with the multilevel explanation of what is to be considered, in a naturalist perspective, as an essentially physical reality. Where Husserl saw the necessity for a fundamental epistemological discontinuity, the contemporary scientific context in our opinion offers on the contrary the possibility of establishing a no less fundamental continuity.

The soundness of this hypothesis is by definition largely dependent upon the success of further investigation. Time will tell. However, every hypothesis also requires a critical examination of its realizability. And in this regard a reflection about the possible limits of a naturalization of Husserlian phenomenology is clearly in order. The problem derives precisely from the fact that Husserlian phenomenology is not only a non-naturalist kind of inquiry, but also an antinaturalist one. Even if it can be argued, as we do here, that today the evolution of science makes it possible to dispute this antinaturalist position, it is a legitimate suspicion that the heterogeneity introduced by Husserl between phenomenological and natural properties might on certain points run so deep that it is unclear how it could be overcome. More precisely, it is unclear how it could be overcome without losing precisely what makes the naturalization of Husserlian descriptions an attractive goal. The rejection of the concept of cause in favor of the notion of motivation provides a clear example of this difficulty: a motivational characterization of mental processes in the Husserlian sense of the term is definitely more at odds with the general conception of natural processes than a causal one.

It certainly is not a matter of repeating the traditional philosophical error—previously criticized (see 1.2.2)—of pronouncing a priori impossibilities, but on the contrary of not falling into the opposite one of adopting a dogmatic attitude on the naturalization of Husserlian phenomenology. The issue is all the more important that it continues to feed skepticism, a skeptical position clearly illustrated by some of the contributors to Part III of this book. Although it is not discussed in full detail, like the other two foundational issues previously mentioned, we have no intention of ignoring it. These three issues have actually been at the center of several discussions of the research group at the origin of this publication.[43]

7. OVERVIEW OF THIS BOOK

Before embarking on its detailed contents, the reader will find here a brief overview of what is to come. We only provide the broadest structure without entering into the details of individual contributions and their conceptual interdependencies.

PART I: INTENTIONALITY, MOVEMENT, AND TEMPORALITY

Intentionality: David Smith, Jean-Michel Roy, and Elisabeth Pacherie

The essays in Part I focus on the general structures of intentionality and their naturalization. David Smith argues that the concept of naturalization involved in contemporary debates is inadequate for naturalizing intentionality: naturalization should not be seen as a transformation of mental properties into the natural properties introduced by the physical sciences, but as the homogenization of heterogeneous categories by means of an appropriate formal ontology based on the Husserlian one.

Jean-Michel Roy and Elisabeth Pacherie raise the same issue in different terms: how can a representational analysis of intentionality account for the direct character of many of our intentional states? They also follow a similar strategy of using certain aspects of Husserl's theory of intentionality in their effort for solving it. Although their conclusions are different, they both illustrate a way of putting Husserlianism to the service of a naturalized intentionalism.

Movement: Evan Thompson, Alva Noë, Luiz Pessoa, Bernard Pachoud, and Jean-Luc Petit

The remaining essays in Part I focus on case studies, that is, on specific topics and themes anchored in some aspect of Cognitive Science and simultaneously animated by a phenomenological perspective. These are simply the themes chosen by the contributors themselves, and they thus represent what is most attractive or tractable at the present time, nothing more or less. We made no plan or overall scheme into which contributions had to fit. As a consequence, absent from this list of specific topics are at least two major dimensions of study which have received some attention in the past and which are surely essential: imagination and fantasy, as well as the integration of sensory modalities.

This section opens with a contribution by Evan Thompson, Alva Noë, and Luiz Pessoa which studies in great detail the available data in neuroscience and cognitive psychology concerning the well-known visual effects of filling-in, where a contour or an edge appears vividly although there is no physical correlate of such discontinuity. The effect itself is ideally suited for naturalization, since by its very nature, this is an aspect of appearance that cannot be left out of the analysis. They conclude by postulating that all current accounts excluding filling-in phenomenological data as unnecessary (such as Dennett's) are untenable.

Bernard Pachoud examines one of the main contributions of the Husserlian analysis: a view of perceptual intentionality that highlights the role of anticipation in perceptual experience, thereby clarifying how a transcendent object can be grasped within the immanence of a perceptual experience. The result is a dynamical conception of intentionality where the intentional object (or the meaning) remains a presumption, waiting for confirmation by the future course of experience. This dimension of anticipation, based on a teleological conception of intentionality according to Husserl, characterizes primarily perceptual experiences. A number of contemporary naturalistic theories have revealed a similar anticipatory structure in practical (praxis) intentionality, thereby inviting comparisons between these two kinds of intentionality as well as convergences with these naturalistic approaches.

Jean-Luc Petit juxtaposes a Husserlian account of intersubjectivity via the self-image and lived body and the recent discovery by Giacomo Rizzolatti of mirror neurons. These are unique sites in the brain which are activated not when an animal moves its own body but when *another* animal in its presence moves its body, a neurobiological suggestion of the other-as-self. The intriguing consequences of this case are discussed by Petit on the basis of a hypothesis of isomorphism (see 5.2).

Temporality: Tim van Gelder and Francisco J. Varela

Both van Gelder and Varela independently make a sustained attempt to link the Husserlian analysis of temporality with modern-day concepts of the dynamical approach to Cognitive Science. Van Gelder argues mostly for a dynamical interpretation of retentional trajectories and shows how such an argument precludes the Brentano-Meinong interpretation of retention as remembrance. In his conclusion he insists that phenomenological data can actually constrain and guide the choice of scientific explanation, excluding, for example, computational accounts.

Varela takes up the same topic but draws on the neurodynamics of brain assemblies as correlates of temporality. His analysis of retention is similar to van Gelder's, but he extends his discussion into the asymmetrical relationship between protention and retention, and relates this asymmetry to the affective dimension of absolute flow uncovered in Husserl's late work on time. He concludes by proposing new figures of time where genetic and static analysis can be joined as constraints on external analysis.

PART II: MATHEMATICS IN PHENOMENOLOGY

There are three main reasons for devoting a substantial portion of this book to formalization and mathematical issues. First, Husserl's contributions to formal ontology is, in our opinion, decisive for the mathematization and therefore the naturalization of a number of cognitive phenomena. Indeed, Husserlian formal ontology is not purely set-theoretic. It is a theory of constructing principles of objects, and as such in many respects more adequate to cognitive facts. Second, as we already argued at some length in this essay, mathematical modeling has in our opinion a key role to play in any attempt at naturalizing phenomenological data. Finally, mathematics always played an essential role in Husserl's phenomenology, which was first developed as an answer to the turn-of-the-century problem of the foundations of arithmetic. Thus, if this book is to clarify the real nature of the Husserlian enterprise in order to assess its relevance to contemporary Cognitive Science, it should therefore address the general issue of its relationship with mathematics.

Formal Models: Barry Smith, Jean Petitot, and Roberto Casati

These papers speak to the first two reasons given for devoting part of this book to mathematization and formal issues. In his paper Barry Smith makes a link between the Husserlian phenomenology of perception and the ecological viewpoint developed by Gibson. This leads him to a general theory about the segmentation of spatially extended entities, a theory which is formally related to mereology and to a realist ontology of boundaries and frontiers.

In a text essentially devoted to the morphodynamics of perception, Jean Petitot shows how the tools provided by modern differential geometry make it possible to formalize the eidetic descriptions of the third logical investigation as well as of *Ding und Raum*. After discussing several physico-mathematical models of segmentation, he offers a geometrization of the relation between visual field and kinesthetic control and analyzes different models of perception by sketches.

Roberto Casati's paper shows how one can axiomatize a phenomenology of motion and an associated mereology. In this Casati is representative of a host of current studies on mereo-topology.

Phenomenology and Mathematics: Dagfinn Føllesdal and Giuseppe Longo

The contributions by Føllesdal and Longo speak to the third reason, the historical relationship between phenomenology and mathematics. Føllesdal comments on the importance that Kurt Gödel attributed to Husserlian phenomenology. After discussing Husserl's thesis of the ideality of mathematical forms, he shows how the Platonic realism of Gödel is inspired by phenomenology. He lays special emphasis on the links between eidetic intuition in Husserl and the objectivity of mathematical meaning in Gödel.

Giuseppe Longo retakes the most vital aspects of the problem of the formalization of the continuum and offers an analysis of how mathematics transforms the originary intuition of the continuum into proof principles.

PART III: THE NATURE AND LIMITS OF NATURALIZATION

The papers in Part III extend the discussion of the general issues addressed earlier in the book from specific thematical or methodological perspectives. Their ambition is to examine in more general as well as more philosophical terms the very possibility of the project of naturalizing Husserlian phenomenology.

Philosophical Strategies of Naturalization: Ronald McIntyre, Juan-Jose Botero, and Natalie Depraz

First comes what might be seen as a group of purely philosophical definitions of this project. Ronald McIntyre tries to clarify its specificity through a critical account of the recent attempt by Fred Dretske to offer a naturalist account of qualia. Natalie Depraz attempts to show that there is no insuperable obstacle to reconciling the transcendental position of Husserl with a naturalist concern in the area of cognition. Juan-José Botero offers an analysis of the Husserlian notion of the immediately given and explores its implications for a naturalizing perspective.

Skeptical Attitudes: Jean-Michel Salanskis, Maria Villela-Petit, and Renaud Barbaras

These contributions illustrate a more skeptical attitude about the very possibility of naturalizing Husserlian phenomenology. Jean-Michel Salanskis and Maria Villela-Petit argue on the basis of a close examination of Husserl's theory that Husserlianism cannot be naturalized without losing precisely what makes it valuable from either a descriptive or a philosophical point of view. Renaud Barbaras brings into the book the important Merleau-Pontian line of analysis in an explicit and original manner. His main thesis is that beyond the lived body (*corps propre*) one should seek the basis of perceptual life in the very status of the living being, thereby arguing for the elimination of the naturalism versus idealism opposition.

Jean-Pierre Dupuy closes the discussion with a historical account of the relationships between the sciences of cognition and Husserlian phenomenology. He provides crucial elements for a better understanding of how and why the question of naturalization of the latter has finally come to the foreground of the philosophy of cognitive science.

PART ONE

INTENTIONALITY, MOVEMENT, AND TEMPORALITY

CHAPTER TWO

Intentionality Naturalized?

DAVID WOODRUFF SMITH

> With all its eyes the natural world looks out into the Open.
> Only our eyes are turned backward, and surround plant,
> animal, child like traps, as they emerge into their freedom.
> —*Rainer Maria Rilke*

1. INTRODUCTION

1.1. INTENTIONALITY IN NATURE

We must open up the conception of nature and naturalism au courant in the philosophy of cognitive science. Consciousness and its intentionality are part of nature. But their essence is not exhausted by physical composition or causal role or neural function or computation (classical or connectionist)—as important as these are to their implementation. We must widen "naturalism" accordingly so that our theory of mind and cognition incorporates the characters of consciousness and intentionality that are the hard-earned results of phenomenology and ontology.

To that end I shall outline an ontology that distinguishes diverse *categories* of the world and carves a place for consciousness and intentionality in the world of nature. Intentionality will be categorized within the world of nature and "naturalized" in that way, without reducing consciousness or its intentionality to a causal or computational process along the lines envisioned by current cognitive science.

The guiding assumption, which I shall call *unionism*, holds that there is but one world, ordered and unified as "nature." That world includes us, our conscious intentional experiences, and a host of other things, from rocks, trees, and bees to families, symphonies, and governments. These things belong to diverse substantive or "material" categories such as Body, Mind, and Culture, which are ordered by diverse "formal" categories such as Individual, Quality, State-of-Affairs, and so on. The world is unified by the systematic ways in which formal categories link together and govern material categories.

This proposed unity does not preclude diversity of categories (think of the classifications in biology, the table of elements in chemistry, the fundamental forces and particles in physics). Yet diversity does not require disjoint realms of beings delimiting, say, bodies, minds, and cultures (à la dualism, materialism, idealism, historicism). In this way the world enjoys categorial complexity without substance dualism. From quarks to quasars, from consciousness to volition to cultural institutions, there is ontological complexity, but all within this one world.

Among the formal categories of the world, I shall claim, are Intentionality and Dependence. But if these are distinct formal categories, it is a mistake in fundamental ontology to identify intentionality—or consciousness itself—with a structure of causation, or dependence, realized in a brain or computer. The life of mind is more complicated than that, categorially.[1]

1.2. NATURALISM IN PHENOMENOLOGY AND COGNITIVE SCIENCE

Some ninety years ago Edmund Husserl developed a philosophical account of consciousness and cognition in *Ideen* I (1912–13) on the heels of his *Logische Untersuchungen* (1900–1901). Husserl held that "intentionality" is the central feature of consciousness (it was Husserl who coined the term "intentionality"). His account of intentionality—including cognition in perception and judgment—was the foundation of "phenomenology," Husserl's new science of consciousness. With Husserl the theory of intentionality and intentional content thus came into its own, after a long prehistory.

Some twenty years ago, at the heart of the emerging discipline of "cognitive science," Jerry Fodor outlined a philosophical account of cognition in *The Language of Thought* (1975). Fodor held that "mental representation"— what Husserl called "intentionality"—is the central activity of mind and analyzed its structure as symbolic computation in "the language of thought." More recently, Fodor and his foes have debated whether this computation is "connectionist" in form, that is to say, implemented by neural networks in the human brain. Fred Dretske, on the other hand, in *Knowledge and the Flow of Information* (1981), emphasizes, rather, the flow of physical "information" in perception and knowledge between environment and organism.

But Husserl and Fodor et al. take opposite positions on naturalism. Expressing today's conventional wisdom, Fodor in *The Elm and the Expert* (1994) says any "serious psychology" must be naturalistic. In kindred spirit Fred Dretske in *Naturalizing the Mind* (1995) seeks to show how consciousness might be captured in naturalistic terms. Husserl, however, argued that any "rigorous science" of consciousness must reject naturalism. Of course everything depends on how naturalism is defined. If intentionality is naturalized in the way of Fodor and Dretske, then I stand with Husserl against "naturalization." But if naturalism is defined in the way I shall propose, as unionism in a system of ontological categories, then I accept a "naturalized" intentionality, and I think that in today's debate Husserl could as well.

In *The Elm and the Expert* Fodor updates his account of mental representation, now adopting Husserl's term "intentionality" and drawing what he thinks are consequences of naturalizing the theory of mind and intentionality. In *Naturalizing the Mind* Dretske proposes to explicate the crucial features of consciousness, including intentionality, qualia, and introspection, in terms of external relations our experiences have to relevant objects in the environment, relations consisting in the causal flow of physical "information." Where Fodor, Dretske, and others would outline a theory of mind within the bounds of a naturalism stressing computation and causation, I want inversely to outline a form of naturalism within the bounds of a theory of mind (*inter alia*), stressing its place in the categories of a phenomenological ontology.[2]

The term "naturalism" outlives its usefulness, however, if it is taken to mean nothing more than "scientific." My aim here is to get beyond such labels and dig into what would be required of an ontology adequate to the phenomenology of consciousness and its intentionality.

2. OUTLINES OF A PHENOMENOLOGICAL ONTOLOGY

2.1. ONTOLOGICAL CATEGORIES

Systematic ontology begins by distinguishing fundamental kinds or *categories* of things in the world. Plato distinguished forms from the particulars that exemplify them (to various degrees of imperfection). Aristotle, master classifier and proto-biologist, framed a more down-to-earth ontology of "categories" (launching this term of art in philosophy: *kategoremata*, literally "predicates"). Aristotle distinguished the following categories:

> Substance, including Primary Substance (Individual Thing) and Secondary Substance (Species), Quantity (Discrete or Continuous), Quality (Condition, Capacity, Affective Quality, or Shape), Relative (better Relation), Where, When, Position (Posture), Having, Doing (Action), Being Affected (Being Acted Upon)

If Plato's forms reside in a heaven far above the world of particulars, Aristotle's categories—starting with Substance—are meant to structure things in nature. Thus Aristotle went on to distinguish matter and form within the constitution of a primary substance.

For our purposes let us simplify and update Aristotle's system of categories, as follows:

Individual, Species, Quality, Relation, Location, Quantity, Intentionality

Species include natural kinds and, if you like, artificial kinds. Relations form their own category (by contrast, many philosophers sought to reduce relations to monadic properties). Space and time fall under location. Quantity leads into other mathematical structures (details to be specified). Intentionality—following Brentano and Husserl—covers not only purposeful action (and inversely, being acted upon), but perception, imagination, thought, and so on (significantly widening Aristotle's niche for acting and being-acted-upon).

We shall consider increasingly complex systems of categories, using this modified Aristotelian scheme as a prototype and foil for further reflections. The issue, as we proceed, will be the niche of mind in a world framed by ontological categories. If Brentano was right that intentionality is the distinguishing mark of the mental, then of course mental phenomena would simply fall under Intentionality. But life is more complicated than that, as we shall see.

Classical nominalism began in Ockham with the goal of having only the category Particular, or Individual, what Aristotle called "Primary Substance": all else becomes mere ways of talking or thinking (for Ockham, thinking in a mental language). While I cannot argue the case here, I think nominalism—better named particularism—is orthogonal to naturalism. Our theory of nature assumes the categories Species, Spatiotemporal Location, and more. But whether these categories could be somehow eliminated, or reduced to the category Individual, is a further issue and would survive the denial of naturalism—as we saw in Berkeley's ontology of idealism (which would recognize only minds and ideas, two kinds of particular).

Aristotle conceived his categories as the most general yet disjoint kinds of things there are. This would seem to mean that the categories themselves fall under the category Species. But that is not right. The categories are not *summum genera*, species at the highest level in the genus-species hierarchy: they are not species at all. Dog is a species of Mammal, but Species, Relation, and so on, are not species: they are *categories*. Thus, a more systematic account of categories is needed, along the lines charted by Husserl.

2.2. FORMAL AND MATERIAL CATEGORIES

Husserl drew a distinction (with a nod to Leibniz) between formal and material ontology, thereby distinguishing "formal" and "material" categories.[3] While the distinction is not easy to draw in general terms, it becomes clear in particular systems of ontology, where it has sharp consequences for the ontology of mind. When we begin to think in such terms, as we shall see, the reduction of intentionality to causal-computational process looks like a serious category mistake.

According to Husserl, *material* ontology recounts material categories of things according to their specific characters or "essence," while *formal* ontology recounts formal categories that apply to things of any material category. If you will, formal ontology posits *forms* of things in the world, and material ontology posits "matters" or domains to which forms may apply. In this sense formal categories are topic-neutral. Indeed, Husserl sometimes spoke of the ideal of a *mathesis universalis* (Leibniz's term), suggesting that formal ontological structure is to be described ultimately in a unified mathematical framework. However, a formal ontology is formal because it describes ontological form, not because it may ideally be expressed in a symbolic or mathematical language, and not because forms are identified with mathematical entities such as number or set.

For instance, if Descartes were right that minds and bodies belong to two distinct realms, both realms would still be characterized by the formal distinction between substances and their modes (things and their properties). Applying Husserl's distinction to Descartes's ontology, we would say that Mind and Body are two material categories, while Substance and Mode are two formal categories that apply to each of these material categories. Thus the mental divides into mental substances (minds) and mental modes (modes of thinking), while the bodily divides into corporeal substances (bodies) and corporeal modes (modes of extension).

Or consider Husserl's ontology.[4] He recognized three material categories—Nature, Culture, and Consciousness—and several formal categories, including Individual, Species, and State-of-Affairs. In Husserl's system, the material categories are the highest genera under which species can fall, and the formal categories are forms that apply within each material category, so that an individual's belonging to a species (which falls under the genus Nature or Culture or Consciousness) forms a state of affairs. Thus each of the "regions" Nature, Culture, and Consciousness is structured by the "forms" Individual, Species, and State-of-Affairs.

In Husserl's ontology the category State-of-Affairs (*Sachverhalt*) is formal and has a "syntactic" structure combining individuals and essences. Wittgenstein adopted a similar view in *Tractatus Logico-Philosophicus* (1921). According to Wittgenstein, the *form* of the proposition "*aRb*" is shared by the state of affairs (*Sachverhalt*) that objects *a* and *b* stand in relation *R*—and the form of an object is the possibility of its occurrence in various states of affairs. Wittgenstein's famous Tractarian ontology is thus a formal ontology in Husserl's sense and indeed is centered on the ontological form State-of-Affairs. Thus, the Tractarian forms Object, Relation, and State-of-Affairs would apply to any domain—mind, nature, culture, or whatever material ontology posits.

Issues in philosophy of mind take their place in such an ontology of formal and material categories. Thus, for Husserl, unlike Descartes, material categories do not define disjoint domains of "substances," but rather different ranges of essence, or species. Accordingly, for Husserl, the same individual can belong to different species (have different essences) under different material categories. Notably, "I"—this one individual—am a physical organism in Nature, a person in Culture, and an ego in Consciousness. More precisely, the individual I includes these three different aspects or "moments" (particularized properties) that fall respectively under the material categories Nature, Culture, and Consciousness. And there are *dependencies* among these moments, as my state of consciousness depends on what my brain is doing and what my culture has done. Consequently, Dependence is a *formal* feature of entities falling under these three *material* categories and holds even between entities in different material categories.

Furthermore, in Husserl's scheme, *intentionality* (being-conscious-of-something as well as being-an-"I") belongs to animal organisms in Nature, to persons in Culture, and to "pure" egos in Consciousness. It follows that Intentionality is a *formal* feature of entities bearing these three different *material* essences. Husserl does not explicitly classify intentionality as a formal feature, but I shall later consider reasons why it should be so classified.

For Husserl, intentionality is "pure" in consciousness but also "bound" into nature and culture. Of course, intentionality is realized in nature, not in rocks, but only in certain physical systems including animal organisms. And intentionality is realized in culture, not in buildings or machines, but only in the persons who build and use them. In this view intentionality is a formal property, in the sense that it applies to things in different "material" domains. It is not, however, "formal" in the sense of a syntactic form of physical symbols. To say with Husserl that intentionality is a formal feature in a formal ontology is not to endorse (with Fodor and many others) the computational theory of intentional content as a syntactic form of physical symbols processed by a brain or a computing machine. Quite the contrary, as we shall see.[5] Ontological form is not the form of symbols, but the form of entities—which may be represented by symbols in virtue of *their* form (the structure of such representation being the purview of semantics).

In logic we assume a distinction between logical forms and the expressions to which they apply in forming more complex expressions. For example, the logical form "p and q" applies to different sentences that may fill the positions of p and q; or the logical form "the F" applies to definite descriptions that may be formed from different predicates F. The distinction between formal and material ontological categories is like a projection of this logical distinction onto the world—or vice versa, pace Wittgenstein! But the point is that this distinction applies to structures of the world as opposed to structures of language. In the spirit of W. V. O. Quine, we might hold that our language and its logic go hand in hand with our ontology, so that both are subject to revision in light of advancing theoretical inquiry. Nonetheless, our ontology is a further thing, and in the spirit of Husserl formal and material categories together structure the world.

Within the structure of language, Quine distinguishes, like Bolzano, between logical forms and the expressions to which they apply. The correct logical forms, for Quine, are those in natural language as regimented by first-order logic. According to Quine, the ontological commitments of our language are expressed only by bound variables, or pronouns: only expressions of that logical form genuinely posit entities; only through so positing entities do we "reify" and individuate objects.[6] So Quine's position yields in effect a *formal* nominalism, holding that all entities in the world have the form specified by the logical form of variables, thus recognizing only the formal category Individual. Husserl would say other forms of language also carry ontological commitment, as predicates may refer to essences or species and sentences to states of affairs. So Husserl's formal ontology is wider, recognizing the formal categories of Essence or Species, State-of-Affairs, and Individual—which involve other formal features, among them Dependence and Intentionality.

The formal/material distinction is not the analytic/synthetic distinction. Quine argued against a sharp distinction between analytic and synthetic statements, the former true by virtue of meaning alone. Yet he held to a distinction between logical and nonlogical statements, the former true by virtue of logical form alone. Where Quine applied the logical/nonlogical distinction to expressions in a language, Husserl applied the formal/material distinction to objects in the world and to grammatical categories in language as a special case. For Quine our ontology is projected from our language, from our bound variables, and logical form is a matter of convention. (The category of terms may be hardwired into human language ability, thus Quine once remarked, "Man is a body-minded animal.") For Husserl our ontology is projected from our intentional experience, expressed or expressible in language, and that ontology applies to language and intentional experience and content as well as to other kinds of objects in the world.

Philosophers have often thought of the logical or conceptual as prior to the empirical, and along these lines one might be tempted to think of formal ontology as prior to material ontology. However, we must instead posit formal categories together with material categories, in a unified ontology. For in practice we abstract formal features from material features of things, and if we revise our material categories sufficiently we may revise the formal categories that govern them. Similarly, Quine holds that our logical and mathematical idioms are most central in the language expressing our web of beliefs, yet even they are subject to revision.[7] Indeed, some say quantum mechanics may require a different "logic" than everyday affairs. Moving to the level of ontology, our formal categories are more central and less variable than our material categories, yet the formal and material work together, and our ontology as a whole is subject to revision as need be.

2.3. THE ONTOLOGY OF NATURE

As we distinguish formal and material categories, let us look toward a categorial ontology of nature. Think of the material categories implicit in physics and the formal categories that might govern these. As a model (subject to revision) contemplate the following categorial ontology of the physical world, the domain of physics:

Formal Categories

Individual, Species, Quality, Relation, Location, Quantity, Dependence, Intentionality, State-of-Affairs

Physical Material Categories

Body, Wave, Mass, Force, Space-Time, Gravitation, Electromagnetism, Quantum Field, Wave-Particle

What I want to stress is the *architecture* or *systematics* of such an ontology, where the nature of things physical is structured by the interaction of formal and material categories. On such an ontology, the world has a systematic unity that consists in the way entities under material categories are governed by formal categories that weave together in an ordered way. In the ancient idiom "nature" (*phusis*) meant the order of things, and ontological systematics focuses on such order, framed here by a system of formal and material categories.[8]

These formal categories are those recounted earlier as an updated Aristotelian scheme, but supplemented here with the categories State-of-Affairs and Dependence. The category State-of-Affairs serves to bind together entities of other formal categories, as states of affairs are formed by individuals of various material categories having appropriate qualities, relations, locations, and so on. Thus, in its formal structure the world is a world of states of affairs (following Husserl, Wittgenstein, and others).[9] But the world is also bound together by dependencies. In this ontology Dependence is posited as a formal category that may govern material causal relations defined in terms of physical force, wave activity, and so on. Thus, A depends on B if and only if A cannot exist or occur unless B *does*; this structure is realized in causation between physical things or events in virtue of the mass, force, and so on, they involve. (Aristotle assumed such a notion in defining qualities of substances, but it was Husserl who developed the ontology of dependence in a detailed way.)[10] Note that Intentionality is posited as a distinct *formal* category, a point to which we shall return.

In the Cartesian and Husserlian ontologies sketched earlier, the formal categories apply in the same way to entities in each material category. In the present ontology, however, the relation between formal and material categories is more complicated, with certain formal categories applying to entities in certain material categories. Thus, a body is an individual with a mass in a gravitational field, but an electromagnetic wave is an individual with a certain mode of propagation in an electromagnetic field. States of affairs are formed in various ways from formal categories: as individuals belonging to species or having qualities or standing in relations, or as entities depending on other entities.[11] The laws of physics, according to such an ontology, describe intervolved formal and material features. For example, "$f = ma$" describes a relation among quantities correlated with a certain force, the mass of a certain body, and the rate of change of its location in spacetime. Certain of the entities involved are "formal" and others are "material."

The categories of physics are subject to raging controversies, specifically, in the interpretation of quantum mechanics. Under material categories, are there waves only, particles being illusions created by interference of observation? Or are there particles only, determinate elements in eigenstates following the collapse of the wave function? Or are there only superpositions forming wavicles, neither particles nor waves in themselves but only relative to observation or the absence thereof?

It remains unclear exactly which ontological categories are best suited to current physical theory; however, the point here is not to settle such issues, but to indicate the relevance of the distinction between formal and material categories—and, more generally, the importance of "systematics" in ontology. However these controversies in the foundations of physics turn out, would the formal distinction between Individual, Quality, and Relation be abandoned? Is this much not presupposed by the most basic structures of mathematics, recognizing things and functions (with or without a strongly realist interpretation of mathematics)? It is hard to see how the different versions of quantum mechanics, or other parts of physics, could do without such a distinction.[12]

In this category scheme, Intentionality is posited as a formal category because it may be required by the material categories presupposed by quantum physics. For on the Copenhagen interpretation of quantum mechanics, observation causes the collapse of the wave function in a quantum system. But if observation is an intentional event (as it is), and intentionality has a distinctive formal structure (as it does), then quantum mechanics (on that interpretation) presupposes the formal category Intentionality. Thus, the ontology of the physical world may require the category Intentionality even before we look at the categorial structure of mind per se.

2.4. THE ONTOLOGY OF MIND IN NATURE

Now let us turn to the ontology of mind. An adequate ontology must be *phenomenological*, in the sense that it recognizes structures of experience, notably consciousness and intentionality, as well as structures of stones, gravity, quantum states, and so on. On the present approach, a phenomenological ontology would be articulated within a scheme of formal and material categories.

For the sake of argument, assume the formal categories already given. What material categories should an ontology of mind assume? They might be the same as those applied to physical entities: this would be a form of physicalism, but the characters of consciousness and intentionality would have to take their place somehow in the category scheme. Or in a plural-aspect scheme like Husserl's, the formal categories would apply to, say, the material categories of Bio-Matter, Culture, and Consciousness. Each of these material categories would be characterized by diverse properties, but each would be governed by the formal categories of Individual, Species, and so on.

Rather than begin with the material categories of physics, however, our theory of mind and cognition must begin with categories of things in the everyday world of common sense—what Husserl called the life-world, that world which lies between quarks and the cosmos.[13] We do not begin our ontology of the world-around-us by dealing with bosons and black holes, or neurons and neural nets, abstracting so far from our familiar concerns that we no longer know where we fit in. Rather, we encounter and categorize mental or cognitive activities *in everyday life*: prior to our theorizing in physics or neuroscience, which is constrained by our everyday experience and answers to it in our scientific practice of observing and theorizing. Indeed, our quantum physics and neurophysics must ultimately jibe with everyday experience in such a way that recognizes and accounts for everyday affairs, including our conscious activities of theorizing.

Consider then the following categorial ontology of the world as we know it in everyday life:

Formal Categories

Individual, Species, Quality, Relation, Location, Quantity, Dependence, Intentionality, State-of-Affairs

Everyday Material Categories

Object, Event, Place, Time, Plant, Animal, Human Being, Mind, Action, Practice, Artifact, Institution

Here, an object is an individual that persists relatively unchanged, an event is an individual that transpires relatively quickly in time, and so forth. The formal and material categories interweave so that there is ontological complexity in the world. But there are no separate domains of mental and physical substances, nor a simple division of properties into mental and physical.

In this ontology there is one world that includes mind and culture and "natural" objects or events. Mind takes its place in the order of the world, along with stones, trees, and owls, as well as cities, schools, and stories. A *mental activity* such as a thought, perception, or action is an intentional event: it is categorized materially under Event and formally under Intentionality. In closer detail, a mental activity is experienced by a subject (human or animal), carries an intentional content (a concept, proposition, and so on), and if veridical is directed to an object (the object of thought). There may be collective as well as individual intentional activities, such as collective beliefs or group intentions. The salient mental events are conscious: we *experience* these and build our ontology around them among other familiar things. Now, *cultural* entities also take their place in the world. A hammer is an artifact: categorized formally under Individual and materially under Artifact. A political party is an institution, classified under Individual and Institution; a song is something we write and perform, an artifact, and so forth. *Cognition*, then, consists in a mental activity of perceiving or thinking being intentionally directed to an appropriate entity, which may be an object, an event, a plant, a hammer, and so on. Notice that some features of mind or cognition are formal and some are material, instances of formal or material categories, respectively. And notice, roughly, how the formal and material categories work together in these formulations.

These categories structure the things we deal with every day in our niche in the human world within the natural world. There are vital differences among the objects of everyday human life in the stone age, the agricultural age, the industrial age, and now the age of air travel, telecommunication, and computers. Yet the formal categories of Individual, Species, and so on, seem to apply to things under everyday material categories in any of these ages. And the everyday material categories of this scheme seem appropriate to different cultures of humans, ancient and modern. Our categories are not written in stone (or iron or silicon), but we must revise them cautiously.

Unionism—the formal ontological backbone of an appropriate naturalism—requires that the world of nature be one world including quarks, quantum wave collapses, and black holes along with human beings and conscious intentional experiences and political scandals. Thus, the present ontology is unionist. As Husserl stressed, there must be dependencies of consciousness and human affairs on the basic physical states of things (and perhaps vice versa): dependencies among "moments" that instantiate the relevant categories, formal and material. From quantum mechanics to neuroscience there is much yet to learn about these dependencies. From categorial ontology, however, we draw an approach that systematizes the contributions to "formal" and "material" structures of the world. A unionist ontology would ultimately detail how the ontological structures of things physical, mental, and cultural are all extruded from a unified system of fundamental ontological categories, formal and material. The "correspondence problem" (borrowing the term from physics) is then how precisely to characterize relations among the physical, phenomenological, and cultural aspects of things—which are diverse aspects of things in this one world.[14]

2.5. SUBCATEGORIES FOR CONSCIOUSNESS AND INTENTIONALITY

Within the preceding ontology, under certain categories we may carve out subcategories that structure consciousness and intentionality more specifically, thus refining the formal and material categories that define mind.

Under the formal category Intentionality we specify formal subcategories that structure the intentionality of an experience. These are Subject, Experience, Content, and Intention. Thus, the formal structure of intentionality is that of an *intention*, or "directedness," among subject, experience or "act of consciousness," content, and object. Content is a distinct formal category, since contents—images, concepts, propositions, and so on—are distinguished from species, relations, numbers or quantities, and so on: they are formally their own kind of thing. And Content is a *formal* rather than a material category, since it is plausible, so far as we know, that the same content may be realized or invoked in different material categories, e.g., if extraterrestrials have experiences that are realized differently than experiences in humans or animals. Our brains produce experiences through neural processes, but the extraterrestrial's system produces experiences, say, through gaseous propagation (in a life-world like Jupiter's). This is not the functionalist claim that computation may be executed in different hardware or wetware or gasware. Rather, the claim is that thinking and other kinds of experience may be ontologically dependent on variable kinds of processes—processes that do not reduce to computation.

Cognition—in perception, thought or contemplation, and judgment—is formally classified as a kind of intention, or intentionality, not a structure of dependence. Yet our cognitive activities are materially analyzed as dependent on a causal flow involving the neural activity in our brains and its causal interaction with things in our environment. If this ontology is correct, then the reduction of intentionality or cognition to causal-computational process—as proposed in recent cognitive science—rests on a formal category mistake. It is not just that we happen to talk about intentionality and causality in different ways, even in different grammatical categories, or that we experience them in very different ways. Rather, the point is that we categorize them differently.

From our conscious mental activities, we may abstract material categories of their psychology and phenomenology. These are phenomenological material categories governed by the formal category Intentionality. Thus, under the material category Mental Activity are subcategories specifying phenomenological types, namely, Perception, Thought, Emotion, and Volition. These types of mental activity carry materially distinct types of content: perceptions, images and thoughts (propositions), feelings (and desires), and volitions (or intentions).

Conscious intentional experiences are thus categorized formally under Intentionality and materially under Mental Activity. The category scheme in which they take their place then looks like this (ignoring further subcategories):

Formal Categories

Individual, Species, Quality, Relation, Location, Quantity, Dependence, Intentionality, State-of-Affairs

where "Intentionality" covers the formal subcategories of

Subject, Experience, Content, Intention

Everyday Material Categories

Object, Event, Place, Time, Plant, Animal, Human Being, Mental Activity, Artifact, Institution

where "Mental Activity" covers the material subcategories of

Perception, Thought, Emotion, Volition

Mental life grades off from the conscious into lower levels of awareness and on into the unconscious—and into extraordinary phenomena of split brains, split personalities, hallucinogenic experiences, and highly disciplined states of meditation. We begin our categorization, however, with conscious mental activities familiar in everyday life. Empirical investigation into the less familiar will extend our categories, perhaps modifying them as well.

2.6. NATURALISM, DUALISM, SUPERVENIENCE, FUNCTIONALISM

How does the categorial phenomenological ontology I've sketched differ from extant positions in philosophy of mind and cognitive science?

This ontology posits a diversity of categories in our one world. There are many kinds of things in the world, and many basic categories, even different levels of categories (formal and material). Yet all things are tied into one world: "nature," if you will. This unionist view differs from extant forms of naturalism precisely in its account of categorial diversity.

Like all forms of naturalism, this ontology rejects substance dualism. It does not divide the world of concrete things into two domains, the mental things (minds, souls, spirits) and the physical things (bodies, from quarks to quasars). Rather, mind is part of nature, and so is culture: physical objects and events, mental activities, persons, societies, and cultural institutions all occur in this one world of nature. However, this categorial ontology rejects the simple identification of mind (and culture) with the workings of quarks, neurons, and so on. For it posits a more complex system of ontological categories.

Property dualism takes a step toward categorial diversity in positing two types of properties (as opposed to substances): physical properties (such as mass) and mental properties (such as intentionality). The categorial ontology I propose does not, however, divide properties into just these two categories. Instead, it posits a structured system of categories that divide the world into various groups of things, properties, and so on.

Supervenience theories hold that the mental "supervenes" on the physical—assuming property dualism but denying substance dualism.[15] One form of supervenience is defined basically as the dependence of a mental event on physical events in a brain. Since Dependence is one of the formal categories in our ontology, supervenience can be placed in that ontology. However, dependence alone does not place mind in the world, as shown by the variety of categories we have adduced.

Functionalism takes a different step toward categorial diversity, distinguishing the functional and physical properties of a system, and identifying mind with the computational function of a neural system (at least in humans and other thinking animals on Earth). The functional/physical distinction can be seen as a formal distinction among types of properties. In the categorial ontology above, this distinction would be reconstructed in terms of a temporal sequence of events: a functional property is defined solely by a type of result in a sequence of events. However, this categorial ontology would reject the simple identification of mental event types with functional types. For there is more complexity in the categorial structure of mind (and culture) than function alone. To deny functionalism is not to deny function, but to put it in its place.

The ontology above differs from these prominent approaches to philosophy of mind, then, in seeking a systematic account of the *categorial complexity* of the world and mind's place therein. In the following I explore recent forms of naturalism from this perspective, especially the causal and computational models of mind espoused by Fodor and Dretske.

2.7. INTERNALISM AND EXTERNALISM

Within the preceding categorial ontology, what are we to make of the debate between internalism and externalism in philosophy of mind?

On the *internalist* view of intentionality, what makes a mental activity intentional, or directed toward its object, is the intentional content held in mind, where that content is internal to the mental act. By contrast, on the *externalist* view, what makes a mental act intentional is context, either its physical causal history or its cultural circumstance, whence intentional content must be defined in terms of the act's contextual relations. The classical view is internalist, as found in Husserl and defended recently by John Searle and (with a contextualist reformation) myself.[16] But the predominant attitude in recent cognitive science has been externalist, as expressed by Fodor and Dretske.[17]

However, as we work with the unionist ontology above, it becomes clear that the opposition between internalism and externalism is false. A mental act has both a causal genesis and a phenomenological character. And these two aspects of the act belong to different ontological kinds: the former is an instance of the category Dependence, while the latter is an instance of the category Intentionality (and relevant subcategories). Our ontology must recognize both the genetic tree and the phenomenological character of a mental act, its "clade" and its "phenotype" (to borrow biological idiom)—and neither reduces to the other.

In this ontology, Intentionality and Dependence are distinct formal categories. They must be distinct, since they have radically different ontological structures. Thus, the structure of intentionality is that of an experience (by a subject) intending an object via a content (a concept, proposition, image, and so on). By stark contrast, the structure of dependence is that of one thing's needing another in order to exist. The ontology of these structures is so obviously and fundamentally different that reducing the intentionality of an experience—or its content—to its causal dependence on other things, as externalists sometimes propose, is simply out of the question.

2.8. INTENTIONALITY AS A FORMAL CATEGORY

Our Cartesian heritage shapes philosophy of mind as a choice among *material* categories of substance, so that we think we must say either "All is Body" or "All is Mind" or "All is divided between Body and Mind." Thus the lure of physicalism in the age of physics. Furthermore, the emphasis on empirical ("material") results of recent science—from quantum mechanics to cognitive neuroscience—leads us to overlook distinctions about mind that belong properly to formal rather than material ontology. Thus causal and externalist theories of mind in Fodor, Dretske, and others cathect on material patterns of causation, while functionalist and computationalist models of mind obsess over the marvels of computer engineering (the most "material" of results).

But systematic ontology—ontological systematics—leads us to think about mind in different ways, avoiding the usual suspects of substance dualism, idealism, physicalism, functionalism, and so on.

In an ontology that distinguishes formal and material categories, Intentionality belongs among the formal categories. To justify this assumption in detail would be a long story; we would have to show that the intentionality of an experience is a unique form differing from that of a quality, a relation, a dependence, and so on. To begin the story, the ontological structure of intentionality is reflected in the distinctive "intensional" logic of idioms such as "*A* thinks that . . ."—but we are talking about ontological structures of experiences in the world, not logical structures of our language about experiences.[18] Accordingly, we must distinguish the object of thought from the content, the idea or concept of the object, through which one thinks about it, through which it is "intended" by one's thinking. This structure of intention-via-content is formally unique. Thus, the ontological structure of an intention or intentionality is just plain different from that of a quality, a relation, a dependence, and so on. Hence, Intentionality, Quality, Dependence, and so on, are distinct formal categories.

It is natural to speak of the "intentional relation" between an experience and its object, yet this "relation" is so unusual that Intentionality and Relation deserve the status of distinct formal categories. The formal structure of an intention, or "intentional relation," is that of subject-act-content-object. Thus, a subject has an experience or act that has a certain content which prescribes a certain object (if such object exists); intentionality is this directedness of act by subject through content toward object. Is this the structure of a *relation* among subject, act, content, and object? Either "Yes" or "No" carries problems. If it is a relation, its number of terms varies: sometimes there is no object and it's a three-place relation; sometimes there is an object and it's a four-place relation. This is not normal for relations. As Brentano and Husserl observed, intention is "relation-like" if not a proper relation. If it is not a relation, then what? Then it has its own form, as described, and a distinct category.

The category Intentionality is formal because it may apply to materially different domains. The same form of intentionality, such as perceiving a window, may apply to very different experiences in a fish, a lizard, a parrot, or a cat, not to mention an extraterrestrial. The functionalist, with Fodor, would explain this by identifying mentation with computation, realizable in different physical systems and even through different algorithms. That is not my point. Without reducing mind to computation or function or causal role, we should see that Intentionality is a form that applies to different domains of mental activity just as Relation applies to different domains of individuals. Whence intentionality is a formal, not material, property of thoughts, perceptions, and so on.

What I want to stress is the role of intentionality in an ontology of mind among other things. If we recognize Intentionality as a *formal* category, we shall not be tempted to find the difference between consciousness and, say, electricity in two types of substance called "mind" and "matter." We shall instead articulate a unified world in which such different phenomena take their places.

2.9. PROBLEMATIC FEATURES OF CONSCIOUSNESS AND INTENTIONALITY

Three features of mental activity have been problematic in recent philosophy of mind and in cognitive science. These are intentionality, qualia, and consciousness. Within the ontology I have outlined, where can we place these crucial features of mind?

Consciousness is the great mystery of the day in cognitive science, yet the familiar turf of phenomenology. Now, part of the problem of consciousness is its formal structure and part is its material character. Three crucial aspects of consciousness are intentionality, reflexivity, and qualia.[19]

The *intentionality* of a mental activity, on the above ontology, is a formal feature instancing the formal category Intentionality. The structure of intention (subject-act-content-object) applies to both conscious and unconscious mental activities.

Now, part of the formal intentional structure of a conscious mental activity is its *reflexivity*. When I have a conscious experience, I am reflexively aware of my having the experience. This form may be specified in phenomenological description, articulating content, by saying: "In this very experience I now see that wriggling snake on the path before me."

The prefix "in this very experience" specifies the reflexive structure or content that in part makes the experience conscious. That reflexivity makes it, as Sartre stressed, a "consciousness (of) itself": not a separate act of introspection or reflection on the experience, but a pre-reflective awareness of the experience as it transpires. For Sartre, indeed, this character is definitive or constitutive of consciousness—an insight that cognitive science has yet to appreciate fully, or to rediscover.

Quite a different feature of consciousness is the subjective character of an experience: its "phenomenal" or "qualitative" character, or *qualia* (especially its sensory characters)—in Thomas Nagel's idiom, "what it is like" to have that experience. What makes an experience conscious, I would urge, is the combination of qualitative character and reflexivity, which takes its place within the intentionality of the conscious experience.

To what category do qualia belong? Qualia are properties of an experience or act of consciousness. Their formal category is Quality. Their distinction from other qualities is a material distinction within the domain of conscious mental activities—falling under the material categories Perception, Thought, Emotion, Volition—to which the forms Quality and Intentionality apply. Specifically, they are distinct in type from qualities such as the spiking frequency of a neuron or its receptivity to certain neurotransmitters. The intentional form of an experience must make room for these qualities we call subjective.

Now, if Intentionality is a formal ontological category, and Mental Activity a material ontological category, then an event of cognition has the form of an intentional mental activity with a specific intentional content such as "I now see that snake on the path before me." The event may have the material essence of being implemented by a neural process in a human brain. Or if the event is a thought performed by a being on a distant planet, its material essence may be very different. Whatever its material essence, it may also have a form not of Intentionality but of Dependence: its causal role, which is a form of dependence on past and future events. But since Intentionality and Dependence are different formal categories, there is no temptation to reduce intentionality to a causal-computational role. However, the formal category Intentionality does not apply to every material domain: rocks do not have intentionality, and neither do silicon chips. (This is not to beg the question of whether Intentionality reduces to Causation or Dependence. Remember, the formal properties of intentionality are not preserved by causal reduction.)

Finally, note that consciousness does not reduce to computation. Not all conscious activity is computation; feeling dizzy is not computing. Perhaps, as neuroscience suggests, a certain form of computation is part of the neural activity that implements every state of consciousness. But that is a different matter, a gray matter.

3. CRITIQUE OF NATURALISM

3.1. FODOR ET AL. FOR NATURALISM

Where classical phenomenology, in Husserl and his successors, opposed something called "naturalism," today's cognitive science assumes naturalism as a given—the only option of good science—and seeks to "naturalize" mind and specifically intentionality.

Current attitudes toward naturalizing intentionality run the gamut, however. Quine once rejected the "science of intention" because it does not reduce to physical science and indeed requires a different logic than the rest of natural science. But he now gives our talk of intentional attitudes a place of honor alongside the language of natural science, and he says consciousness is something that must be explained.[20] Jerry Fodor assumes psychology must be intentionalistic—embracing intentionality in belief, desire, and so on—and also naturalistic; rejecting behaviorism and eliminativism along with idealism, he proposes to "naturalize" intentional content in the language-of-thought. Daniel Dennett endorses talk of intentionality, if only as a convenient "stance" toward what is really going on as the brain crunches data; his "explanation" of consciousness explains it (away) as multiple drafts of code in the brain. Paul Churchland and Patricia Smith Churchland have sometimes denounced intentionality as a remnant of folk psychology, superstition rather than empirical wisdom; but they do not now dismiss consciousness itself, the crowning achievement of neural activity. David Armstrong identifies mental activity, including intentionality, with brain activity, and he analyzes consciousness as the brain's monitoring itself. Fred Dretske takes consciousness and intentionality seriously and analyzes their structure as a flow of causal "information" outside the head. Donald Davidson and Jaegwon

Kim, meanwhile, have held that the mental and intentional "supervene" on the physical activity of the brain—a ramified form of physicalism. And Francis Crick (Nobel Laureate biochemist) gives scientific credulity to consciousness and even the "soul" while declaring, "You're nothing but a pack of neurons."[21]

Fodor holds that "naturalizability" is required for any serious science, not just psychology or cognitive science. He defines *naturalism* in effect as the assumption that "everything that the sciences talk about is physical" (Fodor 1994: 5). This assumption boils down to *physicalism*, or *materialism*, the ontological view that everything is physical. When Quine proposed "naturalizing" psychology and epistemology, he urged following the methods of natural science (and expressing its results in first-order logic), thereby securing a physicalist ontology, unless science leads elsewhere. He thus opposed beginning with a "first philosophy," whether a metaphysics (as in Aristotle) or an epistemology (as in Descartes)—or we might add, a phenomenology (as in Husserl).[22] The naturalism in cognitive science today assumes both ontological and methodological positions, but I want to focus on the ontological.

Fodor thinks a naturalistic intentional psychology requires two doctrines:

(1) *causalism*, the view that intentional content (and also linguistic meaning) is "information," in the technical sense of a physical structure transmitted by a causal flow; and

(2) *computationalism*, the view that thinking is computation, in the technical sense of computer science, namely, an algorithmically defined process in either a digital computing machine or a neural network in a brain.

(The labels "causalism" and "computationalism" I introduce here for convenience.) Causalism—championed by Dretske with Fodor following suit—is a variety of

(3) *externalism*, the view that content or meaning is defined by its external relations to physical (or on some views social) relations with what lies "outside the head" and indeed outside the given intentional state.

And computationalism, of course, is a variety of

(4) *functionalism*, the view that thinking is wholly defined by its function in a physical system as it interacts causally with other processes of thinking and ultimately with processes in the physical environment.

Classical computationalism also assumes

(5) *syntactic formalism*, the view that the properties of thinking that count are formal, syntactic properties of physical symbols processed in brains or computing machines.

An alternative to classical computationalism is

(6) *connectionism*, the view that the properties of thinking that count are vector distributions of relevant properties in dynamic networks of neurons in brains, which can be modeled or perhaps shared by computer systems with parallel distributed processing.

Some connectionists consider this view a paradigm shift away from classical computationalism (assuming syntactic formalism) and thus from the computer model of thought. Fodor, however, counters that the form of the computation, whether logico-syntactic or connectionist, is merely a matter of implementation.[23] And the implementation of computation, whether classical or connectionist, lies in causal processes. Hence causalism remains in force. Dretske, however, downplays computation inside the brain and stresses the causal flow of "information" outside the organism. So the project of naturalizing the mind, for Fodor and Dretske, is to show how intentionality and other features of mind can be accounted for in a way consistent with causalism, hence externalism—all in the service of naturalism, and ultimately physicalism.[24]

Unfortunately, neither causalism nor computationalism (nor connectionism) preserves the properties of consciousness and intentionality. The phenomenological character of consciousness (beginning with qualia) is not preserved, and intentionality is not simply identical with the structure of a causal process—whether realizing a connectionist or a classical computational architecture. Within philosophy of mind, in the cognitive science tradition, Searle has argued clearly and effectively the inadequacy of the computationalist view: syntactic form alone does not yield intentional content or meaning—neither, we might add, does connectionist form. Consciousness and intentionality, Searle holds, are irreducibly subjective properties of mental states, realized somehow in our brains.[25] Earlier, within the phenomenological tradition, Husserl, Sartre, Merleau-Ponty, and others charted the properties of consciousness and intentionality in great detail, always distinguishing them from various natural, physical properties of human bodies.

The properties of intentionality do not fit into the causal-computational view Fodor prefers. Fodor's task in *The Elm and the Expert* is to bite the bullet and try to make his preferred view amenable to the basic features of intentionality. But Fodor recognizes that his favored naturalizing gets wrong the basic properties of intentionality. How does he justify going on with his approach? He says the problem cases—Frege cases and Twin cases—don't happen very often. That means his theory is wrong: they happen and his theory cannot handle them. On consciousness he is silent, beyond saying it is not tractable in his kind of research program.

Dretske in *Naturalizing the Mind* bites the bullet in closer detail, recasting the features of conscious experience as external and causal. He treats intentionality as natural "indication": a perceptual state indicates its object as a speedometer indicates the speed of the automobile (all these things being physical entities). In effect Dretske builds in causal terms a replica of the structure of intentionality, as well as one for qualia and for introspection. That gets the structure right but applies it to the wrong phenomena. By tracing the causal flow of physical "information" that gives rise to the important features of consciousness, intentionality, qualia, and introspection, Dretske shrewdly tracks the causal preconditions of such phenomena. But he identifies the *physical structures* called "information" in information theory with the *intentional contents* called "information" in everyday talk about contents of thought or speech. Now, intentional "information" in one's thought may well depend on physical-causal "information" in one's environment and indeed in one's brain. But the two things have very different properties.

While it may seem that causalism combined with externalism or computationalism combined with functionalism serves the needs of naturalism and current cognitive science, neither is compatible with prior results of phenomenology and indeed ontology. Phenomenology, in concert with ontology, has detailed the structures of consciousness and intentionality in well-defined arguments from well-defined observations. These are sound results achieved by basic principles of rational inquiry in good philosophy or good science (as detailed, notably, by Quine in his general epistemology).[26] Yet externalism—the broad assumption behind causalism, computationalism, and functionalism—does not jibe with a phenomenologically sensitive account of intentionality in perception and other indexical forms of intentionality, as I have argued in a detailed study of acquaintance.[27]

Fodor says, "I'm not going to fuss about ontology except where it matters" (1994: 3). Unfortunately, a full theory of intentionality and consciousness requires more ontology than is countenanced by Fodor and most philosophers of mind in cognitive science.

Nor do Fodor et al. fuss about phenomenology, even where it does matter. Consciousness has become a hot topic in cognitive science ever since neuroscientists declared it worthy of study.[28] Yet the writings of Fodor et al. show little awareness of the extant results of phenomenology. Owen Flanagan's *Consciousness Reconsidered* is advertised with the proclamation that its author "examines more problems and topics associated with consciousness than any other philosopher since William James"; yet the book makes no mention of Husserl, Sartre, or any other phenomenologist, even though Flanagan wants to make room for phenomenology in cognitive science.[29] In a recent issue of *Scientific American* philosopher David Chalmers, writing in the new wave of consciousness-raising, says that conscious experience might yet be explained not by neuroscience, but by "a new kind of theory" that gives new fundamental laws about subjective conscious experience.[30] Aptly he broaches the need to distinguish between subjective and objective aspects of "information." Of course, that "new" kind of theory is called phenomenology, and it has been a going concern for nearly a century. Many of its laws about intentionality, content, sensation, temporal awareness, consciousness of one's experience, one's body, oneself and others, and so on, are already in place.

If psychology is to be set within the bounds of naturalism, naturalism must be set within the bounds of an adequate phenomenology and ontology. To this end there is much to be learned from Husserl.

3.2. HUSSERL ET AL. AGAINST NATURALISM

Husserl opposed naturalism as an ontology that would reduce the essence of consciousness and intentionality to physical-biological properties. Today he would have opposed, with Searle, their reduction to causal or computational properties, as opposed to intrinsically subjective characters of experience. But Husserl's antinaturalism was part of a systematic phenomenological ontology whose details he developed in the first and especially the second books of *Ideen*. Husserl opposed naturalism on methodological as well as ontological grounds, since he sought foundations for natural science in a "first philosophy" that began with reason and ultimately grounded all knowledge in phenomenology. Here I shall focus only on the ontological issues. (Other phenomenologists, from Heidegger to Sartre, have also rejected naturalism. Here I shall draw on my own reconstruction of Husserl's account of mind and body sans idealism.)[31]

Husserl posited three "regions" of being, which he called Nature, Spirit or Culture, and (Pure) Consciousness. These regions are not domains of individuals or events; they are species or "essences." They are the highest "material" essences or genera to which individuals or events may belong. Nature is characterized by physical properties including spatiotemporality, mass, causality, and life. (Under Nature Husserl distinguished the living from the merely physical, and my "living body," or *Leib*, from my "physical body," or *Körper*.) Culture is characterized by persons in communities holding values and making history. And Consciousness is characterized by the subjectivity of experience and the central feature of intentionality. Importantly, one and the same individual or event may be characterized by all three essences. For instance, I am a biological organism of the species *Homo sapiens sapiens*, and thus under Nature; I am also a person teaching philosophy, and thus under Culture; and I am as well an ego experiencing this event of thinking, and thus under Consciousness.

More precisely, bringing in Husserl's ontology of dependent parts or "moments" (what some philosophers today call "tropes"): the same individual, called "I," has distinct *moments* that are particularized instances of the essences Consciousness, Culture, and Nature—say, my moments of thinking, being a teacher, and being over six feet tall. Moreover, there are relations of ontological dependence among such moments or tropes. Thus, my thinking depends upon—cannot occur without—certain activities in my brain and other activities in my culture. (There lies a specific doctrine of the "supervenience" of the mental on the physical and cultural. But that is another story.)

Since the same individual can fall under these three essences, Husserl is a monist about substrates but a pluralist about essences. In today's terms his metaphysics is a plural-aspect view: a form of substance-monism and property-pluralism—or essence-trialism.

According to Husserl's account, intentionality is a property of consciousness, or part of the essence Consciousness, whereas force and mass and energy and causation are properties of nature, or part of the essence Nature, and value and empathy and community are properties of culture, or part of the essence Culture. Husserl's "transcendentalism" boils down to just this distinction among three irreducibly distinct essences and the properties that characterize them. According to Husserl, the "transcendental" region of consciousness does not reduce to the "natural" region of physical causation or to the "cultural" region of community. For Husserl, these three ranges of essence are presented through three distinct ranges of sense or noema expressed in three distinct ranges of language about the intentional, the physical, and the cultural. There are thus three grades of "transcendental" involvement: at the levels of language, sense, and essence.

Given Husserl's ontology, what is wrong with the causal-computational view of mind is that it wrongly identifies two "moments" of an event of thinking: those of its intentional character and those of its causal-neuro-computational character. These two moments may be parts of the same event, and even interdependent, but they are numerically distinct. Notice that it matters not whether the computational architecture is classical or connectionist.

In Husserl's idiom, "naturalism" is the ontology that reduces the essence of consciousness to the essence of "nature," reducing the property of intentionality to a form of spatiotemporal-causal connection between act and object of consciousness. Naturalism in that sense Husserl rejected, violently. There is, however, a different ontology of nature and consciousness, and thus a different conception of "naturalism," that fits well with principles of phenomenology and ontology along the lines articulated by Husserl and facilitates the results of cognitive neuroscience. In the first section of this essay I sketched a model of such a phenomenological ontology.

3.3. "NATURE" REBORN WITH CONSCIOUSNESS AND INTENTIONALITY

The ancient meaning of "nature" survives today in the distinction between "nature" and the "nature of things." Originally, "nature" (*phusis*) meant the nature of the world (*kosmos*). The earliest Greek philosophers posited an order to things in the world—the primordial assumption that became science. Today "nature" means the world so ordered, and its order is detailed by the "natural" sciences.

Where nineteenth-century naturalism stressed the organic character of the world and our place in it, late-twentieth-century naturalism has stressed the physical character of the world, including the biological, along with the methodology of the physical sciences. Yet "naturalism" in current philosophy of mind (in Fodor, Dretske, and many others) takes a much more specific form: embracing not only physicalism, but computationalism, causalism, and externalism. What we need now, to accommodate the results of both phenomenology and cognitive neuroscience, is a naturalism endowed with metaphysical imagination.

The proper conception of nature begins with the recognition that our intentional states of consciousness are part of nature, with the characteristics uncovered by phenomenological ontology. To see this we must recognize two points not adequately addressed by Fodor et al.: first, that we *experience* states or events of consciousness, notably intentional states; and second, that events of consciousness enter into *relations of intentionality* as well as relations of causation. The first point is the crux of phenomenology, the second its cognate in ontology. We must recognize unconscious intentional states as well, but here let us focus on the conscious ones.

The fundamental insight of naturalism should be the view that there is but one world, ordered and unified as nature. This view I have dubbed *unionism*. The traditional term "monism" stakes a different claim, that there is only one substance or one kind of substance. Unionism, by contrast, says there is only one (actual) world.[32] Within the order of the world, however, there may be different categories of things, including fundamentally different kinds or properties. When we turn to mind, we find that consciousness and intentionality are fundamentally different in character from processes of causation and computation, and we should not shoehorn them into the wrong category. Consciousness and intentionality depend on and enter into causal processes, both inside and outside the brain: notably in perception and action. And intentionality, at least in some forms, involves computation. But while perfectly "natural" and part of this one world, consciousness and intentionality do not consist simply in causal or computational processes, as Fodor et al. hoped. As with life in general, ontology is complicated and phenomenology plays its role.

Searle has rightly stressed that the properties of consciousness and intentionality are irreducibly subjective properties that nevertheless occur in nature in biological events in human and animal brains.[33] They are not merely syntactic properties (whatever that may mean for neural events as opposed to our linguistic symbols); indeed, syntax itself is a matter of convention. Consciousness and intentionality have "internal" properties of representation, properties that do not reduce to causal sequence or the transmission of physical structures called "information." Their essence is not wholly "external," or "outside the head," in either causal or social relations.

First, we must recognize the existence of consciousness and its phenomenological structure; this requires the practice of phenomenology (by whatever methodology works: let us not bog down over "*épochē*," "hermeneutics," and so on). Then we must place consciousness and intentionality into the proper categories of our ontology. To distinguish "subjective" properties of consciousness and intentionality from "objective" properties of stones and quarks is not to lapse into a dualism of mental and physical substance. It is rather to chart the distinctive features of things, recognizing a pluralism of categories of properties of various things—all in the one world in which we live.

The naturalizing of mind proposed by Fodor, Dretske, et al. would reduce intentionality and consciousness to the flow of physical "information" through a brain or through a computer. What could motivate the picture of mind—our own experience—as nothing but bits in the void? I suspect two assumptions of perennial philosophy: (1) there are only particles in the void; and (2) all else is illusion. The first assumption is a simplistic materialism, the second a foolish metaphysics. Both have ancient roots.

But consciousness is not an illusion.[34] And intentional structure in belief, desire, and so on, is not (as the Churchlands used to suggest) a theoretical illusion, an old wives' tale from ancient folk theory. Conscious intentionality is in fact the medium of illusion: an illusion is the presentation of something in consciousness that does not exist (outside the "intention"). If we know anything at all, it is that we have conscious intentional experience of this and that. Such is the subject matter of phenomenology, and to deny it is folly. We cannot deny consciousness and its intentionality in the name of science, one of the great achievements of human consciousness, any more than we can deny human language, the medium in which science is carried out. What we can do instead is wonder how consciousness—along with language and thinking-in-language—is realized or implemented in the order of nature described by recent science.

And twentieth-century physics, its foundations still unsettled, strongly suggests that the world-order is not that of particles in the void. In relativity theory, space-time itself has topological structure—it is not a "void." And in quantum mechanics, the things in quantum systems are not "particles," but things in wave-like states that may collapse into particle-like states. These eigenstates, for that matter (pun intended), may even be states of consciousness: that much is perfectly compatible with quantum physics. And on some interpretations of quantum mechanics, the collapse of the wave function is itself triggered by an observation, an act of consciousness: in which case consciousness is implicated in the structure of physical states below the level of what normally we call causal processes.

I do not mean to suggest that proponents of today's naturalism are ignorant of twentieth-century physics, not to mention biology and neuroscience. Quite the contrary. My point is that considerations of phenomenology and ontology along with physical and cognitive science lead to a very different view of the role of consciousness and intentionality vis-à-vis causal and computational processes.

I do mean to suggest that we all carry vague background assumptions that shape our theorizing in less than obvious ways. These attitudes are part of the "background" of intentionality, unearthed by phenomenological reflection on intentionality itself.[35] Perhaps they have the status of "memes," cultural ideas passed on like genes in the cultural realm.[36] And I do mean to suggest that the reigning form of naturalism is led by such background attitudes into the untenable reduction of the properties of consciousness and intentionality to causal or computational properties.

What we need instead is a wider ontology behind naturalism, a unionism that places mind in nature without losing the distinctive characters of consciousness and intentionality. This requires a sensitive metaphysics, an ontology with appropriate formal, material, and phenomenological categories.

4. CONCLUSION

4.1. ONE WORLD, WITH CONSCIOUSNESS AND INTENTIONALITY

I have outlined a categorial phenomenological ontology according to which consciousness and its intentionality, reflexivity, and qualia are part of nature yet carry their own distinctive characters. In such an ontology the world has a certain *unity*, articulated by formal and material categories, within which consciousness takes its place. Everything there is, from quarks to consciousness to governments and black holes, takes its place within this *one* world.[37]

The lesson for philosophy of mind, from phenomenology to cognitive science, is that "naturalism" looks dramatically different when we look to such a phenomenological ontology, wherein mind cannot be "naturalized" by reducing consciousness or intentionality to a causal or computational process. Yet only through such an ontology can we ever hope to understand the phenomena of consciousness and intentionality and their role in the natural order of things.

CHAPTER THREE

Saving Intentional Phenomena: Intentionality, Representation, and Symbol

JEAN-MICHEL ROY

1. INTENTIONALITY AND SEMANTIC PROPERTIES

Is a mental representation a symbol?

This problem has not yet been given the attention it deserves. Its importance derives mainly from the contemporary revival of representationalism in the study of cognition. Indeed this revival raises three essential problems:

1. Is it scientifically relevant and philosophically legitimate to introduce a representational level in the explanation of cognitive phenomena?

If it is,

2. How can such a representational level be naturalized?
3. How should it be analyzed in the first place? In other words, how are a representation and a representational process to be defined at the mental level itself?

The question of whether a mental representation is a symbol clearly belongs to this last problem. Contemporary representationalism is faithful to a long philosophical tradition going back to the seventeenth century when it asserts that it is, but it does so without reflecting much on the legitimacy of such an identification. For most philosophers and cognitive scientists, the point seems self-evident; but like so many other points that seem self-evident, it demands in fact careful examination.

Such an examination seems all the more in order for these various contemporary research programs seeing in representationalism a way of naturalizing intentional explanation. In order to transform intentional explanation into a natural and consequently bona fide scientific one, they consider it necessary to adopt a twofold strategy: first to reconstruct intentional explanation in representational terms, and then to naturalize this representational reconstruction itself. The strategy is probably best illustrated by the classical computational interpretation of intentionalism. According to this interpretation, a system whose behavior is amenable to intentional explanation is indeed nothing more than a physical system of representations understood as symbols, that is, a symbolic system constituted of physical entities pertaining to the ontology of fundamental sciences of nature. The implications for such a strategy of the question of the mental definition of representation are clearly of most dramatic proportions. Any error slipping in at this level can either block the representational reconstruction of intentionalism or the naturalization of this reconstruction, or even both.

As a matter of fact, one can legitimately wonder whether the obstacles encountered since the mid-1980s by the attempts to naturalize the so-called semantic properties of mental representations might not partly derive from the fact that their authors resort with undue haste to a concept of mental representation that is, in fact, inadequate to the task. Similarly, it is arguable that many contemporary reconstructions of intentional concepts in representational terms are running against difficulties stemming from the same source and which have so far unfortunately received but very little attention.[1]

The most important of these difficulties is the question of how an intentional relation can be both direct and symbolic. Indeed, on the one hand, a symbolic-representational conception of intentional states seems to require that every intentional relation be indirect by virtue of the very nature of a symbol. However, on the other hand, it seems no less necessary for any intentionalism really concerned with adequacy to intentional phenomena to introduce a distinction between a direct (as illustrated by the traditional notions of intuition and acquaintance, either sensory or intellectual) and an indirect type of intentionality.

This is the issue I wish to address here. My ambition, however, will be less to offer a solution than to make clear the full complexity of the difficulty by means of a confrontation between Fodor's and Husserl's theories of intentionality. I will first contend that Fodorism, taken as a paradigm of contemporary attempts at naturalizing intentionalism by means of a symbolic conception of mental representation, results in an unsatisfactory reconstruction of the notion of an intentional state because of its inability to accommodate the distinction between direct and indirect intentionality.

I will then turn to the concept of intentionality delineated by Husserl in his *Logische Untersuchungen* of 1900–1901 and *Ideen* I (1913) with a view to assess to what extent it can be instrumental in removing the difficulty facing Fodorism. As a matter of fact, the theory of intentionality developed by the early Husserl offers the quite interesting property of granting a key role to the opposition between direct and indirect intentionality, and at the same time advocating a representational analysis of the most general structures of an intentional state. More interesting still, a close examination of the theory shows in my opinion that Husserl also was strongly tempted, in a way quite revealing of the depth of the issue at stake, to assimilate the notion of mental representation with that of a symbol. Accordingly, his work seems to offer a remarkable case of an attempt to reconcile a symbolic-representational conception of intentional states, which I will label crypto-semantic for reasons to appear, with the acknowledgment of the necessity for a distinction between direct and indirect intentional states. It seems, therefore, most appropriate to inquire whether this attempt is successful, and if it is, whether it gives us a way to rescue the symbolic-representational strategy of naturalizing intentionalism exemplified by Fodorism, in spite of Husserl's strongly antinaturalist orientation (and assuming of course that the second phase of this strategy, which once again rests upon the assimilation of a mental symbol with a physical one and which will not be addressed here, is itself unproblematic).

In an effort to sketch an answer to this question, I will finally argue that a symbolic conception of mental representation seems to preclude any distinction between a direct and an indirect kind of intentionality, and that Husserl's theory actually fails to show how to make these two claims compatible with each other. Indeed, Husserl resorts in fact to a further distinction between two kinds of indirectness: a properly representational one, which is viewed as a common feature of all intentional states, and another one specific to the symbolic and expressive mode of intentionality. In other words, I will conclude that, appearances notwithstanding, his theory of the general nature of the intentional state is not really symbolic. However, this further distinction is introduced in a fairly surreptitious way, and its content stands in need of clarification. In my eyes, it nevertheless opens up an interesting line of investigation, one that should not be neglected if we are to successfully reconstruct intentionalism in representational terms, assuming of course that a representational approach to the problem is well conceived.[2] That question I do not even raise here, not out of dogmatism, but only because the question of the relevance of representationalism itself depends on a preliminary clarification of the nature of mental representation.

Such a confrontation between Fodor's and Husserl's theories of intentionality clearly illustrates how Husserl's phenomenology can become a key instrument of investigation in the search for a naturalized theory of cognition, even though it does not yet address the crucial issue of how Husserlian descriptions can themselves be naturalized. But before wondering how a Husserlian description can be naturalized, we should first determine whether it is worth doing so.

2. AN OBSTACLE TO FODORIAN REPRESENTATIONALISM

2.1. NATURALIZING INTENTIONAL REALISM

Jerry Fodor's philosophical investigations center around a single fundamental issue: giving a fully scientific status to that specific form of psychological—and especially cognitive—explanation he calls intentional realism.

According to Fodor, a psychological theory counts as a case of intentional realism if it meets three conditions.

1. It must be an explanatory mentalism, that is to say, it must grant explanatory relevance—in the general sense of scientific explanation, whatever its specific definition may be—to mental elements, either as *explananda* or as *explanantes*. In other words, it must not make use of a purely behavioral or neurobiological conceptual apparatus.

2. These mental elements must include mental states, and especially mental states endowed with that property labeled intentionality since the Middle Ages and which Fodor, faithful to the analytic tradition, sees as a special kind of relation, the relation of being about something. As a first approximation, the notion of intentional content designates what an intentional state is about, the referent of the aboutness relation. As such it is to be contrasted with the type of an intentional state, that is, the property of being a belief, a desire, a wish, and so on. Intentional content and intentional type vary independently.

3. It must grant causal efficacy to such intentional states, and in particular to their intentional contents. By doing so it makes use of the following, and fairly familiar, general form of explanation: X does y because she wants z and believes that if she does y, she will get z. According to intentional realism, a psychological process, and especially a cognitive one, is thus essentially a causal sequence of intentional states. More specifically, Fodor distinguishes among three kinds of causal relations: "the causation of behavior by mental states; the causation of mental states by impinging environmental events (by proximal stimulation as psychologists say); and . . . the causation of mental states by one another" (1987b: 12).

The familiar aspect of intentional realism is a consequence of its proximity to folk psychology, that is, to the mode of explanation we naturally and regularly put to use in order to explain both our behavior and that of others, and even to a certain extent, that of nonhuman organisms. In Fodor's opinion folk psychology is actually the best incarnation of intentional realism. This is why his endeavor to give intentional realism a scientific status is in fact nothing less than an attempt to transform folk psychology into a scientific kind of psychology.

Such a project includes two main tasks. The first is the somehow purely technical requirement of improving inaccurate, hasty, and uncertain intentional generalizations of psychological common sense and of replacing them with nomic propositions that are fully specified and as rigorously established as the experimental method makes it possible in the realm of mental phenomena.

The second is a more philosophical undertaking. Commonsense psychology resorts to the conceptual framework of intentional realism but is quite unable to define it precisely or justify its use. However, a scientific discipline that adopted the same attitude would remain much too vague and uncertain, and therefore imperfect.

The most important element of this second task of a clarificatory and justificatory nature is the necessity to naturalize the fundamental tenets of intentional realism. Indeed Fodor shares the conviction that no nonformal knowledge can claim to be scientific if its object of investigation does not belong to the domain of the physical sciences. In other words, mental properties, and that property of being in an intentional state in the first place, are not scientifically acceptable in his opinion unless they can one way or another be transformed into natural properties, that is to say, into properties homogeneous with the properties of physical reality as it is understood by physical scientists. The main philosophical requirement confronting the scientific rescue of intentional realism is therefore to answer the following question: how can a causal sequence of intentional states also be a physical process?

Fodor, however, is also a firm believer in the failure of modern reductionism, according to which such naturalization could be achieved through the identification of all mental properties with substantial or first-order physical properties. Accordingly, the adequate formulation of the central point of his philosophical investigation is better phrased as: how can a causal sequence of intentional states also be a physical process, given that the defining properties of an intentional state cannot, or at least cannot all, be identified with physical first-order properties?

In order to solve this problem, Fodor seems to alternate between two distinct lines of investigation. They differ from each other both in the priorities they establish and in the methods they use.

The first one grants priority to the naturalization of the causal efficacy of intentional states, and of their intentional content in particular: to what physical mechanism can correspond the fact, for instance, that believing that the sun is shining makes me want to go out without an umbrella? Its objective is not, however, to elaborate a solution for this problem, but only to examine whether existing psychological theories, and most of all contemporary information-processing psychology, contain such a solution and to clarify its nature. This is the line of investigation that Fodor terms "speculative psychology" in his 1975 book *The Language of Thought*, which also offers the best illustration of it. The strategy of speculative psychology consists in laying bare the general conception of the explanation of mind (and of cognition in particular) which underpins a region of contemporary psychological research and in assessing to what extent it corresponds to a form of naturalized intentional realism.

By contrast, the second line of investigation favors the naturalization of the states composing intentional processes over the naturalization of intentional causation. Its central concern is to answer the following question: what is an intentional state if it is to count as something physical? In addition it does not try to achieve this objective through the analysis of available experimental psychology, but through an exercise of conceptual construction that can be appropriately labeled "philosophical psychology."

These two sorts of inquiries are obviously complementary, and each one of them successively goes through two similar steps. In the first step the intentional element (causation or state) to be naturalized is transformed into a representational one; in the second step the representational reconstruction thus obtained is naturalized.

2.2. THE DOUBLE REDUCTION

My critical examination of Fodor will be entirely focused on the first step of the philosophical line of investigation: that is, on the philosophical reconstruction in representational terms of the notion of intentional state, and especially of its distinctive property of intentionality. Limiting even further my scope of inquiry, I will deal in fact only with a specific form given by Fodor to this first step.

2.2.1. The Structure of the Double Reduction Strategy

Indeed, Fodor sometimes characterizes the representational reconstruction of the intentional state with which the philosophical approach to the naturalization of intentional realism begins as a reductionist move, in the limited sense that it reduces intentional states to mental representations.

This reductionist move is part of a more complex one taking linguistic meaning as its point of departure and successively reducing the relation between a linguistic symbol and its content to the relation between an intentional state and what it is about, and then the relation between an intentional state and what it is about to the relation between a mental representation and its content. It is therefore the second stage of a "double reduction."

This double reduction strategy is best exposed in his article "Mental Representation: An Introduction": "The idea," Fodor writes, "to put it in a nutshell, is that it might be possible to pull off a double reduction: First derive the semantic properties of linguistic symbols from the intentional properties of mental states; then postulate a population of mental symbols—*mental representations as one says*—and derive the intentional properties of beliefs and desires from these. Practically every major twentieth-century philosopher, at least in the Anglo-American tradition, has taken it for granted that such a double reduction is out of the question. But it increasingly appears that they were all wrong" (1987a: 116).

Let us examine more closely the nature of each of these two reductive moves and the arguments supporting them.

The first one is based on the observation of a similarity. Fodor contends that symbols, linguistic symbols in particular, are the only entities besides intentional states that have both causal properties and properties of aboutness, commonly referred to as semantic properties. Comparing the belief that the cat is on the mat with the sentence expressing it, he writes about the latter:

> On the one hand it is a physical object. . . . Qua physical object it has an indefinite complex of . . . causal properties. For example it exerts a certain gravitational force upon the moon, it reflects light in various complicated ways. . . . But on the other hand, this sort of physical object is special in that it also has a bundle of intentional properties, much as we have seen that beliefs and desires do. So in particular it looks to be about something (viz. the cat, or where the cat is, or the fact that the cat is on the mat . . .). (1987a: 111)

Like the mental state of believing that the cat is on the mat, the sentence expressing that the cat is on the mat is about a certain state of things, which in addition seems here to be identical in both cases. This initial observation can be summarized as in Figure 3.1.

About'
(Mental aboutness)

T1' ⟶ T2'
(Intentional state)   (Intentional content)

About"
(Semantic aboutness)

T1" ⟶ T2"
(Linguistic symbol)   (Semantic content)

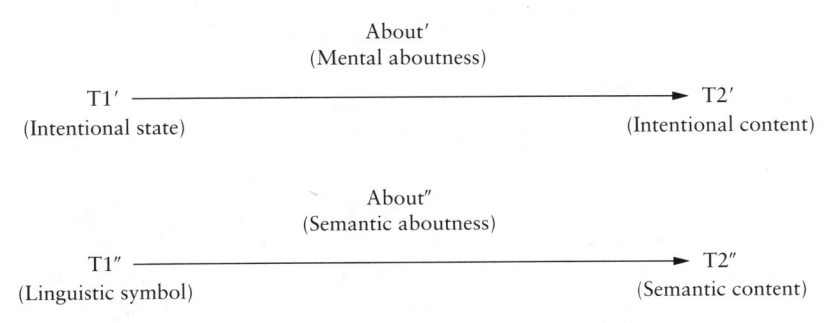

FIGURE 3.1. Fodor's parallelism between mental and linguistic aboutness.

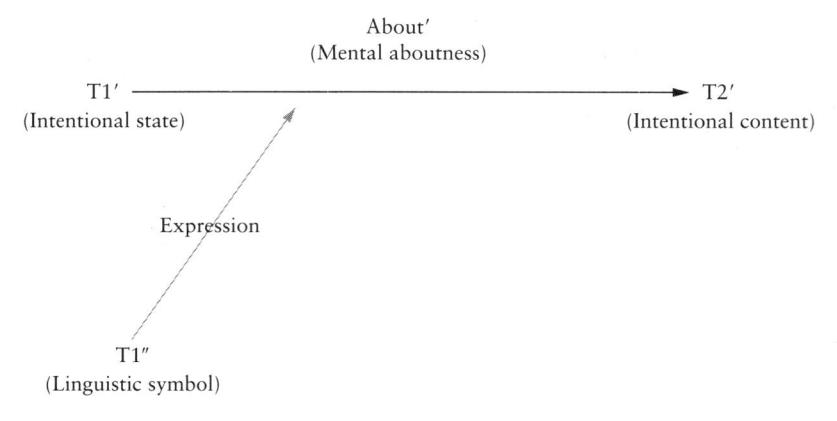

```
                     About'
                (Mental aboutness)
T1' ─────────────────────────────────► T2'
(Intentional state)                    (Intentional content)
              ↗
             /
            Expression
           /
          /
        T1"
   (Linguistic symbol)
```

FIGURE 3.2. The first step of the Fodorian reduction.

Arguing that such a parallelism is "too striking to be accidental," Fodor immediately draws the conclusion that it is a rational move to try to reduce these two similar properties of aboutness to a single one. The reduction he opts for has two aspects. First, he identifies the contents of the two relations of aboutness (T2" = T2') and then suggests that the linguistic sentence is about this common content only in a secondary or derivative way, thanks to the relation of expression it has with the intentional state—a relation of expression of which he offers no detailed analysis. In short, in Fodor's opinion we express what we think about, and we can do so because we are thinking about it. This quite traditional approach to the language/thought problem is recommended in his eyes by the failure of the numerous endeavors to reverse it on the part of contemporary philosophers. It can in turn be schematized as in Figure 3.2.

The second step of the double reduction consists in similarly establishing a relation of partial identity as well as a relation of derivation between the intentionality of the mental state and the representational capacity of a mental representation. It is quite important to emphasize that mental representations are immediately characterized as mental symbols, and even more specifically, as mental symbols of the same nature as linguistic ones, in short, as mental words. By virtue of this second reduction:

> We can think of beliefs and desires as inheriting their semantic properties from those of mental representations, just as we have been thinking of linguistic symbols (e.g. English sentences) as inheriting their semantic properties from the intentional properties of the beliefs that they are used to express. On this view, the semantic properties of mental representations are at the very bottom of the pile. It is mental representations that have aboutness in the first instance;

everything else that is intentional inherits its intentionality, directly or otherwise, from the intentionality of mental representations. (1987a: 115)

The second step should, however, not be seen as a mere repetition of the first. Fodor insists that the existence of mental representations, unlike that of linguistic symbols, must be postulated. In the first step the reduction is suggested by the observation of a parallelism, in the second it is suggested by the first reduction itself and it is necessary to hypothesize the term of the reduction, namely, mental representations. Besides, a difference remains between the linguistic symbol and the mental state from which it "inherits" its intentional capacity, and consequently the two intentional relations cannot be totally identified. On the contrary, the intentionality of the mental state is nothing more than the intentionality of the mental representation. Accordingly, the mental representation must be understood as being a part of the mental state, and a proper schematization of the second step of the double reduction looks like Figure 3.3.

2.2.2. Consequence: The Semantic Conception of Intentionality

The fundamental consequence of such an identification of mental intentionality with the semantic properties of a mental representation viewed as a mental word is to give birth to a symbolic picture of intentional realism.

It is, however, important to distinguish this symbolic picture of intentional realism from the language-of-thought hypothesis. The latter is a special case of the former; it does not derive in any immediate or necessary way from such a symbolic picture and introduces the further idea that a system of mental symbols is endowed with the same kind of internal organization as a formal language. This thesis should not be confounded with the more fundamental assertion that a representation is nothing but a mental word in the sense of a word-like symbol. This assertion alone captures the essence of representationalism sensu stricto. In turn, the language-of-thought hypothesis should be distinguished from the computational hypothesis, which is no more than a particular version of it. In short, even though a mental representation is a sort of mental word, the representational reconstruction of

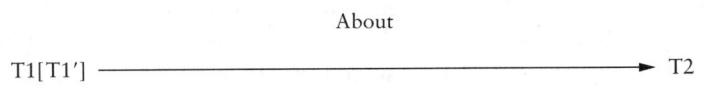

$$T1[T1'] \xrightarrow{\text{About}} T2$$

FIGURE 3.3. The second step of the Fodorian reduction.

intentionalism is conceptually different from both the language-of-thought hypothesis and the computational theory of cognition.

In this regard, the exposition of the double reduction to be found in "Mental Representation: An Introduction" is not worded with sufficient care, since it conveys the impression that the immediate consequence of the double reduction is not sheer representationalism—that is, once again, the symbolic picture of intentional realism—but the language-of-thought hypothesis itself. The risk of confusion is reinforced by the way Fodor uses the expression "representational theory of mind," by which he usually means not representationalism sensu stricto but the language-of-thought hypothesis, to which he also famously subscribes. In other words, he himself wrongly uses the name of the genus to designate what is no more than one of its species. Only in the later context of his critical analysis of connectionism does he come to realize the importance of distinguishing between representationalism and the language-of-thought hypothesis, and consequently between the two elements associated with the expression "representational theory of mind." According to this analysis, the opposition between classical cognitivism and connectionism is indeed to be understood as an opposition between two kinds of representationalism, one subscribing to the idea that the system of mental representations has a language-like structure, and the other rejecting it, but both accepting the more fundamental premise that a mental representation is a symbol.

It is thus fairly difficult to locate in Fodor's work an adequate statement of how representationalism should be sensu stricto understood. The best approximation to it is probably the definition offered in the first chapter of *Psychosemantics*, where representationalism is characterized as the thesis that an intentional system is a system endowed with a set of representations constituting both "the immediate objects of the propositional attitudes and the domains of mental processes" (1987b: 17). This thesis has two implications.

First, an intentional mental state should be seen as a relation between such a system and a complex representation having the property of being about an object (or state of things) in the same way that a linguistic symbol is about what it is the symbol of. In other words, an intentional system S is, for instance, in the state of believing O, if there is in S a complex mental representation M that has a semantic relation R (representing) with an object O external to the system S, and if this representation M stands in a certain relation R^* (belief) with S. The R^* relation is thus the element corresponding to the intentional notion of type, while the R relation corresponds to the notion of intentionality. This reconstruction can be schematized as in Figure 3.4.

```
                    R*                    R
System ─────────────→ M ─────────────→ Object
```

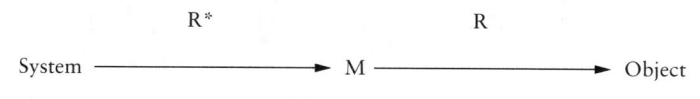

FIGURE 3.4. Fodor's symbolic analysis of the intentional state (1).

Second, an intentional process of S should in turn be conceived as a causal sequence of (complex) mental representations standing in R^* relations with S and in R semantic relations with certain objects. Fodor writes: "Mental processes are causal sequences of tokenings of mental representations" (1987b: 17).

The symbolic view of intentional realism resulting from the first step of the double reduction strategy therefore advocates what Fodor calls a polyadic conception of the intentional state, in the sense that its property of intentionality is separated from its other properties, and a semantic conception of intentionality, identifying intentionality with the semantic properties of a wordlike mental entity.

If it is crucial to distinguish this semantic conception of intentionality from the language-of-thought hypothesis, however, when it is complemented by this hypothesis, the theory of intentionality advocated by Fodor becomes a semantics in the full sense of the term. As a matter of fact Fodor designates it with the revealing term of "Psychosemantics." When considered in its full extension, his theory of intentionality is therefore nothing else than the semantics of a primary language on which all other kinds of semantics are based. It is interesting to note that, within Psychosemantics itself, Fodor finds it necessary to distinguish between the problem of defining the general nature of a mental symbol, delineating what he calls "the theory of meaning" and sees as a philosophical kind of investigation, and the problem of the compositionality of meaning, corresponding on the contrary to a second and purely psychological part of the psychosemantical inquiry.

2.3. LIMITATIONS OF THE SEMANTIC CONCEPTION OF INTENTIONALITY

The problem I wish to discuss is whether such a semantic conception of intentionality is acceptable, disregarding the analysis of the notion of intentional type also being proposed. Accordingly, my objective is not to assess, like in so many discussions of Fodor, the success of his naturalization of representationalism, but that his prior representational reconstruction of intentional realism.[3]

2.3.1. The Requirement of Adequacy to Intentional Phenomena

Among the various criteria by which such a success is to be measured, adequacy to the phenomena that representationalism is intended to capture is undoubtedly of crucial importance. Accordingly, one of the main questions to be addressed is whether Fodorian representationalism yields a form of intentional realism adequate to intentional phenomena.

In the context of Fodor's investigation, the notion of intentional phenomena refers primarily to folk psychology. Folk psychology can aptly be considered a conceptual system, evidenced by logical data such as attributions of intentional states, and referring to nonlogical ones such as behavioral data and first-person data. In the strict and traditional sense of the term, only such nonlogical elements are appropriately labeled phenomena. However, these are but a small portion of what Fodor's naturalization enterprise wants to account for. Indeed, his symbolic representationalism claims to reconstruct commonsense intentional realism, not only to be an alternative and more adequate conceptualization of the same domain of nonlogical data.

As a result, the naturalization project amounts to the transformation of one conceptual system (folk psychology) into another (a naturalized version of it). As such it can be usefully compared to an intertheoretic reduction. In both cases indeed the problem is to redefine a set of concepts on the basis of a number of primitive notions. The specificity of the Fodorian transformation lies in two distinctive features already mentioned. It is a two-step procedure, reconstructing folk psychology in terms first of a representationalist as well as a realist intentionalism, and then of a naturalist version of it. And it involves a process of scientization: its ambition is not simply to replace one scientific conceptual system with another, but to replace a prescientific conceptual system with a scientific one.

By nature, an intertheoretic reduction must meet certain criteria of adequacy: an arbitrary redefinition of the concepts to be reduced is clearly out of order. It is no less clear that these criteria of adequacy mainly include the preservation of a number of properties of these concepts. This conservative dimension is a general feature of all intertheoretic reductions and it is well illustrated by the classic case of the Fregeo-Russellian logicization of mathematics. Russell and Frege offer, for instance, to redefine the concept of integer as the set of all classes equivalent to a given class, and one of their major arguments in favor of such a definition is that it does preserve all well-established properties of integers.

In the same manner, the Fodorian naturalization of folk psychology has to save a number of its properties; although, because of the naive character of folk theories, this constraint is more flexible than in the case of two scientific theories. Among the properties to be preserved, Fodor explicitly mentions the fundamental principle of the parallelism of causal and semantic properties of intentional states (1987b, chap. 1), the distinction between type and content (1981a), and even a number of specific intentional generalizations.[4]

In short, what the Fodorian reconstruction of intentionalism is after is a *substitute* for the conceptual system of folk psychology, and one meeting in addition the general requirements of scientificity. Its goal is to modify, in a realist, representationalist, and naturalist way, this system while retaining some of its aspects. It is in other words necessary, to paraphrase Plato's famous injunction to the astronomers of Antiquity revived by Pierre Duhem (see *"Sozein ta phainomena": To Save the Phenomena*, Duhem 1985) that the Fodorian transformation be capable of saving intentional phenomena. SOZEIN TA STOCHASTIKA PHAINOMENA:[5] such is Fodor's own injunction to the cognitive scientist of his time. And indeed he sometimes uses such a Platonic-Duhemian terminology. He writes for instance in "Propositional Attitudes" that "it would be nice if [the Representational] theory of belief permitted us to save the appearances" (1981a: 178).

It is consequently quite important to assess the extent to which the semantic conception of intentionality resulting from the double reduction strategy fulfills the constraint of adequacy to intentional phenomena that it sets for itself. In other words: is the identification of the intentionality of a mental state with the aboutness of a wordlike mental representation capable of saving its appearances?

2.3.2. The Directness of Intentionality

It is precisely arguable that the semantic conception of intentionality does not do justice to two crucial types of intentional phenomena, closely connected with each other and difficult to dismiss.

As Figure 3.4 clearly shows, the Fodorian representationalist reconstruction of the intentional state transforms every intentional relation with an object into a symbolic one. As a result it apparently excludes all possibility of introducing a distinction between symbolic and nonsymbolic intentional states. It looks, nevertheless, extremely difficult to do without such a distinction: is it not clearly one thing for a mental state to relate to an object by means of a symbol, and another one to relate to it without any symbolic mediation? The opposite view should at least be carefully established.

It could obviously be retorted that the possibility remains of considering a specifically symbolic intentional state as a sort of higher-degree generically symbolic one. In addition to providing a highly questionable definition of symbolic intentionality, this move is of no help for the notion of nonsymbolic intentional state itself. Because it is no less clear—and this is the second one of the two intentional phenomena mentioned—that the states falling into this category are apprehended as directly related to their intentional correlates. On the contrary, attributing to the intentional state a basic symbolic structure makes every intentional relation an indirect one.

Unless, of course, we reject one of the most intuitive as well as time-honored elements of the definition of the nature of a symbol, namely, the idea that it first and foremost is an *aliquid quod stat pro aliquo*, something that stands in place of something else. There are indeed two main aspects in this definition. One is the ability a symbol has of referring beyond itself to another object, its ability to be "in place of something else," which is commonly designated as the aboutness of the symbol; the other one is the property of being an intermediary, of being "something that stands." A symbol makes a relation with something else possible. But in order to be able to do this, it has to be an intermediary element in the very relation it makes possible, and consequently this relation cannot be anything but an indirect one. These two properties are clearly epitomized in the notion of substitute. A symbol is a substitute, in the sense in which an ambassador is a substitute for a nation. The government deals with a foreign nation through its ambassador, because it is a convention that the ambassador stands in front of us in place of his or her nation. It is therefore important to underline that a symbol is not only the *terminus a quo* of a relation with an object but also the partial *terminus ad quem* of this relation. A symbol stands for something else, but there it stands, and accordingly it is also what we are dealing with when we relate with an object symbolically.

Now what Fodor seems to have forgotten is precisely the fact that, inasmuch as it is something standing for something else, a symbol presupposes an element x—an *interpretant* in Charles S. Peirce's terminology—as the source of the symbolic relation and therefore plays itself the role of an intermediary entity. Consequently, the schematization of the Fodorian definition of the intentional state in Figure 3.5 looks more adequate, since it makes the mediating nature of the mental representation fully manifest.

How can such a schematization, however, be reconciled with the idea that some of our mental states are intuitive, or to put it in Russellian terms, are of an acquaintance type? Is it not the hallmark of intuition to be a direct relation with an intentional object? It can certainly be defended that intuition does not exist and that a version of intentional realism excluding all intentional states of this kind is a sound one—a position frequently held in contemporary philosophy. However, such a claim stands in need of detailed ar-

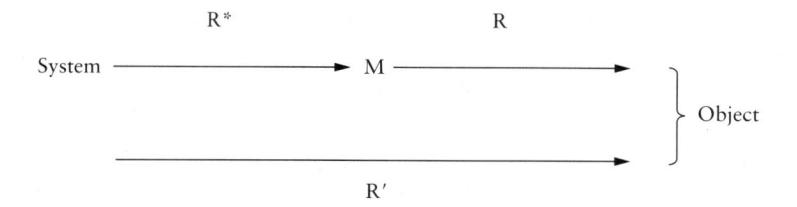

FIGURE 3.5. Fodor's symbolic analysis of the intentional state (2). The additional arrow indicates that the mental representation M, when considered as a symbol, not only is about the Object, but also plays an intermediary role in the establishment of the intentional relation between the System and the Object.

gumentation in view of the fact that it violates our most immediate apprehension of intentional phenomena and also has substantial cognitive and epistemological implications.

Besides, even if it is granted that intuition is a fiction, it remains that many other kinds of intentional states do not fit within a symbolic framework of intentionality. When I feel a desire to drink a Petrus and when I am in the state of understanding the phrase "drink a Petrus," I most probably stand in an intentional relation with the same object or state of things, namely drinking-a-Petrus. However, that this relation can in each case be characterized at a certain level of generality as a relation of being about the same state of things does not mean that it is identical in both of them. If it is natural to see it as an indirect relation in the case of understanding, this has to be seriously argued for in the case of desiring, to say the least. It clearly sounds much more adequate to consider the state of desiring to drink a Petrus as a case of direct intentionality.

As a matter of fact, it is quite difficult to accept that when I say that my desire is a desire of X, or more generally that my belief is a belief of X, my willing is a willing of X, etc. . . . it can be legitimately understood that my desire, my belief, or my willing, in any proper sense of the term, stands for what it is the desire, the belief, or the willing of. It sounds more appropriate to say that my intentional state is about something, but is not the substitute for anything, and in this regard is quite different from a symbol. And therefore that the relation of aboutness itself is in each case different.

The symbolic definition of an intentional state resulting from the double reduction makes it thus necessary to treat intentionality as a relation with an object always mediated by a substitute for this object, a constraint whose power and signification apparently elude Fodor, who does not even make it explicit. Because of these implications the symbolic definition offers too narrow a framework for accommodating the distinction between symbolic and nonsymbolic intentionality, as well as the apparently direct character of numerous intentional states.

2.3.3. Objections

Several objections can be made to this criticism of the Fodorian semantic conception of intentionality. It is, unfortunately, impossible to review them all here, and I will concentrate on the most important one.[6]

It is tempting to argue that if the Fodorian definition does not allude to the notions of substitution and indirectness, it is actually because they are not involved in it. In this perspective, which amounts to a literal reading of Figure 3.4, the intentionality of the mental state is reducible to the aboutness relation R between the mental representation and the object, which is of a direct nature.

However, such a reading makes the adequacy of the Fodorian definition not simply problematic, but plainly impossible.

As this same Figure 3.4 clearly shows, intentionality would thus be too sharply dissociated from the other properties of the intentional state. For in such a perspective, the fact of being a desire, or a belief . . . is not a property of the intentional state qua intentional state. An intentional state would be on the one hand a desire, a belief, . . . and on the other hand the representation of such and such an object. Consequently, the mental state of desiring to drink a Petrus should be characterized as the fact of desiring (to be defined in causal functional terms according to Fodor) a certain symbolic formula, which itself symbolizes a state of things. As far as the property of intentionality per se is concerned, there is therefore no difference between desiring to drink a Petrus and imagining oneself drinking a Petrus: the only difference lies in the relation between the symbolic formula and the system, while the aboutness relation remains unchanged.

According to the most spontaneous and obvious analysis of intentional phenomena, it looks, however, as if the differences corresponding to the distinctions between a belief and a desire . . . have to do, at least in part, with the property of intentionality itself. By reflecting types of intentional states, these differences reflect types of intentionality. It is the intentional content itself that seems to be the object of a desire qua desire, the object of a belief qua belief. . . . The desire to drink a Petrus is apprehended as a desire to drink a Petrus and not as a desire for the formula symbolizing the state of drinking a Petrus! Making a literal reading of Figure 3.4 amounts to saying that the full expression in natural language of such an intentional state should be: "I desire the mental sentence 'drinking a Petrus,' and this sentence represents for me the state of drinking a Petrus." Except in very exceptional circumstances, I cannot accept the idea that such are the objects of my numerous appetites. It is quite difficult to find a more inadequate attempt at saving intentional phenomena. Consequently, Fodor should not be credited with such a theory, even if some of his formulations can be seen as confusing. Indeed, he writes on some occasions that mental representations are the "objects" of propositional attitudes.[7]

A naturally inviting way of making the Fodorian theory reasonably adequate to the intentional appearances it intends to save is by interpreting it in such a way that my desire for a drinking a Petrus is a desire for drinking-a-Petrus, that is, a desire for what is represented by the symbolic-representational formula "drinking a Petrus."[8] But this means treating a mental representation as a substitute; and consequently falling back on the schematization of Figure 3.5 without resolving the difficulties associated with it which have just been pointed out.

Further investigation would also permit in my opinion the claim that Fodor nowhere justifies the assimilation of a mental representation with a symbol and that the double reduction itself is also logically disputable.[9]

2.4. TOWARD A NATURALIST APPROPRIATION OF HUSSERLIAN INTENTIONALISM

Several attitudes are patently possible for those who accept this conclusion while sharing Fodor's concern with naturalizing intentional realism. One could simply give up on folk psychology and resign oneself to the frustrating idea that at best only an imperfect symbolic-representational substitute for it can be naturalized. On the other hand, one could maintain the requirement of adequacy to folk psychology but renounce reconstructing it in representational terms and search for a strategy of naturalization more adequate to intentional phenomena. However, nothing in the criticism put forward justifies such extreme solutions at this point, and it looks more appropriate to first investigate the possibility of reconciling a representationalist version of intentional realism with intentional phenomena. Two main options are open for working in that direction. The first one consists in looking for a way of somehow forcing intentional phenomena into the symbolic-representational framework. The second one is to try to dissociate the two notions of mental representation and symbol.

Both these options must start with pushing the analysis of intentional realism itself further. An important weakness in Fodor's overall strategy is indeed its attempt to naturalize right away an intentionalist and realist interpretation of folk psychology that is only roughly characterized: this leads him to further adopt a form of representational reconstruction of this interpretation that recommends itself more for its naturalizability than for its adequacy to intentional phenomena. However, before transforming a conceptual system, this conceptualization must be given a form that is both accurate and sufficiently rigorous.

And it is at this very point that Husserlian phenomenology can recommend itself. For one thing it is probably one of the most complete and systematic theories of intentionality in twentieth-century philosophy, if not in the whole history of the discipline. For another, it is mainly concerned with providing as rigorous a description of intentional phenomena as possible, even if it makes use of the notion of phenomenon in a very idiosyncratic way (see Chapter 1 of this book) and at any rate in a way quite different from the Fodorian one (see 2.3.1).[10]

There is nevertheless another, more important motive for turning to Husserl. On the one hand, his theory of intentionality grants a key role to the distinction between symbolic and nonsymbolic intentional states, and construes the distinction as an opposition between a direct and an indirect type of intentionality. On the other hand, it also advocates a representational conception of the general structures of the intentional state. Furthermore, it turns out that this representational approach does in fact take the notion of symbol as a model for its analysis of the nature of representation. Consequently, the question is naturally raised whether Husserlianism can provide an illustration of the first one of the two ways previously mentioned of possibly reconciling representationalism with intentional phenomena, and thus offer precious help on how to elaborate an appropriate solution along those lines.

A worry could immediately be voiced about the compatibility of such a line of inquiry with a naturalist perspective. Isn't Husserl's phenomenological theory of intentionality after all based entirely upon the assumption that a truly adequate characterization of intentional phenomena can only be achieved by renouncing all forms of naturalism, both ontological and epistemological?

If this really is the price to be paid for reconciling intentionalism and representationalism by Husserlian means, I agree it is too high. The real challenge, in my opinion, lies on the contrary in sacrificing neither of the two complementary aspects of the project of naturalizing intentional realism, or for that matter, intentionalism *tout court*, namely, fully accounting for intentional phenomena *and* explaining how a material entity such as a living organism can be endowed with such intentional properties. Today a number of critiques of Fodorism complacently oppose the richness and subtlety of intentional theories belonging to the Husserlian tradition to the simplistic and quite deflationary aspects of the symbolic and computational approach to intentional phenomena. However, they generally remain silent on the fact that these descriptions are for the most part associated with an ontological and epistemological perspective precisely rejected by Fodorism and they fail to provide any argument in its favor. But advocating the higher adequacy of a non-naturalist theory of intentionality over a naturalist one without making a case for antinaturalism is clearly unacceptable.

Accordingly, the real problem is to clarify the extent to which the Husserlian theory of intentionality can be instrumental for an appropriate naturalization of intentionalism, and more specifically of a realist version of intentionalism. This of course requires not only a determination of whether Husserl's theory can solve the difficulties of adequacy just pointed out, but also of whether the solution possibly obtained can be naturalized. In short, what is to be investigated is no less than the possibility of a naturalist appropriation of Husserlian intentionalism, and this involves four major tasks:

1. Providing an interpretation of the theory;
2. Assessing its adequacy to phenomena;
3. Establishing the possibility of its naturalization; and
4. Discovering the appropriate way of carrying out such a naturalization.

The point to be discussed in the next section is mainly an interpretive one. I want to examine whether the content of Husserl's analysis of the intentional state offers a possible way out of Fodor's difficulties. And if it does, whether it is indeed by successfully reconciling a symbolic conception of mental representation with a distinction between symbolic and nonsymbolic intentional states, or by renouncing in fact the assimilation of the two notions of symbol and representation and by offering in this manner a nonsymbolic version of representationalism.

In order to reach a sufficient degree of technicality in my analysis, I will limit its scope to the first stage of the development of Husserl's reflections on the general structures of intentionality as they are presented in the second edition of his *Logische Untersuchungen*: Given that this second edition came out at the same time as the first volume of *Ideen* and that Husserl himself considered these two pieces to be largely homogeneous in spite of the well-known introduction of transcendentalism in the latter, my analysis will in fact deal more comprehensively with the 1901–13 published part of his research. Such limitation also answers philosophical motives. Although the modifications to be found in Husserl's theories after 1913, or in fact also in some unpublished material of the 1901–13 period, are sometimes interpreted as a radical departure from an early and official representationalist phase, it is obviously necessary to examine this early representationalism closely. It is only under this frequently unfulfilled condition that the problem raised by the interpretation of the unpublished material as well as of the subsequent developments of his thought can be fruitfully approached.

3. A DILEMMA FOR HUSSERLIAN REPRESENTATIONALISM

3.1. THE PERSISTENCE OF REPRESENTATIONALISM

One point at least is beyond dispute: the theory of intentionality put forward in the second edition of the *Logische Untersuchungen* does constitute a form of representationalism. At least this is what Husserl himself claims from the very first steps of the analysis of the general structures of the intentional state he initiates in the fifth logical investigation. This analysis is mainly conducted in the form of a criticism of the theory propounded by Brentano in *Psychology from an Empirical Viewpoint* (1874). After modifying Brentano's definition of the intentional object, Husserl criticizes in the third chapter of that same investigation another important thesis of his to the effect that "every intentional state is either a mere representation or has a representation as its necessary basis."[11] In no way does Husserl reject this principle, but only the interpretation given to it by Brentano. The term "representation," like the whole terminology of descriptive psychology, looks to him loaded with several intertwined meanings and therefore badly in need of systematic disambiguation. This laborious task concludes with a distinction between no fewer than thirteen different possible meanings, usefully summarized in the closing chapter, and which can be aptly sorted out into two different categories: those dealing with general components of the intentional state, and those referring to specific types of intentional state. Two of the notions falling into the first category are of special importance.

In a first sense of the term, a representation (*Vorstellung*) is nothing else than what Husserl calls the *matter* of an act. In §20 of the fifth logical investigation, after successively introducing against Brentano the idea of the transcendence of the intentional object as well as a distinction between a properly intentional part or *act* (the *noesis* in the terminology of *Ideen*), and a nonintentional part (the *hyle* in the terminology of *Ideen*) within the intentional *Erlebnis* or state,[12] Husserl separates the intentional act itself into two components: the matter (*Materie*) and the quality (*Quälitat*). The matter of an act is defined as the element responsible for establishing the intentional relation with an object, and an object specified in a particular way (§20, p. 221). The less clearly delineated concept of quality designates a number of features of the act having the common property of being irrelevant to the individuation of the intentional object (p. 219).

Since a matter is included in every act, and an act is included in every intentional state, all intentional states are clearly representational for Husserl, in the sense that each is based on a *Vorstellung*: "It is obvious that every intentional state has a *Vorstellung* as a basis; it is obvious that we cannot judge without having a representation of what we judge and the same is true about interrogation, doubt, supposition, desire" (§27, p. 457; my translation).

Out of this first concept of representation, Husserl then derives a second one (only made fully explicit in the sixth logical investigation) for which he specifically reserves the word *Repräsentation*. A *Repräsentation* is the conjunction of the matter of an act with the nonintentional part of the intentional state that Husserl also labels the "representative content" (cf. especially §26).

This representational structure of the intentional state can be summarized as in Figure 3.6.

It is thus clear that the Husserlian theory of intentionality offers an important point of agreement with the Fodorian representationalist reconstruction of intentionalism.

3.2. THE "EIDETIC BARRIER" BETWEEN SYMBOLIC AND INTUITIVE INTENTIONALITY

It is no less beyond dispute that Husserl's theory of intentionality is based upon a fundamental cleavage between intuitive and symbolic types of intentional states, a cleavage without which his epistemology falls apart, and which is repeatedly and insistently reasserted throughout his work. On the occasion of his critical examination of the symbolic theory of perception, according to which sensible qualities of spatial things are signs of the mathe-

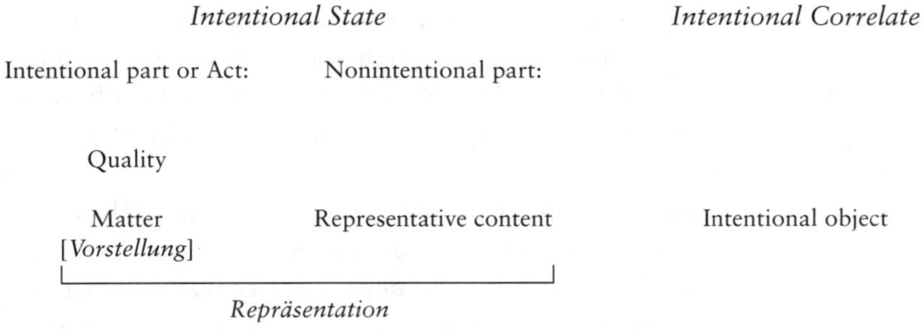

Intentional State		Intentional Correlate
Intentional part or Act:	Nonintentional part:	
Quality		
Matter [*Vorstellung*]	Representative content	Intentional object
└─────────── *Repräsentation* ───────────┘		

FIGURE 3.6. Husserl's general analysis of the intentional state (1).

matical attributes uncovered by physics, Husserl even goes as far as writing in §43 of *Ideen* I that "there is an insuperable eidetic barrier" between "perception on the one side and symbolic representation on the other" (p. 99, my translation).

If on the one hand every intentional state includes a matter and a *Repräsentation*, and on the other hand, the difference between symbolic and intuitive intentional types is irreducible, it is natural to assume that neither the *Repräsentation* nor the matter of an intentional state should be identified with a symbol. Indeed, this seems to be the position indirectly defended by Husserl in the first logical investigation, which is dedicated to the description of symbolic intentionality, considered as a specific kind of intentionality.

It is important at this point to stress a peculiarity in how Husserl elaborates his theory of intentionality in the *Logische Untersuchungen*. He does not start with a phenomenological description of the most general structures of intentionality and then engage in a study of their various possible specifications, including the symbolic one. Instead, he starts with a description of the symbolic kind and only at a later stage, in the fifth and sixth logical investigations, does he try to work out a general definition of intentional state. This priority given to the description of symbolic intentionality is not only a matter of exposition (*ordo exponendi*) but also of investigation (*ordo investigandi*). It is correct to say that Husserl himself acknowledges a "zigzagging" structure in his investigations and that the first logical investigation makes use of concepts explicitly introduced in the last two. But the status of these concepts is then more that of a descriptive hypothesis than that of a presupposition in the strong sense of the term, as it should be if the priority in question were only one of an *ordo exponendi*.

3.2.1. Indirectness as the Essence of Symbolic Intentionality

The explicit goal of the first logical investigation is to inquire not into the most general nature of symbolic intentionality, but only into that of its most important species from the point of view of logic, namely linguistic or expressive (because it makes use of a linguistic expression or *Ausdruck*) intentionality. It is clear, however, that its ambition is also to lay bare those features which any intentional relation must possess in order to be a symbolic one.

Expressive intentionality is described as a complex intentional state composed of two simpler and hierarchized states also intentional, and having for an intentional correlate that equally complex entity we ordinarily call a meaningful word. The more basic of these two components is an intuition (either perceptive or imaginative) and it establishes an intentional relation with a written or spoken linguistic expression. The second one, which Husserl calls the *signification intention*, is nonintuitive and is correlated with another object, namely the referent of the expression (this is of course a simplification, Husserl being a notorious intensionalist). Although both of these intentional correlates are themselves only parts of a large and complex one, the referent is apprehended as the more important. This primacy of the referent over the word in linguistic intentionality is described by Husserl as a phenomenon of attention distribution: when we are in a linguistic intentional state, Husserl writes, "we do not live" in the intuition of the symbol, but only in the nonintuitive apprehension of the referent. The intuition of the symbol is, however, indispensable according to the first logical investigation. Without it we would not relate intentionally with the referent of the symbol, which is exactly what we want to be intentionally related with. Accordingly, the specificity of expressive intentionality lies in its *indirectness*: we intuit one object in order to reach another, and the only function of the first is to be a *substitute* for the second. Husserl's description is captured in Figure 3.7.

Clearly this analysis is general enough to be easily extended to all symbolic forms of intentionality. As a matter of fact it is perfectly consonant with the general definition of the symbol given by Husserl as early as his *Philosophie der Arithmetik*: "A symbolic or improper representation is, as the word itself already indicates, a representation by means of signs. If a content is not given to us *directly* as it is, but only *indirectly* by nonambiguous signs, then, instead of a proper representation, we have a symbolic one" (chap. 11, p. 215, my translation). And he insists: "Consequently, a symbolic representation is a temporary substitute, and even sometimes a nontemporary one, when the object is not accessible in itself."[13]

It should be underlined that because it is established by means of a substitute, a symbolic intentional relation with an object is also, in Husserl's eyes, a relation with something absent for the subject (unless this object is

Intentional State   *Intentional Correlate*

                                                             S

Intention of signification ──────────────── Y ⟶ Referent

                                                             M

                                                             B

Intuitive state ─────────────────⟶ O

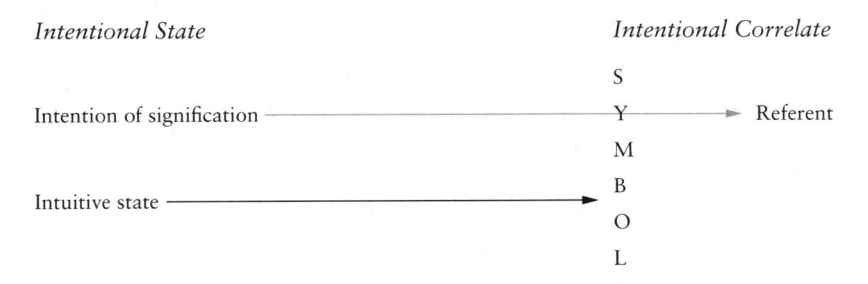

                                                             L

FIGURE 3.7. Husserl's analysis of expressive intentionality.

also apprehended intuitively in an additional act, as it happens in perceptual judgments): what is present to the subject is the substitute for the object, not the object itself. On the contrary, an intuitive intentional relation is direct, and in this sense it is a contact with the object itself, which is therefore present itself for the subject.

3.2.2. Inadequacies of the Definition

This first definition of symbolic intentionality is, however, quickly put into question by the further development of the *Logische Untersuchungen*. It implies with absolute necessity that every expressive intentional state is a complex act based upon the intuition of an object playing the role of a substitute. As Husserl reiterates in the sixth logical investigation: "[The intention of signification] cannot exist all by itself . . . it is always combined with an intuition on which it is based" (§25, in *LU* II/2, p. 619, my translation). Nevertheless, §19 of the fifth logical investigation brings in a curious note of contradiction. In a complement to his earlier description, Husserl writes: "The physical expression, the verbal sound, may seem unessential to this unity, and it is unessential inasmuch as any other verbal sound might have replaced it and done duty for it: *it could even have been wholly dispensed with*" (p. 583). But how could the symbol reasonably disappear if it really is essential for a symbolic intentional relation to rely on the mediation of another intentional object? There are only two possible solutions to this quandary: either Husserl's remark is a slip, or the first logical investigation fails to reveal the full generic essence of symbolic intentionality. Fortunately, the sixth logical investigation provides a clear-cut answer to the question. In §15 Husserl quite explicitly acknowledges the existence of what he calls "signitive [*Signitiven*] intentions beyond the limits of the meaning-function": "Countless signitive intentions lack either a fixed or a passing tie with expressions, though their essential character puts them in a class with signification-intentions" (p. 717). Paradoxically, among these intentions are first to be counted some of the components of external intuitions (either perceptive or imaginative). Indeed, according to Husserl's famous thesis that a spatial object can only be intuited in a fragmentary way, the central part of an intuitive state is always surrounded by other states intentionally correlated with the not-yet-intuited determinations of that object. In other words, not all determinations of the object of an external intuition are effectively intuited, and there is no such thing as a pure external intuition. And these peripheral intentional components of an intuitive state are for Husserl signitive ones. According to the formula introduced in §23 of the sixth logical investigation, an external intuition = $i + s$, where i refers to the set of purely intuitive components of the intuitive state and s to the set of its signitive components. In addition to signitive intentionality, Husserl mentions in §13 a number of cases where signification intentions of the very same nature as those involved in the symbolic kind of act described in the first logical investigation can exist without the support of any symbol. In sharp opposition to what he contended, Husserl thus undisputedly accepts the possibility of having a symbolic intentional relation with an object without using any symbol at all, and the description of the first logical investigation therefore does not grasp the truly essential component of symbolic intentionality. Accordingly, this essential component is to be preferably put into light through an analysis of signitive intentions, or of those cases where the intention of signification is dissociated from the intuition of a symbol.

3.2.3. Blurring the Eidetic Barrier

It is not thereby implied that indirectness could not be the hallmark of the symbolic intentional relation: it is apparently sufficient to locate this indirectness at a deeper level in the intentional state. And such is indeed the direction taken by Husserl in the last two of his logical investigations, where he tries to define the opposition between symbolic and intuitive intentionality as a difference of *Repräsentation*. In order to fully understand this definition, it is first necessary to further analyze the nature of the *Repräsentation* itself.

The matter and the representative content of an act have quite distinct roles. The first constitutes the very heart of the intentional state: it is that which makes the intentional relation possible, whereas the second is incapable of referring by itself to anything else. Representative content is nevertheless indispensable: the matter of the act needs its mediation in order to relate intentionally to an object. In other words, in a *Repräsentation* the matter establishes an intentional relation with an object by means of a representative content. More precisely, Husserl describes the relation between the matter and the representative content as an "animation," an "apperception," or also an "apprehension" (*Auffassung*). The previous schematization of the general structure of the intentional state can thus be complemented as shown in Figure 3.8.

The additional arrow immediately reveals that a *Repräsentation* offers *at its most general level* the very same sort of indirectness that was supposed to capture the specificity of the symbolic kind of intentionality according to the first logical investigation (see Figure 3.7).

```
                     Intentional State                    Intentional Correlate

Intentional part or act:    Nonintentional part:

                  Quality

                     Matter            Representative content
                     [Vorstellung]
                                                                    → Intentional object
                     |_____|
                                  Repräsentation
```

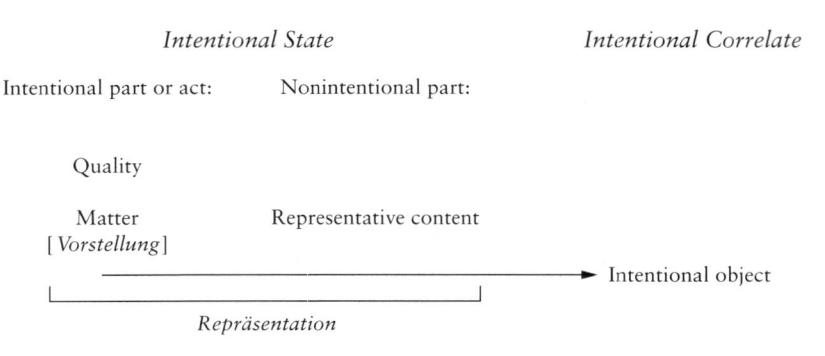

FIGURE 3.8. Husserl's general analysis of the intentional state (2).

As a matter of fact, at this point Husserl also explicitly describes the relation between matter and representative content in terms of interpretation:

> One sees at once that the very same thing which, in relation to the intentional object, is called its representation, i.e. the perceiving, remembering, picturing, symbolizing, intention directed toward it, is also called an *interpretation* [*Deutung*] in relation to the sensations really present in this act. (Fifth Investigation, §14, p. 568; translation modified)

Furthermore, the matter of an act receives a meaning-giving function identical with that of the signification intention in an expressive state, so that a representative content can be said to carry a signification or to be interpreted in the same way a symbol is: "It is the act's matter that makes its object count as this object and no other, it is the objective sense [*Sinn der gegenständlichen Auffassung*], the apprehensive sense [*Auffassungssinn*]." [14] In other words, something of the essence of symbolic intentionality as presented in the first logical investigation seems to belong in fact to every intentional state, inasmuch as every intentional state is conceived as a relation with one entity mediated by another. The matter of an act is related with the representative content, but it is so related in order to be able to reach the intentional object itself.

It cannot be objected that the assimilation of the structure of *Repräsentation* with that of symbolic intentionality as described in the first logical investigation is not faithful to Husserl's thought and results from an overinterpretation of the use of similar terms in different contexts. Indeed Husserl himself makes this assimilation perfectly explicit in a crucial moment of that same fifth logical investigation:

> The grasp [*Auffassung*] of understanding, in which the meaning of a word becomes effective, is, *in so far as any grasp is in a sense an understanding and an*

interpretation, akin to the divergently carried out "objective interpretations" in which, by way of an experienced sense-complex, the intuitive presentation, whether percept, imagination, representation ... of an object, e.g. an external thing, arises. ... If we imagine a consciousness prior to all experience, it may very well have the same sensations as we have. But it will intuit no things, and no events pertaining to things, it will perceive no trees and no houses, no flight of birds nor any barking of dogs. One is *at once tempted to express this situation by saying that its sensations mean nothing to such a consciousness, that they do not count as signs of the properties of the object itself, that their combination does not count as a sign of the object itself.* They are merely lived through without an objectifying interpretation derived from experience. Here, therefore, we can talk of signs and meanings just as we do in the case of expressions and cognate signs. (§23, p. 309; translation modified)

In no way does Husserl assert here that a *Repräsentation* is identical with a signification intention, but he introduces between them an analogy, that is to say, an identity within a difference, which can be summarized as in Figure 3.9.

The difference between these analogous relations lies in two correlated points, which will later be revealed to have a dramatic importance. In the case of *Repräsentation* we are dealing with a single state, while the symbolic relation involves a complex one where the signification intention interprets an element belonging to an associated intuitive act. In addition the element interpreted by the matter of the act in a *Repräsentation* is internal in the sense of being an intrinsic part of the state; on the contrary, what is interpreted by the signification intention is an intentional correlate and is therefore external to the state in question itself.

3.3. SYMBOLIC *REPRÄSENTATION* AND INTUITIVE *REPRÄSENTATION*

3.3.1. A Contradictory Requirement

If Husserl does uncover a deeper form of indirectness within the *Repräsentation* itself, it turns out that he does so in fact to make indirect-

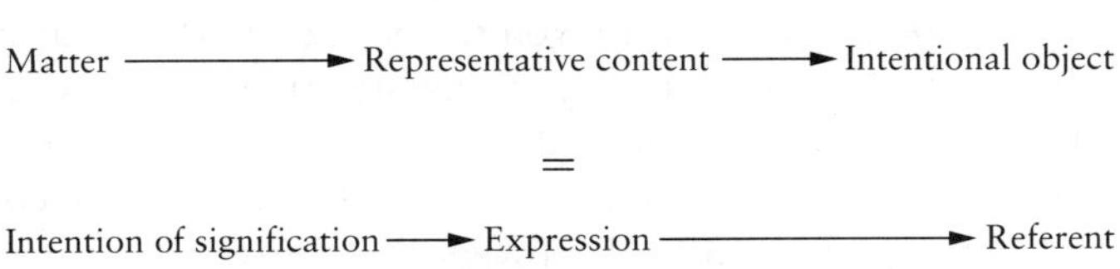

Matter ⟶ Representative content ⟶ Intentional object

=

Intention of signification ⟶ Expression ⟶ Referent

FIGURE 3.9. Husserl's analogy between general and expressive intentionality.

ness one of its generic features, and not anything specific to its symbolic species. But how then can the distinction between symbolic and intuitive intentionality be maintained? The difficulty is twofold. It first derives from the fact that the distinctive property of the first of these two kinds of intentionality has been transformed into a generic one, and cannot consequently be deemed as distinctive anymore. However, this problem is not the most pressing one: the idea of a generic indirectness of *Repräsentation* can be reconciled with that of a specific indirectness of symbolic *Repräsentation* by invoking for instance a difference of degree. The real difficulty lies in the necessity for reconciling the generic indirectness of *Repräsentation* with the direct character of specifically intuitive intentionality. The theory is confronted with two seemingly contradictory requirements, and therefore with a dilemma. And this dilemma is in fact no different from the obstacle confronting Fodorism.

As a general matter, there are only two ways to resolve a dilemma: one is to show that the dilemma itself is an illusion, the other is to renounce one of the two claims responsible for its emergence. The second strategy clearly seems more promising in this case. It requires that Husserl either abandon the "eidetic barrier" put forward between the symbolic and the intuitive, or give up the idea that the specificity of intuitive intentionality lies in its directness (and accordingly that the specificity of symbolic intentionality lies in its indirectness).

It is nevertheless impossible for Husserlianism to renounce the distinction between symbolic and intuitive intentional states without turning its whole analysis of knowledge upside down. This is why *Logische Untersuchungen* unsurprisingly opts for the second solution and by the middle of the fifth logical investigation ends up addressing the following question: wherein lies the difference between a symbolic *Repräsentation* and a nonsymbolic *Repräsentation*, given that every *Repräsentation* has that indirect structure which, at a first level of phenomenological description, seems to be the specific feature of the symbolic intentional state?

3.3.2. Arbitrariness as the Real Essence of Symbolic Intentionality

I will ignore the slow and convoluted process by which an answer is finally reached in §26 of the sixth logical investigation and concentrate on the basic ideas of the solution proposed.

Husserl first clearly distinguishes between the question of the content of the difference between the two kinds of *Repräsentation* and the question of its origin, and starts with answering the second question first.

A natural supposition is that the difference is rooted in the more important of the two components of the *Repräsentation*, namely the matter of the act. This supposition is, however, quickly rejected. In Husserl's eyes it is an unquestionable phenomenological datum that an intuitive *Repräsentation* and a symbolic one can have the very same matter, and therefore be related with one and the same object apprehended under identical perspectives.[15]

Accordingly, it seems more appropriate to try to derive the difference between the two sorts of *Repräsentation* from a difference in their respective representative content. And Husserl actually defends the idea that the representative content of an intuitive *Repräsentation* has that special property of being a "fullness" (*Fülle*), that is, a representative content whose determinations correspond to the determinations of the intentional object of the *Repräsentation* to which it belongs. He also variously calls representative contents of this kind "presentative contents" (*darstellenden*) (sixth logical investigation, §22) or "purely intuitive contents" (§23), and sorts them out into two categories: phantasms (*Phantasmen*) or analogizing presentative contents, and sensations or strictly presentative contents (§22). When I see, for instance, a red house, something in the representative content of the *Repräsentation* of my perceptive intentional state must correspond to the redness of the house being perceived. The redness of my representative content and the redness of the house are, however, two quite irreducibly different things.[16] And an intuitive intentional state is adequate when there is in its representative content a determination that corresponds to each of the determinations of the object.

This difference nevertheless remains insufficient. If every intuitive intentional state must contain a full representative content, every intentional state containing one is not intuitive; it is indeed another unquestionable datum for Husserl that "the same [representative] content can at one time carry a signification, and at another time an intuition."[17] The representative content of a certain shade of red, conjoined with the same matter of act, can for instance give birth to a symbolic *Repräsentation* as well as to a nonsymbolic one of the same red intentional correlate.

There are consequently two main possibilities left: either the difference between a symbolic *Repräsentation* and a nonsymbolic one originates from the interaction of the *Repräsentation* with an element external to it, or it is a matter of the union of its two components. Opting for the latter possibility, Husserl finally contends that it corresponds to two different ways the matter of the act can interpret or apprehend a representative content. A confusion should be carefully avoided here. Indeed, a difference in the sense given by the matter of the act to a representative content (*Auffassungssinn*) is also a difference in the way of interpreting it; but these two kinds of difference are of a different nature. The *Auffassungssinn* somehow exists independently of the representative content interpreted, while the type of modality of interpretation at stake in the second case results entirely from the union of the matter of the act with the representative content. This means that the representative content, as well as the matter of the act, are individually neutral with regard to the opposition between the intuitive and the symbolic. Husserl calls the property of the union of the matter of the act with the representative content, where this opposition is finally stemming from, the "form of the *Repräsentation*," or also, in order to contrast it directly with the sense of apprehension, the "form of the apprehension [*Auffassung*]." [18] He writes for instance in §27 of the sixth logical investigation: "It depends on the form of the apprehension whether the object is represented in purely signitive or intuitive, or mixed fashion" (p. 743; translation modified). Finally he also assigns the same origin to the difference between the imaginative and the perceptive kinds of intuition: "The sole difference is that imagination treats the content as likeness or image, whereas perception looks on it as a self-revelation of the object." [19]

Because the difference between a symbolic *Repräsentation* and an intuitive one has its source in the form of apprehension of the representative content by the matter of the act, its content can in turn only be grasped in the corresponding difference between intentional objects; in other words in the results of the two forms of apprehension.

In §23 of the sixth logical investigation, Husserl writes about the perceptive kind of intuitive intentionality: "As a *Repräsentation*, perception grasps the presentative content in such a way that in and with itself the object itself appears as given" (p. 734; translation modified). According to this remark, to apprehend a representative content intuitively means to interpret it in such a way that the resulting intentional correlate is considered the object itself. In turn, this means that this object is apprehended as being present. But how is the notion of presence to be understood here? In a perception the object perceived is first present in the temporal sense of the term. But this is a feature specific to the perceptive sort of intuitive intentionality; it therefore cannot be considered as a relevant criterion for specifying the opposition in its full generality. It is, on the other hand, tempting to consider that the object is present in the sense of being the immediate or direct term of the intentional relation, as suggested by the analysis of the first logical investigation (cf. 3.3.1). But it is precisely the observation that an intentional relation with an object can be symbolic but not involve the mediation of a symbol that has given a new impetus to the search for the essential nature of the difference between symbolic and intuitive intentionality. Finally, it is therefore only in the sense that it is there itself, "in person" as Husserl likes to put it, that the object of the intuitive intentionality is grasped as being present. But it should be immediately added that this "in person" character cannot be understood anymore as the opposite of a mediated presence, since once again, Husserl acknowledged the possibility of a symbolic intentionality not mediated by a symbol, and on the other hand intentional relations of all kinds are based on the mediating role of a representative content.

How should the in-person feature specific to all forms of intuitive intentionality be thus positively determined? The answer given by Husserl to this question in the fifth logical investigation is *in fine* the following: a *Repräsentation* is of an intuitive nature when the matter of its act apprehends its representative content in such a way that *all the determinations attributed to the intentional object (by virtue of the Auffassungssinn) are considered as having a corresponding element in the representative content.* This is why the representative content of a *Repräsentation* must be a *Fülle*, that is, must be such that each one of its determinations corresponds to a determination of the intentional object. However, it is clearly insufficient that such a correspondence exists. It has to be so to speak recognized in order for the *Repräsentation* to be an intuitive one. In other words, its full representative content has to be apprehended as such.

The symbolic *Repräsentation* can now be characterized in direct opposition to the intuitive one. Its most fundamental feature is that the determinations of its representative content are not apprehended as corresponding to those of its intentional object: "Signitive representation institutes a contingent, external relation between matter and representation content, whereas intuitive representation institutes one that is essential, internal."[20] An extreme case would be that a correspondence does exist but is not recognized, although in most cases of symbolic apprehension it is of course absent since it is not necessary. In fact the very advantage of the symbolic mode of intentionality is to enable the establishment of an intentional relation with an object on the basis of any kind of representative content. As Husserl says: "Significative matter has a general need for supporting content, but between the specific nature of the former and the specific being of the latter no bond of necessity can be found. . . . The case of purely intuitive *Repräsentation* is quite different. Here there is an internal, necessary connection between matter and representing content, fixed by the specific stuff of both."[21] While the relation between the determinations of the representative content and those of the intentional object must be apprehended as a correspondence—and consequently must be treatable as such—this relation is only apprehended as an arbitrary one in the case of symbolic intentionality. And in this arbitrariness lies its truly essential feature.

Lacking the correspondence element of intuitive *Repräsentation*, a symbolic *Repräsentation* also lacks the necessary basis for apprehending the intentional object as present in the sense of being there in person. And indeed the intentional object of a symbolic intentional state is, according to Husserl, apprehended as absent in the sense of not being there itself, in person. But here again the property of not being there in person cannot be defined as that of being indirectly there, by means of a substitute. For what Husserl has come to realize with the case of "signitive intentions" is precisely that not every intentional relation with an absent object takes the form of an intentional relation mediated by a second present object (a symbol). For a *Repräsentation* to be symbolic in the purest and most general sense of the term, it is enough that the matter of the act does not apprehend the determinations of the representative content *as corresponding* to the determinations of its intentional object.

This new way of drawing the line clearly eliminates the notion of indirectness from the generic essence of symbolic intentionality and thus necessarily modifies the general import of the first logical investigation. As a matter of fact, in a revealing comment made in §34 of the sixth logical investigation, Husserl quite explicitly specifies that the symbolic dimension of an expressive intentional relation does not lie in the fact that it is mediated by a symbolic object, but in the fact that it is thereby arbitrarily mediated, given that the symbol has nothing to do with what it stands for. What makes an expression an expressive kind of symbol is its substitutional nature, but what makes it a symbol is the arbitrariness of the substitution.

3.4. THE PERSISTENCE OF THE DILEMMA

3.4.1. A Crypto-Semantic Theory

These developments show that the Husserlian theory of intentionality stumbled from its very beginning on the same difficulty as Fodor's representational reconstruction of the intentional state: how can a representational conception of intentionality be reconciled with a distinction between symbolic and nonsymbolic intentional states if, on the one hand, this distinction is equated with an opposition between a direct and an indirect kind of intentionality, and on the other hand a mental representation is assimilated with a symbol in the traditional sense of the term, that is to say, is understood as a substitute for the intentional object?

The difference, however, is that Husserl sees the problem and tries to solve it. To this end he modifies his initial characterization of the opposition between intuitive and symbolic intentionality by dissociating it at its most general level from the opposition between direct and indirect intentionality. This opposition is then reconstrued as a difference between a nonarbitrary and an arbitrary form of apprehension of the representative content, and correspondingly associated with a modified interpretation of the contrast between the presence and the absence of the intentional object. As a consequence, every intentional relation is indirect because it includes a *Repräsentation*, without being for that matter of a symbolic nature; similarly, *Reprä-*

*sentation*s are indirect in the sense of involving the mediation of a representative content, but their indirectness no longer prevents them from being intuitive.

In spite of these comforting conclusions, it is far from certain, however, that the dilemma has really vanished.

In the first place, if the opposition between direct and indirect intentionality does not coincide anymore with the distinction between intuitive and symbolic intentionality considered at its most general level, it nevertheless remains a valid one at the more specific level of the classification of intentional states. A large number of intuitive states, and chief among them the perceptive ones, do have for Husserl an intentional relation with an object that is present not only in the sense of being there in person, but also in the sense of being directly there, without any intermediary, even if they are not intuitive qua direct intentional states but only perceptive. Similarly, the description of expressive intentionality as an intentional relation mediated by a symbolic object is not rejected, even if it is not symbolic qua mediated intentional relation but only expressive.

In the second place, the similarity between the indirectness of the general structure of *Repräsentation* and that of the expressive kind of intentionality as described in the first logical investigation has not been put into question. Therefore, the general nature of *Repräsentation* seems to retain the very feature that characterizes a symbol according to the traditional and Fodorian definitions of it as a "something" standing for something else. In other words, Husserl apparently maintains at the heart of its generic definition of the nature of intentionality the key element of the generic definition of symbolic intentionality that he rejects. In order to emphasize the deep continuity thereby maintained with the Fodorian theory, I suggest that the Husserlian theory be called a crypto-symbolic, or more precisely still, a crypto-semantic theory of intentionality; by this I mean a theory of intentionality that explicitly rejects the identification of intentionality with semantic properties of a symbol, but de facto retains its most essential element.

It follows immediately from these two observations that Husserl apparently remains committed to asserting that some intentional relations are direct and that every intentional relation is indirect or crypto-semantic by virtue of the general structure of *Repräsentation*, and therefore to denying that there is any contradiction between these two assertions. In other words, his theory of intentionality cannot be consistent unless it not only avoids the dilemma between the nature of *Repräsentation* and the generic nature of intuitive intentionality—as we have just seen it does through a redefinition of the intuitive genre—but also overcomes the persistent dilemma between the nature of *Repräsentation* and that of certain specific forms of intuitive intentionality.

3.4.2. Two Notions of Indirectness

To what extent does Husserl's theory of intentionality really manage to be consistent, thereby possibly offering a way out of the difficulties of the Fodorian representationalist reconstruction of intentionality?

It is quite clear in my opinion that it fails if indeed its analysis of *Repräsentation* is a crypto-semantic one. It is obviously a contradiction in terms to distinguish between a direct and an indirect kind of intentional relation and simultaneously maintain that any matter of act interprets a representative content in the same way as a signification intention interprets a symbol. How could an intentional relation be at the same time both direct and indirect in an identical sense of the notion of directness? If this is really what Husserl's theory maintains, in perceptive intuition I would apprehend a substitute for the intentional object (the sensory representative content) in such a way that I would end up relating directly, without any intermediary, to this object. This is enough of a feat to deserve careful explanation for fear of eliciting strong skepticism. And the truth is that Husserl's investigation is quite disappointing in this regard: he claims the direct character of perceptive intentionality to be an irreducible phenomenological datum but does not try to elucidate its possibility.

It is thus a logical reaction to question the accuracy of his description of *Repräsentation* in semantic terms (or better said, in crypto-semantic terms). And the most natural solution that comes to mind is to call for a distinction between two different notions of indirectness: the indirectness involved in expressive intentionality as a specific kind of symbolic intentionality, and the indirectness at work in the interpretation of the representative content by the matter of any act. The only sensible way to reconcile the idea that there is a direct form of intentionality with the idea that every intentional relation has a fundamentally indirect structure is to suppose, contra Husserl, that the matter of the act does not interpret a representative content in the same way as a signification intention interprets a symbol. In other words, a *Repräsentation* is to be conceived as something quite different from a symbol understood as something standing for something else.

It would be quite surprising if Husserl, with all his fondness for sophisticated distinctions, had not in fact recognized this necessity as early as the *Logische Untersuchungen*. When he introduces his analogy in §23 of the first logical investigation (cf. 3.3.3), he actually takes care to emphasize that the general structure of *Repräsentation* does not, strictly speaking, correspond to that of an expressive intentional state. However, none of the various differences that can be invoked in order to clarify the nature of this disparity seems to have a sufficient degree of radicality to amount to an essential distinction between two kinds of indirectness. In addition, at no time in the *Logische Untersuchungen* or even in the first volume of *Ideen* does Husserl explicitly set out to work out any such distinction.

Although it certainly does not receive the treatment it calls for, the only one of these differences mentioned by Husserl himself nevertheless deserves a second look. As already mentioned, he observes that the representative content interpreted by the matter of the act does not have the status of an intentional object. In the same spirit he also insists on several occasions that we are not conscious of our sensations in perception.[22] The remarks contained in §23 itself of the first logical investigation are probably his clearest statements on this point: "The phenomenological structure of the two sorts of 'grasp' is however somewhat different. . . . [T]he above talk should not be misread as implying that consciousness first looks at its sensations, then turns them into perceptual objects, and then bases an interpretation upon them, which is what really happens when we are objectively conscious of physical objects, such as, for example, sounded words, which function *as signs in the strict sense*. Sensations plainly become presented objects in psychological reflection: naïve, intuitive presentations may be components of our presentative experience, parts of its descriptive content, but are not at all its objects" (p. 309).

In fact, this difference of status between a representative content and a symbol cannot but be connected with a difference of nature in the indirectness of the intentional relation. It would seem at first glance to be no more than a variation in the distribution of attention similar to the variation accounting for our lack of consciousness of the expressions we use (cf. 3.3.2). However, the transparency of the word obtained in this manner is quite different from the transparency of representative contents: even if a word no more exists for us than a representative content does (a sensation in the case of perception for instance), the function of the latter in the intentional state is not identical with the function the former has in an expressive state. While a word plays the role of an *intermediary intentional correlate*, a representative content is an intermediary *without being an intentional correlate*. By introducing this distinction Husserl rejects the idea that representative contents can be seen as relays of intentionality *in the sense of intended objects* (cf. 2.3.4). But this rejection is as much a confirmation of the fact that if the role of a representative content is to be understood as that of a relay of the intentional relation, then it has to be conceived as something other than a symbol, at least in the sense of a symbol as a something that stands for something else, because a symbol is itself an intended element. Representative contents are for Husserl like glasses through which we see the world, and not like pictures of things in the world that we cannot see directly. To put the matter more generally, Husserl's real conclusion in this perspective is that postulating a system of representations is not the same thing as postulating a system of symbols, at least if this system of representations should also be capable of being treated as an intentional system.

4. HUSSERL'S CONTRIBUTION

In spite of his insistence on the parallels that can be drawn between a *Repräsentation* and expressive intentionality, Husserl's theory of intentionality finally turns out not to be crypto-semantic. It more likely rests upon a distinction between two forms of indirectness which, although not well defined or established, does not look a priori incapable of making a representational reconstruction of intentionality compatible with the difference between a direct and an indirect intentional state. This is why, as meager as it might seem at first glance, this Husserlian contribution to understanding the relation between a symbol and a mental representation could end up being fairly fruitful for the contemporary representational approach to the naturalization of intentionalism. In order to test whether it does have such a capability, this difference will first have to be spelled out in a satisfactory way, a task beyond the interpretive limits of this essay. Even if it does, it will remain in any case necessary to investigate the extent to which the resulting sort of representationalism can be naturalized, and if so, in what manner.

Husserl's contribution is not limited in any case to this conceptual point. It also has to do with how his investigation perfectly illustrates the depth, subtlety and resistance of the difficulty. Even though he never discusses it in the full sense of the term, Husserl shows with great clarity how even a very careful descriptive analysis of the phenomenon of intentionality is naturally tempted to model it on a linguistic symbol, and how delicate a task it is to remedy the inadequacies of this symbolic modeling.

Finally, I believe that the interpretation of the early Husserlian theory of intentionality defended here is not without interesting implications for the assessment of the analytical and cognitivist readings of Husserl (cf. section 4.1 of Chapter 1 in this book), although I cannot do more than allude to them.

Those who swiftly reject the analytical reading of Husserl's theory of intentionality often argue that the necessity for distinguishing specifically mental notions of meaning and interpretation is a major claim of the hermeneutical tradition, and that the intellectual closeness of Husserlian phenomenology to this tradition is already well established. However, these critics usually fail to account for that important part of the phenomenological description of intentional phenomena which shows how difficult it was for

Husserl to break with the symbolic dimension of the representationalist tradition,[23] and they also fail to appreciate the theoretical interest of this difficulty. I think that one of the merits of the above analysis is its effort to give full recognition to what can be appropriately called the crypto-semantic temptation of Husserl (he himself stresses how natural it is to see the connection between the matter of the act and the representative content as a symbolic interpretation) and for unfolding its general implications for the theory of cognition.

On the other hand, these developments also indicate that, by focusing on the notion of noematic meaning, the semantic interpretation of Husserl put forward by Dagfinn Føllesdal and Jaakko Hintikka does not go far enough in its parallel between the analysis of intentionality and the analysis of symbol in Husserl. It is not only at the noematic level, but first and foremost in the analysis of the relation between the matter of the act and the representative content that the intentional relation is modeled by Husserl on semantic properties. In other words, the famous extension of the concept of *Sinn* to the noema in §75 of *Ideen* I is itself a consequence of a prior extension of the analysis of expressive intentionality of the first logical investigation to the general structures of *Repräsentation* in the *Logische Untersuchungen*.

However, these developments also make clear the limitations of a semantic reading of Husserlian theory, even when formulated in this more radical way, because such a semantic reading does not take into consideration the fact that Husserl finally acknowledged the necessity for distinguishing between two forms of indirectness and interpretation. They also imply that Hubert Dreyfus's assimilation of Husserlian and Fodorian representationalisms rests on an oversimplification, and they open a new perspective on the relations between these two theories.

CHAPTER FOUR

Leibhaftigkeit and Representational Theories of Perception

ELISABETH PACHERIE

I would like to examine in this essay a particular problem confronted by theories of perception that operate within the framework of naturalistic representational approaches to the mental. This problem concerns the capacity of such theories to account for a characteristic that Husserl considered the hallmark of perception, namely what he called the *Leibhaftigkeit* of the object in perception, that is, the fact that the object in perception appears as given in person or, to put it otherwise, as bodily present. Perceptual intentionality is presently the focus of a great deal of attention in the analytic philosophy of mind and more generally in cognitive science. Why this is so has a direct bearing on what is at stake with the problem of the *Leibhaftigkeit* of perception. Indeed, the *Leibhaftigkeit* of the object in perception can be thought to constitute a difficulty for a representational approach to perception. This difficulty may not be insuperable, provided one relinquishes a narrow, static, and punctual conception of representation in favor of a more dynamic approach to perception and perceptual representation. In fact, it may be that the analyses Husserl offers in *Ding und Raum* provide us with valuable indications of which representational capacities are needed in order to account for the *Leibhaftigkeit* of perception.

1. INTENTIONAL REALISM, NATURALIZATION, AND PERCEPTION

A majority of philosophers in the analytic tradition working within the framework of a naturalistic approach to the mental advocate a form of intentional realism.[1] According to intentional realism, intentionality is an objective fact, that is, there exist mental states that have "intrinsic" or "original" intentionality in the sense that their intentionality is conceived as independent of any interpretative attitude. Moreover, these intentional mental states are assumed to play a role in bringing about behavior, and the role they play is assumed to be a function of their intentional properties or content. Therefore, a philosopher willing to defend both intentional realism and a naturalistic theory of the mental confronts the problem of explaining how material systems can have such intentional states.

In analytic philosophy of mind, attempts to carry out this program of naturalization have typically adopted a representationalist stance. In other words, the question of whether or not a material system can have intentionality has been construed as the question of whether such a system can have representations of its environment or whether states of such a system can be representational states. However, in recent years, there has been an evolution of this representational approach with a more pronounced interest for the perceptual level and a realization that an account of perceptual intentionality constitutes a crucial step toward a naturalization of the mental. This renewed interest for perception is in part the result of the difficulties encountered by attempts to account for the intentional relation between mind and world in a naturalistic way.

Intentional realism was developed mainly within the framework of the cognitivist paradigm, characterized by its adherence to functionalism, computationalism, and a conception of mental representations as symbolic representations.[2] That is, mental representations are viewed as sequences of symbols manipulated according to purely formal rules. The advantage of such an approach is that it allows one to exploit the advances in the theory of formal systems and the theory of calculability in order to describe the relations between the semantic and the material levels. The connection between these two levels is assumed to be mediated by a syntactic level. However, the cognitivist paradigm in its classical form appears quite helpless when confronted with the problem of accounting for the origin of the semantic properties of symbols and of explaining how their meanings get anchored in the world.

In short, the cognitivist paradigm may well offer a possible solution to the mind/body problem, but it does nothing to uncover the mystery surrounding the problem of intentionality conceived as the problem of the relations between mind and world.[3] This major weakness of cognitivism has led a number of philosophers to exploit the resources of information theory in their attempts to naturalize intentionality.[4] The fundamental idea underlying this type of approach is that information is an objective resource definable in purely physical terms. Therefore, if we succeed in defining the intentional relation as a specific type of informational relation—and this implies that the specific constraints it must satisfy should be formulated in nonintentional terms—we will have taken a major step toward the naturalization of intentionality.

According to information theory, the existence of informational relations depends on the existence of lawful correlations between states of structures or systems. These correlations are typically, although not necessarily, conceived of as causal correlations. Very schematically then, the core ideas exploited by information-based theories of intentionality are (1) that an informational relation is the converse of a lawful causal relation and (2) that intentional relations somehow reduce to informational relations. As philosophers involved in this project have learned to their cost, the main difficulty of the task consists in specifying how exactly intentional content is supposed to reduce to information. It is in particular necessary to account for the fact that intentional content, by contrast with merely informational content, exhibits strong properties of intensionality and robustness. An intentional content is also intensional insofar as it represents what it represents in a certain way, under a given mode of presentation. Two representations can represent the same thing and yet differ in their mode of presentation of what they represent.[5] Intentional content is robust in the sense that it can remain fixed even though representations with this content get caused in all sorts of ways. The possibility of error, our capacity to think about things in their absence or to think about things that do not exist or are even impossible are all illustrations of this robustness of intentional content and testify to the difference between meaning and information. As Jerry Fodor aptly put it, "The trick in constructing such a theory is to explain how the meaning of a symbol can be insensitive to the heterogeneity of the (actual and possible) causes of its tokens even though, on the one hand, meaning is supposed somehow to reduce to information and, on the other hand, information varies with etiology" (1990: 90).

Attempts to articulate information-based theories of intentional content have revealed the primacy of perceptual intentionality. Roughly, these theories say that the content of a type of experience is conferred by its typical distal cause, that is, whatever property of the environment typically causes experiences of that type is the property the experience represents. But as Colin McGinn (1989) has remarked, insofar as a variety of properties are instantiated along the causal chain from world to mind, an informational theory must specify what sort of causal relation it is that confers content. In the case of conceptual semantic properties, one may well answer that the semantic relation of reference is based on the relation of perception. We can say for instance that our thoughts of "F" are typically produced by our perceiving instances of F and that this is what explains why "F" refers to F. Thus, these theories can explain one relation, reference, in terms of another, perception. In other words, semantic content can be fixed by reference to perceptual content. This account is not circular insofar as the perception relation is more primitive than the semantic relation it explains. But it would be wrong to believe that we have thereby given a naturalistic account of intentional content. As McGinn insists, an experience cannot count as a perception of something unless it has some suitable representational content. But if the capacity to perceive requires the capacity to represent perceptually, we cannot use the perception relation to explain what it is for an experience to have content.[6] In order to break the intentional circle, we need to give a naturalistic account of perceptual intentionality. Thus, the development of a naturalistic theory of perceptual intentionality appears to be a fundamental requirement if we want to pursue the program of a naturalization of the mental realm.

2. *LEIBHAFTIGKEIT* OF PERCEPTION AND REPRESENTATION

The present interest for perception in the analytic philosophy of mind is thus linked to the realization of the key role played by perception with regard to the problem of mind-world relations—a realization that, as Jacques Bouveresse (1995: 27) notes, was probably hindered as a result of the preeminence attached for a long time to the philosophy of language. By acknowledging the primacy of perceptual intentionality and its foundational role to higher forms of intentionality, analytic philosophers of mind come close to Husserlian analyses concerning the foundational relation of perceptions as primary forms of objectification to higher forms of objectification. This renewed interest in perception goes together with a greater concern for problems linked to the qualitative dimensions of mental life. These qualitative dimensions have been neglected for a long time by a majority of analytic philosophers of mind and of cognitive scientists in favor of the purely cognitive aspects of the mental in the vain hope, on the part of some, that the problems they pose would simply dissolve as research advanced. Instead, research has shown that these qualitative dimensions could not be eliminated or treated as epiphenomenal. For instance, phenomena such as blindsight suggest that perceptual awareness plays an important role in our cognitive life.[7] Thus, perception appears to be at the crossroads, since, on the one hand, the whole project of a naturalization of the mental depends on the possibility of a naturalistic account of perceptual intentionality and since, on the other hand, perceptual experience is a paradigmatic illustration of the importance of the phenomenal and qualitative dimensions of mental life. Indeed, it is in a theory of perception that a divorce between an account of the cognitive aspects and an account of the qualitative dimensions of the mental seems least admissible. It is therefore crucial to examine whether by insisting on an informational and representational approach to perceptual intentionality, one does not contribute to the prolongation of this outrageous situation. I shall examine here a single but important aspect of this question, recently discussed by Bouveresse.

Bouveresse (1995) notes that Husserl brings to the fore an essential feature of perception when he insists on what he calls the *Leibhaftigkeit* of the object of perception. *Leibhaftigkeit* is, according to Husserl, a fundamental property of perception that refers to the very specific form the relation between the subject and the object of the attitude takes in this cognitive mode. Husserl describes this relation as follows:

> The object stands before us in perception as bodily present, as, to put it more precisely yet, actually present, as given *in propria persona* in the actual present. In imagination, the object does not stand before us in the mode of bodily presence [*Leibhaftigkeit*], of reality, of actual presence. Certainly, it stands before our eyes, but as an object that is not actually given now. It might be thought of as now present or as simultaneous to an actual present, but this presence is a presence in thought, not the presence that belongs to bodily presence, to the presence of perception. (*Ding und Raum* [hereafter cited as *DR*], §4, pp. 14–15)[8]

Bouveresse (1995: 52–54) wonders whether the contrast pointed out by Husserl between a situation in which an object is perceived and a situation in which it is simply represented (including represented as given here and now) doesn't cast doubt on the well-foundedness of representational approaches to perception. Such theories could hardly account for the *Leibhaftigkeit* of the object of perception, Bouveresse suggests, since "if, as we may suppose, our idea of mental representation is inspired by our idea of a material image, in which the represented object is not given in person and what is given in person is not the object itself, it is unlikely that we can manage in this way to give a satisfactory account of what perceiving an object consists in" (1995: 54; my translation). Let us note first, with Bouveresse, that from the fact that perception appears to us as immediate, it does not follow that it is. The direct corollary of this is that explaining what makes it seem to us that perception is immediate is not tantamount to showing that perception is indeed immediate.

Similarly, as Husserl himself points out, the *Leibhaftigkeit* of the object in perception should not be understood to imply that the object in fact exists and is actually present, or else the idea of an illusory perception would be self-contradictory. *Leibhaftigkeit* is a property of the phenomenon of perception: "The essential character of perception is to be a consciousness of the bodily presence of the object, that is, to be its phenomenon" (*DR*, §4, p. 15).[9]

As a result, a theory of perception cannot be adequate unless it explains how perception can seem to be immediate, how the object in perception can appear to be given *in propria persona*; in other words, it cannot be adequate unless it explains how perception can have those phenomenal properties of immediacy and *Leibhaftigkeit*. What Bouveresse worries about is whether a representational theory of perception is capable of accounting for this subjective feeling of immediacy and *Leibhaftigkeit*. Bouveresse's disquiet is motivated, I think, by deeper reasons than the simple fact that such theories claim that perception is mediated; what really worries him is the fact that representations are assumed to be in charge of the mediation.

It is important to distinguish clearly between three different problems. The first two problems concern the pertinence of the analogy between mental representations and material images. First, this analogy almost immediately evokes the idea of the mind's eye contemplating the representation produced and producing in turn another representation, thus leading to a well-known infinite regress. In order to avoid the threat of infinite regress or to avoid what is sometimes called the homunculus fallacy, it is necessary to define a notion of mental representation that is clearly different from a material image in that it involves no duality between representation and beholder. This is not the point I want to focus on, however. Theoreticians of mental representations, including perceptual representations, are well aware of this difficulty and are sufficiently warned—or so I hope—against the homunculus fallacy. It is to the credit of the computational systems from which they draw their inspiration that they at least show us how to do without such homunculi.

Second, the analogy with the material image seems to be a main source of the seemingly natural and almost unavoidable temptation to view the idea that perception involves the construction of representations as tantamount to the claim that the things we are directly aware of are in fact representations. In other words, this analogy makes it seem that holding a *representational* thesis is tantamount to holding a *representationalist* thesis, that the very endorsement of the claim that perception involves the construction of representations is enough to make perception an indirect affair: we are aware of a representation and infer on that basis the existence of the public object whose representation it is. To rebuke representationalism by saying that although perception requires the construction of representations, once they are constructed we have them and we do not need to perceive them, would, according to Bouveresse, constitute a dubious attempt to solve the problem through a bit of verbal trickery. Such a solution may indeed appear purely verbal as long as mental representations are conceived of on the model of material representations. Given the informational loss that material images involve and given the external nature of the relation between such kinds of representations and their objects, we indeed have to infer the existence of the represented objects. In order to dispel the feeling that we are faced with a dubious trick, we need to define a notion of mental representation that is much richer informationally.

The third, more general problem confronted by representational approaches to perception is that typically representations do not exhibit the kind of directness and immediacy that is associated with perception. It should be remarked that the absence of those features constitutes the general case and is quite independent of the analogy with the material image. Symbolic mental representations, which in classical cognitivist models are thought to be the vehicles of the contents of propositional attitudes, are conceived of on the model of linguistic rather than image-like or figural representations, yet they exhibit no such features as immediacy or directness. It is indeed possible to account for the difference between, on the one hand, cognitive attitudes such as beliefs, desires, and intentions—what are called propositional or sentential attitudes—and on the other hand, cognitive modes such as perception, imagination, or "iconic" memory in terms of a difference in representational codes: quasi-linguistic, conceptual, or symbolic representations in the former cases and sensory, image-like, or figural representations in the latter.[10] But this distinction between representational codes does not allow us to account for the differences between perception, imagination, and iconic memory. As a consequence, one of the most pressing questions a representational theory of perception is confronted with concerns its capacity to account for the kind of immediacy and directness of perception not shared by representations in general. In other words, what we should ask is whether it is possible to spell out specific constraints such that representations satisfying those constraints will exhibit those features and thus present their objects as given *in propria persona*.

3. *LEIBHAFTIGKEIT* AND REPRESENTATIONAL DYNAMICS

I would like to suggest that with respect to the problem of *Leibhaftigkeit*, a representational theory of perception may not be in a desperate position, provided that it takes into account the temporal dimension of perception and does not proceed to the reductive abstraction that makes perception something punctual and static.[11] The idea that should be exploited is that perception has both a static simultaneous structure and a dynamic temporal structure, that there is a narrow link between the *Leibhaftigkeit* of the object in perception and the temporal dynamics of perception, and finally, that the nature of our perceptual relation to the object gets displayed mainly in the flux of perception, that is, in its temporal dynamics.

Before I present this proposal in more detail, I would like to examine briefly some elements of the analyses developed by Husserl in *Ding und Raum*.[12] Husserl's aim in this book is to investigate the conditions under which perceptual experience can give rise to an awareness of space and spatial items. In other words, he aims at providing an analysis of the constitution of space and spatial objectivity. His analysis follows the method of phenomenological reduction, a method he had discovered in the summer of 1905 and which consists in "bracketing" or refraining from positing the existence of the natural world around us. The first element in Husserl's analyses that I would like to bring out is the famous thesis that to perceive an object is for a profile or an adumbration to appear. In other words, it is constitutive of the mode of being given of the object in perception that only one side of it genuinely appears to me. Thus when I see a house, only the side that faces me constitutes a "genuine appearance." By contrast, my awareness of the other sides is nongenuine or inauthentic insofar as it is not based on any sensations. This one-sidedness of external perception is, according to Husserl (*DR*, §16, p. 51), a radical incompleteness. This incompleteness is necessary and belongs to the essence of external perceptions. This essential inadequacy of singular external perceptions is, on the one hand, a consequence of the necessary transcendence of the object whose mode of givenness excludes what Husserl calls self-position (*Selbststellung*). But on the other hand, this inadequacy also has the consequence that, in order for what is thus inadequately given not to remain radically indeterminate, we need to consider not isolated perceptual moments but perceptual series that allow for an increasing specification and determination of the way the object looks and thus provide us with something akin to a substitute for the self-position of the object.

This leads me to a second essential aspect of Husserl's analyses, namely, his insistence on the importance of the temporal dimension of perception and its role in the determination of the perceived objects. As Husserl points out, a temporal dimension is intrinsic to perception: "A sort of connection of perceptions belongs to the essence of every perception; that is, to its essence belongs a certain (temporal) extension" (*DR*, §19).[13]

In a nexus of perceptions there is a continuous transition from one appearance to the next of an object: we become fully aware of far sides of the object of which we had only empty perception and there is a converse transition from full perception to empty perception. The perceptual synthesis that operates on these series of appearances allows for a more precise specification and determination of the object. In dynamic perception, we do not merely have a perceptual experience as of sides of an object, we have perceptual experience as of the object. But what makes it possible for the unity and identity of the object to be experienced in such a synthesis? First, the transition from one appearance to the next is typically continuous. As Husserl (*DR*, §30) points out, the ordered series of appearances is a continuous series and thus we have an effective order and not a mere collection of elements permutable at will. This does not mean that there are no discontinuities or variations in the presentative contents or that such discontinuities or variations don't have an important role to play, but their values depend precisely on the presence of a background of continuity. The presence of this continuity in the multiplicity of profiles is necessary for the emergence of an awareness of the unity of the object: "It is only when, in the unity of experience, the continuous transition from one perception to the next is warranted that we can talk of the evidence that identity is given. The unity of the object only certifies itself as such in the unity of a synthesis that continuously ties together the multiple perceptions" (*DR*, §44).[14]

However, the object should not be equated with the unity of a given continuous series, but since it can in principle be perceptually given in a multiplicity of ways, it should be identified with the higher-order unity of all the actual and possible series of appearances through which it can be given. Thus, taking as an example the perception of a square, Husserl writes: "All these continuous series stand to one another in a lawful essential relation. They are continuously interrelated and it is only in the all-encompassing unity of these series that the square actually comes fully, 'all-round,' to givenness. It is what it is only as the identical in the systematic unity of these appearances or possibilities of appearances" (*DR*, §30).[15]

Finally, there is a third element in Husserl's analyses that I would like to bring out. The fact that the temporal series of appearances exhibit an effective order is not by itself a sufficient condition for the phenomenal constitution of space and spatial objects. In order to account for the constitution of space and things in space, one must also consider the role played by kinesthesis. According to Husserl, "All spatiality is constituted, comes to givenness through movement, the movement of the object itself and the movement of the 'ego' with the change of orientation it yields" (*DR*, §44).[16]

Although we normally have representations as of an objective three-dimensional space containing three-dimensional objects, visual contents by themselves cannot account for the fact that it is our normal perceptual condition. There are two main reasons for this. First, although the simultaneous unity of visual sensations in a visual field is what, according to Husserl, makes visual sensations fit for the exposition of space and things in space, the unity of an object is given in a temporal series. It is legitimate to posit such a unity only insofar as the continuous transitions from one appearance to the next determine a unique synthesis. But changes in the visual field do not determine a unique synthesis. In order to determine whether a series of appearances should be interpreted as the perception of an object in motion or as the perception of an object at rest seen from a changing perspective, the series of kinesthetic circumstances must be taken into account. To put it briefly, visual contents by themselves do not ensure the unity of a synthesis, such a unity is guaranteed only by the correlation—the functional dependence—between determinate series of kinesthetic circumstances and determinate series of visual appearances. As Husserl (*DR*, §54) puts it, the thing as a unity is given in a series of appearances motivated by a kinesthetic series.[17] The second reason why purely visual appearances by themselves do not explain why we enjoy representations as of an objective three-dimensional space, is that items in the visual field are only "surface beings." According to Husserl, certain types of motion are necessary for the constitution of three-dimensional space. More precisely, the correlations between ordered series of visual appearances and ordered series of kinesthetic circumstances when moving toward or away from an object or moving around it make possible "a new dimension, that makes a thing out of a picture, space out the oculomotor field"[18] (*DR*, §67).

The few Husserlian theses I have chosen to present here in a very succinct manner give only a very imperfect idea of the richness of Husserl's analyses in *Ding und Raum*. The reason why I concentrated on them is that the specific characteristics of the mode of givenness of the object in perception that they emphasize seem to me to be closely related to the phenomenon of *Leibhaftigkeit*. To summarize them briefly: (1) it belongs to the essence of the mode of givenness of the object in perception that it be given as a series of profiles or appearances; (2) as a consequence, a certain temporal extension is constitutive of perception or, to put it otherwise, perception is essentially dynamic, and static content is a mere abstraction from dynamic content; (3) only creatures endowed with a capacity for movement can enjoy perception as of an objective three-dimensional world, and this perception is made possible by the functional dependence between series of visual appearances and series of kinesthetic circumstances.

I shall now abandon the Husserlian terminology in favor of the jargon of the analytic philosophy of mind I am more familiar with. Falling back into my naturalistic prejudices and ignoring the restrictions imposed by *épochè* and the methods of phenomenological investigations, I henceforth concern myself with assessing the prospects of possible naturalist or "genetic-causal" explanations of phenomenal aspects of perception. I turn back to my initial problem, namely, whether the *Leibhaftigkeit* of the object in perception actually constitutes a fundamental difficulty for a representational theory of perception set in a naturalistic framework.

Borrowing from Husserl's analyses, I would like to suggest that what characterizes perception and accounts for its distinctive character is the fact that it exhibits a temporal organization the dynamics of which is under the dependence of both the object and the subject's activity of perceptual exploration. The object is given *in propria persona* insofar as the lawful organization of the perceptual sequence constitutes a test of its presence. Briefly put, the fact that in perception the object appears given *in propria persona* results from the conjunction of the following three conditions: (1) the temporal dynamics of the sequence of perceptual moments does not depend entirely on the perceiver, (2) what depends on the perceiver is correlated with his perceptual-motor exploration activity,[19] that is, with an active perceptual exploration of the scene presented, and (3) what in this dynamics is not under the control of the perceiver nevertheless exhibits a lawful character. I contend that in the other cognitive modes, the three conditions are not simultaneously satisfied. In particular, those other modes display no systematic correlations with the motor activity of the subject. I can, for instance, close my eyes and imagine a cube, I can even imagine myself turning around the cube, I can during this exercise move my head and my body in different ways, but unless by a coincidence or because of my deliberately intending it to be so, my movements will not be correlated with the sequences of images of the cube that I imagine I am moving around.

Thus it seems that we might be able to account for the *Leibhaftigkeit* of the object in perception in the framework of a representational theory of perception, provided that we make use of a richer notion of representation. In other words, this seems to be possible, provided that, as a first condition, the notion of representation used covers both sensory representations taken in the static way and sensory properties taken in a dynamical way. It is important to note that a dynamic sensory representation is not merely a temporal sequence of static representations, but that it is a representation of the relationships between the successive representational moments. The order of complexity of dynamic representations is thus higher than that of static sensory representations. This means that dynamic representations require more sophisticated representational mechanisms that can extract relations between representational moments in a perceptual sequence. Although necessary, this condition is not yet sufficient. If the sketch I gave of an analysis of *Leibhaftigkeit* is correct, then to enjoy *Leibhaftigkeit*, an organism must also be able to discriminate between those relations that depend on his activity and those that do not. Thus it is necessary to allow for a further mechanism, the function of which will be to discriminate between those two types of relations by extracting correlations between the dynamical properties of perceptual experience and the motor activity of the organism. In Husserlian terms, this means that we need a mechanism capable of detecting and exploiting the correlations between ordered series of visual appearances and ordered series of kinesthetic circumstances.

Concerning the connection between perception and action, three points should be noted. First, research in the neurophysiology of action suggests that besides kinesthesis conceived as a peripheral sensory mechanism giving us feedback information about the consequences of our motor actions, centrally generated corollaries of motor commands play an important role in the modulation of afferent information. In effect, a large number of data support the hypothesis that when the brain sends out motor commands it also sends corresponding signals to the parts of the brain involved in sensory processing, so that analysis of stimulation may be adjusted accordingly.[20] Second, it is not necessary that the motor information be consciously represented. It is in fact likely that this information is processed by mechanisms operating at subpersonal levels. Third, the fact that perception as of an objective three-dimensional space populated by physical objects depends on correlations between visual and motor information does not mean that such correlations should obtain in each particular act of perception. That there be such a correlation is an ontogenetic necessity. In other words, it is perfectly possible that in various circumstances, visual information unaccompanied by motor information gives rise to the perception of a spatial object. But this is only possible if in the past experience of the subject correlations between visual and motor information have been established.

Let us now go back to the discrimination of the relations between perceptual moments that do depend on the activity of the perceiver and those that do not. This discrimination will also yield a distinction between the different perceptual modes of givenness of an object. The object is given *in propria persona*, through those relations between perceptual moments the lawful character of which is not ascribable to the motor activities of the perceiver. But simultaneously, what distinguishes the different sensory modalities is the type of correlation they exhibit between the dynamic properties of the perceptual sequence and the sensory-motor activity of the organism. In other words, what perceptual sequences it is possible or typical to experience depends on constraints ensuing both from the nature of the object experienced and from the nature of the sensory modality involved. To put it roughly, each sensory modality has its own exploratory modes that impose constraints on the nature of possible or typical perceptual sequences in the modality.

Assuming that the brief sketch I have offered of a possible explanation of the *Leibhaftigkeit* of perception is correct or, say, points approximately in the right direction, this property should not constitute an insuperable difficulty for a representational theory of perceptual experience. It should be noted that the tentative account I offer is far from downplaying the role of representational capacities in the explanation of *Leibhaftigkeit*; on the contrary, it requires that we postulate the existence of sophisticated higher-level representational mechanisms. A corollary of this is that *Leibhaftigkeit* may not be a primary feature of all forms of perception, but rather the hallmark of highly evolved forms of perception. Organisms endowed with rather primitive perceptual capacities, directly coupled with behavioral output, have an experience (or a lack thereof) that is likely to be closer to the experience of patients with *blindsight* than to the experience we enjoy of the *Leibhaftigkeit* of the perceived object. It would then be mistaken to believe that in order to account for the *Leibhaftigkeit* of the object in perception one must tighten the links between perception and action to the detriment of representational mediations.

CHAPTER FIVE

Perceptual Completion: A Case Study in Phenomenology and Cognitive Science

EVAN THOMPSON, ALVA NOË, AND LUIZ PESSOA

Cognitive science, in its aim to be the science of the *mind*, cannot avoid taking account of how human beings experience themselves and the world. Yet precisely how should cognitive science go about taking account of human experience? One proposal, growing out of the work of Daniel C. Dennett (1991), advises cognitive scientists to construct a preliminary description of human experience from the third-person perspective, and then to interpret and evaluate this description in relation to an account of the brain. Within this proposal there is no place for the autonomous investigation of human experience, that is, for the conceptual and reflective examination of human experience as it is lived, independent of scientific accounts of the brain. We think that this lack of concern for the autonomy of human experience is unacceptable: cognitive science must include reflective examinations of human experience in addition to causal-explanatory theories (Varela, Thompson, and Rosch 1991). In this essay, we shall argue that proposals such as Dennett's rest on a mistaken conception of the relation between the person or experiencing subject and the person's brain—the brain is treated as if it were the proper subject of experience, when the proper subject is rather the person. As a result of this misconception, Dennett and others are led not only to misdescribe the character of perceptual experience, but also to misjudge the conceptual and empirical significance of issues in visual science about perceptual completion. Furthermore—and this is striking in the context of Dennett's dismissal of phenomenology[1]—these mistakes were long ago identified as such within the phenomenological tradition. By drawing on the resources of this tradition, we hope to show the importance of phenomenological reflection and conceptual clarification for empirical research in cognitive science.

1. PERCEPTUAL COMPLETION: THE BASIC ISSUES

Figure 5.1 illustrates the so-called neon color illusion: a red diamond is seen where there is only a lattice of red line segments. The term "neon color spreading" (van Tuijl 1975) is often used to describe this phenomenon: the figure seems to result from the color having leaked from the line segments into the background. The color is said to "fill in" the background, thereby forming the figure. Nevertheless, one does not see any spreading or filling-in process; one sees only the figure. What line of reasoning, then, lies behind the description of such figures as having been "filled in"?

Visual scientists use the terms "filling-in" and "perceptual completion" to refer to situations where subjects report that something is present in a particular region of visual space when it is actually absent from that region, but present in the surrounding area. The idea is easiest to understand in the case of the blind spot. We have a blind spot in each eye corresponding to the region where the optic nerve leaves the retina and there are no photoreceptors. In everyday perception we are never aware of the blind spot. The blind spots of the two eyes do not overlap, and something that falls on the blind spot of one retina will fall outside the blind spot of the other. Even under monocular viewing the blind spot is not easily revealed. Close one eye and focus on a point on a uniformly colored piece of paper: there is no experience of any gap or discontinuity in the visual field. Now follow the instructions for the

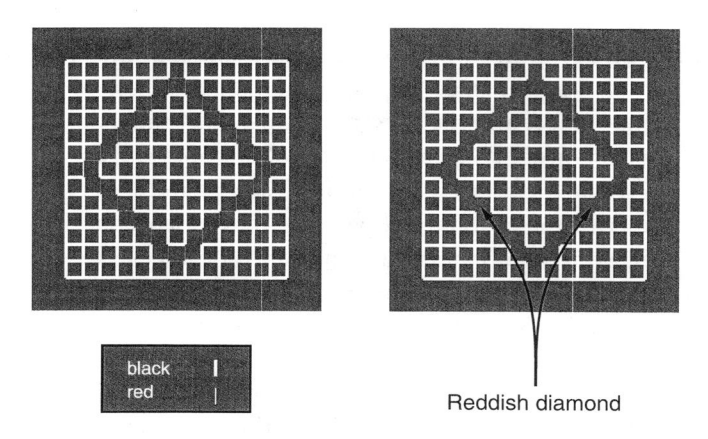

FIGURE 5.1. Neon color illusion. When the segments in the diamond are red and the matrix is black (left), the entire diamond appears reddish even though only the segments are physically colored red (right).

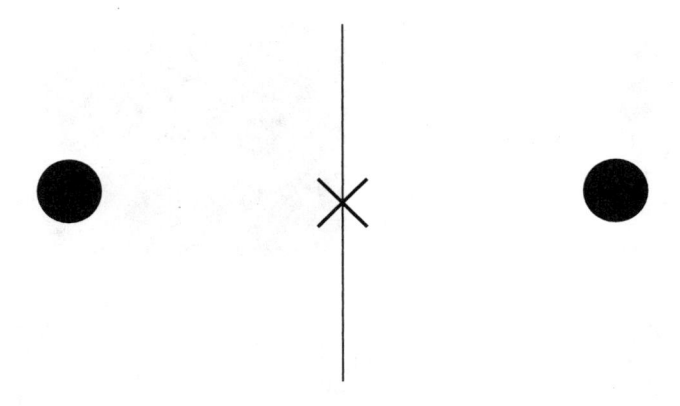

FIGURE 5.2. Blind spot demonstration. Close your right eye while fixing on the cross. Adjust the distance of the page in front of you until the left dot disappears (start at a distance of about 8 inches). Repeat with the left eye closed.

blind spot demonstration in Figure 5.2. The left dot disappears and one perceives a uniform expanse of brightness and color. This is an example of *perceptual completion* or visual *filling-in*: the color and brightness surrounding the area corresponding to the blind spot are said to "fill in" that area so that a uniform expanse is perceived.

The existence of such perceptual completion phenomena at the subject-level is uncontroversial. The term "filling-in," however, is often used in a controversial sense that goes beyond what subjects report. In this controversial sense, the term "filling-in" suggests that certain kinds of subject-level, perceptual completion phenomena are accomplished by the brain's providing something to make up for an absence—by the brain's actively filling in the missing information. Whether there is *neural filling-in*, however, is a matter of great debate in visual science. We will argue later that there is considerable evidence for neural filling-in, but that great care needs to be taken in thinking about the relation between neural filling-in and subject-level perceptual completion.

To appreciate the debates about filling-in it is necessary first to review certain facts about vision and second to discuss certain conceptual and methodological points.

Consider that many of the objects we perceive have roughly uniform regions of surface color and lightness. Now consider two facts. First, neurons in the visual system do not respond strongly to uniform regions, but rather to luminance discontinuities (Hubel and Wiesel 1962, 1968).[2] In other

(A) (B)

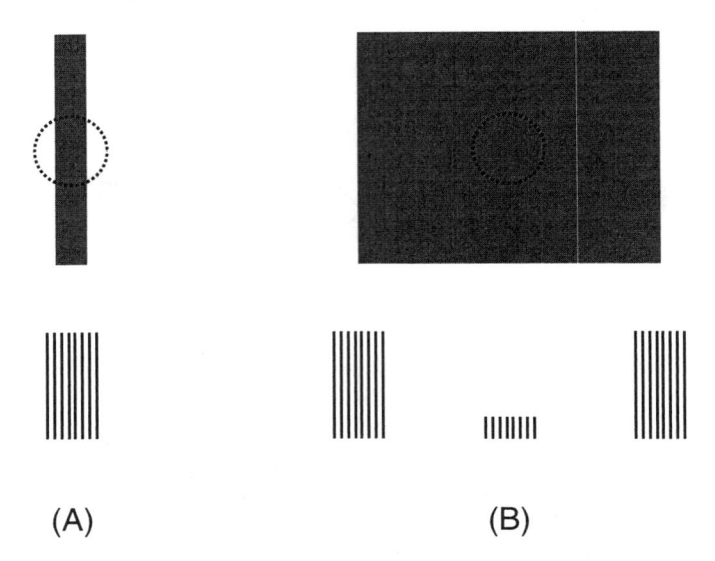

FIGURE 5.3. Schematic representation of cellular responses to boundaries and regions. *Left*, an edge stimulus elicits strong responses when stimulated by an edge (a moving edge typically produces even vigorous responses). The circle denotes the receptive field of the cell, indicating the portion of visual space that can potentially affect a cell's firing. *Right*, a large "surface" stimulus evokes strong responses only at its borders. Weak (or no) responses are produced for internal regions away from the borders. Note that given the receptive field size (circle) it is possible to stimulate the cell without including any stimulus edge.

words, most neurons respond strongly only to boundaries (or edges), and do not produce vigorous responses to regions or surfaces (large expanses of stimulation) (Figure 5.3). Second, psychophysical experiments—for example, with stabilized images—have shown the importance of boundaries for proper surface perception (Krauskopf 1963; Yarbus 1967). In the classic study by John Krauskopf (1963), an inner green ring was surrounded by a red annulus (Figure 5.4). When the red-green boundary was stabilized on the retina (so that it always maintained a fixed position on the eye), subjects reported that the central disk disappeared and the whole target, disk plus annulus, appeared red. (This is another case of visual filling-in: Krauskopf's observers perceived the central area as having the red of the surround even though "green" light was striking the corresponding region of the retina.) These and other results (e.g., Land 1977) suggest that even under natural viewing conditions the perceived color of a surface depends not only on the

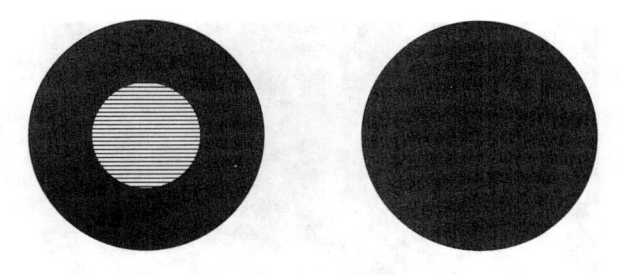

FIGURE 5.4. Fading of stabilized images. *Left*, the boundary between a red ring (gray) and a green disk (hatched) is stabilized on the retina. *Right*, after stabilization, a large red disk is seen.

light reflected from the surface but on the *change* in light across the boundary of the surface.

If boundaries are so important, how is the brain able to determine the color and lightness of continuous regions? In other words, if continuous regions carry weak (or zero) physical signals, how do we see object surfaces (and not only boundaries)? Is there an active filling-in process at the neural level that provides for the immediate lack of physical signals at certain image regions (away from surface borders)? Some visual scientists have developed theories and models based on the idea of a neural filling-in process that involves activity-spreading, diffusion, and other forms of neural completion. Others have argued against this idea, suggesting, for example, that contrast measures at borders can be used to assign surface features. We argue later that in the case of brightness perception there is good evidence for neural filling-in that involves spatially propagating activity.

The filling-in controversy is not only empirical, however, for it involves fundamental conceptual and methodological issues about the proper form of explanation in visual science, as well as deeper philosophical issues about the nature of visual perception, issues especially familiar to philosophers and psychologists in the phenomenological tradition.

To appreciate the methodological issues it is necessary to introduce the concepts of the *bridge locus* and *neural-perceptual isomorphism*. The best way to do this is with an example. Figure 5.5 presents another case often discussed in connection with filling-in, the Craik-O'Brien-Cornsweet effect (Craik 1940; O'Brien 1958; Cornsweet 1970). Two largely uniform regions of different brightness are seen while most of the corresponding stimulus regions have exactly the same luminance. In fact, the two regions differ only in the luminance distribution at the "cusp" edge separating the two regions. Why, then, do we see a brightness step?

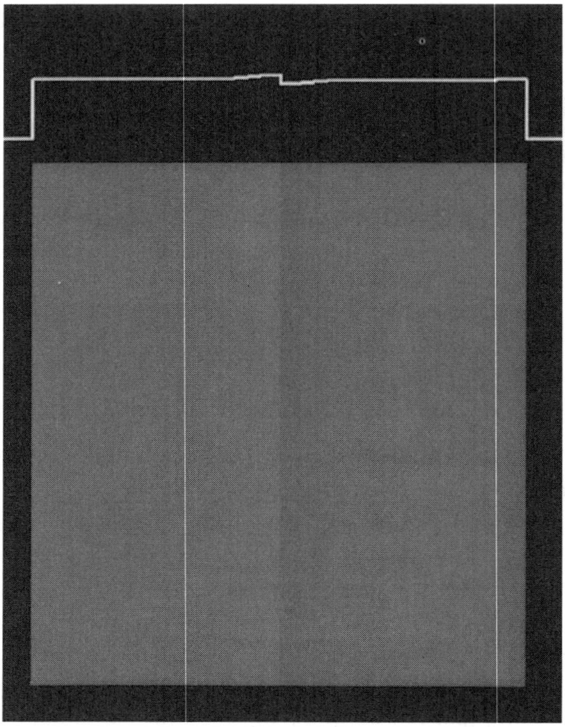

FIGURE 5.5. Craik-O'Brien-Cornsweet display. The luminance of the two rectangles is identical, except in the vicinity of the common border, where there is a luminance cusp. For appropriate display conditions, the left and right regions appear to have uniform color and the left appears uniformly brighter than the right. Above the figure we show a cross-section of the luminance distribution of the figure below.

Here is one route leading to an answer to this question that appeals to neural filling-in (Todorović 1987). Suppose one assumes that activity of a particular type in a specific set of neurons is necessary and sufficient for the occurrence of the Craik-O'Brien-Cornsweet effect. These neurons would form the "immediate substrate" for the perceptual effect. Visual scientists use the term *bridge locus* to refer to this idea of a particular set of neurons "whose activities form the immediate substrate of visual perception" (Teller and Pugh 1983: 581). Now suppose one also assumes that there must be a one-to-one correspondence between the perceived spatial distribution of brightness in the effect and the neural activity at the bridge locus. In other words, just as the perceptual content consists of two uniform regions with a brightness step, so too the immediate neural substrate must consist of spatially continuous activity and a step difference. In short, suppose one assumes that there has to be an *isomorphism* between the perceived brightness distribution and the neural activity at the bridge locus (Todorović 1987). One would then arrive at the following sort of explanation of the effect: the brain takes the local edge information and uses it to fill in the two adjacent regions so that the region with the luminance peak (left) becomes brighter than the region with the luminance trough (right). The end result is the perception of a brightness step in the absence of any corresponding luminance step.

Two basic ideas are involved here. The first is that the way things seem to the subject must be represented neurally in the subject's brain. The second is the idea that, in analyzing visual perception, one must arrive at a "final stage" in the brain—a bridge locus—where there is an isomorphism between neural activity and how things seem to the subject. (The isomorphism can arise at some earlier stage of visual processing, as long as it is preserved up to the bridge locus [see Teller and Pugh 1983: 586; Teller 1984: 1242; Todorović 1987: 550].) We will refer to this idea as *analytic isomorphism*. When applied to perceptual completion phenomena, such as the Craik-O'Brien-Cornsweet effect, analytic isomorphism entails that there *must* be neural filling-in to make up the difference between how things are and how they seem to the subject.

Analytic isomorphism is essentially a conceptual or methodological doctrine about the proper form of explanation in cognitive neuroscience. The doctrine is that it is *a condition on the adequacy of an explanation that there be a bridge locus where an isomorphism obtains between neural activity and the subject's experience*. Furthermore, the isomorphism is typically taken to hold for spatial or topographic properties, thus suggesting that vision involves representations having the form of an "internal screen" or "scale model" that preserves the metric properties of the external world (O'Regan 1992).

In this essay, we argue that analytic isomorphism should be rejected. Nevertheless, we believe that the *empirical* case for neural filling-in remains strong.

Enter the philosophers. Dennett (1991, 1992) has tried to brand "filling-in" the "F-word" in cognitive science. He thinks that the sort of reasoning epitomized by analytic isomorphism, and hence the idea that there must be neural filling-in, depends on a fundamentally mistaken conception of consciousness. Dennett calls this conception "Cartesian materialism." In the stereotypical version of Cartesian materialism, there is a place in the brain—a "Cartesian theater"—where contents become conscious as a result of being presented to an inner "audience" or homunculus—a viewer of the panoramic "internal screen" (O'Regan 1992). Everybody agrees that this idea is totally wrong. Nevertheless, most scientists and philosophers do not correctly understand exactly why it is wrong. As Dennett observes, the real mistake is a *conceptual* one: the mistake is to assume that consciousness is a property of individual contents in the way that truth can be considered a property of individual sentences. Given this concept of consciousness, it would seem that there must be a determinate spatiotemporal point in the brain where a content "enters consciousness." Dennett thinks that this concept of consciousness is incoherent and offers in its place the idea that "consciousness is a species of mental fame" (Dennett, forthcoming). Just as it is impossible to be famous for a second, or to become famous in a second, or to be famous when there are no other people around, so it is impossible for a single, momentary, isolated content to become conscious: "Those contents are conscious that persevere, that monopolize resources long enough to achieve certain typical and 'symptomatic' effects—on memory, on the control of behavior and so forth" (Dennett, forthcoming). In short, for Dennett, consciousness is constituted through the joint interaction of spatially and temporally distributed information-processing systems.

Dennett argues that to claim that there is neural filling-in "is a dead giveaway of vestigial Cartesian materialism" (1991: 344). Like a number of visual scientists, he believes that there is no reason to suppose that the brain fills in the regions; the brain simply represents the fact that regions are filled in without itself doing any filling in. For Dennett, perceptual completion is a case of the brain's "finding out" or "judging" that certain features are present, without the brain's having to "present" or fill in those features.

Dennett has done a service by showing how the filling-in idea often depends on Cartesian materialism and analytic isomorphism (see also O'Regan 1992). But we disagree with Dennett's positive view that perceptual completion is always just a matter of the brain's "finding out." In the course of this essay, we will argue for three main points: (1) The idea of neural filling-in has to be separated from Cartesian materialism and analytic isomorphism. Dennett is right to reject the latter but wrong to reject the former. (2) There is evidence in visual science to support the idea of neural filling-in. Contrary to Dennett, filling in is not always just finding out. (3) Dennett misunderstands the relation between perceptual content and brain processes. The misunderstanding leads him to neglect precisely what phenomenologists routinely practice—the careful conceptual and phenomenological study of lived experience—and to offer instead statements about perceptual experience motivated entirely by subpersonal considerations about the brain. As a result, Dennett seriously distorts the conceptual and phenomenological character of visual perception. In contrast, we argue for the need to pursue careful conceptual and phenomenological studies of perceptual experience as a complement to scientific research.

2. FILLING IN VERSUS FINDING OUT: DENNETT ON FILLING IN

In this section, we present the details of Dennett's position on filling-in. Dennett makes two kinds of points about filling-in, one conceptual and the other empirical.

The conceptual points depend on distinguishing clearly between the *content* of a representation and the *vehicle* or *medium* of representation. Suppose one sees a colored region. This is one's perceptual content. Dennett assumes that there must be states or processes in the brain that bear this very content. (As we will see later, this assumption is problematic.) But he observes that this could be accomplished by the brain in a number of different ways. First, there could be a representation of *that* region as colored, or a representation of *that* region could be *absent*, but the brain *ignores* that absence. The point here is to distinguish between the *presence* of a representation and *ignoring the absence* of a representation (Dennett 1992: 48). Second, suppose there is a representation of that region as colored. This too could be accomplished by the brain in different ways: for example, the representation could be spatially continuous or pictorial, or it could be symbolic.

These conceptual points show up the main mistake made by analytic isomorphism. Analytic isomorphism holds that there must be an isomorphic neural representation for each conscious perceptual content. As Dennett correctly observes, however, there need be no isomorphism between perceptual contents and neural representations, for some perceptual contents might correspond to neural processes that ignore the absence of neural representations, or they might correspond to symbolic representations.

Take the blind spot, for example. From the fact that one has no awareness of a gap in one's visual field, it does not follow that there must be a neural representation of a gapless visual field, for the brain might simply be ignoring the absence of receptor signals at the blind spot. Nor does it follow that the blind spot must be completed with spatially continuous representations, for the region might simply be designated by a symbol.

Dennett's conceptual points still leave open the empirical matter of just what the brain does to accomplish perceptual completion. Here Dennett is not entirely clear about what he means when he says that the brain "jumps to a conclusion."

In the case of the blind spot, Dennett asserts that the visual cortex has no precedent of getting information from that retinal region, and so it simply ignores the absence of signals from that area. The moral of this story is that the brain does not need to provide any representation for perceptual completion to occur; completion can be accomplished by ignoring the absence of a representation (cf. Creutzfeldt 1990: 460). The contrast, then, is between *providing a representation* and *jumping to a conclusion, in the sense of ignoring the absence of a representation*. According to this story, the brain does not need to fill in the blind spot in the sense of providing a roughly continuous spatial representation, nor does it need to label the blind-spot region—the absence of any representation for the blind spot region is simply ignored or not noticed in subsequent visual processing. Notice that this is a case of providing content; the point is that there is no representational vehicle specifically devoted to the blind spot.

On the other hand, Dennett sometimes contrasts providing a roughly continuous spatial representation with labeling a region. And he says that "filling in" means the former. Here the contrast is between, on the one hand, *providing a spatial representation of each sub-area within a region*—filling-in—and on the other hand, *jumping to a conclusion, in the sense of attaching a label to the region all at once*. In this story the brain provides both content for the blind-spot region and a representational vehicle devoted to that region, namely, a label.[3]

Dennett's slogan is "The brain's job is not 'filling in.' The brain's job is *finding out*" (1992: 47). The principle of brain function being assumed here Dennett calls "the thrifty producer principle": "If no one is going to look at it, don't waste effort providing it." For example, to see a region as colored, all the brain needs to do is to arrive at the judgment that the region is colored. Whether Dennett thinks that the brain accomplishes this by ignoring the absence of a representation or by providing a label ("color by number"), he clearly thinks that filling in the color of each sub-area ("color by bit map") is not the thriftiest way to do it.[4]

3. DENNETT'S CRITICISM AND VISUAL SCIENCE

In visual science there has been a great deal of debate about filling-in in relation to the broader topic of neural-perceptual isomorphism. Our main aim in this section is to establish a connection between these long-standing debates in visual science and Dennett's more recent treatment of filling-in.

3.1. LINKING PROPOSITIONS AND ISOMORPHISM

In 1865 Ernst Mach stated what has since become known as "Mach's principle of equivalence":

> Every psychical event corresponds to a physical event and vice versa. *Equal* psychical processes correspond to *equal* physical processes, *unequal* to *unequal* ones. When a psychical process is analyzed in a purely psychological

way, into a number of qualities *a, b, c,* then there corresponds to them just as great a number of physical processes α, β, γ. To all the details of psychological events correspond details of the physical events. (Mach 1965: 269–70)

Thirteen years later, in 1878, Ewald Hering (1964) asserted that the neural-perceptual parallelism was a necessary condition of all psychophysical research. G. E. Müller (1896) then gave a more explicit description of the neural-perceptual mapping. He proposed five "psychophysical axioms" that postulated a one-to-one correspondence between neural and perceptual states (see Teller 1984 and Scheerer 1994). In particular, his second axiom stated that perceptual equalities, similarities, and differences correspond to neural equalities, similarities, and differences. This axiom was not offered as a solution to the so-called mind-body problem, but rather as a methodological principle that could be a guide in inferring neural processes from perceptual experiences (Scheerer 1994: 185).

Wolfgang Köhler accepted this idea, but thought that Müller's axioms were not comprehensive enough because they did not include occurrent perceptual states, but covered only the logical order between neural and perceptual states (Scheerer 1994: 185). In 1920 he proposed what he would later call the principle of isomorphism (Köhler 1920), building on Müller's earlier formulation, as well as Max Wertheimer's (1912). In his 1947 book *Gestalt Psychology*, Köhler wrote: "The principle of isomorphism demands that in a given case the organization of experience and the underlying physiological facts have the same structure" (Köhler 1947: 301).

There are several points about Köhler's principle of isomorphism that deserve mention. First, by the phrase "have the same structure" Köhler had in mind structural properties that are *topological*. Although the concept of neural-perceptual isomorphism has often been taken to mean a geometrical one-to-one mapping, Köhler clearly intended the isomorphism concept to have a topological sense. For example, he argued that spatial relationships in the visual field cannot correspond to geometrical relationships in the brain; they must correspond rather to functional relationships among brain processes (Köhler 1929: 136–41; 1930: 240–49).

Second, Köhler did not hypothesize that neural-perceptual isomorphism obtained for all properties of perceptual experience. In particular, he did not extend the principle of isomorphism to sensory qualities, such as brightness and color (Köhler 1969: 64–66, as quoted in Kubovy and Pomerantz 1981: 428). The principle was restricted to "structural properties" of the perceptual field, that is, to characteristics of perceptual organization, such as grouping and part-whole relationships.

Finally, it is not clear whether or not Köhler espoused what we are calling analytic isomorphism. Two considerations suggest that he did not. First,

Köhler upheld a nonlocalizationist view of brain function, in which field physics was the main analogy for the underlying physiology; hence the notion of a privileged site of perceptual experience in the brain seems foreign to his way of thinking about the neural-perceptual relation. Second—and this is more telling—he seems to have held (at least according to one interpreter) that the isomorphism principle "is not an a priori postulate, but 'remains an hypothesis which has to undergo one empirical test after the other'" (Scheerer 1994: 188).

In recent years Davida Teller has reintroduced some of these issues into visual science (Teller 1980, 1984, 1990; Teller and Pugh 1983). According to Teller, acceptable explanations within visual science have the following form: "If the question is, what is it about the neural substrate of vision that makes us see as we do, the only acceptable kind of answer is, we see X because elements of the substrate Y have the property Z or are in the state S" (Teller 1990: 12).

This formulation leaves open another question about form: what is the relation between the form of a given neural response and the form of the corresponding visual appearance? Answers to this question invoke linking propositions—propositions that relate neural states to perceptual states. By analyzing how visual scientists reason, Teller (1984) formulated five families of linking propositions called Identity, Similarity, Mutual Exclusivity, Simplicity, and Analogy.

The Analogy family is the one that concerns us here. It is a "less organized" family of propositions whose form is as follows:

$$\Phi \text{ "Looks Like" } \Psi \rightarrow \Phi \text{ Explains } \Psi$$

where "Φ" stands for physiological terms, and "Ψ" stands for perceptual terms. The arrow-connective "$\rightarrow$" has a conditional sense, thus the formulation reads: If the physiological processes (events, states,) "look like" the perceptual processes (events, states), then the physiological processes explain the perceptual processes.

The arrow is not the connective of logical entailment. It is heuristic, and is meant to guide one to the major casual factors involved in a given perceptual phenomenon. Thus the term "explains" on the right-hand side is really too strong—the idea is that "Φ" is the major causal factor in the production of "Ψ": "If psychophysical and physiological data can be manipulated in such a way that they can be plotted on meaningfully similar axes, such that the two graphs have similar shapes, then that physiological phenomenon is a major causal factor in producing the psychophysical phenomenon" (Teller 1984: 1240).

The Analogy family of linking propositions is similar to Köhler's principle of isomorphism but more general. Isomorphism in Köhler's sense can be seen as a particular instance of the Analogy idea, one in which "looks like" is taken in the sense of structural correspondence. In visual science today, this idea of a one-to-one structural correspondence is often taken to mean a spatial correspondence, so that, for example, spatial variations of brightness in the visual field are explained by analogous spatial variations of neural activity (Todorović 1987: 548). As we discussed in section 1, it is this assumption of spatial isomorphism that typically lies behind the appeal to neural filling-in, in visual science.

3.2. CRITICISMS OF ISOMORPHISM AND FILLING-IN

When Dennett says that the brain doesn't really fill in, it only "finds out," he is implicitly rejecting the principle of isomorphism applied to perceptual completion. In other words, he is rejecting the hypothesis that perceptual completion depends on neural completion processes that are structurally isomorphic to the perceptual phenomena. In visual science there has been a great deal of debate about such hypotheses, and the debates all predate Dennett's treatment (Ratliff and Sirovich 1978; Grossberg 1983; Bridgeman 1983; Todorović 1987; Kingdom and Moulden 1989; see also O'Regan 1992). In fact, in 1978, Floyd Ratliff and Lawrence Sirovich argued against the need for a neural filling-in process in an argument similar to Dennett's. They argued that to assume that there must be neural filling-in to account for the homogeneous appearance of bounded regions is to misinterpret Mach's principle of equivalence as requiring that there be an isomorphic mapping from the form of the neural process to the form of the perceptual response. But such an isomorphism is not logically necessary. Therefore, neither is a neural filling-in process (see also Bridgeman 1983; Kingdom and Moulden 1989).

Ratliff and Sirovich went on to make some remarks that are interesting in relation to Dennett's discussion of Cartesian materialism:

> The neural activity which underlies appearance must reach a final stage eventually. It may well be that marked neural activity adjacent to edges [rather than neural filling-in between the edges] . . . is, at some level of the visual system, that final stage and is itself the sought-for end process. Logically nothing more is required. (1978: 847)

This point is similar to Dennett's that once discriminations have been made, they do not need to be re-presented to some central consciousness system—a "Cartesian theater" (1991: 344). But there is a dissimilarity too: as Dennett's critique of Cartesian materialism and his alternative "multiple drafts" model of consciousness makes plain, the notion of a "final stage" may have no application at all. In fact, given the dense connectivity of the brain, with reciprocal forward and backward projections, it is not clear what "final stage" could mean in any absolute sense (see section 5.1). For this reason, Dennett's discussion of filling-in represents an advance over Ratliff and Sirovich's.

Although neural filling-in may not be logically necessary, whether there is neural filling-in has to be an empirical question. Ratliff and Sirovich admitted this: "We cannot by any reasoning eliminate a priori some higher-order stage or filling in process. . . . But parsimony demands that any such additional stage or process be considered only if neurophysiological evidence for it should appear" (1978: 847). Dennett too admits this (1991: 353; 1992: 42–43). What sort of evidence is there, then, for neural filling-in?

4. EVIDENCE FOR NEURAL FILLING-IN

Dennett subjects a rather large variety of visual phenomena to his "thrifty producer principle"—blind spot completion, apparent motion, peripheral vision, neon color spreading—as well as nonvisual phenomena such as the phoneme-restoration effect. The conceptual point he wishes to make is well taken, but the phenomena have to be considered in a case-by-case way.

We would like to draw attention to three cases here—the blind spot and motion aftereffects, illusory contours, and the temporal dynamics of brightness and color induction. All three provide vivid counterexamples to Dennett's assertion that perceptual completion is accomplished by the brain's ignoring an absence. Furthermore, for the temporal dynamics of brightness at least, and very likely also for illusory contours, the brain does not seem to be providing content by assigning a label, but rather by making use of a *spatially* organized representational medium.

4.1. THE BLIND SPOT AND MOTION AFTEREFFECTS

If one visually adapts to a screen containing moving dots, and then views a screen containing stationary dots, one will typically perceive the stationary dots to be moving in the opposite direction. This is known as the *motion aftereffect*. What happens if you adapt monocularly to moving dots that traverse your blind spot? Does the blind spot region—which contains no photoreceptors and so is not stimulated—also generate an aftereffect?

Ikuya Murakami (1995) addressed this question in an intriguing study. Instead of directly assessing whether a regular aftereffect is produced, he assessed the *interocular transfer* of the effect, that is, whether the motion aftereffect could be measured at the corresponding visual field of the other eye. It is well known that a standard motion aftereffect transfers interocularly. Murakami found that in the blind spot case the aftereffect also transfers interocularly. In other words, adaptation to filled-in motion at the blind spot of one eye can cause a motion aftereffect at the corresponding visual field of the other eye. This result provides evidence for the perception of real motion and the perception of filled-in motion sharing a common neural pathway early on in the visual system.

This study is directly relevant to Dennett's position. Why would the motion aftereffect transfer if the brain had just "ignored the absence" of stimulation? If the brain treated perceptually completed motion at the blind spot and real motion differently, then one would not expect the motion aftereffect to transfer. Murakami's study thus provides a *measurable effect* of what appears to be the brain's having taken the trouble to fill in the motion at the blind spot (though not necessarily in a topographic manner).

4.2. ILLUSORY CONTOURS

Figure 5.6 shows the famous "Kanizsa triangle" (Kanizsa 1955, 1979). In the figure there are illusory contours—clear boundaries where there is no corresponding luminance gradient—and a brightening within the figure.[5]

FIGURE 5.6. The Kanizsa triangle. Illusory contours are seen forming a triangle-shaped region although there are no corresponding luminance changes. Note also that the illusory figure is brighter than the background.

The illusory contours and the central brightening are said to be "modal" in character (Michotte et al. 1964): they are perceptually salient and appear to belong to the figure rather than the ground.

Several researchers have suggested cognitive theories of illusory contour perception, most notably Richard Gregory (1972) and Irvin Rock (Rock and Ansen 1979). In these theories, illusory contour formation is largely the result of a cognitive-like process of postulation. Illusory contours are viewed as solutions to a perceptual problem: "What is the most probable organization that accounts for the stimulus?" Although there is ample evidence for the role of cognitive influences in illusory contours, current studies point to the importance of relatively low-level processes in the formation of illusory contours.

Two lines of evidence point to an early neural mechanism for illusory contour completion: (1) neurophysiological data and (2) psychophysical studies of the similarities between real and illusory contours.

4.2.1. Neurophysiological Evidence

In an influential paper, Rudiger von der Heydt and colleagues (von der Heydt, Peterhans, and Baumgartner 1984) presented results from single cell recordings in alert macaque monkeys that suggest neural correlates of illusory contours in area V2. Among other things, they studied neural responses to notch stimuli—dark rectangles with parts missing, forming an illusory rectangle. Cellular activity fell off with increasing notch separation and was greatly reduced when only a single notch was present, in parallel with the perceptual disappearance of the illusory figure. In all, the cellular recordings of von der Heydt, Peterhans, and Baumgartner revealed cells whose responses to illusory contour variations resembled human psychophysical responses to similar variations (see also von der Heydt and Peterhans 1989; Peterhans and von der Heydt 1989; for similar results in the feline visual cortex, see Redies et al. 1986). Although some have described these findings as the discovery of "illusory contour cells" (Lesher 1996), von der Heydt, Peterhans, and Baumgartner (1984) tried to draw a clear distinction between the stimulus-response relationship, on the one hand, and perceived entities, on the other. For instance, they used the term "illusory contour stimuli," rather than "illusory contour cells," and they introduced the term "anomalous contours" to define a stimulus property without reference to perception.[6] Although making a link between single cell activities and perceptual phenomena is problematic (see Pessoa, Thompson, and Noë, in press), the evidence here nevertheless seems to suggest that the perceptual completion of boundaries involves the neural completion of a presence, rather than "ignoring an absence." Moreover, the neural completion appears to be spatially organized, instead of symbolic (accomplished by a label).[7]

4.2.2. Psychophysical Evidence

Many psychophysical studies have provided evidence for a common early treatment of both real and illusory contours by the visual system (see Lesher 1996; Spillman and Dresp 1995). For example, A. Smith and R. Over (1975, 1976, 1977, 1979) have revealed similarities between the two types of contours in the realm of motion aftereffects, tilt aftereffects, orientation discrimination, and orientation masking.

Tilt aftereffects are particularly interesting. A tilt aftereffect will occur if one adapts for a few seconds by looking at lines oriented counterclockwise from the vertical, and then one is exposed to a test stimulus of vertical lines. The latter will appear to be tilted clockwise, away from the adapting orientation. There is compelling evidence from recent studies showing that tilt aftereffects cross over between real and illusory contours (Berkeley, Debruyn, and Orban 1994; Paradiso, Shimojo, and Nakayama 1989). Thus adaptation with real lines can affect the perception of illusory contour orientation and vice versa.

An important question concerns the level at which real and illusory contours have similar status. Motion and tilt aftereffects are often attributed to short-term habituation in early visual cortex (Barlow and Hill 1963; Movshon, Chambers, and Blakemore 1972). Thus the evidence from psychophysics is that real and illusory contours share internal processes at an early level of the visual system. In fact, there is considerable evidence pointing to the functional equivalence of real and illusory contours in the operation of the visual system (see table 1 of Lesher 1996; Spillman and Dresp 1995: 1347). Hence psychophysical evidence reinforces the point that, in the case of illusory contours, the brain does not appear to be "ignoring an absence," but rather completing a presence in a way similar to the case of real contours.

4.3. TEMPORAL DYNAMICS OF BRIGHTNESS AND COLOR INDUCTION

There is an enormous literature on the spatial variables determining brightness and color induction. In contrast, there are considerably fewer studies investigating temporal variables (Boynton 1983; Kinney 1967; see Heinemann 1972). But there are a few studies with results that speak directly to the question of evidence for filling-in.

Michael Paradiso and Ken Nakayama (1991) used a visual masking paradigm to investigate two issues—first, the role of edge information in determining the brightness of homogeneous regions and, second, the temporal dynamics of *perceptual* filling-in. They reasoned that if the filling-in process involves some form of activity-spreading, it may be possible to demonstrate its existence by interrupting it. If boundaries interrupt filling-in, what happens when new borders are introduced? Is the filling-in process affected before it is complete?

Figure 5.7 shows the paradigm they used as well as the basic result. The target is presented first and is followed at variable intervals by a mask. For intervals on the order of 50–100 msec, the brightness of the central area of the disk is greatly reduced. If the mask is presented after 100 msec, the brightness of the central region is largely unaffected. The most striking result was that the brightness suppression depended on the distance between target and mask. In particular, for larger distances maximal suppression occurred at later times.

Paradiso and Nakayama's results are consistent with the hypothesis that brightness signals are generated at the borders of their target stimuli and propagate inward at a rate of 6.7–9.2 msec/deg. The idea that contours interrupt the propagation is perhaps clearest for the case where a circular mask is introduced, resulting in a dark center, for the brightness originating from the target border seems to be "blocked." Paradiso and Nakayama discuss several alternative accounts, such as lateral inhibition processes, but do not consider them to be plausible explanations of their findings.

In this context, it is worth pointing out that the filling-in model of brightness perception proposed by Stephen Grossberg and Dejan Todorović (1988) has been shown by Karl Arrington (1994) to produce excellent fits to the data from Paradiso and Nakayama (1991). This sort of close link between psychophysics, neurophysiology, and modeling seems especially promising for investigating the mechanisms responsible for perceptual completion.

Another relevant study comes from R. De Valois, M. Webster, and K. De Valois (1986). They employed center-surround standard (reference) and matching (variable) stimuli, similar to the ones used in classic contrast studies. They compared the results of direct changes in brightness (or color) where the center of the standard pattern was modulated (as was the matching pattern), to the changes that occurred when the surround was modulated sinusoidally while the center was kept constant at the mean level. (In other words, they compared the perception of direct changes in luminance to the perception of changes in brightness produced by luminance changes in a sur-

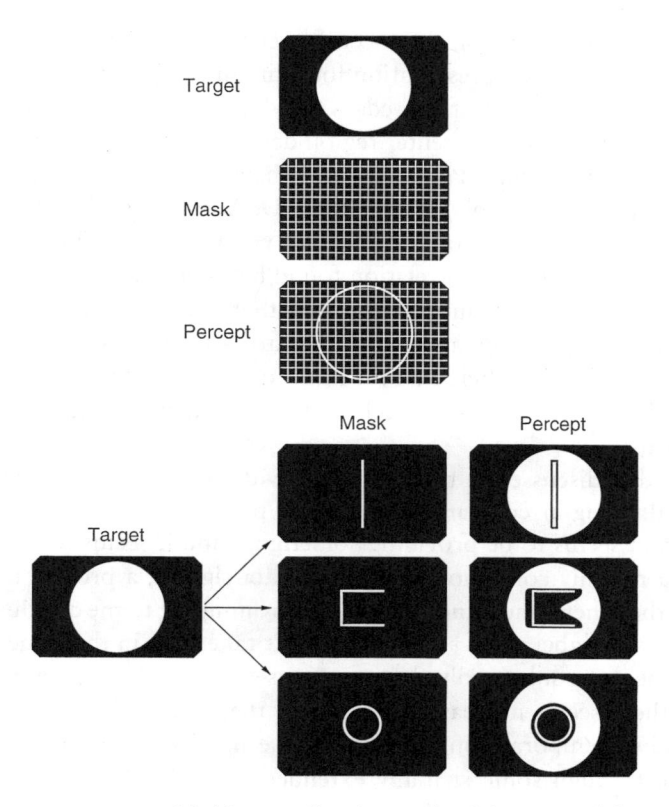

FIGURE 5.7. Masking paradigm in a study of the temporal dynamics of brightness (Paradiso and Nakayama 1991). *Above*, brightness suppression of a disk-shaped target by a mask consisting of a grid of thin lines. The target and mask are each presented for 16 msec. Optimizing the temporal delay between the stimuli yields a percept in which the brightness in a large central area of the disk is greatly suppressed. *Below*, brightness suppression is highly dependent on the arrangement of contours in the mask.

rounding area—this is a temporal version of the classical simultaneous contrast effect.) Their studies revealed two main findings: (1) The temporal frequencies studied had little effect on the apparent brightness change in the former, direct condition (color variations were present but small). (2) In the latter, induced condition, the amount of brightness change fell drastically as the temporal frequency increased (see Pessoa, Thompson, and Noë, in press, for further discussion). These results can be interpreted in terms of a spreading mechanism of induction that occurs over time, one that would provide a spatially continuous representation for filling-in. Brightness and color signals would be generated at the edges between center and surround, and would propagate inside the center region determining the appearance.

A. F. Rossi and Michael Paradiso (1996) have replicated the brightness induction results of De Valois, Webster, and De Valois (1986) and have studied the role of pattern size on the effect by varying the spatial frequency of the inducing pattern. The correlation found between spatial scale, degree of induction, and cutoff frequency indicates that there is a limited speed at which induction proceeds and that larger areas take more time to induce. Rossi and Paradiso conclude that the limits on the rate of induction are consistent with an active filling-in mechanism initiated at the edges and propagated inward.

The studies discussed in this section provide strong evidence for the sort of featural filling-in contrary to Dennett's position.[8] In brightness filling-in, the brain seems to be providing something, and it seems to be doing so through a roughly continuous propagation of signals, a process that takes time. On the other hand, ignoring a region by jumping to the conclusion that it has the same label as its surround doesn't take time in the same way: although labeling would involve brain processes with their own temporal limitations, there seems no reason to suppose that it would be subject to the same kind of temporal constraints as those involved in signals having to propagate through some spatially extended area. As Dennett himself has said: "You can't assign a label to a region *gradually*, and it is hard to think of a reason why the brain would bind the 'gradually' label to a process that wasn't gradual" (1993: 209).

5. FILLING-IN WITHOUT ANALYTIC ISOMORPHISM AND CARTESIAN MATERIALISM

We now return to the conceptual issues surrounding the neural-perceptual relation. We have seen that there is considerable evidence for neural filling-in. The main point of this section is that the existence of neural filling-in does not entail analytic isomorphism or Cartesian materialism.

Discussions of neural filling-in have been closely tied to the doctrine of analytic isomorphism. Visual scientists sometimes interpret the evidence for neural filling-in within the framework of analytic isomorphism (see section 5.1). On the other hand, Dennett rejects Cartesian materialism and with it neural filling-in: although he appears to concede that neural filling-in is an "empirical possibility" and says that he does not wish "to prejudge the question" (1991: 353), he nevertheless asserts that the "idea of *filling in* . . . is a dead giveaway of vestigial Cartesian materialism" (p. 344).

We agree with Dennett that a particular conception of consciousness—"Cartesian materialism"—motivates analytic isomorphism and its argument for neural filling-in. We also agree that any argument for neural filling-in based on Cartesian materialism should be rejected. (We too think that Cartesian materialism is fundamentally misguided, though not for the reasons that Dennett thinks: see section 6.) But the *empirical case* for neural filling-in as discussed above is entirely separate from such philosophical considerations about consciousness. This means that theories and models in visual science that appeal to neural filling-in need not be motivated by Cartesian materialism. One must distinguish sharply between the existence of neural filling-in as an empirical matter and Cartesian materialist interpretations of filling-in. Visual scientists are mistaken when they interpret the evidence for neural filling-in within the framework of analytic isomorphism, but Dennett is equally mistaken when he says that talk of filling-in reveals a commitment to Cartesian materialism.

5.1. ISOMORPHISM AND THE BRIDGE LOCUS

As we discussed in section 3, the term "isomorphism" first gained prominence in visual science through the work of Wolfgang Köhler. Although the isomorphism concept has often been interpreted to mean a spatial or topographic correspondence, Köhler held that neural-perceptual isomorphism should be thought of as topological or functional. Our view is that there is nothing conceptually wrong with these sorts of isomorphism as such. Whether there are either spatial/topographic or topological/functional neural-perceptual isomorphisms in any given case is an empirical question for cognitive neuroscience to decide.

What we find problematic is the doctrine of analytic isomorphism, which holds that cognitive neuroscientific explanation requires the postulation of a "final stage" in the brain—a bridge locus—where there is an isomorphism between neural activity and how things seem to the subject. There are two critical points to be made here, one concerning the role played by the concept of the bridge locus and the other concerning the concept of isomorphism.

Davida Teller and E. N. Pugh Jr. (1983) introduced the term "bridge locus" in their framework for mapping between the neural and the perceptual domains:

> Most visual scientists probably believe that there exists a set of neurons with visual system input, whose activities form the immediate substrate of visual

perception. We single out this one particular neural stage, with a name: *bridge locus*. The occurrence of a particular activity pattern in these bridge locus neurons is necessary for the occurrence of a particular perceptual state; neural activity elsewhere in the visual system is not necessary. The physical location of these neurons in the brain is of course unknown. However, we feel that most visual scientists would agree that they are certainly not in the retina. For if one could set up conditions for properly stimulating them in the absence of the retina, the correlated perceptual state would presumably occur. (Teller and Pugh 1983: 581)

This passage expresses a number of different ideas that need to be disentangled. First, Teller and Pugh state explicitly that a particular pattern of activity at the bridge locus is *necessary* for the occurrence of a particular perceptual state. But at the end of the passage they also explicitly state that *retinal stimulation* is probably *not necessary* (assuming one could stimulate the bridge locus neurons directly), thereby suggesting that the bridge locus activity pattern is *sufficient* for the perceptual state. Therefore, it seems that part of what they mean by the "bridge locus" is a particular set of neurons having a particular pattern of activity that is necessary and sufficient for a particular perceptual state. Second, in calling the bridge locus a particular "neural stage," and in saying that this stage is not likely to be found in the retina, Teller and Pugh seem to be conceiving of the bridge locus in a localizationist manner as a particular cortical region or area.

Analytic isomorphism relies on the concept of the bridge locus. Consider the following statement by Todorović (1987: 549): "A logical consequence of the isomorphistic approach is that a neural activity distribution not isomorphic with the percept cannot be its ultimate neural foundation." By "ultimate neural foundation" Todorović indicates that he means the bridge locus. The doctrine of analytic isomorphism states that it is a condition on the adequacy of cognitive neuroscientific explanation that there be an ultimate neural foundation where an isomorphism obtains between neural activity and the subject's experience.

We are suspicious of this notion of the bridge locus. Why should there have to be one particular neural stage whose activity forms the immediate substrate of visual perception? Such a neural stage is not logically necessary; moreover—to borrow Ratliff and Sirovich's point about neural filling-in—parsimony demands that any such stage be considered only if neurophysiological evidence for it should appear. On this score, however, the evidence to date does not seem to favor the idea. First, brain regions are not independent stages or modules; they interact reciprocally because of dense forward and backward projections, as well as reciprocal cross-connections (Zeki and Shipp 1988). There is ample evidence from neuroanatomy, neurophysiology, and psychophysics of the highly interactive, context-dependent nature of visual processing (DeYoe and Van Essen 1995). Second, cells in visual areas are not mere "feature detectors," for they are sensitive to many sorts of attributes (Martin 1988; Schiller 1995). One of the main ideas to emerge from neuroscience in recent years is that the brain relies on distributed networks that transiently coordinate their activities (Singer 1995; Vaadia et al. 1995), rather than centralized representations. Finally, Dennett and Kinsbourne (1992) have argued that the notion of a single neural stage for consciousness hinders our ability to make sense of neural and psychophysical data about temporal perception.

Some of these critical points could perhaps be met by relying on a less localizationist conception of the bridge locus, which as Todorović (1987: 550) observes, is probably an "oversimplified notion," for "there is no compelling reason to believe that the bridge locus is confined to neurons of a single type within a single cortical area."[9] Although this is a step in the right direction, the term "bridge locus"—defined as "the *location* [our emphasis] at which the closest associations between Φ [physiological] and Ψ [psychological] states occur" (Teller and Pugh 1983: 588)—does not strike us as particularly useful for thinking about the distributed neural correlates of perceptual experience. For example, such correlates might involve neural assemblies where membership is defined through a *temporal* code, such as response synchronization (Singer 1995; Varela 1995). For this reason, we think that the concept of the bridge locus should be abandoned.

To abandon the concept of the bridge locus means rejecting analytic isomorphism, for analytic isomorphism depends on this concept. Some visual scientists, however, reject analytic isomorphism while nevertheless adhering to the concept of the bridge locus. For example, Ratliff and Sirovich (1978) denied analytic isomorphism but asserted that the neural processes involved in perception "must reach a final stage eventually." The notion of a "final stage" seems equivalent to the notion of the bridge locus. We would reject any framework that depends on the concept of the bridge locus, whether isomorphic or nonisomorphic.

We now return to the concept of isomorphism. A good example of what we object to in analytic isomorphism can be found in a statement made by Todorović (1987) in his discussion of "isomorphistic" versus "nonisomorphistic" theories of the Craik-O'Brien-Cornsweet effect (see Figure 5.5). Todorović admits that any mapping from neural to perceptual states "is an aspect of the notorious mind-body problem," but then goes on to say, "conceptually the idea of an isomorphism between certain aspects of neural activity and certain aspects of percepts may be more acceptable [than a nonisomorphic mapping], at least within a general reductive stance that assumes that, at some level of description, perceptual states *are* neural states" (1987: 550). We disagree. On the one hand, as Todorović recognizes, and as Köhler himself observed over thirty years ago (Köhler 1960: 80–81), the thesis of neural-perceptual isomorphism does not logically entail mind-brain identity. On the other hand, suppose one does assume that "at some level of description, perceptual states *are* neural states." Even then, neural-perceptual analytic isomorphism would be plausible only if perceptual states were *strictly identical* to neural states (that is to say, if each type of perceptual state were identical to a particular type of neural state). But isomorphism would not be plausible if the identity is weak, that is, if perceptual states are multiply realizable with respect to neural states (so that, although every perceptual state is identical to some neural state, one and the same type of perceptual state can be realized in many different types of neural states, or in many different types of non-neural physical states for that matter). This issue of strong (or type) identity versus weak (or token) identity is indeed "an aspect of the notorious mind-body problem," and nothing that Todorović says favors the strong identity thesis. Hence no basis has been given for the a priori claim that isomorphism is conceptually preferable to nonisomorphism in cognitive neuroscientific explanation.

6. RECOVERING THE PERSONAL IN COGNITIVE SCIENCE

The final matters we wish to discuss concern the conceptual and phenomenological issues about perception raised by Dennett's treatment of filling-in.

Dennett thinks that the notion of filling-in falls into the trap of Cartesian materialism. We agree that the analytic isomorphism argument for filling-in that we have rejected does involve Cartesian materialism: analytic isomorphism holds that filling-in has to take place so that there can be a neural-perceptual isomorphism at the bridge locus; Cartesian materialism holds that brain contents taken on their own are either conscious or not conscious, and for a neural content to be conscious it has to arrive at a privileged site in the brain. But we disagree about the consequences of denying analytic isomorphism and Cartesian materialism. Dennett thinks it follows that filling-in is unnecessary and that the brain jumps to conclusions instead. As we have seen, however, although neural filling-in is not logically necessary, there is nonetheless plenty of evidence for it in visual perception.

Dennett's rejection of neural filling-in is motivated by general philosophical considerations in addition to his wish to dispel Cartesian materialism. In our assessment, Dennett recognizes an important conceptual point about perceptual content, but then misconstrues its significance, especially for understanding the relation between the perceptual experience of the person and brain processes.

The important conceptual point is the following. Suppose one has a perceptual experience that there is something red in front of one. It is normally assumed that the brain represents *that there is something red there*. But nothing whatsoever follows about the nature of the neural representation of this situation. For example, it does not follow on logical, conceptual, or methodological grounds that there is a spatial or pictorial representation of the red region in one's brain. In general, one cannot infer anything about the nature of the neural representational medium from the character of the perceptual content.

One of Dennett's favorite examples for making this point is parafoveal vision (1991: 354–55; 1992). Suppose someone walks into a room covered with wallpaper whose pattern is a regular array of hundreds of identical images of Marilyn Monroe. The person would report seeing that the wall is covered with hundreds of identical Marilyns. But the person can foveate only a few Marilyns at a time and the resolution of parafoveal vision is not good enough to discriminate between Marilyns and colored shapes. One can conclude that the brain represents *that there are hundreds of identical Marilyns*, but not that there is a spatial or pictorial representation of each identical Marilyn (see also O'Regan 1992: 474–75, 481). Once again, there is no logical route from the content of perception to the representational vehicles of perception in the brain.

We think that the full significance of this point has to do with an important distinction that Dennett himself has emphasized in his writings—the distinction between the personal and the subpersonal. For Dennett, the personal is discerned from "the intentional stance," whereas the subpersonal is discerned from "the design stance" (Dennett 1987). When one adopts the intentional stance toward an animal or a system, one is interested in it as a whole interacting in its environment, but when one adopts the design stance one is interested in its internal functional organization.

In visual science, the importance of drawing this kind of distinction between the personal and the subpersonal has been emphasized in ecological and active approaches to vision (Gibson 1979; Ballard 1991; Thompson, Palacios, and Varela 1992; Thompson 1995). For example, many years ago J. J. Gibson wrote: "In my theory, perception is *not* supposed to occur in the brain but to arise in the retino-neuro-muscular system as an activity of the whole system" (1972: 217). "Perceiving is an achievement of the individual, not an experience in the theatre of consciousness" (1979: 239). One does not have to agree with Gibson's specific hypotheses about how visual perception works to see the main point being made here: the proper subject of perception is not the brain, but rather the whole embodied animal interacting with its environment.

Despite his own personal/subpersonal distinction, Dennett does not embrace wholeheartedly the point that it is the person or animal that is the proper subject of perception. In saying that there is no logical route from personal-level perceptual content to neural representation, Dennett acknowledges one side of the point, the side facing from the personal to the subpersonal. But he does not embrace the other side, the side facing from the subpersonal to the personal. Dennett holds that although there is no logical route from personal-level content to subpersonal representation, there is a logical route in the other direction, from subpersonal representation to personal-level content. Indeed, the route could not be more direct, for Dennett treats personal-level content as if it were entirely *constituted* by subpersonal content, with the result that there can be no difference in kind between perceptual content and neurally represented content. This assumption is fundamental to his approach to consciousness, according to which the truth-values of third-person descriptions of perceptual experience are ultimately to be evaluated in relation to the scientific account of brain processes.

We think that this way of thinking leads Dennett to misdescribe certain perceptual situations that demand careful conceptual and phenomenological study. This is best seen in his discussion of parafoveal vision.

In the Marilyn wallpaper case, after asserting that the brain just "jumps to the conclusion that the rest are Marilyns, and labels the whole region 'more Marilyns' without any further rendering of Marilyns at all," Dennett writes: "Of course it does not seem that way to you. It seems to you as if you are actually seeing hundreds of identical Marilyns" (1991: 355). Dennett clearly implies that he thinks there is a sense in which you are *not* seeing hundreds of identical Marilyns, that in some way your seeing hundreds of identical Marilyns is an illusion (see also Blackmore et al. 1995). But what exactly does he mean?

The first thing to be noticed about these remarks is their indifference with respect to the personal/subpersonal distinction. When Dennett says "Of course it does not seem that way to you," what way does he have in mind? The immediately preceding sentence is a description of how the brain jumps to a conclusion "without any further rendering of Marilyns at all." Does he mean, then, that it does not seem to you that your brain jumps to a conclusion? Of course, this is true: it does not seem to *you*, the *person*, that *your brain* labels the whole region "more Marilyns." But so what? Suppose your brain does propagate a high-resolution, foveated Marilyn image "across an internal mapping of an expanse of wall." Still it would not seem *that way to you either*. After all, one of Dennett's points is that one cannot read the character of the neural representations off of one's experience as a perceptual subject.[10]

On the other hand, the sentence immediately following the remark "Of course it does not seem that way to you" does refer to your perceptual experience: "It seems to you as if you are actually seeing hundreds of identical Marilyns." But in what sense does Dennett deny that you are actually seeing all those Marilyns? Here is what he goes on to write:

> In one sense you are: there are, indeed, hundreds of identical Marilyns out there on the wall, and you're seeing them. What is not the case, however, is that there are hundreds of identical Marilyns represented in your brain. Your brain just somehow represents *that* there are hundreds of identical Marilyns, and no matter how vivid your impression is that you see all that detail, the detail is in the world, not in your head. (1991: 355)

This passage misdescribes the perceptual experience of the *person* on two counts. First, Dennett describes your perceptual experience as if it involved seeming to see all the details in your head. As he says several pages later: "The hundreds of Marilyns in the wallpaper seem to be present in your experience, seem to be in your mind, not just on the wall. . . . But why should your brain bother importing all those Marilyns in the first place?" (pp. 359–60). This description is completely unfaithful to the character of perceptual experience: the Marilyns do not seem to be present in your experience or in your mind (whatever that might mean); they seem to be present there on the wall.

Second, Dennett says that, in looking at the Marilyns, it seems to you that you see all the detail. This too is mistaken. Although you do seem to see all the detail in the sense that the wall seems to you to be covered with hundreds of identical Marilyns, you do not seem to see each Marilyn equally well. At any given moment of your perception, the Marilyns straight ahead seem clear as day, while those off to the side appear less distinct, and those in the periphery seem barely noticeable. Of course, at any time you can turn your head to look at the others: in the example as Dennett describes it, "you walk into a room" and notice the wallpaper; thus you are an active, moving perceiver, able to scan the environment, not an experimental subject being instructed to fix a point in your visual field while sitting still. Nevertheless, in turning your head, some Marilyns will come into focus and others will become indistinct, though still seen as present on the wall. Thus Dennett's account conflates two different things—your seeming to see *that there are hundreds of identical Marilyns on the wall* and *your seeming to see all of them in full detail so that each is equally distinct*. Not only can you seem to see that there are hundreds of identical Marilyns without your seeming to see each Marilyn in full detail, but there is a sense in which it is necessarily the case that your visual experience of the Marilyns will be vague or indistinct in just this way. The reason is that this kind of vagueness, blurredness, or indistinctness in the visual field is an ineliminable feature of visual experience. Hence Dennett, in presupposing that the visual experience of the Marilyns could have presented each Marilyn clearly and distinctly, seems to be disregarding the very nature of the phenomenon.

This sort of indeterminacy in perceptual experience was the subject of extensive philosophical investigation early in the twentieth century, not only by Edmund Husserl and Maurice Merleau-Ponty, but also by Ludwig Wittgenstein during his "middle period" (1975). (It was discussed even earlier by William James.) In Wittgenstein's case, one important point of departure was the recognition that one cannot see, for example, a gaggle of geese flying overhead as a gaggle of, say, one hundred and twenty-seven geese, for one cannot visually distinguish the latter from a gaggle of one hundred and twenty-five geese. It can make no sense (at least in normal contexts) to say that someone noticed one hundred and twenty-seven geese fly by, where what is meant is that the person's visual experience represented just that number of geese and no other. According to Wittgenstein, this kind of consideration reveals something essential about the nature of visual experience; in particular, it shows that intrinsic to visual experience is a particular kind of vagueness or indeterminacy. To use one of Wittgenstein's examples, because one cannot by looking distinguish a row of thirty identical pencils marks from a row of thirty-one, it follows that there is no such thing as a visual image of precisely thirty identical pencil marks (1975: 258, 268). Consider another of his examples: it would make no sense to say of a visual figure (i.e., a figure in visual space) that although it seemed to be a circle, it was in fact a thousand-sided figure. The reason is that there is no *visual* criterion that would enable one to distinguish a circle from an appropriate thousand-sided figure (1975: 266). Therefore, there is no difference between these two visual figures. For Wittgenstein, each of these cases exemplifies a respect in which there is an ineliminable, irreducible lack of determinacy to visual experience:

> The moment we try to apply exact concepts of measurement to immediate experience, we come up against a peculiar vagueness in this experience. But that only means a vagueness relative to these concepts of measurement. And, now, it seems to me that this vagueness isn't something provisional, to be eliminated later on by more precise knowledge, but that this is a characteristic logical peculiarity....
>
> Admittedly the words "rough," "approximate," etc. have only a relative sense, but they are still *needed* and they characterise the nature of our experience; not as rough or vague in itself, but still as rough or vague in relation to our techniques of representation. (1975: 263)

Contrary to what Dennett seems to imply, then, the inability to see each Marilyn clearly and distinctly should not be seen as a contingent feature of perceptual experience, one that might have been otherwise. Rather, the indeterminacy of the Marilyns on the periphery of the visual field, compared to those in the center, is essential to the nature of the experience as a *visual* experience.

In the phenomenological tradition, this kind of indeterminacy has been discussed in connection with the perceptual organization of the visual field and the embodied character of perception. Building on Gestalt psychology, phenomenologists have discussed at great length the figure-ground structure of both static and dynamic perception, in which the figure is typically clear while the ground recedes eventually into an indeterminate background (Husserl, *Ideen* I, §35; Merleau-Ponty 1962: 4–6; Köhler 1947: 173–205; Gurwitsch 1964). As Merleau-Ponty discusses at the very beginning of his *Phenomenology of Perception*, the basic tenet of Gestalt theory is that the simplest thing that can be given in perceptual experience is not a simple sensation or quale, but rather a figure on a background. But whereas the Gestalt theorists took this to be an empirical, psychological fact, Merleau-Ponty argues that "this [figure on a background] is not a contingent characteristic of factual perception. . . . It is the very definition of the phenomenon of perception, that without which a phenomenon cannot be said to be a perception at all" (1962: 4). From the vantage point of phenomenological reflection, the figure-ground structure (in which as a matter of formal necessity the ground becomes increasingly indeterminate in contrast to the figure) is an invariant feature of perception as a type of intentional experience, and is known to be such a priori. The basis for this claim involves a particular aspect of the phenomenological method, known as "ideation through imaginative variation." Very roughly, the idea in the present case is that, no matter how one imagines the perceptual situation to be varied, the figure-ground structure always remains as a formal, constitutive feature of perception, while on the other hand, imagining the figure-ground structure to be absent is tantamount to no longer imagining a case of *perception*.[11]

Phenomenologists make the same kind of point about the essentially embodied character of perception. Perceptual experience involves the tacit, background awareness of one's body, but this feature is not a contingent one; it is a formal invariant of perception, and is known a priori to phenomenological reflection. For something to be a possible object of perceptual experience it must be the kind of thing that can be experienced as being situated in relation to the spatial vantage point provided by one's body. Indeed, the spatial position of one's body determines in part the figure-ground structure of perception: the figure corresponds to the focus of one's gaze and the ground to what one sees in the surroundings. Furthermore, the perceptual surroundings can be differentiated into the immediate spatial context of the figure, on the one hand, and the indeterminate background of the periphery, on the other, with the indeterminate background including the marginal presence of one's own body. Thus the background awareness of the body turns out to be essential to the figure-ground structure of perceptual experience: the perceptual object not only stands out against an external background; it is situated within an implicit bodily space. In Merleau-Ponty's words: "One's own body is the third term, always tacitly understood, in the figure-background structure, and every figure stands out against the double horizon of external and bodily space" (1962: 101).

With respect to the Marilyn example, the same kind of point emerges from these phenomenological considerations as did earlier in our brief discussion of Wittgenstein: there can be no incompatibility between the indistinctness of parafoveal vision and actually seeing that the wall is covered with hundreds of identical Marilyns. The reason, for the phenomenologist, is that the indistinctness of peripheral vision—although empirically explicable in terms of the anatomy and physiology of the retina—is based on something a priori, namely, the figure-ground structure and the embodied character of visual perception. Merleau-Ponty's statement of this point is worth quoting at length:

> To see an object is either to have it on the fringe of the visual field and be able to concentrate on it, or else to respond to this summons by actually concentrating upon it. When I do concentrate my eyes on it, I become anchored in it, but this coming to rest of the gaze is merely a modality of its movement: I continue inside one object the exploration which earlier hovered over them all, and in one movement I close up the landscape and open the object. The two operations do not fortuitously coincide: it is not the contingent aspects of my bodily make-up, for example the retinal structure, which force me to see my surroundings vaguely if I want to see the object clearly. Even if I knew nothing of rods and cones, I should realize that it is necessary to put the surroundings in abeyance the better to see the object, and to lose in background what one gains in focal figure, because to look at the object is to plunge oneself into it, and because objects form a system in which one cannot show itself without concealing others. (1962: 67–68)

In speaking of the "fringe" of the visual field in the first sentence of this passage, Merleau-Ponty is drawing on an idea that goes back to William James. What James recognized, which Husserl later discussed in great detail, is that one's field of vision is situated within and bounded by a "horizon" (this term is Husserl's), and that the outline or boundary of the visual field is indistinct, having the experiential character of a *fringe*. For James, as for Husserl and Merleau-Ponty, to neglect the phenomenon of the fringe is to seriously distort the nature of experience: it amounts to the assumption that the concept of determinacy one finds in geometrical representations of space and physical objects is applicable in stating the character of experience.[12] Hence James, when discussing the fringe, writes: "It is, the reader will see, the reinstatement of the vague and inarticulate to its proper place in our mental life which I am so anxious to press on the attention" (1961: 32). Merleau-Ponty echoes the idea in the early pages of his *Phenomenology of Perception*: "The region surrounding the visual field is not easy to describe, but what is certain is that it is neither black nor grey. There occurs here an *indeterminate* vision, a vision of *something or other*, and, to take the extreme case, what is behind my back is not without some element of visual presence" (1962: 6).

"We must recognize the indeterminate as a positive phenomenon," he also says, and this we cannot do as long as "we are caught up in the world and . . . do not succeed in extricating ourselves from it in order to achieve consciousness of the world" (p. 5). What he means is that the sort of determinateness one finds in physical objects must not be assumed a priori to be applicable to perceptual experience, in particular to the experiential character of the visual field.[13] Dennett, however, seems to do exactly that: he treats the indeterminateness of visual experience as though it were merely contingent, thereby supposing that all the determinate individual Marilyns on the wall *could* have been present in your field of vision with that very same determinateness.

There is another way of formulating Merleau-Ponty's point about not being able to recognize the indeterminate as a positive phenomenon as long as one is caught up in the world, a formulation that brings us back to the distinction between the personal and the subpersonal levels. The point is that the kind of determinateness that one finds in scientific accounts of the world, in particular in *subpersonal* accounts of the physiology of vision, is not applicable to the perceptual experience of the *person*.

Dennett's mischaracterization of the person's perceptual experience in the passage about the Marilyns cited above seems to involve a general confusion about the relation between the personal and the subpersonal levels. Dennett implies that although you seem to see all the detail, you do not actually see it, because all the detail is not represented in your brain. Notice what this means: the Marilyns are actually there on the wall, you seem to see that there are hundreds of identical Marilyns there on the wall, and you correctly judge that this is so on the basis of your visual experience. Nevertheless, you do not really see them because they are not all represented in your brain, the implication being that if they were all represented in your brain, then you would really see them.

We have already discussed how there can be no incompatibility between the indistinctness of parafoveal vision and actually seeing that the wall is covered with hundreds of identical Marilyns. But there is a more general problem with Dennett's position. Dennett appears to be making the following inference: you seem to see, but you are not really seeing, because your brain has merely jumped to a conclusion. This inference is a non sequitur that confuses the subpersonal and the personal levels: there is no reason to suppose that the brain's jumping to a conclusion is incompatible with the person's actually seeing the Marilyns. If Dennett is right that the brain jumps to a conclusion in the Marilyn case, then the proper thing to be said is that the person actually sees that the wall is covered with hundreds of identical Marilyns, and that this is accomplished subpersonally by the brain's jumping to a conclusion. What is striking is that Dennett seems prepared to deny that one sees that the wall is covered with hundreds of identical Marilyns, even though one forms the judgment, on the basis of looking, that this is the case, and even though the judgment happens to be correct.

Why does Dennett adopt such an implausible view? It would appear that there is an unstated assumption at work in Dennett's reasoning, one every bit as contentious as the doctrine of analytic isomorphism. The assumption is that for an experience to be nonillusory a necessary condition is that it depend on a neural state that has the very same content. For example, to be really seeing hundreds of identical Marilyns (or even, for that matter, for it to seem to one that one sees them) there would have to be hundreds of high-resolution Marilyn representations in one's brain. Or, to take another more general example, for consciousness to be really continuous, the subpersonal neural representations would have to be continuous, but they are not, and so the continuity of consciousness is an illusion: "One of the most striking features of consciousness is its *discontinuity*. Another is its *apparent* continuity. One makes a big mistake if one attempts to explain its apparent continuity by describing the brain as 'filling in' the gaps" (1992: 48). What is striking about this assumption is how close in its logical structure it is to analytic isomorphism: analytic isomorphism assumes that there must be an isomorphism between neural activity and perceptual experience; Dennett assumes that there must be a *correspondence of content* between neural representations and visual perception, otherwise one is not really seeing, or between neural representations and experience in general, otherwise one's consciousness is not really continuous.[14]

Dennett criticizes those who invoke filling-in for relying on a Cartesian materialist conception of consciousness. *But Dennett actually shares the correspondence of content doctrine with Cartesian materialism.* According to this doctrine, there is no difference in kind between neural content and perceptual content because the former entirely constitutes the latter. According to Cartesian materialism, neural content at the bridge locus or in the Cartesian theater constitutes the subject's conscious perceptual content. According to Dennett, there is no Cartesian theater; rather, spatially and temporally distributed, subpersonal neural content constitutes perceptual content at the personal level. We think that both the Cartesian materialists and Dennett are mistaken, for we hold that there is a difference in kind between neurally represented content and personal-level perceptual content.

Dennett's doctrine of the correspondence of content follows naturally from his account of the relation between the personal and the subpersonal. For Dennett, the person or animal is no more than a logical construct of subpersonal brain states and processes, just as the British empire at the time of the War of 1812 was a logical construct of the king, the members of Parliament, various officials and subjects of the Crown, and so on:

> We think that certain sorts of questions about the British Empire have no answers, simply because the British Empire was nothing over and above the various institutions, bureaucracies, and individuals that composed it. The question "Exactly when did the British Empire become informed of the truce in the War of 1812?" cannot be answered. The most that can be said is "Sometime between December 24, 1814, and mid-January, 1815." . . . Similarly, since You are nothing over and above the various subagencies and processes in your nervous system that compose you, the following sort of question is always a trap: "Exactly when did I (as opposed to various parts of my brain) become informed (aware, conscious) of some event?" Conscious experience, in our view, is a succession of states *constituted by* various processes occurring in the brain and not something over and above these processes that is *caused by* them. (Dennett and Kinsbourne 1992: 236, emphasis in original; see also Dennett, forthcoming)

We think that this is a distorted and unacceptable treatment of the relation between the personal and the subpersonal. The person is an embodied being embedded in the world, not a logical construction of brain states (Merleau-Ponty 1962; Varela, Thompson, and Rosch 1991). We cannot present the step-by-step argument for this position here, so we shall simply list the main reasons as they apply to perceptual experience (see McDowell 1994; Noë 1995; Sedivy 1995; and Thompson 1995: 286–303). First, perception is an ability of the animal, and its causally enabling mechanisms are perceptuo-motor processes occurring in the animal and its environment considered as an interactive unit (Merleau-Ponty 1963; Gibson 1979; Ballard 1991; Thompson, Palacios, and Varela 1992; Thompson 1995: 215–42; McClamrock 1995; Noë 1995). Second, although brain processes play the main causal role in enabling perception, they are not the proper bearers of perceptual content; the bearer is the animal as a whole interacting in its environment. Third, subpersonal neural content and personal-level perceptual content are not of the same kind: the former pertains to the functional organization of the nervous system insofar as it causally enables the animal's perceptual abilities; the latter pertains to the animal's dealings with its surroundings and depends on viewing the animal as a rational or intentional being (an "intentional system," to use Dennett's term). In particular, personal-level perceptual content is constrained by understanding, in the sense that it has a rational bearing on thought and action, whereas the content of subpersonal states does not: brain states have contents that outstrip the conceptual skills of the person, and they have only a causal bearing on thought and action, not a rational/normative one (Noë 1995, 1997).

We believe that Dennett's account of perceptual experience goes astray because of his neglect of the personal/subpersonal distinction. Whereas the Gestalt and the phenomenological psychologists insisted that careful descriptions of perceptual experience without any preconceptions about causal mechanisms are needed to complement causal-explanatory theories, Dennett forgoes such careful descriptions and in their stead offers statements about perceptual experience motivated entirely by subpersonal considerations, thereby distorting the conceptual and phenomenological character of that experience.

In the end, Dennett's treatment of perception goes astray on a fundamental conceptual point obvious to phenomenologists. To see what we mean consider Mach's attempt to draw his visual field with his right eye shut (Mach 1959: 19; see Fig. 10.1, p. 325). From his position lying on a divan, he sketched the outline of his nose, his beard and stomach bulging upward, and his legs stretched out. The striking defect in the drawing is at its outer limits, where he attempted to depict the indeterminacy at the periphery of his visual field by means of fading to white. The visual field is indeterminate in various ways, as we discussed in the Marilyn example. But these indeterminacies cannot be depicted in a drawing. In general, it seems to be a conceptual/phenomenological truth that one cannot represent the visual field (Wittgenstein 1975: 267; Noë 1994). Any attempt to depict the visual field will be a depiction of what is seen, not of the way it seems.[15] Mach did not draw his visual experience of the room; he drew the room as it looked to him from where he lay. The conceptual point of these considerations is that how things seem to one can never be just a matter of whether one has a picture in one's head corresponding to how things seem. Pictures cannot do that job. But Dennett's criticism of filling-in would appear to rest on the idea that they can, for the reason he gives for why one does not actually see hundreds of identical Marilyns on the wall is that there is no such picture in the brain. It would seem that Dennett has lost sight of the conceptual autonomy of perceptual experience at the personal level in relation to subpersonal neural processes.

To uphold the conceptual autonomy of the personal level means treating our understanding of ourselves as conscious perceptual subjects as a distinctive form of understanding, one that can be brought into "mutual accommodation" (Varela, Thompson, and Rosch 1991) or "reflective equilibrium" (Flanagan 1992) with cognitive science, but that cannot be reduced to an understanding of ourselves as logical constructions of brain states. Once the conceptual autonomy of the personal level is acknowledged, then Dennett's exclusively third-person approach to experience becomes unacceptable. As we have tried to illustrate here, however, it is possible to pursue the descriptive, conceptual, and phenomenological study of personal-level experience in tandem with psychophysical and cognitive neuroscientific research. As phenomenologists have long recognized, whenever we attempt to understand and explain our perception, we do so on the basis of our lived, perceptual experience of the world. Unless this experience has been conceptually clarified and systematically described, our scientific explanations will always be incomplete.

CHAPTER SIX

The Teleological Dimension of Perceptual and Motor Intentionality

BERNARD PACHOUD

Our object is to examine a set of convergences between phenomenology and theories of a naturalist type (emanating from empirical or formal research) concerning intentionality, which both perspectives, phenomenological and naturalist, agree is an essential property of consciousness or more generally of mental states. We will concentrate on an aspect of intentionality that Husserl considered central, namely, its teleological character. This type of teleological structure is, moreover, not at all unfamiliar to naturalist theories; indeed, it is a central feature of various models of mental activity, in particular those which Husserl accounts for in terms of intentionality (notably perception). What is the real nature of this convergence of ideas between the phenomenological approach and naturalist theories? Are we facing a single set of theoretical conclusions obtained by fundamentally different methods? Can these two types of statements be substituted for each other in such a way that, in the end, the phenomenological position can be replaced by a reductionist form of naturalized phenomenology? And more generally, what implications for phenomenology, on the one hand, and naturalism, on the other, follow from these convergences? And above all, what type of relation do these convergences invite us to entertain between phenomenology and naturalist approaches?

We will begin by reminding ourselves of the sense in which anticipation plays a crucial role in the Husserlian theory of intentionality. The importance of anticipation implies that this theory is a dynamic and temporalized conception of lived experience, since it is only through the unfolding of lived experience that something like an objective unity, an "apprehension of the object," can be grasped.

There are a number of reasons why we should emphasize the teleological dimension of the activity of consciousness. In the first place, it is in Husserl's opinion what accounts for the enigma of the intentionality of consciousness, that is, its ability to apprehend a transcendent object at the very heart of the immanence of consciousness. The importance of this aspect of the Husserlian theory of intentionality has been in my opinion underestimated and at times even misunderstood by Husserl's analytical or cognitivist readers. On the other hand, this teleological dimension sets the Husserlian conception apart from most contemporary philosophical theories of intentionality developed from a naturalist standpoint, with the exception of John Searle's, whose formal conception of intentionality is explicitly derived from his teleological theory of meaning.[1]

Finally, the teleological structure inherent in intentional experience is in fact primarily the structure of action. One is thereby led to inquire into the existence of a link between intentionality in Brentano's sense (i.e., the property of representations to relate to an object) and intentionality in the ordinary sense of the term, as a property of an action, an action whose end is anticipated. Even more, one is prompted to envisage a possible proximity, even an interdependence, between intentional lived experience in general and the domain of motor action. For if Husserl lays special emphasis in his studies of intentionality on the analysis of perceptual experience, he nonetheless recognizes that perceptual experience itself depends heavily upon motor functions. In *Ding und Raum*, he undertakes a phenomenological investigation of the role of motor functions (and the experience one has of them) in perceptual activity. On this point, a comparison with naturalistic contributions, in particular those of neurophysiology, is interesting, since it enables us to articulate more exactly some of Husserl's theoretical claims, which in turn will lead us to inquire into the nature of the relation between phenomenology and contemporary naturalistic approaches.

1. THE STRUCTURE OF ANTICIPATION INHERENT IN THE HUSSERLIAN CONCEPTION OF PERCEPTUAL INTENTIONALITY

The Husserlian conception of intentionality is best approached through the study of perceptual experience. From the time of his first analyses bearing on perception, in the fifth logical investigation, Husserl insisted upon the distinction that has to be drawn, within experience, between the appearance of the object (potentially multiple) and the appearing object (unique). He never ceased to stress the fact that the perceptual experience (in particular the visual) of a spatial object can never be an adequate representation of it: the thing is not fully given in experience; it is present only in intuition through one of its profiles or, taking account of duration and our movement around the thing, through a succession of profiles. Nevertheless, even though what he calls the actual content of our perception (that is to say, what is strictly speaking perceived: the profiles of the object) never ceases to be modified (as a succession of profiles), we never cease to perceive one and the same object, which allows us to claim that the object appearing "across" the multiplicity of its profiles is not "actually" contained in the lived experiences but precisely transcends them. (What is immanent, contained in the lived experience, are the perceived profiles of the object; but since all these profiles refer to one and the same object, something is thereby apprehended which is perceptually richer, which lies beyond these experiences, which is transcendent to the experience.) All that remains is to specify the regulated relation obtaining between the lived experiences and that which appears in them, or more explicitly, between these profiles and this unique object to which they all refer. In the end, it is a matter, as Husserl put it in *Ding und Raum*, of understanding how "objectity is constituted in and through the lived experiences."[2]

One already finds the sketch of an answer in the sixth logical investigation:

> It may happen that we are not satisfied with "a single look" and that, on the contrary, we envisage the thing from all sides in a continuous flux of perceptions. . . . This continuous flux of perceptions also shows itself as a fusion of partial acts in one single act and not as a complete act founded in partial acts. . . . Perception is as it were dilated. . . . In the dilated act we are directed towards nothing new, objectively speaking, but always towards this same object already envisaged across its partial perceptions. (§47, p. 677)

The unity of partial perceptual acts in "one perception" of the same object results from their being fused, and this is made possible, as Husserl explains in *Ding und Raum*, by the invariant structure of the object (i.e., its essence), detectable in the succession of its profiles whose variation is regulated by this invariant structure. The perceived transcendent object is nothing other than this "identity of what is perceived here and there" (*Ding und Raum* [hereafter cited as *DR*], §10, p. 26). Also, access to the transcendent object presupposes the temporalization of perceptual experience which Husserl calls "dilated perception," enlarged to include retentions. As for this fusion of acts, it depends upon "detecting" an identity in the content of this lived experience (and this identity is that in which their essence consists).

> The perceptions which we call perceptions of the same object make themselves known as such in the unity of the consciousness of identity, which later is founded in their essence . . . it is in virtue of their essence that they are adapted to one another in the unity of a consciousness of identity, the possibility of just such a unification being founded a priori in their essence. (*DR*, §10, p. 28)

What is therefore present in the singularity of each perceptual experience is a profile of the object, while the thing itself is not effectively given save in the flux of its changing appearances whose pole of identity it constitutes, an identity experienced (detected) across "the syntheses of identification amongst these appearances." So, the thing is the synthetic unity of its multiple appearances. It depends upon the flux of consciousness but does not belong to it. This is the sense in which it is transcendent (outside consciousness), even though apprehended in the immanence of lived experience.

Understood in this way, the givenness by adumbrations (by profiles) of the spatial object, a givenness which is always inadequate and partial, far from being an inconvenience, proves on the contrary to be that which makes it possible for us to accede to a transcendent object. The access to that which, strictly speaking, lies "beyond" what is given (the profiles), to the object "transcending" the perceptual data, is accomplished by means of an act of anticipation, which in *Ideen* I Husserl calls the apprehension of a meaning:

> In principle a physical thing can only be given "one-sidedly." . . . A physical thing is necessarily given under simple modes of appearance . . . but what is "actually" predelineated is accompanied by a horizon, by a more or less vague zone of indeterminateness. By indeterminateness is meant the possibility of determining a rigourously prescribed style, a possible diversity of perception whose phases are founded in the unity of one perception. (§44, p. 100)

This indeterminateness obliges us to anticipate nonapparent but possible determinations, determinations compatible with those which do appear. This horizon of possibilities is therefore constrained, prescribed as it is by the essence of the concept of perception, which ensures a consciousness of identity vis-à-vis these possible modes of the appearing. This essence of the thing (i.e., its invariant spatial structure), which Husserl calls its "noematic sense," "points ahead to possible connections of perceptions merging continuously to make up the unity of one perception" (p. 101).

Finally, this structure of anticipation inherent in the perceptual act by reason of its inadequateness is developed further by Husserl in *Cartesian Meditations*: "Every actuality involves its own potentialities. Far from being absolutely indeterminate potentialities, the latter are intentionally predelineated in respect to content" (§19, p. 81).

We even find here "a new feature essential to intentionality." As Husserl puts it: "Each state of consciousness possesses an intentional horizon which refers to potentialities." "Thus for example, in each external perception, the sides of the object which are actually perceived refer to sides which are not yet perceived but which are only anticipated . . . as aspects 'to come' in perception" (*Cartesian Mediations* [hereafter cited as *CM*], §19, p. 82).

There is, therefore, a continuous anticipation in perception, since the identification of the object in its three-dimensionality is implicitly an anticipation of its other profiles. The course of experience will either confirm or negate this anticipation and, by the same token, this three-dimensional identification. It is interesting to note that this apprehension of what is not strictly speaking present (or given) is conceived by Husserl as the intending or determining of a meaning, which is no way arbitrary, since as an anticipation, it is constrained by the essence of the given (the invariant spatial structure of the object).

This is how we understand that "any cogito, as a consciousness, is indeed, in the broadest sense, a 'meaning' of its meant, but at any moment this meaning means something more than what is given at the moment" (*CM*, §20, p. 84). It is in this going beyond, beyond what is strictly given, that the perceptual act "transcends," accedes to something that it does not itself contain (which is transcendent in relation to the immanence of the lived experiences of consciousness) and which nevertheless it constitutes. As for this transcendent thing, it is nothing other than "the intentional unity, that is, the unique and identical term at which consciousness arrives across the flux . . . which makes up the diversity of perception, provided only that it passes from one form to another" (*Ideen* I, §41, p. 94).

This transcendent thing (the spatial object) is only completely given "by means of certain connections at the very heart of experience" (*Ideen* I, §49, p. 116), and it is nothing other than "the intentional unity which in principle cannot be given save as that unity which links these multiple modes of the appearing" (§42, p. 98).

This perceptual act, which constitutes the transcendent object as the unity of its appearances, makes it possible for consciousness to be the consciousness of something, makes it possible for consciousness to accede to something which exceeds it, namely, the transcendent object. Nevertheless, this "transcendent" act has a price, since the anticipation of the object is subject to being confirmed or disconfirmed by the course of experience.

The emphasis is therefore on the continual flux of appearances, linked among themselves by syntheses of identification which ensure that these appearances are related to an object (an invariant pole of determinations). Henceforward, the inadequateness of perception (its finitude) should not be understood as deficient with regard to an adequate perception (which is impossible in principle) but, as Rudolf Bernet puts it, "as a function of the unlimited character of the multiplicity of appearances relating to the same thing. . . . The inadequateness which pertains to any knowledge of a transcendent object . . . is evident in the form of the impossibility of concluding, that is, of bringing the progress of this knowing process to a definitive conclusion" (Bernet 1994a: 129–30). It follows that the telos (the ideal, the completed accomplishment) of perception should not be understood as the adequate givenness of the thing (impossible in principle), but as the idea of an infinite progress in the givenness of the thing, one which is, in consequence, always susceptible to complementary determinations. What is implied in this structure of anticipation is the necessarily presumptive character of the meaning (or the knowledge) awaiting validation or invalidation in the course of experience. Husserl himself insists on this presumptive character of external perception: "I exist for myself with an apodictic necessity while the world . . . only enjoys the meaning of presumptive existence. The real world only rests upon the constantly prescribed presumption that experience will constantly continue to unfold in accordance with the same constitutive style" (*Formale und Transzendentale Logik*, §99, p. 222). Certainty is only to be had in the apprehension of an identity of lived experiences and so presupposes not merely the connections between such experiences but also their temporalization, that is, their enlargement into retentions, thereby allowing for the apprehension of identity.

It is worth underlining, as Husserl does himself, that this finitude is not that of our cognitive resources but is linked to the very essence of perception and in this respect applies to every perceiving being (or system), even a divine subject. It follows that perception can only be a dynamic and therefore temporalized process.

The main aspects of this phenomenological analysis of perceptual experience can be summarized as follows:

1. Perceptual experience has to be conceived as a dynamic process, which in consequence has to unfold over a certain period of time and is not a strictly instantaneous phenomenon.

2. Perceptual consciousness is a flux of lived experiences at the heart of which objects are apprehended thanks to the perception of an objective identity over and beyond the multiplicity of the object's modes of appearing. So perception proceeds from a range of mental activities that, so to speak, tests the reality of the object and is not a sort of passive and instantaneous reception of the object. This "confirmation" (of the reality of the object) results from the concordance, at the heart of the experience of the subject, of aspects under which the object appears to him (the apprehension of the object is always presumptive and is confirmed through the unfolding of experience). It might be said that the central principle of perception is that of the concordance of the flux of experience.

* * *

This concordance, which turns out to be one of the great principles of mental functioning (indicative of reality), can be found again at the level of the integration of different perceptual modalities (for example, between sight and touch, even between sight and hearing). This multimodal sensorial integration is another indication of the reality of what is thereby perceived by different senses. And it is the concordance of the diversity of these perceptual data (each of which only apprehends one aspect of the object) which is the index of the reality of the object.

2. THE DIMENSIONS OF PERCEPTUAL EXPERIENCE NECESSARY FOR THE APPREHENSION OF THE OBJECT IN ITS MATERIAL CONCRETENESS

The analysis of perceptual experience just presented is still partial and insufficient to the extent that it has not really done justice to the specific property of perception as a conscious relation to an object, namely, the fact that in perception the object is apprehended in its reality, in its material concreteness, or as Husserl is wont to say, is given to us "*leibhaftig,*" "in flesh and blood" according to Paul Ricoeur's translation.

Indeed, it has done no more than account for our apprehension of the invariant spatial schema of the object, over and above the multiplicity of its appearances, as Husserl recognizes explicitly in *Ideen* II: "A spatial body having a qualitative fulfillment is not yet . . . fully a thing . . . in the normal sense of a material reality" (§14b, p. 37). And as if to underline this character of apparently simple unity, without any indication of reality or materiality, on many occasions Husserl calls the invariant spatial schema of the thing a "phantom." This follows simply from the fact that perceptual experience is indeed much richer and more complex than what has been described so far. In fact, in order to describe the elements of this experience, phenomenological analysis has to distinguish the levels or the dimensions involved in perceptual experience and, in the first stages of the analysis, leave some of them out of consideration with a view to reintroducing them later, in particular if they prove necessary to account for the apprehension of the object in its materiality (i.e., in its *Leibhaftigkeit*). Adopting the transcendental point of view on constitutive activity, Husserl prefers to conceptualize this plurality of levels in terms of strata, these different strata indicating the different constitutive operations phenomenological analysis seeks to distinguish, even though they are present as superimposed in lived experience. These strata of experience have not been mentioned so far and they now have to be reintroduced as Husserl himself reintroduces them at §§15, 16, and 18 of *Ideen* II.

2.1. "THE THINGLY ENVIRONMENT" AT THE HEART OF WHICH THE OBJECT IS APPREHENDED

The first aspect of reality Husserl acknowledges leaving out of consideration in the analysis to an object of perception is the "thingly" environment in which this object is apprehended: "Thus far we have taken the thing in isolation. But it is relative to circumstances that the thing is what it is" (*Ideen* II, §15c, p. 41). This co-apperception of the context of a thingly world to which the thing belongs proves to be necessary for the apprehension of the thing as such, that is, to its material existence:

> Adopting the hypothesis . . . whereby we take the thing out of its context, we are unable, once the experience has run its course, to determine in an evident way whether the thing we have just experienced effectively exists or whether we have been the victims of a simple illusion, the thing then being a pure and simple phantom. (*Ideen* II, §15b, p. 40)

> The thing which appears as being at rest and qualitatively unchanged does not "show" more than can be gleaned from its schema or rather from its appearance, even though it is, at the same time, apprehended as a material thing. But from this point of view, it does not show itself, it does not, strictly speaking, confront us, does not make itself available for an original givenness. (*Ideen* II, §15b, p. 37)

That by means of which the thing is apprehended as a material thing "that does not show itself" does not correspond to any supplementary qualitative datum, at least from a visual standpoint; whence the difficulty of doing justice to it, phenomenologically speaking. This apprehension of reality rests in fact on certain elements of the experience, in particular the fact that the object is apprehended as one object among others with which it enters into definite relations. It could simply be a matter of their spatial relations, which might remain invariant if the objects are immobile. It could also be a matter of relations of interaction between these objects, relations which would be interpreted as causal relations. It is in a certain sense its insertion into a world of real objects through definite relations that confers upon the object its value as a reality: "The reality properly speaking, here called materiality, is not to be found in the simple sensible schema . . . rather it is precisely to be found in this relation to circumstances, and this with the mode of apprehension which corresponds to it" (*Ideen* II, §15c, p. 41). The thingly context therefore proves to be necessary to the apprehension of the reality of the thing in interaction with other things.

2.2. THE BODY OF THE PERCEIVING SUBJECT

Among the co-apprehended objects in perceptual experience left out of consideration is one that has a very special status, namely, the body of the perceiving subject. But the body plays a central role in perception and, in a more general way, in the apprehension of reality, and this for a number of reasons.

In the first place, the body of the perceiving subject is the means by which any perception takes place, for all perception is necessarily mediated through the organs of sense, even if this mediation is not as manifest in the case of vision as it is in that of touch.

The special status of the body of the perceiving subject also follows from the fact that it is always and necessarily co-apprehended in perceptual experience and even more when situated in a phenomenologically invariant and eminent spatial position, since it serves as a point of reference for the phenomenological system of spatial coordinates. Husserl acknowledges that he has left the body of the perceiving subject out of consideration in the greater part of his analyses of perception: "In general we have not taken into account the own-body, which, however, even if only partially, is a thing which appears. . . . We have acted as if the "I" was a spirit furnished with eyes but a disembodied spirit" (*DR*, §83, p. 273). A complete phenomenological theory of perception must therefore allow for the perceiver's own body, which requires that we consider its special mode of constitution and the role which it plays in perceptual experience.

Furthermore, among the objects of consciousness, and especially perceptual objects, the perceiver's own body enjoys a special status for a very specific reason. The experience one has of one's own body is, so to speak, double. It is true that one can always perceive one's own body like an object in the world among other objects, from the outside so to speak, as when one looks at one's hand for example; but it is not primarily in this way, as a thing (*Körper*), that our own bodies appear to us, but rather as living bodies (*Leib*) which we are and not objects which we have (*Ideen* II, §§35–42). This duality in the apprehension of our own bodies, both as objects (of perception) and as subjects (as the seat and the instrument of perception), results from the dual manner in which we constantly apprehend them. We, at one and the same time, perceive them from the outside as objects and from the inside "in the first person." The Husserlian concept of *Leib*, of the perceiver's own body, refers back to this double dimension, subjective and objective, to this dual and concordant experience that we have of our own bodies. This experience of our own bodies plays a central role in constitutive activity. In particular, in virtue of the dual structure of the perceiver's own body, vested with an interiority and an exteriority, it plays a role in the apprehension of the other as another subjectivity, founded in the apprehension of the other's body as another *Leib*, perceived from the outside but referring to an inside similar to the perceiver's own. Thus, by virtue of this coincidence of the subjective and the objective in the apprehension of the body, objectivity can never be apprehended save at the heart of subjective experience.

Finally, if the perceiver's body intervenes as an instrument of perception, it does so not only as an organ of perception but just as much as an organ of movement, thanks to which the subject can transport himself toward objects. As for the apprehension of one's own body, it is as a body capable of self-movement that this is brought about. Even though movement is intrinsically linked to the perceiver's own body, the importance of this dimension for the apprehension of reality deserves separate development.

2.3. THE PERCEPTION OF ONE'S OWN MOVEMENTS

Movement is a dimension, or a stratum, of perceptual experience that is still more immediately important than the two previous ones, since it is already required by the apprehension of the sensible schema (and not simply by the apprehension of the materiality of the object), as Husserl shows in *Ding und Raum*. In fact, if the object is constituted (is apprehended) as the principle of unity for the multiplicity of its appearances, what is necessary for this constitutive operation (or apperceptive synthesis) is the variation of the appearances of the object and, in consequence, a movement which moreover can either be the movement of the object or that of the subject.

> In isolated appearances there is nothing which makes it possible for the identity of the appearing object to be effectively disclosed.... It is only when, in the unity of experience, the continuous passage from one perception to another is guaranteed that we can talk of the evidence in accordance with which identity is given. The unity of the object is only validated in the unity of the logical synthesis, that of identification.... The identical-unchanged spatial body [of the object] is only validated as such in a kinetic perceptual series which continuously allows its different sides to become apparent. The body [*Körper*] (of the thing) must turn and be displaced, or I have to move. (*DR*, §44, p. 155)

So, movement proves to be an essential component in the sense of being necessary to the apprehension of the spatial object; something Husserl insists upon on several occasions:

> All spatiality is constituted, is brought to givenness, in movement, in the movement of the object itself or in the movement of the I. (*DR*, §44, p. 154)

> Rest and movement, the changing and the unchanging, find their meaning in the constitution of thinghood as reality, in which such events play an essential role. (*Ideen* II, §18b, p. 62)

So what we now have to do is clarify the Husserlian analysis of the role of movement in the perceptual apprehension of the object, and especially in the apprehension of reality (or of materiality).

3. PHENOMENOLOGICAL ANALYSIS OF THE ROLE OF MOVEMENT IN THE SPATIAL PERCEPTION OF OBJECTS

If, from a phenomenological point of view, one considers the role of movement in the perception of spatial objects, one is immediately referred to the question of determining how movement is given to us phenomenologically; in particular, how does movement appear to us in visual perception? Certainly, we "see" movement whenever a displacement of the sensible schema of the object in the visual field occurs; but since the movement can affect the object just as well as the subject, the question remains, what enables us to distinguish, phenomenologically, between a movement on the part of the object and a movement on the part of the perceiving subject. Again, the reply seems evident: it is through the perception of the movements of his own body, and thanks to what Husserl calls "kinesthetic sensations," that the perceiving subject distinguishes movements that affect objects from movements that affect his own body or, more exactly, which he initiates and of which he is the subject. A first and important conclusion for the phenomenological analysis of the constitution (or the apprehension) of the object is therefore that the strictly visual modality of perception proves to be insufficient for removing the ambiguity that surrounds the visual perception of movement and therefore is not sufficient to constitute spatiality. Recourse is needed to another sense dealing with the perceiving subject's own movements.

> It turns out that visual contents are incapable of assuming by themselves the function of expository contents for visual space and for thinghood in general....
>
> I have in mind here sensations of movement. They play an essential role in the apprehension of every external thing but are not apprehended in such a way as to permit the representation of matter.... They do not form a part of the projection of the thing, nothing qualitative corresponds to them in the

thing.... This means that the extensional moment of visual sensation, as also that of tactile sensation, certainly offers a spatial outline but does not however suffice to render the constitution of spatiality possible.... New sensations are needed, and we are talking here of sensations of movement.... They make the manifestation of space possible, but without manifesting themselves. (*DR*, §46, pp. 159–61)

And to emphasize the fact that these sensations of movement concern the perceiver's own body, Husserl calls them "kinesthetic sensations." As for the necessity of such kinesthetic sensation for the perception of space, Husserl tries to make this apparent by envisaging ambiguous (visual) perceptual situations in which these kinesthetic sensations are needed to eliminate the ambiguity.

> At first sight, and taking into account the case where, while the eye and the body remain completely immobile, a thing—at rest or in movement—can appear, one might think that kinesthetic sensations are inessential for the constitution of the thing. In such a case nothing changes from the kinesthetic point of view. It would then seem that what the purely visual field offers as a means of discrimination suffices to constitute a thing's appearance. It has to be admitted however that this line of thought is unacceptable when one compares the cases where the field of objects is at rest and where only the eye moves and those where the eye is at rest and where the field of objects moves. For it is possible that exactly the same change in the visual field takes place. (*DR*, §50, p. 175)

In other words, one and the same change in the visual field can correspond to a movement of the subject or to a movement of the object. Husserl also envisages the reverse perceptual ambiguity where there is no phenomenal change, where nothing moves in the visual field—which can however correspond to two situations: either both the subject and the object are immobile, or the subject and the object move concomitantly and in parallel with each other and in such a way that the visual field remains invariable and immobile.

> With a visual field that remains unchanged, things can appear both in movement and at rest. This shows us that purely visual indications do not suffice for apprehension, that they are not capable of differentiating between immobile and mobile appearances. This implies that the constitution of objective place and of objective spatiality is essentially mediated by the movement of the body, in phenomenological terms, by kinesthetic sensations. (*DR*, §50, p. 176)

This line of reasoning regarding the need for kinesthetic sensations (and so of motor functions) in the constitution of space (and beyond that in the apprehension of reality) merits a remark regarding the Husserlian way of doing phenomenology. It consists in envisaging ideal possibilities, proposed as various kinds of thought experiments, rather than in deepening the phenomenological description of experiences whose course it seeks to retrace. Finally, it is by comparing experiences that are only imagined or remembered that Husserl brings out the significant and distinctive features of these experiences.

To return to the role of movement in perception, Husserl restricts himself to simply mentioning the existence of perceptual illusions linked precisely with the visual perception of movement. But it is interesting—and altogether convincing concerning the role of kinesthesia in the apprehension of spatiality—to consider carefully a genuine experience of ambiguity or of perceptual illusion in relation to movement, which takes place precisely when most kinesthetic sensations are absent.

For example, one can consider the perceptual illusion of movement we have all probably experienced when, seated in a train standing in a station, we get the impression that it is the train in which we are seated that is starting up, since the contents of our visual field have been rearranged, even though, in reality, it is the neighboring train which is leaving in the opposite direction. It is noticeable that this illusion is shattered as soon as we look at the solid background (for example, the station), which, if it is immobile, cancels our impression of being in motion and, at the same time, makes it appear that it is the neighboring train that has started up. This solid background is, however, one of the strata of perceptual experience which Husserl recognizes as essential, even if most of his earlier analyses leave it out of consideration (*Ideen* II, §15c).

Husserl also invokes a situation comparable to displacement in a train or a car when he considers the substitution of a passive movement for the active movement of the subject. Schematically, he seems to think that kinesthetic information linked to the active movement of the perceiver's own body is in a certain sense replaced by sensations linked to the displacement of the vehicle, a little as if the perceiver's own body extended its "referential axis" to the vehicle.

> Exactly the same final result would have been achieved if I had run alongside the car (or the train) in movement. . . . The series of appearances are exactly the same, only, in place of the kinesthetic motivation of the running, there is now the vibration of the car, the noise from the running of the wheels, etc. . . . We have to note that the term kinesthetic motivation also covers very different series of movements. (*DR*, §83, p. 283)

So it seems that Husserl means by "kinesthetic sensations" the sensations derived from active movements without his ever specifying exactly, at least in *Ding und Raum*, to what these kinesthetic sensations correspond.

This leads to our second remark, namely, that Husserl's own descriptions of kinesthetic sensations appear all the more unsatisfactory today in the light of the fact that they can be more precisely described thanks to the development of the neurosciences. For example, in the case of the visual illusion of movement (which we have just considered), extravisual information exists which can resolve the ambiguity, namely, vestibular information by means of which we perceive the linear acceleration affecting our body. In this text, Husserl makes no mention of this when he considers the perception of movement. We will return to the neurophysiological contributions that make it possible for us to determine not simply the kinesthetic sensations themselves but also the mechanisms upon which they depend, and we will see how the alteration of these mechanisms can make it impossible for the subject to decide whether the movement comes from him or from the world, or in other words, whether the movement is objective or subjective. And the question for us will then be to determine whether this specification of kinesthetic data is in principle possible for phenomenology, whether the phenomenological approach can come to terms with it or whether, at this stage, the matter has to be handed over to a naturalist approach.

Before we take account of these naturalist contributions, and with a view to emphasizing the role of motor activity in the apprehension of space and of things, we will consider another illustration of the Husserlian claim according to which spontaneous motor activity is necessary for perceptual intentionality, or alternatively, to the apprehension of the object as a reality. Think of watching the countryside go by through the window of a train. How do we know, phenomenologically speaking, what it is that makes it possible for us to perceive the countryside as real and not, for example, as if it were a mere image, as when one watches a film. In other words, what is the phenomenological difference between "seeing the countryside go by through the window of the train" and "seeing the countryside go by at the cinema," and this in a comparable situation where the camera would be installed in the train in place of the passenger and where the going by of the countryside would be filmed through the window.

If one abstracts from certain layers of perceptual experience which have not been taken into consideration up to now, namely, the co-apperception of the thingly context (among other things, the perceiver's own body) and the real/causal circumstances of experience (to put it concretely: if one abstracts from the fact, co-perceived in reality, that one is seated in a moving train or, on the contrary, in a cinema), and if one limits oneself to the visual experience of the "going by of the countryside," what (in this sense) makes the phenomenological difference, is that despite the irrepressible flight of the countryside, we are still, in the actual viewing of the countryside, at liberty to fasten upon and follow this or that detail of the countryside, to temporarily retain this object in our visual field, thanks to our motor activity (to the motor activity of the eye which constantly intervenes, but eventually also to movements of the hand and upper body, even to the possibility of leaning out the window to keep some object in view a little longer), while this very liberty, this freedom to initiate motor action is almost entirely denied us in the viewing of a film, a situation over which we have hardly any control, hardly any scope for initiating the flux of phenomena which we can only "follow" passively. What phenomenologically speaking makes the difference between these two situations would be our motor activity in the perception of the real world, by contrast to our quasi passivity in the viewing of a filmed representation of the world, which is betrayed, phenomenologically, by the absence of kinesthesia.

One can, for example, ask what our experience in the train would be if we were paralyzed and deprived of all motor activity, even the ocular. Surely our experience of the countryside going by would be denied the possibility of a verification that allows for ocular focusing (which vouches for the objective unity and the stability of the object in spite of the variation of its appearances). From a strictly visual point of view, one could even ask whether this experience would be distinguishable from the viewing of a filmed countryside. Since this possibility of paralysis is difficult to conceive imaginatively, one can imagine a device by which, while still being in the train, we would only have access to the countryside through a porthole which, moreover, would be situated at a distance from us and in such a way that ocular movements would be virtually ruled out for fear of losing the porthole at the center of our visual field. It seems that in this situation we would not be able (or at least it would be much more difficult) to discriminate between the going by of the real countryside and the going by of a filmed countryside. In other words, it seems that the initiation of motor activity, even limited to ocular motor activity, plays an essential role in the perception of reality.

3.1. IS AN EXPERIMENTAL PHENOMENOLOGY CONCEIVABLE?

The examples we have just advanced do not arise out of ordinary situations, and the fact that this is so raises a series of questions. It seems that at a certain point in phenomenological analysis, if one wants to bring out certain components of lived experience, one has to turn to exceptional situations such as experiences of ambiguity or of perceptual illusion, which allow us to disassociate and to identify the components of lived experience and to bring their role to light. Why not henceforward conceive these situations in a quasi-experimental way, by controlling, even by manipulating, the physical parameters of the situation? In other words, why not have recourse to what might be called "an experimental phenomenology," which would certainly continue to describe experience, or its lived contents, but in circumstances whose parameters would be controlled?

Such a project might at first sight appear to be in contradiction with the methodological requirement proper to phenomenology, that of suspending any belief, and so a fortiori any knowledge regarding external reality, with a view to founding the description solely upon what appears. Is it not contradictory to want both to suspend all knowledge regarding the external world and at the same time to control certain parameters? To this objection one might reply by insisting that nothing requires that we put these two requirements, that of an experimental control of the situation and that of the phenomenological *epochē*, into operation at the same time. On the contrary, one can perfectly well envisage, in the first instance, a determination of the "experimental situation," certain of whose parameters would be controlled, and then, later on, adopt a phenomenological attitude with regard to the latter by strictly limiting one's attention to the lived experiences themselves. One could even go so far as to insist that any phenomenological analysis in the end actually does proceed in this fashion, by first choosing, within the natural attitude, some experience to which the phenomenological analysis will then direct its attention. The Husserlian descriptions themselves bear on lived experiences that are in fact selected and characterized first of all in the natural attitude, before the operation of a "reduction" then makes it possible to consider them from a properly phenomenological point of view. There is therefore no difficulty in principle in restricting, even in manipulating in advance, the situation the experience of which is going to carry the phenomenological description, since in any case this experience arises initially as the result of a selection operative in the natural attitude.

4. NEUROPHYSIOLOGICAL CONTRIBUTIONS TO THE SPECIFICATION OF KINESTHETIC DATA

The theme of the visual perception of movement, and even of the role of motor activity in perception, is by no means confined to phenomenology. It is the object of a variety of research undertaken in an empirical perspective, and especially in neurophysiology. The specificity of Husserl's analysis lies in the theoretical implications attributed to it, in making it a condition of the apprehension of space, and thereby of thinghood, and finally of intentionality in general.

We will restrict ourselves to mentioning some contributions of a neurophysiological kind bearing upon the perception of movement and in particular upon the role of kinesthesia, insofar as the latter are specified in this way. It will transpire not only that these naturalist contributions are compatible with those of phenomenology but that they can be employed to complete the Husserlian positions or to render them more precise. As a result, not only will the inadequacies of phenomenological analysis become apparent, in addition, its fundamental positions will be justified, especially with regard to the interdependence of motor activity and perception and with regard to the role of anticipation.

The physicist E. Mach, in his work of 1875 on the sensations of movements, was interested in the perception of the displacement of the perceiver's own body in space insofar as the latter is based on visual information. He gave the name "vection" to those phenomena involved in the transformation of the visual scene which inform us of such movements. And it has now been established by neurophysiology that two kinds of systems contribute to the perception of the movements (linear and angular) of a body in space: vision on the one hand (in particular by means of vection phenomena), and the vestibular system on the other, which constitutes an inertial center and furnishes information on the linear and angular accelerations of the head (Berthoz 1997; see esp. chap. 2). A large number of studies have sought to specify the respective weight of these two types of information and the ways in which these kinds of sensorial information are integrated in a perceptual judgment bearing on the movement of the body.

If one retains the nomenclature of "kinesthetic sensations" to refer to sensations relative to the movements of the perceiver's own body, this in conformity with the Husserlian definition, then the following can be claimed quite properly to belong to kinesthetic sensations: (1) vision, and especially the phenomena of vection; (2) vestibular information; and (3) proprioception, which provides us with knowledge of the relative position of our limbs in space and of their movements, thanks to a system of articular, muscular, and tendinous receptors.

Finally, we draw attention to the central role, for vision, of ocular motor functions. This raises the question of the kind of kinesthetic information available to us concerning eye movements. Is it not indirectly, through the displacement of our visual field, that we become conscious of what we are looking at? Have we a sensation of the position of our eyes comparable to that which we have, through proprioception, of the position of our arms?

This question is not new and has already marked the history of neurophysiology, since Helmholtz raises a related question when he asks how it is that, when we move our eyes, the world remains stable even though our retinal images move. Which is as much as to ask (and Helmholtz does also put the question in these terms): when the retinal image moves, how do we know if the movement can be attributed to our eye or to the object, if the movement comes from us or from the world? It is interesting to note that this question is curiously similar to that posed by Husserl when he affirms that the same displacement of the objective field can correspond to a movement on the part of the objects or to a movement on the part of the perceiving subject and to which he replies by invoking the determining role of kinesthetic sensations (*DR*, §49). What is at issue here is nothing other than the objectivity (i.e., transcendence) of the appearing movement. In other terms, something happens, an event, a movement, and it is a question of knowing whether this movement comes from us or from the external world, whether we are its author or whether we are simply affected by it, whether it is a movement of the subject or a movement of the object. In the case of the displacement of the visual content, what guarantees the exteriority of the event, when movement occurs, is not the invariance of the appearances (since in every instance what is perceived is "an" object which appears to move) but knowing whether this movement comes from me or from the object. The discriminating element is therefore "the sensation of the movement of my eyes," the kinesthetic sensation, and the whole problem is one of knowing the relationship between this sensation and the ocular motor functions. It cannot be a question of proprioception or, strictly speaking, of sensation, but only of information linked to motor command (one might talk of motor intentionality). The arguments in this direction are the following:

This information is wanting whenever a passive movement is imprinted on the eye—though a mobilization can be marginally initiated by pressing the globe of the eye sideways with the finger, which provokes a displacement of the retina and correlatively of our perception of the world.

Helmholtz also took note of the fact that the efforts required by patients suffering from ocular paralysis to effect ocular movement left the eye immobile but created the impression that objects in the world had been displaced in the direction of the effort. From which Helmholtz concluded: "These phenomena make it impossible for us to doubt that we estimate the direction in which we look by way of that effort of will by means of which we try to change the position of our eyes.... We therefore feel what willed impulses, and how strong, have to be applied to our eyes to turn them in a given direction" (von Helmholtz 1866; quoted in Jeannerod 1983: 132). The sensation invoked here is conceptually linked to what Maine de Biran called the "sentiment de l'effort," which constituted for him the subjective criterion of voluntary action, even of the intention to act. Today we know what makes up the neurophysiological substrate of this mechanism as a result of the research of Roger Sperry (1950) and especially of Erich von Holst and Horst Mittelstaedt (1950). It is now admitted that when the motor centers send a motor command to the effector systems they also send a copy of this command to the sensorial center concerned with movement, in the case of ocular motor functions, to the visual centers (whence the name given to this re-afferent information: "re-afference copy" or "corollary discharge"). In the case of ocular movements, this information, this copy of motor commands, would make it possible to compensate for the displacement of the retinal image linked to the movements of the eye, thereby ensuring the stability of the retinal image. It is moreover remarkable that this process of adjustment of representation as a function of movement takes place, according to the theorists who describe it, by anticipating the consequences that follow from motor functions. Sperry, for example, argues that in order for this compensation for the displacement of the retinal image to take place immediately "it has to be assumed that, in the visual centers, an anticipatory adjustment takes place, one which is specific to the direction and the speed of each movement" (Sperry 1950; quoted in Jeannerod 1983). This mechanism not only is valid for the stabilization of the visual image but also proves to be a general mechanism involved in the control of motor functions. The principle of this control rests on an anticipation of the effects of movement, an anticipation that is at every instance compensated for by the observed effects of the movement and which allows for its continuous adjustment in the very course of its accomplishment. This process of anticipation is also emphasized by Marc Jeannerod, who claims that "the brain dominates the situation since it 'knows' what is going to result from its own action. It anticipates the effects of its own movements with a view to maintaining its environment invariant" (Jeannerod 1983). It is a matter of what cyberneticists have called a mechanism of *feed-forward* control, that is, one founded on anticipation. That this type of process intervenes in the control of all motor functions suggests that such a mechanism of anticipation constitutes one of the major principles regulating the functioning of the nervous system. But we have seen that this process of anticipation also plays a decisive role in perceptual experience, which only really gains access to the *profile* of an object and so only apprehends it in its totality by anticipating its other modes of appearing.

This efferent copy mechanism finally plays a crucial role in the awareness of action and especially in our awareness of the voluntary character of action. It can be shown that it is by virtue of this mode of control, and of the continuous adjustment of action, that the latter is appropriated in an intentional mode. In fact, the greater part of our actions are assured by the release of routine motor functions, a release that can take place in a voluntary way, deliberately, but also quite frequently in an automatic way, released by certain stimuli in the environment. This neurophysiological mechanism of efferent copy is therefore indispensable if we are to "feel" ourselves to be the initiators of our acts (a fortiori when it is a question of the automatic release of routine motor functions) and consequently also the subject of our acts (in this respect, it plays a central role in the constitution of subjectivity). So this mechanism proves to be one of the essential components of what is globally designated by Husserl as "kinesthetic sensations," and is in particular the component relevant to the active and intentional movements of the subject's own body.

The pertinence of this mechanism (of this aspect of kinesthetic experience) for the question of the apprehension of the object (and of its external reality) becomes clear in the light of what happens when this mechanism is altered or damaged in some way by a pathology. A certain number of experimental arguments support the hypothesis that the malfunctioning of this mechanism might be at the origin of a number of psychotic phenomena, the most typical of which would be the "passivity experiences" such as the delusion of external control. In experiences of alien control, patients lose the feeling of being the initiators of their acts or their thoughts, or to put it otherwise, lose the feeling of intentional control over their behavior, to the point where they attribute the initiative to an alien force that exercises control over them. This dysfunctioning of the processes of motor control (i.e., of this kinesthetic modality) also constitutes one of the best hypotheses available to cognitive psychopathology for accounting for hallucinatory phenomena, primarily auditory hallucinations conceived as subvocal productions on the part of the subject which he fails to recognize as his own (Frith 1992).

It is remarkable that these psychopathological hypotheses are perfectly congruent with the Husserlian theses concerning the necessary role of kinesthetic data in the constitution not simply of space but also of things or, in other words, of the apprehension of the materiality of the thing. It is also not surprising that any such deficiency in kinesthetic experience should have repercussions for the constitution of the perceiver's own body experienced in a profoundly altered way as disassociated or split in schizophrenic pathology.

From these convergences between the Husserlian theses concerning intentionality and contributions of a naturalist kind (neurophysiology), it can be argued that the naturalist approach comes to take over, so to speak, from phenomenological analyses, whose theses are thereby corroborated, but also and especially, completed and made more precise, particularly with regard to the mechanisms brought to light by naturalist research. For example, the emphasis placed on the role of kinesthetic sensations in the constitution of spatiality and thinghood can be regarded as an important result of Husserlian phenomenological analysis, but this kinesthetic information remains insufficiently defined by Husserl. Could the phenomenological analysis be taken still further? No doubt it could be deepened but it inevitably encounters a limit in the exploration of acts. The process of motor control, for example, made possible by the mechanism of "re-afference copying," whose place and importance at the heart of the kinesthetic system (invoked in a general way by Husserl) have already been demonstrated, can only be described and specified by a naturalist approach, which in this case appears to take over, and necessarily so, from phenomenological investigation.

5. SHOULD MOVEMENT RATHER THAN PERCEPTION BE CONSIDERED THE PARADIGMATIC EXPERIENCE OF MENTAL INTENTIONALITY?

As has already been emphasized, it is remarkable that in *Ideen* I, the work in which phenomenology is presented in a systematic way, Husserl conducts his analyses primarily from the standpoint of perceptual experience, more precisely of visual perception, thereby making it appear as the paradigm for all conscious lived experience. This primacy accorded to perception is all the more noticeable, since in his earlier works and lectures, Husserl based his analyses on a variety of other types of lived experience, experiences of imagining, remembering, speaking, judging, counting. All the same, the priority accorded to perception appears perfectly comprehensible in *Ideen* I, where Husserl seeks to render intelligible this fundamental eidetic property of consciousness which is intentionality and, what is more, in a transcendental perspective, thereby bringing to light the constitutive activity of consciousness. The privilege accorded to perception relates to the fact that it constitutes the exemplary experience of the relation to the object, or more exactly, the experience in which the object is apprehended, since it turns out that in perception consciousness is not affected passively. It is equally striking that in the context of *Ideen* I Husserl hardly ever explores the role played by movement at the center of perception, whose importance he had nevertheless already brought to light in *Ding und Raum*. To be sure, this dimension is reintroduced in the second volume of *Ideen*, but the latter was not published during his lifetime and it is significant that Husserl should have decided to postpone, to demote so to speak, this dimension so closely linked to motor functions, thereby reinforcing the primacy of perception and its status as a model for intentional lived experience. Moreover, Husserl makes this quite explicit when he undertakes to present perceptual experience as the point of departure for rendering intelligible the totality of intentional experience: "What has been established in some detail by according a special status to perception is now valid for all kinds of intentional lived experience" (*Ideen* I, §91).

It is precisely this primacy accorded to perception which looks as though it should be called in question if one is going to draw the consequences of what has been established phenomenologically by Husserl himself, namely, that perception is inseparable from movement and not merely in a factual but also in a necessary, and therefore essential, way, since the apprehension of the object as a unity presupposes a variation of its appearances—and therefore movement. If all perceptual activity is necessarily associated with a motor function, then we must ask which of these two dimensions, perceptual or motor, should be regarded as dominant. This comes down to asking whether it is legitimate to privilege the perceptual dimension as Husserl does in fact do in *Ideen* I, and this at the cost of abstracting perception from the conditions of its realization, notably the motor dimension. Would it not be better, on the contrary, to question this primacy accorded to perception and so to privilege the dimension of movement?

A choice of this kind is not without its consequences. It requires us to see in movement, or in action, rather than in perception, the model on the basis of which to think intentionality. This decision also determines the choice of the experiences taken as exemplary, and upon which phenomenological analysis will accord preferential status. The primacy of perception leads one to take as paradigmatic the perceptual experience of an immobile object, thereby making the perception of movement appear as a special case, a more complex case, and one which has to be considered in consequence as secondary. But if, as we have seen, movement is in fact necessary for perception, should we not rather regard the perception of an immobile object as a particular case of the perception of movement and of change? In this way, we bring back to the fore the crucial distinction the subject must be capable of drawing between a displacement of the visual scene brought about by his own movement and a displacement which is independent, in other words, between an objective movement (of the object) and a subjective movement (on his part). This suggests that it is in the experience of movement that the division between the subjective and the objective has to be effected. Finally, if all perceptual activity is indissociable from motor activity (even if the latter is reduced to visual exploration through ocular movements), then every perceptual experience is at the same time a motor experience, one which can not be passed over by phenomenological analysis without exposing the latter to the criticism of being radically incomplete. Henceforward, why not regard perceptual activity as integrated into motor activity, at the center of which perception necessarily intervenes (at least in the control and the adjustment of movement to its environment). This results in a reversal of the order of priority between movement and perception. Movement now has to be considered as the paradigmatic experience on the basis of which intentionality is to be understood and within which perception must itself be integrated.

This idea concerning the primacy of movement, or at least of a privileged relation between movement and the intentionality of consciousness, that is, the ability to posit objects and, over and beyond that, a world, has already been advanced and developed by certain phenomenologists, notably by Maurice Merleau-Ponty and Jan Patočka. Even though it is opposed to what we have called the "primacy of perception" in *Ideen* I, this idea nevertheless can still be found in the work of Husserl, who seems himself to subscribe to just such a thesis when he writes, in *Ideen* II, that it is only on account of the perceiver's own body, particularly its capacity for self-movement, that a world can be constituted for a subject: "The own body is the organ of the will, it is the one and only object which can be put into movement in a spontaneous and immediate way by the will of the ego. . . . Only bodies are capable of immediately spontaneous (free) movements. It is thanks to such free acts that an objective world can be constituted for this ego . . . a world of spatio-corporeal things" (*Ideen* II, §38, pp. 151–52). In other words, the ego is only constituting when it is capable of movement, which presupposes its embodiment.

With Patočka one finds, very clearly expressed, the claim that the intentional structure at work in perception, as a teleological structure, only really finds its complete fulfillment in movement and in action. In the perceptual act, in fact, the apprehension of the object remains presumptive and so always incomplete; even if it never ceases to be validated, it always remains open to a possible invalidation. On the other hand, it is not until, in action, this teleological structure attains its goal that the coincidence between the aim, or the anticipation, and its fulfillment is experienced. The success or the failure of the act brings the presumptive aim to a close.

> Perception, no less than the other dimensions of objectification, never reaches its goal, is always dispersed in new references; for it, being is never grasped in a definitive and exhaustive fashion, in its in-itself, but remains in its perspectives. On the other hand, movement poses being directly. . . . Movement presupposes that there is a direct coincidence between the subjective and the objective, which latter is only possible by way of a body which responds to our subjective "I can" and "I do." . . . A leap into being is accomplished in such a movement. . . . It is an act in the full sense. It is not a perspective on something objective: it itself creates the objective as such, in person. (Patočka 1995: 17; our translation)

> In contrast to perception or objectification, which turns around being without ever entirely reaching it, movement coincides perfectly with what is experienced. It is a realization and, in this respect, real. If the subjective and the objective coincide here, it is not because it is a matter of an experience as an experience (one could say the same of anything subjective), but inasmuch as the act does not stay in the realm of the subjective, inasmuch as it has precisely a route, a consequence, and a sediment in the external world. (Ibid., p. 19)

It is basically for this reason that the paradigmatic experience of intentionality, as a relation to the world and to objectivity, seems to us better represented by movement than by perception. In fact, it is only in movement that experience and reality fully coincide, that the subjective and objective phenomena, which are perceived quite differently but as referring to the same reality, fall together. This is the reason why, by virtue of its incarnation in the subject's own body, movement can be considered as the paradigmatic experience for intentionality.

Translated by Christopher Macann

CHAPTER SEVEN

Constitution by Movement: Husserl in Light of Recent Neurobiological Findings

JEAN-LUC PETIT

For Husserl, the movement of an organism, as oriented by its tendencies toward some vital aim from whose attainment it draws satisfaction, is an operative factor in the process of the subjective constitution of the world. First of all, effort and practice are required for the articulation and mastery of the integrated system of kinesthetic and hyletic circuits that make up the organism itself. Then, the constitution of the meaning of the being of the physical things situated in the physical space surrounding this organism calls for the regulated play of motivating kinesthesia and expository sensations. Finally, the constitution of an intersubjective world of communal life can only be understood in relation to the organism's capacity to empathize with the activities of other organisms, whether human or not.

The primacy of movement in constitution is confirmed when we turn from the transcendental viewpoint of phenomenology to the naturalistic viewpoint of the neurosciences. As expected, the primacy of movement in constitution was first confirmed by biomechanical studies (developed in the Soviet Union and the United States in the 1970s and 1980s) on the postural body schema and the experimental disassociation of the perceived and "real" positions of the body or limbs under artificially induced kinesthetic illusions. But it has received a new and more unexpected confirmation from findings in the study of the bioelectrical activity of cortical neurons, which without recourse to elementary reductionism, has actually succeeded in bringing to light the neural basis of the practical understanding of the meaning of our own movements and the movements of others.

1. THE THEORY OF CONSTITUTION

The world, Husserl insists, was not made all by itself without any active, driving participation on the part of the organism for which it exists. Such an apparently trite remark turns out to be a real challenge for the philosopher insofar as Husserl seeks to make him see how everything is brought into being in and through the absolutely constitutive movements of the organism, presupposing nothing in advance of itself except inherited instincts. Rather than an obvious mistake, this turns out to be a truth confirmed in the experience every living being has of itself. What is critical to phenomenology is that, from the standpoint of the organism, things are endowed with meaning and value only through the comportment adopted toward them and in accordance with how such things appear to the subject.

As to "being," we should make it clear that from now on we shall only be concerned with its *meaning* as sustained by acts that radiate out from some subjective center, namely, that of the organism itself. There is no point in inquiring into the constitution of any other type of being, except perhaps to show that in fact what one has in mind when one thinks about the meaning of "objective" or "absolute" being is derived from what one has in mind when one thinks about the meaning of subjective being. For all that, the program of constitution is not limited to instrumental things located in the world around us—a quite trivial model for the meaning of being. By right, it extends from the organism's sense of its own being—so much so that the "I" is not exempt from the necessity of having to constitute itself—to the meaning of the being of a common world, as well as to that correlational sense of being which arises out of their interactions and which is bestowed by the latter upon the organism itself as well as upon things and the world.

1.1. SOLIPSISTIC CONSTITUTION: MOVEMENT AND KINESTHESIS

In manuscripts dating from the 1930s, Husserl addresses the problem of the incarnation of the Cartesian subject. Investigating the rootedness of the acts of the subject in underlying strata of motivation, he took up again the traditional concept of instinct and interpreted it in terms of his intentional psychology. The development of a new theory of pulsional intentionality made possible a transition from, on the one hand, the dynamism of instinctive impulses and the fundamental inertia of the organism as immediately affected by itself—which has nothing to do with the subject or the pure act—to, on the other, the spontaneous activity of the I, which makes itself known well before conscious representation and voluntary action.

Pushing intentionality back toward the source of action and, in so doing, overcoming the obstacle represented by his own Cartesianism, which as he was well aware, "created a breach between affection and action," he worked out a concept of affection as "provisional action," as an "invitation, a call to the I to act." He had no hesitation in bringing the vocabulary of affection and action together in such a way that "in consequence, no distinction could be drawn between desiring and willing and, furthermore, no distinction could be conceived between willing in general and acting."[1]

But the elimination of this essential phenomenological distinction only means that what prevails before action in the more primordial strata of the organism's constitution, what precedes the active intervention of the I, is movement, an ability to move itself experienced internally by that very organism which is motivated by desire. Before becoming, in the full sense of that word, an acting subject, the subject of its acts, the organism, is already "on the move," because only as already on the move is it capable of finding out about itself, discovering its own capacities and mastering them, and indeed of becoming for itself the pole of its own acts, if not a subject."[2]

However, we should not draw premature conclusions from the fact that in this context he fell back upon the term "kinesthesia." To the best of my knowledge, Husserl did not take part in the famous—and probably mistaken—"Williams Debate" (Wilhelm Wundt vs. William James) on the question whether all that we know about our movements is based, a posteriori, upon afferent and therefore peripheral information—as James's kinesthesia theory would have it—or whether, on the contrary, it is based a priori on a central corollary efference of the motor command, as indicated by Wundt's *Innervationsgefühl*. As a phenomenologist, Husserl sticks to the experience of the organism, a subjectively lived experience that keeps the organism constantly informed of the position and movement of its body and limbs. Whatever the origin (central or peripheral) of this information, our movements are no less related to the I, when they are our acts (whether instinctive or voluntary), and to the not-I, when they are passively undergone. As to the neurophysiological controversy, recent data would lead us to believe that the attack launched by James might not have been brought to as definitive a conclusion as some psychologists have claimed (Gandevia and Rothwell 1987: 1117–30). What can reasonably be said of Husserl's use of the term "kinesthesis" is that this use of the term is essential to his theory of constitution, even if it preserves a phenomenological neutrality with regard to the dispute over the source of the internal knowledge of our own movements.[3]

In the course of this so-called genetic line of research, references to child psychology are to be found, references that emphasize the continuity and gradualness of intentionality ranging from instinct, "a mode of empty effort lacking any representation of the goal" (C 16, 4: 11), right up to a willing whose intentions are oriented by just such a representation. In this way, the hierarchy of the intentional strata leading up to willed action is brought to light. At the lowest level, we find the simple alternative of an empty intentional desire, together with its satisfaction in pleasure. Then, this alternation forms a chain of intentions and fulfillments that can in their turn be posited as the goal of an intentionality that is less bound by immediacy. From there on, gratification can be ever more deferred until desire is transformed into a "preoccupation" that extends to a subject's entire life, and even beyond, as the indefinite openness of a project that appears to be foreshadowed by instinctive impulses.

Such an intentional regression toward the origin finds its inaccessible limit in "hereditary factors" characterized by Husserl as an "empty horizon"[4] symmetrical with that other empty horizon which characterizes the totality of all the means of action available to humanity. These two horizons delimit our life world as a practical field. Their "emptiness" does not imply any lack of determination but the sedimented foundation of phylogenetic experience,[5] from which nothing stands out at first, even though this horizon is still needed as the indispensable background for our acts. For even if the structural constraints of the species are to be located in it, some activity on the part of the organism is required to expose these constraints.

Husserl even goes so far as to outline a phenomenology of fetal experience, claiming that the "child in its mother's womb already has kinestheses and through this kinesthetic mobility, its things." So that, at birth, the child "is already an I with a high level of experience (since) such an experience has already been acquired in its intrauterine existence" (*Zur Phänomenologie der Intersubjektivität* [hereafter cited as *ZPI*], part 3, p. 605). He also gives us some indication of the importance of a neonatal phenomenology of movement and kinesthesis for the constitutional process. A "genetic" sequence leads the organism from primitive activities motivated solely by the instinct of self-preservation to activities by means of which the organism works toward its own being-constitution. The intentional analysis of the sucking reflex in babies brings to light an instinctive impulse, that of drinking, which is aroused by a specific stimulus, the smell of the mother's breast, and whose strictly prescribed satisfaction is dictated by the sensation of lip contact. Here, Husserl says, there is no room for maneuver, the kinesthesis which is brought into action being "originally adapted." Nevertheless, continuing with his intentional analysis, he takes note of an important new stage in the process of constitution. Starting out as a simple instinctual vector, the movement in question becomes an object of enjoyment for its own sake. Rather than go into raptures over the apparently gratuitous playfulness of the baby's contented activity, Husserl sees in it an attempt to actively integrate the kinesthetic systems of different organs of motion with a view to bringing them under control. It is as if the child does not so much agitate its limbs by chance but in order to explore the extent of its freedom of articulation or to bring different forms of movement under its control through repetition:[6] "We may therefore conclude that that instinct which is exercised in kinesthetic activity leads, in the end, to the possibility of being able to reproduce any posture as the unity of an always available structure" (C 16, 4: 15).

Thus, from its ontogenetic origins, and in the most obvious way, movement is what makes the organism self-constituting. Relying on the limited fulfillment of instinctual functions, an ever more agile and precise rhythmic movement is set up, a choreography of the living organism in the very process of discovering its own body, a body which it has before it takes possession of it, and whose typical possibilities of moving about have to be acquired through experience. For there is a world of difference between the carrying out of a movement by one who is not aware of being constrained and the carrying out of the "same movement" by one who lets its actions be constrained by a just and well-founded sense of its insurmountable restrictions.

1.2. STATIC AND DYNAMIC CONSTITUTION: PERCEPTION AND ACTION

The term "aesthetic" is normally used to refer to sensory impressions impacting upon the organism from the environment. The term "practical" is used to refer to spontaneous activity. To be sure, no organism can be exclusively receptive or passive or exclusively active. However, philosophical tradition has separated aesthetics, or the theory of perception, from the practical, or the theory of action, even while common sense allows for a continuity between feeling and acting and considers the perceived world and the world of action one and the same. Husserl made an attempt to remedy this state of affairs by reintroducing "praxis" and "kinesis" into "aesthesis." For even if in the realm of the absolute the world is in no way dependent upon us, the same does not hold for "the world of our experience." The theory of the constitution of the spatial thing will give us an insight into our active contribution toward the making of this world.

The problem was to transform the analysis of the conditions of the possibility of external experience, our Kantian heritage, into an analysis of the practical conditions under which an object and a world are effectively constituted for an organism, which latter also constitutes itself correlatively. But the organism is not an aggregate of faculties: sensation *plus* intellectual syntheses, but an entity sensorially affected by what is not itself and whose acts include, no doubt, intellectual syntheses but also acts of attention, decision, and effective intervention in its surroundings.

Freeing the structure of our experience from the classical representation of the world that obscured matters for Kant, Husserl reevaluated that primary strata of subjective life which is determinative for the shaping of this experience as one in which sensoriality and activity coexist and are interwoven. His analysis of a priori structures begins with an almost geometrical description of concrete spatiotemporality. This "eidetics of experience" can be found in the *Lectures on Inner Time Consciousness* of 1905 (constitution of the temporal object—a sound, a melody) and in the *Lectures on the Thing and Space* (*Ding und Raum*, 1907) (constitution of the spatial thing).

The Kantian tradition provided the human subject with a faculty of sensation structured in accordance with the infinite, one-dimensional series of time intervals that clocks measure and the infinite, tridimensional, homogeneous, isotropic space of surveyors and astronomers—both being required for localizing every possible object and measuring the intervals between them, their trajectories, and so on. Believing that in this way he had laid bare the formal structure of any experience, Kant claimed "that the absence of space can never be represented."[7]

Husserl took up this implied challenge. Embarking upon a program of constitution of the spatial thing, he admitted that this spatiality is a product of the process of constitution, therefore, that empirical space is not originary but secondary with regard to a pre-empirical, quasi space. The assertion that this quasi space is constituted by the movements of the organism seems absurd if one presupposes the priority of ordinary space but not if, like Husserl, one is only concerned with movements experienced from within, in the act itself, thanks to the kinestheses of the organs responsible.

Phenomenological analysis brings to light a primary stratum of experience that precedes objective time and space, that is, which does not entail this time or this space. On the other hand, it does entail some more primitive "field" of experience that is encompassed by the acts of an "I," from which action emanates and which is affected in turn by its contact with this field. The formal properties of this field differ significantly from those of classical time and space. Never empty because it is always centered on some object constituted therein, this space can not pretend to be all-inclusive. What is given to us in it is, first of all, mere appearances (*Erscheinungen*): transient or recurring, they tend to be recognized, at most, as being of "the same thing," a thing which does not as yet exist outside the series of its appearances. The same appearances are finally subject to synthesis, that is, to an active grasping on the part of the I which itself only becomes apparent through its active relationship to this object.

Let us take some examples: a sound seems identical to me although in fact it changes constantly from the moment I first hear it to the moment when it fades away entirely; I see only the red sides of a cube which I anticipate as being red all over while still allowing for the possibility that the sides I do not see are blue—a qualification that in no way obliges me to revise my estimation of the cube as the "same" cube.

These appearances or ways things are given are not distributed in an isotropic space but include some privileged modes (the optima of each domain in question) and some defective modes (the corresponding extrema). For the optical field, the optimum is the focal center, the point at which the internal determinations of the thing are most apparent. The extremum is the edge of the field, where the details fade away, lose all sharpness and distinction. Alternatively, the optimum is the ideal visual proximity, the extremum, the horizon of perspectival distancing. For the temporal field, the optimum is the "living present," the threshold of the ongoing activity of the I, with two extrema representing the limits of my retention of the "just having been" and of my protentional orientation toward the "about to be."

But this list of properties of the perceptual field is a static one. It does not give us the thing we have to deal with practically in experience but a "linear manifold [*Mannigfaltigkeit*] extracted from a pluri-dimensional multiplicity."[8] It is up to my mathematical colleagues to determine the legitimacy of Husserl's barely concealed borrowing of Riemann's term from his *Mannigfaltigkeitslehre*. If space is Euclidean, the pre-spatial field might be Riemannian. And there might be some mathematical operation, fundamental to the constitutional process, which would account for the conversion of the field into a space. Intuitively, the manifold that interests us here, a pre-empirical foreshadowing of the thing, is that of the virtual object synthesizing the information given to us by the infinity of the appearances of a given object seen from all possible points of view. One is reminded of the representations of analytic cubism, exactly contemporary with *Ding und Raum*: a bottle on a table, a guitar, a portrait of Ambroise Vollard, and so on. This kind of "objectivity" is nothing but the objective correlate of all the possible ways of gaining access to the object subjectively, ways that are prescribed in advance in the very structure of the perceptual field—rather like a geometrical schema embodying the more general axioms characterizing the properties of perceived objects.

Let us try applying our reductive method by effecting a provisional reduction, through abstraction, of our visual experience to the "oculo-motor field" by placing in suspense any information that might be made available to us through the movements of our head or of the rest of our body and considering simply what the movements of our eyes enable us to see. The perceptual multiplicity that would be given to us in this way possesses surprising properties. It would be given as being neither three-dimensional nor impenetrable. Appearances pass through each other without obstruction as ghosts pass through walls. They enter the perceptual field at one edge, leave by another, without it even being possible for us to keep them within the bounds of the field. There would no doubt be curved surfaces, but no object would possess a closed surface, since the side on which it rested could not be seen.

So before we have to do with things in space possessing the full status of physical realities, we are confronted with appearances in the perceptual field, with phantoms. Static phenomenology is limited to determining the properties of fields that are unknown to classical space, with a view to bringing to light the strata subtending the perceptual experience before the manifold gets brought together in the perceived object. "Genetic" phenomenology goes from this analytic cubism to a synthetic cubism. It follows up the process by which, on the basis of the regularly stratified a priori constraints inherent in multiple fields of appearance, the spatial thing, in the normal sense of that word, gets constituted. This dynamic integration requires the activity of an I that has to intervene in perception not only as the unique pole from which all points of view on a thing radiate out but as an organism capable of bringing about the necessary coordination between this multiplicity of perceptual appearances and another equally powerful multiplicity (*von gleicher Mächtigkeit*)[9] which is also dependent upon the I in order to be put in action, and which consists in the system of kinestheses based on the motor or sensori-motor organs of the I, a system that has to be integrated in parallel with the former.

At first Husserl conceived of this perceiving activity of the I as essentially determined by the epistemological ideal of the perfect givenness of the thing under all its aspects, a givenness that fulfills the truth intention of empirical judgment. But he never held the view that perceptual intentions can get to their object without being brought to them by some movement on the part of the perceiving organism.[10] If "I want to know more about" appearing things, I bring into play my kinestheses, and the aspects concealed in the original, initial presentation forthwith make their appearance. Which presupposes that the objective aspects of things and the kinestheses accomplished by my organs of sense are so tightly interlaced that we can speak, interchangeably, of the self-givenness (*Selbstgegebenheit*) of things or of their "creation" (*Schöpfung*) through the movements accomplished by the organism—even (and Husserl is ready to abuse language in this way) of the "creation of nature by consciousness" (*DR*, §49, p. 175). Seeking to establish his theory of constitution on this basis, Husserl advanced the rather bold thesis that the normal match between external sensations and kinesthetic sensations was a one-to-one correlation between two continuous multiplicities. "If the stream of kinaestheses K is an alteration stream $K_0 \cap K_1$, then each difference in the process of alteration motivates a corresponding difference in the alteration of the 'intention to'" (§54, p. 188).

With the result that, taking account of the complex system integrating the kinesthetic circuits of all the organs of the organism (not just the eyes but also the neck and the rest of the body), one is led to the conclusion that every kinesthetic alteration of a given organ motivates an alteration in the sensorial field associated with it. A closed kinesthetic series, starting out from kinesthetic immobility and coming back to immobility across the intermediary degrees of tension, therefore yields a perceptual multiplicity which is nothing other than the "thing itself" constituted in the corresponding layers of the complete kinesthetic system. But with regard to the constituting process that mobilizes this complete system, this thing is not the thing in the ordinarily "objective" sense of that word. It is for example nothing but a simple "ocular-motor thing," something we are obliged to relativize as a transitional phase in the appearing of a thing endowed with a much richer, multidimensional meaning just as soon as we take into account the kinesthesia furnished by the movements of the neck and the rest of the body, the impact of the global posture of the organism on the perceived world. A something that only retains this meaning on the basis of the well-organized complexity of all the movements that an organism is capable of deploying once its interest is aroused by it and it gets involved with it in a practical way.[11]

Perhaps there is room here for a distinction between "kinesthetic constitution" and "practical constitution." The first would stand in much the same relation to the second as ocular-motor constitution does to constitution by the totality of kinesthetic data, a simple sedimented layer in the constitution of the objective thing. In which case, in addition to the kinesthetic motivation of fields of images whose intentionality is guided simply by the desire to know more about the object, the constitutive process would require that the thing be really invested with signification, that it be the goal of practical activity which bestows meaning upon what it utilizes, produces, or transforms while withdrawing such meaning from things it rejects or destroys. It is perhaps the bringing of action (in the strong sense) into the very heart of the theory of constitution that distinguishes the analyses of human praxis in the life-world, taken from the manuscripts of the 1930s, from the formal and almost mathematical analyses of perceptual multiplicities to be found in *Ding und Raum*, which is itself written very much in the spirit of the *Logische Untersuchungen*.[12]

It is practical activity alone that is capable of introducing new layers of meaning, layers of meaning that are not attributable solely to the vital drives of the isolated organism and which also allow for social meaning—inconceivable as long as the role of intersubjectivity in the process of constitution has not first been determined. For the world contains more than the "world of things" opened up by perception, and access to this something more is afforded by action. "Without my practical intervention, the world would be a world of things. It pertains to the full reality of our world that it is for us a practical world" (D 12, 2: 32).

If we bear in mind that, from my point of view, all my movements unfold in a continual adjustment such that in learning that "the same thing" seen this way from this angle, is seen that way from that, I at the same time learn that its identity manifests itself in the fact that it "stands out against" this entire series of modifications. I derive therefrom the feeling of a continuous and harmonious transition from one modification to another, accompanied henceforward by kinesthetic sensations, sensations that I am even able to anticipate by way of a movement that is itself continuous and harmonious. Hence, by deploying in advance the possible appearances of the thing, I am able to project it from points of view that have yet to be assumed, points of view that open up on latent possibilities—and this merely by giving free play to my activity. This intimate adjustment of movements, inaugurated by the I and the objective movements of the thing, confers upon the latter a certain ontological consistency in the face of the I—a consistency for which the I is nevertheless responsible, though not in an arbitrary or capricious way.

Henceforward, one might say, the thing possesses "in itself" the norm regulating its movements, its possible appearances and disappearances. The vectors of its displacements and transformations are attached to it. The axes of its rotations and reversals are inscribed in it, not ascribed to the I. It has acquired objectivity to the extent that I grant to it, without qualification, an "absolute" meaning of being, a meaning which must not be confused, of course, with the independence and the personal autonomy of those very special things which are the bodies of other I's.

1.3. INTERSUBJECTIVE CONSTITUTION: EMPATHY WITH THE ACTIONS OF OTHERS

From the start, the generalization of the theory of constitution to the other is confronted with the difficulty of distinguishing the appearances that found the "introjection" of lived experience into bodies other than my own from all other appearances and modes of givenness. Such a distinction was not to be found in the positivist analysis of sensations that, in many respects, anticipate that of phenomenology. Ernst Mach (1886) and Richard Avenarius (1912) could only see such an introjection as a intrusion of the "metaphysical dualism" into our "natural concept of the world," because they held to Hume's atomistic conception of experience with its bias in favor of the priority of the simple (assumed to be homogeneous) vis-à-vis the complex (and the heterogeneous). Free from this prejudice,[13] as well as from the opposite prejudice voiced by Heidegger, Husserl had no objection to the notion of *Einfühlung* introduced into psychological aesthetics in 1903 by Theodor Lipps (1903a: 185–204), who was the first to describe the phenomenon of active participation through our kinesthesia in the movements and actions of others, and this in the very act of perceiving the latter (cf. his famous example of the spectator at the circus and of the trapeze artist on his wire in Lipps 1903b: 185–204). On the contrary, he was able to make use of this idea to provide a legitimate phenomenological content for the empty notion of introjection offered by Avenarius.

Why does intersubjectivity, or introjection, appear so early in Husserl's writings and even in a "formalist" context—that of *Ding und Raum*—where, as he says himself: "This already escapes from our line of thinking"?[14]

Because if he had not taken steps to accommodate it at a sufficiently early phase in his development, the specifically phenomenological experience would never have been other than his alone, given that there is only one way to understand subjective activity—whether understood as movement or action—even if I experience it as an effective intervention in the surrounding world. This way goes by way of my body whose perceptual and practical kinesthesia have to be mobilized again and again, drawn out of rest into activity, if I want to know what it is to "fasten upon," "follow," "apprehend," "push," "thrust," "resist," "get up," "walk," and so on.

Up to this point, it is perfectly in order that the interpretation of action should be *solipsistic*. Moreover, it runs the risk of remaining so unless and until, situated and stabilized within this primordial layer, a body other than my own arises in the world of objects, a body the experience of which forces its way through this solipsistic enclosure. At first sight such an eventuality seems improbable. For every "external" body owes its meaning of being to the fact that it is presented in a specific "mode of givenness" as an experience lived out passively in a sensational affection or lived out actively on the basis of kinesthetic sensations whose measure of intensity is my own willing, and that these lived experiences are necessarily my lived experiences unfolding in the temporality of my subjective life. However, I also have to take into consideration the narrowness of my basis of observation up to this point, if only with reference to the sphere of my full primordial experience, which is not limited to the strictly defined continuity of that presence of myself to myself which reaches out from my intentions to my kinesthesia and from my kinesthesia to the sensational material that results from my being affected by objects.

A real discontinuity prevails between myself and the other self. I can no more have the experiences of the other than he can have mine. Nevertheless, when I am in the presence of an other, I do not normally take him to be an object, a simple external body. For that body over there "reminds" me of my own. I put myself "in his place." "Empathy" (*Einfühlung*) enables me to experience directly in the other whatever I might have been able to experience in the way of affections and kinesthetic data, as if it were I who governed in his body. My primordial experience, however reduced it might be, is not just that of a consciousness isolated in a world peopled by inanimate objects. We do actually have an experience of the other. To be sure, although I am denied all access to the perceptual intuiting of the other, I am nevertheless in a position to *appresent* in some kind of ideal intentionality the lived experiences of the other through empathic *presentification*. My experience contains the bodies of others in such a way that the experience of each is opened up onto a world of experience alien to itself and which is based upon this body as being that of another.

From this moment on, the perceptual and practical world is peopled by a multiplicity of actors in constant interaction, an interaction mediated by the bodies that each claims as its own. When "I push," I feel another who "resists me." My action is not simply confronted with an inert and lifeless obstacle against which I exhaust my strength in vain. Rather, "I struggle," I feel him "giving way," I "carry the day" or alternatively, "he recovers"; "I am beaten" by the action of an other with whom I can also elect to join forces with a view to attaining a common goal, the goal of an action which is itself common—sometimes even in its very intentions.[15]

For all that, I am ready to admit that empathy does not yield everything. It does give us the possibility of replaying the kinesthetic circuits furnished by the organs of perception and of movement mobilized by others with regard to their acts (as are ours with regard to our own) and so of recognizing in the general flux of experience those intersubjective unities which are "actions." In this way, and to the extent that the external world, however external it is in its spatiotemporal exteriority, is also (and even especially) composed of human actions (or at least of objects constituted in human action), we obtain a world which is, in a certain sense, *practical*.[16]

But we cannot yet be said to live in such a "practical world." This world in which we posit actions and which we people with our productions remains as external to us as the world of the objects of perception. The intersubjectivity that results looks more like a multiplicity of interconnected points of view, where each remains an observer of what he does (or of what others do) rather than an actor. We still have to render intelligible the synthesis of these points of view in a communitarian "we" that can be set up as the subject of its own world of praxis—but without either detaching itself from or overseeing the latter—because it is integrally constituted in, and indeed at the very same time as, this latter world.

The critical question is that of determining whether just such a phenomenology of praxis is capable of crossing the divide that separates a plurality of subjects (each of which has access to the lived world of the other by way of reciprocal empathy) from a community in the strong sense of that word, one that cannot be reduced to the individuals it contains. As a perceptual subject, it is possible for me to empathize with the interior life of the other. I am free to carry through (or not) the act by means of which the alien I is presentified, as it overlaps my perception of a certain body that reminds me of my own. But nothing links me empathically in a more special way with "my" other. On the other hand, a community is a humanity linked together by a concordant course of life.

But surely, whatever holds for perceptual praxis should also hold for social praxis. In perception, I anticipate an object as "the same," and I link its various aspects under the rule of this presumptive identity—at least until an unassimilable disagreement forces me to try out a new identity. In my social conduct, I have faith in the presumed agreement of the course of existence—at least until an anomaly disrupts this unity. The communalization (*Vergemeinschaftung*) of intersubjectivity therefore depends exclusively on the continuity of the life led in connection with others with mutual preoccupations and interests, such that the "we" which we form together finishes up by being written into the practical world as an object that endures even while continuing to experience itself as the subject who is familiar with this practical world, who acts in it, who has in it his familiar ways of being and who continually enriches his world with novel productions (*ZPI* III, 23, p. 394). But we must be careful not to construct a supra-individual subject equipped with faculties of perception and action in the image of the individual subject.

A "we" is formed when, together with others as co-subjects in a community of understanding based on regular interaction, I establish certain connections with persons based on *social acts*, acts that are defined by virtue of the fact that their realization, as acts, consists uniquely in the establishment of the very links which they constitute as social acts. Here, the praxis in question has nothing to do with natural objects and takes as its object the perpetuation of its own existence. Henceforth, action is no longer confined to the body of each individual actor but is deployed as "our action" bound by social connections in a new environment, the domain of what exists for us in a practical way. This domain must not be confused with the external world as the locus of the goals of actors. For, from now on, these actors, linked together by a social act, constitute themselves as their own goal and therefore no longer have their field of activity outside of themselves but participate in this field both as the source and as the goal of a common action; or if you prefer, figure both as subjects and as objects (*ZPI* III, 14, pp. 208–9).

The interiorization of praxis into a world constituted by the actors themselves marks a new phase in the intersubjective understanding. While empathy could at most penetrate the subjective life of the other, so to say, against his will, I am obliged to awaken in the other a specific intention to communicate in order to have access to his communicable contents. An infinite reflexivity of intentionalities begins to get tied together, transforming subjects opposed to one another (as I and not-I) into an "I" who addresses a "Thou" who is for himself an "I" having the first "I" as his "Thou." Hence the "constitution of a 'we,' acting as a personality of a higher order, as the unity of a, so to speak, *multi-headed subject of action*" (*ZPI* III, 29, p. 478).

Action becomes communicational, a kind of "multilayered" (*mehrschichtige*) action which lies at the root of any sociability. I want to get the other to do or to think certain things. But I cannot give him orders in the absence of an already existing convention of obedience, a convention whose existence cannot simply be assumed as already binding upon myself and the one I address. In such a situation, communication occurs just as soon as the other understands what I want and this understanding proves capable of being a sufficient motive for doing what I want him to do. If in addition, the communicating subjects are also speaking ones (communication does not have to be verbal—in this regard Husserl appeals to Wolfgang Köhler's apes; see *ZPI* III, 29, p. 478), *discourse* results, a discourse the other understands as such, as addressed to him and as expressive of my intention relative to our mutual behavior (p. 474). This community of discourse and its reception functions as a new mode of overlapping between myself and the other. Action has definitely been socialized, since "the acts of one I are reciprocated in the acts of the other I" (p. 477). On this basis, the habits of the one confirm those of the others "from within," creating an enduring suprapersonality, which in turn becomes the source of further acts, concordant or not. Since, in addition, social acts are objective, that is to say, since social acts are "as real events experienced by each perceiving subject in a preconstituted *intersubjective field of experience*, events in which several human subjects participate" (p. 478), all the essential conditions are met for the constitution of *social groups* (a household, a friendship, an association) in a life-world, a common culture (p. 479).

2. PHYSIOLOGICAL FINDINGS

2.1. KINESTHETIC ILLUSIONS AND THE CORPOREAL SCHEMA

Taking advantage of the circumstance—scarcely philosophical—that certain states are sufficiently powerful to be able to devote a part of the resources they squander in rivalry on medically supported athletic competition or the conquest of space, one scientific discipline, the biomechanical physiology of movement has developed an original experimental program aimed at bringing to light, under laboratory conditions, the phenomenon of kinesthetic perception of bodily posture and this by dissociating it from the real anatomical position of the organism through the creation of kinesthetic illusions. What relevance does this have for the philosophical themes discussed here?

A moment's thought enables us to conclude that kinesthetic posture is founded on *Leib*, anatomical position on *Körper*. At first sight it would seem that this school of physiology has done nothing other—whether deliberately or not—than what phenomenology does (even though by appealing simply to an analysis of the meaning of experience), namely, struggle against the widespread confusion between *Leib* and *Körper*, between the living organic body and the physical body-thing. In which case we would have hit upon an exceptional instance where instrumental intervention in the external and physical conditions of action (by employing physio-therapeutic vibrators, tables of force, virtual reality helmets, parabolic flights, recumbent rotating devices, and so on) would confirm the sense in which the organism exists as a unity and a totality; an instance where the artificial production of illusions would have helped us understand the normal mode of access of the subject to his body.

The first half of my thesis therefore indicates that the biomechanical physiology stemming from the years 1970–80 can, as a technology of perceptual movement, be understood as *applied phenomenology*. Let those who are not aware of the relativity of the terms "pure" and "applied" in science suspect me of nourishing goodness knows what imperial ambitions on the part of phenomenology with respect to science. I am not talking here of an unconscious phenomenology, a naive or even primitive phenomenology; for the Russian doctors in question are cultivated gentlemen and their not-infrequent references to Maurice Merleau-Ponty—our French "last Husserl"—alongside the great classics of humanistic physiology (Lord Adrian, Nicholas Bernstein, Duchêne de Boulogne, and so on) prove that they were not entirely naive about the philosophical significance of their research.

If Husserl had done nothing more than underline the constitutive role of kinesthesia for the "body scheme" and the relation of the organism's constitution to its environment, his theory would already have the value of an intuitive premonition. In fact, after a lapse reaching from the beginning of the century to the 1970s, physiologists have been brought to revise their attitude (Goodwin, McCloskey, and Matthews 1972: 705–9, 738–45). Against the traditional division of the "five senses" they are now committed to a rehabilitation of kinesthetic sensations, reviving the idea of a sixth, "muscular" sense so dear to Sir Charles Sherrington (1900). The sense of movement and the sense of position have been recognized as irreducible sensorial modalities, notwithstanding the identity of their peripheral receptors. Muscles have been raised to the rank of full-fledged sense organs, the seat of both kinesthetic reception and the emission of sensorimotor messages directed toward the brain by way of the afferent (not the efferent, motor) nervous system. Kinesthetic and tactile sensations have been pronounced just as essential to the sense of the body as to its orientation in the surrounding world, thereby unifying personal and extrapersonal space (Roll 1993: 75–90).

A classic experimental formula developed from the work of G. M. Goodwin, D. I. McCloskey, and P. B. C. Matthews, of the Physiological Laboratory at Oxford (1972) requires that one apply a mechanical vibration of low intensity just above the elbow while pressing the head of a physiotherapeutical vibrator against the skin covering the tendon of the biceps (alternatively, the triceps).[17] The vibrated arm is immobilized and the subject's eyes are covered with a blindfold. He is asked to use his free limb to "accompany" the other if he feels it moving under the effect of the vibration. We know that the application of such a vibration to the biceps produces a reflex contraction of the upper arm. This contraction is usually "isotonic," that is, takes place without any increase in tonicity but with a shortening of the muscle—whence the movement of the upper arm. The immobilization of the arm renders it "isometric," the resistance opposed to the movement constraining the muscle to contract without shortening, even while increasing its tonicity (Goodwin, McCloskey, and Matthews 1972: 720).

Under these conditions, the subject experiences not a contraction but an *extension* of his upper arm and, according to the instructions, he extends the other (by several tens of degrees) with reference to the immobile arm subject to vibration, while continuing to believe that he is keeping them parallel. With regard to the position and the movement of his arm, he is the victim of an illusion, an illusion which would be reversed if the vibration were applied to the triceps rather than the biceps. The proof: his surprise when one removes the blindfold from his eyes.

A highly systematic reading, carried out later by James Lackner of Brandeis University, using the same method of illusion (to cite only this for want of space), has brought to light an illusion of falling forward caused by the vibration of the Achilles tendon, an illusion of falling backward caused by the vibration of quadriceps, an illusion of longitudinal rotation of the body caused by the vibration of the buttock muscles, in addition to a host of illusions of bending, extending, or rotating the head caused by the vibration of the neck muscles (Lackner and Levine 1979).

But the most elegant experiments are still those conducted by Victor Gurfinkel, of the Moscow Academy of Science, who managed to derive every possible variety of illusion from the influence of the position of the head with regard to the body on the reflex extension of the knees under a vibration applied to the Achilles tendon (Gurfinkel and Levick 1991: 147–62). Not only does he succeed in showing that the rotation of the head inhibits the extension of the leg on the side to which the head turns (while it aggravates the extension of the other leg); he also shows that this asymmetry persists as an illusion of movement when one immobilizes the leg while applying vibration to the Achilles tendon, and when the head is immobilized but subjected to an illusion of rotation provoked by applying vibration to the neck. He even succeeds in demonstrating that the asymmetrical reaction of the legs is never so strong as when it is "caused" by the illusory perception of the movement of the head (rather than its "real" movement).

From a phenomenological point of view, the most interesting theoretical interpretation to be drawn from this mass of findings on kinesthetic illusions is Gurfinkel's own. He is much more emphatic than the other researchers on the need not to reduce postural organization to an agglomeration of isolated local reflexes, still less to the product of an association of kinesthetic signals. And if, on occasion, he is willing to make use of cognitivist language to talk about an "internal representation in the central nervous system including a list of the parts of the body," his use of this language is only a way of distancing himself from the associationism of behavioral reflexologists. He is as concerned as his American counterpart Lackner[18] with rejecting the "naive objectivism" (this expression is not his) of those who confuse the body scheme with schemas for the activation of those somatotopical sensorial charts plotted by single-neuron recordings. For in such schemas he sees only static structures incapable of reacting to the continual changes provoked by the stimuli that accompany the movement of the organism.

So his conception of the bodily schema as "a process rather than a structure" comes close to the Husserlian conception of the multidimensional multiplicity of kinesthetic motivation: "a supra-modal organisation containing information about the cinematic structure of the body, and about the dimensions of its links and their mass-inertial characteristics synthesizing the different types of afferent signals, and presenting the results of this synthesis in the form of spatial coordinates and trajectories of body parts" (Gurfinkel and Levick 1991: 152).

I hope my unwillingness to take part in a scientific squabble has not exposed phenomenology to charges of favoring this typically "holistic" physiology by supporting what some call its conservative resistance to the elementary determinism (neuronal in particular) of a more recent physiology. Be that as it may, if what we are looking for is a neurophysiological interpretation of the Husserlian theory of constitution, it is clear that we are already provided with at least a valid approach. Along with the *body scheme*, this research into kinesthetic illusions underpins the theory of constitution with a respectable empirical foundation.

2.2. NEURAL CORRELATES OF THE UNDERSTANDING OF ACTIONS

The challenge we face is that of trying to interpret the theory of constitution in terms of recent neurophysiology. With the aid of the computer, new techniques have been developed for taking encephalographic recordings through micro-electrodes implanted in an active and conscious animal, and these techniques have made it possible if not to "look" into the brain—pace Wittgenstein—at least to "listen" to the bioelectrical activity of single neurons while carrying out specific tasks. And to such an extent that this approach has even seemed to be doomed to inquire into "grandma's neuron," the selective destruction of which, neurophilosophers have predicted, would make it impossible for you to recognize your grandmother.

In fact, it seems that such an atomistic reductionism has not proved fatal. The totality and complexity of the organism has been rediscovered, less in the "parallel distribution" model suggested by the engineering of artificial neural networks than in the anatomical and functional hierarchy that obtains between the regions of the cerebral cortex, depending on whether they enclose "low level" neurons, which encode the movements of the organism in their full detail, or "high level" neurons, which encode actions independently of their concrete modes of realization.

More especially, I would like to draw the attention of phenomenologists to a recent discovery the philosophical importance of which is likely to be missed because of the poor state of interdisciplinary communication at this time. At the level of the individual neuron, biological support has been uncovered for the *understanding* of the *intentional signification* of the *actions* of *another agent*. One might have thought—indeed the first part of my paper might have led you to believe—that such a dimension could only feature as an emergent property, making its appearance solely on the plane of the whole person engaged in communitarian interaction (linguistic and cultural) with other persons.

What makes the corporeal rootedness of such an understanding even more profound is undoubtedly that its origin is neither representational nor "cognitive" but practical. To the extent that an organism is capable of understanding the intentional signification of its own actions, it acquires the possibility of immediately understanding the signification of the actions of others, that is, without the mediation of any perception of an initially non-interpreted bodily movement followed by a judgment that attributes meaning on the basis of a special interpretation. But despite being noninferential and pre-predicative, this understanding still has no less an access to the supposedly "grammatical" aspects of the encoding of the meaning of actions in categories expressing vital values.

From now on it will not be possible to hold that action is a "grammatical fiction," a composite product devoid of ontological reality, a simple linking of associative reflexes or automatic reactions to external stimuli. Rather, these reactions require integration into a whole that certainly contains the individual organism (in the first instance, a certain collection of neurons in its cerebral cortex) but is not limited either by it or by its social or intraspecific grouping. Its boundaries are to be fixed by a natural hermeneutics of the intentionality of actions, classified according to the type of meaning they convey in the context of a teleology of living beings in their environment. In the same way, just as not every objective movement is understood as action nor, one may assume, will the actions of species too far removed in the phylogenetic tree be so understood, and going still further in the direction of lifeless artifice, we already know that a "hand" seen in "virtual reality" is not perceived as accomplishing actions, at least in this sense, that it does not affect the cerebral metabolism as does the perception of a real hand.

Giacomo Rizzolatti and his team from the Institute of Human Physiology at the University of Parma discovered in 1992 in the pre-motor cortex of the macaque monkey (area F5, the equivalent of the Broca's area in human beings) a class of neurons which they themselves described as "surprising" (Rizzolatti et al. 1992: 176–80; Rizzolatti 1994: 220; Rizzolatti et al. 1995). The characteristic of these "mirror-neurons" is that they are activated, and display the same structure of activity, *both* when the animal accomplishes certain hand movements directed toward some goal *and* when he observes the experimenter in the process of accomplishing what one is obliged to call *the same actions*.

For several years this team has been conducting research into the functional complexity of the neurons of the pre-motor cortex by comparison with those of the primary motor cortex. The neurons in question are not activated when the animal carries out individual, concrete movements—implying privileged nerve pathways and a group of determinate muscles. They are activated only when it carries out an *action*, where the latter is defined as a series of articulated movements aimed at *one and the same goal* no matter what the limb, the muscles, or the detail of the movements brought into play, and no matter what the position of the limbs or of the body required for their activation. And to such an extent that it has been possible to classify these neurons according to the type of action associated with their realization: "grasp with the hand," "grasp with the hand and mouth," "reach," "catch with precision" or "with the whole hand," etc. All the neurons of the same type encode actions that meet the same objective. The authors have suggested that the totality of these neurons make up a vocabulary of all the actions necessary for the animal to "attain, grasp, reach, grasp and bring its food to its mouth."

The conditions under which these neurons are stimulated have turned out to be of a characteristic complexity. The process responsible for carrying through the movements is not directly selected by the stimulus, whether visual or motivational. Rather, it initiates a motor program that ends up eventually in action. With regard to visual stimuli and the neurons responsible for reaching and grasping, the response is not determined by any object presented in any way but is dependent upon the question whether this stimulus does or does not meet a certain expectation on the part of the animal. If it does, it still has to be of the kind "object within reach." It is as if these neurons reacted not to the stimulus as such, that is, to its form or its sensorial appearance, but to its *meaning* for the animal. But reacting to a meaning is precisely what one means by "understanding." Should we not therefore be talking of understanding rather than of simple stimulation?

What is particularly surprising about this discovery by the team from Parma is that one is even more tempted to talk of an "understanding of actions" once one appreciates that an action on the part of the experimenter (and which is observed by the animal) also possesses the power to activate the neurons that code an action of the same kind in the animal itself. Hence the title of the article published in 1992 in *Experimental Brain Research*: "Understanding Motor Events." In the course of a series of tests bearing upon these pre-motor neurons, which are brought into play by, or which modify their activity in the course of, a prehensile movement carried out by the monkey with its hand, it was noted that the experimenter's action in gathering food with his hand had the power of activating these neurons, even in the absence of any movements on the part of the monkey. A class of neurons that fires selectively whenever the monkey takes a sunflower seed or a raisin between the thumb and the index finger fires in just as active a fashion whenever the monkey watches the experimenter doing the same thing. A second class of neurons which displays an intense spontaneous activity and is powerfully inhibited during prehension is similarly affected, and in a quite precise fashion, when the monkey sees the experimenter taking the seed—and this at the very moment when he takes it.

In the course of a systematic study of neurons located in area F5 and affected by different types of manual actions accomplished under the gaze of the animal, it was possible to establish a classification of these neurons as a function of the type of similarity between the action observed and the action carried out by the monkey. First, there was a group which was only activated by strictly *identical* actions: "grasp with the mouth," "grasp with the hand," and so on. Another group allowed for observed actions which bore a *visual resemblance* to those of the monkey: "using the hand to place an object on the table" bears a visual resemblance to "grasping." Yet another group allowed for actions perceived as standing in a *logical relationship* with the actions carried out. "Placing an object on the table" is the necessary condition of "carrying it to the mouth." One last group of neurons answered to the actions of the experimenter, without their activity bearing any relation to the movements of the animal. None of the neurons belonging to any one of these groups can be correlated with simple movements of the hand or of the object, nor with any act of prehension employing instruments.

In a more recent experiment, another monkey was placed in the presence of the one which carried the implanted recording device, and a strictly synchronized firing of the neurons of area F5 was noted each time this other monkey grasped the food offered by the experimenter.

Going further and trying to establish the existence of mirror-neurons in humans, it has recently been discovered (1995) that observing the experimenter grasping an object induced in the subject an increase in the motor potential evoked by magnetic stimulation of the cortex in the muscles that bring into play the execution of the same movement. But in both cases, tomography by emission of positrons shows a "highly significant activation" in Broca's area (Rizzolatti et al. 1995: 13–14). From an anatomical point of view, the F5 area and Broca's area are alike in that they both seem to be responsible for associating a somatotopic representation of the hand—predominant in the monkey—and a somatotopic representation of the muscles of the mouth—predominant in humans.

But then, what are we to make of the functional role of these mirror-neurons in man, neurons whose schema of activation seems capable of representing the identity between the meaning of one's own actions and those of the other but not the emotional state or the predisposition of the subject to action? For Rizzolatti, the answer is to be sought in a recent anthropological theory according to which speech in primates is not derived from the cry (which is not directed toward a determinate fellow creature and depends upon instinctual behavior and the emotional state of the subject) but rather from gestural communication with visual contact, in particular, the smacking of the lips which precedes articulation.

Conclusion: the comprehension of the actions of others lies at the root of speech. We understand each other through language because we have already understood each others' actions. Without pressing too far this question of an "empirical confirmation" of phenomenology, we must at least be prepared to admit that the recent findings of neurophysiology amply justify Husserl's upholding, against Lipps and Max Scheler,[19] the assertion that our empathic experience of the other is an internal imitation of the movement accomplished by the other, and which implies an actualization of the *kinesthetic sensations*—including its neural correlates—corresponding to the movement in question and not its effective execution nor even any affective fusion with the other. In addition, Husserl was also amply justified in upholding against his "former self" the assertion that the world is not constituted by the solipsistic subject and that, as a life-world inclusive of nature and culture, its constitution is intersubjective and practical and not subjective and "cognitive" (representational).

CONCLUSION

In order to clarify my position on the controversial question of the naturalization of Husserlian phenomenology, I am going to make a few simple and obvious comparisons.

To start with, there are those who occupy the foreground in the cognitive sciences and in the neurosciences and who aspire to calling the tune for others to dance to: these are the "model builders." Without even mentioning their overhead projection films and their flowcharts, the value of any segment of which is rarely, if ever, called into question, they are recognizable by the intrepid casualness with which, once they are provided with a functional system, they become indifferent to whether this system applies to collections of neurons in the brain of a primate, human, or otherwise, or whether, on the contrary, it applies to the wiring of a robot or even to an artificial (virtual) network of neurons. To refer to a philosopher who is presently more in vogue than poor Husserl, I would say that they are situated in the perspective of *Tractatus* 4.014: "A gramophone record, the musical idea, the written notes, and the sound waves, all stand to one another in the same internal relation of depicting that holds between language and the world." Against which one has only to appeal to the author of the Investigations, who only admits "the existence of a system of impulses emitted by the brain in correlation with spoken or written thoughts" to the extent that he takes it to be "impossible to read processes of thought into cerebral processes," because he sees "no reason why the system should continue in the direction of the center" ("Why might this order not, so to speak, arise out of chaos?"; Wittgenstein 1980, §903). And one goes on repeating, with a specious air of exhaustiveness, that the central opposition of our time is between two camps and two camps only: the Gestaltists (who nowadays prefer to call themselves "functionalists"), who recommend, if not an isomorphism, at least some kind of program to implement correspondence between all levels, and the Thomists (no relation to the saint), who recommend an order emerging out of chaos.

Husserl (strictly speaking, that aspect of his thought which interests me) does not seem to me to engage his thinking either in the direction of isomorphism (or program), or that of emergentism. His approach zigzags between archaeology and teleology and is based upon a fundamental intuition: the intuition that form, structure, signification, and sense are both prefigured in the being in which they subsist before becoming fully effective and, once they are so prefigured, projected beyond this being into a futural elsewhere where they will eventually cease to exist. Thus, the institutional forms that together mold the culture of each human community are, to the extent that this is possible, meaning-full structures. To view them as an order potentially isomorphic with every other order at every other level of analysis or as resulting from underlying micro-movements which are unpredictable at the macro-level is, in the one case just as in the other, to leave out of consideration the meaning shared by all those who intend these meaning-full structures, to examine them in a cavalier manner from a detached standpoint which is extended to the entire universe, in a word, to objectify an order that is supposed to have been always already in place or which arose fully equipped in some way or other.

Husserl looks at things in a completely different way. His method is to dive right into the lived experience of meaning, even into the flux, not, of course, to risk drowning but to try to draw out of it the meaning, to orient himself with regard to it, to identify its origins ("archai") and its goal ("telos") without any other ambition than to ceaselessly uphold the tension between these two poles of the meaning field. For his intellectual commitment differs radically from that of Köhler, Ferdinand de Saussure, Wittgenstein, Douglas Hofstadter, and so on. It is his conviction that grasping a meaning permits us to actualize the original conditions that make it possible, at the same time that it enables us to accede by right to a world whose horizon is opened up by it. Let me explain. The entire system of human culture is a structure of meaning. To participate in it is possible only subject to certain conditions, which are not satisfied by stones, for example, but are satisfied by humans and certain nonhuman species of animals, in any case always living creatures.

One of the most basic conditions is "our experience of others," that is, that we have an experience of the other which is not reducible to the physical thing which its body is. Empiricism cannot uncover this experience because it limits itself to sense data, to the bombardment of our sensory terminals with stimulation. In a certain sense, our experience of the other includes the experience that the other has of itself and of us. This is the *Einfühlung* which was unjustly and erroneously dismissed by Heidegger, who imputed quite wrongly to Husserl's attempt to overcome the solipsism inherent in his own Cartesianism, a point of view which was adopted thereafter, if not by the entire phenomenological tradition, at least by those who command the heights in my country. The only way of getting back to the impulsional intentionality of intersubjectivity, located in our dispositions, tendencies, and empathic or intropathic kinesthesia, is by getting around any objectifying consciousness or willful interpretation of action. By becoming aware of the fact that we are responsible for the meaning of the being of the other and by being ready to make a heroic effort to get past positions which could have been—and may still be—held against him in order to render intelligible this very awareness (Cartesian subjectivism, Kantian transcendentalism, Fichtean idealism, etc.), Husserl remains exemplary.

However, empathy is a concept borrowed by early phenomenologists from empirical psychology (Lipps). This means that there are psychological, psycho-physiological, vital, and natural sources of meaning. Meaning does not arise in being by accident, like a face seen in the clouds or on the sand only to be blotted out soon after without ever recurring. Nor is it eternally imprisoned in a labyrinth of mirrors in which images are reflected back and forth indefinitely. As against Descartes's conception of the man-machine (or the brain-machine of those of his ungrateful beneficiaries, who accuse him of making a "mistake" without taking the trouble to read him), our body is, for Husserl, an organism, *Leib*, not *Körper*. It "makes sense of," is "oriented toward something (or someone)." The living being which we are cannot exist without feeling something at some level no matter how "elementary"—except perhaps the molecular, if not the cellular level. To examine these conditions (mirror-neurons, etc.), whether they be ontogenetically acquired or phylogenetically written into the organism, to examine the "living experience of meaning," which may help to explain the meaning-giving activity of the subjective and intersubjective being which this organism is, both this organism and those other organisms it encounters in its environment, this, it seems to me, opens up a legitimate way of understanding "naturalization."

I therefore have no hesitation in averring that those who seek in Husserl's own declarations grounds for objecting to "naturalism" in psychology and in the other natural sciences (statements which can easily be found in *Logische Untersuchungen, Ideen* I, and *Krisis* and which, as it happens, I am well aware of) fail to make a case which presents any serious objection to this kind of "naturalization." Phenomenologists should not need to be reminded that this program of naturalization presupposes an intentional and phenomenological psychology, not a behaviorist psychology, still less that of cognitivists who mistakenly suppose that they have moved beyond behaviorism. More particularly, it demands a biology capable of surmounting the obstacles represented by the objectivism and the mechanism of the "model-builders," all of which takes us in the direction of that hermeneutical anthropology of the life-world of human communities which has been sketched out in Husserl's manuscripts since the 1930s. Since no one is the master of the meaning words assume, I am ready to admit that my own words can also be taken in a sense other than that I intended (that, for example, of W. V. O. Quine)—which gives me the right to decline all responsibility for what others may chose to make of my present claims.

Translated by Christopher Macann

CHAPTER EIGHT

Wooden Iron? Husserlian Phenomenology Meets Cognitive Science

TIM VAN GELDER

Consciousness has many aspects. One of these is called "time consciousness." This is not consciousness of Time itself, nor is it just consciousness that takes place in time. Rather, to put the point somewhat cryptically, it is consciousness of temporal objects as temporal. A temporal object is anything that exists in time, or endures. Rocks, chairs, conversations, tides, tunes, and empires all endure. In this respect they differ from, for example, numbers. Time consciousness is a special kind of awareness of temporal objects—an awareness of them as enduring. It is the difference between my thinking abstractly of Nirvana's "Smells like Teen Spirit," and my hearing it play on the radio. In the latter case, though not the former, the song actually unfolds in time and my awareness is an awareness of it as happening in time. The situation is essentially similar (though less dramatic) in the case of temporal objects such as chairs, which do not depend on change in time to be what they are.

A little reflection can generate an interesting puzzle about time consciousness. Both the song and my awareness of it happen in time. They are like parallel tracks in the same time frame. However, as we usually think about time, only the present and what is in it actually exist; thus, only a momentary stage of the song and a momentary stage of my awareness exist at any given time. The other stages did exist, or will exist, but do not exist now. It seems plausible, then, that my awareness at this moment of the music must be an awareness of the song now, that is to say, of the current, momentary stage of the music. The other stages do not exist, so how can I be aware of them? And here's the puzzle: if at any given time I am just aware of the part of the song playing now, how can I ever be aware of the song as an integrated piece that takes place over time?

I am not claiming that this puzzle represents some deep metaphysical difficulty. Rather, it is a provocative way to point out an interesting theoretical domain. It is an entry point into serious reflection on the nature of time consciousness. What must be going on in our minds to make time consciousness possible?

Presumably, an understanding of time consciousness should be part of an understanding of the nature of consciousness in general. Our philosophical and scientific tradition offers at least two major approaches to the study of mind and consciousness: phenomenology and cognitive science. These approaches are patently different in almost every important respect: they have their own literature, practitioners, professional meetings, vocabulary, methods, and so on. They have fundamentally different orientations: phenomenology proceeds from the assumption that the study of mind must be rooted in direct attention to the nature of (one's own) experience, whereas cognitive science proceeds from the assumption that a genuine science of mind must be rooted in the observation of publicly available aspects of the minds of others.

To which of these approaches—phenomenology or cognitive science—should we turn for an understanding of time consciousness? They are sometimes regarded as direct competitors. Philosophical arguments have been adduced to demonstrate that genuine knowledge of consciousness can only be achieved by one method or the other. The position taken here, however, is that these conclusions are unwarranted. Phenomenology and cognitive science should be regarded not only as compatible, but as mutually constraining and enriching approaches to the study of mind. I shall attempt here a kind of "proof by example" of this position. It will demonstrate how both phenomenology and cognitive science can shed light on the phenomenon of time consciousness, and how their respective contributions can inform each other. The claim will be that only phenomenology and cognitive science in conjunction can adequately resolve the paradox of time consciousness described above.

1. PHENOMENOLOGY AND TIME CONSCIOUSNESS

The most sustained investigation of time consciousness in the phenomenological tradition was that undertaken by Edmund Husserl. He visited the topic periodically throughout his life, and his written treatments of it are scattered throughout his work.[1] To make matters worse, Husserl's writings are notoriously difficult for the nonspecialist. Fortunately, there are now a number of admirably clear and comprehensive presentations of Husserl's thought on time consciousness available in the secondary literature, including especially those by John Brough, Izchak Miller, and William Blattner.[2] The reader is referred to those works for thorough treatments of the topic. In this section, I will relate, in highly simplified form, just enough of Husserl's account for the major purposes of this essay.[3]

The upshot of the paradox of time consciousness is clear. When I am aware of something temporal as temporal, there is more to my awareness than simply a succession of momentary awarenesses of momentary stages. When I hear a melody, I don't simply hear this note now and another note a moment later. Something more is going on—but what could that be?

An all-too-obvious move is to suggest that what we need, over and above the succession of momentary awarenesses, is an additional awareness of all the stages of the temporal object as composing a single temporally extended entity. Husserl, attributing a view along these lines to Alexius Meinong, puts it this way: "There must be an act which embraces, beyond the now, the whole temporal object."[4] Since this additional awareness cannot, by its very nature, take place until all the momentary stages have actually occurred, it must take place at the end of the succession of awarenesses.

Husserl demonstrated that this view cannot be correct, however. For one thing, it is hard to see how this final all-embracing awareness can actually take place, for there is nothing left for it to embrace. By the time the final act takes place, the momentary stages of the object itself and the momentary awarenesses of those stages have been and gone; they are fully in the past, and in that sense no longer exist. One might attempt to remedy the situation by stipulating that one retains memories of the momentary stages of the object, and the final awareness combines those memories into an awareness of the entire temporal object. However, even as amended this way, the Meinongian suggestion falls afoul of another distinctively phenomenological objection. If you attend to your experience of being aware of a temporal object, you find yourself aware of that object as temporal even as time unfolds. When you listen to a melody, you do not have to wait around until the melody is finished in order to hear it as a melody.

The key to solving the puzzle is to realize that, as Husserl put it, "consciousness must reach out beyond the now."[5] Every momentary awareness of the temporal object must be an awareness of more than just the corresponding momentary stage of the temporal object. Consciousness must at that moment somehow relate the momentary stage of the temporal object to other stages, that is, to what went before and what is to come. Husserl's theory of time consciousness is a sophisticated account of how awareness can build the past and the future into the present. It is thus a detailed theory of what is required for there to be any time consciousness (of the sort we have) at all.

The basic insight is that every momentary stage or "act" of time consciousness actually has a triple structure (see Figure 8.1). The centerpiece is a "primal impression" of the momentary stage of the temporal object. This primal impression corresponds roughly to the momentary awarenesses that figured in the Meinongian account. It simply takes in or "intends" what is now, in a way that is completely oblivious of what went before and what is

...Past Stages...Now...Future Stages...

Retention   *Primal Impression*   *Protention*

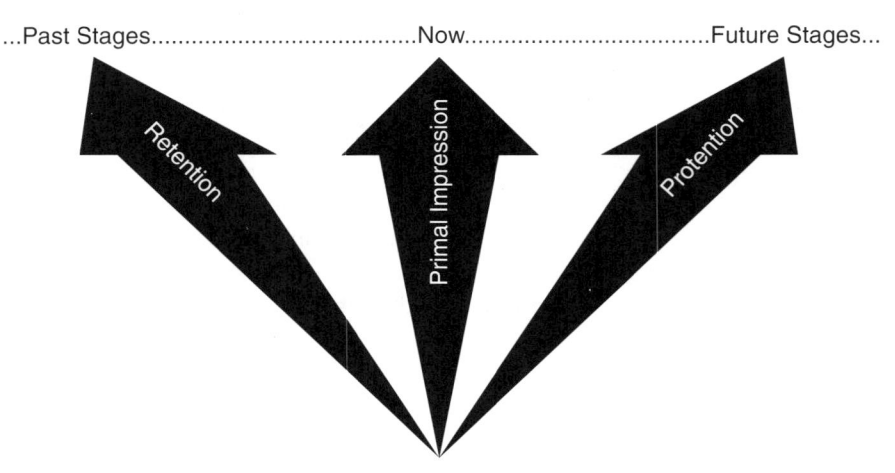

FIGURE 8.1. Husserl's triple structure of time consciousness.

to come. However, on Husserl's theory, primal impressions do not stand alone; they are only part of the triple structure that is essential to any individual act of time consciousness. Put differently, primal impressions are not awarenesses in their own right; they are essential ingredients or "moments" of full-blooded awarenesses of temporal objects.

The other ingredients of time consciousness are retentions and protentions. These are also intendings of stages of the temporal object. What distinguishes them from primal impressions, however, is that retentions are intendings of past stages, whereas protentions are intendings of future stages. For a crude illustration, imagine hearing the tune "Yankee Doodle," and consider your awareness of the tune at the time of the second note, that is, the one corresponding to the "-kee." Roughly speaking, on Husserl's account, your perceptual time consciousness of the tune as a whole at that very moment has a triple structure of intendings: a primal impression of the second note ("-kee"), a retention of the first note ("Yan-"), and a protention of the third note ("Doo-").

Husserl's theory of the triple structure of time consciousness clearly accounts, in broad outline, for how my awareness now can build in the past and the future, and thus be an awareness now of the temporal object as temporal. However, it does so at the cost of invoking what seem to be rather mysterious beasts, retentions and protentions. Why mysterious? Well, go back to the original paradox of time consciousness. What is past has disappeared forever, and what is future has not happened yet. In an obvious sense, neither the past nor the future exist now. The mystery is, how can retentions and protentions "intend" what doesn't exist? Or rather, what are retentions and protentions, such that it makes some kind of sense to say that they do this?

Husserl explores the notions of retention and protention, and their role in time consciousness, in great depth and detail, but it is not obvious that he succeeds in clarifying these notions enough to remove the sense of mystery. I suggest that this mystery can only really be resolved once Husserl's theory is fleshed out by reference to actual models, from cognitive science, of the causal mechanisms underlying time consciousness. Before looking at those models, however, more of Husserl's account needs to be on the table. The following is a simplified and synthesized list of properties that Husserl ascribed to retention:

1. Retentions happen "now"; they are components of the current phase of consciousness even though they are directed upon stages of the temporal object that are "now" in the past.

2. Retentions present past stages "as past to some degree." In order to have a coherent awareness of a temporal object, we must somehow assess the "pastness" of past stages; the temporal relations among the stages must be preserved. It is only because retentions present past stages "as past to some degree" that when I hear the third note of "Yankee Doodle," my awareness of the tune includes retentions of both the first and the second notes, but the retention of the first note presents it as further in the past than the retention of the second.

3. Retentions are formed from primal impressions. A primal impression at one moment becomes a retention at the next. A primal impression is, by its very nature, directed upon the current momentary stage of the temporal object. As soon as that stage is past, the intending of it which is a necessary part of time consciousness has become a retention. This might be put by saying that retentions are impressions that are past their prime.

4. In a given act of time consciousness, retentions, the primal impression, and protentions form a "continuous manifold." That is, there are an infinite number of retentions and protentions directed at vanishingly small past and future slices of the temporal object. In fact, it is probably misleading to talk of retentions and protentions at all. Rather, there are retentional and protentional regions of the whole intentional manifold that composes the momentary act of time consciousness.

5. Retention and protention do not extend infinitely far into the past and future. One retains and projects only stages of the temporal object within limited bounds of the current moment. When in the middle of a Mahler symphony (which can seem to go on forever), one's awareness of the music does not (typically) include the opening notes or anticipate the final ones.

6. Retention is not a memory, an image, or an echo. It is tempting to think of retention as consciousness of something which does exist now, and

which has the function of (re)presenting something else that no longer exists. Husserl, however, is adamant that this is not how retention intends past temporal stages. Retention is not a matter of having images of a past stage. Retention is not a matter of having memories that re-create the past as if it were now; nor is it like echoes still hanging around in the now. As Brough puts it: "Retention does not transmute what is absent into something present; it presents the absent in its absence" (1989: 276). Retention reaches out directly into the past. It is more like perceiving than representing.

7. One might object that retention cannot be perceptual in character because the temporal stages upon which it is directed in an important sense no longer exist. The past has been and gone, and so cannot be literally perceived. Husserl was aware of this difficulty. Of retention, he says: "But 'perceived past,' doesn't that sound like wooden iron?"[6] Husserl's way of dealing with this problem appears to come down to sticking to his guns and denying the assumption that perception must always be of something that exists at the time of the perceiving itself. Retention is, allegedly, the direct intending of what is past.

Retention, then, is the current, direct, and "perceptual" intending, within finite limits, of past stages of the temporal object as past to some degree. Husserl is, effectively, describing an aspect of consciousness that is, theoretically, entirely novel. It is difficult to grasp clearly the nature of retention because it is essentially unlike any mental act as delineated by more familiar taxonomies (e.g., our everyday or "folk" sense of the kinds of mental acts that there are).

Protention is basically the symmetrical opposite of retention, directed toward the future rather than the past. The major difference, of course, is that whereas the past has happened, and in that sense is fixed, the future is still open; there is certainly no way in which one can know what it will be. How then, one might ask, can protention—intendings of the future, modeled on perception—possibly exist? This really is very mysterious. Husserl had relatively little to say about it, except to suggest, in a quite unsatisfactory manner, that protention is somehow both determinate and open at the same time.

2. COGNITIVE SCIENCE AND TIME CONSCIOUSNESS

How does cognitive science deal with time consciousness? Truth be known, the topic has never been high on the cognitive science agenda. There are various sorts of investigations of time-related issues, but they tend to sidestep the issue that so concerned the phenomenologists, namely, the internal structure of the mental acts involved in being aware of temporal objects as temporal.[7] Fortunately however, cognitive scientists have been paying increasing amounts of attention to some aspects of cognition that are closely related to time consciousness. One example is auditory pattern recognition, a special case of which is the recognition of music. An essential feature of auditory patterns is that they happen in time; the particular way they unfold in time is what makes them the pattern that they are. Moreover, our perception of auditory patterns, such as melodies, is a classic case of time consciousness. If we can understand the mechanisms that enable us to recognize auditory patterns, we might obtain insight into how it is that, more generally, we can be aware of temporal objects as temporal.

Cognitive scientists try to understand the causal mechanisms responsible for a given phenomenon by producing and analyzing *models*. There are at least two fundamentally different kinds of models, corresponding to what is arguably the deepest division between kinds of research in cognitive science. That is the division between the computational approach, on one hand, and the dynamical approach on the other. Computationalism has dominated cognitive science since the discipline emerged in the 1950s and 1960s and is still the mainstream or orthodox approach.[8] It takes cognitive systems to be computers, in the quite strict and literal sense of machines that manipulate internal symbols in a way that is specified, at some level, by algorithms. Computers in this sense are exemplified by Turing machines. Cognition, according to this approach, is the internal transformation of structures of symbolic representations. A classic example of mainstream computational modeling is the SOAR framework developed by Newell and others, within which detailed models of a wide variety of aspects of cognition have been developed.[9] Since cognition is taken to be the behavior of a computer, computer science provides the general conceptual framework within which cognition can be studied. Standing behind this approach to cognition is long philosophical tradition, stretching from Plato through Descartes, Leibniz, and Kant, and culminating in contemporary philosophers such as Fodor, which assumes that the essence of mind is to represent and reason about the world.

What do computational models of auditory pattern recognition look like? At the most generic level, they work by applying recognition algorithms to symbolic encodings of the auditory information. This implies a two-stage process; one in which the auditory signal is encoded, and another in which the encoded information is analyzed. As a consequence, there is a structural feature that all computational models share: the buffer. This is a kind of temporary warehouse in which the auditory information is stored in symbolic form as it comes in, in preparation for the recognition algorithms to do their work. This is achieved by sampling the auditory signal at a regular rate, that is, using an independent clock to pick out points of time and measuring the signal at those times, then storing in the buffer symbolic representations of those measurements together with the time they were taken.

The dynamical approach to cognitive science takes cognitive systems to be dynamical systems rather than computers.[10] In this context, a dynamical system is a set of quantities evolving interdependently over time. The solar system is the best-known example of a dynamical system; it consists of the positions and momenta of the sun and planets, all of which are changing all the time, in such a way that the current state of every quantity affects the way every other one changes. In cognitive science, most (though by no means all) dynamical models of cognition are neural networks, in which the set of interdependently evolving quantities are the activity levels of the neural units. According to the dynamical approach, cognition is not the manipulation of symbols but rather state-space evolution within a dynamical system, and the emergence of order and structure within such evolution. The relevant conceptual framework is that of dynamics (dynamical modeling and dynamical systems theory), which may well be the most widely used and successful explanatory framework in the whole of natural science. Standing behind the dynamical approach is an alternative philosophical tradition, from Heidegger and Ryle earlier in the twentieth century to contemporary figures such as Dreyfus and Varela, which takes the essence of mind to be ongoing active engagement with the world.

What do dynamical models of auditory pattern recognition look like? At the most generic level, they work by having the auditory pattern influence the direction of evolution within the dynamical system. It will be useful to describe one such dynamical model in just a little detail. This is the Lexin model for auditory pattern recognition developed by Sven Anderson and Robert Port.[11] It is a neural network in which each of the system variables (neural units) changes its activity level as a function of the current activity of the other variables and the connections between them in a way that is determined by differential equations. For the general architecture of the network and the form of the governing differential equations, see Figure 8.2.

There are many subtleties about the particular organization and behavior of this network, but for current purposes we only need to understand its operation in the most general terms. The total state of the network at a given time is the set of values of each of the neural units. This total state corresponds to a point in a geometric space of all possible total states. Every neural unit is continuously changing its activity under influence from other units, and so the total state of the system is itself continuously changing. This change constitutes a particular trajectory through the state space, which can be schematically depicted by means a curve on a plane (Figure 8.3).

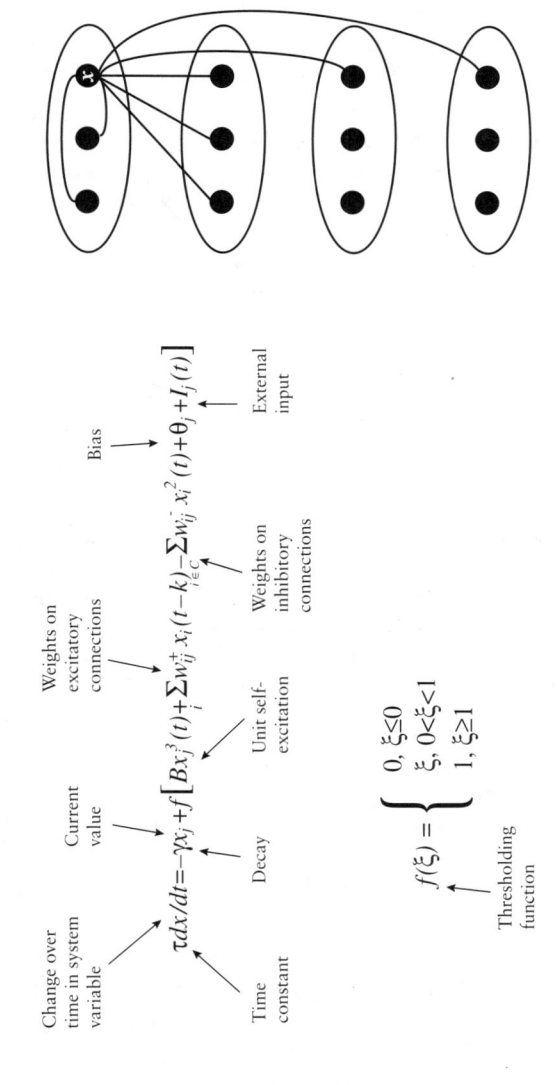

FIGURE 8.2. The Lexin dynamical model of auditory pattern recognition developed by Robert Port and Sven Anderson. On the right is a schematic depiction of the neural network architecture. Units inhibit each other within a cluster but excite units in other clusters. On the left is the general form of the differential equations that govern the evolution of individual variables and hence change in the system as a whole.

$$\tau dx/dt = -\gamma x_j + f\left[Bx_j^3(t) + \sum_i w_{ij}^+ x_i(t-k) - \sum_{i \in C} w_{ij}^- x_i^2(t) + \theta_j + I_j(t)\right]$$

$$f(\xi) = \begin{cases} 0, & \xi \leq 0 \\ \xi, & 0 < \xi < 1 \\ 1, & \xi \geq 1 \end{cases}$$

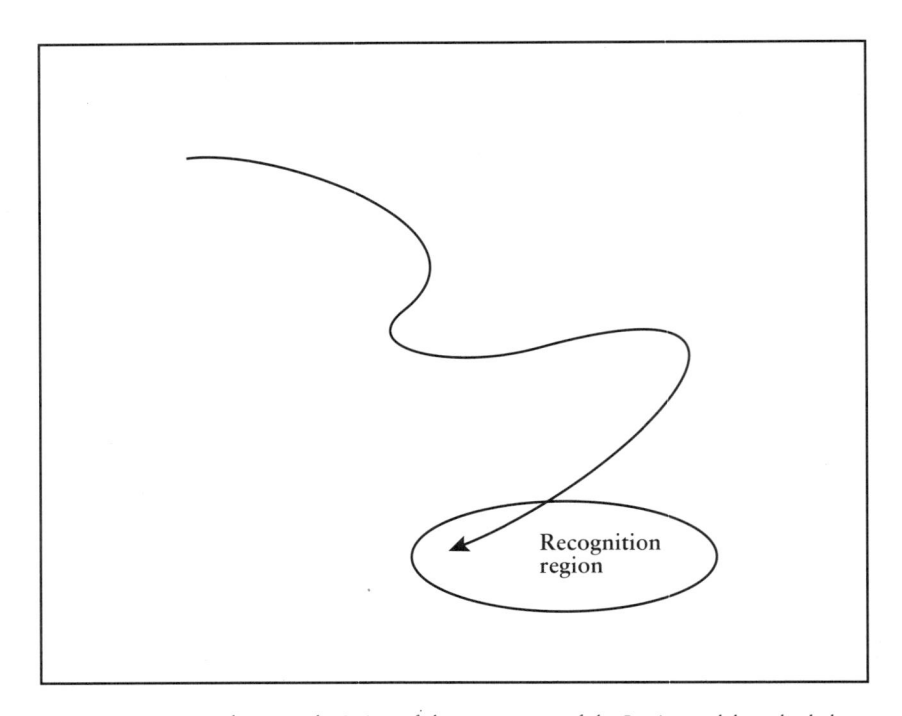

[Figure: A rectangular box containing a curved trajectory line that winds down into an oval labeled "Recognition region" with an arrow pointing into it.]

FIGURE 8.3. A schematic depiction of the state space of the Lexin model, and a behavioral trajectory. Each point along the curved line represents a state of the system at a particular time. The shape of the curve is determined by a combination of the system's intrinsic behavioral tendencies and external influences. In this case, the system passes through the recognition region and thereby recognizes the external influences as constituting a familiar pattern. A successful auditory pattern recognition system of this type is one that will pass through the recognition region if, and only if, a familiar pattern is presented.

What determines the shape of this trajectory (i.e., the behavior of the system)? At one level, it is the intrinsic structure of the neural network itself—roughly, the way it is built. If we take two sets of electronic components and hook them up in different ways, electrical currents will flow within them very differently. One might function as a radio receiver, the other as a metronome. Similarly, the behavior of a (real or physical) neural network is a matter of how its particular neural components are wired together. At a more abstract level—the level of mathematical description—the shape of the trajectory is determined by the form of its governing equations and the values of the parameters they contain. For example, the behavior of the solar system is described (to a good approximation) by Newton's equations of motion. A different set of equations would of course describe very different patterns of motion. Newton's own equations contain a parameter g, the gravitational constant. The behavior described by the equations depends on the value of this parameter. If it were somewhat larger, the equations would predict planets spiraling into the sun. Neural network equations typically have many parameters, but the most obvious are those corresponding to the "weights" determining the extent to which one neuron can influence another through a given connection.

Think of all the possible behaviors a given system might exhibit. Each of these is a distinct trajectory through the space of possible system states, corresponding to a distinct curve in a state-space diagram. Collectively, they constitute what is known as the system "flow." The shape of the flow is determined by the system's intrinsic *dynamics*—the "forces" that push the system state in one direction or another, depending on where it happens to be. They can be thought of as constituting a kind of landscape over which the behavior of the system "flows." For a crude but compelling analogy, imagine a marble allowed to roll from various points on a smooth but very uneven floor. The hills and valleys form the landscape that shapes all the paths the marble might take.[12]

Some dynamical systems are entirely self-contained. They are completely insulated from the outside world, and any change in state is dictated solely by their intrinsic dynamics. More commonly, behavior within a system can be influenced by external events. There is an important distinction between two ways this can happen. The first is direct intervention in the current *state* of the system—like picking up the marble and setting it down somewhere else on the floor. The other is more subtle. The current state remains the same, but the dynamical *landscape* changes. Since the landscape determines how system state changes, the state will then head off in a different direction. This would be like getting the marble to go where you want, not by touching the marble but rather by changing the shape of the floor. When there is a change in the dynamical landscape, of course, this affects every possible path (i.e., the entire flow). Sometimes, these changes result in the emergence of a *qualitatively* distinct dynamical landscape. We saw an example above: if one could increase the gravitational constant enough, the planets would no longer be in stable orbits but would spiral into the sun. The situation where changes in the parameters of a system result in qualitative changes in dynamical landscape is known as a *bifurcation*.

Let us return to the Lexin model and auditory pattern recognition. Lexin is a neural network dynamical system whose state continually evolves in a way determined by the system's dynamics. This dynamics depends in part on the current settings of all system parameters. Some of these parameters correspond to auditory input ($I_j(t)$ in the equation). Their values at a given time are determined by the nature of the auditory input at that stage. The Lexin system, after a program of "training," has come to be wired up in such a way that for each distinct tone, there is a single unique point attractor in the dynamical landscape of the system. This is a state of the system such that wherever the system happens to be, it will head toward and eventually end up in that state. When the system is "hearing" one tone, it will head in the direction of the attractor for that tone. When another tone is presented, the system bifurcates; the previous attractor is replaced by another in a different location, and the system then heads off toward the new attractor. Thus, as the auditory pattern unfolds over time, it causes a series of bifurcations which result in the system state being pulled first in one direction, then another. It is as if a marble were rolling around on a floor whose hills and valleys were constantly changing. This process of "attractor chaining" results in a system trajectory whose shape directly reflects the nature of the auditory pattern. Note that in this process the system usually never actually *reaches* an attractor, and does not need to do so. Like a dog chasing first one car then another without ever catching up, it will weave an erratic path shaped by the pattern in external events.

Now, how can an arrangement of this kind be understood as recognizing auditory patterns? Recognizing a class of patterns requires discriminating those patterns from others not in the class, which must somehow be manifested in the behavior of the system. One way this can be done is by having the system arrive in a certain state when a familiar pattern is presented, and not otherwise. That is, there is a "recognition region" in the state space which the system passes through if and only if the pattern is one that it recognizes. Put another way, there is a region of the state space that the system can only reach if a familiar auditory pattern (sounds and timing) has influenced its behavior. Familiar patterns are thus like keys that combine with the system lock to open the door of recognition.

The remarkable fact is that dynamical systems can in fact be configured to exhibit exactly this kind of response. This is what the Lexin model does with a small repertoire of relatively simple patterns. If this model is along the right lines, this is what our own auditory systems do with the vast repertoire of complex and subtle patterns that we can discriminate from the sea of noise around us.

3. PHENOMENOLOGY INFORMS COGNITIVE SCIENCE

We thus have two general approaches to the study of cognition, which have issued in two very different kinds of model of auditory pattern recognition. Which of these kinds of models is to be preferred? Their value is ultimately a matter of how they match up against all the relevant empirical data. It is difficult at the moment (and especially difficult for someone standing outside this particular discipline) to deliver any definitive judgment here. However, it is possible to make a more limited point of comparison, one that is directly relevant to the major aims of this essay. In this section I will suggest that phenomenological evidence weighs in on the side of dynamical models as opposed to computational models (at least as those two classes are sketched above).

An obvious and superficially plausible objection to the computational approach in general has always been that cognition does not seem to be a matter of manipulation of symbols inside the head. When one introspects on one's own thought processes, one generally doesn't observe the symbols and transformations that are alleged to constitute those processes. The standard way in which mainstream computational cognitive science has dealt with this objection is to suggest that the posited computational processes are *subconscious*, and so the phenomenology does not directly bear on the issue. This strategy is not simply a matter of self-serving selection of the kinds of evidence to be taken into account. There is no reason to assume that the phenomenology of a mental process should somehow give direct insight into the nature of the causal processes that subserve that phenomenology. By analogy, the picture on television gives no insight into the causal mechanisms that give rise to that picture (except, perhaps, in the very special case in which the program on television happens to concern how televisions work). In a certain sense, we "see through" the screen to the content that is conveyed by the television. In a similar way, we "see through" the mechanisms responsible for our cognitive processes.

Unfortunately, computationalists have, by and large, gone on illegitimately to assume a general license to ignore phenomenological data of *any* kind whenever it is convenient to do so. Their models are generally evaluated only by whether they match the measured performance data, and not by whether they make any sense in terms of our own observations of our experience. In the long run, however, this attitude cannot be sustained. Phenomenological evidence—both the everyday kind and the theoretically sophisticated deliverances of Husserl and others—is one source of relevant constraint among others. Like any other data, phenomenological evidence must be treated with care, but no theory of mind and cognition would be complete unless it could properly integrate causal mechanisms with phenomenology. Although phenomenological observation cannot, in general, be presumed to give *direct* insight into the nature of the mechanisms responsible for experiential phenomena, there must ultimately be an account of why those phenomena are the way they are given (at least partly) in terms of the nature of those mechanisms. For this reason, the nature of our experience should be regarded as having the potential to constrain our theories and models in cognitive science.

Now, the phenomenological observation that is relevant here is simply a relatively obvious point on which Husserl relied when criticizing the Meinongian theory of time consciousness. Recall that according to that theory, time consciousness is made possible by the presence of an additional mental act that surveys all the momentary stages and synthesizes them into a single apprehension of the object as a temporal whole. This act can only take place once all the momentary stages have occurred. However, attending to the nature of the experience involved, it seems clear that we do not have to wait until the temporal object is over before we can perceive it as a temporal object. I don't have to wait until the end of "Smells like Teen Spirit" before experiencing it as the song that it is; indeed, I don't have to wait until the end of even a single bar. After perhaps an initial delay, every sound, on a moment by moment basis, is perceived as part of that tune. In short, time consciousness unfolds in the very same time frame as the temporal object itself.

How does this observation bear on the difference between dynamical and computational models? Well, notice that computational models have the same temporal structure as the Meinongian account of time consciousness. In computational models, the auditory pattern is first encoded symbolically and stored in a buffer. Only when the entire pattern has been stored in the buffer do the recognition algorithms go to work; and it is only when those algorithms have done their work that the system could be said to have any kind of awareness of the pattern as such. It follows, therefore, that computational models are open to the same objection as the Meinongian account. The fact is, in order to recognize a tune as such, we don't (as computational models suggest) have to wait until the end of the tune. I hear the tune as a tune even as the tune is playing.

On the other hand, dynamical models exhibit exactly the kind of simultaneous unfolding that phenomenological observation suggests. The state of the system is always changing, and from the onset of the very first sound, the system is evolving in a direction that reflects both the auditory pattern itself and the system's familiarity with that pattern. In other words, the system begins responding to the pattern as the pattern that it is from the moment it begins.

Clearly, then, dynamical models fit much better with the nature of our experience than computational models do. Other things being equal, this gives us good reason to prefer dynamical models over computational models; and if we accept this, then we have accepted that phenomenology can substantially constrain cognitive science.

How might computationalists respond? One possibility is to deny or reinterpret the phenomenological evidence. Perhaps it merely seems that our experience of a tune unfolds while the tune is playing. Perhaps in fact all we have, while the tune plays, is a momentary awareness of the sound playing at each instant, and only when the tune is over do we comprehend the tune as a temporal whole. Perhaps, in Dennett's terms, the mechanisms of time consciousness do an Orwellian rewrite of the temporal history of our experience.

Perhaps. Note, however, that there is no particular reason to believe this other than a desire to save computational models in an ad hoc way. We should presumably prefer a kind of explanation which does not require us to suppose that we are systematically deceived by our experience over one that does require this. Note also that the standard strategy employed by computationalists to discount phenomenological evidence, however plausible it might be in other cases, is not persuasive in this particular case. The actual time-course of my experience—how it happens in time—is not so obviously something that is conscious or subconscious in the normal sense. In any case, presumably the phenomenological conclusion can be tested by psychological ("third person") experiments that shed light on the actual temporal frame of experience and can indicate whether our sense of awareness of a temporal object as it unfolds is an illusion or not.

Another kind of response would be to deny that a Meinongian structure is *essential* to computational models. Certainly, it is possible to imagine some kind of parallel-processing computational architecture which begins pattern recognition from the very moment the auditory event commences. This would be a major structural departure from current computational models, and parallel processing is always much easier envisaged than actually achieved. Perhaps it is not, after all, *essential* to computational models that they be broadly Meinongian. However, what is essential is that there be two theoretically distinct processes, one in which the auditory pattern is symbolically represented, and one in which algorithms operate on that symbolic representation. It is no accident that this theoretical distinction is universally reflected in the actual temporal structure of computational models; to avoid a Meinongian structure is to work against the computational grain. In the long run, if what you need in your system is simultaneous coevolution, you may as well go with one that has it as a standard feature rather than with one that can only get it as an expensive aftermarket accessory.

4. COGNITIVE SCIENCE INFORMS PHENOMENOLOGY

We have just seen how phenomenology can be relevant to cognitive science, giving a basis for preferring one kind of account of the underlying causal mechanisms over another. What about the other direction? How can cognitive science inform phenomenology?

The main claim of this section is the bold one that cognitive science can tell us what retention and protention *actually are*, and in that sense deepen our understanding of them and of time consciousness in general. The case is parallel to that of genes. The theory of heredity effectively dictated that there must be some mechanism of transferal of information from one generation to another, and specified the general properties that it must have. It was then up to the molecular biologists to find the mechanism itself. Likewise, Husserl's phenomenological theory specifies that time consciousness requires retention and protention, and the general properties they must have, and cognitive science uncovers the actual mechanisms that underlie time consciousness and instantiate retention and protention. In discovering what retention and protention actually are, we deepen our understanding of the phenomenological theory and may even be able to alter and improve that theory.

When we understand how dynamical models of auditory pattern recognition work, we are (without realizing it) already understanding what retention and protention are. When we look at schematic diagrams of the behavior of these models, we are (without realizing it) already looking at schematic depictions of retention and protention. The key insight is the realization that the state of the system at any given time models awareness of the auditory pattern at that moment, and that state builds the past and the future into the present, just as Husserl saw was required.

How is the past built in to current awareness? In a dynamical system, there is only one way in which the past can be retained in the present, and that is by making a difference to the current state of the system—that is, to the location of the current state in the space of possible states. Thus in the Lexin model, the awareness of the current stage of the music builds in the past by occupying one location (and hence changing in a certain direction) rather than another, and it occupies that particular location only because it happened to trace out the particular trajectory that was shaped by the prior inputs. It is that location, in its difference from other locations in the context of the intrinsic dynamics of the system, which "stores" in the system the way in which the auditory pattern unfolded in the past. It is how the system "remembers" where it came from. Note that in such an arrangement, the past intrinsically and automatically flavors the awareness of the current stage. In this kind of model, momentary awareness (Husserl's "primal impression") is essentially shaped by retention of the past.

How is the future built in? Well, note that a dynamical system, by its nature, continues on a trajectory from any point. This is true even when there is no external influence. The particular path it follows is determined by its current state in conjunction with its intrinsic dynamics. Thus, there is a real sense in which the system automatically builds in a future for every state it happens to occupy. Now, if the current state is one that results from exposure to a particular auditory pattern, the future behavior of the system will itself be sensitive to that exposure. In other words, the system will automatically proceed on a path that reflects the particular auditory pattern that it has heard up to that point. Thus, protention is *also* a geometrically describable property of dynamical systems. Protention is the location of the current state of the system in the space of possible states, though this time what is relevant about the current state is the way in which, given the system's intrinsic dynamics, the location shapes the future behavior of the system. The current location of the state of the system is what stores the system's "sense" of where it is going. Note that, as with retention, protention is an essential aspect of current awareness.

The best way to tell whether these theoretical identifications are really appropriate is to compare retention and protention on the dynamical interpretation with the list of properties that Husserl ascribed to retention and protention. And in fact, they turn out to fit like hand and glove. Almost every description Husserl gave of retention and protention finds a natural interpretation in terms of the current location of a dynamical system capable of auditory pattern recognition such as the Lexin model. Again, consider retention first:

1. The dynamical interpretation of retention identifies it with an aspect of the current state of the system, rather than any past or future aspect of the system.

2. In these kinds of dynamical auditory pattern recognition systems, the location of the current state of the system reflects not just what previous sounds it had been exposed to, but also the order in which it was exposed to those sounds—or, more generally, how long ago it was exposed to them. Therefore, there is a clear sense in which retention, on this interpretation, intends the past as past to some degree.

3. A primal impression is that "moment" of time consciousness which intends the current stage of the temporal object. In the case of tune recognition, it is the aspect of one's awareness of the tune as a whole which is awareness of the current note. On the dynamical account, awareness of the tune as a whole is identified with the current state of the auditory recognition system. The nature of these dynamical systems is such that current inputs act as parameters that influence how the system changes its state. More crudely, they push the system in one direction or another. The primal impression should therefore be identified with the way the system is currently changing under the influence of the current sound input. This gives us a clear interpretation of the claim that retention is modification of primal impression, for the locations of subsequent states of the system result directly from the way

it is changing at any given time. Current change transmutes into future location.

4. Dynamical auditory pattern recognition systems such as the Lexin model are continuous, both in the sense that the space of possible states is continuous and that their state changes continuously in that space in response to inputs which affect it continuously in time. Since retention is identified with a system's occupying its current location in state space, and this location reflects past inputs, it makes sense to say that retention builds on the past in a continuous way. However, on this interpretation of what retention is, we find the very same awkwardness in using the term "retention" as a singular term as we found in the phenomenological account. There are no separate "retentions" distinct from each other and from the primal impression. The very idea of a *manifold* is an attempt to move from a set of things to an unbroken continuum, but we can now see that this term is unnecessary. Rather, there is a continuous retentional aspect to the current state of the system.

5. It is a fact about these dynamical models that influence is "washed out" in the long run. Generally, the longer the state of the system is buffeted about by current inputs, the less the influence of a past input is discernible in the current state. There are no strict limits here, but it is clear that the current state does not retain the influence of inputs arbitrarily far in the past; thus, the current interpretation confirms the phenomenological insight that retention is *finite*.

6. Clearly, retention as explicated here does not relate to past stages of the temporal object via some other current mental act, such as a memory or an image or an echo. There is no space for any such additional acts in the model. In that sense, retention is *direct*.

7. A strength of the dynamical interpretation of retention is that it does not underwrite exactly that aspect of retention which Husserl found most difficult to deal with and concerning which he was the least persuasive. In other words, if retention is the current location of the system, considered insofar as that current location reflects the past inputs, there is no clear way to make sense of retention as somehow perceptual in any substantial sense, and especially not perceptual with regard to something that no longer exists. The verdict must surely be that Husserl was *mistaken* in attempting to describe retention on a perceptual model. His own sense that "perception of the past" was tantamount to "wooden iron" turns out to have been accurate. From the perspective afforded by the dynamical interpretation, we can see both why Husserl felt compelled to talk that way—he had no better model of how something could "directly intend" the past—and yet encountered such difficulty in explaining just what this mysterious form of perception is.

What about protention? Recall that on this account, protention is identified with the system's occupying its current location, since it is that location (in combination with the system's intrinsic dynamics, and keeping external influences fixed) which determines the future behavior of the system. As with retention, this account makes sense of protention as current, intending future stages as future to some degree, as a continuous "manifold," as finite, and direct. Again, however, it demurs on Husserl's interpretation of protention as perceptual in character. Again, this is surely a *strength* of the account, since it removes precisely that aspect of protention which was most mysterious. That is, when we interpret Husserlian phenomenology in the light of dynamical models of cognitive processes, we can see what is going on in such a way that we can make sense of protention as intending a possible future, but without doing so on a perceptual model, which does away with the need to wonder how a protention can intend what might never even take place.

Do these dynamical interpretations reveal what retention and protention actually are, or do they really show there is (after all) no such thing? This is a judgment call; which way we should go depends on the extent to which the properties Husserl ascribed to retention and protention are exhibited by the corresponding features of the dynamical models. My own opinion is that there is such a strong match that the right answer is that cognitive science is indeed giving an alternative account of the very same theoretical postulates. However, this judgment requires rejecting one significant aspect of Husserl's interpretation of time consciousness, namely his idea that time consciousness requires, in some sense, the direct *perception* of the past and future. Rather, we can now understand better what retention and protention actually are, and can see how they can *intend* the past and future without perceiving them. Since this was the most problematic aspect of Husserl's account, this demonstrates how cognitive science can not only flesh out phenomenology, but actually improve it.

5. RELATED WORK

While drafting this essay I was not aware of other attempts to provide a scientifically grounded naturalization of the Husserlian theory of time consciousness. As it turns out, however, Francisco Varela was at the same time engaged in the same project, and he has developed an account that is similar in broad outline (Varela, this volume). One fundamental point of agreement is that phenomenology and the sciences of the mind/brain do not conflict or even compete with each other; rather, each is essential, and each constrains and enriches the other. Another is that the phenomenology of time consciousness can only be naturalized in the context of a dynamical understanding of cognition. In other words, cognition in general and time consciousness in particular are essentially dynamical phenomena. At a slightly more detailed level, both accounts agree that the threefold structure of time-consciousness (retention, primal impression, and protention) can be interpreted in terms of properties of dynamical systems; that retention is a matter of how the current state of the system depends on the trajectory of the system through a sequence of instabilities (bifurcations); and that protention is a matter of how the current state in a particular dynamical landscape shapes future behavior.

Beyond these points of agreement lie many contrasts. Some are due to the greater complexity in Varela's treatment of both the phenomenology of time consciousness and the neural mechanisms of cognition and do not amount to genuine differences. There is, however, one substantial point of methodological difference. Whereas Varela's work relates Husserl's phenomenology to (cognitive) neuroscience, in the treatment here it is related to cognitive science. Varela describes his general research project as "neurophenomenology"; in a similar vein, these ideas might be regarded as belonging to "cognophenomenology."[13]

What is the difference? Originally, cognitive science was conceived as the science of cognition conducted at a relatively high level, at which the underlying implementation details (whether neuroscientific, silicon-digital, or whatever) are safely ignored. Recent years have witnessed the emergence of another discipline lying between cognitive science and neuroscience, called—not surprisingly—"cognitive neuroscience." This is the study of cognition in terms of the known details of the actual neural mechanisms underpinning cognition in humans and other animals. Meanwhile, the term "cognitive science" has expanded in meaning to include cognitive neuroscience.

The development of cognitive neuroscience does not entail that "good old-fashioned" (high-level, implementation-independent) cognitive science is defunct or obsolete. The proliferation of "special sciences" over and above atomic physics indicates that scientifically describable order in nature occurs at many levels. Some aspects of cognition find their best explanations in cognitive neuroscientific terms, while others are best explained at higher levels. In the current case, we have two parallel dynamical explanations of time consciousness, one focusing relatively more on an abstract account of the kind of dynamical mechanisms that might underpin time consciousness in any cognitive system, the other focusing relatively more on the actual mechanisms of time consciousness in brains as they are in fact found here on planet Earth.

The former kind of account buys a kind of generality through its simplicity, and its distance from the neuroscientific details. The same account may well carry over to time consciousness in an intelligence implemented in optical circuits or plasma flows. Much of Varela's neurophenomenological story, by contrast, is applicable only to intelligences implemented in neural circuitry capable of sustaining integration through phase locking. An additional advantage of taking a "cognophenomenological" approach is that, by simplifying and abstracting, it becomes easier to build an actual mathematical model, in the specific sense of a specified set of variables evolving in accordance with a set of equations which can be written down and simulated on computer (e.g., Lexin). Varela offers us a complex sketch of the neural mechanisms involved in time consciousness, but (in this volume's essay at least) stops short of specifying a full mathematical model.

Both these forays into the naturalization of the phenomenology of time consciousness are just initial explorations. Only sustained investigation will clarify the benefits, and relative merits, of each approach. In the meantime, a certain measure of comfort can be drawn from the fact that two independent efforts have arrived at the same basic conclusion: that time consciousness—an essential element of a fully aware "self"—is a fundamentally dynamical phenomenon.

CHAPTER NINE

The Specious Present: A Neurophenomenology of Time Consciousness

FRANCISCO J. VARELA

1. SETTING THE STAGE

My purpose in this essay is to propose an explicitly naturalized account of the experience of present nowness based on two complementary approaches: phenomenological analysis and cognitive neuroscience. What I mean by naturalization, and the role cognitive neuroscience plays, will become clear as this essay unfolds.[1]

It would be foolish to claim that one can tackle this topic and expect to be satisfied. The experience of temporality addresses head-on the fundamental fact that we exist within a transparent web of time. The elucidation of the experience of temporality occupies a central place in the history of thought altogether, and most certainly in the phenomenological tradition. Many have referred to St. Augustine's *Confessions* (specifically book 11) on the paradoxes of a past-containing nowness (*distentio animi*), or more recently to the pragmatic psychology of William James as found in the famous *Principles of Psychology*, where the apt expression "specious present," which gives this article its title, first appeared in print.[2]

Edmund Husserl considered temporality a foundational axis of his phenomenological research: all other forms of mental activity depend on temporality, but it depends on none of them. He worked on these questions until his death (see Appendix A). Unlike his illustrious predecessors, who never pursued their descriptions far enough, Husserl *did* manage to make real progress in the formulation of the basic structures of intimate time.

I will start by drawing from the phenomenological account developed by Husserl, fully aware that I am stepping right into a complex debate within phenomenological research. My decision to start with his texts on time has nothing to do with proving or disproving a point about Husserl's thought. I prefer to take my cues from Husserl's *style* as an eternal beginner, always willing to start anew; this is the hallmark of phenomenology itself (but it has not always been the case in practice). What interests me most are the unrealized implications of his writings: only in their turns and jumps do we get a glimpse of how his descriptions contains a dynamical bent, which is key, I will argue, for a naturalization project. This dynamical bent will provide the bridge from pure phenomenological inquiry to recent results in neural dynamics, to include the discovery of large-scale neural assemblies.

I take quite literally the importance of seeing experience as a *firsthand* description. As Bernard Besnier has recently remarked, we should not "neglect this essential guiding principle of phenomenology, namely, that it advances by description . . . of an experience that one must therefore *re-do*."[3] It is on the basis of such active involvement in the phenomenology of time that I introduce some plausible *additions* and interpretations to the current discussion.

In brief, I approach temporality by following a general research direction I have called *neurophenomenology*, in which lived experience and its natural biological basis are linked by mutual constraints provided by their respective descriptions (Varela 1996). This also means that I will not hesitate when necessary to mix both modes of discourse as if they were partner in a dance, as if they were one, for that is what a naturalized account of phenomena means, and only in action can we see it happening. Given the importance of the topic of the experience of temporality, let it be clear that I consider this an acid test of the entire neurophenomenological enterprise.

2. LIVED TIME IS NOT PHYSICAL-COMPUTATIONAL

Like any other true phenomenological study, the exploration of time entails the gesture of reduction and the identification of descriptive invariants. Phenomenological reduction is a topic that I cannot expand upon here, for justifying reduction philosophically does not serve my purpose. The actual practice of phenomenological reduction does.[4] For the reader unfamiliar with this terminology let us at least say that reduction starts by a disciplined suspension of one's habitual attitudes, a bracketing of what we seem to know. This bracketing provides the opportunity for a fresh look at phenomena, in this case temporality as it appears directly to our flesh-and-bone selves.

As soon as we enter a study with this kind of authentic philosophical attitude, it becomes apparent that the familiar account of time inherited from our modern Western cultural background is inadequate. In fact, we have inherited from classical physics a notion of time as an arrow, as a constant stream based on sequences of finite or infinitesimal elements, which are even reversible for a large part of physics. This view of time is entirely homologous to that developed by the modern theory of computation. As a refined expression of general computation, the writing head of a Turing machine inscribes symbols one by one in an infinite string, giving rise to time as a sequence-stream, exactly as in classical mechanics.

As computational views entered into cognitive science in the form of the computationalist (or cognitivist) viewpoint, computational time was unquestioningly used in the cognitive study of time. Some research continues to base experimental studies on an "internal timer" that gives rise to duration at various scales. A (hypothetical) clock emits pulses that translate into behavior; judgments on duration depend on pulse counting and are reflected on memory and decision (Church and Broadbent 1990). This strict adherence to a computational scheme will be, in fact, one of the research frameworks that will be *abandoned* as a result of the neurophenomenological examination proposed here. But I will return to this conclusion later, after presenting my main argument.

Even under a cursory reduction, already provided by the reflections of Augustine and James, time in *experience* is quite different from time as measured by a clock. To start with, time in experience presents itself not only as linear but also as having a complex *texture* (evidence that we are not dealing with a "knife-edge" present),[5] a texture that dominates our existence to an important degree. In a first approximation this texture can be described as follows: There is always a center, the now moment with a focused intentional content (say, this room with my computer in front of me on which the letters I am typing are highlighted). This center is bounded by a horizon or fringe that is already past (I still hold the beginning of the sentence I just wrote), and it projects toward an intended next moment (this writing session is still unfinished). These horizons are mobile: this very moment which was present (and hence was not merely described, but lived as such) slips toward an immediately past present. Then it plunges further out of view: I do not hold it just as immediately, and I need an added depth to keep it at hand. This texture is the raw basis of what I will be discussing in extenso below. In its basic outline, we shall refer to it as the *three-part structure of temporality*. It represents one of the most remarkable results of Husserl's research using the technique of phenomenological reduction.

Another important complementary aspect of temporality as it appears under reduction is that consciousness does not contain time as a constituted psychological category. Instead, temporal consciousness *itself* constitutes an ultimate substrate of consciousness where no further reduction can be accomplished, a "universal medium of access to whatever exists. . . . Constitutive phenomenology can well be characterized as the consistent and radical development of this privilege of consciousness into its last ramifications and consequences" (Gurwitsch 1966: xix). We find a converging conclusion in

James concerning the apparent paradox of human temporal experience: on the one hand, there is the present as a unity, an aggregate, our abode in basic consciousness, and on the other hand, this moment of consciousness is inseparable from a *flow*, a stream (chapter 9 of *Principles*). These two complementary aspects of temporal consciousness are the main axes of my presentation.

This rough preliminary analysis of time consciousness leads us, then, to distinguish three levels of temporality:

1. A first level proper to *temporal objects and events* in the world. This level is close to the ordinary notions of temporality in human experience, which grounds the notion of temporality currently used in physics and computation.
2. A second level, which is quickly derived from the first by reduction, the level of *acts of consciousness* that constitute object-events.[6] This is the "immanent" level, the level based on the "internal time" of acts of consciousness. Their structure forms the main body of the phenomenological analysis in Husserl's *Lectures*.
3. Finally (and this is the most subtle level of analysis), these first two levels are constituted from another level where no internal-external distinction is possible, and which Husserl calls the "absolute time constituting *flow of consciousness*" (p. 73).[7]

3. THE DURATION OF OBJECT-EVENTS

3.1. DURATION: THE EXPERIENCE OF VISUAL MULTISTABILITY

The correlate or intentional focus of temporal consciousness is the temporal object-event. Time never appears detached from temporal object-events; indeed, temporal object-events are what these acts of consciousness are *about*. Unlike the psychologist or the neuroscientist, the phenomenologist finds the content of the object less important than the manner of its appearance.

At various points in his research Husserl returns to the basic observation that what is proper to temporal objects is their double aspect of *duration* and *unity* (PZB, pp. 23, 113–14). Duration is correlative to the intentional direction: I am walking by *this* house, *that* bird flew from here to there. These are actual durations and refer to the object having a location in time. Unity is correlative to the individuality of the object-events in question, to the extent that they stand out as distinct wholes against the background of other events. Thus a temporal object-event is a complete act that covers a certain span *T*. However, the entire act is a continuous process in the course of which *moments of nowness are articulated*, not as a finished unity but in a succession. It is this mode of constitution of object-events, whatever their duration T and their content, that interests me here. It must be the case that consciousness of succession is derived from the structural features of the acts of consciousness. Our problem is how to characterize these structures.

In his writings Husserl is characteristically sparse with examples. In *PZB* he uses one recurrent illustration: listening to a melody (a choice most later commentators have followed as well). I think it is important to examine this issue more carefully for various reasons. First, because Husserl introduces his example, strangely enough, as an un-situated subject, in an abstract mode: he does not give us the circumstances under which the music is being listened to (alone, in a concert hall?), or the quality of the listening experience (is it a moving piece, is he familiar with it?). These circumstances are not incidental details; without these particularities the mode of access to the experience itself is lost.

We still lack a phenomenology of internal time consciousness where the reductive gestures and the textural base of the experience figure explicitly and fully. The entire phenomenology of internal time consciousness must be rewritten with the precision of a mode of access to experience that serves as support for reduction; what transpires in Husserl's writing often falls far short of such a standard.[8] In what follows I depart from custom by inviting the reader to perform specific tasks of multistable visual perception that will provide the reader and the author with explicit common ground for discussion. Multistable perceptions make good case studies: they are precise and complex enough for analysis while still providing corresponding neurocognitive correlates. Indeed, multistable visual perception phenomena are deceptively clear. See, therefore, the experiment outlined on page 271.

The instructions for this experiment turn the subject into an active agent in the constitution of meaning, as it is illustrated here in a minimal case. There is a lot more to explore in this experiment concerning the perceptual horizon used for changing perception, as well as the strategy of language (the naming of the alternative, the "aiming" at the other possibilities).[9] But let me stay with the temporal aspects of this perception. We notice, as it has been known since the gestaltists, that as we acquire proficiency in this maneuver, reversing the image can be accomplished with little effort and upon request. It is also clear that the reversal has in itself a very complex dynamic that takes on a "life" of its own (more on this later). We also notice that the gesture of reversal is accompanied by a "depth" in time, an *incompressible* duration that makes the transition perceptible as a sudden shift from one aspect to the other, and not as a progressive sequence of incremental changes.

Granted, such "Necker" phenomena are not common in ordinary life. Consider the following, more realistic example: I open a door, and as I move

> ### A Task in Visual Perception
>
> Consider the following image: 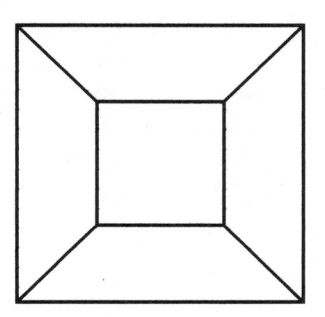
>
> Out of context, most Western subjects naturally see either a "pyramid" or a "hallway": 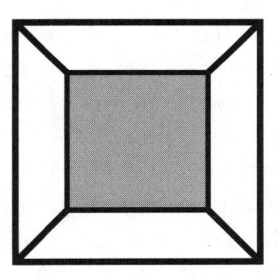 
>
> Suspend habitual interpretations and consider multiple variations together. We may infer that since the upper image depicts neither pyramid nor hallway, it is an ambiguous or multistable perception.
>
> These variations can be *practiced* by the following strategy:
>
> 1. Fix on the center of the figure.
> 2. Blink your eyes.
> 3. "Aim" at its alternative.

across the threshold I run into somebody who is standing directly in front of me. Through both body motion and visual orientation the person's face comes spontaneously into focus. I recognize a colleague and thrust out my hand for a greeting. Both examples, the multistable visual perception and the vignette just presented, are very different from physically passive object-events such as listening to music.

In the example of multistable perceptions we do not need to move our entire body. However, an important layer of motion is actively present, whether in head adjustment, frowning and blinking, and surely, in eye movements of various kinds. This is important, for little can be concluded from cases where all motion is absent. As phenomenological research itself has repeatedly emphasized, perception is based in the active interdependence of sensation and movement.[10] Several traditions in cognitive research have, as well and in their own way, identified the link between perception and action as key.[11] It is this *active* side of perception that gives temporality its roots in living itself. Within this general framework, I will concentrate more precisely on the structural basis and consequences of this sensori-motor integration for our understanding of temporality.

3.2. THE NEURODYNAMICS OF TEMPORAL APPEARANCE

My overall approach to cognition is based on situated, embodied agents. I have introduced the name *enactive* to designate this approach more precisely. It comprises two complementary aspects: (1) the ongoing coupling of the cognitive agent, a permanent coping that is fundamentally mediated by sensorimotor activities; and (2) the autonomous activities of the agent whose identity is based on emerging, endogenous configurations (or self-organizing patterns) of neuronal activity. Enaction implies that sensorimotor coupling modulates, but does not determine, an ongoing endogenous activity that it configures into meaningful world items in an unceasing flow.

I cannot expand this overall framework more extensively,[12] but it is the background of my discussion of temporality as a neurocognitive process. Enaction is naturally framed in the tools derived from dynamical systems, in stark contrast to the cognitivist tradition that finds its natural expression in syntactic information-processing models. The debate pitting embodied dynamics against the abstract computational model as the basis for cognitive science is still very much alive.[13] For some time I have argued for the first and against the second, and this choice justifies the extensive use of dynamical tools in this paper (see Appendix B).

From an enactive viewpoint, any mental act is characterized by the concurrent participation of several functionally distinct and topographically distributed regions of the brain and their sensorimotor embodiment. From the point of view of the neuroscientist, it is the complex task of relating and integrating these different components that is at the root of temporality. A central idea pursued here is that these various components require a *frame or window of simultaneity that corresponds to the duration of lived present*. In this view, the constant stream of sensory activation and motor consequence is incorporated within the framework of an endogenous dynamics (not an informational-computational one), which gives it its depth or incompressibility. This idea is not merely a theoretical abstraction: it is essential for the understanding of a vast array of evidence and experimental predictions.[14] These endogenously constituted integrative frameworks account for perceived time as discrete and nonlinear, since the nature of this discreteness is a horizon of integration rather than a string of temporal "quanta."

At this point it is important to introduce *three scales of duration* to understand the temporal horizon just introduced: (1) basic or elementary events (the "1/10" scale); (2) relaxation time for large-scale integration (the "1" scale); and (3) descriptive-narrative assessments (the "10" scale). This recursive structure of temporal scales composes a unified whole, and it only makes sense in relation to object-events. It addresses the question of how something temporally extended can show up as present but also reach far into my temporal horizon. The importance of this three-tiered recursive hierarchy will be apparent all through this essay.

The first level is already evident in the so-called fusion interval of various sensory systems: the minimum distance needed for two stimuli to be perceived as nonsimultaneous, a threshold that varies with each sensory modality.[15] These thresholds can be grounded in the intrinsic cellular rhythms of neuronal discharges, and in the temporal summation capacities of synaptic integration. These events fall within a range of 10 msec (e.g., the rhythms of bursting interneurons) to 100 msec (e.g., the duration of an EPSP/IPSP sequence in a cortical pyramidal neuron). These values are the basis for the 1/10 scale. Behaviorally, these elementary events give rise to micro-cognitive phenomena variously studied as perceptual moments, central oscillations, iconic memory, excitability cycles, and subjective time quanta. For instance, under minimum stationary conditions, reaction time or oculomotor behavior displays a multimodal distribution with a 30–40 msec distance between peaks; in average daylight, apparent motion (or "psi-phenomenon") requires 100 msecs.

This leads us naturally to the second scale, that of long-range integration. Component processes already have a short duration, on the order of 30–100 msec; how can such experimental psychological and neurobiological results be understood at the level of a fully constituted, normal cognitive operation? A long-standing tradition in neuroscience looks at the neuronal bases of cognitive acts (perception-action, memory, motivation, and the like) in terms of *cell assemblies* or, synonymously, *neuronal ensembles*. A cell assembly (CA) is a distributed subset of neurons with strong reciprocal connections.[16]

CAs comprise distributed and actively connected neuronal populations (including neocortical pyramidal neurons, but not limited to them). Because of their presumably strong interconnections, a CA can be activated or ignited from any of its smaller subsets, whether sensorimotor or internal. One of the main results of modern neuroscience is to have recognized that brain regions are indeed interconnected in a reciprocal fashion (what I like to refer to as the Law of Reciprocity). Thus, whatever the neural basis for cognitive tasks turns out to be, it necessarily engages vast and geographically separated regions of the brain. These distinct regions cannot be seen as organized in some sequential arrangement: a cognitive act emerges from the gradual convergence of various sensory modalities into associational or multimodal regions and into higher frontal areas for active decision and planning of behavioral acts. The traditional sequentialistic idea is anchored in a framework in which the computer metaphor is central, with its associated idea that information flows upstream. Here, in contrast, I emphasize a strong dominance of dynamical network properties where sequentiality is replaced by reciprocal determination and relaxation time.

The genesis and determination of CAs can be seen as having three distinct causal and temporal levels of emergence: an ontogenetic level, which organizes a given brain into circuits and subcircuits; a second, developmental-learning level consisting of sets of neurons whose frequent co-activation strengthens their synaptic efficacies; and a third level of determination, that of the CAs' constitution. The third level is the faster time scale of the experience of immediate daily coping, which manifests at the *perception-action* level, having a duration on the order of seconds.

In the language of the dynamicist, the CA must have a *relaxation time* followed by a bifurcation or phase transition, that is, a period within which it arises, flourishes, and subsides, only to begin another cycle. This holding time is bound by two simultaneous constraints: (1) it must be longer than the time of elementary events (the 1/10 scale); and (2) it must be comparable to the time it takes for a cognitive act to be completed, namely, on the order of a few seconds, the 1 scale) (Varela et al. 1981; Pöppel 1988). In brief, as we said before, the relevant brain processes for ongoing cognitive activity are distributed not only in space but also over an expanse of time that cannot be compressed beyond a certain fraction of a second, the duration of integration of elementary events.

In view of the above, I will now introduce three interlinked, but logically independent, working hypotheses:

HYPOTHESIS 1: *For every cognitive act, there is a singular, specific cell assembly that underlies its emergence and operation.*

The emergence of a cognitive act demands the coordination of many different regions allowing for different capacities: perception, memory, motivation, and so on. They must be bound together in specific groupings appropriate to the specifics of the current situation the animal is engaged in (and are thus necessarily transient), in order to constitute meaningful contents in meaningful contexts for perception and action. Notice that Hypothesis 1 is *strong* in the sense that it predicts that only *one* dominant or major CA will be present during a cognitive act.

What kind of evidence is there to postulate that every cognitive act, from perceptuo-motor behavior to human reasoning, arises from coherent activity of a subpopulation of neurons at multiple locations? And further, how are such assemblies transiently self-selected for each specific task? Since this will be a recurrent topic for the remainder of this essay, I'd like to formulate it as the second of my working hypotheses. The basic intuition that comes from this problem is that a specific CA emerges through a kind of temporal *resonance* or "glue." More specifically, the neural coherency-generating process can be understood as follows:

HYPOTHESIS 2: *A specific CA is selected through the fast, transient phase-locking of activated neurons belonging to sub-threshold, competing CAs.*

The key idea here is that ensembles arise because neural activity forms transient aggregates of *phase-locked* signals coming from multiple regions. Synchrony (via phase-locking) must *perforce* occur at a rate sufficiently high to permit the ensemble to "hold" together within the constraints of transmission times and cognitive frames of a fraction of a second. However, if at a given moment, several competing CAs are ignited, different spatiotemporal patterns will become manifest, and hence the dynamics of synchrony may be reflected in several frequency bands. The neuronal synchronization hypothesis postulates that it is the precise coincidence of the firing of the cells that brings about unity in mental-cognitive experience. If oscillatory activity promotes this conjunction mechanism, it has to be relatively fast to allow at least a few cycles before a perceptual process is completed (e.g., recognition of a face and head orientation).

Recently this view has been supported by widespread findings of oscillations and synchronies in the gamma range (30–80 Hz) in neuronal groups during perceptual tasks. The experimental evidence now includes recordings made during behavioral tasks at various levels, from various brain locations both cortical and subcortical, from animals ranging from birds to humans, and from signals spanning broadband coherence from single units, local field potentials, and surface-evoked potentials (electric and magnetic) (see Singer 1993 and Varela 1995 for a history and summary of this literature). Figure 9.1 provides a sketch to help clarify these ideas.

This notion of synchronous coupling of neuronal assemblies is of great

Activity

head motion and fixation   recognizes form

Duration

cognitive present   cognitive present   [seconds]

ca. 500 msec   ca. 500 msec

Coherence of phase

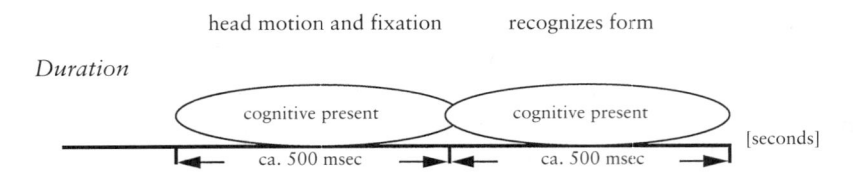

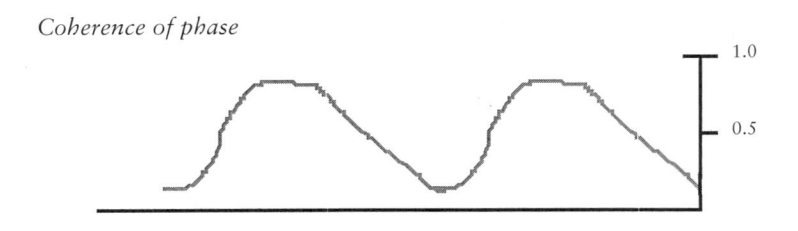

1.0

0.5

Topography of synchrony

○ = brain region   ——— = strength of synchrony

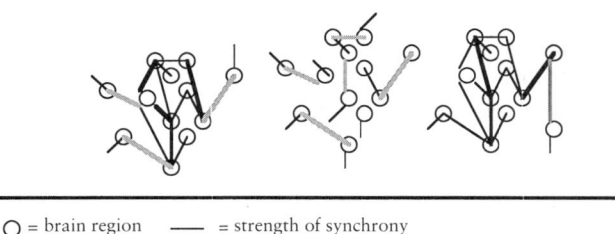

FIGURE 9.1. A diagram depicting the three main hypotheses. A cognitive activity (such as head turning) takes place within a relatively incompressible duration, a "cognitive present." The basis for this emergent behavior is the recruitment of widely distributed neuronal ensembles through increased frequently coherence in the gamma (30–80 Hz) band. Thus, the corresponding neural correlates of a cognitive act can be depicted as a synchronous neural hypergraph of brain regions undergoing bifurcations of phase transitions from one cognitive present content to another.

importance for our interpretation of temporality, and we will return to it repeatedly below (see also Appendix C). Here is the point where things get really interesting in our development of a view of cognition that is truly dynamic, one that makes use of recent advances in both nonlinear mathematics and neuroscientific observations.

Thus, we have neuronal-level constitutive events that have a duration on the 1/10 scale, forming aggregates that manifest as incompressible but complete cognitive acts on the 1 scale. This completion time is dynamically dependent on a number of dispersed assemblies and not on a fixed integration period; in other words it is the basis of the origin of duration without an external or internally ticking clock.[17] These new views about cognitive-mental functions based on a large-scale integrating brain mechanisms have been emerging slowly but with increasing plausibility.

Nowness, in this perspective, is therefore presemantic in that it does not require a rememoration (or as Husserl says, a presentification) in order to emerge. The evidence for this important conclusion comes, again, from many sources. For instance, subjects can estimate durations of up to 2–3 seconds quite precisely, but their performance decreases considerably for longer times; spontaneous speech in many languages is organized such that utterances last 2–3 seconds; short intentional movements (such as self-initiated arm motions) are embedded within windows of this same duration.

This brings to the fore the third duration, the 10 scale, proper to descriptive-narrative assessments. In fact, it is quite evident that these endogenous, dynamic horizons can be, in turn, linked together to form a broader temporal horizon. This temporal scale is inseparable from our descriptive-narrative assessments and linked to our linguistic capacities. It constitutes the "narrative center of gravity" in Dennett's metaphor (Dennett 1991), the flow of time related to personal identity (Kirby 1991). It is the continuity of the self that breaks down under intoxication or in pathologies such as schizophrenia or Korsakoff's syndrome.

I am now ready to advance the last step I need to complete this part of my analysis:

> HYPOTHESIS 3: *The integration-relaxation processes at the 1 scale are strict correlates of present-time consciousness.*

We are thus referred back to the experiential domain, and the nature of the link asserted in Hypothesis 3 is what we need to explore carefully. Distinctions between ongoing integration in moments of nowness, and how their integration gives rise to broader temporal horizons in remembrance and imagination, are at the core of the Husserlian analysis of intimate time, to which we now return.

4. THE JUST-PAST IS NOT MEMORY

Temporal objects appear to us as such only because of the correlative *acts* of consciousness that have specific modes of appearance that are at the very heart of the issue of immediate temporality. Normally we designate these modes by the terms "present," "now," "past," and "future." Beyond this cursory designation, however, reduction clearly points to the mode of "now" as having a unique or *privileged status* (*PZB*, p. 35). Two lines of analysis lead to this. First, the texture of now, which James calls specious. In effect, now is not just a mere temporal location, it has a lived quality as well: it is a space we dwell in rather than a point that an object passes by or through. Second, it is in relation to the rich structure of present nowness that all other modes of temporality take form. Both of these lines of analysis will be explored here.

To start, in spite of Husserl's own descriptions and geometric depictions, "nowness" is not a point or an object but a location, a field with a structure analogous to the *center and periphery* structuring of the visual field. Husserl himself speaks of nowness as a "temporal fringe" (*PZB*, p. 35). In other words, the very mode of appearance of nowness is in the form of extension, and to speak of a now-point obscures this fact: "Present here signifies no mere now-point but an extended objectivity which modified phenomenally has its now, its before and after" (*PZB*, p. 201). Husserl is grappling here with one of the antinomies of time: it is always changing and yet in some sense it is always the same. A temporal object-event such as my identifying the figure as a pyramid has a unity that first appears as present nowness. It then slips away when it appears anew as a hallway. The previous recognition (and its givenness) has now sunk into the past, as when an object moves from center to periphery in space. This marks the beginning of the resolution of the apparent contradiction between sameness and difference, constancy and flow, which we will elaborate more below. To do so, I must now move to another level of detail in the study of the structure of consciousness, one which is constitutional (in Husserlian jargon), insofar as it provides the temporal features of mental acts that unify them into a single *flow* of consciousness.

The key issue in this stage of my examination of temporality is the contrast between the mode of appearance of now and that of the just-passed, the act which reaches beyond the now. As Husserl points out, commenting on similar reasoning in Brentano: "We could not speak of a temporal succession of tones if . . . what is earlier would have vanished without a trace and only what is momentarily sensed would be given to our apprehension" (*PZB*, p. 397, my translation).

But how can this structure of the time perception be constituted? What is preserved is also modified. If when I see a pyramid, I could still hold unchanged the nowness of when I saw the hallway, all temporal structure would disappear. The relation of the now to the just-past is one of slippage organized by very strict principles: "New presentations each of which reproduces the contents of those preceding attach themselves to the perceptual presentation, *appending* the continuous moment of the past as it does so" (*PZB*, p. 171; my emphasis).

This phrase expresses the intuitions behind the analysis of *dynamics intrinsic to these slippages of appearance*, as developed in the following section. It is key for my search for bridges between naturalization and the texture of temporal experience.

What form does this slippage from nowness to immediate past take? Is it another emergent aggregate of the temporal horizon, similar to the one we assume (Hypothesis 3) underlies the experience of nowness? This was Brentano's postulate: the constitution of the past is re-presentation or memory presentification of what preceded. In several remarks dispersed over the years, Husserl actually gets close to a demonstration that the slippage from the now to the just-past is not the same as immediate memory retrieval or *presentification*.[18] To the appearance of the just-now one correlates two modes of understanding and examination (in other words, valid forms of donation in the phenomenological sense): (1) remembrance or evocative memory and (2) mental imagery and fantasy.

There are at least two main arguments for Husserl's observation. First, memory retrieval happens in the present, in the "now," and there is surely a nowness to the act of remembering. Thus we cannot account for the past with an act that is supposedly happening in the now. Second, when I remember having seen the hallway (as opposed to being in the embodied situation of seeing it now) the past and the successive past that receded into oblivion have an immediacy, an "evident-ness" to them. In the present I "see" what just passed; in memory I can only hold it in a representation as if through a veil. Thus memory and evocation have a mode of appearance that is qualitatively different from nowness.[19]

Let us return to the visual task and resume our examination. As I look at the pyramid at that moment of now, I experience both its near side and the entire pyramid as a durable unity (the pyramid is namable). This reveals the play between the primal impression of the near side of visual perception-action and the constituting unity that make an identifiable object-event appear. It is the manifold of retentions, as illustrated by the exercise, that makes sense of the entire event: the now is experienced in an "original" way.

> For only in primary remembrance do we see what is past; only in it is the past constituted, i.e. not in a representative but in a presentative way. . . . It is the essence of primary remembrance to bring this new and unique moment to primary, direct intuition, just as it is the essence of the perception of the now to bring the now directly to intuition. (*PZB*, p. 41)

Accordingly, Husserl makes a disciplined distinction between impressional as opposed to representational consciousness. In impression an object is originally constituted and is thus given as present (I am now looking into the page and I see the pyramid). Representation represents an object-event already given to impression (I evoke seeing the pyramid a little while ago for the first time). The Ur-impression is the proper mode of the now, or in other words, it is where the new appears; impression intends the new (I was not counting on seeing the pyramid as I looked). Briefly: impression is always presentational, while memory or evocation is re-presentational. Besnier remarks: "This is what is usually expressed by saying that retention belongs to a 'living present' (*lebenhaftig* or *lebendig*). But there is something that retention de-presents [*démomentanéise*], which one could translate by *Ent-gegenwärtigung*, but this choice might create confusions."[20]

Similar conclusions can be drawn from neurocognitive evidence. For a long time cognitive psychology has distinguished between evocative memory as implied above and other forms of immediate retention, such as short-term, working, or iconic memory. I am taking these as correlates of the just-past. Interestingly, the chronometric studies of brain correlates of memory draw a clear distinction between impressional perceptual events and perceptual events requiring the mobilization of memory capacities. For instance, comparing rote versus elaborate mnemonic recollection of items yields a substantial (200–400 msec) shift in the corresponding ERPs (event-related potentials; see, e.g., Rugg 1995). More recently, brain imaging methods have begun to establish that quite different structures are mobilized during active presentational tasks according to whether these presentations are memories (episodic, operational) or products of the imagination. All these presentational tasks mobilize a whole new set of capacities that add to the flow of time but are obviously not required for it.

5. THE DYNAMICS OF RETENTION

5.1. THE FIGURES OF TIME: RETENTION AS PRESENT

Husserl introduces the terms *retention* and *protention* to designate the dynamics of impression. Retention is the attribute of a mental act which retains phases of the same perceptual act in a way that is distinguishable from the experience of the present (but which is not a re-presentation, as we just saw). The key feature of retention that is its direct contact with earlier impressions making perception at any given instant contain aspects that show up as temporally extended. As we discussed, under reduction, duration has a speciousness, it creates the space within which mental acts display their

The Specious Present 281

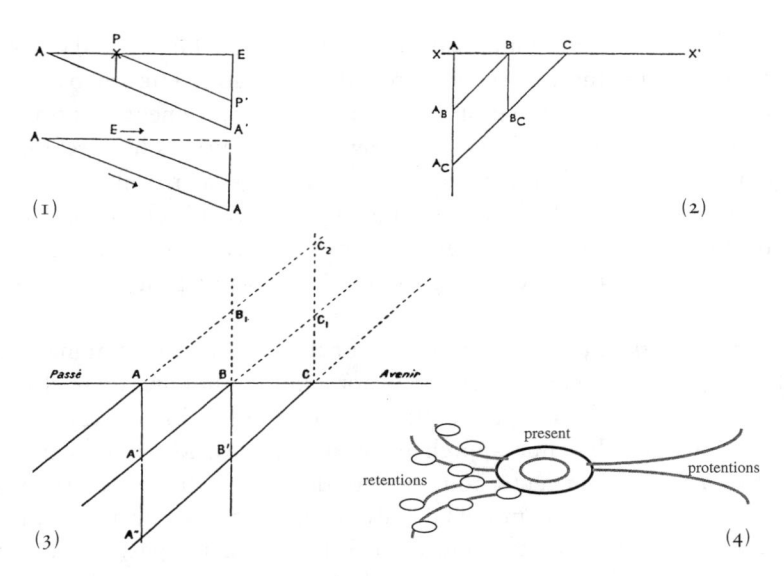

FIGURE 9.2. The "figures of time," as introduced by Husserl. (1) The diagram chosen by Stein and published in *Lessons* (PZB, p. 28); (2) one of several variants kept by Husserl after 1905 (PZB, p. 230); (3) the rendition by Merleau-Ponty (in Merleau-Ponty 1945: 477), which prolongs the lines into retentional time, as Husserl himself suggested (cf. PZB, p. 331); and (4) my own rendering of Merleau-Ponty's later critique of this diagram (Merleau-Ponty 1945: 479).

temporality. Similarly (but not symmetrically) another aspect contains future threads or *protentions*. This is the three-part structure that transforms an intentional content into a temporal extension. Figure 9.2 reproduces a sketch, one of the "figures of time" taken from the 1905 lectures, a geometrical depiction of the three-part structure of temporality. The now and the degrees of pastness are what Husserl refers to as *Ablaufsmodi*, slippages or elapsing modes, and which are depicted in reference to a source-point, whence the discreteness in this diagram. The use of lines and points is unfortunate, since it distracts from Husserl's remarkable insight; one might guess this is an echo of his training as a mathematician. The fate of these figures of time has been curious. Since they are easily grasped, they have been used extensively as summaries of Husserl's position. Yet these "figures of time" hardly do justice to the scope of his explorations; at best they illustrate an earlier and static view.[21] The appeal of the diagrams came through in Maurice Merleau-Ponty's *Phenomenology of Perception* (1945: 477) where the author comments approvingly on these depictions. However, Merleau-Ponty was well aware of the shortcoming as he added next to the diagram: "Time is not a line but a network of intentionalities." Further on, he wrote:

"The emergence of a present now does not *provoke* a piling behind of a past, and a pulling of the future. Present now *is* the slippage of a future to the present, and the just-past to the past: it is in one single movement that time sets in motion in its entirety" (p. 479). However, many writers have referred to this and several other diagrams in Husserl's writings uncritically.

In brief then: "Primal impression intends the new and actual phase of the temporal objects-events, and presents it as the privileged now. Retention presents just elapsed phases and presents them as just past in various degrees" (Brough 1989: 274).

Retention is then a specific intentional act intending the slipping object constituting it as just past. Retention is not a kind of holding on to the now by its edge; it is an active presentation of an absence that arises from the modifications and dynamic apprehension of the now. Metaphorically it is more like moving from center to periphery than the aftereffect of an image, which is like the present modified only in intensity. But in the temporal realm, it is a curious structure indeed: it is present-living past. Or, as Husserl quipped in a handwritten marginal scribbling on his working notes: "But 'perceived past' doesn't that sound like a 'wooden iron'? [*hölzernes Eisen*]" (*PZB*, p. 415).[22]

5.2. RETENTION AS DYNAMICAL TRAJECTORIES

It is indeed a wooden iron, unless we take a dynamical view of how the origin of the now can be formulated on the basis of our three working hypotheses. The use of "append" and "slippage" in the phenomenological description already evokes this view, but it needs to be developed fully. Besides the fact that there is substantial experimental support for these hypotheses, it is essential to recognize that we are dealing with a bona fide candidate for the synthesis of a temporal space where cognitive events unfold. The discussion that follows requires at least some understanding of the dynamics of nonlinear phenomena as applied to cognitive events. The reader not familiar with basic notions can turn to Appendix B for a sketch.

Let us be more specific. Large-scale phenomena seen in the nervous system as long-range integration via synchronization of ensembles cannot be dissociated from intrinsic cellular properties of constituent neurons. Intracellular recordings studied in in vivo and in vitro slices of various brain regions, of both vertebrates and invertebrates, have shown the pervasive presence of intrinsic, slow rhythms mediated by specific ionic gating mechanisms (Llinás 1988; Nuñez, Amzica, and Steriade 1993). In other words, what we have are large arrays of neural groups that because of their intrinsic cellular properties, qualify as complex nonlinear oscillators (see Appendix C for an explicit account of fast-slow nonlinear oscillators).

Why is this of importance here? Because it leads us directly to an explicit view of the particular *kinds* of self-organization underlying the emergence of neural assemblies. These arise from collections of a particular class of coupled nonlinear oscillators, a very active field of research (see, for example, Mirollo and Strogartz 1990, Winfree 1980, Glass and Mackey 1988, and Kelso 1995). These dynamical processes, in turn, illuminate the mechanisms whereby neuronal assemblies "now" possess a three-part structure.

The key points to keep in mind for our discussion are the following. First, self-organization arises from a *component* level, which in our case has already been identified as the 1/10 scale of duration, and reappears here as single or groups of nonlinear oscillators. Second, we need to consider how these oscillators enter into synchrony (see Hypothesis 2) as detected by a *collective* indicator or variable, in our case relative phase. Third, we need to explain how such a collective variable manifests itself at a global level as a cognitive *act*, which in our case corresponds to the emergence of a percept in multistability. This global level is not an abstract computation, but an embodied behavior subject to initial conditions (e.g., what I "aimed" at, the preceding percept, etc.) and nonspecific parameters (such as changes in viewing conditions and attentional modulation). The local-global interdependence is therefore quite explicit: the emerging behavior cannot be understood independently of the elementary components; the components attain relevance through their relation with their global correlate.

What have we gained? Very simply that in these kinds of emergent processes there can be a natural account for the apparent discrepancy between what emerges and the presence of the past. In effect, the fact that an assembly of coupled oscillators attains a transient synchrony and that it takes a certain time to do so is the explicit correlate of the origin of nowness (Hypothesis 3). As the model (and the data) shows, the synchronization is dynamically *unstable* and will constantly and successively give rise to new assemblies. We may refer to these continuous jumps as the *trajectories* of the system. Each emergence bifurcates from the previous ones given its initial and boundary conditions. Thus each emergence is still present in its successor.

To bring this idea closer to firsthand experience let us perform a second task in visual perception (p. 284). After following the instructions, observers have reported that the positions at which the perceptual switches occur do not coincide but are lengthened in either direction of the image sequence.

When this is analyzed from a dynamical point of view, the following account is plausible: The extremes of the series ("female," "male") are closer

> ### A Second Task in Visual Perception
>
> Consider the series of images below (Fisher 1967):
>
> Practice the following task:
>
> 1. Starting with the male image on the upper left, slide your eyes sequentially over the figures until you reach the female image at the bottom right.
> 2. At some point, the perception of a male face will have switched to one of a female body. Mark the point at which this has happened.
> 3. Starting at the opposite end, repeat the process in reverse. Mark the point at which your perception switches.

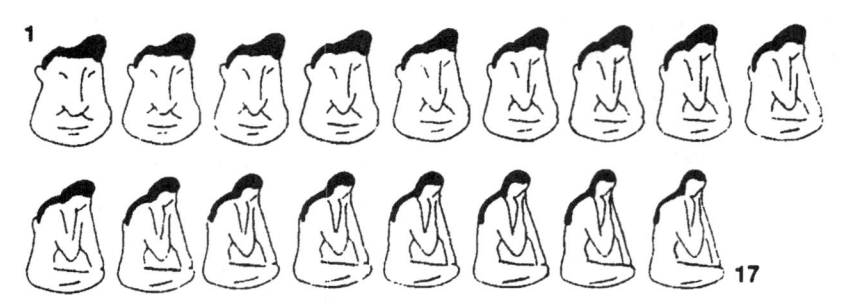

to a stable attractor basin corresponding to a single percept. When the ambiguity has increased sufficiently (when the observer has moved to a position sufficiently advanced in the series), we pass through a bifurcation or phase transition and the emergence of a new percept becomes possible. Note, however, the system tends to stay close to the fixed point of origin, as if this point had an active residue (hysteresis, in technical jargon) for the trajectory, an appended remnant (to use Husserl's term). The order parameters constrain the trajectories, the initial percepts hover around the stable percepts, but these trajectories may wander to different positions in phase space.

This behavior embodies the important role of order parameters in dynamical accounts. Order parameters can be described under two main aspects:

1. The current state of the oscillators and their coupling, or initial conditions; and
2. The boundary conditions that shape the action at the global level: the contextual setting of the task performed, and the independent modula-

tions arising from the contextual setting where the action occurs (namely, new stimuli or endogenous changes in motivation).

This second visual task makes it is clear that we are not dealing with an abstract or purely syntactic description. Order parameters are defined by their embodiment and are unique to each case. The trajectories of this dynamic, then, enfold both the current arising and its sources of origin in one synthetic whole as they appear phenomenally. A wooden iron indeed.

5.3. THE DYNAMICS OF MULTISTABILITY

The kinds of specific dynamics we have brought to bear on the understanding of retention and the just-past are not simple. Arrays of coupled oscillators are particularly interesting because they do not in general behave according to the classical notion of stability derived from a mechanical picture of the world. Stability here means that initial and boundary conditions lead to trajectories concentrated in a small region of phase space wherein the system remains, a point attractor or a limit cycle. In contrast, biological systems demonstrate *in*stability as the basis of *normal* functioning rather than a disturbance than needs to be compensated for, as would be the case in a mechanical system.

Let us return once again to our experiential ground of visual multistability. As we saw in the example of Fisher's figures, multistability is the result of properties that are *generic* to coupled oscillators and their phase relations. In other words, their mode of appearance is an invariant under certain conditions with reporting subjects. This is further clarified by recent experiments performed to study the dynamics of multistability in visual perception. As shown in Figure 9.3, J. Scott Kelso and colleagues (1994) presented observers with *variant perspectives* of the classical Necker cube, a close relative of our first visual task. By asking the observer to push a button when the perceptual reversal occurs, one obtains a time series of reversal which obeys a stochastic distribution (a gamma function with a mean at around one second). Kelso and colleagues, however, requested observers to perform the same task of time measurement while noting separately the time series as a function of perspective, which is thus used as an order parameter.

The interesting observation is that, again, at the extremes of the images (the "hexagon" mode, and the "square" mode), the distribution of reversal intervals is considerably flattened. The subject is more likely to have sporadic figure reversal, or to be "fixed" on one mode for a longer duration. At these extremes subjects report getting "blocked" by an interpretation. As before, one can think of these results as the way the coordination of a wide ar-

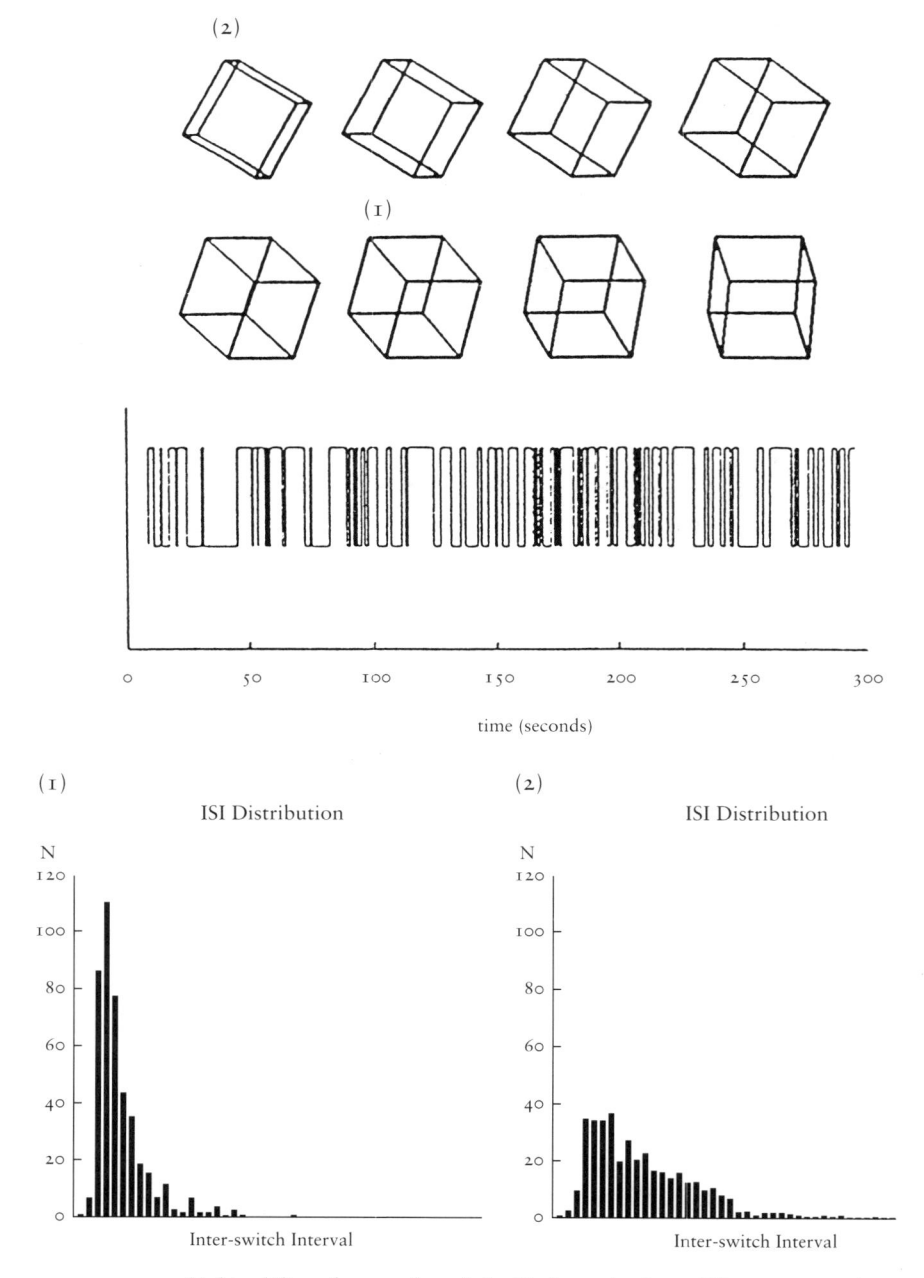

FIGURE 9.3. Multistability of perception of the Necker cube from different perspectives, used here as an order parameter. When the cube is reversed from projection (1), the time intervals between spontaneous inversion are shown in the lower diagram, with an upward trace each time a reversal is perceived. This interswitch reversal time series has a probabilistic distribution shown below, a distribution that is considerably spread when the viewing projection is changed to (2). In this latter case the switch is more difficult, and the observer is "struck" with one interpretation for longer periods of time. (Kelso et al. 1994: 219–21)

ray of oscillators appears via a common variable of phase. By introducing perspective variants, the location in phase space is accordingly modified, and new dynamical modes appear, in this case revealing a saddle instability (Figure 9.4, p. 293).

That this dynamical interpretation is actually linked to neuronal ensembles as we have been assuming here is shown by recent experiments (Leopold and Logothetis 1996). A monkey was rigorously trained to voluntarily "aim" at reversing a set of ambiguous figures (binocular rivalry, a visual task known to be similar to Necker cube or Fisher figure reversal), and then to indicate the moment at which this reversal appeared for his perception. At the same time, the firings of individual neurons were recorded from a number of its visual cortical areas. The authors report that in motion-sensitive area MT, a percentage of neurons correlate with reversal and can be modulated by the perceptual requirements of the tasks; this percentage is diminished in primary regions V1/V2. This kind of evidence strongly supports the notion that multistability arises through the large-scale collaborations among neurons at many different places in the visual cortex and elsewhere in the brain, a concrete example of an emerging CA for a specific task which has perceptual and phenomenal correlates.

Elsewhere in this volume, Tim van Gelder also discusses the three-part structure of time from a dynamical cognitive science viewpoint. It is quite reassuring that we have independently reached converging conclusions concerning the key role of dynamical interpretation in a research program of naturalized phenomenology, and more particularly concerning the re-understanding of the three-part structure of time. However, our views differ in some significant aspects, which are worth underlining here for the reader.

In his discussion van Gelder grounds his analysis on "Lexin," a connectionist network developed by Philip Anderson and Robert Port for auditory pattern recognition. As in a large class of connectionist work, Lexin changes its connection according to a training period, following which a sound input triggers a dynamical trajectory that approaches an attractor, a unique location in state space. Lexin's architecture has its roots in work of the early 1980s, which made popular the standard view of neural networks as dissipating dynamical processes governed by point attractors and limit cycles or, as they are usually called, attractor neural networks (ANNs; Amitt 1991).

In contrast, in more recent, biologically oriented dynamical studies, the generic role of instabilities has been stressed, a needed expansion of results in neural networks and connectionism. ANNs have played a role in our understanding of biological circuits and, more important, in the development of artificial intelligence. In the hands of the engineer, motion and perceptual devices that mimic some living behavior have provided impressive performances (see Arbib 1995 for a recent overview). Lexin in particular is meant to retrieve a learned set of auditory patterns. However, only with a dynamical description that incorporates *in*stability as having a role can we satisfactorily account for enactive cognition such as the three-part structure of time. In this class of dynamical systems, the geometry of phase space needs to be characterized by an infinity of unstable regions, and the system flows between them spontaneously even in the absence of external driving forces. There are no attractor regions in phase space, but rather ongoing sequences of transient visits in a complex pattern of motion, modulated only by external coupling.

Auditory perception, particularly in mammals, is so rapid (some mammals can make individual sound discriminations in the order of 2–3 msecs on the 1/10 scale) that it is far from clear how a slowly converging ANN could be a good model. More important, any model based on point attractors will surely lack the intrinsic interest of endogenous instabilities proper to brain dynamics. This is, again, one of the reasons we stay close to biologically inspired, coupled, nonlinear oscillations and frequency binding as a source of dynamical correlates proper to complete cognitive acts.

Van Gelder's analysis and mine coincide, however, on the intuition of the pertinence of dynamical views for the illumination of retention. Unlike him I have my reasons (discussed in section 7) for seeing protention as quite asymmetrical from retention, and as not having, as retention does, a constrained path in phase space.

6. THE DYNAMICS OF FLOW

6.1 THE GENETIC ANALYSIS OF TEMPORALITY

I need to turn now to the final step in my analysis, a step that is taken on far less trodden ground than the intentionality of object-events and retentional dynamics, two "classical" topics in phenomenology since the time of Husserl. Because the discussion so far has been concentrated on a particular kind of intentional act, retentional dynamics still belongs to the type of constitutional analysis referred to as "static," the classic level at which most commentators of Husserl's time analysis remain. It is called static because it is intentionally directed to object-events and to what appears (either as being an external process or as having immanent duration, such as the completion of a movement). In other words, so far we have considered the more accessible levels of temporality, the appearance of object-events and the acts of consciousness that constitute them.

Husserl brings to the fore a third and final level of analysis that has been less explored by later work. This is "the absolute time-constituting flow of consciousness" (*PZB*, p. 73). In the context of the present use of dynamical ideas it is interesting that Husserl's choice to refer to this level of study as the "flow" is suggestive: "It is absolute subjectivity and has the absolute properties of something to be denoted metaphorically as 'flow' [*Fluß*] as a point of actuality, primal source-point, that from which springs the 'now,' and so on" (*PZB*, §36, p. 368).

The idea of flow opens up to two less "classical" issues that I will dwell on here: (1) the *genetic constitutional* analysis of time, just introduced above as the flow of absolute time, and (2) its close relative, the *affective* dimension (see section 7). Husserl established the distinction between static and constitutional analyses of time during the years 1917–23. These topics are notoriously more difficult to explore, not only because they are grounded in Husserl's later work (see Appendix A), but also because they touch on subtle areas, which is what makes them more attractive. Accordingly, the reader is asked to consider what I propose in the remainder of this text as a *sketch* of future work more than anything else.[23]

Return to the first visual task (it is important that you actually do this). Choose one of the percepts, "aim" at changing it to the other one, then return to the one you chose first. The result is clearly two distinct experiences that are similar in content. The link joining them demonstrates the basic fact that there is an underlying temporalization that is relatively independent of the particular content of the views. As Husserl concisely remarks: "Every experience is 'consciousness' [*Bewußtsein*] and consciousness is always consciousness-of. . . . Every experience is itself experienced [*selbst erlebt*] and to that extent also intended [*bewußt*]. *This* being intended [*Bewußt-sein*] is consciousness of the experience [*Erlebnis*]" (*PZB*, p. 291).

The link is a *reflection*, which is not always present but may always be put into action, for it accompanies all my acts. This reflection is temporal, since experiences *are* (immanent) object-events with duration: they appear already slipping into the past and gradually disappear into the fringes of time. It is against this background of the flow of experiencing that the duration of object-events and the experience of temporality is constituted. This underlying flow raises then a new apparent paradox: it can be detached from the temporal object-events but at the same time it appears inseparable from them, since without object-events there is no flow.

The nature of this immanence is taken up again by Husserl in the following (remarkable) passage which summarizes his previous analysis: "I may express the situation thus: What is perceived, what manifests [*selbstgegeben ist*] as an individual object, is always given in unity [*Einheit*] with an absolutely non-manifest domain [*nicht gegeben Mannigfaltigkeit*]" (*PZB*, p. 284; translation slightly modified).

Proper immanent temporality is that of lived experiences themselves.

Here we reach what might rightly be perceived as the second aporia of temporality: the coexistence of permanence and change. Consciousness is a constant background against which distinct temporal acts and events appear. Around 1911 Husserl introduced the term "double intentionality" (*PZB*, pp. 80, 379) for this articulation, since there is not only a retention (of the object event) but also a *retention of retention* (a reflective awareness of that experience). These two sides of intentionality work together and are inseparably interwoven into the unitary flow of consciousness. Consciousness could not exist apart from the acts it intends or experiences, but it remains distinct from them, a pregnant unity of appearance and nonappearance.

We may now ask what avenues of access or exploration are available to study the immanent flow? As discussed before, one main source is the *reflexive* act, the becoming-aware of experience as temporal. This is quite immediate, and the most convincing argument to establish that flow is an essential phenomenon. However, although accessible, immediate reflection is a task made difficult by the simple fact that to provide description we need to keep up with the shiftiness of changing experience. As we have said, shifts take mere fractions of a second, and even diligent observation makes it hard to provide useful distinctions.[24]

The second royal avenue of access to the flow is remembrance, if we understand that such presentification must be done in a "pure" manner, with a view to its nature and not its specific content. I can very clearly relive the last visual percept in the task. But this evocation is complete only when it pulls with it the embodied context in which that image arose (my posture, the car passing in the background, the concurrent fragments of ideation as I was doing the task). In other words, although an evocation intends an object which it brings to presence in a specific mode (see section 4), it does so as a field: the intended object is a center, but it is also a periphery full of the context of the embodied experience. This fringe, although not intended, is, nevertheless, brought to life by remembrance: "In order to examine properly (in its 'genetic' constitution) the temporality of immanent experience, it is necessary to direct one's reflexive focus during an experience of *Erinnerung* on the experiences that are re-produced by themselves. This is difficult" (Besnier 1993: 347).

Indeed it is, but at least it is feasible enough so that we can concur that there is such a thing as the bringing into life the fringes of a memory. Where one could have found an isolated item sought by remembrance, we find, without specifically looking for it, the appended relived threads of the experience itself. Or if I may speak more figuratively: in remembering an intended object, it comes out bristling with retention threads of the original experience. Stated positively: what makes remembrance have such a retentional fringe must be *the manner in which these very retentions were constituted*.

In our attempt to naturalize acts of retention, we attempted to solve the "wooden-iron" nature of the past-always-present (see section 5). Further examination of the mode of appearance of immanent temporality confronts us again with a new apparent paradox, not unlike that of the wooden iron. The process of slippage itself (that is, de-presentation, *Entgegenwärtigung*, *démomentanéisation*) has the marks of being an active or even self-generated process. Can there be a process that is a cause of itself? In this case the paradox takes the more classical form of a *regressum ad infinitum*. Is there an angle to illuminate this second apparent contradiction?

6.2. THE GEOMETRY OF NONLINEAR FLOWS

An answer to these questions has already been sketched in passing, and it now needs to be unfolded more fully. The neurodynamics of time we have been pursuing is essentially based on nonlinear coupled oscillators. As we saw, this class of dynamical systems finds its wealth of behavior in the fact that constitutional instabilities are the norm and not a nuisance to be avoided. The case of multistability makes this quite evident experientially: the percepts flip from one to another (depending on order parameters; see Figure 9.3) by the *very nature* of the geometry of the phase space and the trajectories.

This is a widespread characterization applicable not only to this study case. Complex, nonlinear, and chaotic systems in general provide a self-movement that does not depend (within a range of parameters) on where the systems are. In other words, whether the content of my visual percept is a man or a woman or a pyramid or a hallway, the intrinsic or immanent motion is *generically* the same. If the specific place in phase space is a correlate of the intentional content of an object-event, the system never dwells on it, but approaches, touches, and slips away in perpetual, self-propelled motion. Cognitively, this corresponds to the observation that in brain and behavior there is never a stopping or dwelling cognitive state, but only permanent change punctuated by transient aggregates underlying a momentary act (at the 1 scale of duration; Hypotheses 1–3 above). Formally, this is expressed by the pervasive presence of stable/unstable regions, so that any slight change in initial and boundary conditions makes the system move to a nearby stable/unstable region.

This notion has been and is still explored by dynamicists under various guises. In the specific case of multistability of the Necker cube (see section 5.2), we assume the coordination of a wide array of oscillators via a common variable: phase. By introducing perspectival variants, the dynami-

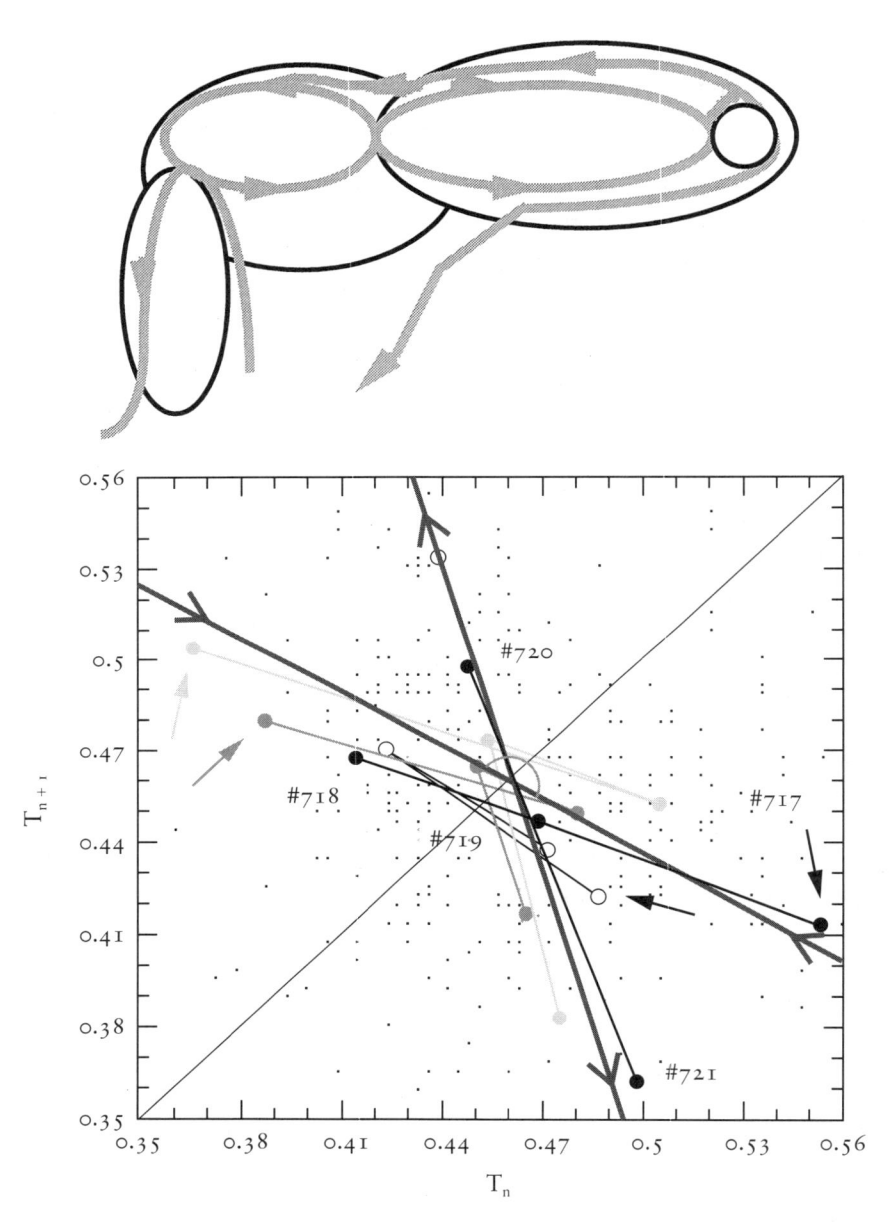

FIGURE 9.4. *Top*, a highly schematic diagram of the current view that a complex, chaotic dynamic should be regarded as having a geometry in phase space where multiple instabilities are found locally (gray lines). A system's trajectory shifts (in black lines) constantly from one local instability to another, in an unceasing flow, under the modulation of boundary conditions and initial conditions. *Bottom*, experimental evidence for local saddle instabilities in the time series from the cortex of an implanted epileptic patient. The peaks of the local discharge in the temporo-occipital cortex are followed in their return map or Poincaré section

cal landscape is accordingly shifted to new dynamical modes appearing in the phase portrait. This saddle instability implies that at that point there is mixture of tendencies to be attracted into that position or to move away from it, and the slightest perturbation will push and pull the trajectories along.

More generally, many apparently "noisy" natural events (such as the transition times between Necker cube reversals) have recently yielded unexpected deterministic patterns under nonlinear dynamical analysis beyond the reach of traditional linear analysis (see Appendix B). The main feature of these methods is to give us a view of dynamics based not only on trajectories but also in the more encompassing frame of *the geometry of the phase space landscape* (see Figure 9.4).

This is not merely a formal description. These geometrical patterns can be studied even in a highly localized grouping of neuronal activity such as that measured by an electrode on the surface of the brain (a few cubic millimeters of cortex). For instance, in a local temporal epileptic focus, which seems like a noisy oscillation, we have found evidence for such multiple determinism and instabilities (Le Van Quyen et al. 1997a, 1997b). While his brain was being recorded, a subject was asked to perform simple visual and auditory discriminations. We then studied the interval between these discharges much like the time series from Necker cube reversals. This provided consistent indications these temporal dynamics cannot be characterized as a simple "noisy" periodicity. Even a simple first-return map (the value of one time interval plotted against the value of the following one) reveals detailed changing geometrical patterns depending on experimental conditions, but shows consistent evidence of a saddle instability with stable and unstable manifolds. This observation suggests that the phase space landscape can be characterized by *departures from strict periodicity in a nonrandom manner* (Auerbach et al. 1987). In particular, the different perceptual discriminations "pull" this local dynamic toward a distinctly unstable periodicity. Although the positions of the periodic points are shifted between the behavioral conditions studied, the related slopes of approach to the instabilities appear as invariant features of the dynamics for all our experimental conditions (Figure 9.4).

T_n plotted against T_{n+1} indicated by the background points. We may investigate further the structure of the trajectories by examining individual short sequences of points around the diagonal. A typical example of recurrent observed trajectories is shown, displaying the sequence of points numbered 351–55. From points 351–54, the state of the system is drawn toward the diagonal (that is, a strictly periodic regime), but after point 354, it diverges away from the diagonal with a different linear slope. The slopes for the approach and divergence are regular and thus an invariant of the system's dynamical geometry. (Le Van Quyen et al. 1997b)

In this case study we stress the relevance of local nonlinear properties in brain events that are often lost when global, averaging methods (like spectra, or even dimension estimators) are applied. There is a surprising degree of detail displayed by the trajectories or orbits of the epileptic dynamics as modulated by perceptual tasks. A paradigmatic manifestation of this is the fact that a chaotic trajectory typically includes an *infinite* number of unstable periodic orbits. These orbits are unstable in the sense that the smallest deviation moves the state away from the periodic orbit. Thus, a nonlinear deterministic (or chaotic) system never remains long in any of these unstable motions but continually switches from one periodic motion to another, thereby giving an appearance of randomness (Artuso, Aurell, and Cvitanovic 1990).

6.3. DOUBLE INTENTIONALITY

We have gained, then, a new intuition to resolve the riddle of this second wooden iron of the mixture of passivity and activity, of invariance and change, of double intentionality. "The self-appearance [*Selbsterscheinung*] of the flow does not require a second flow, rather it constitutes itself as phenomenon itself [*in 'sich' selbst*]" (*PZB*, p. 381). Merleau-Ponty refers to this paradoxical aspect of reductive description by saying that to exist, time "must be already in me [*fuse en moi*]," and as it arises as a flow of retentions, it also self-manifests (*Selbsterscheinung*).[25] In fact: "I have not chosen to be born, but once born, time must already permeate me [*le temps fuse a travers moi*], whatever I do."[26]

Husserl develops his descriptive account of this paradoxical appearance of "double intentionality" in the notions of transverse and longitudinal intentionality (*Quer-* and *Längsintentionalität*).[27] The first is retentional dynamics—the static constitution. Longitudinal intentionality, in contrast, is the genetic constitution of the temporalization (self-manifestation) of experiences themselves. These are necessarily interdependent, but their mode of dependence and the root of their difference is what is difficult to express: "For all of that we have no names" (*PZB*, p. 371).

Longitudinal intentionality acts by an integration from within the now itself; it provides an unchanging substrate from which the flow emerges. As Besnier remarks (1993: 350), there is a great temptation to transpose the analysis of perceptual intentionality by envisaging this as a "pure" substrate or *Ur-hyle*. I do not have to enter into the thorny technical debate this mode of analysis has produced since Husserl (Depraz 1996b). My contribution is to bring to the fore the intuition derived from the generic nonlinear flows, following our hypotheses. Self-manifestation appears in our analysis as self-motion or generic instability, which is not a mere artifact of description, but an invariant formal description for self-organization. Thus its relevance to temporality is appropriate. The flow, in the neurodynamical sense, is precisely a wooden iron that exists as flow only to the extent that it is constituted in individual trajectories (not an inert geometrical magma), which, as ongoing, self-propelled, and transient, visit various regions in phase space (corresponding to an intended object-event, an appearance).

The inseparability of these two intentionalities here is not only descriptively accurate but part of the intrinsic logic of complex nonlinear dynamics. It would be inconsistent to qualify the self-motion as a "deeper layer" of the dynamical process and to describe these trajectories as mere appearance (Gallagher 1979). Mutatis mutandis, it seems illusory to isolate a "deeper" layer of genetic constitution where experience would be constituted from an absolute time, and only then made manifest in conscious intentionality. What is deep is the *link* between self-motion (immanence) and trajectories (appearance).

Enough has been said about the immanent or absolute flow to suggest its importance and perspicacity. It is surely a topic that needs exploration, and it is the natural ground for bridges to other varieties of experience and to other traditions concerned with human consciousness.[28] Indeed, this level of analysis touches more than any other on the ground of self, pure ego, or basic consciousness. Brough (1989: 288) summarizes:

> And thanks to the infinite horizon opened up by the absolute flow, we can be sure that we can go right on changing and accumulating a past, while still remaining the same. There is a fissure, then, in consciousness. Thanks to this fissure, any one of my acts, asserting itself and holding sway for a more or less brief time . . . is able to "slide off" without taking my whole self with it. If my internal awareness were glued without gap to my fleeting experiences, the passage of time would rip my ego to shreds.

But we must now leave these considerations and turn to our last topic, which is the closely related issue of the appearance of this self-motion from the perspective of affect.

7. PROTENTION: TRANSPARENCY AND EMOTIONAL TONE

7.1. IMMANENT TEMPORALITY AND AFFECT

Return again to the first task and reexamine more closely the nature of the switching as it happens. One essential component of the experience is that the shift is sudden and accompanied by a (more or less distinct) emotional change when the visual perception shifts abruptly. Thus the mode of slippage of the now into the just-past, the retentional trajectory, not only appears as the presence of the past in a way that is distinct from representational memory but also gives us the cue that the *emotional tone* is an integral part of the phenomenon. What is the role of emotion or affect in the self-movement of the flow? And what is its role, if any, in protention, the anticipation of what is to come?

In Husserl's published texts, protention is not extensively analyzed, and I have the impression that he implicitly assumes a certain symmetry with retention, as if the same structure of invariance for the past could be flipped toward the future. But protention intends the new prior to an impression and thus can only be a prefiguration. Husserl speaks of "empty constitution" (*PZB*, p. 52), but it is not expectation or anticipation in the sense of containing a representation of what the next now will bear. To see why this is so, one need only to apply the same arguments that were used for distinguishing retention from evocative memory. Indeed, protention has a mode of openness: "The only thing definite is that without exception something will come"; in listening to a melody (his example) there is a predictable side to protention since it intends further phrases of the music (*PZB*, pp. 84, 106). These and similar remarks from the *PZB* seem to have provided the basis for the symmetrical view of the three-part structure of time, and as indicated in the oft-used figure of time discussed earlier (see Figure 9.2).

This analysis can be substantially enriched. There are at least two main sources of evidence to conclude that protention is generically *not* symmetrical to retention. The first is, precisely, that the new is always suffused with affect and an emotional tone that accompanies the flow. In fact, protention is not a kind of expectation that we can understand as "predictable," but an openness that is capable of self-movement, indeterminate but about to manifest. In this quality it provides the natural link into affection or, more aptly, with some form of self-affectedness (see below). The second is that retention has the structure of a continuum, but protention can only be a bounded domain, since we cannot anticipate that which is yet to come. While the threads of retention set the stage for protention, protention cannot modify the retentional threads retroactively.[29]

Time and affect were never systematically treated by Husserl. A substantial part of his notes is still unpublished or is accessible only from secondary sources (see Appendix A). However, a deepening of his later analysis of time makes it possible to trace some important fragments of a view of affection as initiating the drive of the lived flow itself, as Natalie Depraz (1994) points out (linking it to the parallel question of the constitution of space, p. 70). My propositions in the remainder of this section are not entirely at variance with Husserl's later research and thus in continuity with what has been already developed here. As he says: "How is the self [*Ich*] the center of this life it experiences? How is it experienced? It is affected by that which consciousness is conscious of [*Bewußtsein bewußt ist*], it follows affect, or still it is attracted, held, taken in by that which affects it" (MS C III/1).

Husserl's notes contain recurrent references to this primordial aspect of the child's early life where one finds an "instinctive" intentionality (*Triebsintentionalität*). As Depraz remarks: "Affect is thus this non-form which makes constitution of the self by itself, that affects it in the strict sense of structure, that of constitutive temporality.... Affect is there before being there for me in full consciousness: I am affected before knowing that I am affected. It is in that sense that affect can be said to be primordial" (1994, pp. 73, 75).

How is this pertinent to the three-part structure of time? Husserl remarks that during a melody the sounds affect me differently as it creates its retentional threads, an attentional tendency (*eine Tendenz der Zuwendung*). Or we may say it provides a *disposition* that is marked by gradual intensities. This temporalizing effect puts protention at the center stage: "It is not only the impressions from hyle that affect, but already 'hyletical anticipations of data'" (Depraz, 1994, p. 79).

Philosophy did not abandoned time as a royal road to the study of affect after Husserl. Heidegger and Merleau-Ponty both have a great deal to say about the topic. The main innovation in their philosophies is the treatment of time as self-affectedness. As Merleau-Ponty says: "Le temps est 'affection de soi par soi,'" and notes that the expression derives from Kant as modified by Heidegger in his *Kantbuch*.[30] Self-affectedness becomes a key insight into the nature of consciousness: "Even the most precise consciousness of which we are capable is affected by itself or given to itself. The very word consciousness has no meaning apart from this duality" (Merleau-Ponty 1962: 488).

With Emmanuel Levinas (1988), a further sphere of affection, hetero-affection, is brought to the fore: alterity is the primary clue for time's constitution. We are affected not only by representations and immanent affection ("affection de soi par soi"), but by alterity as inseparable from the sphere of an ego-self. In this move the very distinction between auto- and hetero- ceases to be relevant, since in all cases it all is brought down to the same manifestation: it is a question of "something other," the experience of an alterity, a difference in the identity of the present, whether by the inevitable slippages to retention, or by the anticipations in protention.

But these philosophical discussions are not central for us here in all their detail (Depraz 1998). We are seeking to move beyond the apparent paradox between an original impression in time that would be colored by affection, or conversely, the primacy of affection that would underlie temporality. We seek a nondual synthesis whereby affect is constitutive of the self and at the same time contains a radical openness or unexpectedness concerning its occurring.

7.2. TRANSPARENCY AS DISPOSITION FOR ACTION

In order to move further we need to have a concrete base for our examination, much as the visual tasks provided the basis for the static analysis. Many alternatives exist, but I have chosen to explore the role of affection in the constitution of time in the context of active involvement in the world and through the dispositional quality of affect and its gradations. From the point of view of enactive cognitive neuroscience, coping plays a central role (see section 2.2). It should be kept in mind, however, that focusing on this region of affect is by no means exhaustive.

From the perspective of phenomenology, we are referring to the phenomenology of *immediate coping*, which finds its first expression in the study of affectedness (*Befindlichkeit*) as one of the constitutive moments of Dasein that Heidegger described in *Sein und Zeit* (division 1, especially chapter 3). As it is well known, Heidegger studied most particularly our involvement with the surrounding network of tools and equipment, in order to discover what kind of beings humans must be that such encounters are possible.

I am not going to repeat the key points of the constitution of Dasein, but examine more closely the observation that *both* equipment *and* the user show up as transparent in immediate coping. It is at this point that Heidegger's analysis is much more helpful than Husserl's. Heidegger calls this stance *Umsicht*, a kind of seeing that is not reflective or thematized in any way.[31] How is the user's transparency shifted to a conscious mode that brings nowness to the fore? As he says:

> Being in the world, according to our interpretation hitherto, amounts to a nonthematic, absorbed transparency [*unthematische, umsichtige Aufgehen*], in activities that are constitutive for the network of equipment at hand. Our concerns [*Besorgen*] appear the way they do because of the familiarity with the world. In this familiarity Dasein can lose itself in what it encounters within the world. . . . How can the worldliness of this familiarity be illuminated [*erleuchten*]? How can entities at hand be thrust to the fore by the possible breaks in the network of equipment being handled in which transparency "operates" [*die Umsicht sich "bewegt"*]?[32]

Heidegger points to how intentionality, in its traditional sense, can interrupt a flow of action. If, as I write this, I hit a control key, and I am shown a message saying "Do you really wish to erase this text?" I find myself deliberately avoiding pressing the "OK" button, in an emotional tone of hope and tension. The awareness of the possibility of making a fatal mistake breaks into the present, triggering a (more or less marked) shattering of transparency. In parallel, a new stance in ongoing coping emerges: I deliberately click on the "Cancel" button.

Thus Dasein is absorbed in the world, but malfunctions and breakdowns of various kinds can shift it back out of it. I use the word *transparency* here to indicate precisely this unreflective absorption. Transparency is but a description of that which can be broken in the flow of experience, hence its interest for our purposes here.[33]

When the carpenter hammers, the hammering action and its objects are transparent. Transparency is what it is because it is eventually broken, as when the hammer slips and lands on the finger. Such a breakdown brings the transparent equipment into view, and a new set of action-assessments begins. This standard Heideggerian vignette can be extended to all embodied actions, that is, actions in a fluid context where there is always a mixture of immediate coping and concurrent secondary activities of language and mental life. It is a disposition for involvement. Transparency is therefore always in the context of a series of ongoing action-behaviors. It is related neither to content nor to efficacy (cf. my faulty typing, or the carpenter's mistake). However, transparency is not obligatory, since an attentional tendency can produce its disappearance at various degrees of abruptness. In contrast to a breakdown in equipment, attention can also be *endogenously* motivated in a reflective gesture motivated by a critical review and design. The carpenter may stop to evaluate the quality of the wood before using it, or his relationship with his employer. Notice, in passing, that the gesture of carrying out phenomenological reduction is a loss of transparency by self-motivation. This can be seen as the form reduction takes in the Heideggerian lineage of phenomenology.

Transparency, then, is a readiness or dispositional tendency for action in a larger field of specific *ontological readiness*, that is, an expectation about the way things in general will turn out. For this very same reason transparency has everything to do with habitus, the recurrence of our lives. Learning a skill is a prototypical example of transparency acquisition. However, the temporal constitution of transparency is not limited to individual actions: it extends to the full span of human life, into history altogether. In the Heideggerian jargon, transparency and its dispositions extend into historicality.[34]

The loss of transparency is never distant from a dispositional affective tone, as we have seen. But we can now see that different degrees of breakdown in transparency and the multiple manners in which it happens opens a panoply of affective tonalities: fear, jealousy, anger, anxiety, self-assurance, and so on. Accordingly, the word "emotion" is used here in its specific sense: the *tonality of the affect that accompanies a shift in transparency*. Affect, on the other hand, is a broader dispositional orientation which will precondition the emotional tone that may appear. This is quite essential.

As I write now, I have a dispositional attitude that engages me in a anticipation of writing and shaping my thoughts into sentences. As I write this word now, the disposition is colored by an emotional charge, a moderate resentment for not finding the proper expression. But that emotional tone appears against a background of the exalted mood of a productive day devoted to finishing this text.

More explicitly, I want to distinguish three scales for affect, homologous (but not isomorphic) to the three scales of temporality used above. The first scale is *emotion*: the awareness of a tonal shift that is constitutive of the living present. The second is *affect*, a dispositional trend proper to a coherent sequence of embodied actions. The third is *mood*, which exists at the scale of narrative description over time.

7.3. EMOTIONAL TONE AS DYNAMICAL LANDSCAPING

Examined from this perspective, emotions cannot be separated from recurrent constitution, since the transparency of recurrent constitution is not deliberate, but part of unthematic coping. The embarrassment that accompanies a loud belch in a French restaurant is entirely transparent to a European; it seems the "natural" reaction to have. This unreflective appearance of embarrassment as affective tone is only perceived when, say, on a trip to the Middle East. The entire social phenomenon of eating and manners is cultural-historical, but this does not contradict the visible signs of bodily emotions that go with embarrassment—redness of the face, change of breathing, and tightness of facial muscles.

For the ethologist, affect and emotions are a relatively small repertoire of immediate dispositions that are physiologically inscribed in a species inheritance, although in most mammals, habit and sustained learning may shape this inheritance significantly.[35] Neurobiologically, affect and emotions can be associated with a relatively stable set of neural correlates (see, e.g., Damasio 1994). Studies of human emotional responses, even in relatively artificial situations, reveal the extent to which the biological endowment of "basic" emotional patterns is enfolded in the historical individual. Individual habits, historicity and language, constitute the palette of human emotional life incorporating the biological makeup to an end that is individually unique.[36]

Homologously, we can say that the experience of time has a biological base in elementary events (1/10 scale), but this basis is enfolded with other structures of temporalization into the specious present that is our theme. To deny that such a deeply rooted biological basis plays a role in the appearance of temporality is fruitless. Similarly, I am not reducing emotions to their empirical correlate in a reductionistic move. As considered here, emotions are an integral part of an ontological readiness. However, this should not obscure the fact that such an ontological constitution has roots in basic emotional dispositions inseparable from our history as living beings and from minute events in brain physiology.

When I induce a break in transparency following reduction when looking at the visual image of our task, I bring to it an emotional disposition which prefigures the change in my perception. In saying "I expect to see," I also provide exogenous, additional order parameters that alter the geometry of the phase space. This process of "sculpting" a dynamical landscape is intrinsically distinct from the trajectories that move within it, but form an inseparable unity.

In fact, it has been known for some time that the intention to carry out a movement is coupled with a change in emotional tone that varies in degree. As a global variable, induced changes in the dynamical landscape can be detected. One well-known case is the readiness potential. For a finger movement, a large, slow electrical potential can be measured over the entire scalp which *precedes* by a fraction of a second the beginning of the motion, and the subject's ability to report that he has decided to initiate the movement.[37] This is not a correlate of intention (as it is sometimes described), but it does give a concrete idea of how vast a reconfiguration of a dynamical landscape is involved at the origin of a fully constituted now (moving the fingers). In the results of Leopold and Logothetis (1996) already mentioned, a similar reconfiguration of the disposition for firing of individual neuronal responses is visible some 100–200 msecs *before* the monkey indicates that it has switched to a new percept.

Why is all this relevant here? Because it is direct evidence of the manner in which emotional tonality plays into the dynamics of flow. Emotional tonality is, by its very action, a major boundary and initial condition for neurodynamics. This diffuse, constitutive effect is in accord with the mechanism of action via neurotransmitters that have been known for some time to condition the modes of response at the neuronal level, as the body of knowledge of psycho pharmacological agents attests.

This sketch of the nature of protentions via affective tonality has taken us to a third and final step of what seems to be, in formal terms, a genetic constitution of temporality. I have introduced a final dynamical principle that applies to neurocognitive dynamics as well. I refer to the mutual bootstrap between the phase space landscape and the specific trajectories that move in it, and the fact that the very same trajectories provide the very conditions for an embodied coupling, since through their coupling they shape their dynamical landscape. Metaphorically, the walker and the path are intrinsically linked.

This bootstrap principle seems to be present in a variety of natural systems and has recently been referred to as "operating at the edge of chaos," or "self-organized criticality." For example, this idea provides a renewed view of evolution, since it provides an answer to the old nature (genetic expression) versus nurture (environmental coupling conditions) dilemma. In this synthetic view (cf. Kauffman 1993) the relation between natural forms (the *Baupläne* of organisms) and the selection process in their ecological embeddedness is not one of contradiction but precisely a mutual imbrication when seen through dynamical glasses.[38] This built-in shiftiness, enfolding trajectories and geometry, gives a natural system a possibility of always staying close to regions in phase space that have multiple resources (e.g., at least two in bistable visual perception).

To conclude: The generic structure of double intentionality proposed by Husserl is, I submit, of this class of dynamical bootstrap, and the analysis of affect and emotional tonality can give the evidence for it.

8. NOWNESS: NEW FIGURES OF TIME

To gather all the threads that have been developed here, and to echo the tradition started by Husserl himself, I would like to propose a new figure of time, the *fourfold structure of nowness* (Figure 9.5).

This is not so bold or far-fetched. By now it seems clear that the point-by-point, linear time depiction at the base of the figures of time is insufficient. One major improvement is to introduce, then, not lines but flows, *dynamical* trends. A second major improvement is to take into explicit account what surfaced in the later work of Husserl himself, the central role of double intentionality, static constitution, and genetic constitution. This final ingredient gives to the homologies between the constitution of space and time the preeminence they deserve. I do this by taking the *center/fringe* structure as the very core of a new figure of time. Once these three basic aspects have been incorporated a new representation falls into place quite naturally.

1. To start, let us consider the role of dynamics that has been central in our development, and hence move away from the use of discrete points in a line as in the traditional diagram. Not only do we leave behind a line geometrical figure, but we must introduce an *asymmetry* into it. Concerning static constitution, we have discussed two different kinds of dynamical ideas:

I
Static Constitution—Transversal Intentionality—Three-part Structure of Temporality

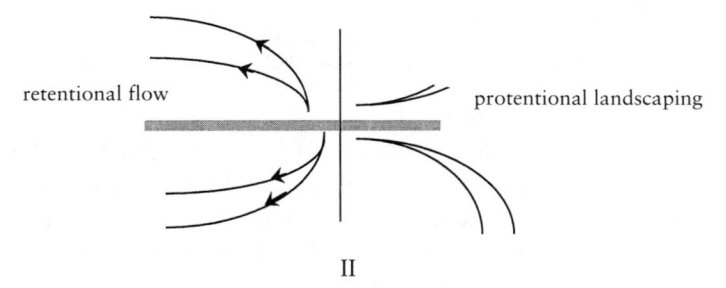

retentional flow — protentional landscaping

II
Genetic Constitution—Longitudinal Intentionality—The Flow

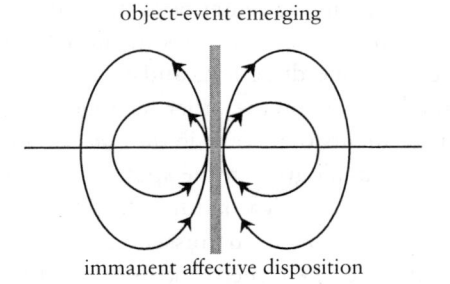

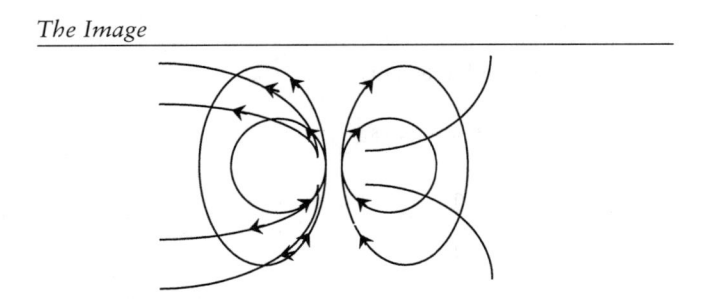

object-event emerging

immanent affective disposition

The Image

FIGURE 9.5. The fourfold structure of nowness. The new figures of time resulting from the neurophenomenological analysis presented here. For an explanation, see section 8.

retentional trajectories (the past) and order parameters for anticipation (the future). In the new diagram the dynamical quality is displayed by arrows on lines, as is traditional in mathematics, but I distinguish trajectories from anticipatory landscaping by dropping the arrowheads in Figure 9.5 (I). Concerning genetic constitution, we also have two distinct ideas: the immanent temporalization of self-motion and the directed intentionality relative to a position in phase space.

	Dynamical Ingredients	
trajectories of retention	order parameters of anticipation	*Static* *past/future*
transient attractors intentional content	self-motion of generic instabilities	*Genetic* *change/permanence*

2. Next we consider the spatial ingredients, that is, the role of a center-periphery configuration at the core of temporalization. Concerning static constitution, we of course recover the retention-protention axis. Again, these are asymmetrical, since retentions recede into past, but the protentional fringe is an open horizon of anticipation. Thus we find again that the center-periphery structure does not provide all the necessary distinctions, since the fringes as they move away from the center become qualitatively different. As to genetic constitution, the fringe reappears in the preconscious, affective substrate (permanence) on one direction, and in the conscious, embodied ego, aware of emotional change on the other (change).

We thus arrive at ingredients that come in *two sets of four*. The center/periphery configurations are analogous in the spatial and dynamical schemes, since they underscore the paradoxical nature of past in the present, and of change within permanence that puzzled Husserl (and many others) throughout his work. These pairs are, then, the wooden irons of the figure of time. I

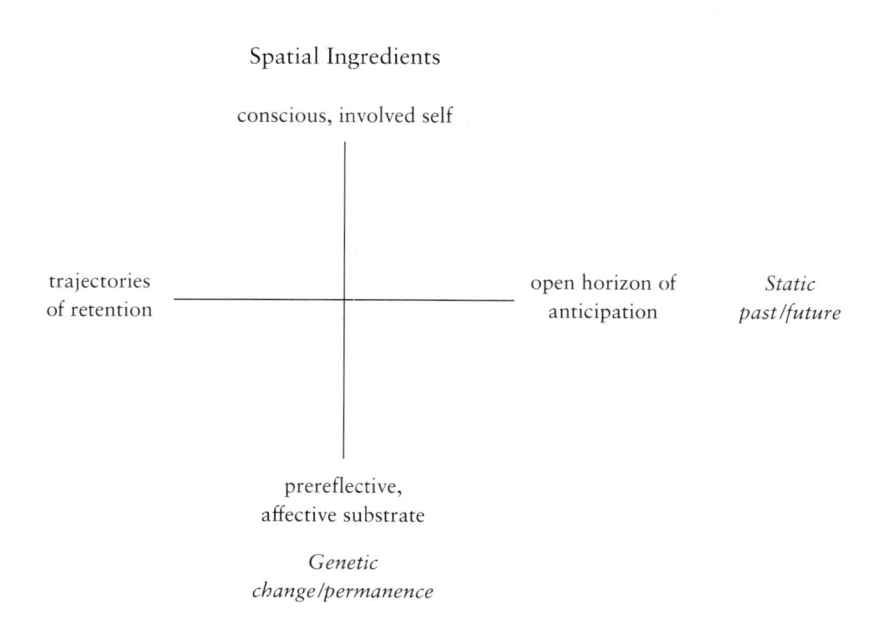

Spatial Ingredients

conscious, involved self

trajectories of retention | open horizon of anticipation | *Static* *past/future*

prereflective, affective substrate

Genetic *change/permanence*

do not presume to have resolved these paradoxes, only to have given new insights into them.

Fundamentally, there is an added insight that comes from the fact that the component ingredients have a *generic* link between them, an internal interdependence that has been explored throughout this essay. In other words, not only are the new figures of time graphical combinations of items, but they display links that are not only descriptive but effective. Phenomenologically, I have stressed the full *interdependence* of both intentionalities, the inseparability of the static and genetic analyses, and the mutual determination of instinctive and cognitive constitution of self. In parallel, the trajectories and the landscape of their phase space are a unity in a complex nonlinear system. Correspondingly, we have examined the many aspects under which determinism, the trajectories, regions in phase space, and adaptive geometrical landscapes are complementary. I consider these mutual interdependencies and their role in the constitution of temporality the most immediate insight that naturalization can provide.

With these elements in position, time, as I said, falls naturally into place. Figure 9.5 places these ingredients in relation to one another, both in terms of the role of dynamics and space, and with regard to the circular causality for the longitudinal but not for the transversal intentionality. Since the order parameters for protention do not influence retroactively the system's history, we arrive at an asymmetrical fourfold figure of time.[39]

We are now in a position to stand back and reconsider our analysis of temporality. Has neurophenomenology passed the acid test? Let us return to the neurophenomenological research program: the circulation between the external and the experiential. In Varela 1996 the neurophenomenological working hypothesis was stated as follows:

> *Phenomenological accounts of the structure of experience and their counterparts in cognitive science relate to each through reciprocal constraints.*

On the one hand, we are concerned with a process of external emergence with well-defined neurobiological attributes, on the other, with a phenomenological description that stays close to our lived experience. The nature of the sought-after circulation one seeks is no less than that of *mutual constraints* of both accounts, including both the potential bridges and contradictions between them. What is the specific nature of the passages between these two accounts in the case at hand? What have we learned in the specific case of immediate temporality?

One thing is clear: the specific nature of the mutual constraints is far from a simple empirical correspondence or a categorical isomorphism. Three ingredients have turned out to play an equally important role: (1) the neurobiological basis, (2) the formal descriptive tools mostly derived from nonlinear dynamics, and (3) the nature of lived temporal experience studied under reduction. What needs to be examined carefully is the way in which these three ingredients are *braided together in a constitutive manner*. What we find is much more than a juxtaposition of items. It is an *active* link, where effects of constraint and modification can circulate effectively, modifying both partners in a fruitful and complementary way.

A proper analysis of this relationship cannot be done here, and I must close by referring the reader elsewhere for its presentation (Varela 1997). But at least it could be said that the neurophenomenological research program that emerges from this study reaches beyond hopeful declaration to reveal an open road for exploration.

Appendix A: Edmund Husserl's Research on Time Consciousness

Husserl's work on time has been a difficult and active field of investigation for phenomenologists for half a century. Since the avatars of the publication of Husserl's work and the secondary literature is of some significance for us here, I will briefly outline it. The saga unfolds in four acts.

1. THE *LESSONS* (1928)

In 1917 Husserl requested his assistant Edith Stein to prepare his work on temporality for publication. He provided her with texts from his 1905 seminar, but included some from as far back as 1901 and as late as 1917. Stein carried out her task during 1917, putting aside more than half of the sources and rewriting the texts extensively, including titles and section headings. She turned her work in to Husserl in September 1917. But, as was often the case with Husserl's requests to his assistants, he then decided to introduce new, significant revisions and postponed its publication. It was only in 1927, after discussing with Heidegger the imminent publication of *Sein und Zeit*, that Husserl apparently went back to Stein's work and sent it to Heidegger. Although Heidegger added only minor changes, the book appeared under his nominal editorship with the title *Vorlesungen über das innere Zeitbewußtsein aus dem Jahre 1905* (Halle 1928). (The English translation by J. S. Churchill, *The Phenomenology of Internal Time Consciousness*, appeared in 1966.)[40] For modern presentations based on this early material, see McInerney 1991 and Miller 1984.

2. THE BOEHM EDITION (1966)

The *Lessons* can adequately be described as Stein's very personal rendition of the original texts. Shortly after publication, several readers realized to what extent her influence had marked the only available material of Husserl's research. The French translator of the *Lessons*, Henri Dussort, had already raised this issue but could not complete a new edition closer to the originals. In 1966 Rudolf Boehm produced a critical edition, available as Husserliana X, *Zur Phänomenologie des inneren Zeitbewußtseins (1893–1917)* (abbreviated here as *PZB*). Boehm's work provided the public with a wider selection of writings, a careful chronological analysis of the 1928 edition, and several unpublished appendices and sketches. Rudolf Bernet has also provided some comments on the complementary texts to the Boehm edition (Bernet 1985), with some new indications about dating and an introduction. This edition provided for the first time a broader reading of his work, and it has been the main source of virtually all published work since. It is also the main source for this essay, along with the excellent introduction by Brough (1989) who has provided an English translation of *PZB* (1991).

3. THE BERNAU (1917–18) MANUSCRIPTS

Interestingly, Husserl wrote a significant amount of work during 1917–18 in Bernau. Sometime later (in 1928?), he turned his notes over to his assistant Eugen Fink for revision. Revising these *Bernauermanuskripten* was to take Fink from 1928 to 1935, a long adventure indeed and one that can now be traced in detail thanks to the meticulous work of Richard Bruzina (1993, 1994) and that constitutes in itself a rich source of information about the research carried out jointly by Husserl and Fink. Fink kept these manuscripts until his death, and they were not available at Louvain for Boehm's edition in 1966. A critical edition is not yet available (but is in preparation by Iso Kern and Dieter Lohmar); some texts also appear in *Analysen zur passiven Synthesis (1918–26)*, Husserliana 11, 1996.[41]

4. THE "SPÄTEN ZEITMANUSKRIPTEN" (1929–35)

The so-called late manuscripts are the last addition to the saga we are tracing. They compose Husserl's last corpus of work on time, space, and intersubjectivity. They are as yet entirely unpublished, and correspond to Group C of the manuscripts in the Husserl Archives in Louvain. Nevertheless, important extracts have been made available in books by Gerhard Brand (1955) and Klaus Held (1966). For this essay, I have relied on Depraz's (1994) discussion on temporality and affect in these late manuscripts.

Appendix B: Nonlinear Dynamics and Neurocognitive Events

This is a bird's-eye view of nonlinear dynamics from the point of view of its relevance to neuroscience. It is intended only as a complement for the readers of this essay for whom this is an entirely foreign domain of modern science. For further reading, Port and van Gelder 1995 and Arbib 1995 are excellent recent sources; Ott, Sauer, and Yorke 1993 is more technical but of great value.

1. BRIEF HISTORY

Probably the first to see the difficulties and possibilities of chaotic dynamical systems was Henri Poincaré at the turn of the twentieth century when he was working on the problem of three celestial bodies under mutual gravitational attraction. Poincaré analyzed orbits resulting from sets of initial points and found very complicated behavior, which we would call chaotic today. Despite theoretical work on chaotic dynamical systems by several mathematicians (like Stephen Smale or the Soviet school of A. N. Kolmogorov in the 1950s), it took a long time for researchers in other fields to recognize the "reality" of chaos in nature and to turn their attention to the strange behavior of some nonlinear dynamical systems. Milestones on the way toward public recognition of the new phenomena in the 1970s were articles by Edward Lorenz (on the weather), Robert May (on animal populations), and Otto Rössler (on chemical reactions), who announced their findings with titles like "Simple Mathematical Models with Very Complicated Dynamics." The accent was on the fact that these systems produced irregular and almost random-*looking* behavior though they are perfectly deterministic. Immediately the question arose, how many of the observed irregularities found in nature were due to such nonlinear motion, that is, follow deterministic rules despite their random appearance.

2. BASIC CONCEPTS

Nonlinear dynamics (= chaos theory = complexity theory) is a recent field of research rooted in mathematics but also in physics and other natural sciences. Rigorous definitions have only evolved with the discovery of more and more surprising dynamical effects.

It is perhaps best to start with the notion of a *state or phase space*: a domain of variables or measurements which attempts to completely specify a given process. Such specification is a law or a *rule*, and these systems are therefore *deterministic*, in contrast to random dynamical systems. The sequence of subsequent states evolving according to the dynamical rule describes a *trajectory* in state space. In the case of continuous time, the system is defined as a *flow*,

$$f: S \to S \quad z_{t+1} = f(z_t)$$

Smooth flows can be differentiated with respect to time, giving a differential equation

$$\frac{dz}{dt} = F(z, t)$$

The number of first-order differential equations, or equivalently the *dimension* of the state space, is referred to as the order of the system, sometime as its number of degrees of freedom. A *periodic* point is one to which the flow or map returns after some time. Experimentalists are mostly interested in dynamical systems defined on a state space $\Re^n$ (n real-valued measures) or subsets thereof, since these state spaces have been proved useful for the description of natural phenomena. We distinguish finite dimensional systems, which may be defined as maps or ordinary differential equations and infinite dimensional systems, defined for example by partial differential equations or time-delay differential equations.

We speak of *linear dynamical systems* if the function F is linear, that is, if

$$F(\alpha x_1 + \beta x_2) = \alpha F(x_1) + \beta F(x_2)$$

holds. Stated in ordinary language: for linear systems the whole *is* the sum of its parts. Solutions that move away from the origin exponentially in time are called *unstable*, while solutions converging exponentially toward the origin are called *stable*.

All dynamical systems which are not linear are called *nonlinear*. This name by exclusion might seem surprising. As Stanislav Ulam is said to have remarked: "Calling a science 'nonlinear' is like calling zoology 'the study of non-human animals.'" Yet the distinction has been necessary in the natural sciences, which is so accustomed to linear systems. The discovery of new forms of dynamical behavior unrestricted by linearity is one of the greatest achievements of the twentieth century.

3. DEFINING CHAOS

There is as yet no universally accepted definition of chaos. Typical characterizations of chaos are based on low-dimensional (i.e., not higher than five or six), bounded dynamics with sensitive dependence on initial conditions. The bounded region where the dynamics turns may not be decomposable into separate parts. Note that the first two parts of this description are common. Linear systems with stable dynamics remain bounded in phase space; linear systems with unstable dynamics show sensitivity to initial conditions. What makes a system chaotic is the combination of the two. This combination can only be obtained in nonlinear systems.

The mathematically rigorous definition of chaotic behavior in deterministic systems still raises problems, particularly since not all kinds of behavior that would intuitively be called "chaotic" are known yet. For example, the older definition of chaos requiring a dissipative system with a strange attractor is out of date. As more and more of the unexpected behavior of nonlinear dynamical systems is found, the mathematical concepts eventually will converge. In fact, the science of nonlinearity resembles a sea of ignorance with some small islands where results are known and applicable, as shown in the sketch below (which I owe to Thomas Schreiber).

Apart from the basic ideas sketched above, in the study of neural systems some tentative ideas (some indicated in the chart below) have proved quite important for neuroscience and are used in the present study as well. In fact, when considering a large ensemble of complex interacting components such as the brain, one is quickly confronted with the issue of *self-organization*. These are distinguished, salient states of motion in phase space which arise from the *reciprocal or collective cooperation between components*, quite independently of outside inputs. These patterns can be modeled by the same tools as other dynamical systems, and are constrained by order parameters (such as initial and boundary conditions). An explicit example is found in Appendix C, and a less formal description in the way in which visual multistability was presented earlier in this essay. These large collective ensembles are typically quite *unstable*, as we saw before (see Figure 9.4). This instability leads to more or less frequent shifts from one pattern to another, and these transitions are a topic of intense interest today. These are referred to as *bifurcations* (from a given state), or as *phase transitions* (see Figure 9A.1).

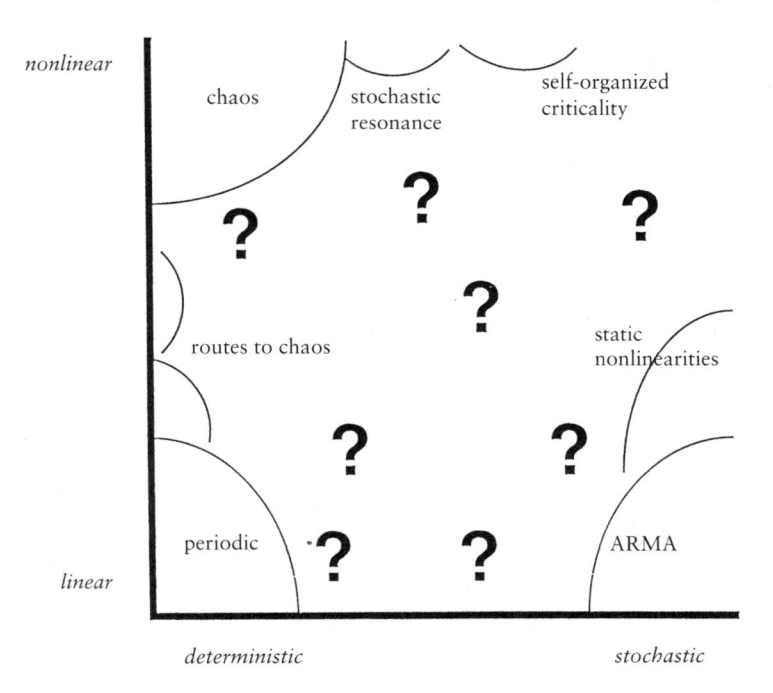

FIGURE 9.A1. Dynamics: a current cartography.

4. A BRIEF SKETCH OF SOME LINEAGES IN NEURODYNAMICAL RESEARCH

The use of dynamical tools in cognitive neuroscience has come from several relatively independent lineages of research.

The early tradition of Gestalt psychology founded by Wolfgang Köhler and W. F. Koffka is explicitly dynamical although they did not couch their results in that language. But their influence has echoes even today. One of the influential representatives is René Thom with his neo-gestaltist ideas issued from his work in bifurcations, and elaborated extensively by Jean Petitot.

A second lineage comes from the interest of physiologists working in motion and behavior. In the early 1950s in Russia, A. Bernstein produced the first fully dynamical account of coordination on neural terms, and at the same time in Germany, Erich von Holst provided pithy detailed examples that were among the first to incorporate phase portraits and instabilities. This tradition is still active today in the work of J. J. Gibson and J. S. Kelso, for example.

A third trend issued from the early cybernetics movement in the 1950s in the United States, especially from the influential work of Warren Mculloch, Arthur Rosenblatt (who is the pioneer of modern connectionist views), and Heinz von Foerster. From this lineage we owe the inspiration of Walter Freeman, who was the first to explicitly introduce the notion of ensemble synchrony and phase coherence as a key mechanism in neurocognitive pattern formation.

Appendix C: Neuronal Synchrony via Coupled Oscillators

To make my ideas quite precise, it is important to work on the basis of an explicit dynamical model for the emergence of synchronous neuronal assemblies. The model introduced here focuses on a subset of middle-layer pyramidal neurons known to play a role in cortical coherences: the intrinsically bursting cells (IB).[42] The IBs are distinguished by their ability to generate clustered bursts of several spikes riding upon a slow depolarization wave, followed by a large hyperpolarization. Since the IBs possess an extensive tree of divergent axons extending far into the horizontal dimension of layers IV–V, they are likely to contribute to an excitatory interconnected network responsible for the organization of large numbers of neurons into macroscopic space-time patterns of transiently coherent activity. Furthermore, many of the cells in layer V can generate rhythmic bursts in the range of 4–10 Hz and are believed to play a significant role in cortical rhythmogenesis.

Relatively little attention has been paid to the possible significance of such slowly bursting components for temporal binding. We suggest that populations of interacting bursting neurons with slow rhythms, such as IBs, are a natural candidate for the generation of synchronous assemblies. Our analyses of synchrony among a network model of intrinsically bursting neurons demonstrate that cellular discharges can aggregate into separate phases and display regular time lags between their rhythmic spike trains. Global feedback inhibitions associated with the tonic depolarization of the coactivated bursts play a leading role in the phase aggregation by the sculpturing of the activities with hyperpolarization. If our conjecture is relevant, various brain oscillations (including the gamma range, 30–80 Hz) may be considered as time sequences of more elementary components, as discussed in section 2.2.

Two basic questions are raised by our view. First, how can the slow rhythmic bursting neurons become mutually synchronized fast enough, and, second, how can coexisting synchronous aggregates be distinguished or labeled for further integrative processes? IB cells are characterized by two distinct time scales of the membrane potential: a slow dynamic corresponding to the smoother phases (bursting and the quiescent repolarization), and a fast one corresponding to the sharp transition between them. Generically, systems that exhibit such behavior can be characterized as relaxation oscillators. The Fitzhugh-Nagumo equations (FN) are representative of this class and provide a mathematical formulation of IB intrinsic rhythmicity on the basis of ionic gatings. Basically, these two-dimensional equations describe the repetitive interplay between fast and slow time scales in biological membranes:

$$\frac{dV}{dt} = f(V) - u(t) + I(t)$$

$$\tau \frac{du}{dt} = aV - (1-a)u$$

where V denotes the mean membrane potential, $u(t)$ is a slow component of the membrane currents, $I(t)$ represents the sum of synaptic and external currents entering the cell, t is a time constant specifying the scale difference between fast and slow time scales, and $f(V) = V(V - 1)(V + 1)$ is a nonlinear function that mimics the N-shaped relationship between the fast membrane currents and the cell potential V. In the phase plane (V, u), V increases during the upper solution of u (depolarization) and decreases during the lower stable solution (hyperpolarization). When either end of the bistable region is reached, V abruptly jumps to the other branch, the transitional points being given by the nullclines $dV/dt = du/dt = 0$.

A realistic feature of this model is that when the oscillator is perturbed by an arriving spike, the oscillation may be rapidly reset via the fast jump onto a new phase, depending on the moment of arrival of the perturbation. A phase resetting can be induced by briefly making I negative during the depolarization: the key consequence of this inhibitory pulse is to displace the nullcline $dV/dt = 0$ in the space (V, u) of the oscillator, and therefore modify the position of its transitional regions, leading to a premature hyperpolarization. Because of their sudden-transition possibilities and because the rate of change of the slow variable $u(t)$ before the sudden transition is less than after the jump, a spike shared by two oscillators can readily induce a quick phase-locking of their activities.

In brief, this dynamical behavior means that neuronal relaxation oscillators (such as cortical IBs) naturally afford a mechanism for synchronization as a consequence of various excitatory and inhibitory feedbacks mediated by recurrent local circuitry. In fact, fast GABA-mediated inhibitory interneurons are known to play an important role in the organization of local coherence in the neocortex. This synchronization of ensembles is validated by simulations concerning populations of IB-like neurons randomly connected with varying degrees of strength in connectivity, and all under a common GABA-like common inhibitory control. Increased common inhibition increases the degree of spatial synchronicity, that is otherwise patchily distributed over the array of simulated neurons. Recent results from hippocampal slices confirm this idea quite elegantly (Traub et al. 1996).

PART TWO

MATHEMATICS IN PHENOMENOLOGY

CHAPTER TEN

Truth and the Visual Field

BARRY SMITH

In this study I use the tools of mereotopology (the theory of parts, wholes, and boundaries) to work out the implications of certain analogies between the "ecological psychology" of J. J. Gibson and the phenomenology of Edmund Husserl. I present an ontological theory of spatial boundaries and spatially extended entities. By reference to examples from geography I show that both boundaries and extended entities fall into two broad categories: those which exist independently of our cognitive acts (for example, the planet Earth, its exterior surface); and those which exist only by virtue of such acts (for example: the International Date Line, the state of Wyoming). The visual field, too, can be conceived as an example of an extended entity that is dependent in the sense at issue. I here argue that we can extend this analogy by postulating entities that would stand to true judgments as the visual field stands to acts of visual perception. Such a "judgment field" can then be defined as that complex extended entity which comprehends all entities that are relevant to the truth of a given (true) judgment. The work of cognitive linguists such as Leonard Talmy and Ronald Langacker, when properly interpreted, can be shown to yield a detailed account of the structures of the judgment fields corresponding to sentences of different sorts. Such an account can serve as the basis for a new sort of correspondence-theoretic definition of truth for sentences in a natural language.

PREAMBLE: GIBSON AND PHENOMENOLOGY

This study is part of a larger project designed to exploit the ecological psychology of J. J. Gibson to yield a new, naturalized interpretation of Husserlian phenomenology. The world, as Gibson points out, is a complex hierarchy of internested levels: molecules are nested within cells, cells are nested within leaves, leaves are nested within trees, trees are nested within forests (Gibson 1979: 101). Each type of organism is tuned in its behavior to entities on a specific level of granularity within this complex hierarchy, to entities which together form what Gibson calls an "ecological niche." A niche is that into which an animal fits; it is that in relation to which the animal is habituated in its behavior (Gibson 1979: 129). A niche embraces not only objects of different sorts, but also shapes, colors, textures, tendencies, and boundaries (surfaces, edges, and contours), all of which are organized in such a way that they enjoy affordance-character for the animal in question. That is, the given features of the entities in the niche motivate the organism; they intrude upon its life; they stimulate it in a wide range of different though characteristically understandable and familiar ways. The niche shared by all human beings—called by Husserl the "life-world"—is thus such that its basic organizing features are intrinsically comprehensible to the human organism (yielding what Husserl calls the "a priori of the life-world"). These basic organizing features include simple geometrical and topological relations and relations of identity, part, and whole, as well as relations between qualities of different sorts (B. Smith and Varzi, in press [a]).

According to Gibson, human beings, like other animals, are integrated into the world order via their perceptions and actions in virtue of the fact that these perceptions and actions are pre-tuned to the characteristic shapes and qualities and patterns of behavior of the respective environments. In the case of human beings this mutual embranglement is extended further through cultural phenomena, above all through language and its associated institutions. To learn a language is in part also to extend the range of objects in relation to which we are able spontaneously to adjust our behavior. Just as our experiences of objects of perception in our everyday environment are characteristically and for the most part not subject to deliberation, so our experience of the words of a language we thoroughly understand is spontaneously bound together completely with our grasping of the associated meanings and thereby also with our being spontaneously directed toward corresponding objects in the world.

The concept of niche can be extended and generalized beyond the basic level of the life-world of common sense in other ways as well. A humanly extended niche might include, for example, the interior of a cockpit, the floor of a stock exchange, or the environment of a keyboard and computer screen; it might include a library or a highway system, or it might include the world of a scientific theory or of some other specialist activity (for example, of measuring or legislating) in which a human being feels at home. For as Gibson himself intimated, and as Husserl argued in detail in the second book of his *Ideas* (see also the extremely provocative Katz 1987), the activity of scientific theorizing on the part of different specialist sciences can be compared in important respects to the behavior of animals and humans in their respective natural environments. There is a deep-rooted analogy between the relationship of animal or human behavior to niche or life-world on the one hand, and the relationship of the scientist (or a specialist community of scientists) to the corresponding scientific subject matter on the other.

The basic axiom of Husserl's constitutive phenomenology is this: that all objects refer back to corresponding acts in which they are (or can be) given. All entities, on whatever level, are correlates of corresponding acts, and each subject is directed in its acts toward a corresponding world of correlates: "As person I am what I am (and each other person is what he is) as subject of a surrounding world. The concepts of ego and surrounding world are related to one another inseparably" (*Ideen* II, §50). The world of common sense is the accomplishment of a community of persons recognizing one another (or better: taking one another for granted) as being in agreement. The things of the commonsense world are direct correlates not of abstract, theoretical experiences, but of intuitive experiences; they are "things we see, grasp, and touch, just as we, and other people, see them, grasp them, etc." (*Ideen* II §62; see also B. Smith 1995).

From the basic axiom it follows that physical things, too, can be nothing other than the correlates of certain acts, namely of the theoretical acts of physicists. Physical nature is then for Husserl the common "surrounding world" of physicists, precisely as they know of it in their theories and conceived as infinitely extended in perfect regularity. Other such special "surrounding worlds" can be distinguished also. Thus, for example, there are the worlds of mathematical or legal objects, of financial instruments, of chess, and so on. Each such realm of objects is, from Husserl's point of view, an interpersonal, cultural accomplishment, presupposing a certain association of human beings. It is a product of "constitution."

The Gibsonian perspective has obvious implications for our understanding of the theories of the life-world (or of *Umwelt* or "bodily space") put forward, not only by Husserl, but also by Scheler, Heidegger, Merleau-Ponty, and other phenomenologists in their various writings. This same perspective yields also, however, a radically new, realist interpretation of Husserl's "constitutive phenomenology": for constitution is not, from the Gibsonian point of view, the creation of a new domain of entities in some spurious "transcendent" realm: rather, it is the carving out of a new sort of niche from within the already existing surrounding world of the relevant subject or specialist community (B. Smith, forthcoming).

The Gibsonian perspective has implications also for our understanding of the relation of individual acts to their corresponding objective correlates. Thus consider once again the analogy between the relationship of animal or human behavior to niche on the one hand, and the relationship of the specialist community of scientists to its corresponding scientific subject matter on the other. This same analogy can be applied not merely to global behavior-patterns but also to specific acts: an act of visual perception stands to a visual field as an act of (true) judgment stands to a fact or state of affairs. I devote the bulk of what follows to working out some of the implications of this latter analogy.

1. TYPES OF BOUNDARIES

We most commonly demarcate reality along what we might call natural or bona fide boundaries. The most prominent (and most salient) examples of such natural boundaries are the outer boundaries of objects in space and processes in time. Such natural boundaries are boundaries in the things themselves. They would exist even in the absence of all articulating activity on our part. The natural boundary of you is (roughly speaking) the surface of your skin.

We can also recognize internal natural boundaries—for example, the boundaries around your heart, lungs, and other organs. But we can recognize unnatural boundaries as well, that is to say, boundaries, both internal and external, which correspond to no genuine heterogeneity (natural articulations) on the side of the bounded entities themselves. The boundary of Utah corresponds to no local physical discontinuity, and to no qualitative heterogeneity (of material constitution, color, texture, etc.) in the world itself.

Let us call inner and outer boundaries of this second sort fiat boundaries, a terminology that is designed to draw attention to the sense in which the latter owe their existence to acts of human decision or fiat or to cognitive phenomena of associated sorts (B. Smith 1994; B. Smith and Varzi, in press [b]). The plausibility of extending our ontology by acknowledging fiat boundaries in this way lies first of all in the fact that all of the standard distinctions we can make between types of natural boundaries can be straightforwardly applied to their fiat counterparts as well. Thus we can distinguish between natural and fiat boundaries of different numbers of dimensions: the equator, like the edge of this table, is a one-dimensional boundary; the North Pole, like the corner of this table, is a zero-dimensional boundary. We can distinguish between complete and incomplete boundaries, whether natural or fiat: the Western Front (anno 1916) and the boundary between France and Germany are examples of incomplete fiat boundaries, in the sense that they do not of themselves serve to demarcate any object in the way in which this is done, for example, by the equator (which demarcates the two hemispherical surfaces of the Earth) and by the boundary of my body (which demarcates the corporeal me). We can similarly distinguish between enduring and transient natural and fiat boundaries: the Western Front, again, is an example of a transient fiat boundary, the boundary of Iceland (modulo the movement of tides) is an example of a (relatively) enduring fiat boundary, and the boundaries of this cloud and of that stone are transient and enduring natural boundaries, respectively. We can distinguish equally between crisp and fuzzy natural and fiat boundaries: the equator is crisp and the product of fiat; the boundary of this cone of light is crisp but exists as part of the natural world; the boundary of Asia is fuzzy but it is still (we can suppose) a product of fiat; the boundary of the polar ice cap is likewise fuzzy but a product of nature. Deserts, valleys, dunes, and so on, are delineated not by crisp outer boundaries but rather by boundary-like regions that are to some degree indeterminate (Cohn and Gotts 1994). Most peninsular objects (including fingers, hands, arms) are characterized likewise by the possession of indeterminate boundaries in the area where they abut their larger hosts. (We leave to one side here the question whether, as quantum physics seems to suggest, there is an additional type of boundary indeterminacy that pertains to all material objects given in our normal experience.)

2. FIAT OBJECTS

Once fiat boundaries have been recognized, then it becomes clear that the opposition between bona fide and fiat can be drawn in relation to objects also (B. Smith 1994). Fiat objects are those objects which exist only by virtue of the fact that some corresponding (complete) fiat boundary has come to be drawn. Examples of genuine objects are you and me, the planet Earth. Examples of fiat objects are all geographical entities—Dade County, Florida, the United States, the Northern Hemisphere—which are demarcated in ways that do not, or do not everywhere, respect qualitative differentiations or spatiotemporal discontinuities in the underlying territory. And then, not the least important reason for admitting fiat objects into our general ontology turns on the fact that most of us live in one (or in what turns out to be a nested hierarchy of such objects).

Clearly, most geographical fiat objects will have boundaries that involve a combination of bona fide and fiat elements: the shores of the North Sea are bona fide boundaries, not, however, its boundaries at those points where it abuts the Atlantic. The Western Front was built out of bona fide stretches, where opposing armies faced off against each other in more or less linear fashion, knitted together by interspersed fiat stretches, generated algorithmically, by joining up the dots (roughly: a front line is the shortest distance transecting the region separating two neighboring but opposed infantry companies). We might in light of this example distinguish between the following:

1. Fiat boundaries, every portion of which is laid down by explicit human fiat (for example, by treaty, or by drawing lines on a map)
2. Fiat boundaries, stretches of which are determined in whole or in part in relation to natural boundaries (or to preexisting fiat boundaries) on the basis of geometrical algorithms (most determinations effected by boundary commissions are of this sort, for example, when a boundary is specified as lying in the middle of a river bed)
3. Fiat boundaries determined algorithmically not in relation to boundaries but in relation to other, real properties of the underlying subject matter: the boundaries depicted in dialect and electoral atlases are of this sort, as are the transient boundaries depicted in weather maps

3. FIAT BOUNDARIES AS CREATED ENTITIES

What begins as a fiat geographical boundary may evolve over time into a natural boundary, reflecting not merely new features of the landscape but also differences in the language or dialect or trading habits of those who live on either side—all of which suggests that we develop a view of geographical boundaries as created entities, entities subject to the vagaries of history. Thus fiat boundaries seem to have a beginning in time, and geographical boundaries in general are such as to instantiate one of a number of characteristic patterns of boundary evolution (Prescott 1978).

Against this, however, is an alternative view according to which spatial boundaries are merely abstract mathematical constructions and are thus not the sorts of things that can be subject to historical change. Boundaries are not created, on the given view, but discovered or picked out from the infinite totality of all geometrically possible alternative ways of dividing up (say) the surface of the earth. Utah, on the given reading, existed long before its boundaries were first picked out by the responsible administrators, and it may similarly continue to exist for long after human beings have ceased to occupy this planet.

Are fiat boundaries, and the fiat objects they circumscribe, discovered or created? The former view has in its favor the virtue of ontological parsimony: only one sort of boundary needs to be admitted into our ontology, where on the latter view we should have to admit in addition to purely geometrical boundaries also certain historically determined boundaries that coincide with these. An argument in favor of the existence of historically created boundaries can however be formulated as follows. We note, first of all, that "Hamburg" is an ambiguous term, standing on the one hand for a certain city (Hamburg-Stadt) and on the other hand for a certain administrative entity (Hamburg-Land), which is one of the constituent Länder (states, cantons) of the German Federal Republic. Hamburg-Stadt and Hamburg-Land are distinct entities, which happen to coincide spatially. On the geometrical account of boundaries (boundaries are discovered, not created) Hamburg-Stadt and Hamburg-Land have identical boundaries; on the alternative, historical reading, they have boundaries which are distinct from each other and from the underlying geometrical boundaries, even though all three sets of boundaries happen to coincide spatially.

Why on earth, now, should we not embrace the more parsimonious reading and save ourselves the embarrassment of, in this case, three complete sets of boundaries in the very same place? The answer to this question turns on the possibility of divergent histories. The boundary of Hamburg-Stadt might, after all, have lain elsewhere. Each geometrically determined boundary is, however, as a matter of necessity exactly where it is. If, therefore, the boundary b of Hamburg-Stadt were identical to (and not merely contingently such as to coincide with) a certain geometrical boundary, then we should have to swallow the simultaneous truth of (1) b could have lain elsewhere and (2) b is as a matter of necessity exactly where it is.

One must reject the temptation to suppose that we are confronted here with a mere verbal dispute, which could be resolved by some alternative choice of words. For consider the in-many-ways-analogous case of Bremen. "Bremen," too, is ambiguous; it refers on the one hand to a certain city, and on the other to a certain Land. In this case, however, the boundaries of Bremen-Stadt and -Land do not coincide. And of course something analogous might hold in the case of Hamburg, too: it would be an administrative act of no great difficulty to bring it about that, as of tomorrow, the boundaries of Hamburg-Stadt and -Land should likewise be distinct or be, in however subtle a fashion, differently defined. This implies, however, that already today we are dealing with entities that could have distinct histories, and this is possible only if the entities themselves are already distinct.

4. FIAT OBJECTS IN PERCEPTION

Geographical boundaries such as those of Hamburg-Stadt and -Land are, if the argument above can be accepted, human creations that are subject to the vagaries of history. It is as if, through the evolution of our political and administrative and legal practices and through practices relating to property law, new boundaries come to be inscribed in reality in addition to the natural boundaries in relation to which these supernumerary fiat boundaries are constructed and in terms of which they are defined. As will already have become clear from some of the examples mentioned above, however, we are confronted in our everyday experience also with a great wealth of such supernumerary boundaries of a more transient sort, boundaries created by our acts of perception and by human cognitive processes of other sorts. Imagine, for example, that I am outdoors on a clear day looking out over the landscape. One prominent object in the visual field hereby determined is my present horizon, a transient and incomplete and roughly linear boundary between earth and sky, whose existence and nature are determined not by any simple act of decision or fiat on my part but by my very existence as a visually perceiving subject in a given location at a given time, as also by the perimetric properties of my visual system, by topographical features of the location, and by the laws of optics. Note, however, that even in this case there is a residual element of human decision at work, namely, the decision on my part to turn my head in a given direction at a given moment.

The horizon is a component object of the visual field, and the latter may be defined, with Ewald Hering, "as the totality of real objects imaged at a given moment on the retina of the right or left eye" (1964: 226). Let us assume that the eye sees in normal fashion, that it is not momentarily startled, and that there are no tricks, mirrors, or special equipment, and no clouds, fog, stained glass, or the like, in its way of seeing given objects. The depictions of the visual field provided by Ernst Mach (1959: 19; see Figure 10.1) and by Gibson (1979: 118f.) tell us that the objects making up the visual field according to Hering's definition are primarily the surfaces of three-dimensional entities (the surfaces of walls, trousers, bookends, etc.). In fact we can distinguish three sorts of component object: (1) two-dimensional surfaces (with their own intrinsic curvature in three-dimensional space); (2) the boundaries of these two-dimensional surfaces (both one-dimensional edges and zero-dimensional vertices; both fiat and natural boundaries: the horizon is an example of a one-dimensional fiat boundary in the interior of the visual field); and (3) the one-dimensional psychologically induced fiat outer boundary of the visual field itself. The boundary of the visual field is a complex, subtle, ever-changing and gappy patchwork of physical surfaces and other components. The patchwork is "open," topologically speaking: its external boundary is not a part of the visual field itself (as death is not an event in life). The patchwork is organized further in terms of an opposition between entities ("figures") in the focus of attention, which characteristically manifest determinate boundaries, and entities which have indeterminate boundaries and which are experienced as running on (as "ground") behind them.

FIGURE 10.1. The visual field. (Mach 1959)

5. LANGUAGE-GENERATED FIAT OBJECTS

A further important class of transient fiat boundaries are those effected through our everyday use of natural language. As Talmy puts it, drawing attention to a hitherto insufficiently studied analogy between the articulations effected by the descriptive use of language and those effected by acts of visual perception: "Linguistic forms can direct the distribution of one's attention over a referent scene in a certain type of pattern, the placement of one or more windows of greatest attention over the scene, in a process that can be termed the windowing of attention" (1996: 236). Common to all such processes is the determination of a boundary, which might be a sharp line or a gradient zone, and whose particular scope and contour—hence, the particular quantity and portions of material that it encloses—can be seen to vary from context to context.

The characteristics of such boundaries are described by Talmy as follows:

> First, the material enclosed within the boundary is felt to constitute a unitary, coherent conceptual entity distinct from the material outside the boundary. Second, there seems to be some sense of connectivity throughout the material enclosed within the boundary and, contrariwise, some sense of discontinuity or disjuncture across the boundary between the enclosed and external material. Third, the various portions of the material within the boundary are felt to be co-relevant to each other, whereas the material outside the boundary is not relevant to that within. (Talmy 1996: 240; compare the characteristics of the ecological niche as set forth in B. Smith and Varzi, in press [b])

As Talmy and Langacker have shown in great detail, and as the phenomenologist Johannes Daubert emphasized in the "delineationist" ontology of states of affairs he developed in the early years of the twentieth century (Schuhmann and Smith 1987), the very same material can be subject to such windowing or profiling in different ways, amounting, in our terms, to the inscription within one and the same whole of internal fiat boundary-structures of different sorts. Thus to take one very simple example, the very same totality of objects and processes is windowed in different ways by "Blood flowed from his nose" and "He was bleeding from the nose."

The thesis that the windowing effected through a complete linguistic act is a matter of the drawing of a topologically complete fiat boundary around a given portion of worldly material then allows us to develop a sort of topological grammar, a grammar that exploits the formal tools of the topologist (more precisely: of the mereotopologist; see Simons 1987, Varzi 1994, B. Smith 1996, and B. Smith and Varzi, in press [a]), in giving an account of the ways in which, through language, we effect systematically different sorts of windowing or profiling of reality (or fail in the attempt). Thus, for example, we can associate different sorts of incomplete or syncategorematic expressions ("John caused . . . ," "John closed . . . ," "John . . . quickly," and so on) with different sorts of incompleteness on the side of the corresponding fiat boundaries. There are then incomplete boundaries, analogous to the geographical cases of incompleteness previously referred to, in the linguistic sphere as well.

A further type of articulation, in some sense complementary to the addition of fiat boundaries within the interiors of objects, arises where bona fide interior part-structure is as it were stripped away, as occurs, for example, when an extended entity with genuine interior boundaries is treated as if it were a homogeneous whole. One variety of this phenomenon in the linguistic sphere might be called fiat continuity, which occurs where natural language sanctions the use of mass terms ("water," "sugar," "luggage") to refer to entities that are in fact made up of discrete units in such a way that they come to be treated as continuous. It is here that we encounter the granularity that is characteristic of all phenomena of natural cognition: only those extended parts of objects and processes which enjoy a certain minimal extent come to be counted as parts within natural language fiat articulations. (See Ojeda 1993 and Habel 1994.)

There is one important difference between the views of Daubert on the windowing of language, and those of Talmy and Langacker, however. Daubert very clearly saw the boundaries in question—by analogy with the geographical case—as boundaries in reality, although generated by human fiat. In this he was struggling against the "constitutive phenomenology" of his master Husserl (Schuhmann and Smith 1985). Talmy and Langacker, in contrast, with their talk of "conceptual boundaries," of "boundaries in conceptual reality," of boundaries in "our concept of reality," and so on, seem unclear whether language-induced boundaries would be drawn within the mind or in exterior reality or in some other not clearly specified "conceptual realm." The motivation for this unclarity is understandable: it derives from the desire to develop a theory of linguistic usage that would apply equally to all the myriad different sorts of objects to which our sentences relate. Thus as Langacker points out:

> We are capable of constructing conceptual worlds of arbitrary complexity involving entities and phenomena that have no direct counterpart in peripherally connected experience. Such are the worlds of dreams, stories, mythology, mathematics, predictions about the future, flights of the imagination, and linguistic theories. All of us have constructed many conceptual worlds that differ in genre, complexity, conventionality, abstractness, degree of entrenchment, and so on. For many linguistic purposes all of these worlds are on a par with the one we distinguish as "reality." (1987/1991, 1: 113)

Note, however, that constructing these worlds is not comparable to what some might argue is the most important of all linguistic purposes, namely that of giving an account of how, through language, human beings are able to become related to peripherally connected reality at all. Note, further, that if reality (or what Langacker calls "reality") is regarded as a mere constructed world, then one runs the risk of flouting our normal distinction between objects and concepts (for example between rabbits and our concepts of rabbits), with much confusion as its consequence:

> A person's conception of reality is itself a conceptual world that is built up from peripherally connected experience through complex sequences of mental operations. We construct our conception of the "real world" bit by bit, stage by stage, from myriad and multifarious sensory and motor experiences. . . . It

is our conception of reality (not the real world per se) that is relevant to linguistic semantics. (1987/1991, 1: 114)

In the eyes of the cognitive linguist, it would seem, our natural language sentences about rabbits are not about rabbits (per se) at all; rather they are about conceptual rabbits that we ourselves have constructed bit by bit. The whole thrust of cognitive grammar à la Talmy and Langacker is unfortunately to minimize in this fashion the ontologically crucial differences between human concepts and reality.

6. TRUTH

What I now want to claim is that the construction of transient sentence-generated fiat boundaries of the sort described by Daubert, boundaries *in reality*, is pervasively involved in all descriptive statement-making uses of language, that there are transient fiat boundaries in the judgmental sphere analogous to the transient boundaries of visual fields associated with acts of visual perception. In this connection it is important to bear in mind that truth for empirical sentences has classically been understood in terms of a correspondence relation (that is to say, of some sort of isomorphism) between a judgment or an assertion on the one hand and a certain portion of reality on the other. The central difficulty standing in the way of this classical theory turned always on the fact that reality evidently does not come ready-parceled into judgment-shaped portions of the sort that would be predisposed to stand in relations of correspondence of the suggested sort. The theory of language-induced fiat boundaries can, however, allow us to treat judgment itself as a way to draw fiat boundaries around entities in reality of the appropriate (truth-making) sort. In this fashion it yields a way of putting the world back into semantics, or of anchoring true judgment to a reality of exactly the sort required by the correspondence theory (Smith 1993).

Let us define the *judgment field* as a portion of reality, a fiat object, that is demarcated by the transient fiat boundary associated with a given true empirical judgment. A judgment field is then a certain region of reality through and around which the relevant judgmental fiat boundary is drawn. As such it exists in and of itself, regardless of our judging activity. The judgment field—called by Daubert the state of affairs or *Sachverhalt*—is, however, also in a certain sense dependent on our judgment. For in the absence of the judging activity, an entity of the given sort would in no way be demarcated from its surroundings, nor would it have the internal demarcation-structure which it comes to have by virtue of the sentence forms employed. In this way, then, cognitive linguistics can replace its confused notion of conceptual reality with the geographer's notion of reality as subject to fiat articulations. It will then be in a position to exploit its remarkably sophisticated resources for the analysis of the grammatical structures at work in natural language in order to produce a truly adequate account of truth for natural language in correspondence-theoretic terms.

CHAPTER ELEVEN

Morphological Eidetics for a Phenomenology of Perception

JEAN PETITOT

We tackle the problem of naturalizing phenomenology by proceeding from examples. These belong to the phenomenology of perception and bear on, first, the theory worked out by Husserl in the third logical investigation, which deals with the relation of dependence between spatial extension and sensible qualities; second, the links between geometry, vision, and kinesthetic control analyzed in *Ding und Raum*; and third, adumbrative perception as described in *Ideen* I. Geometrical models are worked out for each of these examples. They share rather sophisticated concepts of differential geometry, such as those of smooth manifold, fibration, calculus of variations, stratification, control, and singularity. Our main epistemological claim is that naturalizing phenomenology is an enterprise that has to be carried out in two steps, the first of which concerns the mathematical schematization of the eidetic descriptions, and the second, the implementation (e.g., neural) of the resulting algorithms.

1. INTRODUCTION

1.1. ORIENTATIONS FOR NATURALIZING PHENOMENOLOGY

I will try to tackle the difficult problem of naturalizing phenomenology by proceeding from technical examples.[1] To do so, I will adopt the following strategy.

1. The naturalization of phenomenology must be grounded in a *natural* science whose object is the phenomenal appearing itself, considered as a *natural* process.
2. The link between naturalist explanations, mathematical models, and computer simulations on the one hand, and phenomenological eidetic descriptions on the other, can be set up by viewing the latter as constraints on the former.
3. The key point is the mathematical schematization of phenomenological descriptive eidetics, that is, the elaboration of a *mathematical* descriptive eidetics (which Husserl thought impossible in principle).[2] For us, to natu-

ralize an eidetics consists in implementing its mathematical schematization in natural substrates (e.g., neural nets).
4. This epistemological position can be summarized with two slogans: "Every description is the name of a problem." And, "Every concept is the name of an unknown algorithm."

1.2. EIDETICS OF SENSIBLE SCHEMATA

We chose our examples to illustrate different phenomenological problems and mathematical tools. They concern essentially the phenomenology of perception and the relationship between its morphological basis and the semantic levels of predication and judgment. It would be relevant here to give a detailed account of Husserl's concept of noema. But it would take too long. We refer only to the bibliographical items and to Rudolf Bernet's 1991 paper "Le Concept husserlien de noème." In Husserl's 1906–1908 lectures on the theory of knowledge and the theory of meaning and in *Ideen* I, Bernet distinguishes three dimensions of noematic ideality:

1. The noematic appearance:[3] the object as it is intuitively and immediately given (by direct acquaintance) in the constituting multiplicity of its adumbrations (*Abschattungen*). It is not itself an intentional meaning but a presentation, a display (*Darstellung*) of the object.[4] Its ideality is morphological.
2. The noematic meaning: a syntactically structured categorial content associated with judgment. Its ideality is logical.
3. The noema as object = X: of a constitutive rule, identity pole, or synthetic unity of appearances. Its ideality is transcendental.

It is, of course, essential not to confuse these three different dimensions. It would be an amphiboly in Kant's sense.

2. THE TRANSCENDENTAL TURN IN THE PHENOMENOLOGY OF PERCEPTION

Let us begin by reminding ourselves of certain aspects of the phenomenology of perception, e.g., in Husserl's 1907 lectures *Ding und Raum*.

2.1. PERCEPTION AND REDUCTION

In a transcendental perspective, the phenomenology of perception aims at clarifying the way the world of three-dimensional "things" constitutes itself as a transcendent world in the immanence of lived experiences and intentional acts.

In as much as the transcendental reduction brackets objective space and time, pure lived experiences can no longer be identified with psychological events (i.e., mental contents, acts and processes, or private feelings). Thus transcendental reduction reveals perceptual intentionality as a "constitution" of external objects.

The eidetic structures of perceptive experience are rooted in the rule-governed stream of consciousness. By its rules, the immanent temporal order of lived experiences constitutes objectivity. In that sense, the *passive synthesis* of the sensible *ante*-predicative manifestation is the ultimate ground of logical and predicative acts.

Such an analysis of perceptive evidence, and especially of the correlation between sensorial hyle and immanent lived experiences, on the one hand, and on the other, the objective properties of transcendent objects, raises a new de jure question: "How are evidential statements bearing on an objectivity which is not effectively given in the phenomena, possible?" (*Ding und Raum* [hereafter *DR*], §7, p. 19).

2.2. SELF-POSITING VERSUS EXPOSITING (DISPLAY), IMMANENCE VERSUS TRANSCENDENCE

The transcendental reduction reduces perception to immanent pure experience, which, contrary to things, states of affairs, and events of the external world, depends upon a consciousness of absolute givenness excluding any doubt and even any "doxa." This does not hold for the "exposition"—display, *Darstellung*—of a thing. The givenness in person (*Leibhaftigkeit*) of a thing does not possess any absolute character and is coupled with doxic modalities (*Glaubhaftigkeit* or propositional attitudes).

This opposition between "absolute data" (immanence) and "exposition" or "presentation" (transcendence) corresponds to that between *self-posited* immanent perceptions and presentational ones. Self-posited perceptions give their object in an *adequate* and *complete* way. This is not the case with presentational perceptions, which give only partial aspects (adumbrations) of the objects and need therefore an "*identification synthesis*" or a "*consciousness of identity*" unifying the different adumbrations as adumbrations of one and the same object (noema as object = X in the transcendental sense).

As the symbolic correlate of noetic syntheses, the object cannot therefore be a *real* component of the lived experiences adumbrating it. It can only be an *intentional* component. The givenness of an object is never absolute, never carried out "in the mode of a self-posited object" (*DR*, p. 30). Its essential inadequation and incompleteness constitute the *phenomenological origin of perceptive intentionality* as pointing toward an external world.

2.3. LIVED EXPERIENCES AND SPATIALITY

We will see that one of the main difficulties faced by Husserl was the impossibility of conceiving *geometrically* of a spatial extension different from objective physical space. Of course, every perception possesses an extensional moment, but "space is the necessary form of thingness, and not the form of 'sensible' experiences" (*DR*, §14, p. 43). For Husserl, space always belongs to transcendent objects. As the form of any external transcendence, it is adumbrated and constituted in specific experiences. But these are not themselves objectively spatial. How then to conceive of their "immanent" spatiality?

2.4. PRESENTATION (*DARSTELLUNG*) AND APPREHENSION (*AUFFASSUNG*)

The intentional relation of immanent perceptive contents to the transcendent objects they adumbrate depends upon their *apprehension*. *Auffassung* is a *process* operating on sense data: "It is by their apprehension that they [the sense data], which per se are dead stuff, acquire a sense which gives life to them, in such a way that an object can be displayed" (§15, p. 46).

We meet here the four main terms of the noetico-noematic correlation: hyletic data are animated by an "intentional morphe" (noetic syntheses = apprehension) that converts them into noematic appearances that adumbrate objects. Apprehension is always an *interpretation*. Husserl's concept of meaning is therefore an active one. It concerns effective cognitive algorithms processing hyletic data and converting them into presentational adumbrations.

Now, insofar as it is impossible to reduce the appearance of any object to one adumbration alone (it would have to be a complete givenness), there always exists a co-givenness of an infinite number of adumbrations of one and the same object. In that sense, the appearing always goes beyond what is intuitively given. It necessarily implies some reference to other, counterfactual possibilities of display.

2.5. EIDETIC CHARACTERS OF SENSIBLE SCHEMATA

Perception constitutes what Husserl calls a regional ontology. He considered it the most basic regional ontology, the one upon which the others are built up. In *Ideen* I and II, Husserl describes the sensible objects as "archiobjects" given "in person" pre-judicatively in an aesthesic noetic synthesis. This mode of appearing is not that of concrete material things, but that of sensible schemata constituted in the temporal flow of adumbrations.

There exist three main phenomenological characters of sensible schemata.

1. *The relation of foundation of sensible qualities in their spatio-temporal extension.* The spatiotemporal extension of a sensible schema—what Husserl calls its "spatial body"—constitutes its "characteristic eidetic attribute," "an eidetic form of all real properties." The spatial body is filled in by sensible qualities (colors, textures, roughness, etc.). It is an originary datum of any perceptive experience.
2. *The saliency of the form (the gestalt) so qualified.* It is necessary for catching the form and is realized through qualitative discontinuities.
3. *The adumbrative perception.* A sensible schema gives unity to different aspects. This adumbrative mode of manifestation is originally characteristic of perception and is "different in principle from the manifestation of real properties [material properties of things]" (*Ideen* II, §32, p. 131).

3. THE THIRD LOGICAL INVESTIGATION AND THE MORPHOLOGICAL ANALYSIS OF IMAGES

After these theoretical preliminaries we come to our first example. It concerns the naturalization of a very simple eidetic description, namely, the morphological description of a form, of a visual gestalt, given by Husserl in the first chapter of the third Logical Investigation. This text has been carefully analyzed by Kevin Mulligan, Barry Smith, and Peter Simons.[5] We also commented on it elsewhere.[6] It brings into action two fundamental gestaltist concepts, namely, that of merging (*Verschmelzung*) and that of segmentation (*Sonderung*), which are closely related to those of covering (*Überdeckung*) and fulfillment or filling-in (*Erfüllung*). In general, any mereological structuration of a whole in parts is the result of segmentation processes merging some moments and separating others.

3.1. THE HUSSERLIAN DESCRIPTION OF THE DEPENDENCE RELATION "QUALITY → EXTENSION"

Husserl begins to develop the key points in §4 of the third Logical Investigation, referring to Carl Stumpf's works.[7] As a "corporeal figure," the extension of an object is a primary quality filled in by sensible secondary qualities. As it is explained in *Ding und Raum*: "Any body, and more precisely any sensible schema of full corporeality, is a spatial corporeality (a spatial figure) 'over which' or 'in which' sensible qualities spread" (p. 297). Husserl distinguishes carefully a quality as *abstractum* and "the immediate moment which refers to it in intuition."[8] He calls the latter an "ultimate specific difference." The relation between a particular spatial extension and its immediate qualitative moments is a "functional dependency," whereas that between the kinds of extension and quality is an "eidetic law" that legalizes these functional dependencies.

Husserl then works out an *objective* and *a priori* conception of the dependence law: "Obviously, this is not a mere empirical fact, but an *a priori* necessity, which is grounded in pure essences [*in den reinen Wesen*] (*LU* III, §4, p. 237).

In §§ 5–7 this point is elaborated. The dependence/independence distinction is *objective*. It is given in an "apodictic evidence" and ruled by an "objective legality." It is free from any link to any effective psychological consciousness, to the "facticity of our subjective thought" (§6, p. 242). We meet here a typical example of a *synthetic a priori* principle.

3.2. ANALYSIS OF THE DESCRIPTION

Many other Husserlian texts, in particular *Ding und Raum* and *Ideen* I, deepen the analyses of the third Logical Investigation in what concerns the filling-in of spatial extension by sensible qualities.

3.2.1. Extension Is a Universal Topological Format for Qualities

Husserl emphasizes the fact that it is the cohesion of extension (its spatial "order," its topology) that confers unity upon qualities.

> Color data are not scattered and without connection. They share a fixed unity and a fixed form, the form of a pre-phenomenal spatiality. (*DR*, §21, p. 69)

> The privilege of the spatially distinctive mark is that its continuity corresponds to the continuity of qualities: different qualities (visual, tactile), lacking connections in themselves, receive from it their unity. (p. 346)

Spatiality is a universal format for sensible qualities.

3.2.2. The Primacy of Extension and the Dependency "Quality → Extension"

There exists, therefore, a primacy of extension: the dependence relation "quality → extension," even if bilateral (an extension can exist only if it is qualitatively fulfilled, and a quality can exist only if it fulfills some extension), is so fundamentally *asymmetric* that it can in fact be considered *unilateral*: "Places don't receive their order from colors, but, on the contrary, colors from places" (*DR*, p. 347). The spatial figure prescribes its rule for qualitative filling-in and for its variations according to "typical laws of filling-in." It is in this way that "pure spatiality" can be acquired "as a fundamental form of thingness" (§78, p. 264).

3.3. SEGMENTATION AND MERGING: CONTINUITY AND QUALITATIVE DISCONTINUITIES

The intuitive qualitative moments can be apprehended only if they form a global unity which stands out against a background (what Husserl calls a *phänomenale Abhebung*). In order to be grasped, a phenomenon must be "salient." How can such a saliency be obtained? To explain this key point, Husserl introduces, following Stumpf, "the difference between contents *intuitively 'separated'* from their neighbors, and contents *merged* with them" (*LU* III, §8, p. 247).

Merging (*Verschmelzung*) of neighboring contents yields an effect of wholeness,[9] a passage from local to global. On the contrary, segmentation (*Sonderung*) is an obstacle to merging and limits parts in wholes. Husserl emphasizes the fact that it is rooted in the concept of *discontinuity*: "Sonderung beruht . . . auf *Diskontinuität*." And he summarizes the process in the following way (his emphasis): "*Two simultaneous sensible concrete realities form necessarily an 'undifferentiated unity' when all the immediately constitutive moments of the first pass continuously over into the constitutive moments of the second*" (§8, p. 248).

Qualitative discontinuities are sharp transitions between ultimate specific differences. They are discontinuities of the functional dependency "quality → extension." They structure the covering (*Deckungszusammenhang*) of extension by quality. They can be grasped only if they are contiguously unfolded "against the background of a continuously varying moment, namely, the spatial and temporal one" (§9, p. 250). In short, spatio-temporal extension has to be the medium of a spreading (*Ausbreitung*) of qualities. It is from this spreading that Husserl derives the following definition of the gestaltist concept of qualitative discontinuity: "It is from a limit of space or time that one jumps from one visual quality to another. In this continuous transition from one part of space to another, one doesn't progress also continuously across the covering quality: at some point, neighboring qualities present a finite (and not too small) gap" (§9, p. 250).

And Husserl significantly adds that spatiality operates in this eidetic description not only as a "*sensible* moment" whose "objective apperception constitutes the phenomenal spatiality" but also as an "*intentional* moment" where the objective spatial figure is intuitively displayed. Space possesses, therefore, a noetic face (format of passive synthesis) and a noematic one (pure intuition in Kant's sense).

This analysis is made more precise in *Ding und Raum*. For objects to appear, some "lines of discontinuity" or some segmenting "lines of pre-phenomenal delimitation" must exist: "Without qualitative discontinuities separating it from its surroundings, no image can be salient, and focus attention" (*DR*, §53, p. 185).

Segmentatibility is a "characteristic" of the visual field closely related to its spatial "order" (its topology). It provides a pre-phenomenal mereology, that is, individuated two-dimensional constituents that can adumbrate three-dimensional objects.

3.4. THE CONFLICT BETWEEN THE SYNTHETIC-MATERIAL-MORPHOLOGICAL AND ANALYTIC-FORMAL-LOGICAL LEVELS

Morphological essences belong to the regional ontology of perception—which Husserl calls "material"—and not to formal ontology. The dependence law "quality → extension" is *synthetic a priori* and not analytic. One of the main problems is then to know what its *mathematical* status can be. Concerning this point, Husserl remains rather ambiguous. The reason is that, according to him, only analytic laws "can be completely 'formalized.'" And any analytic law, as he puts it in the third Logical Investigation, "is built up on formal logical categories and categorial forms" (§12, p. 260). Accordingly, in the second chapter of the same investigation, Husserl develops a general axiomatics of dependence relations.

To understand this crucial point, which engages the scientific destiny of phenomenology, we must take into account the Husserlian incompatibility between the "vague morphological essences" of sensible intuition and the mathematical idealities, especially the geometrical ones. For Husserl, the essences abstracted from intuitive data are not "exact and ideal concepts" and, therefore, cannot be mathematical:[10] "Essences apprehended by direct ideation [*Ideation*] in the intuitive data are 'inexact' and must not be confused with 'exact' essences, which come from a *sui generis* 'idealization' [*Idealisierung*]" (§9, p. 249).

According to Husserl, there cannot exist any morphological geometry and, therefore, any morphological schematism of the dependence relation "quality → extension" that could play the role of a transcendental schematism for the morphological synthetic a priori laws.

As we showed elsewhere,[11] this rejection of any morphological schematism is catastrophic for the scientific project of phenomenology because it leads to a drastic opposition between descriptive eidetics and science: "The descriptive concepts of any pure description, that is, of a description which immediately and faithfully conforms to intuition [*Anschauung*], and therefore of any phenomenological description, are for reasons of principle different from the determinant concepts of the objective sciences" (§9, p. 245).

3.5. THE MORPHOLOGICAL SCHEMATISM OF THE DEPENDENCY "QUALITY → EXTENSION"

This very elementary (but fundamental) example shows us what might be meant, from a cognitive point of view, by a naturalized phenomenology. The eidetic description we just sketched out is a noematic one. It concerns the simplest and most primitive component of sensible schemata. To "naturalize" it we apply the following strategy. First, we convert the phenomenological descriptive eidetics into a geometrical one. The geometrical schematization of synthetic a priori laws is the key to naturalization. It does indeed provide a non-naively formal version of noematics. Once we have worked this out, we have to implement it in natural processes, for example, in macrophysical theories of self-organized complex systems (the "external" side of naturalization) or neural nets (the "internal" side of naturalization).

The key Husserlian concepts that have to be geometrically schematized are essentially the following: (1) space-extension; (2) concrete quality / abstract quality, species, kind; (3) dependence/independence, inseparability/separability; (4) unilateral functional dependency "quality → extension," covering, filling-in; (5) merging / segmentation of neighboring qualities; (6) continuity/discontinuity; and (7) diffusion, spreading (*Ausbreitung*).

4. THE RELATION OF FOUNDATION "QUALITY → EXTENSION" AND THE CONCEPT OF FIBRATION

4.1. THE PRE-PHENOMENAL SPATIAL ORDER AND THE CONCEPT OF A SMOOTH MANIFOLD

To work out the geometric schematization, we must of course link the pre-phenomenal intuitive and continuous spatial order with a geometrically well-defined structural level. This cannot be the topological level, which is too soft: topologically continuous structures, such as fractals, can have an infinite internal complexity. Nor can it be the metrical level, which is too rigid and characteristic of objective physical space. We have therefore to assume that the relevant level is an intermediary one. We choose the *differentiable* one.

Such an hypothesis can be historically confirmed. Indeed, the Stumpfian concept of *Verschmelzung* used by Husserl comes from the German psychologist Johann Friedrich Herbart (1776–1841), who developed a *con-*

tinuous theory of mental representations. Essentially in the same vein as Charles Sanders Peirce after him, Herbart was convinced the mental contents are vague and can vary continuously. For him, a "serial form" (*Reihenform*) is a class of mental representations which undergo a graded fusion (*abgestufte Verschmelzung*), gluing them together through continuous transitions. He coined the neologism *synechology*[12] for his metaphysics (Peirce's neologism *synechism* is clearly similar). It is not sufficiently well known that Herbart's point of view greatly influenced Bernhard Riemann when he was elaborating his key concept of a Riemannian manifold (*Mannigfaltigkeit*).[13] Even if Riemann did not agree with Herbart's metaphysics, he stoutly proclaimed that he was "a Herbartian in psychology and epistemology." Erhard Scholtz has shown that in Riemann's celebrated *Über die Hypothesen, welche der Geometrie zu Grunde liegen* (1867) "the role of topological space [is] taken up in a vague sense by a Herbartian-type of 'serial form,' backed by mathematical intuition" (1992: 23). Now, the "intuitive" space underlying a Riemannian manifold is a smooth manifold. It must also be emphasized that the modern concept of a manifold was elaborated by Hermann Weyl, the great mathematical genius who was Husserl's philosophical disciple.[14]

4.2. THE CONCEPT OF FIBRATION

From our point of view, the schematization of the foundational law "quality → extension" has to correspond to a *category* (a type) of mathematical structure. This category must correspond to the "essences" governed by the law. And as for the specific mathematical structures belonging to it, they must correspond to models of phenomenal instantiations of the law (tokens).

We will show that the relevant category of structure is that of *fibration* or of *fibered space*.[15]

Intuitively, a fibration is a differentiable manifold E endowed with a *canonical projection* (a differentiable map) $\pi : E \to M$ over another manifold M. M is called the *base* of the fibration, and E its *total space*. The inverse images $E_x = \pi^{-1}(x)$ of the points $x \in W$ by π are called the *fibers* of the fibration. They are the subspaces of E that are projected to points in M.

In general, a fibration is required to satisfy the two following axioms:

(F_1) *All the fibers E_x are diffeomorphic with a typical fiber F.*

(F_2) *The projection π is locally trivial, that is, for every $x \in M$, there exists a neighborhood U of x such that the inverse image $E_U = \pi^{-1}(U)$ of U is diffeomorphic with the direct product $U \times F$ endowed with the canonical projection $U \times F \to U$, $(x, q) \to x$. (See Figures 11.1 and 11.2.)*

340   *Jean Petitot*

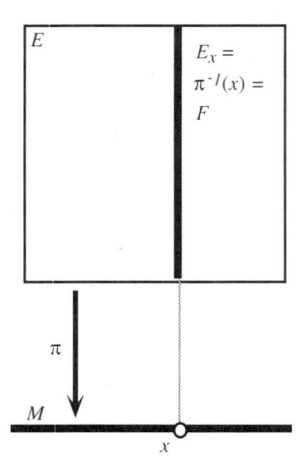

FIGURE 11.1. The structure of a fibration. M is the base space, E the total space, π the structural projection, $E_x = \pi^{-1}(x)$ the fiber over the point $x \in M$. All fibers are isomorphic to a typical fiber F.

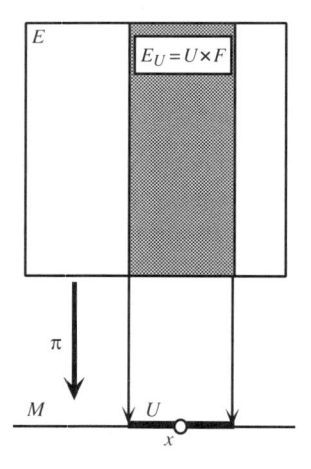

FIGURE 11.2. Local triviality of a fibration. Every point $x \in M$ of the base space possesses a neighborhood U such that $\pi^{-1}(U)$ is isomorphic to the trivial fibration $p: U \times F \to U$ (the projection of a Cartesian product onto its first factor).

In our case, the base manifold M is the ambient space of the substrate's extension W, and the fiber F the space G of the kind of sensible qualities under consideration (e.g., the color space). It is the canonical projection π that schematizes geometrically the law of foundation. It introduces a dissymmetry between the base M and the fiber F: the base is an "external" extensive space, the fiber an "internal" intensive one. The very fact that π projects E on M expresses the unilateral dependency of the intensive magnitudes and secondary qualities relative to the extensive magnitude and the primary space quality: the external space *controls* the internal state.

Even if we cannot develop this point here, we must emphasize the fact that the concept of fibration is required by neurophysiological as well as by technological implementations. Indeed the orientation hypercolumns of the visual cortex (which associate each retinal position with the whole space of directions) implement a fibration.[16] It is the same for a computer screen: to each pixel ($w \in M$) are associated one to three bytes coding the gray levels or the RGB colors (fiber F).

4.3. THE CONCEPT OF A SECTION OF A FIBRATION AND HUSSERL'S FUNCTIONAL DEPENDENCIES

The general structure of a fibration allows for an easy mathematization of the Husserlian concept of functional dependency. Let $\pi : E \to M$ be a fibration and $U \subset M$ an open subset of M. A *section s* of π over U is a map $s : U \to E$ which *lifts* U to E. This means that s associates to every $x \in U$ an element $s(x)$ of the fiber E_x over x. We get therefore for the composed map $\pi \circ s : U \to E$ the identity of M. If there exists on U a local trivialization $\pi_U : E_U \cong F \times U \to U$, it transforms s in a classical map $x \to [f(x), x]$ of U into the direct product $F \times U$, where $f : U \to F$ is a map (a "function") of U into the fiber F. Therefore, the concept of section generalizes the classical concept of map, that is, of functional dependence. In general s is supposed to be continuous, differentiable, or analytic. It can present discontinuities along a singular locus. (See Figures 11.3 and 11.4.) It is conventional to write $\Gamma(U)$ for the set of sections of π over U.

A section of a fibration therefore exactly expresses a specific functional dependency of the qualitative moments (the fiber) relative to the extension (the base). We therefore retrieve exactly the "pure" Husserlian description and thereby "prove" that it is indeed mathematizable.

4.4. MORPHOLOGIES AND QUALITATIVE DISCONTINUITIES: THE WAY FROM HUSSERL TO THOM

Qualitative discontinuities that make a phenomenon salient are discontinuities of sections. Let $q_1, \ldots, q_n$ be the sensible qualities that can fill in the external space W. They belong to space kinds $G_1, \ldots, G_n$ (colors, textures, etc.). Let $s_1(w), \ldots, s_n(w)$ be the sections expressing the filling-in of W by the q_i (that is, $s_i : W \to E_i$ is a section of the fibration $\pi_i : E_i \to W$ with fiber G_i). This allows us to schematize the concept of phenomenological

342   Jean Petitot

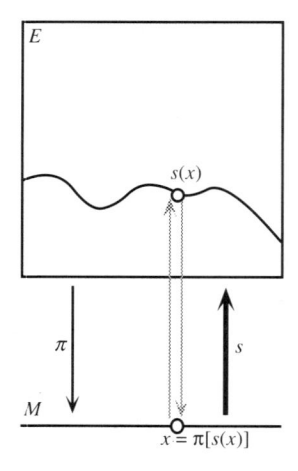

FIGURE 11.3. The concept of a section s of a fibration π. The section s associates to every point x of $U \neq M$ a point of E lying over x that is a point of the fiber E_x. Therefore, $\pi[s(x)] = x$.

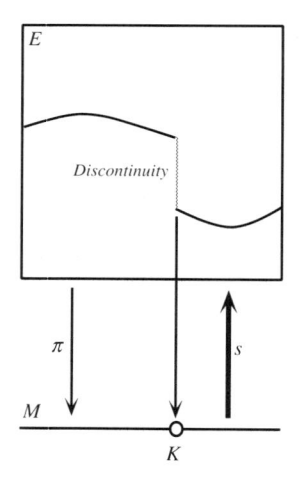

FIGURE 11.4. A section of a fibration can be discontinuous along a singular locus K.

saliency constitutive of the concept of morphology. One of René Thom's major merits was his understanding of this point.[17] Thom calls a point $w \in W$ where all the sections $s_i(w)$ are locally continuous a *regular* point. Regular points form an open subset R of W.[18] Let K be the complementary closed set $K = W - R$. K is constituted by special points—called *singular*—where at least one of the sections $q_i(w)$ is discontinuous. It realizes a morphology whose phenomenological saliency corresponds exactly to Husserl's pure description.

4.5. THE CATEGORIZATION OF THE QUANTITATIVE SPACES

It must be added that qualitative kinds G are generally categorized in different species ("essences"). This means that (1) the space G is decomposed in domains (categories) $p_1, \ldots, p_k$ by a system of boundaries Σ (this is called a *stratification*), and (2) there exist in these domains *prototypes* corresponding to "central values."[19]

The existence of such categorizations entails extra qualitative discontinuities. In addition to the discontinuities proceeding from those of the sections $s_i(w)$, there exist those due to the fact that the values $s_i(w)$ change category. They can exist even if the sections s_i are continuous. (See Figure 11.5.)

4.6. MORPHOLOGICAL SCHEMATISM AND DESCRIPTIVE EIDETICS

Morphological schematism allows us to mathematize all eidetic components of the phenomenological description.

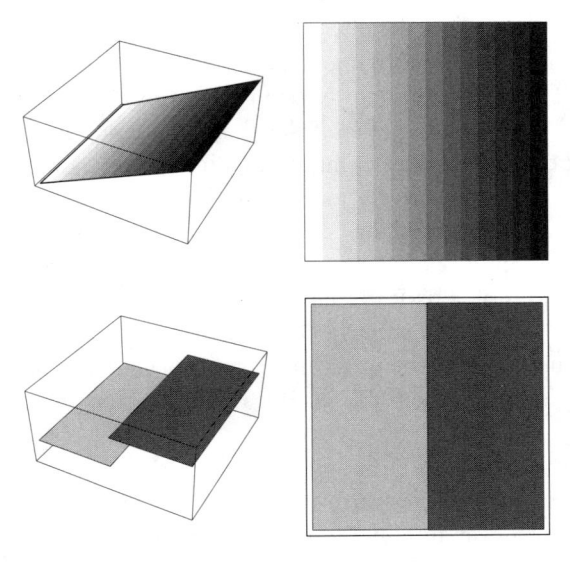

FIGURE 11.5. When the fiber of a fibration is categorized (here a "continuum" of gray levels is categorized into two discrete values) a continuous section becomes a locally constant one presenting qualitative discontinuities.

1. The functional dependencies determined at the level of minimal specific differences correspond exactly to *particular* sections $s : W \to E$ of *particular* fibrations $\pi : E \to W$.
2. The qualitative salient discontinuities are modeled by discontinuities of sections $s \in \Gamma(U)$.
3. The eidetic law "concretely determined by its material contents" corresponds to a particular fibration $\pi : E \to W$ of fiber G but without any particular given section. π implicitly contains an infinite universe of potential functional dependencies, namely, all the sets of sections $\Gamma(U)$ for $U \subset W \subset M$. Such a fibration models a first level of abstraction: the global extension M and the qualitative kind G are determined, but not the particular domain W or the section s.
4. The synthetic a priori law of dependence "quality $\to$ extension" corresponds to the general mathematical structure of a fibration. It concerns the most abstract kinds—the essences—of space and quality (this is a second level of abstraction).
5. Last but not least, the "analytic axiomatization" of this synthetic dependence law in the framework of formal ontology corresponds to the *axiomatics* of fibrations, that is, to the *category* (in the mathematical sense) of fibrations.

4.7. THE PROBLEM OF ABSTRACTING QUALITIES

It is possible to confirm the phenomenological relevance of such a "fibrational" schematization by looking at the way it solves the difficult Husserlian problem of abstracting qualities from pre-empirical coverings.

At a (naive) level, one could consider that a "simple" (i.e., constant, uniform) color such as "red" is a common quality shared by all red things. But even if traditional, this naively extensional point of view is not convincing. First, it takes for granted the "atomist" nominalist axiom of the primacy of individuated things. Now, things result from highly complex noetico-noematic processes of constitution and are by no means primitive data. Second, it does not take into account the fact that, in a covering, quality can vary continuously. Hence the question: "Isn't the general use of the concept of quality made possible only by an idealizing concept formation?" (*DR*, p. 363).

Husserl's answer is quite subtle. It is based on the concept of *localization*, that is, of restricting coverings to "small pieces of the surface": one divides the extension into domains where the covering quality can be considered "simple": "Every coloration which is not the extension of a simple quality is decomposed by a space partition into partial colorations of different simple qualities" (p. 363). If the coloration varies a lot, then one must take the *limit* of a decomposition into small domains, and "the simple quality becomes the filling-in of a spatial point" (p. 363).

4.8. SIMPLE QUALITIES AS GERMS OF SECTIONS

We will see later (in section 6.2) that for Husserl the points of the prephenomenal spatial order are not ideal mathematical ones, and are only defined at a certain scale or resolution. But let us suppose for the moment that they are limits of smaller and smaller domains. The problem is the following.

If we admit that the fiber G of the fibration $\pi : E \to M$ *is already known*, and if we consider a section $s \in \Gamma(U)$ over U, then we can of course consider its value $s(w)$ at every point w of U. In particular, for every element p of G—namely, for every "simple" quality—we can consider the *constant* section s_p defined by $s_p(w) = p$ for every $w \in U$. The problem is that knowledge of G *presupposes* the idealizing abstraction of qualities. This confusion between what is constituting and what is constituted is one of the worst phenomenological mistakes.

We must therefore suppose that *we don't already know* G and dispose only of coverings, that is, sections $s \in \Gamma(U)$. How it is then possible to reconstruct G from these data alone?

The first idea is precisely that of localization, that is, of the *restriction* of a section defined over an (open) set U to an (open) subset V of U. Restrictions are transitive. Husserl was aware of this fact. After having explained how spatial continuity confers its unity upon qualitative determinations (see section 4.3), he claims, "But all this is still not enough, and hides something" (*DR*, p. 346), and refines his description: "Color covers extension and forms or orders itself in it. To every fragment of extension there corresponds a fragment of coloration, and also again to each fragment of fragment. And all the partial colorations are ordered in the unity of the global coloration, whose form of order is precisely the global extension" (p. 346).

Through localizations and restrictions, it is possible to shift from the global level to the local one. Reciprocally, it is possible to shift from the local level to the global one by *gluing* local restrictions.

The second main idea for reconstructing the fiber G only from sections is to take the limit of localizations whose domain becomes "point-like." It is Husserl's idea to define a "simple quality" as "a filling-in of a spatial point."

Technically, let $s \in \Gamma(U)$ be a section of π over U. To define its value at $w \in U$ *purely in terms of sections*, we look at the (open) subsets V of U containing w. They form a structure known as a *filter*, and it is possible to take the *limit* of the restrictions of s relative to this filter. In this way we get what is called the *germ* of the section *s* at *w*. It localizes *s* to an "infinitesimal" neighborhood of *w*. And Husserl's eidetic description has been retrieved.

5. PHYSICO-MATHEMATICAL MODELS OF THE THIRD LOGICAL INVESTIGATION

Let us now go on to the possibility of naturalizing this geometric schematization of Husserl's eidetic description by using physico-mathematical models. We will sketch out two examples. They identify the *Verschmelzung* and *Sonderung* noetic syntheses with effective algorithms processing signals (hyletic data).

5.1. THE MUMFORD-SHAH MODEL

One of the main problems of natural and computational vision is to understand how signals can be transformed into geometrically well-behaved observables. The key point is the segmentation process. Let therefore $I(x, y)$ be a rough image. It is an unstructured hyletic datum without any geometrical structure. The question is: how can we go from it to a morphologically organized perceptual image? What "geometry machine" provides its morphological formatting?

More than a thousand segmentation algorithms have been recently worked out which merge local data in homogeneous regular regions and separate the regions by regular crisp edges. The main problem is that two-dimensional regions and one-dimensional edges are *in competition* and, moreover, are geometrical entities of *different dimensions* which interact very subtly. In fact, underlying this proliferation of models there exists a deep unity. As was emphasized by Jean-Michel Morel, "Most segmentation algorithms try to minimize . . . one and the same *segmentation energy*" (Morel and Solimini 1995). Such segmentation energy allows us to compare one segmentation with another and to measure how well it approximates the rough signal. The most popular model for doing so is the Mumford-Shah (David Mumford won a Fields Medal in algebraic geometry and became a specialist in the study of vision).

In a recent paper, "Bayesian Rationale for the Variational Formulation" (Romeny 1994), David Mumford emphasizes that "one of the primary goals of low-level vision is to segment the domain W of an image I into the parts W_i on which distinct surface patches, belonging to distinct objects in the scene, are visible." The mathematical problem is to use low-level cues "for *splitting* and *merging* different parts of the domain W."

In these models, there exist *two parts*: a *prior* model and a *data* model. Actually, the prior model takes as an a priori the phenomenological *Verschmelzung / Sonderung* complementarity (even if there exists of course no reference to phenomenology in computational vision). It imposes the constraint of approximating the signal I by piecewise smooth functions u on W–K, which are discontinuous along the regular edges K.

Now, we pass from the eidetic description to a true mathematical modeling by introducing a way of *selecting*, from among all the allowed approximations (u, K) of I, the best possible one. For this, Mumford used a *functional* $E(u, K)$, which allows the comparison between two segmentations $E(u_1, K_1)$ and $E(u_2, K_2)$. E must contain at least three terms: (1) a term that measures the variation and controls the smoothness of u on the connected components of W–K; (2) one that controls the quality of the approximation of u by I; and (3) one that controls the length, the smoothness, the parsimony, and the location of the boundaries, and inhibits the spurious phenomenon of oversegmentation.

The "energy" E proposed by Mumford and Shah (1989) is:

$$E(u, K) = \int_{W-K} |\nabla u|^2 dx + \int_W (u - I)^2 dx + \int_K d\sigma$$

Minimizing E is a compromise among the following:

1. The homogeneity of u on the connected components of W–K: if $u = cst$ then $\nabla u = 0$ and $\int |\nabla u|^2 dx = 0$, and therefore minimizing this term forces u to be as constant as possible.
2. The approximation of I by u: if $u = I$ then $\int (u - I)^2 dx = 0$, and therefore minimizing this term forces u to be as close as possible to I.
3. The parsimony and the regularity of the boundaries: they are measured by the global length L of K, $L = \int_K d\sigma$, and therefore minimizing this term avoids oversegmentation.

The model can be interpreted probabilistically, using the equivalence $E(u, K) = -\log[p(u, K)]$, p being a probability defined on the space of possible segmentations (u, K).

Such a variational algorithm optimizes the way in which neighboring pixels can be merged in homogeneous regions separated by qualitative discontinuities. It provides, therefore, a *variational* approach to Husserl's *Verschmelzung / Sonderung* duality. It transforms the segmentation problem into a particular case of what is called in physics a "free boundary problem." It is an extremely difficult problem; in fact, it is not yet completely solved.

5.2. MULTISCALE ANALYSIS AND ANISOTROPIC DIFFUSION EQUATIONS

The Mumford-Shah model is variational and global. It is possible to construct other models of the *Verschmelzung / Sonderung* complementarity which are more local and based on anisotropic nonlinear partial differential equations.

The first move consists in interpreting *Verschmelzung* as a *regularization* or smoothing process, which filters the signal by convoluting it with Gaussian profiles. The different widths of the Gaussian profiles correspond to different scales. Such a process is more plausible neurophysiologically, for it is well known that there exist, in the visual system, fields of neurons whose receptive fields are Gaussians. But Gaussians being the kernel of the heat equation, it is possible to interpret the *Verschmelzung* process as the application of a *diffusion equation* to hyletic data in a scale space.[20] The equation is

$$\partial_s I_s = \Delta I_s = \text{div}(\nabla I_s)$$

where I_s is the image blurred at scale s, ∂_s the partial derivative of I relative to s, Δ the Laplace operator, div the divergence, and ∇ the gradient operator.

The problem is that the heat equation is isotropic and homogeneous and cannot, therefore, be *morphological*. It is adapted to the regularization of the image (*Verschmelzung*) but not to its segmentation (*Sonderung*). It also blurs the boundaries. To be morphological, a diffusion equation must preserve boundaries from blurring. Indeed, it should even *enhance* them. This may seem quite impossible because merging and splitting are opposite processes. But it is nevertheless possible if the diffusion equation is *anisotropic*.

Several solutions to this problem have been worked out. The initial key idea was contributed by Jitendra Malik and Pietro Perona and consists in inhibiting the diffusion near the boundaries, that is, in zones of large gradients. It leads to equations of the type

$$\partial_s I_s = \text{div}[g(\nabla I_s) \cdot \nabla I_s]$$

where g is a decreasing positive function such that $g(x) \xrightarrow[x \to \infty]{} 0$.

But the most radical solution is to use a diffusion equation that inhibits the diffusion transversely to the level lines of the image. We get (P.-L. Lions, J.-M. Morel, L. Alvarez) the equation

$$\partial_s I_s = \Delta I_s - \frac{H(\nabla I_s, \nabla I_s)}{|\nabla I_s|^2}$$

where H is the Hessian of I_s (the quadratic form given by its second partial derivatives).[21] It is uniformly parabolic along the level curves of I but totally degenerate in the gradient direction. It makes the level curves evolve as fronts with a normal velocity equal to their curvature (it is the problem known as "curve shortening," "flow by curvature," and "heat flow on isometric immersions").

This example makes still clearer what might be meant by the naturalization of phenomenology (see section 3.5). The eidetic description provides synthetic a priori laws of perception as the foundation law "quality → extension," the complementarity *Verschmelzung / Sonderung*, and so on. These laws shift from a descriptive status to an explicative one by being translated as structural design constraints for effectively implementable algorithms. In this way, we get physico-mathematical models that are naturalist models of noetic synthesis operating on hyletic data and generating a noematic structuring of the phenomena (in this case morphological segmentations).

6. GEOMETRY AND VISION IN *DING UND RAUM*

6.1. THE TWO-DIMENSIONAL SPATIAL ORDER OF THE VISUAL FIELD

Let us come now to our second example. It concerns Husserl's description of the two-dimensional spatial order of the oculomotor field and of its kinesthetic control.

6.1.1. The Basic Character of the Visual Field

Husserl devotes extremely precise analyses to the visual field M considered as a pre-empirical extension endowed with a spatial order. This field is basic because all the adumbrative contents of things are fragments of it. It raises (at least) four questions concerning (1) its structure; (2) its kinesthetic control; (3) the phenomenological constitution of the global space "coperceived" in every perception (it is the phenomenological origin of transcendental aesthetics); and (4) the constitution of "the astonishingly separated position of the ego" as a correlate of the surrounding world. This ego and its lived body allow us to convert pure lived experiences into "internal," psychological, and neurally implemented ones.

6.1.2. The Finiteness of the Field and Space as Manifold (*Mannigfaltigkeit*)

The field's extension is *finite*. This has two main consequences: first, the impossibility of a complete and adequate presentation of a thing (we have already seen that this lies at the root of perceptual intentionality); and second, the synthetic a priori necessity of gluing different fillings-in of the field in order to constitute the temporal flow of perceptive adumbrations in a global space.

The field is structured by the *fixed order* of its positions: "Visual space is the idea of a two-dimensional manifold consisting, to a certain extent, in pure fixed points" (*DR*, p. 313). Its position in the field is therefore a fundamental determination of any element of sensation. It provides its "qualitative particularity" and converts it into what Hermann Lotze called a "local sign" (p. 364).

But the different positions are all equivalent and can be commuted: "The visual field is a two-dimensional manifold which is congruent with itself, continuous, simply homogeneous, finite and, of course, delimited" (§48, p. 165). This is an excellent picture of the characteristic properties of the visual field as a two-dimensional manifold endowed with its group of automorphisms. To summarize:

1. It is a metrically bounded Riemannian manifold (its finiteness is what is called a compacity property).
2. It is a multiscale two-dimensional manifold with varying resolution, fine-grained at its center and coarse-grained at its periphery.[22]
3. It is a homogeneous space whose group of automorphisms acts transitively (it can exchange any two points).

6.1.3. Dimensionality and Stratification

It is well known that it is extremely difficult to define correctly the concept of dimensionality. The standard mathematical definitions are not phenomenologically relevant, for they are abstract and ideal, not intuitive. Phenomenologically, the only intuitive data are fragments of coverings of extension by qualities. Just as Husserl resorted to the iteration of fragmentation to define what can be a "simple" quality (see section 4.5), he resorts to a new remarkable geometrical intuition to define dimension. "Bi-dimensionality means that every fragment of the field is delimited by dependent limits, which themselves are in turn fragmentable continuous manifolds.... But now the limits are no longer fragmentable, they are simple elements of extension, namely, 'points'" (*DR*, §48, p. 166). Since then, this intuition has been formalized, essentially by Hassler Whitney and René Thom, under the name of *stratification*.

Let us consider a domain D of M (an open, connected, and simply connected subset of M equal to the interior of its closure). D has the same dimensionality as M. It has a *boundary* $B = \partial D$. Husserl implicitly assumes that the boundaries are regular (piecewise smooth submanifolds). His first fundamental intuition is that the boundary of a manifold of dimension n is of dimension $n - 1$, that is, that the boundary operation ∂ drops the dimension by 1. His second intuition is that it is possible to iterate the operation ∂ and to consider $\partial^k D$ for $k = 1, 2, \ldots$ His third intuition is that points are nonfragmentable, without boundary, and therefore of dimension 0.

These three key intuitions allow us to define without difficulty the dimension of M. One considers all the possible domains $D \subset M$ and computes the minimal number k of ∂-operations necessary to reach points; k is the "phenomenological" dimension of M.

6.2. THE CONCEPT OF MULTISCALE FIELD

Another fundamental Husserlian intuition concerns the multiscale character of the visual field.

6.2.1. Visual Atoms and Scale Invariance

With regard to the concept of fragmentation, Husserl analyzes the phenomenological relevance of the concept of "point." The question is to know what *"visual atoms"* are and, more precisely, "whether fragmentation, which leads to *minima visibilia*, provides essentially ultimate elements in this way, and if points are therefore the same thing as visual atoms" (*DR*, §48, p. 166). Husserl goes thoroughly into this intuition by emphasizing even the self-similarity and the scale invariance of the pre-phenomenal continuum. He notes "the essential similarity to itself of the visual field, on a large and small scale" and explains that "it is obviously this immanent similarity which, as evident generic similarity, justifies the transposition of the eidetic relationships discovered, so to speak, in the macroscopic universe, to the microscopic 'atoms' situated beyond divisibility" (§48, p. 166).

Husserl therefore introduces the idea that for "visual atoms" a base scale can be established. We find the very same idea in recent theories of vision with the implementation of resolution in the receptive fields of retinal ganglionary cells. Husserl also introduces the idea (largely confirmed by the work on multiscale differential geometry) that classical geometry is an *ideal-*

ization transposing to an infinitesimal scale the eidetic structures drawn from the perceptive scales.

6.2.2. CHANGES OF SCALE AND INTENTIONALITY

Husserl also uses the concept of scale when he analyzes the fact that the field is not really translation-invariant, the images located at its periphery being "less differentiated" than those located at its center (*DR*, §55, p. 193). Resolution is weak (coarse-grained) at the periphery and strong (fine-grained) in the foveal zone. Peripheral images share a "poorer internal differentiation" and "less and less separated parts will be extracted" (ibid.). On the contrary, central images share a "richer" internal differentiation.

In image processing and the neurophysiology of vision, this corresponds to filtering techniques by "pyramidal" (or multiscale) algorithms. One smoothes the optical signal by convoluting it with (for example, Gaussian) filters (see section 5.2). If I_0 is the initial signal (the brute image, the "hyle"), and if one smoothes it at scale s, one gets an image I_s. If $s' > s$, $I_{s'}$ is "poorer" and I_s "richer." One shifts from I_s to $I_{s'}$ by convolution (this is very easy) and, reciprocally, from $I_{s'}$ to I_s by deconvolution (this is very difficult).

This idea is explicit in Husserl. Focalization—a cognitive process linked with attention and interest—allows us to shift continuously from the "poorest" images to the "richest" ones. We will see later that Husserl conceives of the *identifications* between the different parts of the field (when its contents change according to its kinesthetic controls) in terms of "intentional rays" "going through" the images and their presentational contents. He very accurately describes the processing of scale change. Passing to a finer scale enriches the presentational content. This is an "ex-plication" of the image, an increase of differentiation. When a "poor" image differentiates itself into a "richer" one, "every intentional ray divides . . . itself according to these internal differences, and develops itself [*explizierend*]" (§55, p. 193). Such an "ex-plication" reaches a *maximum* in the central region of finest scale. Maximally "ex-plicated" intentions "don't admit any supplementary ex-plication" (p. 195).

Reciprocally, when a "rich" image becomes "poorer," it "de-differentiates" itself. Its presentational capacity becomes weaker. Intentionality no longer "ex-plicates" but "im-plicates" itself.

Husserl introduces here a new key idea, that of a *retention* (a sort of short-term memory) of the "rich" image in the "poor" one. What is distinctly apprehended through attentional focusing "is intentionaly maintained and serves to enrich implication" (*DR*, p. 340). For Husserl, it is because apprehension is susceptible to such "enrichments" and "explications" that it is necessarily intentional. The "rich" retained intention "permeates" "the series of poorer images from which the movement of images flows" (*DR*, §55, p. 194). Accordingly, "the differentiated detail means ... more than what it displays" (§55, p. 195). Exposition is no longer fully explicit, but in part implicit. We meet here a new aspect of this characteristic of intentionality that a perception never reduces to a mere presentational display and is always co-given with an infinite nexus of systematically connected presentations. Not only does there exist for every transcendent object a continuous infinity of co-given adumbrations, but for even a single adumbration there exists a continuous scale of ex-plication. Every object is noematically the unity of an infinity of multiscale aspects, and the fact that infinitely many different images are in fact co-given in any single image implies an intensional (in the pragmatic sense), symbolic, and indexical structure of any perceptual display. The latter is richer than the strict display. It contains potential dimensions to which it refers in a no-longer immediately intuitive but mediately *symbolic* way.

In that sense, there always exists a "semiotic" dimension in perception, each actual perceptual display pointing as a sign—as a Peircean index—toward a potential infinity of other actualizable ones.

6.3. THE CONSTITUTIVE ROLE OF KINESTHESES

6.3.1. The Primacy of the Continuum and the Kinetic Synthesis

For Husserl, the problem of the kinesthetic control of perception belongs to "the great task ... of penetrating as deeply as possible into three-dimensional phenomenological 'creation,' or, in other words, into the phenomenological constitution of the identity of the body of a thing through the multiplicity of its appearances" (*DR*, §44, p. 154). According to him, it would be a "monstrous presumption" to believe there exist simple answers to these problems, for "[they] count among the most difficult questions bearing upon human knowledge" (§44, p. 156).

"The effective identity of the appearing object" cannot result from isolated presentations. As a "meaning identity" linking the different perceptions adumbrating a single thing, it is of a logical nature. But it presupposes the possibility of flowing *continuously* from one adumbration to another: "It is only when, in the unity of experience, the continuous flow from one perception to another is warranted, that we can speak of the evidence according to which an identity is given" (§44, p. 155). In other words, *logical identity depends upon continuous variability*, and according to Husserl, this is the very origin of synthetic a priori laws. The logical synthesis of identity presupposes continuous synthesis, which is the only kind that corresponds to originary intuition. But in so far as continuous synthesis is always temporal, it is in fact a *kinetic* synthesis. It rules phenomenologically temporal series corresponding to three classes of movements, namely, those of the eyes, the body, and objects.

6.3.2. The Kinesthetic Sensations

But here again, it is essential not to confuse the constituting level with the constituted one, and, adopting the natural attitude, consider that the movement of external objects is the most primitive one. For it too results from a constitutional process. In a correct eidetic description, the phenomenological source of movement has to be found not outside but *within* the internal *kinesthetic sensations*.

Husserl starts from the evidence that "the extensional moment of visual sensation . . . is not sufficient for making possible the constitution of spatiality" (DR, §46, p. 160). Kinesthetic sensations are absolutely required. They share a very peculiar status. Indeed, they belong to the "animating" apprehension (the intentional morphe) resulting from noetic syntheses, but without possessing a proper presentational function: they make possible the presentation of external objects without being themselves presentational. We will see that they act as *controls* on the visual field.

Besides their "objectivizing" function, kinesthetic sensations share a "subjectivizing" function that lets the lived body appear as a proprioceptive embodiment of pure experiences, and the adumbrations as subjective events.[23]

6.3.3. The Control Space of Kinestheses and Its Paths

The space $\mathcal{K}$ of kinesthetic controls is multidimensional and hierarchized. It includes varying degrees of freedom for movements of eyes, head, and body. These controls exert their "objectivizing" function through *temporal paths* k_t in $\mathcal{K}$. They "build continuous unities only in the form of paths, where a linear [i.e., one-dimensional] submanifold of the global manifold of kinesthetic sensations [$\mathcal{K}$], superimposes itself, as a filling-in continuum, on the continuous unity of the pre-empirical temporal path" (DR, §49, p. 170).

6.3.4. The Kinesthetic Control and the Relativity of Movement

There exists an obvious equivalence between a situation where the eyes move and the objects in the visual field remain at rest, and the reciprocal situation where the eyes remain at rest and the objects move. But this trivial aspect of the relativity principle is by no means phenomenologically trivial, at least if one does not confuse what is constituting and what is constituted. Relativity presupposes an *already* constituted space. At the pre-empirical constituting level, one must be able to discriminate the two equivalent situations. The kinesthetic control paths are essential for achieving such a task.

6.3.5. The Kinesthetic Control Is Not Directly an Associative Link

Husserl starts with the simplest situation where, the body being fixed and the objects remaining at rest, the control reduces to the correspondance $k \leftrightarrow i$ between the purely ocular kinesthetic sensation and the visual image i. A temporal series $t_1, \ldots, t_n$ entails a series of correspondances $k_1 \leftrightarrow i_1, \ldots, k_n \leftrightarrow i_n$, and a temporal flow, a continuous correspondance $k_t \leftrightarrow i_t$.

Husserl then analyzes the nature of the dependence relation $k \leftrightarrow i$ and shows that it cannot be an associative one (in the sense of reinforcement learning). Obviously, a control k cannot determine any particular image i. Any control k can be linked with any image i. There exists therefore no association, no "empirical motivation," between k and i. What can be the nature of the link?

6.3.6. Kinesthetic Controls Act as Operators on Paths

Husserl's idea is the following. Let us consider an initial link $k' \leftrightarrow i'$ and another image i'' (compatible with i'). To each visual path i_t going from i' to i'' corresponds a kinesthetic path k_t going from k' to another control k'', which will settle a new (final) link $k'' \leftrightarrow i''$. In other words, "associated with the representation of an image movement $i' \leftrightarrow i''$, I immediately get the representation of a kinesthetic flow $k' \leftrightarrow k''$, as a flow belonging to it" (§51, p. 179). This eidetic description can be modeled in the following way. Let $\mathcal{F}$ be the "space" of visual images. Ideally (that is, if one doesn't take into account the pixelization of images), it is a functional space of infinite dimension. $\mathcal{K}$ *controls* $\mathcal{F}$ in the sense that the *paths* in $\mathcal{K}$ operate on the *paths* in $\mathcal{F}$. More precisely, let $k \leftrightarrow i$ be an initial link and k_t a path with origin k in $\mathcal{K}$ (an ocular movement). The k_t determines a movement in $\mathcal{F}$ (an image movement) i_t and, moreover, with the same temporal parametrization. This correlation is sufficiently strong to allow the visual system to solve the *inverse problem*, namely, to retrieve the path k_t from the given path i_t.

But this clarification is not sufficient. The movements i_t are variations of

356 *Jean Petitot*

the contingent filling-in of the visual field M. And the problem is to understand the nature of the link between $\mathcal{K}$ and M themselves. There exists a "fixed association," not between any $k \in \mathcal{K}$ and any $i \in \mathcal{F}$ but between M and $\mathcal{K}$ *as such*, that is, between "the entire extension" and "k in general." And Husserl asks "how to understand and describe more exactly the phenomenological situation" (§51, p. 180) constituted on the one hand by the fixed association $M \leftrightarrow \mathcal{K}$ and, on the other hand, by the nonassociative correlations $k_t \leftrightarrow i_t$?

6.3.7. Kinesthetic Controls Are Gluing Operators

Husserl discusses the elementary example of a square S with corners a, b, c, d. His description can be formalized in the following way. Let us suppose for simplicity that the field M is a simple domain D (a disk). To focus on the point a means that D is centered on a. (We also assume that the square is sufficiently small relative to D; if this is not the case we have to consider sufficiently many intermediate points). (See Figure 11.6.)

To each position $p = a, b, c, d$ corresponds a token D_p of the field D. And if the figure i_a filling in D_a can "refer" to the figure i_b filling in D_b, it is because D_a and D_b *overlap*, and are *glued* together through their intersection $U_{ab} = D_a \cap D_b$. This means that there exists a local gluing isomorphism ϕ_{ab}: $U_{ab} \subset D_a \to U_{ab} \subset D_b$ identifying the intersection U_{ab} viewed as a subdomain of D_a with the same U_{ab} viewed as a subdomain of D_b. In the continuous limit, there exists a temporal series D_t with gluing operators $\phi_{tt'}$ for t and t' sufficiently near. This spatiotemporal series is filled in by the image series i_t.

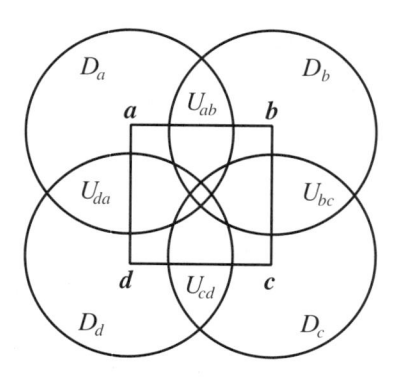

FIGURE 11.6. Scanning square S with corners a, b, c, d. To each position p corresponds a token D_p of the visual field D centered on p (focalization on p). The neighboring D_p overlap.

To say that the "pointing" of each i_t to other $i_{t'}$ is *intentional*, or that intentions "go through" the series i_t, is to say that intentionality corresponds to gluing operators identifying different points of the visual flow as the same. This interpretation will be confirmed later (in section 6.3.9) when we will see Husserl introducing "intentional rays going through the images" to identify the corresponding points of different images (point tracking).

More precisely, intentionality corresponds to the realization in consciousness of the gluing operators.[24] Once again, it is essential here not to confuse, as the natural attitude does, the constituting level and the constituted one. For the latter there exists a priori an ambient global space where the continuous series of the D_t and of the fillings-in i_t are embedded. *But in absence of such a space, only the D_t and the gluing operators $\phi_{tt'}$ remain, and one shifts from the local level to the global one by gluing local charts all identical to D.* The gluing operators must therefore be realized in consciousness. This is the main role of kinesthetic controls: *the k_t are gluing protocols.*

We have therefore to distinguish three levels: (1) kinesthetic controls k_t, which are paths in $\mathcal{K}$; (2) manifolds resulting from gluing identical D_t according to the k_t (namely, by identifying corresponding points through "intentional rays going through the images"); and (3) qualitative fillings-in i_t of the D_t.

It is through the D_t that the k_t control the i_t and $\mathcal{K}$ controls $\mathcal{F}$. The temporal paths in $\mathcal{K}$ act on $\mathcal{F}$. Let $k_0 \leftrightarrow i_0$ be an initial link and let us consider a path k_t in $\mathcal{K}$ with origin k_0. k_t acts as a gluing protocol for the flow D_t of the visual field. D_0 is filled in by i_0, D_t by i_t, and the gluing of the D_t induces the gluing of the i_t in a "glanced over" global image. The spatial gluing of the i_t, and their intentional referring presupposes a temporal gluing, an immediate memory, a "retention" of i_t in $i_{t'}$, for t' sufficiently close to t.

6.3.8. The Categorization of $\mathcal{F}$-Paths by $\mathcal{K}$-Paths

Such a schematization (which Husserl could have gotten from Hermann Weyl if he had been less dogmatic) allows us to clarify one of the most difficult paragraphs of *Ding und Raum*, namely §52, where Husserl tries to make more explicit the control $\mathcal{K} \leftrightarrow M$ (M is the true visual field, and D is a simplified version as a two-dimensional disk). First, as we already seen, no association $k \rightarrow i$ can exist between a particular kinesthetic sensation and a particular image. On the other hand, insofar as the pre-empirical field M is a system of fixed places, it cannot admit any association $k \leftrightarrow M$ either. The manifold M "doesn't provide any base for a link $[k \leftrightarrow i]$. For it is precisely always there, always given with any k and therefore with all possible k and

k-paths" (§52, p. 183). The solution to this difficulty proposed by Husserl is quite subtle: "The link can consist only in the *formal unity* of paths" (our emphasis). This means that the paths i_t of $\mathcal{F}$ are grouped in *equivalence classes* $[i_t]$ (that is, categories), which Husserl calls *path types*. It is only with an image path *type* that a determined kinesthetic path can be associated. Between a path type $[i_t]$ and a kinesthetic path k_t an associative link can exist—and does exist effectively—that is, a true control (a motivation). It is the "form"—the type—of paths in $\mathcal{F}$ that is associated with paths in $\mathcal{K}$.

Husserl therefore introduces the profound and beautiful idea that the paths k_t in $\mathcal{K}$ *categorize* the space of paths i_t in $\mathcal{F}$. But this means exactly that the paths k_t act on the paths i_t. Let i_0 be an initial image: k_t defines—through the gluing protocol for the D_t—a path type $[i_t]$, and the image path i_t is the token with origin i_0.

Moreover, we even find in *Ding und Raum* the idea that the image flows i_t are in fact *trajectories of vector fields* in the functional space of images $\mathcal{F}$. Besides the retention in every i_t of the $i_{t'}$ preceding it (for $t' < t$ sufficiently close to t), there exists also a *protention* of i_t in the successive $i_{t'}$ (for $t' > t$ again sufficiently close to t), what Husserl called an "infinitesimal deformation" of i_t. Husserl had a clear idea of what is called a tangent vector to a manifold, since he spoke of "linear direction of change" and of "differential."

6.3.9. Transversal Intentionality and Intentional Rays: From Identification to Identity

We have seen that a thing (at rest) is constituted through "an ideal system of possible continuous series of appearances temporally coinciding with possible, continuous, and motivating kinesthetic series" (*DR*, §55, p. 190). These series are the trajectories $k_t \leftrightarrow i_t$, and the correlated thing is provided by the *unity* of their flow. Now, unity is based on an "intention-toward" (the protention along the temporal trajectory), which is not "delimited": "By virtue of its essence, it doesn't terminate in the determined image.... It goes through it and keeps this character of a transversal element, independently of the way the continuity of appearances can extend" (§55, p. 190).

But what can the nature of this "transversal" intentionality be? It is here that Husserl introduces the concept of *intentional ray*. As he puts it: "Intentional rays which go through the actually given images ... link, in a consciousness of unity, corresponding points of continuously transformed images" (§55, p. 191). Intentional rays process what can be called a "point tracking." They are gluing isomorphisms embedding a part of i_t in $i_{t'}$, Husserl speaks even of a "'mono-univocal' correspondance" (p. 198), what is now called an injection (or a monomorphism). Identity consciousness is based on such operations of identification: "Points located on the same intentional ray display . . . one and the same objective point" (§56, p. 198). Husserl stresses this fundamental fact: "A consciousness setting unit here goes through the pre-empirical temporal continuity, [and] a flow of contents, tracked by the intentional ray, displays, step by step, the same thinglike point" (§56, p. 198).

We show in Figure 11.7 how a global image I with global extension W can be constituted via a window D (a square for simplicity) moving diago-

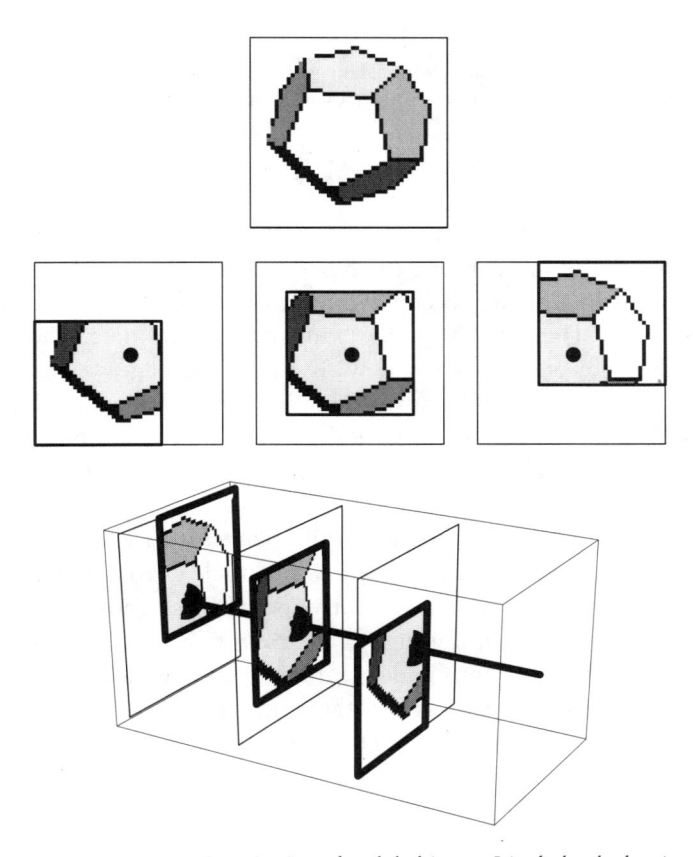

FIGURE 11.7. Constitution of a global image I (a dodecahedron) in a global window W by moving a sub-window D (a square) in W. Top, I in W. Center, evolution of D. A point p occupies different locations in the different tokens of D. Bottom, an intentional ray tracks p and transforms it into an individuated objective "thing-like" point.

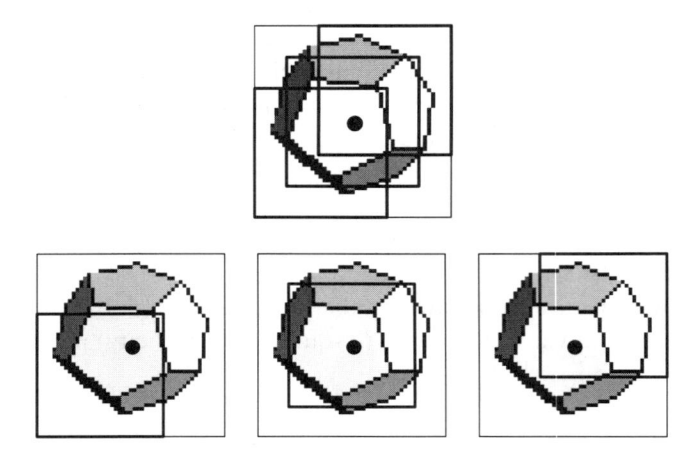

FIGURE 11.8. Once the global image *I* is constituted, we can think of the visual field *D* as a window moving in an objective external ambient space *W*.

nally in *W*.²⁵ In the first image we see *I* in *W*. In the second image we see how *D* evolves. We show in fact the filling-in of three exemplars of *D*. We show also a distinct point *p* occupying three different locations in the three exemplars of *D*. They represent the "immanent" local data whose gluing produces the "objective" extension *W*. In the third image we show the intentional ray tracking *p* and transforming it into an individuated objective "thing-like" point. In Figure 11.8 we show how, once the objective image has been constituted, it becomes possible to think of the visual field as a window moving in *W*.

We grasp very well here the necessarily *noematic* essence of objects as identity poles: a trajectory of identified points tracked from image to image corresponds to one and the same objective point. The condition of the possibility of any transcendent object is that "every point, in its relative place, is set up as an identical [unit] and intentionally maintained as an identical [unit]" (§61, p. 218). We witness here the genesis and the emergence of transcendence out of immanent acts and contents.

6.4. ELEMENTS FOR THE CONSTITUTION OF OBJECTIVE REALITY

Supplied with these basic eidetic descriptions, Husserl tackles the different components of objective reality. We have no room here to discuss this phase of his work. We will simply note that he begins with the constitution of objective *temporality*. That each point possesses its "pre-empirical temporal place" in an image path i_t, implies that the identical objective (thing-like) point associated with a trajectory (a "transversal intentional ray") becomes an *individuated* point *temporally parametrized*. In other words, *once constituted, the noematic identity of the objects*, the trajectories of identification yielded by noetic syntheses, can be interpreted, according to the natural attitude, *as objectively temporal trajectories of individuated objective points*. So, temporality radically changes its status. It shifts from the lived pre-empirical immanence to the objective transcendence it displays.

Husserl also discusses the constitutive role of the different levels of kinesthetic control. Though already rather rich, the previous description concerned only the most elementary case of an object at rest and a kinesthetic control restricted to the oculomotor level. But there exist several coupled kinesthetic systems: eyes, head, body. Moreover, external objects can present different forms of movement: they can move across the visual field, they can approach or recede, they can rotate, and so on. This fact notably complexifies the relations between *k*-controls and *i*-displays but doesn't fundamentally change the principles of analysis.

Husserl also investigates binocular vision and stereopsis, with regard particularly to the constitution of objective three-dimensional space and the three-dimensional objects embedded in it. He emphasizes that stereopsis results from the fact that the two binocular images are not perfectly identical. Their slight discrepancies are *interpreted* by the visual system as relief cues and "depth values" (p. 173) superposed upon qualitative discontinuities.

Here again, Husserl's description is astonishingly modern. Pre-empirical (immanent, noetic) depth has nothing to do with a supplementary third dimension. But it *displays* a noematic properties of objective spatiality, namely the third dimension: "These differences of relief are not at first differences of place, but *they acquire the meaning* of differences of place" (§49, p. 174, our emphasis). It is apprehension (as interpretation and intentional morphe) that after having computed the tiny gaps between the two binocular images, constitutes, constructs cognitively, infers, the third objective dimension.

Studies on stereopsis, from Bela Julesz's pioneering works to Ninio's self-stereograms[26] show that this pure eidetic description is in perfect agreement with the present results of visual cognition.

To bring these few remarks on *Ding und Raum* to a close, we will underline the manner in which Husserl connects the typification of displaying paths (noesis) with objective ontology (noema). The main idea is that *ontological* characters of external objects are correlated to kinesthetically motivated *types* of possible chains of adumbrations. This point is crucial for the naturalization of the phenomenology of perception.

On the one hand, Husserl stresses the fact that the geometrical concepts of point, line, surface, place, figure, size, and so on, used in eidetic descriptions *are not spatial* "in the thing-like sense," since what is at stake is precisely the phenomenological genesis of the objective space. In particular, it is "senseless" to believe that "the visual field is . . . in any way a surface in objective space" (§48, p. 166), that is, to act "as if the oculomotor field were located, as a surface, in the space of things" (§67, p. 236).

But on the other hand, Husserl also explains that the kinesthetic complex, which with its coupled levels, allows us to access the infinite space and an "integral" (but always inadequate) display of the objects, "makes the oculomotor field (eventually enlarged to infinity) the mere projection of a three-dimensional spatial thingness" (§63, p. 227). In other words, once the three-dimensional global space $\mathbf{R}^3$ has been constituted (through two-dimensional gluings and stereopsis), *one can reverse the dependence order* between what is constituting and what is constituted, and act as if (1) the visual field M were embedded as a fragment of surface in $\mathbf{R}^3$; and (2) the filling-in adumbrations were projections on M of objects in $\mathbf{R}^3$, and were therefore *causally* generated by them. As a result, what comes first in the order of phenomenological constitution becomes second in the order of objective causality, and vice versa. We meet here the main example of the inversion of priorities between the phenomenological approach and the objectivist one in the natural attitude. We witness the genesis of objective ontology.

Among all possible paths i_t, only those which are kinesthetically motivated are really possible (Husserl calls them "real possibles"). But this extremely strong constraint imposed by the *kinesthetic control* can also be expressed by *global geometric constraints* on images. The "computation" processed on the i_t through the "circumscribed lawfulness" constraining them, can also be executed from geometrical *transcendent* hypotheses setting a three-dimensional space, external objects, planes and directions of projection, and projections. That is why one can posit spatial three-dimensional objectivity and express the lawfulness of adumbrative flows *as if* it were a consequence. Frontal translations, closeness/remoteness, rotations, changes of orientation, occlusions, and so on, are object transformations that are *encoded* in typical transformations of images. But they are exactly the same as if they had proceeded from projections of Euclidean automorphisms of $\mathbf{R}^3$.

In short, the typification of the temporal flow of paths i_t is actually imposed by the kinesthetic control (the motivation). But it is *also* describable in terms of objective transformations (rotations, etc.) of the noematic invariants extracted from the flow. In that sense, it determines a "thing-like" ontology of external objects.

We see up to what point objectivity is here *transcendental* and not naively ontological. It is the intentional (noematic) *correlate* of eidetico-constitutive rules operating noetically on hyletic data formatted by a pre-empirical transcendental aesthetics.

Let us stress again that an inversion of perspective becomes possible once three-dimensional space and three-dimensional objects become available as constituted entities. One can interpret in an objectivist way the continuous transformation i_t of two-dimensional images as if the body were embedded in objective space $\mathbf{R}^3$, as if the oculomotor field were a piece of surface defined by the position of the body, and as if three-dimensional objects were projected onto it. Husserl claims that "from a formal point of view," these transformations are "exactly" the same as for "projections of a geometrical body on a plane" (§69, p. 241). This claim is essential, for it shows that "from a formal point of view"—that is, from the point of view of *an appropriate geometrical eidetics*—there exists an *equivalence* between the phenomenological-constitutive and the causalist-objectivist approaches. Sharing a *common* formal level, these two apparently opposed perspectives are in fact deeply *complementary*.

We therefore measure the crucial importance of a pure *geometrical* descriptive eidetics. Neutral as to the phenomenology of appearances and the ontology of things, it can be realized in *two* complementary ways: (1) cognitively, and in that case the problems of implementing noetic synthesis will have priority; and (2) objectively, and in that case the problems of physical causality will have priority. In this sense, it is the key to the naturalization of the phenomenology of perception.

7. ADUMBRATIVE PERCEPTION

7.1. IMPORTANCE OF ADUMBRATIVE PERCEPTION

A third remarkable example where Husserl's eidetic description is akin to contemporary cognitive research is that of adumbrative perception. We have already evoked it several times.

In the different elements of *Abschattungslehre* scattered throughout his works, Husserl investigates several problems whose contemporary relevance is striking.

1. The enigmatic *equivalence* between the temporal flow of adumbrations and the object = X as an intentional unity and noematic pole. We have seen that there exist eidetic "chaining rules," that is, a "descriptive composition" and an "internal organization" *prescriptive* for experiences. Such rules are correlative of the noematic unity of the object. They rule its appearing, its mode of display.

2. The incompleteness of adumbrations implies that the complete determination of object givenness can be only *temporal*. Incompleteness and temporality are essentially linked and manifest our cognitive finitude. Constituted in the immanent temporality of the pure Ego, the flow of adumbrations unfolds a dynamic order. Whence the key problematic of *anticipation*. The possibility of ruled coherent anticipations is one of the main characteristics of objective transcendence.
3. The incompleteness of adumbrations also generates a *horizon of co-givenness*: an actual adumbration is inseparable from an infinity of other potential and virtual ones.
4. Incompleteness generates finally the gap between intuition and intention. It produces the intentional meaning of the noematic object. As was stressed by Ronald McIntyre, it is essentially because the complete determination of givenness can only be temporal and grounded in anticipations that noematic rules are *semantic*. This attests to the phenomenological genesis of sense and denotation.

7.2. FLOW OF ADUMBRATIONS AND TEMPORAL SYNTHESIS

7.2.1. Adumbrations and Inadequate Givenness

Each perceptual display giving the object "properly" and "in person" is related to a horizon of other possible "improper" (unfit to match the hyletic data but counterfactually actualizable) displays lacking any presentational content. Each perceptual display is therefore necessarily embedded in a temporal flow of adumbrations evolving continuously "in a merged [*verschmolzen*] unity" out of which noeses extract intentional noematic identities. In every adumbration there is more than the adumbration itself. There is also the referring to (pointing toward) other co-given potential adumbrations.

Improper adumbrations are not intuitively presented but "symbolically" represented. This certainly does not mean that they are imaginary. Imagination is also an adumbrative faculty. The problem is that symbolic pointing is a constitutive part of the immediacy of intuition. The givenness of an object "in person" always acts as a *sign* as well. The direct acquaintance in perceptual evidence is in fact essentially indirect: "It refers, *thanks to its sense*, to possibilities of filling-in, to a continuous-unitary chaining of appearances" (*DR*, §35, p. 124, our emphasis).

7.2.2. Anticipations and Misapprehensions

The essential incompleteness and inadequacy of adumbrative perception implies the a priori synthetic necessity of ruled anticipations. But in-

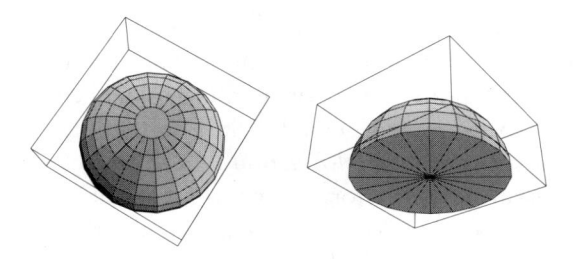

FIGURE 11.9. The problem of generic anticipations. They are nonmonotonic. When we see a spherical form from one vantage point, we anticipate seeing a spherical form from all vantage points. But of course that is not necessarily the case.

sofar as the other co-given adumbrations of the object correspond to non-intuitively filled-in intentions, anticipation can only be an expectation (and not an inference). This means two things.

First, anticipation will be only "*generic.*" It will concern only the most probable and typical expectations. If we look from one viewpoint at what appears to be a sphere (Locke's example used by Husserl), we will assume that it is effectively a uniform sphere. But of course this is not necessarily the case. It could for instance only be a hemisphere. (See Figure 11.9.)

Second, mismatch is therefore possible and anticipations can fail. Generic anticipations are nonmonotonic (in the sense of default logics).

However, even if a fully determined anticipation is impossible, every anticipation remains submitted to the "circumscription," legalizing a priori the concept of an object. A mismatched anticipated adumbration can only be replaced by another *compatible* one.

7.2.3. Generic Anticipations and Typical Adumbrations

In *Ding und Raum*, Husserl analyzes in great detail *generic* anticipations. We have seen that in a flow of adumbrations, there exists a "protentional" "differential of movement" (that is, tangent vectors) defining anticipations and expectations. But among all the possible adumbrations of an object, certain are privileged and display the object in an optimal way.

Husserl introduces the profound idea that the "fullness" of presentation has a "degree." Not all adumbrations are informationally equivalent. The optimal ones are those of maximal degree: "The increase of filling-in or completeness of givenness comes to an end at limit points . . . where the increase becomes a decrease" (§32, p. 107). These "turning points" are "maximal points" of the "fullness of data." Protention (pointing toward) is not only a tangent vector (a "differential of movement") along an adumbrative path A_t. It is also a tendency toward the maximal informational completion.

Everything happens as if one could define, on the functional space $\mathcal{A}$ of adumbrations, a sort of *potential function F* (as in the classical calculus of variations)[27] measuring their informational content (their "degree"), a function whose maxima would select the optimal adumbrations. The idea is that there exists a *variational principle* governing the *anticipated* adumbrative flows (and not of course the effective flow, which is determined by the kinesthetic controls). The best adumbrations then act as *prototypes*, as "*attractors*" attracting the paths A_t.

Husserl is perfectly aware of the mathematical fact that the maxima of F must be *critical points*. We have seen that he speaks of "turning points where the increase becomes a decrease." They produce "preferential" prototypical (but still inadequate) displays. And Husserl concludes that adumbrations "*are themselves adumbrated* in this new sense" (§35, p. 125; our emphasis). The idea is astonishing. These *second-order* adumbrations correspond, in the realm of immanent experiences, to "the consciousness of givenness in its own and par excellence." It is toward them "that tend, in a way, every other display, every other consciousness of givenness, . . . the *intention* in the flow of perceptions" (§36, pp. 125–26).

According to Husserl, there exists therefore a *double* dynamic in the space $\mathcal{A}$. In so far as adumbrations are images ($\mathcal{A} \subset \mathcal{F}$), there exists the kinesthetic control $\mathcal{K}$ whose paths act on paths in $\mathcal{A}$ (see section 6.3). But insofar as each adumbration points spontaneously (without any k-control) toward an optimal filling-in, there exists also an optimization dynamic X on $\mathcal{A}$. X is the gradient dynamic associated with the potential F measuring the informational content (the "degree") of the elements $A \in \mathcal{A}$. The trajectories of X "climb up" F to its maxima (prototypical adumbrations), and $\mathcal{A}$ is so categorized in attractor basins. According to such a variational principle, perceptual intentionality is also always intentional in the sense of *finality*. As is stressed by Husserl, "this consciousness of [maximal] givenness . . . is the end of perceptive movement" (§36, p. 226).

Once again, we verify the extent to which Husserlian intentionality depends upon a continuous synthetic synthesis and a functional geometrodynamical schematism that has absolutely nothing to do with a logical theory of denotation.

7.2.4. Structural Stability and Relevance

Husserl introduces two other important ideas concerning prototypical adumbrations.

The first one is very akin to that of *structural stability*, pervasive in contemporary differential geometry thanks to great mathematicians such as Whitney, Thom, Smale, and Arnold. The prototypical adumbrations (maximal points) are structurally stable—or *generic*—in that they can vary "inside some limits" without altering the apprehension of the object: "noticeable" differences in the appearances are nevertheless informationally "insignificant": "The visual intention enters the privileged zone, but for the filling-in of this intention, every appearance that does not exceed some limit of variation is suitable" (§36, p. 128). In other words, there exists around each maximal point a central domain of strong stability where the quantitative discrepancies are qualitatively (morphologically) negligible.

7.2.5. Typicality, Relevance, Interest, and Conceptualization

Husserl specifies also his idea of "fullness of givenness." The potential F measuring the "fullness of data" (the informational content) depends upon the interest, the relevance, and the attention at stake in apprehension: "The spheres of completeness, the maximal points and zones, do not belong to the essence of appearance as such, but to the interest grounded in it and to the afferent attention" (§37, p. 130). For instance, in the perception of an object there will be an optimal face, an optimal distance, and so on. These optima are preferential in the sense of the modern theory of *prototypes* and *categories*.

Husserl then stresses the fact that this theory of optimal adumbrations provides the ground for "the empirical forming of concepts." *Conceptual generalization is a complex cognitive process rooted in the synthetic a priori laws of perceptual adumbrations.* It is a generalization through typicality. An empirical concept is no longer logically defined by its extension, but functionally as a *type*, as a *schema* in Kant's sense: "The way the concept is oriented is determined by the interest which rules the process of concept formation, the constitution of the consciousness of generality" (§37, p. 130). This very modern approach to concept formation is all the more remarkable, since it was elaborated in a period when the logicist's extensional conception prevailed.

7.3. GEOMETRICAL EIDETICS OF APPARENT CONTOURS

For a long time, I have stressed the link between Husserl's *Abschattungslehre* and many works in differential geometry and computational vision. The case is particularly clear in what concerns the key problem of outlines or *apparent contours* (ACs).

We must first use multiscale segmentation techniques (see section 5.2) for

368 *Jean Petitot*

extracting from the signal geometrically well-behaved boundaries. Then we must use stereopsis and other cues (e.g., shading) to interpret these boundaries as ACs of three-dimensional, external objects. Let us suppose that these (difficult) tasks are already achieved. The remaining problem is then one of an essentially geometrical nature.

Geometrically, the Husserlian problem of the equivalence between a transcendent object T embedded in three-dimensional ambient space $\mathbf{R}^3$ and the family (the functional space) of its adumbrating ACs is an absolutely nontrivial *inverse problem*. The direct problem is: given $T \subset \mathbf{R}^3$ and a projection π (that is, a plane of projection P and a direction of projection δ), build the AC $AC_T(\pi)$ of T to π. It is already nontrivial and requires sophisticated mathematical concepts. Indeed an AC is the projection on P of the *singular locus* S of the restriction of π to T. S is the locus of points x of T where the direction δ is tangent to T and $AC_T(\pi)$ is the projection $\pi(S)$ of S.

In Figure 11.10, we represent in perspective the singular locus S of a horizontal torus T for a direction making a $\pi/12$ angle with the horizontal plane. We represent S alone, and S on the torus. In Figure 11.11 we also represent four adumbrations of T. Finally, in Figure 11.12, we represent eight ACs of T along a rotation path. The key feature is that between the second and the third steps, the AC presents two symmetrical exemplars of a singularity known as a swallowtail, whose unfolding creates two cusp points and a crossing point. We see perfectly well on this example what the optimal AC type is. It is the most complex one in the sense of singularity theory (Figures 11.11 and 11.12.)

Thanks to singularity theory, it is possible to classify the singularities appearing *generically* in ACs. They can visually be detected through fields of neural cells sharing appropriate receptive profiles.

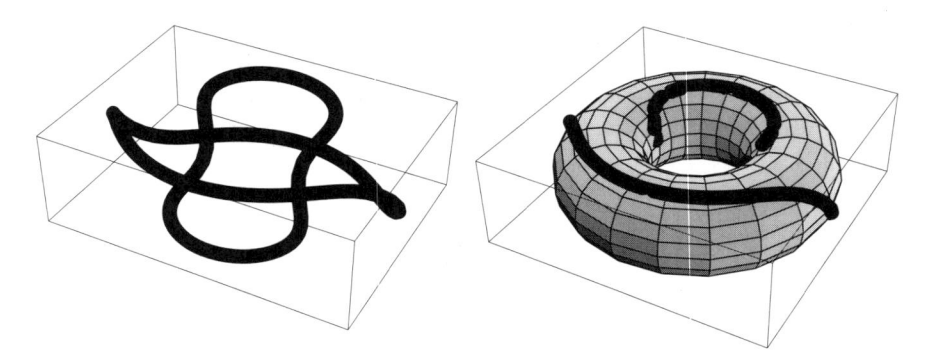

FIGURE 11.10. The singular locus S of an horizontal torus T for a direction making a $\pi/12$ angle with the horizontal plane. *Left*, S alone. *Right*, S on the torus.

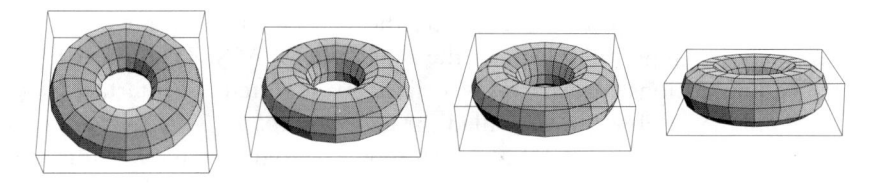

FIGURE 11.11. Four adumbrations of a torus T.

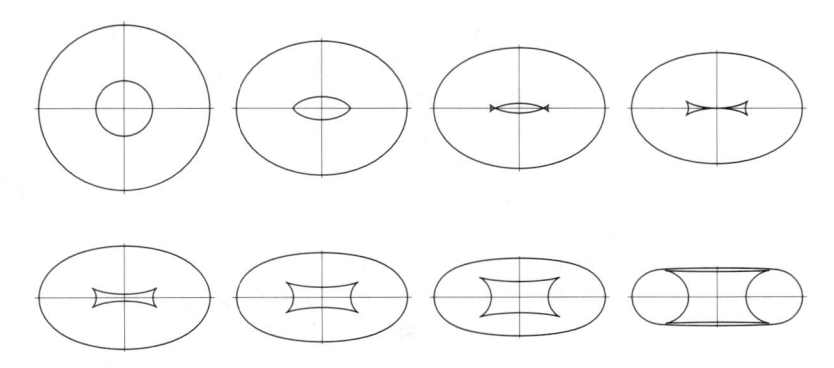

FIGURE 11.12. Eight apparent contours (ACs) of a torus T along a rotation path. Between the second and third steps, the AC presents two symmetrical swallowtail singularities whose unfolding creates four cusp points and two crossing points.

The situation becomes particularly interesting when singularity theory is coupled with the Riemannian geometry of the surface T: elliptic zones (where the points are like those of an ellipsoid), hyperbolic ones (whose points are saddle-like) with their two fields of asymptotic directions, and the parabolic curves separating these two kinds of zones. In accordance with the position of the direction of projection δ relative to these elements, one gets different singularities. For instance, the swallowtails of a torus correspond to the points where δ is tangent to an asymptotic curve at an inflection point (what is called a flecnodal point). The most complex case is that of "Godron points" where δ is a double asymptotic direction tangent to a parabolic curve.

If we consider now the space V of projections π, we can analyze the temporal evolution of the ACs of T along a path in V. This evolution depends on how V is decomposed into domains, each of which corresponds to ACs of the same qualitative type. What is called an *aspect* is a generic central value of a qualitative type. It is exactly what Husserl called a typical adumbration.

We see that the shape of *T categorizes* the space *V* of viewpoints in categories, each grouping the tokens of the same type of ACs. This categorization of adumbrations in aspects is realized by a system of interfaces K_T whose combinatorial version is called the *aspect graph* of *T*: G_T. There exists an *equivalence* between *T* and K_T. *T* allows us to determine K_T: it is the (easy) direct problem. Reciprocally, K_T allows us to reconstruct *T*: it is the (difficult) inverse problem.

The geometric equivalence $T \Leftrightarrow G_T$ is the mathematical version of the Husserlian eidetico-constitutive law. It can be formulated in terms of temporal flows by exploring the categorization K_T through *temporal paths* in *V*. This conversion of a "synchronic" structure into a "diachronic" one is the root of perceptive intentionality. It generates the belief in external reality.

We see the duality correlating the object = *X* as a noematic pole of identity and the adumbrations displaying the different aspects of the object. Every AC has a noetic face (the associated information processing) and a noematic face (its geometry). It is a noematic *appearance* and not a noematic *meaning*, a presentational content and not a propositional one. It can be conceived of in two complementary ways. If one considers it as a projection of an already constituted three-dimensional object embedded in objective space (see section 6.4), then it is an objective datum informing the cognitive system about the external world. In that case it depends upon a causal theory of reference and is a *large* content. On the other hand, if one considers it as an element of a system of other co-given ACs, it is a *narrow* content, functionally determined by its relations with them.

The link between the two perspectives is given by the object = *X* acting as a coherence and identity principle for the considered ACs, warranting a solution to the inverse problem because the aspect graph can be generated by a possible object. The object = *X* can never be displayed in perception. It acts semantically as a denoting symbol, but in a nontrivial way. In fact, it acts *in an intensional, indexical, and pragmatic way*, as a *choice operator* selecting counterfactually an aspect and actualizing it among others, which remain virtual (horizon of co-givenness).

We arrive therefore at the conclusion that there exists what Husserl calls a perceptive "*genealogy*" of denotation. It is only at higher cognitive levels, when objects have been converted into symbols that denotation in its classical logical sense recovers its rights. In the simplest act of denotation, information is processed in a twofold manner: morphologically (as adumbrations, incompleteness, anticipations, and so on) and symbolically (as denotation).

CONCLUSION

It is impossible to tackle here the many other correlated problems. We take the liberty of referring the reader to our other works for the following problems:

1. That of the natural *mereology* of spatial domains filled in by sensible qualities (namely, of sections of fibrations).[28]
2. That of the links between the descriptive eidetics of perceptive morphologies and the syntactico-semantic theory of perceptive *judgments*. Using deep links between formal logic and fibrations and more generally *sheaves* (what is called the *theory of topoi*), it is possible to formalize the *perceptual genealogy of predication* brilliantly worked out by Husserl in *Erfahrung und Urteil* (1939).[29]
3. That of the *internal temporal coding* of the geometry of vision, especially through synchronization processes in the visual cortex. The issue of internal temporal coding raises fascinating questions concerning the neural implementation of the inner consciousness of time.[30]

Anyway, we hope to have shown that contrary to Husserl's constant claim, there *does* exist a *geometrical* descriptive eidetics able to assume for perception the constitutive tasks of transcendental phenomenology and to mathematize the correlations between the kinetic noetic syntheses and the noematic morphological *Abschattungen*. Using such a geometrical descriptive eidetics, the naturalization of phenomenology can be reduced to the problem of implementing effective algorithms. For that very reason we are convinced that morphodynamical functionalism is the key to naturalizing phenomenology.

Translated by Christopher Macann

CHAPTER TWELVE

Formal Structures in the Phenomenology of Motion

ROBERTO CASATI

Husserl wrote that the Ur-Earth does not move, thereby thinking to express one of our pretheoretical, prescientific beliefs—that the Earth does not move. He thought it necessary to talk of an Ur-Earth, because he knew, as we do, that the Earth moves. It is, however, unfelicitous to just swap names, for if the Earth moves, and the Ur-Earth does not, it follows then that the Ur-Earth is not the Earth. But obviously when we jump on the Ur-Earth, we thereby jump on the Earth.

It is not by changing the subject matter of our discourse that we can best capture the form of our pretheoretical beliefs. After all, it is of the Earth itself that we (falsely) believe that it does not move. The ordinary way of speech is already adequate; there is no need to postulate a parallel ur-reality in order to say that we have false beliefs about ordinary reality.

Here we shall investigate the commonsense picture of rest and movement. Our starting point will be some pretheoretical, prescientific beliefs, such as the belief that the Earth does not move. We do have these false beliefs, and we have many more about motion in general, not only about a *particular* moving object. Some of these arise quite directly from the underdeterminacy of perception. The dialectic of rest and motion has a firm perceptual ground; our concepts err because our percepts do. We are unable to perceive the Earth as moving on its axis (over a sufficiently short lapse of time). But error—though sometimes present—is not of the essence. We use perceptually still objects on Earth, such as mountains or coasts, as a frame for locating perceptually moving objects, such as people or boats or goods. We also use moving objects as frames for locating other moving objects. To ascertain whether some of these objects are *absolutely* still or *absolutely* moving may be beyond the limits of common sense (and of phenomenology). Thus, questions about whether some bodies (such as the Earth) are absolutely at rest or in motion, whether space is absolute, or whether it exists at all, may be beyond the limits of phenomenology (in a similar way, there might be no phenomenological answers to questions about mental monism). However, even though common sense has no answers to these transphenomenological questions, it is not thereby blind to some of the concepts that are here at stake—such as that of absolute motion. We propose, methodologically, that we suspend our judgment as to the truth or falsity of certain beliefs about absolute rest and motion of certain objects and consider the structure of these beliefs, the way they are logically and conceptually related to one another. In this spirit, we shall attempt here a reconstruction of the dialectic of rest and motion. We shall proceed step by step, by first investigating *pure*, as it were, notions of rest and motion, and by examining how far we can go in trying to classify intuitive kinds of motion in terms of nonintrinsically spatial or temporal concepts. Space and time are introduced at a further stage, either as examples of reference objects, or by exploiting the theory of localization. (The spirit of this exercise is thus different from that of more traditional axiomatic projects, which offer a formal reconstruction of, say, Newtonian rational mechanics.[1] We are concerned here with commonsense concepts of rest and motion, and of space and time.)

1. THE SIMPLE LOGIC OF MOVEMENT WITHOUT SPACE AND TIME

Although common sense may not choose between a relational and an absolutist conception of space,[2] time, and movement, it is not blind to these notions. Common sense accepts as unproblematic the notions of absolute rest and motion; and these are logically related in a rather interesting way. The following definitions and axioms capture the basic intuitions regarding these notions.[3] Starting from these axioms, one can then add some more specific ones, thereby building a corresponding class of systems. The noteworthy fact about these systems is that they do not use spatial and temporal concepts (that should enter in an exhaustive *definition* of movement, not taken into account here), thus showing the formal structure of space- and time-independent properties of movement. Space will be introduced later, but only insofar as it is a component of the metaphysics of movement, without being in any sense exploited for geometrically characterizing movement. This approach helps testing the limits of a hypothetical core metaphysics of movement, at least insofar as it is recognized by perception.

In our formulation, we shall initially use two primitive predicates: a monadic predicate "Sx," for "x is at rest (absolutely)," and a binary predicate "Sxy," for "x is at rest relative to y." (At a later stage we shall see the interest of reducing the monadic S to the dyadic S.). Using these predicates, we can immediately define corresponding predicates for motion:

$$\text{D1} \quad Mx =_{df} \neg Sx$$
$$\text{D2} \quad Mxy =_{df} \neg Sxy$$

Thus, "Mx" expresses "x is in (absolute) motion," or simply "x moves," and "Mxy" expresses "x moves relative to y." Note that insofar as motion is defined simply by negating rest, no fine-grained distinction between types of motion is made available.

We fix the properties of relative rest and motion by means of the following axioms:

$$\text{S1} \quad Sxx$$
$$\text{S2} \quad Sxy \to Syx$$
$$\text{S3} \quad Sxy \wedge Syz \to Sxz$$

Thus, being relatively at rest is reflexive, symmetrical, and transitive. It follows that being relatively in motion is symmetrical and irreflexive:

$$\text{M1} \quad \neg Mxx$$
$$\text{M2} \quad Mxy \to Myx$$

It is also apparent that M is not transitive: given three objects x, y, and z, it might be the case that Mxy and Myz, but also that Sxz (for instance, because Sx and Sz—only y moves—as when $x = z$).

On this basis, two additional axioms relate absolute and relative rest and motion.

$$\text{A1} \quad Sx \wedge Sy \to Sxy$$
$$\text{A2} \quad Sx \wedge My \to Mxy$$

By A1, if two bodies are absolutely at rest, they are at rest relative to each other. (Newton: "It is a property of rest, that bodies really at rest do rest in respect to one another" [23].) Obviously neither the converse of A1 nor the weaker conditional $Sxy \to Sx \vee Sy$ are true, for two bodies x and y can move together as a single body, or it can be that Sxy, $x = y$, and Mx. As for A2, it says that if a body is absolutely still, and another absolutely in motion, then they move relative to one another. The converse is not true, nor is the weaker $Mxy \to Sx \vee My$, for the two bodies x and y could be both moving.

Axioms A1 and A2 link absolute with relative rest, on the one hand, and absolute rest and motion with relative motion on the other. They have a number of intuitive consequences that highlight criteria for motion and for rest and answer thus the general question: Given our knowledge of the states of (relative or absolute) motion or of rest of certain bodies, what are we allowed to infer about the states of other bodies that are related to the former? We give some illustrations starting from cases in which absolute rest (or motion) is known (i.e., referred to in the antecedent of a conditional), and list the *absoluteness patterns*

T1 $Sx \land Sxy \to Sy$
T2 $Sx \land Mxy \to My$
T3 $Mx \land Sxy \to My$

T1–T3 exhaust the possibilities of determining the absoluteness of motion or rest of any of two bodies that are in various possible relative states; the indeterminate case is that of the situation in which $Mxy \land Mx$, that does not allow an inference to either My or to Sy. In order to infer to absolute rest one has to examine a situation in which something is at absolute rest. The same applies to the following *relativity patterns*:

T4 $Sxy \land Myz \to Mxz$
T5 $Mxy \land Syz \to Mxz$

Again, note that from the conjunction $Mxy \land Myz$ we cannot infer either Mxz or Sxz. In particular, as we said, relative motion is not transitive.

Some generalizations are of interest. For instance, we easily discover that relativity of motion entails absoluteness of motion.

T6 $Mxy \to Mx \lor My$

If two bodies move relative to each other, then *at least* one of them is in absolute motion (this is, straightforwardly, the contrapositive of A1). The converse is not true (it is the contrapositive of the false $Sxy \to Sx \land Sy$), and neither is the weaker $Mx \land My \to Mxy$ (the contrapositive of the false $Sxy \to Sx \land Sy$), for again, two bodies x and y can move as a single body, or it can be that $x = y$. On the other hand, T6 generalizes to

T7 $\exists x \exists y Mxy \to \exists Mx$

We also have the following theorem of absolute rest:

T8 $\forall x \forall y (x \neq y \land Mxy) \to \forall x \forall y (Sx \land Sy \to x = y)$.

That is, if everything moves relative to everything else, then there is *at most* one object that is absolutely at rest (since two objects at rest do not move relative to each other). By contrast, the following registers an important fact about relative rest:

T9 $\exists x S x \to \exists x \exists y S x y$

This theorem is much weaker than its companion for absolute motion. In fact, it is trivially satisfied in a universe where there is a single resting individual. More trivially, it is satisfied in any nonempty universe, since everything is at rest relative to itself by S1.

There is some interest, from an epistemological point of view, in the fact that absolute rest cannot be inferred from relative rest or relative motion (if not in the weak form of T8), whereas absolute motion can (these are consequences of the irreflexivity of relative motion and of the reflexivity of relative rest). For the inference to absolute rest a reference is required to something that is absolutely at rest. On the other hand, various theorems deliver criteria for absolute motion (T2, T3, T6, T7), given some facts about relative rest and motion and absolute rest.

All these theorems constitute relevant epistemological criteria that mimic that part of our reasoning about movement that does not involve space. In the following sections we shall come closer to (absolute) space.

2. OTHER SYSTEMS

2.1. A SYSTEM WITH ABSOLUTE REFERENCE OBJECTS

The foregoing used the monadic predicate for absolute rest as an undefined primitive next to the binary predicate of relative rest. We assumed the possibility that some bodies were absolutely at rest, without explaining this particular property. As an alternative, one could adopt a more structured system, in which there exists one single individual that has the unexplained property of being at rest, call it "s." Under such circumstances, one can then define absolute rest and motion in terms of relative rest and motion with regard to s:

D3 $Sx =_{df} Sxs$
D4 $Mx =_{df} Mxs$

Given D2, one could therefore use "Sxy" as the only primitive predicate, now flanked by a primitive singular term "s." A plausible candidate for s is

Newtonian absolute space, but it could be any reference object. Contextually, *s* is typically the Earth. In any event, absolute rest and motion thus defined become *de re* properties (much in the sense in which *being John's brother* is a property that depends upon John. It remains open whether the *de re* property in question is also *rigid*, in the sense that it depends on the same individual in all possible worlds. *Being John's brother* is rigid).

Given such a redefinition, it is worth observing that a rewriting of the relevant propositions from the system outlined in section 1 shows that A1 and A2 are now derivable as theorems, since the following follow immediately from S2–S3:

A1' $Sxs \wedge Sys \rightarrow Sxy$
A2' $Sxs \wedge Mys \rightarrow Mxy$

The formulation in terms of *s* is thus much more powerful.[4]

Instead of choosing an absolutely resting object and the dyadic relation S as a primitive, one might also choose an absolutely moving object *m* and the dyadic relation S as a primitive, and define M*x* as S*xm*, S*x* as ¬M*x*, and so on. (By contrast, it would not do to choose both *m* and the dyadic M as primitives, for one would not be able to define M*x* as M*xm*, since *x* could be at rest.) There are some reasons for not doing so, though. If one chooses *m* and the dyadic S, a general point is of importance: there is one single kind of absolute rest, but there are many ways of being at motion absolutely or relatively. An object could be moving even though it is not at rest with respect to *m* (they may have, say, different speeds or be moving along different paths). This in turn implies that defining M*x* as S*xm* would have the consequence of constraining the kinematics of *x*. All absolutely moving objects would be moving at the speed of *m* on paths parallel to *m*'s. And we should infer from T7 that in every pair of objects that move relative to each other, one would be moving as *m* does. It is thus apparent that our desire to start from an absolutely still object *s* is all the more motivated if we want to abstract from kinematics. At the same time, this is obviously one point at which the limits of the project of working out the pure, nonkinematical component of motion begin to show up. The commonsense framework is too poor here.

2.2. A SYSTEM WITH ABSOLUTE REFERENCE OBJECTS EXPLICITLY ASSUMED

The above characterization captures the conceptual ties between absolute and relative rest and motion. As such, it is neutral as to the existence of absolute space (or of an individual with the role of a fixed framework). We introduce now a system that explicitly assumes absolute reference objects. In addition to A1 and A2, it has the following axiom:

$$A3 \quad \exists x S x$$

As such, A3 does not guarantee that there is a single individual that plays the role of absolute space; nor that any such individual is what we would like to consider as absolute space. But it is an important step toward the introduction of that very individual. Observe that absolute space does the job nicely—it provides a frame of reference for rest and motion. This is what any object being absolutely at rest can provide—it might thus be considered an absolute reference object. In an absolutist conception of space, space satisfies A3 (and every part or region of space does too), and is thus an absolute reference object.

A system with absolute motion instead of absolute space would assume the M-analog of A3, viz.,

$$A4 \quad \exists x M x$$

2.3. A SYSTEM IN WHICH ABSOLUTE REST IS A CONSEQUENCE OF ABSOLUTE MOTION

This system is based on all of A1–A4. By T7, it has the following theorem

$$T10 \quad \exists x \exists y M x y \to \exists x S x$$

This is a strong, metaphysical claim. It does not simply tell us that in order to *discover* that an object is moving absolutely we need an absolute reference object; it claims that movement itself can exist only if something that does not move exists.

This system is, however, necessary to establish a bridge from absolute rest to absolute motion. The overall (existential) independence of the two notions suggests the possibility of different situations, such as the one described by $\exists x M x \wedge \neg \exists x S x$—a totally dynamical world—or $\forall x S x$; a world that is, according to a Newtonian at least, rather similar to ours should verify both $\exists x M x$ and $\exists x S x$. On the other hand, a nonempty world verifying neither $\exists x M x$ nor $\exists x S x$ is logically excluded; by the same token, worlds are excluded in which movement is relational *only* (see T7).

2.4. ABSOLUTE AND RELATIVE MOTION

Still another possibility is to introduce, along with A1 and A2, the following:

$$A5 \quad Mx \rightarrow \exists y Mxy$$

Given T7, this would have the equivalence

$$T11 \quad Mx \leftrightarrow \exists y Mxy$$

This statement means that there is no distinction between relational and absolute motion. This, again, is a substantial metaphysical thesis.

3. THE MEREOLOGY OF MOVEMENT

Up to this point we were just interested in the fact that some objects move, with no concern for any of the *ways* in which they move. For that reason we have treated the objects in our domain as simple, with no parts, and we have avoided any spatial or temporal description. This may be justified insofar as many bodies move in a straightforward way, by translating on a rectilinear path without undergoing any deformation, rotation, or acceleration. Rational mechanics considers movers as represented by a chosen point—say, their center of mass; and in fact, for most purposes an object's trajectory can adequately be reduced to that of the chosen point. This is hardly the case with commonsense categorizations of movement. Some bodies accelerate, others rotate with no translation—thus being, in a sense, still—and others yet move by changing their shape and volume, like worms.

It is here that we need to introduce spatial and temporal notions. However, it turns out that in order to cope at least with the simplest of these cases, all we need is mereology (and eventually mereotopology). The spatial properties of the parts referred to are not relevant. (As to the temporal dimension, we shall discuss some facts in a moment.)

Let us, then, add the primitive for parthood, P. We shall assume it to be axiomatized as in General Extensional Mereology (GEM),[5] as follows:

$$(P1) \quad Pxx,$$
$$(P2) \quad Pxy \wedge Pyx \rightarrow x = y$$
$$(P3) \quad Pxy \wedge Pyz \rightarrow Pxz$$
$$(P4) \quad \neg Pyx \rightarrow \exists z(Pzx \wedge \neg Ozy)$$
$$(P5) \quad \exists x\phi \rightarrow \exists z \forall y[Oyz \leftrightarrow \exists x(\phi \wedge Oyx)]$$

3.1. WEAK AND STRONG RIGIDITY

The result of combining GEM with the basic theory of section 1 yields a theory we shall label GEMS. This immediately allows us to define an interesting notion of rigidity, or "weak rigidity":

$$D5 \quad WRIx =_{df} \forall y(Pyx \to Sxy)$$

A thing is weakly rigid if it is at rest relative to all its parts. Given the transitivity of S, one might as well say that a thing is rigid whose parts are all at rest relative to one another. We should make a distinction between this weak notion of rigidity and a stronger notion, related to causality. Weak rigidity is neither tensed (something could be weakly rigid at a certain instant, and cease to be rigid immediately thereafter) nor dispositional (for instance, to be weakly rigid is not for something to retain the S relation between its parts in relevant counterfactual circumstances). Weak rigidity sets no dynamical requirements: a loose drop of oil might be rigid, and might be moving rigidly, insofar as all its parts are still relative to the drop itself. In the same sense, a scattered object or aggregate can be rigid (even by sheer chance, as in the case of a heap of bread crumbs on a table). And so can a Husserlian "phantasm," an object that keeps its shape in spite of being immaterial. Frames, in the sense explained below, are rigid.

Strong rigidity entails weak rigidity but is, moreover, causally sustained. It is a property of causally connected bodies or aggregates (on the latter notion, see Casati and Varzi 1994: 125–28). Some scattered aggregates too might be causally connected, as in the case of a planetary system (even though the latter are in general not rigid). Basically, the idea is that the behavior of one part of the strongly rigid object will not, as a norm, affect its S relations with (some relevant, or all) other parts of the same object.

3.2. FRAMES

Given the fact that the relation of relative rest is an equivalence relation, we can build equivalence classes of objects that are still relative to one another and choose one of them when we represent their M or S relation to any other object in the universe. We call any such object a *frame*. A frame is thus weakly rigid. We can also, more comprehensively, define a frame on x as the sum of all objects that are at rest with respect to x:

$$fx =_{df} \sigma y(Sxy)$$

3.3. INTERMEDIATE CASES OF MOTION

In between the two extremes of relative rest and motion there exist some cases of hybrid motion in which, for instance, it is not the whole of the object that moves but only some of its parts (so that the object is not rigid), or the whole of the object moves but the object does not change place (as in the case of the rotation of a disk around its center). We shall now test the expressive power of GEMS with respect to the definability of these movements. In general, intermediate cases of motion occur when different parts of one and the same object behave differently—with regard to S and M—relative to other objects and their parts. The most general case describable in GEMS is *partial motion*, PM:

$$D6 \quad PMx =_{df} \exists y(Pyx \wedge My)$$

An equivalent definition would be

$$D6' \quad PMx =_{df} \exists y \exists z \exists w(Pyx \wedge Myz \wedge Sxz)$$

Note that, in spite of being a monadic predicate, PM hides a relational component. Partial motion is satisfied by any object in a couple of objects that are in relative motion, or by any object that has two parts in relative motion. We want to distinguish between these two cases and define thus the latter, *proper* partial motion, PPM:

$$D7 \quad PPMx =_{df} \exists y \exists z(Pyx \wedge Pzx \wedge Mzy)$$

(As is clear from the definition, proper partial motion is only possible if something is in [relative] motion). A first characteristic example of partial motion is the *blob* movement, BM, in which an object contracts, expands, or spins because some of its parts move but some others do not (in general, when a part of the proper partially moving object is still relative to another part):

$$D8 \quad BMx =_{df} PPMx \wedge \exists y \exists z(x \neq y \wedge x \neq z \wedge y \neq z \wedge Pyx \wedge Pzx \wedge Szy)$$

Another restriction on PPM gives us the notion of *internal motion*, IM:

$$D9 \quad IMx =_{df} \exists y \exists z(Sxz \wedge Pyx \wedge Mzy)$$

An object moves internally if it is at rest relative to some other object but, relative to the latter, some of its parts are in motion.

We introduce here a substantially new possibility, that of an object that is globally still (in a peculiar sense) but whose parts are in motion, relative to another object. One might think of a given amount of water that is gently whirling in a glass; the whole of the water does not move relative to the glass, although most parts of the water do. It is obvious that

> T12 IM$x \to \neg$WRIx
> T13 PPM$x \to \neg$WRIx
> T14 BM$x \to \neg$WRIx

that is, weak rigidity prevents a body from being internally moving (if a given x satisfies WRI, then all of its parts are still relative to x; thus, given a y such that Sxy, by the transitivity of rest all parts of x are at rest with respect to y; hence $\neg$IMx).

3.4. ROTATION

The preceding discussion has some bearing on the difficult topic of rotation. It follows from T10 that the rotation of a rigid circular body a around its center cannot be considered a form of internal movement. At the same time there is a sense in which a circular body x that just spins around its center is not "moving" relative to any other body, say y (the interest of the IM definition). But now one may be tempted to object to this. For consider the matter from x's viewpoint: y will be seen as moving in a circle around x. Thus—relative motion being symmetrical—it really is the case that Mxy. Now we would like to suggest that matters are more complicated. For consider three bodies x, y, and z nonconcentric, such that z is still while x and y rotate on their centers. Thus, ROx and ROy, but x and y do not move otherwise: were it not for the rotation, it would be the case that Sx and Sy; let us provisionally tag this sense of rest by writing "S$'$." If one takes x's viewpoint, it would seem to one that S$'yz$, Mxy, and Myz; symmetrically, from y's viewpoint it appears that S$'xz$, Mxy, and Myz. But from z's viewpoint it holds that S$'xy$, S$'xz$, and S$'yz$. How can we make all these perspectives compatible? For if S = S$'$, a contradiction emerges at once. We do not want to give up the sense S$'$, but this appears to set a limit to GEMS.

4. GOING THE OTHER WAY AROUND AND INTRODUCING REGIONS

One may define an M$'$-kind of motion in the cases at stake by stating that M$'xy =_{df}$ M$xy \land$ S$'xy$. This would be the motion of x with regard to z in the foregoing example. And now the same difficulties we had for the distinction of S and S' arise for the distinction of M and M'. Imagine the following three objects: a still disk x; a disk y that is not translating relative to x, but is rotating on its center (clockwise, say); a disk z that is not rotating but translates relative to x. Thus Mxz holds; M'xy holds, but does Mxy hold? Again, one intuitive way to answer that it does is to take y's point of view; accordingly, x will be seen as rotating counterclockwise around y. This movement, though, seems different from the movement of z relative to x.

If what matters for our purposes is how much of movement can be captured in terms of GEMS, the RO motion lies beyond our expressive power.

The intuitive difference between S and S' or M and M' is that what matters is the space where the objects are located. Rotating objects (in particular, perfectly circular rotating objects) just do not move out of their place. In the last discussed case, the difference between y and z is that the place of y is moving relative to x, whereas the place of z is not. More formally, and using the region functor "r,"[6] it holds that $\forall w(Pwy \rightarrow Mwx)$ (assuming that the middle point of x is not a part thereof—points are provisionally excluded from the domain) and that $\forall w(Pwz \rightarrow Mwx)$; but whereas S(r$y$)$x$, it is the case that M(rz)(rx). Introducing regions increases the size of the ontology, but reduces the size of the ideology: we dispose of M' and S'.

One possibly controversial point is to take regions as movable. That is, we allow the writing of sentences such as M(rz)(rx). How can we *know* whether an object is at (absolute or relative) rest or in motion at a given time instant t? Our theory does not say this; it does not define, for example, motion as a succession over time of states of rest at different places. But it does not thereby introduce dynamical considerations as the distinguishing criterion (for instance, it does not require that, at t, x is in motion if and only if it has a certain *acceleration*).[7]

This is more controversial for regions. For even if we allow for instantaneously moving bodies, we cannot accept that regions move—for they do not move at all, instantaneously or not. Thus, to say that M(rx)y is actually to say that x is at a different region *at different times*, and this sets an important limit to the expressive power of GEMS supplemented with regions.

Appendix: A Note on Newtonian Rest and Motion

In the "Scholium" Newton proposed to distinguish absolute and relative motion and rest "one from the other by their properties, causes, and effects. It is a property of rest, that bodies really at rest do rest in respect to one another" (Earman 1989: 23, cf. A1); on the other hand, "absolute rest cannot be determined from the positions of bodies in our regions" (ibid.). The latter statement is here captured by the weak theorems of absolute and relative rest, T8 and T9. R. F. Muirhead (1887: 476) remarked the trivial A1 → T6. (Newton's first criterion "helps us only in a negative way, by enabling us to deny the attribution of true rest to both of two systems that are moving relatively to each other"). As is well known, Newton also saw the impossibility of distinguishing relative from absolute motion in purely geometrical terms; this is rendered in the present system by the impossibility of defining the relational and the monadic M in terms of each other (only the weak implication T6 holds); definability would deliver a criterion for either type of motion; apparently, it is not geometry that is at stake. Newton introduced dynamical properties as the distinguishing criterion: "The effects by which absolute motion is distinguished from relative are the forces of receding from the axis of circular motion. For there are no such forces in a circular motion purely relative, but in a true and absolute circular motion, they are greater or less, according to the quantity of the motion" (Earman 1989: 24). Now force should be taken into account in a broad phenomenological investigation of movement (and not only for the prospects of physical theory proper); at the same time it is not clear, from the commonsense point of view, whether the dynamical factor is intrinsic to movement.

Newton's distancing himself from common sense should not be overestimated. True, he writes that he does "not define time, space, place, and motion as being known to all" (ibid., 20); John Earman (1989: 7) comments that "Newton is here declaring his own emancipation" "from the primitive notions of everyday life." But the text of the "Scholium" indicates only that Newton is *refining* those concepts. His putative disagreement with ordinary notions concerns the erroneous commonsense belief that motion is only relative motion. Newton proposes to distinguish relative quantities and "quantities themselves," the former being only "measures" of the latter (ibid., 25): "And if the meaning of words is to be determined by their use, then by the names, times, space, place, and motion their [sensible] measures are properly to be understood; and the expression will be unusual, and purely mathematical, if the measured quantities themselves are meant" (ibid.). This would only bespeak Newton's understatement of the plasticity of common sense: absolute motion seems to be clearly conceivable, even though epistemological criteria for it are worth a whole physical theory. At the same time, one should remember that some of the properties that for Newton would characterize the "true" concept of motion are perfectly acceptable to common sense (indeed, A1 is Newton's first principle).

CHAPTER THIRTEEN
Gödel and Husserl

DAGFINN FØLLESDAL

1. GÖDEL'S STUDY OF HUSSERL

It is not widely known that there is a connection between Husserl and Gödel. Husserl never referred to Gödel—he was more than seventy when Gödel obtained his first great results, and he died a few years later, in 1938, without seeming to have taken notice of Gödel's work. And Gödel never referred to Husserl in his published works. However, Gödel's *Nachlaß*, part of which has now come out in volume 3 of Solomon Feferman et al., *Collected Works of Kurt Gödel* (Feferman et al. 1995), shows that Gödel knew Husserl's work well and appreciated it greatly. Thus Gödel writes in a manuscript from late 1961 or shortly thereafter:

> Just because of the lack of clarity and the literal incorrectness of many of Kant's formulations, quite divergent directions have developed out of Kant's thought—none of which, however, really did justice to the core of Kant's thought. This requirement seems to me to be met for the first time by phenomenology, which, entirely as intended by Kant, avoids both the death-defying leaps of idealism into a new metaphysics as well as the positivistic rejection of all metaphysics. But now, if the misunderstood Kant has already led to so much that is interesting in philosophy, and also indirectly in science, how much more can we expect it from Kant understood correctly?[1]

Gödel had started to study Husserl just a couple of years before he wrote this, in 1959 (Wang 1981: 651, and Wang 1987: 12ff.). He found Husserl quite congenial, and he soon became quite absorbed by Husserl's writings. He owned all of Husserl's main works,[2] and his underlining and comments in the margin indicate that he studied them carefully. The comments are mostly in Gabelsberger shorthand, but thanks to Cheryl Dawson, who has very kindly transcribed them, we can see that Gödel's comments are mostly approving, amplifying some of Husserl's points. However, sometimes he is critical, notably in his notes to the *Logische Untersuchungen* (1900–1901) and to some sections of Husserl's last work, the *Krisis* (one part published in 1936, the rest after Husserl's death). Generally, Gödel is most appreciative of the *Ideen* (1913) and the other works written after Husserl's "idealist" conversion around 1907.

Gödel had expressed views on philosophy of mathematics similar to those of Husserl long before he started to study him. What he found in Husserl was not radically different from his own views; what impressed him seems to have been Husserl's general philosophy, which would provide a systematic framework for a number of his own earlier ideas on the foundations of mathematics.

From Gödel's manuscripts and particularly through his notes in his copies of Husserl's works we can see what Gödel was attracted to in Husserl, and how he understood Husserl. It seems to me that Gödel's understanding of Husserl is extraordinary, placing him among the earlier philosopher's foremost interpreters.

I will now first go through very quickly some basic ideas in Husserl and see how they are connected and then turn to Gödel. The interconnection between the ideas in Husserl's work seems to have been one of the features that attracted Gödel. In Gödel's own writings, especially before he read Husserl, we do not find a systematic philosophy. Instead, Gödel has some basic points that he comes back to repeatedly, mainly a kind of realism with respect to mathematical entities and concepts. Gödel also thinks that we have a special kind of insight, or intuition, that is the basis for our mathematical theories. One of our aims is to understand a little better what kind of insight this might be. What is it that Gödel means by intuition? And is it at all possible that one can have that kind of intuition?

Many people get scared off when they open Husserl's books and read about intuition, *Wesensschau*, and other abstruse notions. However, they are not so mysterious. In order to understand them, we have to make use of the notion of intentionality, which is the notion in Husserl from which the others flow.

1.1. INTENTIONALITY

Husserl claimed, following his teacher Brentano, that consciousness can best be characterized by being intentional. Not in the practical sense of our having a plan, or purpose, but in a theoretical sense of directedness toward an object. In the case of perception, we can elucidate this notion of directedness by help of Quine's observation, that what reaches our sensory surfaces is not sufficient to uniquely determine what it is that we perceive. Thus, in the Jastrow/Wittgenstein example of the duck/rabbit, we may see a duck or a rabbit. What reaches our eye is the same in both cases, so the difference must be coming from us. The difference has to do with the different anticipations we have of further experiences when the object moves or we move around relative to the object, when we use our other senses, and so on. We structure what we see, and we can do so in different ways. This is obvious in the duck/rabbit case, but according to Husserl all perception is similarly underdetermined, even in cases we do not consider ambiguous. What cases we regard as ambiguous is largely a matter of past experience, we have come into the habit of structuring our experience one way and are not aware of other possibilities. A person who has grown up in an area where there are no ducks whatsoever, only rabbits, probably would not see much of an ambiguity in the Jastrow/Wittgenstein picture. There is just another rabbit. That other structures are possible is brought home to us in cases of misperception. We become aware of another way of structuring our experience as soon as we discover our mistake. And misperception is always possible.

Consider the following example: there are states in the United States where they try to keep people within the speed limit by posting life-size figures of policemen along the road. If you drive there and are not familiar with this, you are likely to look at the speedometer and make sure that you are within the speed limit. Then, as you come very close, you will see that what you have there in front of you is far too thin to be a policeman, only one quarter of an inch thick. You will then revise your view and impose another structure on what you see, maybe that of a cardboard figure. Once you do this, you will of course not say that there was a policeman there until you came close, and then he was transformed into a cardboard figure. You will say that there was a cardboard figure there all along, but that idea did not occur to you. Once it does occur, it has, of course, to be compatible with all that reached your sensory surfaces from when you first spotted the figure, not just what you are experiencing now. The restructuring hence involves not only what is here now, but also what was here in the past.

1.2. ESSENCES

So far, I guess, everybody could agree. Now we get to that crucial step that involves *Wesensschau*. Given that we can experience a multitude of different objects when we are in a given sensory situation: a duck, a rabbit, but also an ear of a rabbit, an eye, or even the color or the front side of an object, could we not, for example, when we stand in front of a tree just as much concentrate on its shape, its triangularity, for example, if it has a nice triangular shape. And we have anticipations as to how a shape might change if we move around the object. We might expect the circular shape of a coin to look elliptical if we see it from the side. So we have anticipations about shapes as well as about physical objects. A crucial difference between a shape and a physical object is that in the case of a shape, that shape could be had by another object than the one that happens to have it now. So the shape is a general notion, and if we are concerned with a shape, it does not matter whether we replace the particular physical object that instantiates it with another object that instantiates the same shape. The same holds for arithmetic features, couples, triples, etc., we can focus on these general features rather than on the individual physical objects.

The distinction is easy to make precise. If we can take the physical object that we are facing away and put in another one, and still say that we are experiencing the same object now as we did before, for example, circularity or triangularity, we are not experiencing a physical object, but what Husserl calls an *eidos* or an essence (*Wesen*). I think this helps to make Husserl's notion of *Wesen* or essence a little more palatable, because it is not some peculiar feature that is unique to an object and that the object shares with no other object. It is just a feature that the object could in principle share with any number of objects. Mathematical entities are typical of the kind of entity that we are dealing with when we are focusing on essence. For Husserl, mathematics is a typical example of an eidetic science, a science of eidos.

In mathematics one studies certain kinds of essences: numbers in arithmetic and shapes and related features in geometry. Husserl proposes an extension of geometry into a systematic examination of the kind of features one later comes to study under the heading "topology." To give an example of essences, consider a glass, a cup, and a doughnut. If I ask you to pick two of these objects that are similar to one another, many would pick the glass and the cup, because they can both be used for drinking. This is fine. This is an essence instantiated by these two objects and not by the third. There is, however, another eidos that is instantiated by the cup and the doughnut: they are what we could call one-hole objects. We can turn one into the other by transformations of the kind we know from modeling clay: without fusing any openings or tearing anything apart. We have a hole in the doughnut and one in the cup's handle, but no such hole in the glass. Mathematics is the only highly developed eidetic science. There are, however, also other general features of objects that it might be interesting to explore, Husserl says, and he envisaged new branches of eidetic inquiry different from mathematics.

1.3. ANSCHAUUNG, WESENSSCHAU

Husserl insists that he is an empiricist. However, it is a great mistake, he says, to believe that just because we learn about the world around us through our senses, the only objects we can learn anything about this way are physical objects. We can have insight into essences as well as physical objects. As a general term for both kinds of insight Husserl uses the term "intuition" (*Anschauung*), and he divides intuitions into two kinds: perception, in the case where the object is a physical object (in a wide sense of "object," that also includes processes and states), and essential insight, or *Wesensschau*, where the object is an essence. So this is what Husserl means by the mysterious-sounding term *Wesensschau*. One might still claim that there is no such thing, but it is difficult to reject the notion once one agrees that the object of an act is underdetermined by what reaches our senses and accepts the correlated idea of intentionality.

1.4. TRANSCENDENCE

For Husserl there is no difference in principle between experiencing mathematical objects and experiencing physical objects. It is all pretty much basically the same kind of accomplishment: we are structuring the world that we are confronted with, whether it be the concrete world of physical objects or the abstract world studied in mathematics. An eidetic science is exploring the world of abstract entities. All these entities, concrete and abstract, have many features beyond those that meet the eye or those that we are attending to. Husserl uses an intimidating word for that too. He calls them transcendent.

An object is transcendent when it has more to it than what we grasp in any normal process of grasping, for example, in perception. So all physical objects are in that sense transcendent. There is no way of exhausting all the features of a physical object. The transcendence goes beyond the anticipations that are involved in our structuring the world. The anticipations do not fix all the infinitely many properties of an object, only some of them. Many of our anticipations constrain them to a certain spectrum of possibilities. If I see a tree, for example, in New England in the fall, then I might not be sure whether the other side is green or yellow or red. There is a spectrum of possible colors. I would not expect it to be violet, or something like that. On the basis of past experience I have more or less precise anticipations of what is there.

Involved in my notion of a tree is that it has a color. I do not know which. I just know it is within a certain range of the spectrum. But the tree has definite properties that can be determined by exploring them more and more. This is crucial to Husserl's notion of transcendence: the world and its objects have determinate properties that go beyond what we anticipate and are there to be explored. In perception we explore them by walking around, using our various senses, laboratory equipment, and so on. Sometimes our exploration proceeds harmoniously, we get a steadily richer and more refined conception of what the object is like. Other times our further experience violates our anticipations. We have to revise our notion of what the object is like and sometimes have to give up the belief that there is an object there at all.

Similarly, abstract entities, like numbers and other essences, are transcendent too. We can, for example, use different arithmetical expressions and only later find out that they fit one and the same number. Abstract entities, even quite simple ones, have lots of features that we do not yet know. Take as simple an entity as the number two. There is much that we do not know about it. For example, is two the largest exponent n for which Fermat's equation $a^n + b^n = c^n$ is satisfied by positive integers a, b and c, or is there some larger n for which this is the case? This was an unknown feature of the number two until Andrew Wiles recently proved that two has this property. This is typical of objects, that they not only have a richness of features that we know, but also are conceived of as having much more to them than what we know, something that we might want to find out.

One important theme, to which we will return in connection with Gödel, is how we go about studying abstract entities. Here I will mention only one such method that Husserl uses.

1.5. EIDETIC VARIATION

This method, which Husserl calls eidetic variation, is based on an idea which Bolzano used to define analyticity and to develop his theory of probability, anticipating a main idea in Carnap's theory of probability: one tries out various objects that instantiate some essences to see whether they also instantiate others. To use an example from Husserl's teacher Weierstrass,[3] which is originally due to Bolzano: mathematicians long took it for granted that a continuous function will be differentiable in most points. This fits in many instances. However, Bolzano constructed an example of a continuous function which is nowhere differentiable. His result remained unpublished, but Weierstrass thirty years later constructed another (more complicated) function that had the same properties. Husserl often remarked how Weierstrass had elucidated much more clearly than mathematicians before him what is involved in some of the fundamental notions in mathematics, such as continuity.

1.6. THE DETERMINABLE X, INDIVIDUATION

There is one more notion that Husserl discusses and that is often found mysterious. This is what he calls "the determinable X." When we perceive or remember an object all our various anticipations are said by Husserl to be associated with one and the same "determinable X." Some interpreters of Husserl take this determinable X to be something that insures that our experience is of some particular object and not of another one very similar to it. All our anticipations relate to various properties of the object, and they could fit any similar object. However, thanks to the determinable X, the object gets fixed. This interpretation of Husserl is in part inspired by so-called direct reference theories, where the reference of an expression is supposed to be fixed by some direct relation to the object or to some individuating essence. This, however, seems to be a rather strange kind of notion, that can succeed in fixing on one object rather than another even where they seem to be qualitatively indistinguishable.

Another interpretation of Husserl, which fits in better with the text and also seems philosophically more satisfactory, is that the determinable X has to do with reification, or individuation. We structure the world into objects. We are not just experiencing a heap of features, but features of objects. This means that features go together, as belonging to the same object. It also means that we may encounter an object that is very similar to one that we encountered before and still raise the question "Is this the same object, or a distinct one?" And conversely, an object may change its properties, look very different from how it did before, and still be the same object. The notion of the determinable X makes us distinguish pairs of opposites: identity versus distinctness and similarity versus difference. Things may be distinct in spite of similarities. And things may be identical in spite of changes.

Husserl's view here is in my opinion very similar to that of Quine. Quine has permitted me to quote from two of his unpublished manuscripts:

> As Donald Campbell put it, reification of bodies is innate in man and the other higher animals. I agree, subject to a qualifying adjective: *perceptual* reification (1983). I reserve "*full* reification" and "*full* reference" for the sophisticated stage where the identity of a body from one time to another can be queried and affirmed or conjectured or denied independently of exact resemblance. Distinct bodies may look alike, and an identical object may change its aspect. Such discriminations and identifications depend on our elaborate theory of space and time and of unobserved trajectories of bodies between observations. (Quine 1995: msp. 6; the italics are Quine's.)

> I wonder whether a dog ever gets beyond this stage. He recognizes and distinguishes recurrent people, but this is a qualitative matter of scent. Our sophisticated concept of recurrent objects, qualitatively indistinguishable but nevertheless distinct, involves our elaborate schematism of intersecting trajectories in three-dimensional space, out of sight, trajectories traversed with the elapse of time. These concepts of space and time, or the associated linguistic devices, are further requisites on the way to *substantial* cognition. (Quine 1990, msp. 21)

Note how, according to Quine, there is a connection between a schematism of time and space, and individuation of objects. A similar kind of connection is found in Husserl. There is a certain kind of package here of notions that comes together. We cannot have some part of it and not other parts. Space, time, and objects are all involved in the way we structure reality.

1.7. CONSTITUTION: IDEALISM

There is hence a strong Kantian streak in Husserl. We structure reality; even space and time are part of this structure. Husserl called this process of structuring "constitution," and from 1907 on he called himself an idealist. Toward the end of his life he came to see that this label was misleading. Thus in a letter from 1934 he wrote: "No ordinary 'realist' has ever been as realistic and concrete as I, the phenomenological 'idealist' (a word which by the way I no longer use)."[4] Husserl's position does not fit into the usual realism/idealism dichotomy. The more recent label "anti-realism" comes closer to fitting his position.

When we discussed Husserl's notion of transcendence, we noted that according to Husserl, objects, physical things as well as abstract entities, are transcendent. They all have an inexhaustibility in fact of further aspects that we could explore and try to find out about. This gives us a kind of realist or Platonist theory about mathematical entities and meanings. There is in Husserl a combination of a Kantian streak, namely that we structure reality, and a Platonist streak, that this reality is experienced as independent of us. It would be misleading to say that it was there before anybody was ever born, and will stay there long beyond the limits of mankind, for his Platonist reality is timeless. To attribute temporal or spatial location to it is inappropriate.

Very much of what Husserl says about these matters resembles what we find in Frege, and clearly he was inspired in his view by both Frege and Bolzano and also by Cantor, with whom he had long philosophical conversations when they were teaching together in Halle in the 1890s. We have here three typical Platonists in the history of mathematics. But Husserl is not quite like any of them. His position involves an interplay between Kantian and Platonist ideas. This intriguing interplay we also find in Gödel. He is often regarded as a Platonist, but we noted at the very beginning of this paper his attraction to Kant and even more to Husserl.

1.8. INTERSUBJECTIVITY

There are a few more features that I should mention from Husserl before we turn to Gödel. One is that so far I have talked only about subjectivity, and it might seem as if we get the view that every person structures his own world. But Husserl insists that this is supposed to be an intersubjective world. But how can this be? We cannot achieve this just by fiat. Gauss said: "Number is entirely a product of *our* mind." And "The numbers are free creations of *the* human mind." Gödel, too, writes about *the* human mind. Now, who is, or what is this, *the* human mind, or *our* mind? I guess we have one each, I do not think we have a common one. Many philosophers and mathematicians talk that way without stopping and asking what it is that they mean.

Husserl did not ignore this. He saw that it is a serious problem. And he devotes a large part of his years and his writings to discussing how we can achieve a kind of intersubjectivity from a starting point involving a multitude of different subjects. He is very interested in the kind of adjustments that take place between people who try to communicate and who see physical things from different angles. He is also interested in the same kind of adjustments when it comes to abstract entities like those in mathematics. He has, in fact, rather detailed and interesting discussions of the different processes that are involved in such adjustments. Some of these have been collected in three volumes in Husserliana that total about 2,000 pages. But this is only a fraction of the manuscripts he left on this topic.

1.9. THE LIFE-WORLD

Another theme that occupied Husserl, especially in his later years, is that our anticipations and expectations, even though they are joint expectations shared by many people, are largely not noticed by us. I have called them anticipations or expectations. These are unfortunate words, since for Husserl, we never notice most of our so-called anticipations at all.

I will now give an example of a typical anticipation that I think you will all agree that you have, but probably have never thought about. If I interview you before you enter a lecture hall and ask you what you expect when you come in, you may answer that you expect to hear a lecture on a certain topic. You might expect to meet some friends. But you probably would not mention that you expect there to be a floor in the room. The reason that you do not mention it is probably not that you think it will not interest me. Most probably, that thought never entered your mind. However, when I saw how confidently you stepped over the threshold it was quite clear that this was one of your "anticipations." In order to explain your actions in a reasonable way, I would assume that you have such an anticipation. This particular anticipation is due mostly to culture, a culture we are brought up in where, mainly because of lawyers and people like that, one is very careful to lock doors if there is no floor inside. The general notion of culture can to a large extent be elucidated by help of this notion of anticipations that we just take for granted; they become second nature, we never think of them. Nevertheless, these are anticipations that contribute to forming, shaping, the world we live in. The world that is the counterpart to all these anticipations Husserl calls the life-world.

The phrase "life-world" (*Lebenswelt*) is often misused, because so many Husserlians look upon Husserl as a kind of salvation from positivism and scientism and the like. So they think the life-world is the world that we live in, which is not the world of science, but a world we share with primitive people. But it is quite clear in Husserl that the life-world we have is very much a product of our culture. He says explicitly that science and mathematics to a large extent shape our life-world. Even if we are not practicing scientists, results from science seep down into our conception of the world in which we live. Some of this is explicit and thematized, but most of it seeps down unnoticed. For example, without thinking much about it, we all assume that we are living on a spherical planet, one we can travel around. This is all part of our life-world. It was not so for people living long ago nor is it so in all cultures. This is just an example of how our scientific conception of the world gradually seeps down, and leaves its remnants.

"Sedimentation" is the word that Husserl likes to use for this. The fact that he uses "sedimentation" indicates that it has very much to do with past experience. This tones down a tendency one finds in Kant to talk about lots of features of the world as being necessary, at all times, for all people in all cultures. Husserl does talk about the a priori element in experience and about phenomenology aiming at exploring the a priori. This has made many think that his view is very similar to Kant's. However, Husserl gives no transcendental argument to show that something has to be the case. What he means by "a priori" is simply to be anticipated, either consciously or in an unthematized way.

Husserl does not think that we can separate one element in our anticipation that is due to us and one that is due to the world, nor one that is due to linguistic meaning and one that is due to experience. We have a rich set of anticipations, but their genesis is a complex process where the impulses that reach our senses, our structuring activity, and our interaction and communication with others all play important but inextricable roles.

1.10. JUSTIFICATION

Husserl wants to find out more about what is anticipated, he wants to explore what is a priori in this sense. What is a priori may turn out to be false. Even in mathematics one may go wrong.[5] For Husserl there is no realm where one can have rock-bottom certainty. He has a view on justification similar to that of Goodman and Quine, and what Rawls has called "reflective equilibrium."[6] An opinion is justified by being brought into "reflective equilibrium" with the *doxa* of our life-world. Even the most abstract parts of mathematics get their ultimate justification through their connection with the life-world: "Mathematical evidence has its source of meaning and of legitimacy in the evidence of the life-world."[7]

A major puzzle that many might see in this idea of justification is the following: How can an appeal to the subjective-relative doxa provide any kind of justification for anything? It may help to resolve disagreements, but how can it serve as justification? Husserl's key observation, which I regard as an intriguing contribution to our contemporary discussion of ultimate justification, is that the "beliefs," "expectations," or "acceptances" that we ultimately fall back on, are unthematized, and in most cases have never been thematized. Every claim to validity and truth rests upon this "iceberg" of unthematized prejudgmental acceptances we discussed earlier. One should think that this would make things even worse. We fall back not only on something that is uncertain, but on something that we have not even thought about, and have therefore never subjected to conscious testing. Husserl argues, however, that it is just the unthematized nature of the life-world that makes it the ultimate ground of justification. "Acceptance" and "belief" are not attitudes that we decide to have through any act of judicative decision. What we accept, and the phenomenon of acceptance itself, are integral to our life-world, and there is no way of starting from scratch, or "to evade the issue here through a preoccupation with aporia and argumentation nourished by Kant or Hegel, Aristotle or Thomas."[8] Only the life-world can be an ultimate court of appeal: "Thus alone can that ultimate understanding of the world be attained, behind which, since it is ultimate, there is nothing more that can be sensefully inquired for, nothing more to understand."[9]

2. GÖDEL

After this sketch of Husserl's view on mathematical objects and mathematical justification, let us now look at Gödel's view. Gödel addresses the two central questions in the philosophy of mathematics: What is the ontological status of mathematical entities, and how do we find out anything about them? His answers have been widely discussed, and it is interesting to compare his position with that of Husserl.

2.1. REALISM

Gödel had held realist views on mathematical entities since his student days (Wang 1974: 8–11), or more exactly, since 1921–22.[10] It has often been noted that his essay "Russell's Mathematical Logic" (1944) contains a number of strongly realist statements, such as the following about *classes* and *concepts* (p. 137):

> It seems to me that the assumption of such objects is quite as legitimate as the assumption of physical bodies and there is quite as much reason to believe in their existence. They are in the same sense necessary to obtain a satisfactory system of mathematics as physical bodies are necessary for a satisfactory theory of our sense perceptions and in both cases it is impossible to interpret the propositions one wants to assert about these entities as propositions about the "data," i.e. in the latter case the actually occurring sense perceptions.

Gödel expresses similar views in his Gibbs lecture (1951) and also in his unfinished contribution to *The Philosophy of Rudolf Carnap* (Schlipp 1963): "Is Mathematics Syntax of Language?" (Gödel 1953). He there writes the following about *concepts* and their properties (p. 9):

> Mathematical propositions, it is true, do not express physical properties of the structures concerned [in physics], but rather properties of the *concepts* in which we describe those structures. But this only shows that the properties of these concepts are something quite as objective and independent of our choice as physical properties of matter. This is not surprising, since concepts are composed of primitive ones, which, as well as their properties, we can create as little as the primitive constituents of matter and their properties.

Note the comparison between concepts and physical objects in both of the quoted passages. Gödel does not say straightforwardly that the properties of concepts are objective, but that they are *as objective as* the physical properties of matter. This brings him close to Husserl, who as we have seen, held that the abstract objects of mathematics, like other essences, have the same ontological status as physical objects.

Early in 1959, Gödel replied to an inquiry from Paul Arthur Schilpp about the state of his contribution (Gödel 1953) to *The Philosophy of Rudolf Carnap* (Schilpp 1963). Gödel had been working on this essay for several years. In his explanation of why it would not be forthcoming, Gödel says: "A complete elucidation of the situation turned out to be more difficult than I had anticipated, doubtless in consequence of the fact that the subject matter is closely related to, and in part identical with, one of the basic problems of philosophy, namely the question of the *objective reality of concepts* and their relations."[11]

Also in his supplement to the second edition of "What Is Cantor's Continuum Problem?" (Gödel 1964: 272), which Gödel wrote after he had read Husserl, Gödel compares mathematical and physical objects and notes that the notion of objectivity raises a question: "the question of the objective existence of the objects of mathematical intuition (which, incidentally, is an exact replica of the question of the objective existence of the outer world)."

Here Gödel's use of the phrase "exact replica" brings to mind the close analogy Husserl saw between our intuition of essences in *Wesensschau* and of physical objects in perception. In both cases there are complicated processes at work that account for both the independent existence and the intersubjectivity of the objects that are constituted. However, Gödel does not say anything more about objective existence of mathematical objects, but instead goes into the epistemic issues connected with mathematical intuition. On this point, too, Gödel's views are similar to those of Husserl, and the similarity may help us to see what they both are getting at.

2.2. INTUITION

Already in the passage from "Russell's Mathematical Logic" quoted earlier, there is a comparison between mathematical evidence, or mathematical "data," and sense perception. In the article there is also brief mention of Russell and Hilbert's appeal to mathematical intuition. Gödel's own notion of mathematical intuition is discussed in all the other three papers mentioned, and in each of them it is compared to perception. First, in his Gibbs lecture (1951: 30), Gödel states: "What is wrong, however, is that the *meaning* of the terms (that is, the concepts they denote) is asserted to be something manmade and consisting merely in semantical conventions. The truth, I believe, is that these concepts form an objective reality of their own, which we cannot create or change, but only *perceive* and describe."

In his unfinished essay for the Carnap volume (1953: 6–7), Gödel writes:

> The similarity between mathematical *intuition* and a *physical sense* is very striking. It is arbitrary to consider "this is red" as an immediate datum, but not so to consider the proposition expressing modus ponens or complete induction (or perhaps some simpler proposition from which this latter follows). For the difference, as far as is relevant here, consists solely in the fact that in the first case a relationship between a concept and a particular object is perceived, while in the second case it is a relationship between concepts.

Finally, there is the following famous passage from his supplement to the second edition of "What Is Cantor's Continuum Problem?" (1964: 271):

> But despite their remoteness from sense experience, we do have something like a *perception* of the objects of set theory, as is seen from the fact that the axioms force themselves upon us as being true. I don't see any reason why we should have less confidence in this kind of perception, i.e., in mathematical *intuition*, than in sense perception, which induces us to build up physical theories and to expect that future sense perceptions will agree with them.

Gödel leaves it unclear here whether he thinks that the objects of mathematical intuition are classes and concepts (Russell essay), propositions, that is properties of and relations between concepts (Carnap essay and letter to Schilpp), sets (supplement to "What Is Cantor's Continuum Problem?"), or all of these. An answer emerges from Husserl. According to him, as we have seen, intuition, as well as perception, is of objects. There are two kinds of intuition: perception, where the object intuited is a physical object, and categorial, or eidetic intuition, where the object is an abstract entity. Husserl's notion of abstract object, however, comprises all the kinds of entities Gödel mentions: sets, concepts, and propositions. The object, whether it be concrete or abstract, is always intuited as having various properties and bearing relations to other objects.

2.3. INDIVIDUATION

The comparison between Husserl and Gödel throws light on a puzzling passage in the supplement that Gödel added to "What Is Cantor's Continuum Problem?" when it was reprinted in Benacerraf and Putnam, *Philosophy of Mathematics: Selected Readings*, in 1964. Gödel states:

> That something besides the sensations actually is immediately given follows (independently of mathematics) from the fact that even our ideas referring to physical objects contain constituents qualitatively different from sensations or mere combinations of sensations, e.g., the idea of object itself.... Evidently, the "given" underlying mathematics is closely related to the abstract elements contained in our empirical ideas. It by no means follows, however, that the data of this second kind, because they cannot be associated with actions of certain things upon our sense organs, are something purely subjective, as Kant asserted. Rather they, too, may represent an aspect of objective reality, but, as opposed to the sensations, their presence may be due to another kind of relationship between ourselves and reality. (Pp. 271–72)

Charles Parsons, whose work on the philosophy of mathematics I find exceptionally illuminating, states that he finds this passage "quite obscure" (Parsons 1980: 146). However, on the background of Husserl's philosophy I think that there is a way of making sense of the passage, and that it expresses in a condensed way a key to Gödel's philosophy of mathematics.

Gödel's point in this passage is, I think, that what is given in our experience is not just physical objects, but also various abstract features that are instantiated by these objects. Gödel emphasizes in particular the idea of object itself. I take this to mean the features that are involved in individuation of objects, and that we discussed above in connection with both Husserl and Quine. These features, that involve identity and distinctness and thereby counting, and are part of the same package as space and time, are the principal elements studied in mathematics. And they are just as objective as the physical objects studied in natural science.

2.4. HOW DO WE FIND OUT ABOUT MATHEMATICAL OBJECTS?

Gödel's view that we have something like a perception of mathematical objects does not mean that mathematics can achieve certainty. Neither perception nor categorial intuition are infallible sources of evidence. They always involve anticipations concerning aspects of their objects that have not yet been explored, and which may turn out to be wrong. As we have noted, Husserl acknowledges that errors are always possible, even in mathematics and logic.

Gödel sketches four different methods one can use to get insight into the mathematical realm:

2.4.1. Elementary Consequences

Just as we test highly general physical theories by trying to derive observable predictions from them, Gödel noted in his Russell article, as you remember, that mathematical objects "are in the same sense necessary to obtain a satisfactory system of mathematics as physical bodies are necessary for a satisfactory theory of our sense perceptions" (Gödel 1944: 137; p. 128 of the reprint in Feferman et al. 1990).

He also points out that very recondite axioms can have elementary consequences. Thus, discussing various axioms of infinity in "What Is Cantor's Continuum Problem?" Gödel observes that "it can be proved that these axioms also have consequences far outside the domain of very great transfinite numbers, which is their immediate subject matter: each of them, under the assumption of its consistency, can be shown to increase the number of decidable propositions even in the field of Diophantine equations" (Gödel 1964: 264).

2.4.2. "Success"

In "What Is Cantor's Continuum Problem?" Gödel points to another reason we may have for thinking that a proposed axiom is true:

> A probable decision about its truth is possible also in another way, namely, inductively by studying its "success." Success here means fruitfulness in consequences, in particular in "verifiable" consequences, i.e. consequences demonstrable without the new axiom, whose proofs with the help of the new axiom, however, are considerably simpler and easier to discover, and make it possible to contract into one proof many different proofs. The axioms for the system of

real numbers, rejected by the intuitionists, have in this sense been verified to some extent. (Gödel 1964: 265)

So, in this case what matters is not the derivation of new theorems, but that the axiom permits us to derive old theorems in a more elegant way.

2.4.3. Clarification

Sometimes, we find that the axioms we have been setting up so far are satisfiable by two or more quite differently defined classes of objects. Then, by reflecting upon the concepts we are trying to capture by these axioms, we may find that one of these classes does not fit the concept. In "What Is Cantor's Continuum Problem?" Gödel remarks that "it may be conjectured that the continuum problem cannot be solved on the basis of the axioms set up so far, but, on the other hand, may be solvable with the help of some new axiom which would state or imply something about the definability of sets" (Gödel 1964: 266).

2.4.4. Systematicity

In the manuscript from 1961 where Gödel discusses Husserl's phenomenology, he mentions a fourth way in which we can arrive at new axioms, viz., by arranging the axioms in a systematic manner, which enables us to discover new ones:

> It turns out that in the systematic establishment [*Aufstellen*] of the axioms of mathematics, new axioms, which do not follow by formal logic from those previously established, again and again become evident. It is not at all excluded by the negative results mentioned earlier [incompleteness] that nevertheless every clearly posed mathematical yes-or-no question is solvable in this way. For it is just this becoming evident of more and more new axioms on the basis of the meaning of the primitive notions that a machine cannot imitate. (Gödel 1961: 9)

Husserl, who as you remember, had a "reflective equilibrium" approach to justification, attaches great significance to systematization as a way to clarify concepts. It is an important factor in his conception of justification, by way of "reflective equilibrium."

Much more could be said about the relationship between Gödel and Husserl. Gödel, in his 1961 manuscript and in his comments in the margins of Husserl's works has much to say on Husserl's phenomenology as meaning analysis and as a way to gain mathematical insight. However, this will have to suffice for this occasion.

CHAPTER FOURTEEN

The Mathematical Continuum: From Intuition to Logic

GIUSEPPE LONGO

> The conceptual world of mathematics is so foreign to what the intuitive continuum presents to us that the demand for coincidence between the two must be dismissed as absurd. Nevertheless, those abstract schemata which supply us with mathematics must also underlie the exact science of domains of objects in which continua play a role.
> —*Hermann* Weyl, Das Kontinuum, 1918

In this essay we will deal with some foundational problems concerning the mathematical continuum, in relation to phenomenology. There are three main justifications for such an enterprise:

First, as Chapter 1 in this volume has explained, mathematics has always played an essential role in Husserlian phenomenology. In fact phenomenology roots itself in the philosophy of arithmetic.

Second, the question of the *continuum* is central for mathematics (analysis, geometry . . .) and for phenomenology. The flux of phenomenological data, what Husserl calls in *Ding und Raum* the pre-phenomenal space, and internal time consciousness rely upon the originary intuition of the continuum. In what concerns the problematic of transcendental constitution, the link between the intuition and the formalization of the continuum yields the example par excellence of relation between what is constituting and what is constituted. Now it is well known that efforts to formalize the continuum have always encountered, from Aristotle to Weyl, via Leibniz and Cantor, the greatest difficulties. One of the main theses of this paper will be that these difficulties are, so to say, the formal "symptoms" of the intuitive essence of the continuum.

And third, the logical problems concerning formalization and axiomatization play a crucial role in Husserl's *formal ontology*. Husserl's opposition between formal apophantics and formal ontology is parallel to the model-theoretic one between syntax and semantics. But Husserlian semantics is not purely set-theoretic. It wants to be a true formal theory of the principles governing the construction of objects. Now, we will hint that categorical semantics provides a far more satisfactory formal ontology than set theory.

Moreover, we will analyze the correlation between proof principles (formal syntax) and construction principles (categorical semantics). This correlation is analogous to Husserl's noetico-noematic one.

Dagfinn Føllesdal, when discussing Kurt Gödel's and Hermann Weyl's conceptions of the continuum, mentioned several important aspects of Husserl's influence on the thinking of mathematicians. I will approach the discussion of the continuum from the perspective of trying to obtain a *foundation for "mathematical knowledge" as part of our way of interpreting and reconstructing the world, and not just as a "purely logical," (meta)mathematical investigation of mathematics.* Nonetheless, some references to technical work in pure mathematics and mathematical logic will be inevitable.

The starting point for this essay was the comments about the continuum made by Hermann Weyl in the book *Das Kontinuum* (Weyl 1918a). Weyl, a mathematician of great stature, was strongly influenced by Husserl in his numerous foundational and philosophical reflections. In particular the "phenomenology" of the continuum is at the heart of the most interesting, and modern, observations in *Das Kontinuum*. Other important references for these notes will be the articles by René Thom, Jean Petitot, and Jacques Bouveresse in the book *Le Labyrinthe du continu* (Salanskis and Sinaceur 1992), as well as the reflections of Wittgenstein (in different places, to be cited in the text) and in Gilles Chatelet's *Les Enjeux du mobile* (1993).

1. THE INTUITION

Our intuition about the continuum is built from common or stable elements, from invariants that emerge from a plurality of acts of experience: the perception of time, of movement, of a line extended, of a trace of a pencil, and so on.

Time. Weyl considers "time as a fundamental continuum" and the "phenomenal time" of Husserl and Bergson as "conscious experience" of the present which coexists with "memory of the instant gone." Its measure is based on the comparison of temporal segments (Weyl 1918a: 109–11). Weyl describes the intuition of time as a continuous flux, an "experience in transformation." For Weyl, phenomenological time is a duration without points, made out of parts that link together, that are superimposed on each other, because "this is now, but meanwhile now is no more" (Weyl 1918a: 111; see also St. Augustine's *Confessions*).

Weyl's insistence that the continuum is indeed continuous, that there are no parts to which it can be reduced, that the continuum is "noncompositional," develops a fundamental thesis of Husserl's. There is in Husserl an essential opposition between time and space as (pre-)phenomenal life-experiences, which are *constituent* existences, and time and space as *construed* entities. The pre-phenomenal life-experiences, time in particular, cannot be further reduced, whereas the construed entities, as a result of a mathematical construction, are made out of ultimate elements (the points). Weyl accepts the (mathematical) hypothesis that forces a one-to-one correspondence between the real line, as defined following Cantor and Dedekind, and pre-phenomenal space, but he considers unsatisfactory the extension of this correspondence to time.

Movement. We can "see" the continuum in the movement of an object. In physics since Aristotle, time has been seen as presupposing movement: movement gives the measure and even the concept of time. The continuum we derive reminds us again of flux, the passage from the power to the act: but the direct vision of movement has no need to appeal to memory. Weyl then proposes an interesting distinction between the continuous *line* which is there, the "tracks of the tramway" (an image also dear to René Thom, see Thom 1990), and the *curve*, a potential path, "which a pedestrian walks on . . . the trajectory of a point in movement." When this point "finds itself in a determined position, it coincides with a determined point of the plane, without being itself this point of the plane." "In movement, the continuum of points on a trajectory recovers in a continuous monotone fashion the continuum of instants" (Weyl 1918a: chap. 2, par. 8). But this is just superposition: for Weyl the temporal continuum does not have points, the instants are merely "transitions," the present is only possible because of the simultaneous perception of the past and of the future.

The taut string. A thread, a string extended (another of Thom's images), is another experience of the continuum. By its tension, it cannot have jumps or holes.

The pencil on a sheet. This is the most common experience of the continuum: no one entertains discourse or conscious reflection of the continuum before having drawn lines on pieces of paper thousands of times. The experience is neat: a set of black points transforms the curve into a line, in Weyl's sense above. The points are collected in the trace, which makes their individuality disappear. These points become evident again, as isolated points, wherever two lines cross.

Cauchy, in his first demonstration of the theorem of the mean value (see section 2), does not go further than the intuition of the continuum that comes from strings and curves traced by a pencil and their crossings.

Viewing the traces of a pencil over paper suggests from where our intellectual experience of points—isolated and without dimensions—could have come: from the crossing of two lines. Points are not part of our intuition of the continuum, clearly at least not from the temporal continuum, as Weyl tells us, but also not part of the spatial continuum, as Wittgenstein explains. For Wittgenstein, a curve is a *law*, it is not made out of points; "The intersection point of two lines is not the common element of two classes of points, but the *intersection of two laws*" (Wittgenstein 1964; quoted by Bouveresse 1992). If the line or the curve of the movement has only one dimension, that given by the law that describes it, then we are forced to conceive of a point, as the crossing of two lines, as devoid of dimension. This is also suggested by two lines or by pencil traces crossing on a sheet of paper. *The point without dimension is a derived conceptual construction, a necessary consequence of a line as a one-dimensional law.* It is a posterior reconstruction, specific to set theory, which "puts together" the points to reconstruct the line. From this reconstruction comes the set-theoretical inversion of priorities—the continuum as a set of points—an inversion rejected, as we mentioned, by Weyl, Wittgenstein, and Thom alike, although for different reasons.

2. THE MATHEMATICS

One of the most important theorems about the mathematical continuum is intuitively obvious: if on a plane a continuous line has one of its extremities in one side of a right line and the other on the other side of the same right line, then the continuous line cuts through the right line.

> THEOREM OF THE MEAN VALUE. *If the function $f(x)$ is continuous with respect to the variable x between a and b, and if we call c an intermediary value between $f(a)$ and $f(b)$, then we can always satisfy the equation $f(x) = c$, for at least one value of x between a and b.*
>
> PROOF. (Cauchy, 1821) *It is enough to see that the curve which has equation $y = f(x)$ will meet one or more times the line $y = c$, inside the interval between a and b; now, it is evident that this will be what will happen when the hypotheses are met.* QED

This proof is not a proof. It is not that the reasoning is faulty, it is the definitions that are missing: Cauchy does not have (yet) a rigorous notion of continuity or curve (Weierstrass). He appeals to the evidence of threads and pencil traces. Fortunately the theorem itself is true, we can demonstrate it rigorously. In a course in the Ecole Polytechnique in 1815, Louis Poinsot, in his attempt to grasp the mathematical continuum and its relation to differentiability, believed he had demonstrated, in a similar fashion, that every continuous curve is differentiable everywhere, on the left or on the right. The counterexample is well known.

Actually, at the beginning of the nineteenth century, the "intuition" about the continuum in mathematics needed to be made precise. The ether of physics, the archtypical perfect continuum, had permeated the scientific spirit everywhere. There was a choice to be made: in one side Leibniz's infinitesimals, on the other the limits, the continuity in terms of "for all ϵ, there exists a δ" (Cauchy, Weierstrass).

What is invariant, stable, among the many experiences of the world that refer to the continuum? Certainly an *invariance of scale*: all the little bits of time, of a line, even of a string, keep the same properties of that of a longer one (in the perception of continuity as an extended string, we ignore the atoms). In general, the magnifying glass does not change our intuition of the continuum. Or more formally, all homotheties (transformations that enlarge or shrink a mathematical structure) preserve the structure of the continuum. And then, of course, the absence of jumps and holes: the continuum does not stop and resume, nor does it have any holes in which Zeno's arrows can be lost.

Then we had the formidable invention of Cantor and Dedekind. It was to make people forget Leibniz's ideas until the invention of nonstandard analysis, a century later, because of its conceptual simplicity, its precision, its constructivity. Take the totally ordered set of the integers, N, and the rationals, Q, as fractions of integers. The set Q is also totally ordered and has some interesting properties for the continuum: it is in effect a dense order (between any two rationals, there is always a third), hence invariant by homotheties (or by invariance-of-scale) and without jumps. But Q also has an uncountable number of holes or lacunas. Cauchy would have us close these by adding to Q all the limits, in his sense; Dedekind, by defining a real number as the set of rationals that are smaller than itself. These turn out to be equivalent operations. The result is the set-theoretical construction of Cantor-Dedekind which is the standard formalization of the continuum, that of the real line R of analysis. It satisfies the invariance-of-scale requirement and has no jumps or lacunas. Thus a curve in space is continuous if it is described by a law that does not introduce jumps or lacunas and is parametrized by this line R.[1]

2.1. THE IMPREDICATIVE DEFINITION OF THE REAL LINE

There is still a problem with the construction we have sketched: if a real number is the limit of all the rationals that precede it, we are using and we are preparing the ground for a circular definition.

First, there is always an infinity of (positive) rationals smaller than whichever (positive) real: hence we need to use, when defining it, the collection N of all the integers, in its totality. And the classical definition of this totality has the following structure: N is the smallest set that contains zero and which if it contains n it contains $n + 1$. Said in a different way, N is the intersection of all sets that contain zero and which are closed under the successor operation. But the set of all sets than contain zero and are closed under the successor operation contains N itself; thus, the *definiens* uses the *definiendum*.

Second, once the real line has been constructed, whenever we define, for example, least upper bounds or greatest lower bounds, we do so once again using quantifications that can refer to what is being defined (the collection of the upper bounds or of the lower bounds includes the definiendum, the smallest or greatest bound, which is also an upper or a lower bound).

Poincaré and Weyl, who were well aware of these problems in analysis, gave rigorous definitions of "impredicative notion" in mathematics.[2] Poincaré observes that these definitions are not always contradictory, but they always run the risk of being circular. Lebesgue, in 1902, built the general theory of integration over an essentially impredicative definition (the Lebesgue measure). The question was hotly discussed at the beginning of the twentieth century, in particular because of the work of Russell. We will hint at the consequences of this discussion in Weyl's *Das Kontinuum*.

Does this circularity separate the Cantor-Dedekind construction, and hence analysis, from the "intuition of the continuum"? Clearly not. We can see a circularity in the discourse on the continuum as early as Aristotle: the continuum is presented as one "totality already formed, which, on its own, gives meaning to its components" (Panza 1992).

The present time of Weyl is circular in the same way: none of its parts (past, present, or future) has meaning without reference to the others; time itself *is* the simultaneous perception of the past, the present, and the future. The present time that is not here anymore is the past, and the present time that is not here yet is the future, and that we understand only when we are inserted in the whole of time or within a segment of time. The same is true about the continuity of the string or the line, which is not conceived of as a series of points, but globally, or at least through an "enlarged locality." *The impredicativity of analysis permits a possible formalization of this intuitive circularity, in particular of phenomenological time; this is an example of its expressive richness, another point of contact between intuition and mathematics.* Thus, in our view, the apparent seamlessness (or non-compositionality) of time is reflected in the apparent paradoxes of mathematical construction; these circularities need not be avoided but analyzed and developed, in particular by the tools of logic and type theory (see below).

This way the division between time and mathematical analysis, which disturbed Weyl (the absence of points in phenomenological time in comparison with the presence of points in the real line) is in part, but only in part, reduced: the real points can be, a posteriori, isolated, but their definition and their analysis, à la Cantor-Dedekind, requires "a global look" at the continuum, the same way the intuition of the present requires intuitions of the past and future. In *Das Kontinuum*, Weyl is worried, as were most mathematicians at the beginning of the twentieth century, about the lack of rigor in mathematical definitions: too many paradoxes had disrupted the foundational work, definitions tinged with circularity were suspected. For this reason, he tried a novel approach, which avoids impredicativity, since it is based on a predicative approach of mathematical analysis. This attempt was not to affect his concrete work in mathematics (see Chandarasekharan 1986) or his further foundational reflections. Weyl was probably missing, in that temporary restriction of his mathematical tools, a common element between analysis and the intuition of the (temporal) continuum, about which he was particularly concerned. However, given his mathematical talent, his work on this point was to be considered a paradigm by other logicians, who have continued to prefer stratified certitudes to the expressive circularities of impredicativity (see Feferman 1988). But the challenge of his book is primarily his dissatisfaction with the mathematical analysis of the temporal continuum and his critique of the artificial unity of space-time, a very important (and very criticizable) acquisition by the mathematical physics of his time.[3] The continuum of time, by its peculiar unity and because it is irreversible, is very different from that of space, as many thinkers, from St. Augustine to Weyl, have been trying to tell us.

3. BETWEEN INTUITION AND MATHEMATICS

Cantor and Dedekind proposed a precise mathematical formalization of the intuitive continuum, with at least three points of contact with our intuitive demands: the invariance of scale, the absence of jumps, and the absence of holes. This formalization is based on very clear "construction principles": the sequence of natural numbers, quotients, and the limits of convergent sequences. Because *iteration* gives us the integers (we will return to this point) and *quotients* give us the rationals, a *convergence criterion* for a sequence given by a rule gives us a *method for constructing* the reals. A convergence criterion for a sequence, even if the sequence is not known a priori, indicates, without ambiguity, by shrinking the interval, what we define as "the real limit" of this sequence.[4]

The theoretical import of this construction is massive, and its conceptual force rekindles our vision of the world. It does much more than show that the mathematics and its structures are not stratified; it shows that our knowledge is not stratified as well. Once a language and an expressive geometry intervene in the description of the world, they enrich it with forms, which acquire an objective autonomy. This is the basis and the result of intersubjectivity; it emerges from the world; it is full of history and because of this, it is not absolute or arbitrary. But above all it is *this language, this geometry, that will influence our originary intuition*, for a dynamic game is then played. This interplay goes from our intuitions to their formalizations and when it returns to the intuition, it modifies it. A "classical" mathematician does not see a trace of a pencil without seeing the continuum of R, which parameterizes the trace as a curve. He will talk about the continuity of this trace, of space, of time, of movement, directly in terms of his analytical language. The trace over the sheet of paper and the contemplation of movement are instruments for his own reflection, "eyes for the mind," for the construction that he is trying to master, analysis. And, before he resorts to any proofs, he applies his intuition to the mental spaces of analysis and geometry, trying to understand them as he understands a piece of string, as if they were realities of the same order. From this comes the usual Platonic ontology of most mathematicians. It is a formidable help to formulating conjectures and even proofs: Cauchy "saw" the theorem of the mean value. René Thom "lived" for a long time among the continuous and differentiable varieties. His deep immersion in this conceptual space, his mathematical genius, allowed him to "see" first, and then classify the singularities (the catastrophes), an exceptional mathematical (and cognitive) performance. For him, as for many other mathematicians of the continuum, "the Continuum precedes ontologically the discrete," for the latter is merely an "accident coming out of the continuum background," "a broken line . . . the archetypical continuum is a space that has the property of a perfect qualitative homogeneity," hence it gives us a vision, more than a logico-mathematical construction (Thom 1992). Actually Thom goes further: "Any demonstration is a revelation of a novel structure, where the elements solidify the intuition and where the reasoning reconstructs the progressive genesis" (Thom 1990: 560). Such an intuition emerges not from the world but from observation of the universe of mathematics where the "form of existence is without doubt different from the concrete and material existence of the world, but nevertheless subtly and deeply linked to objective existence." For this reason "the mathematician must have the courage of his inner convictions; he will affirm that the mathematical structures have an existence independent of the mind that has conceived them; . . . the Platonist hypothesis . . . is . . . the most natural and philosophically the most economical" (Thom 1990: 560). Dana Scott more prudently said to this author about this hypothesis: "It does no harm." The advantages of the Platonist hypothesis in the "linguistic synthesis" for everyday communication among mathematicians are enormous, due to the efficacy of the objective signification that it can give to the language and to the crucial "scribbles on the blackboard." But the foundational and philosophical drawbacks that it entails are also very important, for all transcendent ontology disguises the historical and cognitive process, the project of intellectual construction, in which mathematics is rich, and in particular the "proof principles" and the "construction principles" that are at its heart.

3.1. OTHER CONSTRUCTIONS OF THE CONTINUUM

Discussing the continuum, we have tried to describe how mathematical intuition is built into our relation with the world, by "these acts of experience . . . within which we live as human beings" (Weyl 1918a: 113). *On the basis of these life experiences, we propose descriptions and deductions, not arbitrarily, but in the full light of history and intersubjectivity, of invariance within a plurality of experiences.* Those descriptions and deductions, those wagers, in a sense, organized in mathematical theories, are our linguistic (algebra, analysis) and spatial formalizations (geometry). *The objectivity, which is transcendental (in the Husserlian sense) but not transcendent, that emerges from these intellectual constructions and which modifies itself and enriches itself in history, will give (mathematical) forms to the world: forms that are not "already there" and which will also modify and enrich our original intuitions.*

These proposals, these constructions, which aim to an objectivity no longer absolute but still strong, still full of intellectual and cognitive paths, theorems, and intersubjective communication, are not unique. In the case of the continuum, Leibniz had proposed another construction, an incomplete and informal one that was unable to resist the very robust construction of Cauchy, Weierstrass, Cantor, and Dedekind. It was necessary to wait for the mathematical logic of the twentieth century, so that an alternative proposal became a new mathematical analysis, nonstandard analysis.[5] The nonstandard analyst describes the continuum differently, along the lines of Leibniz, yet in a formal and rigorous fashion: despite a number of conservative extension results for the new theories with respect to standard analysis (they prove the same theorems, within the standard fragment of the language), his real numbers like "halos of integers" are a different thing altogether and it is possible to demonstrate new theorems for them. The ordered set of nonstandard numbers, the new real number line, loses, for example, the invariance of scale (Hartong), an important characteristic of our different views of the continuum (see Barreau and Hartong 1989). The nonstandard analyst hence views geometrical space, the physical world in effect, in a different way. This change of theory and of intuition of the mathematical continuum seems to offer new insights in mathematical physics (see Cutland 1988 and the articles by Lobry, Lutz, and Reeb in Salanskis and Sinaceur 1992; Salanskis [1991] proposes an epistemological analysis of the nonstandard continuum).

Thom himself does not believe that standard analysis, which is still at the heart of his work, gives a definitive representation of the continuum. Dissatisfied with the arithmetical (and logical) generativity of the (non)standard continuum, exactly like Weyl was by the treatment of the "continuous flux" and of phenomenal time as a set of real points, he has suggested new ideas (see Thom 1992). He audaciously sketches a new conceptual construction. This conception is built from his mathematical experience, which is comparable, for him, in its force and its evidence, to the experience of the world.

But the intuition that is constructed in the praxis of mathematics is different from that which emerges directly from our relation with the physical world, even if they do get mixed up in our working-mathematician minds. The first intuition, the one constructed in the praxis of standard analysis, is based on the Cantor-Dedekind construction and a century's worth of work derived from it. If Cauchy in his "proof" of the theorem of the mean value had referred to well-defined notions of curve and continuity, if he could have appealed to the rigorous mathematical intuition of the standard reals, built over the correct definitions given some decades later, then his proof would have been a proof. He would have used the "informal rigor" of the practice of mathematics. In a somewhat different understanding of this notion from Kreisel, *the informal rigor of mathematics is based on observations "from above and from a distance" of definitions and constructions that we know to be potentially rigorous and then by the development of an informal deduction*: the rigor resides more in the precision of the notions than in the deductions themselves. This intuitive character of this method is typical of work in mathematics because *it is built history and practice*. This mathematical intuition, and the informal rigor which is grounded on it, is not the intuition of the "man in the street" (even less the intuition of Paleolithic man): all training in mathematics, from the student to the researcher, is dedicated to the acquisition of this informal rigor, this difficult balance between intuition and formal rigor, which permits both demonstration and its comprehensible expression.

The merging of these two kinds of intuition, the one of the trained mathematician and the one developed in everyday life, into one single "pure intuition"—which cannot be either purely logical or purely psychological—is the origin of the difficulties of developing a cognitive analysis of mathematics. For the analysis of mathematical intuition, which is neither given nor absolute but rather built into the interplay of acts of experience, language, design, and formalization throughout history, is actually part of the analysis of mathematics as a form of knowledge. And history aside, the confusion between commonsense intuition and the intuition of the experienced mathematician is comparable to the confusion between the objectivity of the physical world and that of mathematics. The "stability" of physical objects and their "invariance" with respect to various forms of perception are at the core of their "objectivity"; similarly, the conceptual stability and invariance of mathematical structures are mistaken, in the Platonist view, for a transcendent objectivity. The fact of one intuition "pure and unique" forces us to believe that to explain any particular question only one theory is possible; this makes it difficult to weigh the merits of different theories, or wagers of representation, that purport to treat mathematically the world and our intuitions of it, especially those intuitions which are as full of history and of questioning as the intuition of the continuum.

4. FROM MATHEMATICS TO LOGIC

Take the subsets, the parts, of the set N of the integers, $P(N)$. If two subsets A and B are strictly included in each other, they differ by a finite or infinite subset, but we would say, in "a discrete way," by successive jumps: it is integers, well-separated ones, that A is lacking to get to B. I hope the reader can "see" this in his head, using his mathematical intuition. But this is not really the case: $P(N)$ contains chains (totally ordered sets) with the same type of order as R (that is, the kind of order of the continuum: dense, without jumps or holes). The proof is easy: Q is countable; choose a bijective enumeration of Q by N and associate to each real number the integers that enumerate its Dedekind cut. Then you have a bijection (an order isomorphism) between R and a chain inside $P(N)$. Our construction principles have given us very rich structures, R and $P(N)$, so rich that they escape the intuitive naive observation. Actually these structures do not exist: the property that we just "saw" is not there, it is not *explained* as we explain a property of the world, *we have demonstrated it*, as we have built these structures, as conceptual constructions. The well-trained analyst can short-circuit this proof and see immediately the continuous chain, for the Dedekind cuts are as concrete for him as this table (to paraphrase Gödel). In any case, to construct the chain in $P(N)$, we have made some "choices." We have presented Q as a set of pairs (fractions) of the integers N. Each rational corresponds actually to an infinity of equivalent fractions; hence to give a bijective enumeration of Q we must enumerate $N \times N$ (easy) and *choose* a representative for each set of equivalent fractions. This choice is effective, for these equivalence classes are decidable—and the theory of recursively enumerable sets (and recursive functions) realizes the axiom of choice.[6] This axiom, this principle, is a construction, or allows a construction, that of the "set of choices," composed of one element for each set in the collection considered (see note 6). Hence it is a *construction principle*, since by using a specific mathematical structure, it allows the construction of new structures. But it is also a *principle of proof*: once presented "in abstracto" (that is, at a formal level, with no intended domain of interpretation, as if it held for all collections of sets, without any hypothesis on decidability or order that allowed the choice of the "first element" of each set) it becomes a purely logical stake: beyond the finite (or decidable or ordered), it completely cuts itself off from the practices of life, and it acquires a level of abstraction that makes it independent of the formalizations "without structure" of mathematics (the *formal set theories*, see section 5). Nonetheless, the trained mathematician uses it every day, without fear of error, knowing without knowing that he's using a powerful proof principle, which only the specific structure of certain constructions makes applicable. And he confuses his cognitive performance, the *vision* of the conceptual structures of his daily intellectual practices, with a mystical ontology.

Let us try again: cardinality is in first approximation the number of elements of a set. Cantor has shown by a simple diagonal construction that R has more elements than N, the integers. The reader clearly sees the real line and the "integer points" well isolated and regularly spaced. The rationals Q are dense and hence give an approximation for each real number. But they are as numerous as the integers. Is it true that if a subset of R "contains more elements" than N or Q then it necessarily has the cardinality of R? What does this observation say about this object universe? What does pure intuition say? Nothing. But still the reals are there, God at least must know them all, with their subsets.

To answer these questions it is necessary to make precise the "frame of the set-theoretical construction," to make precise our "basic principles": if we consider the reals inside the universe of construables of Gödel, we say yes; if we consider the reals inside the set-theoretical universe of Cohen, we say no. We do not know which framework God prefers. The question, from Cantor to Frege, Gödel, Cohen, and Dana Scott has been a key issue in mathematical logic: it is the challenge of the continuum hypothesis. We will refer again to it in section 5.2; but before that we must discuss "iterations" and "horizons."

5. CONSTRUCTION PRINCIPLES AND PROOF PRINCIPLES

One of the "theoretical situations" that gives "certainty" or "structural solidity" in the work of mathematicians and logicians is the joining of different methods, which converge to the same construction. When very different ideas with technical and cultural origins very much apart can be translated into each other, possibly even isomorphically, we can be sure that we have in our hands a significant construction. For these connections, with different degrees of proximity, sometimes just embeddings without isomorphisms, are to be found in all interesting domains of mathematics. That is the *unity of mathematics*: these bridges, these translations, this to-and-from, these intellectual routes through rough tracks, sometimes in parallel, which may arrive by shortcuts to well-known valleys. The audacious explorers (constructors!) will be joined by others, who chose totally different paths, with (sometimes) independent goals.

The relationship between intuitionistic logic and theory of categories (by means of the theory of types) gives one of the more interesting and elegant examples of this kind of correspondence of interrelated, yet independent constructions. A few remarks on this subject will allow us to clarify the notions of "proof principle" and "construction principle," to mention a categorical semantics of impredicative definitions and of the notion of "variation," which are the heart of the analysis of the continuum.

After that, we will briefly return to the axiom of choice and the continuum hypothesis as examples of logical axioms and mathematical constructions.

In our view, the relationship we sketch below may be clarified by (and help us understand) some concepts of Husserl's. First, as we already said, the categorical semantics of formal languages offers a "formal ontology" far more adequate to Husserl's perspective than the set-theoretical one. Category theory is grounded on principles of construction, within a structural understanding of mathematics, which allow us to go far beyond the "pointwise," unstructured, and basically compositional set-theoretical approach. Moreover, *the interplay between proof principles (syntax) and principles of construction (closer to semantics) may be understood by means of a parallelism with the Husserlian correlation noesis/noema*. One has to interpret mathematical constructions as "acts of a subject," in intuitionistic terms. However, *the "objectivity" of these constructions, in our approach, is the re-*

sult of their relation to the regularities of the world and to their "*intersubjective*" content, which is built by and in the dialogue with other subjective experiences. (Of course, this significantly departs from Brouwer's solipsistic philosophy). Thus Husserl's "noeses" may be understood, in mathematics, as systems of rules, possibly implemented in mental acts, and "noemas" are the correlated objectivities, the intersubjective constituents of the mental constructions.

5.1. CONJUNCTION, QUANTIFICATION, AND PRODUCTS

In intuitionistic logic we say we have a "proof" of a *conjunction* $A \wedge B$ (in a unique, canonical way), if we have a proof of A, a proof of B, *and* the possibility of reconstructing from a proof of $A \wedge B$ a proof of A and one of B.[7] Let A and B be two sets, two spaces, any two mathematical structures: what we have just defined is simply the *Cartesian* product $A \times B$ of A and B with its projections, which associate to each element, or proof of $A \times B$, one element or proof of A and one of B. More precisely, it is the category-theoretical version of the Cartesian product, the product invented by the geometers, which thanks to its categorical generalization gives us also the product of two topological spaces, two partial orders, of any two mathematical structures, in their categories (of structures). We have already gone to constructions, having started with proofs: $A \times B$ is the *categorical* (in fact geometric) *semantics* (interpretation) of the intuitionist conjunction $A \wedge B$.

In mathematics, in algebra, in geometry, when we have a construction, we usually have another, its *dual*, for free. Category theory says that it is enough to reverse all the arrows, that is the direction of all morphisms or functions between objects, to obtain the dual of a given construction. In the case of the product, we reverse the direction of the projections. This way we obtain the categorical *coproduct*, which can be constructed in several categories. This corresponds to the notion of intuitionistic disjunction: the famous intuitionistic disjunction $A \vee B$, of which we have a proof if and only if we have a proof of A or a proof of B and we know of which one the proof is. In particular, for this notion of disjunction, $A \vee \neg A$ (A or not A) is not demonstrable: to prove it, we need a proof of A or a proof of $\neg A$, hence the "excluded third option" is not valid. To put this in formal terms, write $S \vdash C$ to mean "S demonstrates C"; then, to state the case as generally as possible,

$$S \vdash A \vee B \text{ if and only if } S \vdash A \text{ or } A \vdash B$$

and hence the theoretic "or" ($\vee$) corresponds to the metatheoretic "or." In a classical system this beautiful intuitionist symmetry of theory and metatheory is lost, for the implication from left to right is false. Hence this intuitionistic "or" is not so odd: it is simply the dual of a very familiar geometric construction, the Cartesian product, and it transfers the metatheoretical disjunction into the theory.

We can also show that the intuitionist implication can be interpreted as the exponential objects in the categories closed under this construction. In intuitionist systems, a proof of $A \to B$ is a "computation" that takes any proof of A into a proof of B or, in type theory, a term of type $A \to B$; informally, it is then a "computable" function from A to B. In category theory, the exponential object, which may also be written as $A \to B$, represents the set of morphisms or functions between two objects of a category.

But mathematics needs variables. The syntactic entities represented by x, y, ..., which are *individual variables* in mathematical logic, are projections in category theory. When they appear within a formula, this generalizes to the notion of *fibration*, a categorical way of talking about *variation*. Thus the universal quantification $\forall x \in B.A(x)$—for all x in B we have $A(x)$—corresponds to a *fibered product* (or pullback), a notion well-established in geometry, a kind of "generalized Cartesian product": actually universal quantification generalizes conjunction, for $A(x)$ must be true at the same time for any x in B. This is an infinite conjunction or a limit: very informally it corresponds to $A(b) \wedge A(b') \wedge \ldots$ for all elements $b, b', \ldots$ in B.

How do we understand the existential quantification $\exists x \in B.A(x)$ (there exists an x in B such that $A[x]$ holds), always in the first-order case (that is, when the variables are individual ones)? The seminal observation of Lawvere is that this is nothing but the dual of the product above, with respect to the operation of substitution (formally $\forall x$ and $\exists x$ correspond, respectively, to right and left adjoints to the substitution functor, see Lambek and Scott 1986). Thus, once more, syntactic principles from logic, indeed Frege's first-order universal and existential quantifications, nicely correspond to actual constructions in geometry.

Matters get more complicated when we consider variables over propositions or sets (we will write them with capital letters $X, Y, \ldots$). Why this extra work? When we discuss the continuum from the logical point of view, this is inevitable: the real numbers of analysis are sets of integers, the numerical codes of (equivalence classes of) Cauchy sequences of rationals. For this reason second-order arithmetic, with variables ranging over propositions, is considered the logical counterpart of Cantor-Dedekind's analysis. Here comes the difficulty: the variables do not vary over a set or predicate, as in $\forall x \in B.A(x)$, but instead they vary inside the collection *Prop* of all the sets or propositions, including $\forall X \in Prop.A(X)$, the proposition that we are trying to define, for $\forall X \in Prop.A(X)$ is in *Prop*. And once more we are faced with the problem of impredicativity. All is not lost. We will sort things out in two different ways: through a normalization theorem (see section 5.3), and through a construction that does not depend on the logic, and which has its origin in geometry (the Grothendieck topos and the ideas of Lawvere). Inside these geometrical categories we can give a structural meaning, as a closure property of certain categories, to this stake that worries many logicians (but very few mathematicians and computer scientists). Briefly, the variation will happen now over a category and not simply over an object in a category, as in the first-order case, for we need to give meaning to the variables over propositions and each proposition is an object; thus it is necessary that this category be closed under products indexed over itself. All this gives a new structure for the variation and a strong closure property. The circularity of the impredicative definitions becomes then a theorem, the closure of certain categories under generalized products, whose origin is geometrical (see Asperti and Longo 1991).

The only difficulty is that the construction cannot be done inside classical set theory (Reynolds 1984); instead, one needs an intuitionistic environment (Pitts 1987; Hyland 1988; Longo and Moggi 1991). Once again, but this is complicated, the geometrical symmetry between $\forall X$ and $\exists X$ can be represented as left and right adjunctions, with respect to a functor that also generalizes the Cartesian product, the diagonal functor.

Here we have an interaction of principles of proof and principles of construction that have very different origins and motivations. We understand proofs through constructions, and this way we obtain one of these conceptual chains that are the kernel of the mathematical conceptual edifice.

In this sketch of a mathematical semantics of proofs we have implicitly used some constructions that take us back to infinity and the continuum. We have touched the continuum in two main ways: the (categorical) semantics of the notion of variation or change, which is one of the elements of the phenomenon of the continuum, and of the impredicative definitions. But there are also passages to the limit, which are implicit in the categorical constructions of the product, as the universal quantification $\forall x \in B.A(x)$ is an infinite conjunction, a categorical limit.

We then go back to infinity, to limits, and to the continuum in mathematics and logic.

5.2. LIMITS AND CLOSINGS OF THE HORIZON

Despite the supporting references to systems of intuitionstic logic, the reader should not suppose that the author is a "devoted intuitionist," although such logicians can still be found (and they are still doing very valuable work) in Northern Europe. The notion of conceptual construction discussed here is the one that emerges from the practice of mathematics, and it is more general than Brouwer's notion or the one formalized by Heyting. The interest for intuitionism is first *mathematical*: these systems have a correspondence in geometry (topos theory), which is hard to find for other logical systems. But the interest in intuitionism is also *methodological*, because of the emphasis it puts on the notion of construction.[8] But we should not make a limiting religion of our extraordinary creative possibilities, when it comes to mathematical constructions. Infinity, for example, has been part of our practices of language and of our perception of space for a long time, too long for us to try and expel it from our mathematical practice or from the logical theorizations.

Consider the sequence 1, 2, 3, . . . that we can iterate without any reason to stop. Its closure, on the horizon, which we call ω, is it not as clear and certain as the finite iteration? Nowadays with computers that do iteration so well, we can observe what happens after iteration more easily than in the past: the finitist engagement in logic this past century is in the origin of (the development of) these formidable digital machines that have changed our daily lives. This finitist effort should remain with the machines! We can continue, as mathematicians have done forever, using this construction, this going to the limit, without fear of losing our "unshakable certainties." And we can state with no problem:

$$\omega + 1, \omega + 2, \ldots, \omega + \omega = \omega \times 2$$

But now the playing is easy, the construction evident:

$$\omega \times 2, \omega \times 3, \ldots, \omega\omega = \omega^2$$

Why not carry on? The rule is there:

$$\omega^2, \omega^3, \ldots, \omega^\omega$$

But we human beings, we find endless iteration boring. This is one of the differences between us and the computers: boredom. Computers don't get bored: iteration is their strongest point. We, once we have understood, once we have detected a regularity, we look further afield, we see the horizon, ω or even ω^ω, as we see the image of poplars in *Les Enjeux du mobile* (Chatelet 1993: chap. 2, page 2): we take in at a glance the range that repeats itself in the direction of the horizon and we project it over an actual infinity. This is a human experience which has gradually been made explicit in concepts through the centuries; maybe it has its origins in the Oriental religions, as Weyl would have it;[9] in any case, this experience has developed because of and within mathematical practice, where religious commitment and Platonist ontology can mix up and justify a conceptual construction, as with Galileo, Newton, or Cantor. But what happens if we continue the iteration of the exponentials? We have ω to the power ω to the power ω ... on the limit, the horizon, this will be simply ω to the power ω, ω times. This ordinal we call ϵ_0; it gives the smallest solution to the equation $x = \omega^x$. Do we need a transfinite ontology to describe and use this construction? No, a simple principle of going to the limit, to the horizon, suffices, if we have an explicit iteration (as in this case) or a criterion of convergence (as in the case of Cauchy sequences). The ordinal ω, or ϵ_0, is not in the world, it is not a convention, nor merely a symbol: *it synthesizes a principle of construction*, a "disciplined gesture" to paraphrase Chatelet, rich in history. Its rigorous use in mathematics has given it a meaning, has inserted it into operative contexts, has shown us its different points of view, has, briefly, found it a place within the conceptual network we call mathematics. This gesture reiterated gives us ... $\omega \times 2$, ... ω^2, ... ω^ω ... ϵ_0. And whatever follows.[10]

The utilization of ϵ_0 in proofs has huge consequences. To begin with, Gerhard Gentzen showed, in 1936, the consistency of arithmetic, by induction up to ϵ_0, hence using methods beyond the finite ones, which are below ω.[11] Next, this "skeleton of infinity" can be found in the minimal construction of a model of set theory: Gödel's constructibles, which takes us back to the continuum. Gödel's idea in 1938 was briefly as follows: starting from the empty set, repeat by induction up to ϵ_0 the constructions formalized by set theory in their language and nothing else.[12] The real numbers built inside this mathematical structure do satisfy the axiom of choice and the continuum hypothesis, for reasons of minimality that we can guess: the sets of real numbers have minimal cardinality (see Jech 1973 and Devlin 1973). Cohen in 1966 proposed another construction for set theory: he added generic or arbitrary elements, whose properties are "forced" bit by bit, during the construction of the model, in a way that *does not realize* the continuum hypothesis (or the axiom of choice).

We normally say that these two major results show the independence of the continuum hypothesis (and of the axiom of choice) from formal set theories (of Zermelo-Frankel, and so on). But this is not the most interesting aspect of this issue: *the meaning of these theorems is in their proofs*. These proofs consist of mathematical (set-theoretical) constructions inside which certain properties are realized, and through this realization they give us precise information about the nature of these properties (in particular about the structure of the continuum and the cardinality of subsets of the Cantorian reals: their cardinality depends on the construction made). The fact that these properties are independent of the formal set theories concerned says nothing about the continuum, but simply underlines the poverty of these formalizations, which are independent of any structure and which were born exactly to answer the questions about the continuum and about choice. Frequently formalism forgets the constructive and structural nature of mathematics: Gödel and Cohen's constructions remind us of this.

5.3. THE INFINITE IN THE TREES

Yet another relevant construction in mathematics is that of the "tree." Mathematical trees have their roots on top: a unique node, which branches downward. A tree is finitely branching if each node has a finite number of nodes below it; a branch is a sequence of consecutive nodes, a path with no interruptions that starts at the root and develops to the bottom. Consider now the following principle, known as König's Lemma: "In a finitely branching, infinite tree, there is an infinite branch."

The reader certainly understands, "sees," this geometrical property of trees: if the infinite tree cannot grow infinitely horizontally (since it is finitely branching) it must grow infinitely vertically. This is an easy observation about the construction of trees, by an "insight" into the plane or the structure of planar trees. However, we cannot, in general, effectively produce (construct by a calculable process) the infinite branch, even if the nodes are labeled and the tree itself is effectively produced (recursively enumerable). More precisely, one cannot create an algorithm, that is to say, write a program that generates the infinite branch, for the computer running this program would have to test each path, erasing and reconstructing its memory in a noneffective way. Hence this principle, even if evident, goes beyond usual effectiveness; it is not intuitionistically acceptable.

Yet this principle has several applications. One is implicit in the categorical analysis of the impredicative definitions mentioned in 5.1: a somewhat similar principle, the uniformity principle (see note 12), is used in the construction of the categories closed under products indexed over themselves (Rosolini 1986, Hyland 1988, and Longo and Moggi 1991; see Longo 1987 for a partly informal exposition). The principle hence contributes to giving structural semantics to the syntax of impredicativity: as we said in section 5.1, we can "understand" the impredicative definitions as closure properties of certain categories. Moreover, the Tait-Girard proof of the normalization theorem for impredicative type theory (see Girard, Lafont, and Taulor 1989) uses König's Lemma and one "comprehension" axiom over the language of sets of the following form:

$$\exists X \in \text{Sets}. \forall x. [x \in X \Leftrightarrow A(x)].$$

The naive Platonists, who accept this axiom, and the limitative constructivists of different schools, who reject it, all attribute to it an ontological content, on the basis of a "prejudice (in fact a medieval one) according to which the *same* logic holds for mathematics and the real world—this implies, as a consequence, that an existential quantification must refer to singular individual entities really existing as separated, independent and transcendent entities" (Petitot 1992a). This mistake, which Petitot describes very well, is based on forgetting the role of proofs in mathematics; it is sufficient to observe closely the argument for "strong normalization" in type theory, in Girard, Lafont, and Taulor (1989: §14) for example, to see that this axiom is simply a *principle of proof*: it "just" permits us to *replace* one variable over propositions (or types) for a given collection of terms, defined during the proof. Where is the ontological miracle?

A major consequence of the strong normalization theorem for Girard's system, and also for other systems starting with Gödel's 1958 system, is a demonstration of the consistency of arithmetic of the first and second orders, and hence of formal analysis (see Girard, Lafont, and Taulor 1989).[13]

In summary, noneffective insights or conceptual constructions are part of mathematical practice and metamathematical theorization and have no need to refer to "ontological" principles. The consequences of an "existentially quantified" assertion (a comprehension axiom, say) are *logical consequences* of possible (or assumed) constructions. Moreover, the geometric insight into trees may be as certain as an effective procedure.

6. THE LOGICAL INDEPENDENCE

The first great result of incompleteness, or of undecidability with respect to an interesting formal system, is Gödel's result, in 1931. In particular, Gödel's "first incompleteness theorem" shows that formal arithmetic, which can code all effective processes, contains an undecidable proposition, call it G, if it is consistent.[14] The second incompleteness theorem says that arithmetic does not show its own consistency. More precisely, the second theorem shows that Gödel's undecidable proposition G is provably equivalent, in arithmetic, to consistency. Hence the second theorem shows that G is true, in the standard model, if we suppose the consistency of arithmetic.

Later, to show the consistency from Gentzen to Girard, it was necessary to come out of effective finitism and make use of stronger principles of proof, as hinted above.

We have also mentioned two other major results of independence, as consequence of Gödel and Cohen's constructions: the continuum hypothesis and the axiom of choice are neither demonstrable nor refutable within formal set theory.

Does this mean that there are mathematical truths that we cannot reach through "demonstration"? How would this be implied by the results of incompleteness or independence, if we just mentioned the existence of proofs or of constructions that *demonstrate* the consistency of arithmetic, of the continuum hypothesis and of the axiom of choice? *There are no propositions that are "true and not demonstrable" in mathematics.* True and demonstrable with respect to what, with respect to which construction and which proof principles? One must make this precise.

There is in the use of the phrase, "true but not provable," a "slipping of meaning," very relevant and typical of naive set theory. We only have a precise notion of the "truth of a proposition" with respect to given mathematical structures (there are in fact several notions: Tarski's, Kripke's, Brouwer-Heyting-Kolmogorov's, among others). But we believe naively that there exists a *set* of true propositions. And hence the mystical reasoning: we move from the *notion of truth* to the *collection*, which exists in God's mind and which contains, one by one, the true propositions, in a well-ordered fashion. Which one, then, the continuum hypothesis or its negation belongs to this collection?

In mathematics when we talk about the truth of a proposition, it is necessary to say what we mean by this (that is, with respect to which notion of truth and with respect to which structures); and moreover, it is necessary to show the truth with respect to this structure, to this notion. That was what Gödel did with the proposition G ("this proposition is not provable"), which he showed to be codifiable and undecidable in formal arithmetic. He also proved that this proposition is true in the standard model *under the hypothesis of consistency*, an obvious consequence of the second theorem of incompleteness (the equivalence, in arithmetic, of consistency and G). But Gödel did not say that the consistency of arithmetic, undemonstrable in arithmetic, is "true": for that it would be necessary to use Gentzen's proof, based on stronger principles. Gödel (and Cohen) later gave us structures for which the continuum hypothesis and the axiom of choice are true (or false) and they *proved it*.

Hence, what is this phenomenon of incompleteness, so important for the treatment of the continuum in logic?

When we discussed the intuitionist conjunctions and disjunctions, we saw a perfect correspondence between proof principles and categorical constructions. But things are not always this perfect. *The incompleteness of a formal theory, with respect to a precise structure, appears when we have a rift, a gap, between proof principles and construction principles.* Formal axioms, abstract principles, syntax for the manipulation of symbols and proofs on the one hand, constructions, in general geometrical or structural ones, on the other. The mathematical and logical difficulty lies in "putting one's finger on" the gap by making precise the proof principles and the construction principles utilized—and by providing theorems that display the gap.

Actually, even once the principles of proof and construction are well described, there is not always a clear demarcation between them; think, for example, of the principle of uniformity or of König's Lemma, or the axiom of choice, which are always between proof and construction. Among the ones we have seen, perhaps only the axioms of comprehension do not look like principles of construction and are pure "proof techniques." Also the rules and the formal axioms of the arithmetic of Peano-Dedekind or the logical systems of first order of Frege and Hilbert, the set theories, are very clearly principles of proof, derived from mathematical constructions (number theory, analysis, and so on). *It is in the difficult-to-detect, but possible, gaps between formal proofs and mathematical constructions, that incompleteness theorems can be found.*

The incompleteness theorems of Gödel (the first: under the hypothesis of consistency, there is an undecidable proposition; the second: the consistency is undecidable) and the consistency proofs from Gentzen to Girard show that in the construction of the integers and their properties we use, or we can use, if we accept them, strong principles, beyond formal arithmetic: we show hence that the consistency is a *true* property over the integers (and hence we show the *truth* of the undecidable proposition given by the first theorem of Gödel, which is nondemonstrable in arithmetic and equivalent to consistency).

The constructions of Gödel and Cohen prove the same thing about the continuum hypothesis and the axiom of choice: they show that they are true (or false in Cohen's case) on certain structures, constructed using certain principles, but that they are nondemonstrable using simply the axioms and rules, the proof principles, of formal set theory.[15] In other words, all these results (and more recent ones, such as Paris-Harrington and Kruskal-Friedman), by proving the truth or validity of certain propositions over *possible* mathematical structures (universes of sets or of numbers) or by proving their unprovability within given formal systems (described by *possible* proof-principles), "simply" display the gap between mathematical constructions (universes of sets, numbers) and formal theories.

Thus, *one should never say in philosophy of mathematics the phrase "there are true but unprovable propositions," for this phrase makes no sense in mathematics*. A working mathematician asks immediately, "*Unprovable* with respect to which system (to which proof principles)? *True* in which structure (using which construction principles and notion of truth)?"

In the twentieth century, formalism, in logic and proof theory, which has found in finitism and formalism its origins, has without doubt helped to answer these questions. But why should logical formalism (and its formal theories), a philosophical method only indirectly descended from mathematical practice, be the ultimate source of our certainties, of our analyses of proof and of construction in mathematics? Foundation is not given by providing the "ultimate" formal theory, but by interrelating (and mutually explaining) the variety of formal and conceptual constructions of mathematics.

The conceptual networks inside which mathematical constructions are embedded do not give us ultimate certainty, but insert each construction within other forms of knowledge. These other forms of knowledge give it a meaning, several meanings, whose connections and compatibilities form the net, relatively solid, of our relation with the world. It is the practical unity of mathematics and its emergence from the world that constitutes its foundations: this frame and the balances of theories, which translate each other, interpret each other, give root to each of its nodes in our forms of knowledge.

The analysis of proofs, proof theory, is one of its instruments. The different structural semantics will provide others. But it is necessary to insert mathematics in the triangular relation of history-individual-world, by reconstructing the cognitive and historic routes and their network of connections at the origin of the mathematical invention and its developments.

The challenge of naturalization, as cognitive analysis, and as analysis of the historical and collective construction of concepts (mathematical ones in particular) consists in finding first a few supporting points for these paths and their network.

7. THREE LEVELS AND THE RICHNESS OF THE CONTINUUM

In this essay we underlined, initially, the non-unicity of the intuition of the continuum. Then we developed an analysis which emphasized three levels: intuition, constructions, and proof principles.

On the first level, the richness of the world and of the points of view from which to observe it, compatible points of view, not isolated, but built from a dialogue with evolution and history, suggests a plurality of intuitive approaches and ground mathematics in our relation to the world. In part we find these points of view in the different mathematical constructions of the continuum, which constitute the second level. These constructions enrich and modify the original intuitions, which are not that simple when the mathematical praxis adds to them its depth. But thanks to logic there is a third level, where the analysis of the proof (as well as the formal set theories, their axioms, their rules of inference) plays an essential role. Clearly, the incompleteness results lie between the second and the third levels, as a precise form of indetermination of mathematical constructions by formal theories.

From a transcendental perspective, mathematical objectivity does not find its origin in the unicity of the intuitive giving, or in the categoricity (or unicity) of the psycho-physical genesis of that one, but instead in the common, historical, and cognitive (hence intersubjective) process of conceptual construction. That is, *in mathematical construction the values and the objective realities are not to be found in the mathematical entities (the integers, the real numbers, ω, or ϵ_0, for example) but in the process of constituting these so-called entities, as conceptual constructions*: the iterations, the passages to the limit, the closures of horizons, the constitutions of invariants.[16] In the case of the continuum, mathematical objectivity is also in the richness of interaction of three levels we mentioned: intuition, mathematics, logic. This interaction is not a vicious circle, but a virtuous one, an extraordinary example of the dynamic character of our forms of knowledge: logic, for example, which only extracts formal rules from the constructive practices of mathematics, offers, thanks to the incompleteness theorems and nonstandard analysis, new mathematical structures, which suggest a new intuition about the continuum. This is a further starting point, through games of dynamic reflection, for other constructions and formalizations.

8. CONCLUSION

The logicist and formalist philosophies of mathematics have, in this century, provided the conceptual philosophical background for major scientific achievements. The birth of computability and, hence, of computer science is one example. Another is the remarkable proposal for a precise notion of mathematical rigor: formal rigor, as the "potential deduction of a theorem by a mechanical (in principle) system of axioms and rules," tells us what it may mean to say that a proof can be carried out with "absolute" certainty. We also know how to construct and recognize a good definition. Now that formal rigor has been objectivized in formalisms (and computers) *we can reconstruct the meaning and the practice of demonstrations and widen our notion of rigor through the use of diagrams, metaphors, and images, in short by trying to understand the role of the "geometric insight."* This is not about replacing the old proof theory with a new one, but about enriching logic and proof theory, about taking it out of the formalist cage that generated the so-called logico-computational hypothesis for human intelligence: "Intelligence

... is effectively defined as that which can be manifested by the communication of discrete symbols" (Hodges 1995). Hence the direct, geometric proof of the Pythagorean theorem does not contain "explicit" intelligence, even less foundational interest for mathematics: intelligence develops only after its translation into finite algebraic languages, if necessary pixel by pixel, over discrete Cartesian coordinates.

We found traces of a different analysis of the foundation of mathematics (and of mathematical intelligence) in the work of logicians who insist on the role of geometry. For example, in the denotational (or categorical, see section 5.1) semantics of Lawvere-Scott for intuitionistic systems (or for programming), geometry and continuity give signification to lists of symbols "without meaning," because "geometry is more compelling," as Dana Scott suggested once. Or also in the geometry of proof nets by J. Y. Girard, where the symmetries and the direct manipulation of images (networks over the plan) come into the play of logical derivations, in an essential way. Moreover, geometry is central in the recent mathematical development of the Husserlian analysis of knowledge, as in Petitot's work.[17] It is perhaps "vision" that is more compelling, as some neurophysiologists claim.

But this widening of proof theory should be more than just a new game of mathematical rules, since this would only give us a new mathematical discipline. Wittgenstein foresaw this happening with the Hilbertian metamathematics (Shanker 1988), and it has in fact happened. Metamathematics became a new and beautiful kind of mathematics, where the principal results have been indirect: a precise notion of formal rigor and computer science, but not the explicit foundation of the mathematical practice, as was Hilbert's dream. We cannot "found" mathematics (its "rules of the game" as Wittgenstein says) only over a mathematical discipline, a logical-mathematical system also made up of mathematical "rules of the game." *There cannot be an internal foundation, purely formal and mathematical, of mathematics: the incompleteness theorems are not accidents, they underline the gap between the metamathematical principles of proof (once transformed into a mathematics of formal rules) and the rigorous practice of mathematical constructions.* It is then necessary to increase the variety of tools for the foundation of mathematics, first by the direct constructions of geometry (which is being done), then with other forms of knowledge; that is, *it is necessary to insert the partial network of mathematical constructions in the wider one of the other forms of knowledge.* The project to aim at should take mathematics out of its "auto-foundational" game (metamathematics as a form of mathematics) and look for its cognitive origins in our relation to the regularities of the world, in the connections to different conceptual constructions, in the mental invariants that we build as living and historical beings.

PART THREE

THE NATURE AND LIMITS OF NATURALIZATION

CHAPTER FIFTEEN

Naturalizing Phenomenology? Dretske on Qualia

RONALD MCINTYRE

Since phenomenological concerns are often perceived as irrelevant to, or even incompatible with, "naturalism" in the philosophy of mind, a naturalistic account of mind that treats such concerns seriously would be most welcome. Fred Dretske's recent book, *Naturalizing the Mind*,[1] promises to offer such an account. The central notion in the book is that of mental representation, and Dretske claims that his "Representational Naturalism . . . provides a satisfying account of the qualitative, the first-person, aspect of our sensory and affective life" (p. xiii).

My discussion has three parts. First, I briefly characterize Dretske's particular naturalization project, emphasizing his naturalistic reconstruction of the notion of representation. Second, I note some apparent similarities between his notion of representation and Husserl's notion of intentionality, but I find even more important differences. Whereas Husserl takes intentionality to be an intrinsic, phenomenological feature of thought and experience, Dretske advocates an "externalist" account of mental representation. Third, I consider Dretske's treatment of qualia, because he takes it to show that his representational account of mind succeeds in naturalizing even the "subjective" features of experience. I argue that Dretske characterizes the notion of qualia in an ambiguous way. I conclude that he succeeds in naturalizing qualia only if qualia are understood as nonphenomenological features of experience and that he therefore has less to say than he thinks about the subjective life of beings like us.

I. DRETSKE ON REPRESENTATION

Phenomenologists who are interested in the philosophy of mind will welcome some features of Dretske's naturalization project. Whereas functionalism, computationalism, behaviorism, and eliminative materialism, for example, ride roughshod over the features of mentality that phenomenologists emphasize, Dretske seems to place them at the very center of his naturalization project. This impression is furthered by what he claims to achieve: a naturalistic understanding of representation, of introspection (including the nature of first-person authority), of consciousness, and of the subjective qualities of experience.

The central notion in Dretske's account is that of "representation." His strategy for "naturalizing" this notion seems to proceed in two parts: first, to describe a natural property—a property that systems which are obviously physical can have—that shares some of the features of intentional experience and thought; and, subsequently, to suggest ramifications of this property that will ultimately describe full-fledged mental representation as it occurs in conscious experience and thought. My focus will be on the first part of this strategy.

Dretske begins with an account of representation appropriate to such nonmentalistic representations as a thermometer's measurement of temperature or a speedometer's measurement of speed: "The fundamental idea is that a system, S, represents a property, F, if and only if S has the function of indicating (providing information about) the F of a certain domain of objects" (p. 2). A system performs its indicating function, Dretske says, by occupying different states corresponding to the different determinate values of the property in question. Thus, if S is an old-fashioned thermometer, the different levels of mercury in its tube correspond to different determinate degrees of temperature. The thermometer, by occupying a specific mercury-level state, thereby indicates that the temperature is a certain value.

Importantly, on this account, a system can *indicate* a property without *representing* it. A thermometer represents temperature, rather than merely indicating it, because indicating temperature is a thermometer's *function*: thermometers are designed to indicate temperature. Thermometers also indicate other things that they are not (ordinarily) designed for. Prolonged readings below 0°C, for example, may indicate that sweater sales will rise, but thermometers (normally) do not have the function of indicating sweater sales and thus do not represent that property. This functional feature of Dretske's notion of "representation" makes it an *intensional* notion and marks it as closer to the mental than mere indication is.

Thermometers and speedometers, like most representational systems, are conventional systems. They are designed by human beings for the specific purpose of indicating some property that they are capable of indicating, and only thereby do they acquire the *function* of indicating that property. But Dretske believes there is also a meaningful notion of "natural representation": a system of indication may achieve, via natural selection or learning, the *natural* function of indicating some particular property. A system does so, he says, when the system's indicating that property is useful to the system, the information thereby delivered up is available for further use by the system and so integratable into its higher-order responses to its environment, and the system's indicating that property is selected for by evolutionary development. (Cf. pp. 9–10, 162–68.)

Dretske takes conscious experience to be a species of natural representation, but he does not identify the two. Conscious experience, he claims, requires a conceptual element that is not generally present in natural representation. I shall not develop this extension of the notion of representation, however, for the features and problems I will be discussing occur at a more basic level.

Even at the basic level of representation, Dretske distinguishes the "sense" of a representation from its "reference." A representational system, typically, represents some *object* as having the property the system has the function of indicating. The represented object Dretske calls the "reference" of the representation; the property it is represented as having—the "way" the object is represented—he calls the "sense" of the representation.

Let us not pass over this sense/reference distinction too hastily, however. Strictly speaking, on Dretske's account of representation, it is *properties* that representational states or systems represent. (Recall: "a system, S, represents a property, F, if and only if . . .") And in the traditional literature on intentionality, that which is intended or represented in an intentional state (that to which the state is "directed") is called the "object" of that state. So, in the traditional terminology we should say that, for Dretske, the property represented in a representational state is the *object* of the representation; and this property, since it plays the role of represented object, should be called the "reference" of the representation. Dretske, however, calls the represented property the "sense" of the representation. (Here is a first indication that Dretske's terms, as he uses them, do not always mean what phenomenologists would most likely take them to mean.)

For Dretske, then, representational systems represent properties; and the property a system represents is called its "sense." But under certain conditions, there is a derivative sense in which the object that has the represented property may also be said to be "represented." A speedometer, for example, represents speed, and when appropriately installed in a vehicle it represents the speed of that vehicle. Installed in my automobile, a speedometer whose needle is pointing to 50 represents *my automobile* as traveling at 50 kph. In that same representational state, but installed in your automobile, it would represent *your automobile* as traveling at that speed. Thus, Dretske says, just which object (if any at all) a representational system represents is purely a contextual matter. The "sense" of a representational system—the property the system represents an object as having—is determined by the representational character of the system; but its "reference"—the object it represents as having that property—is determined by "a certain external causal or contextual relation" (p. 24).

On Dretske's account, then, the "sense" of a representation is *representationally* related to the representation: it is the property that the representation *represents*. The "reference" of a representation, on the other hand, is only *contextually*, and not *representationally*, related to it: in particular, the reference of a representation is not *represented* (in the proper sense of the term, as Dretske uses it).

Dretske's account of representation has the virtue of preserving the possibility of misrepresentation and referential failure. Given the functional account of representation, a speedometer reading of 50 represents a speed of 50 kph simply because of the speedometer's design and calibration. If something goes wrong and the speed of the vehicle in which the speedometer is installed is actually 60 kph, then the speedometer's reading has *mis*represented the vehicle's speed. And since reference, for Dretske, is strictly a matter of context, a speedometer can represent speed even though there is no vehicle connected to it in the appropriate causal and contextual way.

2. DRETSKEAN REPRESENTATION VIS-À-VIS HUSSERLIAN INTENTIONALITY

Dretske's notion of representation exhibits, at least on the surface, some striking similarities to Husserl's notion of intentionality. "Intentionality," of course, is just Husserl's term for the representational character of thoughts and experiences—their characteristic feature of being "of" or "about" things other than themselves. Like Dretske, Husserl distinguishes the *sense* of an intentional thought or experience (let me use Husserl's term "act" for short) from the *object* (or reference) that the act represents or intends: an act intends or represents its object "as" such-and-such. As in Dretske, an act (or representational state) can have a sense without having a reference or can have a sense that *mis*represents the reference.

For Husserl, the intentionality of an experience is a *phenomenological* feature of the experience; indeed, he sees it as the key feature that must be explicated if we are to achieve an understanding of experience from the first-person, phenomenological point of view. Thus, given the apparent similarities between Husserlian intentionality and Dretskean representation, one might think that Dretske's naturalization project (to the extent it succeeds) can shed light on how to understand the *phenomenological* features of experience naturalistically. Unfortunately, however, these features do not play a role in Dretske's project. To begin to see that this is so, let us turn briefly to Husserl's version of the sense/reference distinction.

Husserl's distinction is motivated, in large part, by the fact that one and the same object can be represented in various "ways." Oedipus's complex relationship with his mother dramatically demonstrate this fact: that Oedipus desires to marry the queen does not mean that he desires to marry his mother, for example, despite the fact that the queen *is* his mother. As Husserl explains it, these desires intend or represent the same object, Jocasta (or a state of affairs involving Jocasta), but they represent that object with a different sense ("the queen" in the one case, "my [Oedipus's] mother" in the other).

Following tradition, Husserl uses the term "object" for that which is intended or represented in an intentional state (that to which the state is "directed"). Recall that, for Dretske, *properties* are what representational states represent. For Husserl, however, intended or represented objects are not all of the same kind: intended or represented objects include properties but also physical objects, events, states of affairs, numbers, persons, and whatever else we can bring before our minds.

Unlike the object of an intentional thought or experience, the sense of an act is not itself intended or represented in the act. Rather, it belongs to the "content" of the act: it is part of the internal structure of the act whereby the act achieves its intentionality and so represents its object in a particular way. Senses, for Husserl, are thus not among the entities that we commonly experience in the natural world. (Husserl takes them to be "ideal" or abstract entities.) In particular, senses are not properties of the objects we intend: when we intend a physical object, we have a sense of it as an individual having certain properties; but the sense belongs to the content of the experience, while the properties belong (or are represented as belonging) to the object.

An act is intentional by virtue of having a sense or content, even if there is no object that "satisfies" this sense. Thus, on Husserl's account as well as Dretske's, misrepresentations and referential failures are possible.

So, there are some surface similarities but also some deep differences between Husserl's account of intentionality and Dretske's account of representation. For Dretske, a representation represents its sense and does not (in any literal sense of the term) represent its reference: the reference is only contextually, not representationally, related to the representation. For Husserl, a representation represents its reference and does not represent its sense: the sense belongs to the structure of the representation, not to the reference that is represented by its means. For Dretske, senses are properties of the sort that physical objects have. For Husserl, they are abstract "contents" of intentional thoughts and experiences.

Most important, mental states and experiences on Husserl's account are *intrinsically* intentional: an act is intentional because it has a sense, and its sense is intrinsic to the act. Thus, the intentional or representational character of an act is due to its own internal makeup as the act that it is.[2] For Dretske, however, representational systems (or states) are *not* intrinsically representational. Even if a system's *indicating* a certain property is due to its internal character, its *representing* something is not. A system represents something only if it has the *function* of indicating it, and systems get their functions from the "outside": by being designed, in the case of conventional representations; by their evolutionary history, in the case of natural representations. Dretske does not emphasize this aspect of his theory until his final chapter, but there he is most emphatic. Says Dretske:

> The Representational Thesis is an externalist theory of the mind. It identifies mental facts with representational facts, and though representations are in the head, the facts that make them representations—and, therefore, the facts that make them mental—are outside the head. A state of the brain . . . represents the world in a certain way . . . only if it has an appropriate information-carrying function. Since functions . . . have to do with the history of the states and systems having these functions, mental facts do not supervene on what is in the head. What is in heads A and B could be physically indistinguishable and yet, because these pieces of gray matter have had relevantly different histories, one is a representational system, the other is not; one is the seat of thought and experience, the other is not. (pp. 124–25)

3. "EXTERNALIZING" QUALIA

As "subjective" features of experience, qualia have been thought to pose especially serious problems for any objective, naturalistic account of experience. Behaviorism, functionalism, and computationalism, for example, have all had little success in dealing with the fact (or apparent fact) that qualitatively distinct mental states can be behavioristically, functionally, and computationally equivalent. Accordingly, Dretske sees the problem of naturalizing qualia as a significant test of his representational version of naturalism, and he hails his own solution to that problem as a major triumph for his theory.

> The Representational Thesis is plausible enough for the propositional attitudes [but] less plausible—some would say completely implausible—for sensory affairs, for the phenomenal or qualitative aspects of our mental life. Nonetheless, . . . I concentrate on . . . qualia—that dimension of our conscious life that helps to define what-it-is-like-to-be-us. I focus here because, frankly, this is where progress is most difficult. This, then, is where progress—if there is any—will be most significant. (pp. xiv–xv)

Given that Dretske's Representational Thesis is the key feature in an *externalist* project for naturalizing the mind, his task of naturalizing qualia amounts to giving an "external" account of them, and this is a task that does seem more than a little implausible, as he puts it. As features that distinguish the "subjective feel" of one experience from another, qualia seem to be "internal" characters of experience par excellence. Dretske himself places them among the "qualitative aspects of our mental life," and elsewhere he calls them "qualities of experience" that make up the "subjective life of [a] being" (p. 65). But Dretske's naturalistic account of qualia, as we shall see, locates qualia *outside* the experiencing organism and its experiences, identifying them with properties of the *objects* that the organism experiences.

We get a clue to Dretske's strategy in a casual remark about intentionality: "Intentionality is real enough," he says, "but it turns out, as Fodor . . . suggests it must, to be really something else" (p. 28). In that Fodorian spirit, Dretske succeeds in naturalizing qualia by construing them as "really something else": not "internal," inherently subjective properties of *experiences*, but objective properties of the *objects experienced*. "In accordance with the Representational Thesis," he says, "I . . . identify qualia with phenomenal properties—those properties that (according to the thesis) an object is sensuously represented . . . as having" (p. 73). Given that identification, says Dretske, there is no problem, in principle, with my knowing the quale of your experience, or a bat's or a parasite's, even though I am incapable of having experiences of those sorts. He offers the following example.

Consider a parasite that attaches to its host if and only if the host's surface temperature is almost precisely 18°C. The parasite then attaches to the host when the parasite has an experience that represents the host as being at 18°C; that is, when, to the parasite, the host seems to be 18°C. Now, says Dretske, the *quale* of the parasite's experience of the host is "how the host seems to the parasite," and "how the host seems to the parasite" is "being 18°C." And so the quale of the parasite's experience is the property of being 18°C. That property, moreover, is not something "inside" the parasite or the parasite's experience. Being 18°C is an objective property—a property of the *host*, if the parasite is representing it accurately. As such, it is something that you and I can know even though we cannot examine the parasite's experience. If we know what 18°C is, then we know the quale of the parasite's experience. Says Dretske:

> If you know what it is to be 18°C, you know how the host "feels" to the parasite. You know what the parasite's experience is like as it "senses" the host. . . . All you have to know is what temperature is. If you know enough to know what it is to be at a temperature of 18°C, you know all there is to know about the quality of the parasite's experience. To know what it is like for this parasite, one looks, not in the parasite, but at what the parasite is "looking" at—the host. (p. 83)

Now, Dretske's view here strikes me as strange. For one thing, I am not sure that I do know "what it is to be (or be at) 18°C." Since Dretske's goal is to naturalize qualia, I presume he intends us to understand such properties as "being 18°C" naturalistically and objectively. As an educated person, I have some inkling of what objective temperature is: to be at a temperature of 18°C is, I think, to have a certain mean molecular kinetic energy, but I cannot be more precise than that. And if I were not an educated person, I would not know even this much about temperature—or color, sound, shape, and so on—considered as an objective, naturalistically characterizable quality of things.

More to the point, though, knowing which physical properties constitute the temperature of an object (even of an object represented or experienced as having that temperature) seems simply irrelevant to knowing the qualia that temperature-experiences have. Even if I do not know what temperature is (in the naturalistic, scientific sense), I know how various temperatures typically feel. These various modes of what it is like to feel temperature are what phenomenologists, and I believe most other philosophers as well, mean by temperature "qualia." But qualia so understood do not align one-to-one with the properties objects are experienced as having. The same water can feel cool to one hand and warm to another, as Berkeley famously noted. Yet, science tells us, the natural property that the water itself has—the temperature being experienced in these qualitatively different ways—is the same in both cases. But if such qualitatively different experiences are representations of the same objective property, then qualia cannot be identified with "those properties that ... an object is sensuously represented ... as having," and Dretske's representationalism founders on the same rock as behaviorism, functionalism, and computationalism.

Dretske seems to think that he can avoid this problem by collapsing the distinction between the objective properties of experienced things and the subjective ways things are experienced. "The Representational Thesis identifies the qualities of experience—qualia—with the properties objects are [represented] as having," he says. "Subjectivity becomes part of the objective order" (p. 65). Dretske's remarks, however, seem sometimes to affirm this identification and sometimes to deny it. "If you know what it is to be 18°C, you know ... what the parasite's experience is like as it 'senses' the host," he says on page 83; but on the very same page he admits that "knowing what temperature is will *not* [my emphasis] tell one what it is like ... to *feel* a temperature of this kind." Again on the same page, Dretske apparently *distinguishes* knowing what a phenomenal property is from knowing what it is like to experience that property: "Deaf people can know what sound waves are without knowing what it is like to *hear* sound waves." Later, however, he seems to make the very opposite claim about vision: "A blind person may know what it is like to visually experience [= see?] movement. If he knows what movement is, that is enough" (p. 94). Evidently, there are some tensions, if not outright contradictions, in how Dretske understands the relation between *qualities of experiences (of objects)* and *(experienced) qualities of objects* and the relation of both of these notions to that of *qualia*.

Dretske's blurring of these notions is especially prominent in an argument he offers for identifying qualia with represented properties. The argument is straightforward, and Dretske challenges dissenters to find some flaw in it. He says: "I am merely drawing out the consequences of facts that almost everyone accepts—facts that are quite independent of the representational point of view being defended in these lectures. ... If [the] result is absurd, then one of the ... facts that led to it—not the Representational Thesis—is to blame" (pp. 83–84). We saw Dretske's argument at work in the "parasite" example above. Its main premise, although Dretske calls it a "fact," is actually presented as a definition: "The first fact," he says, "is that qualia are supposed to be the way things seem or appear in the sense modality in question" (p. 83). The argument Dretske builds from this "fact" can be reconstructed as a series of identities:

1. Qualia are the way things seem or appear.
2. The way a thing *seems* or appears in an experience is the way the thing would *be* (that is, the property it would actually *have*) if the experience were veridical.
3. The property a thing would have if the experience of it were veridical is the property that the thing is represented as having.
4. Therefore, qualia are properties that things are represented as having.

The problem with this argument, I believe, lies in that "first fact," Dretske's definition or characterization of qualia as "the way things seem or appear." By "ways of appearing," Dretske clearly means properties that *things* or *objects* appear to have, or are represented as having, in an experience. So understood, however, the first premise of the argument, "qualia are the way things seem or appear," just *means* "qualia are properties that things are represented as having." Taken in this sense, then, Dretske's first premise is not a definition of "qualia" but a stylistic variant of his conclusion. The argument begs the question.

What makes the argument beguiling is that almost anyone, including those who would resist Dretske's identification of qualia with represented properties, could accept his characterization of qualia as "the way things seem or appear." There must, then, be a different way of understanding the phrase "the way things seem or appear." Phrases such as this are in fact ambiguous. Compare, for example: (1) the way things seem or appear to S (= the way things are experienced by S) and (2) the way women were depicted by Degas. In what "way" or "ways" did Degas depict women? *How* did he depict them? The range of appropriate answers depends on just what we take the question to be about. If taken as a question about *women*, as Degas depicted them, one appropriate answer is "as dancers." But if taken as a question about Degas's *depictions* of women, a different type of answer is appropriate: "impressionistically," for example. Thus, taken in one sense, "ways of depicting women" are descriptions that apply to women: "as dancers," "as workers," "as mother figures," "as sex objects," and so on. Taken in another sense, "ways of depicting women" are modes of depicting: "impressionistically," "realistically," "pointillistically," "cubistically," and so on.

Dretske's argument fails because of this ambiguity, I believe. His definition of qualia as "the way things seem or appear" is uncontroversial only if these "ways" are modes of *appearings*—qualities of *experiences* of objects—rather than properties of appearing *things*. But if the first premise must be given this reading rather than Dretske's, the argument fails. And if the first premise *cannot* be given this reading, then the argument seems not to be about *qualia* at all.

While Dretske's argument depends on blurring the distinction between qualities of experiences of objects and qualities of objects as experienced, much of his defense of his account of qualia depends on our recognizing that distinction. The highlight of Dretske's identification of qualia with represented properties is that it entails that anyone can know the quale of a supposedly subjective experience simply by knowing what objective property the experience represents. But here one wants to object that this cannot be correct: to know what property an experience is an experience "of" is not at all the same as knowing what it is like to experience that property. But, as we saw earlier, Dretske simply grants this: "Surely knowing what temperature is will not tell one what it is like (if it is like anything) for a parasite (or even another human being) to *feel* a temperature of this kind. . . . I do not wish to deny this. I am *not* denying it" (p. 83). To understand this response I believe we must make the very sort of distinction that Dretske's argument suppresses.

Let us return to Dretske's parasite, which is sensing its host as being 18°C. Dretske has said

1. "If you know what it is to be 18°C, you know how the host 'feels' to the parasite. . . . You know all there is to know about the quality of the parasite's experience."
2. "Knowing what temperature is will not tell one what it is like . . . to *feel* a temperature of this kind."

In affirming (2), I think Dretske must also mean to affirm

3. Knowing what 18°C is will not tell one what it is like to *feel* a temperature of 18°C.

So Dretske is making our same subtle distinction here. Knowing "how *the host* feels to the parasite when the parasite senses the host as being 18°C" is not the same as knowing "how it feels to *the parasite* to sense the host as being 18°C." We can understand this distinction and also see why Dretske identifies the first, but not the second, with the property of being 18°C. To ask how *the host* feels to the parasite is to ask which property the parasite senses *the host* as having, and in the present case that is the property of being 18°C. To ask how it feels to the parasite to sense the host as being 18°C is to ask, not how *the host* seems, but how the parasite's *sensing* of the host feels to the parasite. Thus, it makes sense to say that knowing what 18°C is suffices for our knowing how the host feels to the parasite but not for our knowing what the parasite's experience of the host feels like to the parasite.

However, if we allow Dretske to distinguish in this way between "how the host feels to the parasite (when the host feels 18°C)" and "what it is like to feel a temperature of 18°C," then he loses the bigger game. "How the host feels to the parasite," on this reading, is objectively characterizable, characterizable in terms of the temperature the host is represented as having. It is, after all, a quality of the *host* (or at any rate, a quality of the host if the parasite's experience is veridical). But that means that this property is trivially "natural"—natural in the very same way that all intersubjectively observable properties are natural.

Dretske's naturalization of qualia would be noteworthy if the "qualities of experience" that he naturalizes were indeed phenomenological features of experience. But the quale of the parasite's experience, in this phenomenological sense, is what having that experience is like for the parasite, and that remains unexamined in Dretske's externalist version of naturalism. One does not naturalize the mind by naturalizing the *objects* that minds represent.

CHAPTER SIXTEEN

The Immediately Given as Ground and Background

JUAN-JOSÉ BOTERO

In a recent paper (Hintikka 1995b) Jaakko Hintikka argues against what he calls "the idea of self-sufficient intentionality," which (according to him) pervades some influential contemporary interpretations of Husserl's phenomenology. That idea consists basically in seeing phenomenology as a restrictive theory of intentionality that confines the study of intentional consciousness to the study of the "bearers" of the intentional meanings, *noemata* (p. 79). Although in his paper he only mentions Dagfinn Føllesdal's work on Husserl as an example of such an approach, I think it is obvious that the scope of his criticism is much broader than that, and perhaps could be best exemplified by a statement like the following, owed to Maurita Harney: "Phenomenology is the description of the structures of intentionality. This . . . means a description of the noematic structure" (Harney 1984). Hintikka's main criticism consists in stressing the risk faced by those who defend such a restrictive conception of intentionality, and of phenomenology generally, of missing what he claims to be the "specifically phenomenological element in Husserl's philosophy," namely, the "search for the basis of our conceptual world in immediate experience" (p. 82). In contrast, he proposes to lay much more emphasis upon a picture of phenomenological, or Husserlian endeavor, as being essentially characterized by the quest of what is immediately given in direct experience as the founding grounds of our conceptual world.

My aim here is not to address Hintikka's ideas directly, but to take them as a pretext to make some claims about such issues as intentionality and the very concept of the "immediately given" in experience. I will do this by examining some possible ways of understanding what is immediately given and how it is immediately given in experience.

I propose to distinguish between two different senses of the expression "immediately given" (may I hereafter refer to it as IG?): the IG as *ground* and the IG as *background*. We can see both of these senses as conveying a sort of "foundationalist" gist, though they are different in character: IG as *ground* has an epistemological flavor in that it is supposed to provide a kind of knowledge that is more basic and genuine than any other, and so justifies or somehow legitimates them; on the other hand, IG as *background* involves something like the meaning of our everyday intentional life. So that, while in the first sense searching for the IG is a clearly foundational attempt to set knowledge and thinking on solid grounds, in the second sense it does not have this justificatory goal and rather implies a task of clarification (the word "explication" can also be employed here) of the meaning of our conceptual coping with the world.

The sense and scope of this distinction is what I want to expound in the following remarks.

1. WHAT IS IG?

The view of the IG as the ground of objective knowledge may be developed in (at least) two methodological strategies: the first one has a Cartesian-Lockean look in assuming that our epistemic structure and contents rest upon an impeccable groundwork that escapes from, or is immune to doubt, precisely because it is "immediately given" to us. The second strategy, more or less Kantian in spirit, seeks to provide a functional (in the Kantian sense)-constitutional analysis leading to the givenness of the so constituted object in immediate experience. I think Husserl occasionally, at different moments of his life, followed one strategy or the other, most often both at the same time, conveniently amended, enhanced, or supplemented. But my aim in this paper is not to give a full examination of Husserl's thought, so I will say no more about this subject for the moment.

Whatever path one follows, we must be allowed, at the end, *inter alia*, to provide a solution to the puzzle of the objectivity of knowledge, that is, how the object can be undoubtedly given to consciousness and at the same time be part of the objective, external world. The preferred way to handle this problem is to focus attention on the "paradigmatic" act of knowledge, namely, *perception*. But what exactly is supposed to be "given" in perception?

1.1. THINGS

Let us first consider what may be seen as a "stylized standard view" of the givenness of things in perceptual outer experience.

At the time of *Logische Untersuchungen* (1901), Husserl thought all intentional acts of consciousness were "objectifying acts" or were ultimately based upon objectifying acts (see the Fifth Investigation, §41). That is supposed to mean that every intentional act involves the presence of the act's object to consciousness. To make present an object to consciousness is what is called "objectifying," which in turn is another name for "representing" (§33). Thus, every intentional act must make present to consciousness the object, or else it has to be founded over another act which itself must be such an objectifying (representational) act.

The intentional act par excellence is what I will call here the *epistemic act*, that is, the act of knowledge. The main feature of this epistemic act is what Husserl calls its "intuitive fullness." Now, an epistemic act (an act of knowing something) is a *synthetic* act that consists in apprehending the objective identity of two intentions of one and the same object: the meaning intention and the fulfilling (intuitive) intention. Merely intending an object is not knowledge. The "empty" meaning intention will become an act of knowledge only when and to the extent that the merely intended object is presented "itself" within a conscious synthesis, that is, only if the object is made intuitively present, and not merely represented, in consciousness by way of another act, the corresponding intuitive act, and if this is made in a conscious synthesis of the identity of the intended and the "intuited" object. But this is also true for the intuitive act as well (since it is intentional). It will be knowledge only insofar as it enters into an identifying synthesis between the object as intended and the object as it is supposed to present itself in the intuitive act. This is also called *evidence*, though not in ordinary English parlance (*Evidenz* as Brentano and Husserl use the term is the intuitive experience—*Erlebnis*—of truth).

The idea of evidence as synthesis is crucial, for it implies the notion that "the givenness of things themselves" refers back to a multiplicity of experiences which are brought together in the synthesis, and not to an instantaneous and unique grasping of the object ("in a flash"). But it also brings forth the problem of the "intuitive *Sinn*," raised by Hubert Dreyfus (Dreyfus 1982): if the intuitive fulfilling act is an intentional act, it must have an intentional content, namely an *erfüllende Sinn*, but as a *Sinn* it too must be fulfilled, and so on, ad infinitum. This coincides with the point made by Hintikka: that according to this account the direct, sensuous experience of the object is never attained, for all we have is an infinite coincidence of (intended) meanings with (fulfilling) meanings.

There are various reasons at this stage of the development of Husserl's phenomenology for attributing a *Sinn* to the intuitive acts. The main reason seems to be his conception of knowledge as a coincidence (*Deckung*) of the intentional essence of the meaningful act and the intentional essence of the intuitive act. What is called "meaning" in the first case must also be found in the latter, for in the fulfilling act the object is given to us "as it has been meant" in the signitive act; therefore, there must be something in the act of perception corresponding to the *Sinn* of the meaningful act (see the Sixth Investigation, §13). Thus, transposing the *Sinn* from the domain of meaning to the domain of perception rests on the possibility of the coincidental synthesis of the two acts.

Later on, when the notion of *Sinn* has been extended to the entire intentional domain, this problem will become the problem of the "perceptual *noema*." In *Ideen zu einer reinen Phänomenologie*, this notion is justified by the "perspectival" character of perception. The object of outer perception always presents itself in the form of *Abschattungen* (adumbrations) pointing beyond themselves to new *Abschattungen* and thus making possible the perceptual experience of a full-fledged object. In order to account for the object identity amid these variations of perspective we seem to need an *idea* of a completely fulfilled sense as the intentional correlate of the perceptual act. So, the "perspectival inadequacy" of the mode of givenness of physical things, and therefore the necessarily synthetic character of outer perception, would be an additional reason for introducing the notion of perceptual *Sinne*, although in the form I have just presented here it would be a reason founded, not in phenomenology, but perhaps in some kind of "transcendental argument." But even from this superficial point of view, this is also a sound "epistemological argument" for rejecting the idea of an adequate evidence of everyday material objects, namely, the idea that outer physical things are capable of adequate givenness, as Hintikka has pointed out. We will see, however, that phenomenologically grounded arguments in favor of this and some other related ideas are stronger because of their radicality.

1.2. THE "IMMEDIATELY GIVEN" AS "IMMANENT"

There could be some confusion, correctly pointed out by Hintikka, over what the reduction to the "immediately given" amounts to. This reduction is doubtless a question about the foundation of knowledge and thinking. But not every foundation will do the job. It is supposed to ground "our conceptual world" in the immediate givenness of the object of knowledge. Yet Hintikka suggests that this is not an "epistemological" grounding. How can we understand this?

Husserl's "great discovery" of the "domain of absolute givenness" is the central theme of *Die Idee der Phänomenologie* (1907, hereafter cited as *Idee* by lesson).[1] In this work, Husserl starts by bringing forth the unavoidable puzzles that arise when one shifts from the natural to the philosophical attitude and considers seriously the question about the possibility of knowledge (*Idee*, First Lesson). These puzzles bear mainly upon the relationship (which is unproblematic for the "natural attitude") between cognitive acts, conceived as subjective lived experiences, and real, independent objects. In his search for a solid starting point for resolving this critical problem, Husserl takes the Cartesian way of doubting and arrives at the *cogito* as the first absolute evidence (Second Lesson). If I focus my reflection on the intentional, object-directed acts of my consciousness at the moment they are taking place, the acts are given to me "in an absolute way" (ibid.). The presence of the correlative object is thus also an "absolute given" that escapes doubt. The reason is that this kind of intuitive knowledge of the *cogitatio* is "immanent," as Descartes had already said. However, a new concept of "immanence" is worked out by Husserl from the presence of the *cogitatio*. This new concept does not set apart objects, but rather serves to characterize the way they are *given*: every object whose presence is authentic and absolute, is immanent; all the others are transcendent.

According to Husserl, one must distinguish "pure immanence" (*Idee*, Fourth Lesson), defined as every genuine and absolute givenness (*absolute Selbstgegebenheit*) constituted in evidence, from "real immanence" in the traditional sense (the self and his experiences). Thus, for instance, the contents of the *cogitatio* are "objective essences" given in pure intuition; as universal objectivities, they are transcendent in that they exceed the real immanent act; but they are "immanent" in that they are immediately given in an absolute way. Husserl thinks of this discovery as having "a decisive impact for the possibility of Phenomenology" (Third Lesson), since it uncovers the domain of absolute knowledge, namely, the sphere of the givenness, where not only singularities, but also "generalities, objects and general states of affairs" (ibid.) are given to us. It is the disclosure of transcendence in immanence or, so to speak, the reduction of transcendence to immanence without loss for transcendence of its character of "otherness."

This is the sense in which the immediate givenness of the object must be understood at this stage: every intentional consciousness is "consciousness-of," and if consciousness is absolutely given, so is the intentional object (the "of") (*Idee*, Fourth Lesson). Thus, this domain of immanence embraces all of intentional contents. We still need to distinguish in the phenomenon the *appearance* (*Erscheinung*) from that which *appears* (*Erscheinendes*): the object which appears is not really immanent for it is not a real part of the appearance; yet it is immediately, absolutely given, and so, it is immanent in the new sense.

The new concept of immanence entails a new concept of transcendence. "Transcendence in general" is defined as that which "does not constitute an evident presence in a genuine sense," as that which "is not absolutely given in pure intuition" (*Idee*, Second Lesson, p. 9) and "is not a real content of a cognitive act" (p. 35). Roughly, every exteriority and "every knowledge deprived of evidence, that is, every knowledge that falls short of the *genuine in-*

tuition of the posited or intuitioned object" (p. 35) is transcendent. The object (the intentional content) is transcendent in a special way, however. It is not part of the real immanence and, therefore, is really transcendent; yet "it is actually contained in an act of consciousness" (p. 35), and hence, its existence is fully warranted by the act's "absolute and authentic givenness" (Fourth Lesson, p. 55). The intentional object's special transcendence participates, so to speak, in immanence: it is the ideal immanence of the object of knowledge (see pp. 55, 35).

According to Husserl in *Die Idee*, the uncovering of pure immanence and of transcendence in immanence, as well as the theory of "reduction," suffices to solve the puzzle about the possibility of connecting consciousness and the objective world.

Now, there are enough reasons for feeling dissatisfied with this "solution," as Husserl himself did. The main reason is that it responds to the requirements of a "theory of knowledge" carried out in an analytical, conceptual style. By following the Cartesian way of access to subjectivity, one gets the evidence of the *ego* but fails to attain the world of experience as the very starting point of transcendental reflection. Thus, the "reduction" is a "reduction proper to the theory of knowledge" that leads "too easily and too fast" to the *ego*, and as a consequence of this "the *ego* appears as something empty of any content at all," as Husserl acknowledges later on in *Krisis* (1936). I stress this point because there seems to be a somewhat widely accepted view according to which the *given* has to be necessarily immanent. This is true for the kind of theory of knowledge sketched in *Die Idee*, since it ends with a plain and simple "immanent perception" that "really" includes its object as it belongs to the inner experience. But this "domain of absolute givenness," as suitable as it may be for the purposes of a theory of knowledge, is not the living *cogito* needed to account for the subjectivity of the transcendental experience. Husserl himself seemed to be aware of this problem, and in the Third Lesson (after having reached the evidence of the *cogito*) he introduces a new reduction (the true phenomenological reduction) in an attempt to prevent a psychological interpretation of the *cogitatio*; but this move is largely insufficient, since it still remains within the limits of the theory of knowledge and of conceptual analysis.

1.3. OBJECTS

Husserl characterizes the intentionality of the "natural attitude" as those prereflective acts in which I am aware of objects, but not of *Sinne*. The first step of the phenomenological reduction involves a "bracketing" of this naturalistic attitude and so opens to reflection the domain of *noemata*. Now, how are these *noemata* related to those objects? Husserl introduces elaborate considerations regarding the structure and functions of the *noema* that I do not need to go into here. We need only to remember that for Husserl every *noema* has a "nucleus," its "noematic *Sinn*," and that it is through this nucleus that the *noema* is related to the object. Here the phenomenological argument, as before, is also centered on *identity*. Though the different *noemata* of the varying acts or modes of apprehension of the object possess different nuclei, Husserl tells us that all of them "close up together in an identical unity" in which "the determinable which lies concealed in every nucleus is grasped as self-identical" (*Ideen* I, §129). The noematic *Sinn* also has a content, the predicates, which can be stated in expressions belonging to the formal or material ontologies; the nucleus is the "something" around which all the predicates gather and thus becomes a "pole of reference," a "subject" for all those predicates. To that which is both a subject of predicates and a unifying center of the varying *noesis*, Husserl gives the name of "the pure X." It is this X that is supposed to secure the objectivity of the *noema* and its *Sinn*.

But as Hintikka has correctly pointed out, the self-identity of the object, the "pure X," is not really intuitively given, because of its synthetic character. Apart from a series of perspective variations, no point of unification, no identical "something" is given in intuition. Furthermore, the series of variable perspectives is infinitely determinable so that the object can never be completely given, as has been already said. The solution suggested by Husserl is to regard this deficiency as a problem of "Reason": reason prescribes an *idea* of complete givenness as an a priori determination of the continuum of appearances, an *idea* "in the Kantian sense" (see *Ideen* I, §143). What is given is thus this *idea*, not the "objective stuff."

Is it? The idea of such an adequately given object, Husserl tells us, serves as "an a priori rule for the well-ordered infinities of inadequate experiences" (ibid.), that is, a rule to make the incomplete givenness adequate. The rule-character of this *idea* "in the Kantian sense" does not make it very Kantian, however. Remember that Kant distinguishes between concepts, which constitute objective knowledge, and Ideas of Reason, which yield only what we may call here pseudoknowledge inasmuch as they refer to a transcendence that can never be intuitively given. Concepts of understanding are derived from the logical forms of judgments construed as transcendental functions of understanding in relation to a possible experience; they may well be seen as rules. Ideas, on the contrary, are postulated by reason and are surely not rules. Husserl does not make this distinction. The *idea* of the adequately given object functions like a Kantian rule-concept in that it prescribes what has to be done in order for consciousness to get that object. Furthermore,

Husserl criticizes Kant's concept of experience because it does not allow for a full account of the role of subjectivity in the constitution of sensuous experience. Thus, the "a priori rule" found by phenomenological reflection is traced back to the operations with the sensuous material that occur "in the depths of the human soul." This is very different from the Kantian Idea, which is conceived of merely as a kind of rational purpose, not based on, nor directed toward, any sensuous material at all. What then is given?

This conception of the given as an *idea* "in the Kantian sense" has been widely interpreted in terms of a teleological principle that is supposed to function as the originary founding sense of, in a restricted version, (scientific) knowledge, and in a more general one, rationality as such (which is identified with "European rationality," as Husserl apparently did). So, according to this view, what is given is the idealized, fully determined object and, in the long run, the ideal of a rational quest of apodictic truth, or something like that. I will not discuss this interpretation here. I prefer to momentarily espouse the somewhat opposed view that exploits the (so to speak) "non-Kantian" gist of the doctrine of the given as an *idea*. In this view, what is given is not the ideal of a "completely determined" object, but just a rather motley mixture of subjective, passive, and spontaneous constituting activities taking place in the realm of consciousness. In other words, phenomenological reflection at this early stage really gives us something. But what it gives us is not an object, not even an idealized one. How, then, is the *noema* related to the object?

1.4. CONSTITUTION

The static analyses of the *noesis-noema* structures in *Ideen* make explicit what could be taken as the very moment of the givenness of the object. The *noema* is but one moment of the correlation; the other one is the *noesis*, the lived experience itself, or the subjective multiplicity in which the object appears to consciousness.

Now, to the "noematic *Sinn*" there correspond the real components of the *noesis*. These are the "matter," or the *hyle*, that is, the multiplicity of sensory data (e.g., color, sound, solidity) through which manifests the noematic *Sinn*. Since the sensory determinations of the object are given through the *hyle*, we can say that the *hyle* gives us the object. But we must bear in mind that the *hyle* is not identical to the sensory determinations, and that it is not by itself intentional. Therefore, if it gives us the object, it does not do so by itself alone. The intentional character belongs only to the noetic moment, which is often named by Husserl the *form*. We must distinguish then within the intentional lived experience between the pure *hyle* (or sensory material) and the *form* (intentional form). It is the unity of these two that constitutes the lived experience as such. Thus, the *noesis* has the function of constituting objectivity by synthesizing the hyletic diversity in the unity of a *Sinn*.

Intentionality, thus, must not be seen as a mere receptacle for static objective relations but instead as an "operation" (*Leistung*), the operation of "constitution." The object of consciousness is not merely passively "given," it is also actively "produced": it is "*erlebt*" (*Ideen* III, §3). In perception, the noetic *Leistung* has the form of "animation" through perceptual apprehension: sensory data are "animated" by meaningful apprehension, which in this way provides representations of the noematic object (*Ideen* I, §85).

Thus, in a sense it is true that the hyletic moments prescribe the object. Yet they are not intentional by themselves. It is the *noesis* that necessarily informs the *hyle* and determines which object will be constituted. Accordingly, the objective *noema* is the outcome of the intentional unification through noetic *Leistungen* of a hyletic diversity. This is the sense in which it can be said that the object is "given" by the hyletic data. Paradoxically, it is the same sense in which it must be said that the object is "constituted" by consciousness.

1.5. THE "INTENTIONAL" OBJECT

Before going further, I want to make here a direct, roughly stated remark about perception which is also a foretaste of my own conclusions. The IG in Husserl seems to be the object of a certain kind of seeing. Thus, the search for a ground seems to come to an end when "something" strikes us immediately as being true. So, it seems that Husserl thought of the grounds, that is, the foundations of conceptual knowledge, as being something of the same character as, or homogeneous to, that which rests upon them, namely, knowledge. In other words, the grounds of knowledge should be knowledge, though more basic than the conceptual knowledge that depends upon it. It is a very peculiar, unique kind of knowledge, indeed, namely, "perceptual evidence."

Why take perception as the ultimate ground of meaning and knowledge?

Perception seems to be the immediate connection through the senses between two separate things, the knower and the world. I think this is a misleading view, because it involves what I believe is the erroneous empiricist conception that there must be a fully knowable genetic thread leading from "surface irritations" (Quine's *motto*) of the senses to perceptions of objects, and from here to meaning and conceptual thinking. And conversely, that meaning and conceptual thinking (namely, "our conceptualized world") can be traced back from words or minds to "surface irritations." That is, "surface irritations" (which in some extreme view would be the IG par excellence) are the ultimate justificatory evidence for knowledge and meaning insofar as the thread leading from them to objects, and thereafter to meaning and concepts, can be successfully and rigorously spun.

But there is a special sense in which we should view perception as always being not only perception-of, but also *perception-of-as*.[2] We perceive things under one aspect or another, always as things or objects (not *sense data*) we are acquainted with. The "of-as" in "perception-of-as" conveys what is often called (perhaps also misleadingly) the "sense" of perceptual experience, that is, its intentional content. But this must not to be taken as if the "sense" had been "constituted" in a "perceptual" act out of surface irritations plus (neuro-)mental processes (a rough way of putting the form-matter theory of the *hyle*), *independently from the rest of the life (activities, skills, interests, and so on) of the perceiver*. It is clear that Husserl invested much of his efforts in trying to describe the complexities involved in the process of constitution, especially the role played in it by kinesthesis and the lived body. This is doubtless an important qualification of the early doctrine of the *hyle*. As I hope to show later on, even more qualifications will be required if we want to provide a suitable account of perception-of-as.

What I wanted to stress is that within the framework considered so far (constitutional noetic-noematic analysis) what apparently supports, as a ground, our entire conceptual world does not seem to be of a kind with what we normally call "knowledge." And particularly not knowledge of any "object" at all. As far as I can see, transcendental reduction leads us precisely to the absence of such an object. All we find in the objective side of the correlation are profiles, partial appearances that the operations of consciousness interconnect and lead to the awareness of an identity,[3] which is then turned into an object. Thus, the very "object" for intentional consciousness is a constituted, represented, or otherwise a "named" object, as it were, and not an object that is "immediately given" sensu stricto.

1.6. EXPERIENCE

It may seem now that an obvious move is to get rid of the notion of IG as a privileged knowledge of some privileged object. As a matter of fact, after *Die Idee der Phänomenologie* (which contains lectures from 1907), Husserl came more and more intently to grips with conscious *experience*, not knowledge, as the subject matter of phenomenology. Unlike knowledge, direct experience is beyond all possibility of further proof or epistemic evaluation and thus seems to be a more suitable candidate for the place of the "domain of absolute givenness."

In *Formale und Transzendentale Logik* (1929, hereafter cited as *FTL*), for instance, Husserl grounded formal logic in transcendental logic, which he called "the logic of experience." The "world of experiences," in turn, is but the ultimate correlate of formal logic. In other words, if logic wants to guide knowledge of things and objects, the way these are given to us becomes the highest priority. That is why the primary evidence is direct experience. At this stage Husserl closely relates "constitution" and "genesis," and thus "genetic constitution" comes to the forefront, taking the place of the alleged constitution based on "essences." Obviously, the deeper genesis to be analyzed involves the "material nuclei," which originate in experience. Genetic phenomenology thus refers back to the analysis of original evidences as the primordial synthesis of consciousness of things themselves. Husserl now can say that the primary theory of judgment is the theory of judgments of evidence, and that the primary task in such a theory is to genetically refer predicative evidences back to nonpredicative evidence, "which now is called experience" (see *FTL*, §85).

This is the sense in which direct experience plays a foundational role in respect to scientific knowledge. Genetic intentional analysis brings to light the anonymous constituting subjectivity and so uncovers the grounding function of everyday experience in the constitution of natural and formal sciences.

1.7. THE LIFE-WORLD

Let us admit, for argument's sake, that the "logic of experience" is to some extent a kind of epistemology. Even then, it seems to me quite obvious that Husserl's concern is now very far from the quest for the IG as "the interface between my consciousness and reality" (Hintikka 1995b), if this is to be understood in an empiricist, Russellian way. Hintikka cautiously declares in his article that the IG includes "the overlap of consciousness and reality, plus of course whatever we do to that immediate experience in order to transform it into the experience of the fully articulated world of objects" (ibid., p. 85). What comes after "of course" in this statement means that the IG sought after by phenomenologists should be found by genetic, constitutional analysis of the experienced world. But as I see it, this task involves a shift from the establishment of a validating ground for knowledge to the explication of its meaning.

Husserl defines "experience" in *Erfahrung und Urteil* as the evidence of individual objects (§6). But the world of experience is now the life-world, a world where objects are taken as existing within a horizon of typicalities in which they are "familiar" to us. Thus, experience as evidence of individual objects is not merely experience of bare, isolated things, but a complex experience of "typical familiarities" within the entire life-world. To be sure, this world is still considered the "ground of validity" of the empirical sciences; but this must not to be understood in an epistemological sense. If the life-world is a ground for knowledge, it is not because it contains its *truth*, but because it is the foundation of its *meaning*, the *Sinnesfundament*.[4] It is not easy to see why this has to be this way, so I will try to state my points as clearly as possible.

2. THE PHENOMENOLOGICAL DIMENSION

2.1. MEANINGS

Unlike Kantian transcendentalism, Husserlian transcendental phenomenology does not have as its starting point a body of scientific knowledge to be grounded on some basic truths and principles. What has been reached via phenomenological and transcendental reductions is the very field of experience, and what has to be found therein is the experiential everyday life of the subject. Transcendental logic is thus transcendental aesthetics in a deeper and wider sense than the Kantian because it is the logic of experience of the life-world or, as Husserl calls it, "proto-logic" (*FTL*, apps. 1 and 9), meaning by that the fundamental and constitutive function carried out by the analysis of the life-world. Now, the analysis of the a priori structure of this experience is tantamount to phenomenologically unveiling and exposing (*aufweisen*) the idealities—logical and mathematical entities as well as essences—present in knowledge and conceptual thinking *and* their genesis in the phenomenological dimension where experience and concept originate, namely, meaning-constituting intentionality.

Insofar as phenomenology is viewed as a description of formal and material idealities, it may well be called a morphological (non-nomological) science of essences. But insofar as it digs up their genesis in subjectivity it no longer has to do with "entities," but rather with constitutive operating intentionalities and therefore with their intentional correlates, meanings. Genetic phenomenology, as radical reflection on the foundations of our conceptual world, should thus be viewed as the elucidation of those meanings by regenerating the constitutive acts in which they are intended.

Let us take logic as an example. In the presentation of his book *Formale und Transzendentale Logik*, written for the M. Niemayer Catalogue, Husserl says that this work must show the relationship of formal logic and positive sciences to intentional subjectivity. The critique of formal logic must help to clarify and overcome psychologism, but also must help mainly to get at "the most radical reflections over the pure sense of that subjectivity from which we say all being for us can only generate its meaning as a being, and as precisely such a being, in the sources of our life of consciousness." Radical reflection on the original sense of traditional logic must make explicit the anonymous subjective functions hidden in logical formations, and through them, relate such formations to their genesis in everyday experience. Thus, phenomenological reflection becomes "original explication of meaning" (see *FTL*, introduction). It is asked to bring to light "the authentic meaning of logic as a theory of science whose task should be to clarify the authentic meaning of science in general, and to theoretically expound it with clarity" (ibid.).[5]

2.2. SUBJECTIVITY

The clarification of the meaning (sense) of formal logic and positive sciences has two consequences:[6] first, to show that all logical concepts, as well as all conceptual knowledge (our "conceptual world"), are founded on the everyday experience of the life-world; and second, to lay bare the transcendental subjectivity in which all meanings have their genesis.

Reductions and *epochē* let us see that all objects, predicates, and seemingly well established factual entities vanish *as self-sustained things* as soon as they are traced back to the pre-logical, pre-scientific, and pre-predicative experience of the life-world. The material essences of the eidetic regional ontologies result from further idealizations performed on this experience of "typicalities." Thus, what is experienced in the life-world are these subject-relative "typicalities" and "habitualities"; these, and not "essences," are what may be properly called the IG. Therefore, at this level ontological affirmations, and a fortiori scientific ontological-oriented language, are not suitable. What we are to talk about are not things, but meanings.

Now, the ground on which those meanings are founded is not, of course, a set of truths, but what is called "transcendental subjectivity," the a priori conditions of possibility of all possible experience. I see this as a structure which a priori determines the general pattern of any possible experience qua experience of the world. Hence, it is not "given," it is properly pre-given as "horizon."

2.3. THE POSSIBILITY OF PHENOMENOLOGICAL DESCRIPTIONS: WITTGENSTEIN'S TURNABOUT

A serious objection can be raised at this point. I have just mentioned it in saying that "scientific ontological-oriented language is not suitable" for describing the level of direct, immediate experience. It seems that it was this very same objection that caused Wittgenstein to turn away from phenomenology. A brief examination of this issue will be in order here.

Phenomenology, as Wittgenstein saw it, is the attempt to describe immediate experience "directly," that is, without any hypothetical additions. This seems very similar, or even identical, to Husserl's definition. Now, how to describe primary experience? How to provide a pure, nonhypothetical description of what is *given* in experience and furnishes a basis for our ordinary talk of physical objects? How to understand the relationship between language and the content of immediate experience?

It is not hard to see where this concern for language comes from. Both everyday descriptions of people and familiar objects and scientific theories presuppose *hypotheses* about the objects in question and thus do not capture what is "immediately given" in present experience. Now, the idea of a description that contains nothing hypothetical seems to be self-contradictory, for a description has to be linguistic, and language cannot avoid bringing in just what is supposed to be excluded from a pure description of immediate experience. Even the most direct language cannot be more than a representation. Thus, the very idea of a direct presentation of immediate experience *through language* appears to be incoherent.

We are even tempted to say here that what appears to be a mere description of experiences, of the "intentional realm," is in fact a projection of the physical world onto the "phenomenal" world. The "immediate pure experience" (containing nothing hypothetical), for instance, cannot give me three-dimensional objects or the "hidden face" of the tree. The immediate experience has no space, no time, "no neighbors," according to Wittgenstein.

And that assertion seems to show that, in fact, perception of the physical world is primary, and prior to any description of experience. That is clear enough. But we really see three-dimensional objects; objects that are not three-dimensional, that is, objects *within* the experience are derivative and only "come through" when our attention is directed toward the experience itself. We see "profiles" or "adumbrations" only when we shift from objects to "intentional objects." I mean: what are you looking at when you see adumbrations? Not the world. You are staring at a present, momentaneous state of your consciousness and at that very instant you see an adumbration. Could you see it as a "profile" without bringing in your worldly experience of three-dimensional objects? You are projecting your worldly experience of physical, three-dimensional objects into your instantaneous inner experience, and that act allows you to see it "as" a profile. It is not only that *describing* intimate experiences of this sort unavoidably projects your worldly experience because there is no pure phenomenological language that allows you to make an object-free description. It is also that, whatever your inner, momentaneous experience may be, it can only "make sense" for you against the background of your overall experience of your living in your world, of your "form of life."

It seems clear that "description" and "immediateness" exclude each other. As said before, our ontological—and also scientifically oriented—language is completely inappropriate to describe the present immediate experience.

2.4. FORMS OF LIFE

Having bumped against the impossibility of a phenomenological language, Wittgenstein came to reject phenomenology and called any supposed description of what one is directly experiencing only "an inarticulated sound" (cf. Wittgenstein 1964: §68). Phenomenology makes no sense because it attempts to go beyond the limits of language to describe the nature of reality. The world of our experience simply cannot be described in language. The self-evident, that is, the IG, "life," cannot be put in words (see §47). Wittgenstein states the ultimate reason for this rejection in a quite striking way: "You simply cannot begin before the beginning" (§68).

It is interesting to note the core of the problem Wittgenstein was facing at this time (1929): like Husserl, he realized that the immediate experience (IG) is the world to which all significant discourse must refer; but, unlike Husserl, he thought that the nature of this primary world of experience eludes description.[7]

Now, although a pure phenomenological language is impossible, we can still talk about the content of experience. Only it has to be done in our present, everyday language. And so the necessity arises to have a clear view of our current use of everyday language. Using everyday language to describe experience makes us realize that what we are describing are not inner experiences but practices, ways of practically coping with the world. The *understanding* of the world and our place in it revealed through these descriptions is not theoretical, conceptual, propositional. It is practical. It is like a game we play. It consists of ways of acting, habits, skills, customs, and *it cannot be completely spelled out in a theory.*

Propositions that describe these experiences do not mean to grasp the "lived inner experiences" but the practices themselves. They are not an analysis in terms of conditions necessary to and sufficient for these practices, either. They simply "try" to describe them and thus they look like a "mythology." This means they do not capture a "knowledge" or a set of beliefs, but a bunch of practices or ways of acting that we could later on state in the form of rules. A serious consideration of our thoughts and language will take this *background* into account but I do not think it would be an *explanation* of them. It would look like the statement of normative rules, but that will not mean our knowledge of these rules would explain our thoughts and our use of language.

"What has to be accepted, the given, is—so one could say—*forms of life*" (Wittgenstein 1953: vol. 2, p. 226). Description of the IG is description of *forms of life*. And this is not an epistemological explanation of the validity of knowledge or a conceptual descriptive analysis of cognition. It is but a way to get *insight* into "the way we see things," or in Wittgenstein's terms, a "synoptic view" (*Übersicht*) that "produces just that understanding which consists in seeing connections." So, to go back to the beginning is to go back to the source or sources of the meanings, conceptual models, and intuitions one is working with in dealing with one's concerns and to get an *Übersicht* on them.

For Wittgenstein, philosophy is not a fact-finding activity but rather a way to understand what is in plain view. It has to deal essentially with meanings.

2.5. THE BACKGROUND

Let us now turn back to Husserl. I will try to take advantage of what I have said so far in order to summarize my views.

I think I have shown why I understand the search of the IG in Husserlian phenomenology as a progressive explication of meanings. For me, this means that the IG sought after by Husserl should be understood as the *background* of our intentional everyday life, instead of as the justificatory *ground* of the validity of conceptual knowledge. Now, I think that something more can be said about the nature of this IG conceived as *background*.

First of all, the life-world must not be conceived of as an abstract world of essences or a formalistic device for generating meanings. The life-world is but the everyday world of our practical life, only under "a change of sign" (cf. Mohanty 1954). According to Husserl, with the *epochē* "nothing is lost": the "content," the "themes," the "objects," even the "interests" of the naive natural attitude and of the life-world are the same; only the subjective attitude toward objectivity has changed.[8] The thesis of the natural attitude is "bracketed" only to be subsequently recovered endowed with its full meaning. So, transcendental subjectivity and empirical consciousness are not two separated domains; the two are *the same*. Transcendental reflection "frees" empirical consciousness from its dogmatic, naturalistic involvement and thus makes it fully aware of its meaning-constituting functions. In doing so, empirical consciousness becomes transcendental consciousness. Between the two, empirical and transcendental consciousness, there is, as Husserl says, a "wonderful parallelism" (cf. Husserl, *Phänomenologische Psychologie*, p. 343).

2.6. PRACTICAL GIVENNESS

If we arrive at the IG, at that which "stands fast" for us and for everybody, then it will be a mistake to depict it in epistemic terms. For the IG does not pertain to the domain of knowledge (to that "language game"); it belongs rather to the realm of its support, which is external to it. Descriptions of the IG in terms of conceptual, representational knowledge is a serious category mistake, and a fatally misleading one.

There are reasons to believe that Husserl thought there was a basic *practical* mode of givenness and so considered the view that, for instance, unique identification of objects (unique reference) is accomplished through practical relationships. According to a report made by Dagfinn Føllesdal (1979), in a manuscript from 1917–18, called "Science and Life," Husserl wrote on the topic of how our practical actions constitute the world. Constitution in the theoretical and in the practical fields work in parallel ways giving rise to extrapolations that make up the *noema* and thereby constitute the object. "Practical extrapolations have to do with the object's 'serviceability' within our web of means and ends" (ibid.). Thus, our actions constitute the world by extrapolation based on similarity in our practical ways of dealing with things. "The beginning is not a matter of fact, but an action," Føllesdal says, quoting Husserl. There are also other places, for example, in *Erste Philosophie*, where we can find similar and related ideas about the practical mode of givenness, that is, of constitution. This may be useful for explaining the failure of "sense-data" theories to come up with an explanation of sensory perception: sense-data are the product of a theoretical analysis of a practically constituted unity; so, any attempt to reconstruct that unity out of the sense-data is doomed to fail.[9]

2.7. CERTAINTY

What lies at the ground of our conceptual activity is our everyday acting in a communal consensus. The IG is nonconceptual, nonrepresentational, and of course nonpropositional. That is why it cannot be true or false. It cannot, not because it is "firmly established knowledge," an "apodictic truth," but because it is not knowledge in the first place. It is not something that can be true or false. It is derived not from any kind of absolutely trustworthy process of exploration that is supposed to lead us to such an "apodictic truth," but mainly from its nonrepresentational character, that is, from the fact that it is practice, human activity of a certain sort.

I think that if it is true that knowledge is susceptible to doubt, then obviously no knowledge could found knowledge by itself. If what we are looking for is *certitude*, something not subject to further justification, that is, the very ground beyond all possibility of further proof and epistemic evaluation, then that thing cannot be of the nature of knowledge. It must be something of a very different nature.[10]

What has been said conforms to a notion of "foundation" understood as "solid ground." Now the real question can be raised: is the attempt to reach the IG some kind of search for ground of that sort? Maybe the question could be easily answered if one could answer another question first: Why must we attempt to reach the IG in the first place?

The answer could be that something which is "immediately given" to us is *certain*, that "immediate givenness" guarantees *certitude*. But this is nothing but another way to say that it is a "solid ground" for knowledge. Thus, the IG would be a firm foundation of knowledge because it is supposed to be a "knowledge" that is *certain*, that is, not susceptible to doubt. As IG, it does not depend on anything else, and hence it cannot be submitted to epistemic evaluation. But then it is not *knowledge*, as it has just been shown.

2.8. GROUNDING CONCEPTUAL KNOWLEDGE

Another question: Why is so important to get to the IG? And what is the relationship between the IG and the rest of knowledge? If we think of the IG as a *ground*, then it seems its relation to the rest of knowledge must be some kind of "subordination": the rest of knowledge "depends on" the IG. What is the nature of this dependence?

It is not, so it could be said by phenomenologists, a relation of logical consequence, or derivability, like that existing in an axiomatic or deductive system. If it is evidential, one can view phenomenology as a method, technique, or procedure for establishing true knowledge on the basis of *certainty* and thus "founding" it.

But to equate the search for *certitude* with the search for a foundation seems to be a *Cartesian* move (remember what has been previously said about *Die Idee*). It consists in searching for an *immediate experience* about which one cannot be mistaken and then to take it (or its description) as a ground level whereon the rest of knowledge can solidly rely. Alternatively, we can also think that the description of the IG, if it is to be foundational, must be of such a kind that its negation would cause a sort of logical and conceptual absurdity leading to a real impossibility to think. But this is another way to state that the IG is not a *ground* (whose negation would not necessarily lead to such an impossibility) but a *background*: thinking, and a fortiori conceptual knowledge, takes place always against a pre-given non-conceptual background.

One important feature of the IG, as I understand it here, is that it is not conceptual. It must thus be "given" to us by some sort of direct contact. Here the word "given" is highly misleading, since it suggests some kind of gap existing between two things that cannot be entirely joined together.

The IG I am thinking of is something we come to be aware of unreflectively and unself-consciously in the course of our daily lives. We get it partly by inheritance and partly by living coupled to an environment where communal practices, especially language, come to model our intimate "picture of the world." Inheritance and basic intersubjectivity are not epistemic performances (though coupling is indeed a cognitive feature)[11] and hence they are not a matter of knowledge, intellection, or ratiocination. That is why the IG is not conceptual or intellectual.

It may be objected that this is not the IG Husserl is searching for. He is searching for that which is IG *in phenomenological reflection*. But again: Why? Is it because phenomenological reflection is supposed to reach, as "immediately given," the "absolute ground" of knowledge? Now, what comes to be reached at the end (let us suppose there is such an end) could perfectly well be the same ground of our daily epistemic and practical performances. Must I say here it *has* to be that? Suppose what is reached is something different, some sort of conceptual ground. It would be IG. Wouldn't it? I think not, unless one is going along in an uncritical *Cartesian* way.

But I think I have sufficiently insisted that what lies at the ground of our conceptual, epistemic life is nothing epistemic in nature (although it is cognitive). It is not a "system of knowledge," but instead it is action. All our epistemic life rests upon a ground of *certitudes* "immediately given" to us because of our immersion in a human community whose everyday activity at the same time creates that very same substratum itself.

What IG, and in that sense our *background*, is, in Wittgenstein's terms, is a "world picture" we all inherit as members of a community.

2.9. COMMON (COMMUNAL) SENSE

Now, what seems to be crucial is that that picture is not a set of beliefs, and thus cannot be rendered by a set of propositions. It manifests itself in action. Thus, the search for the IG should not follow the route of merely "looking inward," but instead that of "looking at acting." Looking at behavior of many sorts. The IG is not a "knowledge about" but a "way of *acting* in respect to."

Must we call the IG world picture a *"commonsense framework"*?

Caveat: The "commonsense framework" is *not* in any sense a sort of "folk theory." If it were, if the inherited background were some kind of "folk theory," then it would be open to revision and even to elimination by science. Which is not the case. The background has no epistemic status. It is not committed to epistemic goals. It is rather something that makes epistemic operations possible.

When we have reached the IG, the substratum or background, then our description has reached the deepest level of description: the *residuum*. It is not possible to go further. And what is it that we have reached? Can we describe it?

What is the kind of thing that could be the inescapable life-world, that is, the background of our epistemic activities? I think it is the fact that we are human beings dwelling in a community wherein those epistemic activities can emerge and take place and at the same time contribute to the constitution of the community itself. Thus, human beings living in a community and contributing to its continuous regeneration is what is reached when we try to give a general description of the background.

Thus, the life of the community makes possible and supports the epistemic operations; but these are essential elements (among others) of that communal life, that is, those epistemic operations essentially contribute to the existence of the communal life that makes them possible.

2.10. ACTION

There is more to say about the idea of a "practical (nonperceptual) mode of givenness": human action. Human action is neither representational nor objective in nature. Perhaps it is worth saying it is "presentational" in the sense in which it is said of a stage actor that he makes a "presentation" when he is acting. Human action is captured by us as observers in the very same way the actor's performance is grasped and followed by the spectators in the theater: objects, persons, everything is what it is as a part of the entire play, and thus what is immediately given to us and what grounds everything is the entire piece of acting that goes on before our eyes. We could, certainly, make a lot of theoretical, conceptual descriptions of the events, persons, objects, and of their relations to our perceptual mechanisms, but none of that would capture what is going on in the acting. What should be described is the entirety of the performance, and this cannot be represented: it can only be *presented*. Actually, the presentation could be "clarified" by way of a further consideration of the characters, the situations involved, the historical and social contexts, and so on; its meaning could be further "explicated" somehow, but no inventory and no reconstruction will be more immediately given than the presentation itself: no atomistic description will do the job. As a way to get a keener view of this, imagine the result if one day the manager of a stage play faced a strike of the actor's union and proposed to the audience that, instead of the presentation of the play, he give them a complete description of it: the characters, objects, all the complicated stuff involved in the *mise en scène*, plus of course the story, the relationships between the characters, their beliefs, desires, emotions, moods, etc., etc. . . . I think something very similar to that is what happens when one tries to account for the background of our knowledge in a theoretical, conceptual way.

To say that *acting* lies at the bottom of epistemic activities could be an alternative formulation of the idea of the community as the "commonsense framework."

2.11. EXPLANATION VERSUS CLARIFICATION

A significant issue could be raised at this point: since it is not made out of conceptualized *facts* (it is made out of embodied meanings), and since it is not a kind of theoretical knowledge, it may be argued that the background should not be the kind of thing that science can investigate. Thus, the investigation of this background ("framework") would not fall within the scope of science, but within that of philosophy.

Let me say at the outset that if the talk of something being "the kind of thing that science cannot investigate" is an empirical proposition, it is a groundless, perhaps a dogmatic prediction. Nevertheless, I also believe that the assertion that the investigation of the background does not fall within the scope of science, but within that of philosophy, could be partially true. In Husserlian terms, that is what is meant by the "change of sign" operated by *ēpochē* and reduction of the natural attitude to the phenomenological, or transcendental attitude. In Wittgensteinian terms, that would mean that scientific explanation and meaning clarification belong to two different, heterogeneous language games.

This allows me to say some final words on the subject of naturalization.

3. NATURALIZATION

3.1. NATURALIZING ESSENCES

Some quite obvious remarks on the issue of naturalization seem to follow directly from what has been said so far. Naturalizing phenomenological conclusions is a very feasible task insofar as the morphological science of essences is brought into focus. I understand essences as being a kind of entity, idealizations of empirical typicalities of the life-world conceived as the world of perceptual reality. I see no a priori contradiction in the idea of natural science investigating the fixed types which characterize the empirical structures of the life-world and thus form the basis of the genesis—through idealizations—of the material essences of eidetic regional ontologies. The process of idealization leading from empirical typicalities to essences is but a method for uncovering the a priori structures in the empirical phenomena, and thus should provide the basis for an accurate scientific handling of the matter. However, one must bear in mind that these structures are the a priori of natural sciences, not of experience itself.

3.2. NATURALIZING THE TRANSCENDENTAL LIFE-WORLD

The most fundamental strata of the life-world constitute what may be called the transcendental a priori structures of experience itself. These structures are an a priori, not in the Kantian sense, but so to speak, in the sense of the embodied outcome of our cognitive history. Radical *epochē* operated on the life-world is what uncovers those conditions of possibility. In this sense, naturalizing them would mean to naturalize the very a priori conditions of possibility of every possible experience. But I think naturalization here should have a specific sense. It should correspond to the radical character of the realized *epochē*. I mean: the transcendental a priori life-world is not the *matter*, but *the horizon*, and thus to describe it requires radical reflection; a naturalized description, as a theoretically oriented task, would not render the specificity of the grasp achieved by radical reflection but at most what I will call here, in very loose and vague terms, some set of "rules of operation" for dealing with those a priori structures. Historicity, causality, intersubjectivity, spatiotemporality, passive associative synthesis, and other structures which constitute the conditions of possibility of any experience qua experience of the world are a sort of "virtuality" which is realized in each world experience. Thus, these structures cannot be fixed as general fixed patterns, but can be used as rules for performing naturalized descriptions of experience. The reason is that the kind of "pure a priori" of this transcendental life-world is, so to speak, co-generated[12] with the experience at the time of each experience. It is thus not exactly pre-given, as Husserl says, but "co-given." That is why naturalization should take a specific form in this case, namely, the form of "rules for description."

3.3. NATURALIZING MEANINGS

All along I have claimed that phenomenological philosophy should be understood as the explication of meanings, and mainly of what I have called "the IG as background." Naturalizing meanings is not a self-defeating proposal, I think, but it is not obvious how we should understand it. I will make only some brief remarks on this subject.

One way of naturalizing meanings is to assume a formalistic stance that consists in providing an account of meanings along functional lines (meanings as mathematical functions from possible worlds to suitable values, e.g., individuals in the case of reference) and then to propose the suitable algorithms for computing such functions. This is the way suggested by Hintikka and others, it seems to me. I think it is a promising way inasmuch as we are dealing with more or less stereotyped, conventional linguistic formations in more or less stereotyped, conventional contexts.

The computational stance is a similar way, but it seems to me it has a far more restricted scope than the formalistic one.

Eliminativism suggests that meanings are directly tied to our "world picture" and thus seems *prima facie* not to challenge substantially the view I am proposing here. Nevertheless, it also suggests that our "world picture" can be entirely naturalized insofar as it is conceived as "mental," that is, psychological structures, which in turn should be reduced to more "fundamental," perhaps neurophysiological processes. But I have claimed that the background is not "mental" in that sense. The background involves all of our everyday social acting and thus is not ontologically reducible to something else. As consisting of natural phenomena, each item of it could be *causally explainable* in terms of, for example, the behavior of the brain and the nervous system, plus a series of naturalized social sciences, but as the background of meaning it is not reducible to them for the same reason one cannot reduce our social interactions to interactions at a "subpersonal" level. One can explain the other, but they are two fully separated phenomena.

3.4. NATURALIZING PHENOMENOLOGY

To close I will take the risk of proposing my own view on this matter. I think we could take seriously the Husserlian thesis about the parallelism between the empirical and the transcendental and the idea that with *epochē* nothing is lost but the entire everyday world reappears with "a change of sign." In this sense, putting the world into brackets is not to glance at another reality; it is rather to delimit what one wants to look at and to indicate the standpoint from which one wants to do it. The world is put into brackets in order to give rise to the meaning it has for us. So, putting into brackets is a kind of questioning: the "change of sign" yields the question of meaning.

That means the background is not something apart from or prior to our lives; it is rather the pattern of those lives themselves, embodied mainly in the flux of ordinary exchanges in everyday communal life. The phenomenologically reduced life-world is but the ordinary course of social life aware of its own functioning as meaning-bestowing.

So, the experience of meaning is just the everyday experience of living. Naturalizing meanings would consist simply in coming back from the transcendental, self-conscious subjectivity to the natural, everyday world and clarifying its meaning.

Phenomenology should be defined as this continuous going back and forth between reflective and natural attitudes.

CHAPTER SEVENTEEN

When Transcendental Genesis Encounters the Naturalization Project

NATALIE DEPRAZ

> It must be confessed, moreover, that perception and what depends on it are *inexplicable by mechanical reasons*, that is, by figures and motions. If we pretend that there is a machine whose structure enables it to think, feel, and have perception, one could think of it as enlarged yet preserving its same proportions, so that one could enter it as one does a mill. If we did this, we should find nothing within but parts which push upon each other; we should never see anything which would explain a perception. —*Leibniz*, Monadologie, §17

1. PHENOMENOLOGY AND THE NATURALIZATION PROJECT

1.1. INTRODUCTION

To want at all costs to uphold the claims of transcendental phenomenology in a historical and intellectual context in which deconstructionist models flourish might seem to amount to little more than fighting a rearguard action, an action hardly capable of nourishing a vigorous debate. To be sure, the power of deconstructionism does indeed stem from the suspicion it casts upon all constituted or self-constituting thought. Joining forces in its own way with Nietzsche's hammer strategy, it thereby becomes an accomplice of the very destructive nihilism in which the author of *The Genealogy of Morals* got caught up even when he claimed to be its destroyer.

To talk of "transcendental phenomenology" is, at one and the same time, to talk of the close link between Husserl's philosophy and Kant's critical philosophy, and also of the rupture of this link. For Kant, "transcendental" designates the level of the conditions of the possibility of all possible experience, most eminently represented by the pure concepts of the understanding. The categorial conditions of the possibility of experience apply to the latter, take account of the latter, but without ever depending upon it. In the same way, for Husserl too, "transcendental" refers to the a priori level of the structures constitutive of all possible experience; but by contrast with Kant, (1) these structures do not have the exclusively formal character of the Kantian categories, their constitutive origin being of the hyletic (material) kind; as a result, (2) they are given intuitively and are therefore capable of appearing as such. To uphold the rights of a transcendental phenomenology consists in bringing to light the very *constitution* of the experience of an object for a consciousness by showing how the object is, in this way, given intuitively to the consciousness. Unlike constitution, condition of the possibility maintains the duality between the phenomenal and that which conditions it. Constitution, on the other hand, rejects just such a duality by engaging phenomenality on the level of its original constitution.

Besides, the later, post-Husserlian versions of phenomenology, the Heideggerian, Merleau-Pontian, even Levinasian versions, whether ontological, hermeneutical, or ethical, have never ceased to react against all forms of transcendentalism; they see it as illegitimate because in their view it is unavoidably tainted with an idealism that cannot be reconciled with the descriptive prescriptions of phenomenology. However, these phenomenologies have, each in its own way, indisputably served to propose a new "construction" of phenomenal experience. Well aware that the constructive strategy is intrinsic to the phenomenological project itself, that is, that the idea of an unadulterated description is a complete illusion (cf. Fink 1988, §7), the prevailing question in this context is that of the intuitive character of the phenomenal structures opened up by the description: how can we be sure that these ontological, hermeneutical, or ethical constructions are capable of doing justice to the phenomenal character of experience, more capable even than any transcendental constitution of experience?

In this perspective, by leading phenomenology back to the primary description of its own sensibly phenomenal foundations, the project of a naturalization of phenomenology has the merit of short-circuiting any risk of an arbitrary construction of the phenomena to be described. To this extent, it brings any speculative tendency to a standstill and so commits itself to a presuppositionless description of a phenomenon which is always particular and has to be grasped across its immanental structures of givenness. We are reminded here of the position adopted earlier by the sociologist Alfred Schütz, that of a "mundane phenomenology" which refuses to raise questions of principle and to seek access to the conditions of the possibility of the experience to be described, with a view to engaging right away in a description of multiple social relations. Anxious to do justice to the structural relations internal to society, Schütz practices what he calls a "natural *épochè*," which seeks to suspend any ambition of uncovering a meaning behind phenomenal multiplicity. In this way he calls for a natural phenomenology, against Husserlian transcendentality. However, he very rapidly turns to ideal types to furnish a flexible way of structuring social reality and which in more than one respect closely resemble Husserl's use of the *eidē* (Schütz 1959), which are themselves employed to open phenomenology up upon a transcendental configuration.

To what extent is a naturalized phenomenology incompatible with the requirements of a transcendental one? If we begin by raising the question in the context proposed by Schütz, it seems that the opposition between the two is so massive that the question is hardly worth considering. Besides the fact (to which we shall return)[1] that Husserl himself offered a critique that was both elementary and radical of any kind of naturalism, it certainly looks as though—this is what we shall have to look into—transcendentalism and naturalism stand opposed to each other on more than one score. But in the final analysis, the most important question remains the following: can a *genetic reformulation of transcendental phenomenology*, one that does not lead back to empiricism pure and simple but which still avoids the formalistic risks of transcendental phenomenology, be brought into relation with some process of *naturalization* (perhaps we should say: phenomenalization) that would not be subject to reductionist dilemmas?

1.2. THE HUSSERLIAN CRITIQUE OF NATURALISM

That the original phenomenology was set up very early on, well before the transcendental turn, and was directed against any dissolution of the a priori lawfulness of experience into the diverse forms of associationism current at the time and in favor of its ideal structuration is too well known to require recapitulation here.[2] The ideality that, as a matter of principle, commands the very possibility of knowledge and of any phenomenological analysis also finds a strictly phenomenological (non-Kantian, non-Bolzanian) formulation very early on in terms of acts of consciousness. Reaching beyond any merely oppositional inscription of consciousness, which, at the time, had crystallized into the a priori / a posteriori duality, the various forms of which we shall find good reason to reject, it is the description of acts and not of objects which lies at the heart of phenomenology as a radically antinatural approach.[3] In the end, the phenomenological attitude corrects any tendency to attribute to acts themselves determinations that are derived from objects in a simple way.[4]

A consequential transcendental phenomenology will, a fortiori, be highly suspicious of any tendency to substantialize the object (no matter what this object might be) aimed at in the description at the expense of the dynamic constitutive of the act of consciousness through which it is brought to light. Moreover, this kind of hypercritical attitude whose methodological nerve center, the reduction, is to be located in the principle of the absence of presuppositions, a principle Husserl formulated as early as 1901 (*Logische Untersuchungen* [hereafter cited as *LU*], II/1, *Einleitung*, §7, pp. 24f.), has to be equally, and indeed especially, vigilant vis-à-vis itself, that is, vis-à-vis its own potential hypertranscendentalism. Before considering afresh the various antiphenomenological attitudes Husserl condemns,[5] it would be worthwhile to examine the residual transcendentalism still at work in every strict and radical transcendental claim. The most stubborn, because the most secret and *the most intimate enemy of transcendental phenomenology, is the transcendentalism that it conceals within itself*.[6] Husserl and Eugen Fink both express grave reservations about this insidious and powerful "transcendental naïveté."[7]

Basically, the transcendentalist threat may assume two forms, which are only apparently opposed to each other: (1) exaggerated claims on behalf of acts of consciousness, henceforward accorded almost substantial (!) status by virtue of having been so thoroughly purified with regard to the object; and (2) a radical dissolution of all substantiality by conferring upon conscious acts an absolute fluidity. When going over the different forms that the phenomenological critique of naturalism took on as we have done in the appendix to this chapter, we have to bear this very risk in mind, not least because it is so closely associated with attitudes castigated in so eminent and paradigmatic a way. In short, the attitude *opposed* to naturalism comes down to the same thing as naturalism.

That logicism can be part and parcel of psychologism, personalism of naturalism, idealism of realism, subjectivism of objectivism, or again, transcendentalism of empiricism, is a deception that can only be accounted for in terms of the naïveté of the oppositions in question. All the same, these oppositions are valuable because they engender a fruitful because exacerbated tension. Only by examining this *tension* will it be possible to place them in perspective, which is what we have attempted only too briefly in the appendix. Each one of the antiphenomenological tendencies to be examined produces its correlate upon the same plane of analysis, but subject to modifications, facelifts, in the light of the continually evolving research of the founder.

1.3. TENSION WITHIN NATURALISM

It might be said that naturalism is also caught in a dual postulation of meaning: on the one hand, it is just one of the poles of the Husserlian critique and as such stands opposed to historicism (from the time of "Philosophy as Rigorous Science" [1911]); personalism (in *Ideen* II [1912–15]), which, in *Krisis*, is indistinguishable from objectivism and psychologism and which generates its own opposite on the same level; and subjectivism—the extension of which leads to a dissolution of the critique. On the other hand, it also serves as a foil for a phenomenology defined in principle as a critical science and which, by virtue of this definition, could find backing in a subtle form of skepticism (*Krisis*, §24).

By an extension of the notions in question, objectivism and naturalism encompass every *naively scientific* form of attitude. Even psychologism and empiricism are consequently remobilized in this extremely large sense. Certain texts, which are more straightforward and also more polemical in character, use these notions in a fairly general and extensive way and so broaden the spectrum of the critique. This is the case with "Philosophy as Rigorous Science" (1911), which draws up a general indictment against any scientific attitude that is not subjectively oriented. It is also the case with the Vienna Lecture of 1935. The polemical character of these manifestos has repercussions for certain globalizing emphases drawn from the beginning of *Ideen* I, then from the general historical analyses of *Erste Philosophie* and of *Krisis*. In losing sight of the limits of the critique of psychologism, of empiricism, even of realism, transcendental phenomenology acquires the stature of a philosophy that is critical of science, that deems science not thoughtful and so rejoins, in this respect, Heidegger's all-encompassing critique of science as technique.

But the very ambivalence of transcendental phenomenology, both a critique and itself subjected to a critique, is the corollary of another tension that inhabits naturalism itself (or psychologism, which no longer has much to do with what Husserl criticized in volume 1 of *Logische Untersuchungen*). On the one hand, naturalism is a pernicious tendency, or a falsification of phenomena as given immanently to consciousness.[8] On the other hand, naturalization (even more than naturalism, moreover) benefits from a positive evaluation just as soon as it comes under the jurisdiction of a process of *constitution*. "Mundanization, monadic constitution, is such that, essentially, it implies the naturalization of each monad, its temporalization in spatio-temporal reality."[9] In a strict sense, naturalization is henceforward transcendental, for the work of constitution presupposes a prior operation of reduction. Naturalization is the constitution of a nature, just as mundanization is the constitution of a world, or again, just as the ego objectifies itself into a soul and into a human being.[10]

1.4. THE ARGUMENTS AGAINST NATURALISM

Naturalization: falsification of the phenomena, or constitution of natural objectivity? A unilaterally explicative apprehension of the base-nature of the phenomena or, rather, conscious bestowal of meaning upon the natural object? Inscribed in a polarity of an axiological order, naturalization conceals an ambivalence. However, the only yardstick by which its axiological neutrality can be measured is the reduction, the only safeguard against reductionism of any kind whatever.

1.4.1 The Reduction as Antireductionism

Far from exercising a limitative ("reducing") function, reduction frees up a field of phenomena that do not differ in content from natural objects but which are apprehended in a different mode. In short, under reduction the same objects are seen differently.

To reduce is to rely upon the sensibly natural reality of the object as upon a necessary posit and to alter it, from within, by looking at it in another way, that is, by eliciting its peculiarly individual mode of appearing.[11] In short, it is to deploy dimensions contained within it, but unwittingly so. The guiding question of reductive consciousness is: how is this objective fact given to me? In this regard, whether the object is posited as external (as in classical science) or whether it is, so to speak, "interiorized," as in contemporary science, changes nothing about the attitudinal modification imposed upon it. Does neurobiology have the same relation to quantum physics that anatomical physiology might have had to Newtonian physics? In the transition from the latter to the former, it is clear that something like an "interiorization" of the object takes place, running right up to its disappearance. The normal perceiving subject no longer sees the atom any more than he does the neuron. For all that, his retreat into invisibility, the correlate of which is a more refined conception of physical, as well as nervous, matter, does not profoundly modify the materialist and positivist options available to science. The atom, like the neuron, remains an objective fact, less tangible but just as positive from the standpoint of a phenomenological attitude directed toward the "how" of their givenness to consciousness. In this perspective, one is entitled to ask whether Husserl's antinaturalism really is limited to the state (superseded) of the positive sciences of his day,[12] or rather reduced to a critique of the philosophy of nature as the bearer of a dogmatic metaphysics. Does this alternative even exhaust the meaning of the antinaturalism in question? In other words, could it be that a critical position of this kind is really transhistorical and, in consequence, strictly methodological? In fact, even if the positive sciences have modified the way in which they pose their questions, the methodological way in which they gain access to experience remains, for the phenomenologist, in principle the same.

Nevertheless, the phenomenologist's question does get raised in a more specific way; it even gets more refined in the passage from one type of science to another. With regard to the physiological anatomist, it becomes the following: what is the mode of givenness of the sensorial organs to consciousness? Or again: what subjective experience do I have of a sensation of color, of contact, of sound, of a perfume or a taste? The reduction is that thanks to which I am able to gain access to my corporeally lived feeling of standing in relation to the basic exteriority of objects. The physical body, even the living physical body (*Körper*) becomes a lived experience (*Leib*). With reference to neurobiology the question rapidly gets more complicated, more ramified—given that I cannot, in the strict sense, perceive the neuronal connections that are established in me beneath the threshold of perception, the critical question for the phenomenologist turns on the discontinuity, in principle, between the lived experience of perceptual consciousness and the material traces of a cerebral (neuronal) order, and this against any ontological monism that might seek, in a more or less subtle manner, to reestablish some form of continuity between the *res cogitans* and the *res extensa* and this, furthermore, on the basis of the *res extensa*.

Starting from this basic prerequisite, the phenomenological question is duplicated, depending on the approach adopted, object or consciousness. From the side of the object: (1) without a surreptitious and unwarranted transposition proceeding from our habitual mode of perception, can we be sure that neuronal activity can be described effectively in accordance with temporal and spatial modes of individuation familiar to us from this particular mode of perception? From the side of consciousness: (2) is our perceptual activity capable of discriminating in us minute sensorial modifications that, for the most part, we are incapable of noticing?[13] In short, what is in question for a reduced consciousness is this: what mode of givenness of the neuronal dynamic is available to me as a consciousness invested with a hypersensitive lived experience?

In other words, the reduction provides a guarantee against any reductionism, including that which might operate surreptitiously at the very heart of the reduction, namely, that of consciousness itself. By bringing into play an eidetic reduction, we avoid the trap of subjectivism; with the transcendental reduction, we circumvent the restriction of the inquiry to the specifically human.[14]

1.4.2. Nature Revisited by Phenomenology

However alive it might be, however incarnate, nature remains a complex of processes and of subtle mechanisms that take place alongside us, or in us, for the most part without our knowledge. Even if we take part in it, or get caught up with it, in a more or less reflective manner, nature's way with us conceals a strange or alien power that never ceases to astonish us, even to escape all conscious control.[15]

However, it is always on the basis of our reflective capacity that we question this enigmatic aspect of a nature that is also part of us. With Husserl, the questioning process, in "Philosophy as Rigorous Science," proceeds on the basis of the duality *Natur und Geist* inherited from Dilthey and whose different constitutive layers are laid out in the second and third books of *Ideen* before being taken up again in the *Lectures* from the 1920s which bear the same title,[16] after which they are finally renamed *Lebenswelt* in *Krisis*. Reproducing for his own account the Diltheyan requirement of a radical distinction between nature and spirit, in accordance with which the superior cannot be explained from the inferior (cf. also "Wiener Vortrag," in *Krisis*), Husserl is led, in the course of the years 1912–15, to set up the constitution of the world of spirit on the basis of the constitution of the material world. To clarify: the constitution in question presupposes a primary stratum that is both sensible and material and superior strata founded upon it. The foundation (*Fundierung*) in question has nothing to do with a rational or a substantial foundation (*Begründung*), still less, obviously, with a causal foundation. Rather, it has to do with a primary mode of appearance on the part of a primary layer which serves as a guideline, as a source of motivation, *and also* provides a founded layer that is not reducible to the founding layer. From this time on, nature and spirit are referred on to their common unilaterality and referred back to their primordial unity, the lived body (*Leib*), corresponding to the constitutively median and originally expressive layer. In the 1930s, it is the life-world which plays the role of this phenomenologically reduced element which generates the opposition of nature and spirit. In this way, *Leib* and *Lebenswelt* play the role of nondual phenomenological expressions of nature and spirit. In other words, the phenomenological method moves in two directions at once, toward a denaturalization of nature and a despiritualization of spirit.

1.5. THE TRANSCENDENTAL LIMITS OF NATURALIZATION

As a result, the term "limit" also takes on two meanings. Evidently, as we have seen, there are the limits imposed by the transcendental reduction itself upon the process of naturalization. But the transcendental realm is also, if not limited, at least constrained by a resistance internal to nature.

To limit what is natural is to take account of it by assigning to it a determinate place, whether by way of an attitude (natural or naturalist) or by way of a region (material regional ontology) (*Ideen* II, first section; ibid., §15;

Ideen I, chap. 2, §33 and passim). The element on the basis of which a relativization of nature becomes possible, a pure reflective consciousness, even a transcendental ego, enjoys an encompassing status, or the status of a source-point, with regard to either the naive attitude or the regional ontology derived therefrom. Only the reflective element can confer meaning upon a nature to the production of which it has already contributed, by envisaging it in terms of the natural/naturalist attitude (*Krisis*, §38) or in terms of the nature-region. Consequently, it is this element and this element alone which is qualified to enjoy a constitutive function with regard to nature.

And yet: *"Drive off the natural and it comes back at the gallop."* This well-known proverb draws attention to the limits, even the difficulties, of a reduction (therefore also a constitution) that seeks to enclose nature within bounds. This unsatisfactory understanding of the reduction is still that of *Ideen* I (§49), and it refers to a static conception of constitution, in accordance with which the object is nothing more than a unity of sense constituted by consciousness but which is quite incapable of undermining, even of affecting, the meaning-giving activity of consciousness itself.

In the "Lectures from the Winter Term, 1920–21," which, for the most part are taken up in the text published under the title *Analysen zur passiven Synthesis* (which corresponds to MS F I 37, 38, 39), Husserl's analysis frequently relies upon the existence in itself of objects (*das Ansich der Gegenstände*) or upon their being true (*Analysen*, §§23–25, §§44–47; *Erfahrung und Urteil*, §7). The critical issue is that of the constitution of an objective nature endangered by the existence of an exteriority stemming from a naturalness that cannot be integrated with the reductive operation. The question is, is there such a thing as a nature that cannot be recuperated in any form whatever, by any form of consciousness whatsoever? There could be a form of nature that is irreducible, "a factual resource [*faktischen Bestand*] which is in itself unintelligible" (*Ideen* II, §61, p. 276), and which provides a source of motivation, a stimulus for the meaning-giving constitution itself. By proceeding toward a distinction between an originary nature and a secondary nature, the locus of our habitus, Husserl differentiates the respective parts played by nature and spirit, but only by pushing back the limits of unfathomable nature (ibid.). In reality, what nourishes this distinction between the primary and the secondary is still a static maneuver involving spatializing delimitation. We are then led to acknowledge the strangeness of nature, its ultimately incomprehensible character, and in return, our own fragility, even our anxious powerlessness in the face of its incommensurable force (Waldenfels 1980; cf. also Husserl, *Phänomenologische Psychologie*, pp. 55–57). Furthermore, this power of nature, this blind resistance on the part of our own natural being calls for a further refinement of the constitutive method itself, to wit, its "genetization," that is to say, correlatively, the recognition of a passivity internal to the reduction itself (cf. Depraz 1995b).

2. GENETIC PHENOMENOLOGY AND THE THEORY OF EMERGENCE

2.1. BEYOND OPPOSING TENSIONS

Given the elementary but radical critique of the naturalism (whether actually operative or merely envisaged as a tendency) inherent in scientific procedure, a critique in which Husserl engages, at first in a more localized and then, as the need arose, in a more global fashion, it is not possible even to think of engaging in discussion with scientists on the question of the status of the real except by basing our inquiry on the complete depositivization of that which calls for such a critique. Here again, clarification is required. Husserl criticizes scientific positivism while claiming for himself the title of a "true positivist" (*Ideen* I, §20, p. 66; §30, p. 63). In so doing, he insists upon the need to faithfully anchor all reflection in what is given (the positum)—good-bye speculative construction!—and to require a correct apprehension of what is given by consciousness in its quite specific mode of appearance. An absolutely nonreductionist scientificity is henceforward the only authorized topic of inquiry for the properly phenomenological philosopher. In fact, a scientific reductionism, even a subtle one, would reduce the phenomenological attitude to a body of dephenomenologized doctrine. The phenomenologization of science is, in other words, only possible (and fruitful) as a function of its dereductionization.

As we have seen, just as naturalism takes on varied and more or less inflexible forms, so reductionism assumes different hues, more or less frank or vociferous. In both cases, it is a matter of an attitude that, more or less subtly, suppresses the differentiations internal to a phenomenon by tracing it back to a pre-given and already available structure. More brutally, it could be said that the naturalist/reductionist attitude is happy with and even takes refuge in the simplicity of existing grids and ignores the non–a priori determinable complexity of the phenomenon. A comfortable but undemanding attitude; an attitude that is sometimes elegant, and even aesthetic, but which is not equipped to confront the nonabsorbable resistance of a recalcitrant reality.

Reductionism takes on forms that range from caricature (Changeux 1982) to the highest finesse. The most dangerous are obviously the most subtle because it would be very easy to be deceived by them and to think, as in connection with the transcendentalism presented earlier, that we had now definitely gone beyond any reductionist tendency. This turns out not to be the case. For the latter keeps on coming back.[17] It has to be hunted down as persistently as dogmatism, even transcendental dogmatism.

If, in a certain sense, we can talk of a "parallel history" of naturalism and reductionism, we have the right to pose the question of the relevance of a project of "phenomenological naturalization" which is subject to a radically nonreductionist requirement. Are we not confronted here with a *contradictio in adjecto*? Any investigation that consists in *potentializing* the connection (or the correlation if you prefer) between the subjectively eidetic experience—which defines phenomenology in its dual rootedness in psychology and logico-mathematics[18]—and the neuronal basis of the organism seems committed to excluding that equivocal notion of naturalization which tends to restrict the lived experience to the neuron.

Over and beyond this extreme form of reductionism, which restricts spirit, even consciousness, to the brain, whether because the latter seems to offer our only positive access to lived experience or because the analysis bearing on lived experience seems to find its ultimate *objectifying confirmation* (its *validation*) in neurobiological analysis, it is evident that cognitive science has, in the course of its development, tried at each step to get a little further away from this residual reductionism: First, the computational branch of cognitivism adopts for mind a computerized model inherited from the advance of cybernetics, and in so doing interprets mental or psychic states as so many formal systems structured in accordance with the rules of logical symbolism. Second, emergentism, dubious about the naïveté (abstraction) of this symbolizing translation, presents the mental as a network of neurons that interact locally with each other, thereby engendering a global cognitive state of a sub-symbolic type whose own intrinsic properties are not reducible to the local properties of the neurons. In this sense, the emergentist attitude insists upon the dynamic through which consciousness is engendered. By basing its analysis on the network formed by the neuronal substrate, emergentism concentrates upon the static and functional basis of connection among neurons and generates, on that basis, the law of the emergence of the global from the local. And third, an enactive attitude, or what might be called incarnate emergentism, displaces the center of gravity of representation to the action of an individual situated in a given environment which, in return, reacts back upon him and leads him to put into effect an incessant dynamic of adaptation which results, not from willed action on his part, but from an assumed passivity.[19]

These three attitudes do not entertain the same kind of relation vis-à-vis one another. While the passage from the first to the second amounts to a break in the frame of reference, the transition from the second to the third can be presented as a deepening *sensu lato* of the analysis within one and the same emergentist framework. Connectionist emergentism and enactive emergentism refer to a distinction that has only recently been drawn and which has not yet been thoroughly clarified. However, as we shall see, the distinction will prove decisive from the standpoint of the different phenomenological emphases the two sorts of emergentism imply.

2.2. THE COMMON GROUND FOR A POSSIBLE AGREEMENT

The phenomenological theory of reduction/constitution and the theory of emergence share two concerns:[20] (1) to differentiate the *distinct levels* of description by refusing to compress them together or to surreptitiously drag one back down to the other and (2) to work out their possible mode of relation on the clarified basis of their irreducible singularity. "Reduce" now means engaging in just such a regulated process of differentiation. Understanding emergence is a matter of taking into account how the different levels are internally regulated.

I now propose to attempt a nonreductionist (as such, phenomenological) analysis of the relation between phenomenological (static and then genetic) and scientific (connectionist and then enactive) methodologies by trying to evaluate exactly what each gains by such a confrontation. A comparative analysis of this kind will proceed in two steps: it will rely in the first instance upon a distinction that relates the two versions of constitution (static and genetic) to the two versions (connectionist and enactive) of the theory of emergence (point A); it will then go on to take account of a second distinction, this time internal to enaction and to the genetic method, which relies upon the differentiation of the genetic method into genesis and generativity, and so raises, for enactive emergentism, a question concerning the possibility of casting light upon the phenomenologically generative dimension (point B).

Let us run the risk of applying the following analogy: *The static method is to connectionism what the genetic method is to enaction.*

In the same way that the connectivist theory stands opposed to an explanatory model of the physicalist and mechanist type (computationalism) (Dupuy 1994: 84–91, 121–27; Varela 1989/1996: 39), so the theory of constitution reacts against an objectivist type of interpretation (sensualism), which would admit the possibility of the existence (transcendent exteriority) of the object or of nature independent of consciousness (*Ideen* I, §76, p. 174).

"The point of view of function is the central point of view of phenomenology" Husserl affirms at §86 of *Ideen* I.[21] But "functional problems" concern the "*constitution of conscious objectivities.*" More exactly, constitution designates the noetic moment of lived experience in which the noetic moment animates the matter of sensation, that is, confers upon it a meaning (*Sinngebung*),[22] which establishes the objective unity as a noematic unity correlative to the noesis. Constitution is that function proper to consciousness which enables it to bring to light the object as a unity of meaning. So it conceals within itself an internal noetic functionality (a meaning), which distinguishes it from any nonstructured combination,[23] and which features as that on the basis of which an objective unity becomes possible as a result of a concordant synthesis of the lived experiences themselves. Any instantaneous and isolated lived experience (hyletic, for example) is thereby subordinated to the synthetic and constitutive noetic totality that is intentional consciousness. So it is the links, or noetic connections (*Zusammenhänge*), internal to (and which make up) consciousness which furnish the constitutive principles for the objective correlates.

The first formulation of emergence as connectionism makes use of the notion of a network in the sense of internal functional relations among the neurons themselves. Thus a certain number of features confirm the functional analysis of constitutive consciousness: (1) the emphasis placed upon internal elucidation and so against any purely external determination; (2) the attention to regulated synthesis, which makes of the whole (consciousness) a dimension that is not reducible to the parts (the matter of sensation/neurons); and (3) the understanding of this synthesis in terms of cognitive connections/noetic links.

One non-negligible point still makes it possible to anticipate a possible bone of contention: while the noeses function in such a way as to animate their sensible materials, the cognitive processes emerge spontaneously from the local connectivity of the neurons. In other words, between constitutive phenomenology and the connectionist hypothesis there is a difference which amounts to nothing less than the significant difference between an involutive transcendental method and an evolutive immanentist method.

But the concept of constitution which we have made use of up till now obviously arises out of a static determination of the phenomenological method, a method which can be understood in terms of three principal traits: (1) *Fundierung* (founding), (2) *Schichtung* (level theory), and (3) *Objek-*

tivierung (objectification). As has been said, founding is not *Begründung* in the sense of a rational, substantial foundation; it simply indicates that there is a datum and that there are acts which are said to be primary because they appear first, and this on account of our sensible constitution, namely, the perceptual act correlated with what is perceived. The other acts are then called secondary, or founded, because their very manifestation presupposes the former (this is the case with memory, imagination, even empathy). This determination of *Fundierung* is laid out as early as *Logische Untersuchungen* and, in the end, it legitimizes what appears, as is the case for example with the intuitive categorial act founded in the individual sensible act (*LU* II/2, §48). The second trait, the stratification by layers, is the salient characteristic of the static method. It is illustrated in an exemplary manner in *Ideen* II, which proceeds toward the constitution of reality by distinguishing different layers, the primary (natural, sensible matter), the secondary (the psyche), and the tertiary (the world of spirit). As for the third trait, objectification, it fulfills the very meaning of constitution as the giving of meaning to an object (*Ideen* I, §117, p. 290; *Ideen* II, §4). With static constitution we are therefore dealing with a process of knowledge which meets the requirements of that which appears to consciousness and which differentiates the levels (the layers) upon which objects are given to consciousness by examining them individually. *Leib* is not reducible to *Körper*, even though it can only appear on the basis of the latter; the *Lebenswelt* is not reducible to the individual psyche, even though it can only make itself known on the basis of the latter. From this point of view, the emergentist hypothesis also attests to this dual trait, the justification of what appears to consciousness and the irreducibility of the conscious level with regard to the neuronal base. Now for the bone of contention mentioned above. To what extent does genetic constitution reduce this fundamental divergence? In what sense does the acceptance of emergence as enaction result in a dissolution of this difference of points of view?

First of all, we should bear in mind that just as the specific point of view of enactive emergence, as the incarnate engagement of an individual taking action in the context of his life, cannot be abstracted from the spontaneous production of a globally unified consciousness on the basis of an interconnected network regulated by the local properties of neurons, so genetic constitution cannot, without undue risk, be freed from its dependence upon static constitution. Not only does it borrow from the latter its structural rules (which are the rules governing any description based upon intuitive givenness and which prevent the analysis from lapsing into an arbitrary construction), but the adoption of this procedure ensures that the concern with immanent lived experiences themselves (rather than with objects or even with acts alone) can only make sense with reference to the appearing of these lived experiences upon a statically constituted plane. In other words, drawing attention to the way the lived experiences are engendered (temporally and associatively) finds support in the objective unities constituted through these lived experiences in as much as the latter support the dynamic of the constitutive process itself.[24]

2.3. GENETIC DYNAMICS AS A METHOD

Let us now turn to a second analogy, this time an incomplete analogy: *Genesis stands in the same relation to emergence (both connectionist and enactive) as does generativity to a new form of enaction which has yet to be defined.*

> In the sensible sphere, in the sphere of the underlying, which has to be conceived in the broadest fashion, we have associations, residuals [*Perseverationen*], determining tendencies [*Tendenzen*], etc. These "make up" the constitution of nature but their role extends much further, given that the constitution of nature exists for spirits too: the entire life of spirit is traversed by the "blind" efficacy [*Wirksamkeit*] of associations, of impulses [*Trieben*], of affects [*Gefühlen*] as excitations [*Reizen*] and as the determining sources for impulses, of tendencies emerging [*auftauchenden*] from obscurity etc., which determine the further course of consciousness in accordance with "blind" rules. (*Ideen* II, pp. 276–77)

Unlike static constitution, genetic constitution is passive. The immediate result of this is that, while justifying its structuring of appearance in terms borrowed from the static approach, it transposes the analysis to the level of the corporeal rootedness of consciousness, that is, to a sensible, practical and pre-predicative level. Such a transposition from the level of the functionally formal to that of the genetically material cannot but affect the legitimacy of the analysis itself. First, the object in its mode of appearing is no longer the same; it is no longer primarily a matter of the objectifying intentional consciousness actively subordinating the hyletic to the noetic but of a passive consciousness which is at one and the same time both hyletic and kinesthetic. In other words, the act has been displaced and resituated on the immanental plane of lived experience. Second, though based on static laws governing appearances, the method of access to this new object must adopt alternative methodological resources that are not reducible to the these static laws. Contrary to static constitution with its successive layers governed by the order of appearances, a progressive method, genetic constitution adopts a regressive or inverted route which de-sediments or dismantles our spontaneous intentional relation to the object with a view to discovering and bringing back to life the immanent lived experience that was its initial impulse. To capture the lived thrust of this act, which is originally of a bodily order and so has to be located beyond the intentional act itself, it is important to disclose the passive foundation of all activity.[25] While carrying over from static constitution the phenomenological gesture of *Fundierung*, genetic constitution digs beneath the noetic-noematic correlation to bring out the corporeal motivation of our acts. So genetic constitution thematizes the constitutive impulse itself, to wit, the *hylē* as a lived experience originally articulated in kinesthesia. In this bringing to light of the dynamic by which our acts are engendered, a central place must be accorded, evidently, to (1) temporal synthesis and (2) associative synthesis in the form of originally immanental links with the sensible corporeal impulsion (cf. Depraz 1995a, chap. 5).

Now, our interest in the dynamic of emergence, even the emergence of consciousness on the basis of neuronal properties, leads us to note, straight off, the parallel that can be seen to exist between the latter and genetic constitution: First, emergence as genesis also lays claim to the passive character of the dynamic in question; consciousness is born spontaneously from local connections, it arises of its own accord, passively, out of sensibly motivating impulses. Second, both processes take on an *immanentist* character, in the sense that consciousness engenders itself as a passive associative synthesis of acts resonating (*Resonanz*) with each other and coupled (*Paarung*)[26] with each other by virtue of the fact that they grow up out of syntheses that were originally temporal syntheses of immanent lived experiences or, taking as our point of departure more local neuronal connections, which cooperate in accordance with a structural linkage and so continually "resonate" among themselves (cf. Varela 1995). And third, their method is regressive in that it is directed toward bringing to light the elementary neuronal cells, the primordial sensible data, in their originally *synthetic* dynamic (cf. Varela 1989/1996). The initial bone of contention seems to have been absorbed or, at least, to have been shared. The genetic path is now defined uncontroversially as an immanentist and evolutive method that upholds (as does emergentism) the irreducible transcendence of consciousness with reference to the sensorial material or the neuronal cells.[27] At this stage, the opposition between immanence and transcendence proves sufficiently artificial for it to be possible to employ Husserl's (non-dual) oxymoron "immanent transcendence."

One basic problem, briefly mentioned above, still remains, a problem that touches the nerve (or the heart) of the confrontation in question: genetic phenomenology can be defined as a "transcendental empiricism" to the extent that consciousness is reproduced in the context of its sensible genesis (cf. Depraz 1998). Nevertheless, the rooting of any phenomenal consciousness in the bodily experience of sensation remains accessible to perception, even to each person's sensational perception. We can feel our bodies move, our eyes see, our ears hear, our noses smell, we can feel ourselves tasting. Our corporeal sensibility participates in this becoming-conscious which is a form of consciousness appropriate to that subjective access to it which each of us can enjoy (cf. Merleau-Ponty 1962 and Barbaras 1996). The question that neuronal emergence poses for the phenomenologist is that, raised early on, of the rupture, of the discontinuity at the very least, which exists between an analysis of subjective feeling (ordinarily dealt with by psychology), and a neurobiological analysis that is, on a priori grounds, inaccessible to perception, and even to sensation. Starting from these premises, a first series of questions can be proposed (from the standpoint of the object): how can there be anything like the phenomenologically modified reproduction of a datum if there can be neither perception nor sensation of this datum? If this genesis of consciousness can effectively be described as an emergence, the question that has still not been answered is that of the *basis* on which such an emergence arises: the genetic constitution of consciousness is a *self-*constitution; which means that the sensible substrate is from the first converted into a lived linkage stuffed with ideality. Can the same be said of cerebral traces? At what cost could they too become the object of an originally ideal conversion? In other words, whereas the immanent genesis of consciousness is transcendental, to what extent can emergence enjoy a status other than that of empirical immanentism? Another series of questions can be raised in the following manner (from the side of consciousness): What sense does it make to talk of a neurobiological correlate if the relation of correlation is not phenomenological, that is, cannot function as such because it cannot be perceived? To reply to this last question, we need to think about a phenomenological categorization that allows for a corresponding modification (mutation?) of the mode of perception. By employing the latter to thematize a "hyper-aesthesia" we are able to gain access to the microkinesthetic and microtemporal levels of the neuronal resonance itself and so to render intelligible this "empirical" level on a phenomenological plane. In other words, only a phenomenologically refined approach could claim to phenomenologize the cerebral traces themselves by introducing the required originary kinesthetic schema.[28]

Hitherto, the genetic approach has been envisaged as a means of elucidating the temporal and associative self-producing and self-engendering character of the hyletic and kinesthetic experiences of an incarnate individual (*leibliches Individuum*); in the same way, the theory of emergence (including the enactive) brings out the importance of the dynamic of the self-development of the living organism by stressing its ontogenesis. Both insist upon (1) the individual and its mode of individuation, (2) its autonomy, and (3) the always available possibility of an evolution of the radically new on the basis of the known.[29]

Genetic phenomenology also covers a multitude of questions that, in biology, stem from philogenesis and which, in philosophy, concern the community and history. Consequently, it would be appropriate to take advantage of its bifid character: (1) the genetic approach is essentially that of *Leib* as incarnate individual psyche (the so-called approach of psychology); and (2) the generative approach is that of the *Lebenswelt* as the practical, historical, and commonly shared world of everyday life (which legitimizes such disciplines as sociology, ethnology, and anthropology).[30]

The principal characteristic of the generative approach is to situate the correlation no longer at the individual level, whether this be qua noetico-noematic consciousness or again qua hyletico-kinesthetic flesh, but *between* the individual and the world. The genetic correlation of the two a prioris represented by subjectivity and world is therefore the primordial law of that generativity at work in *Krisis*, which latter stands opposed to any residual foundational justification (even one linked to the appearing) and situates intersubjectivity at the very heart of the said correlation (*Krisis*, §§46–48; *ZPI* II, suppl. 12, 13, 14). To talk of a universal a priori of correlation does not mean that one term of the correlation is symmetrical with the other, or worse, can be substituted for the other. If the natural world can provide a motivational guideline for consciousness, this is because the latter still is meaning giving. Each term of the correlation preserves its specific functionality. By the same token, to bring to light the "co-emergence of the system of autonomous unities and the world" (Varela 1979: 224) is to avoid, at one and the same time, representational objectivism and solipsistic subjectivism. Does this mean maintaining a radical asymmetry between consciousness and the world?

The radical conversion of representation into action proposed by the "enactive program" (Varela et al. 1991: 23) runs right along with the idea of a co-emergence of the living organism and the world and seems to respond thematically to generative analysis. Two correlated—but distinct—features result from this: (1) the cognitive processes of an individual are not formal but incarnate, that is to say, they are deployed in an environment or in a context which creates a relation of interdependence (Steels and Brooks 1995); and (2) an intrinsic characteristic of the living is that it should evolve, not in accordance with some "optimum adaptation" of a voluntary kind, but "following its course" or again, in accordance with a natural process of derivation marked by an indelible passivity (Varela et al. 1991). These two features evidently cover the intersubjectively generative approach: (1) individual subjectivity is from the outset intersubjectivity, originally engaged with, and altered by others (cf. Depraz 1995a: sec. 2); and (2) the individual is born, dies, evolves, is constantly changing and, at the same time, perpetuates itself in generations to come.[31]

However, generative phenomenology opens up on a double horizon, originally communitarian and historical, while enactive emergentism remains centered around an individual and his ontogenetic history. If genetic constitution can avail itself of both the connectivist and enactive options of emergence, generativity, in the final analysis, discloses a phenomenological dimension to which, up till now, the cognitive sciences, even when nourished by the evolutionist scheme, have not enjoyed the right to appeal.

> The philosophy of life which sees the light here has been developed in opposition to any residual neo-romantic vitalism, for it immediately assumes the form of a "scientific philosophy of life" . . . so the fundamental character of phenomenology is that of a scientific philosophy of life; a science which does not subscribe to the presuppositions, and is not established on the basis of pregiven sciences, but a radical science which takes for its original scientific theme concrete, universal life and its life world, the surrounding world which is effectively concrete.[32]

To found the positive sciences in a radical way by means of an acquired scientific radicality or even an original scientificity since a priori nonpositivist, such is the project which Husserl lays out from 1927 on and which will culminate in (or get lost in) the investigation around *Krisis*.

Henceforward, the question that has to be raised, quite simply, is the following: could a "biological phenomenology" (Varela 1979: 62, 72) or a "neuro-psycho-(evolutionary)-phenomenology" (Varela 1996) meet the requirements of scientific radicality that preoccupied Husserl at the end of the 1920s? Certainly not alone. With reference to other cognitive theories, the theory of emergence in its incarnate version seems to be the most free from any reductionist risk. However, its residual reductionism is the very risk that dynamism bears within itself just as soon as it assumes evolutionary form, that is, the form of a controversial pan-biologism. The Husserlian philosophy of life presented a parallel risk in its day, a risk that could equally be called reductionist. Although he rejects romantic neo-vitalism, it is questionable whether Husserl does not fall back into a subtle form of spiritualism which makes of spirit (*Geist*) the ultimate determination of transcendental philosophy.[33]

A common risk therefore plagues both genetic phenomenology and the theory of incarnate emergence; a subtle (neo-Leibnizian) form of vitalism which can deviate either into neo-Darwinian biologism or into theological gnostic spiritualism. It only remains—by no means an easy task—to establish the ontology (the metaphysics) compatible with the most acute phenomenological insight, an ontology which can be used to reject both (more subtly) reductionist tendencies by exhibiting their fundamental nonduality.[34]

Appendix

NATURALISM AND ITS CLOSE RELATIONS

Naturalism, in the sense in which Husserl understands it, seems at first to be nothing more than one of those many residual tendencies all of which converge in the overlooking of the act in favor of the object and, more exactly, in the analysis of an act that borrows its modes of determination from the object. So Husserl criticizes tendencies rather than positions and what, in the end characterizes these tendencies is their naïveté. If we had to bring them all under one rubric, we might talk of a "naive attitude" as that paradigmatic attitude which completely undermines the act.[35] This is no doubt why naturalism is more than just one tendency among others, more, for example, than this ultimately naive tendency addressed in *Krisis*: it establishes closer links with the natural/naive attitude than the other tendencies, links which rely upon the natural basis they share, but which go further than anything that can be captured by the etymology alone.

The aim of this analysis of naive tendencies is to demonstrate the peculiarities of each in accordance with two parameters: (1) historical, (2) conceptual. Not all of these tendencies can be evaluated accordingly. Psychologism and empiricism are very localized in time and result in a confrontation between contestants who are in every instance quite easily identifiable. Objectivism and naturalism, on the other hand, cover much more extensive ground, and the critique of these tendencies becomes all the more ambiguous the further it is extended. Finally, realism is distinctive in that it is now a matter of a critique of Husserl's *idealist position* and not a criticism of Husserl as such. This last tendency finishes up by bringing to light the ambivalence of the Husserlian critique of antiphenomenological tendencies. So a carefully differentiated examination of all the forms of the naive attitude proves to be necessary if naturalism is to be correctly situated, and if it is to retain the status accorded to it in the Husserlian frame of reference.

PSYCHOLOGISM

As a mathematician formed in the Weierstrass school and as the inheritor of the logical requirements of Friedrich Albert Lange and of Bernhard Bolzano (*LU* I, appendix, p. 226), Husserl, from the very beginning of his *Logische Untersuchungen*, is committed to the necessity of pure logic as the only philosophically scientific discipline. Its principal task consists in an elucidation of the primitive concepts that make possible an organization of the fundamental connections and an elaboration of the laws of thought on this basis (§§67 and 68). Accordingly, the rigor of logical apriority, implicit in the primacy accorded to categorial ideality, is ranged against two other conceptions of logic (powerful at the time), the techno-logical and the psycho-logical. One turns logic into a normative and practical discipline (§§4–16), the other makes the logical laws of thought depend upon the natural psychological structure (*grosso modo* causal) of the subject, that is, by reducing logic to "natural laws" (§§17–20; for the expression, §19, p. 67). Although they are both in agreement in giving up the purity of logic (contaminated downstream by the normative-practical and upstream by the psychological-natural), it is obvious that psychologism is the subtler enemy for Husserl to the extent that psychology claims to offer a theoretical foundation for normative technology itself.[36]

The psychologists' argument,[37] massive but decisive, can be summed up in one phrase: any working out of logical concepts presupposes "functions or psychic products" that are the constitutive properties of the latter. In other words, a psychological dimension is inherent in the very concepts constitutive of logical laws (*LU* I, §18). The counterarguments to this strong thesis root logic in the ethics of a thinking regulated by the normality of correctness and coherence. Laws are logical just as soon as they are "normal." This is just another way of depriving logic of its purity, which depends exclusively on the truth content of propositions. Psychologists could also quite easily point out that the study of normative laws is only a particular case of the study of "natural laws," a field of investigation logicians are ready to relegate to them.[38]

Seeking to follow the path of the "happy medium" by being equally dismissive of psychologism and of normative logic, Husserl concedes, on the one hand, that "psychology does also contribute to the foundation of logic" but, for all that, neither alone nor in any privileged way, and, on the other hand, that "the most important contribution to the truth is to be found on the anti-psychologistic side" (*LU* I, §20, p. 70). In order to do full justice to the truthfulness of pure logic, a critical analysis of psychologism and its consequences (both near and remote) is required. But the first consequence Husserl draws from the psychologistic position is its empiricism (§§21–29). Henceforward, it can be said that the role of psychology as a possible theoretical foundation for the initial development of pure logic should be limited to a radical examination of the empiricist attitude as such. From an epistemological issue concerning the constitution of a discipline, we pass progressively to a fundamental inquiry into its factual status, a process that culminates in the second logical investigation, which is devoted specifically to historical empiricism.

It is evident, in this respect, that the critiques of psychologism and of empiricism imply each other. If the immediate consequence of psychologism is empiricism, the first implication of empiricism is the "psychological hypostasis of the general" (*LU* II, Second Investigation, §7, p. 127). In addition, the slightly more derivative consequences of psychologism, namely, skepticism and relativism, are, to a large extent, equally contained in empiricism (*LU* I, §§41–51; *LU* II/1, Second Investigation, §§38–39 [Hume]). Over and beyond the controversy (whether conjectural or structural) with psychologistic logicians, what is ultimately at stake is the determination of the status of factuality in its relation to categorial ideality. By defining psychology, from the time of the first book of the *Logische Untersuchungen* on, as "a science of facts" equipped with laws that are vague (*vage*) rather than exact (*exakt*) and which are in fact no more than generalizations from experience, generalizations that, in consequence, cannot lay claim to the apodicity of logical evidence (*Evidenz*) (*LU* I, §21). Husserl exacerbates a tension between matters of fact and ideal categories, a tension that will in turn lead to a punctilious examination (throughout the entire length of the second logical investigation) of the logic immanent in the empiricist attitude as such. What is developed in outline from this time on is the very possibility of eidetics as a categorization that is indifferent—because autonomous—to the facts, while at the same time still taking them as exemplary guidelines.

EMPIRICISM[39]

Far from finding its measure in the later, transcendental determination, the Husserlian critique of empiricism, from this second logical investigation on, ranges itself against the specific *abstraction* that, in one form or another, inhabits the infatuation with factual realm. What is meant here by "abstraction"? In the first place, and in a quite general way, a paradox: the investigation of the most concrete element often ends up with an abstraction, or again, the attempt to grasp what is simple can give rise to indefinitely many sophistications. Further, contrary to the gesture which abstracts (*ab-s-trahere*), that is, literally, which draws out of, which cuts up and detaches, which produces partial elements external to each other and as it were juxtaposed to one another, the phenomenologist is concerned with connectedness (*Zusammenhang*), and with the internal links (*Verbindung*) that bind fact and lived experience, and lived experiences among themselves. The focus of the critique can be most clearly expressed as follows: the unilateral attention devoted to the material fact, to the datum of sensation, results in its being cut off from consciousness and in its being situated outside the latter. The result is an atomization of thought, which thereafter, and quite naturally, seeks to fill the vacuum it has itself succeeded in creating by some form of associationism.

What is at stake in the demarcation of phenomenology and empiricism is decisive: to constitute an eidetics on the basis of a comprehension of the kind (*Spezies*) as a concrete unity. A stake of some consequence, since it is the scientificity of the newborn science of phenomenology which is in question. Any response to this question must measure up to the criteria of that pure logic which is founded in categorial ideality even while rooting itself in a study of singular lived experiences, which constitute the object of this new science, if indeed it has one. In fact, the often-noted paradox is that after having dismissed psychology for its inadequately a priori character,[40] Husserl is brought to found his science on a sort of psychology, albeit a new, because eidetic, science of lived experiences.[41] Whence the care he takes to study the so-called "theories of abstraction" in relation to the "ideal unity of the kind."

The important point is in the end located in this distinction between two notions of *abstraction* to which attention is already drawn as early as the second logical investigation (see *LU* II/1, Second Investigation, p. 112). Phenomenological abstraction seeks to grasp the unity of identity, also called specific unity,[42] right up to the appearance of the individual object, which is not itself apprehended directly, even if it appears across the apprehension of the specific. The latter is a mode of consciousness distinct from the mode of consciousness involved in the perception of an individual object. By contrast, abstraction "in the improper meaning of that word" refers back to empirical psychology, which proceeds by a generalization of the act aimed at the particular object and without distinguishing between two types of act. The bringing to light of the act in *Spezie* is basically a first formulation of the act of eidetic variation, other traces of which are also to be found throughout the first chapter of the second logical investigation and which will be formalized in the sixth (*LU* II/1, Second Investigation, §§1–2; *LU* II/2, Sixth Investigation, §26).

At this stage, the demarcation between empirical generalization and eidetic variation is that of *distinct* methods of access to the concretely general. Over and above this point in common with empiricism (which, however, does not see in the apprehension of the general an act of consciousness *sui generis* and so distinct from the act by which the factual individual is apprehended), the critique becomes more precise. Lockean abstraction involves the separation and then the re-joining of what has been separated in accordance with the laws of resemblance and connection (*LU* II/1, Second Investigation, §§9–10); nominalist abstraction, developed in reaction to Lockean generalization and attributed to Mill, is exclusively the work of attention (*LU* II/1, Second Investigation, §§13, 15, 18); Humeian abstraction, finally, emerges as an induction nourished by custom, and sedimented in belief, in accordance with a process that exhibits a sort of genesis, one that Husserl here places out of bounds because this genesis is not rooted in a descriptive analytics governed by an awareness of the act character of consciousness (*LU* II/1, Second investigation, §§32–35, esp. pp. 194–96).

REALISM

While the first two antiphenomenological attitudes mentioned above are rejected by Husserl in the name of the ideality first of the category, then, of a consciousness conceived as a linked connection of acts, realism refers to a first, massively critical reaction against a phenomenology that, in the mean time, was set up, in 1913, as a "transcendental idealism." Is it now Husserl who is guilty of naïveté? What are the arguments advanced by the realists and who are they?

Much has been written on this idealist "turn" on the part of phenomenology, which for many, amounts to a transcendental departure relative to the "metaphysically neutral" project of the *Logische Untersuchungen*.[43] However, the author of *Ideas* himself sought, in *Krisis*, to place the "Cartesian" presentation of the transcendental reduction in the perspective of an abrupt leap to the reduced ego, the first result of which was to deny, purely and simply, the very world, which nevertheless functions first as a sort of springboard, and then as a guideline (*Krisis*, §43). Moreover, as we have seen, idealism does not mean a metaphysical doctrine but a theory of knowledge which posits ideality (the category) as the condition of the possibility of knowledge. In this respect, categorial becomes a first name for transcendental, this last phenomenological qualification, from 1905–7, having the merit of bringing to light the constitutional dynamic of reduced objectivity, which as we have seen, replaces a more Kantian conception set out in terms of conditions of the possibility.

But the realist critique concerns the existential status of the object and, more importantly, of the world. The realists, in the first instance Roman Ingarden,[44] defend the idea that the real external world enjoys an ontological existence totally independent of the position and the apprehension of any subject whatsoever. The Husserlian definition of the thing as noematic correlate and its intentional dependence with regard to constituting consciousness makes up the core of the realist objection, which argues on the contrary for the self-sufficiency (*Selbständigkeit*) of the object (cf. Kalinowski 1992: 57–58). Starting out in 1913 from a healthy distinction between real being (*real*) and pure consciousness, Husserl produces an ontological idealism that reduces the thing to a noematic consciousness. Ingarden condemns Husserl for his flagrant naïveté, the very naïveté of which the latter accused the empiricist in a different context. The question is: how to do justice to the in-itself of nature in the framework of a constitutive phenomenology? Although in *Der Streit um die Existenz der Welt*, Ingarden unfolds the possibility of a transcendental realism where the fact of the existence of the world cohabits with a pure consciousness (cf. Ingarden 1964–65, pt. 2, §77), he does not proceed any further with the development of just such a possibility.

Besides, from the time of the Introduction to the second edition of *Logische Untersuchungen*, Husserl insisted on the distinction between a description of "external events in Nature" situated on the same plane as the psychological description of internal experience and a phenomenological description that excludes the possibility of passing judgment on lived experiences belonging to empirical persons (*LU* I, p. xiii). Only the lived experience in its ideality (later to become the mode of givenness of the object to consciousness) interests phenomenology, not the psychological experience, still less the real (*real*) experience of nature. Psychic and natural reality are here both dismissed as counterparts of each other. The stake is high, since it is the reduction itself, this neutralization (correctly understood as non-negating) of the real existence of the object (and of the world) with a view to disclosing the appearing to consciousness, that is endangered by the realist critique.

With realism, phenomenology no longer appears in the guise of a critique but of that which is *criticized*. Husserl therefore finds himself obliged to make his own positions clearer, notably, by explicating the eidetic and transcendental structure of the appearing to consciousness of an object.

OBJECTIVISM

Starting from when, as a result of having set itself up as an idealism, phenomenology becomes in turn the object of a massive critique by the realists, Husserl tendentiously makes ever more extensive use of his critique of antiphenomenological attitudes, all of which get brought under the term "objectivism." Yet again, and in the same words, we come across the central point of the principal argument: to apply to conscious acts, determinations which are derived from the transcendent real object. While the technical texts (*Logische Untersuchungen*, *Ideen* I) made only limited use of these terms and carefully targeted their critique, objectivism is deployed as a bulwark against any philosophical conception deemed nonphenomenological.

The objectivist attitude is especially called in question in the context of a rereading of the history of philosophy, to which Husserl proceeds (rather somewhat belatedly, it is true) on two occasions, to wit, in *First Philosophy* (*Erste Philosophie*) in 1923–24 and in *Krisis*. The first attempt to establish a historical perspective rejoins many points raised in the critique of the second logical investigation. Nevertheless, it is now objectivism that provides the general rubric alongside, indeed taking over from, the term "dogmatism."[45] The generalization of the critique signifies in a rather ambiguous way both radicalization (in the sense that Husserl braces himself against any tendency to weaken the import of the reduction) and attenuation, because the all-out critique is lacking in sharpness. But it also contains a certain contraction, the search for a way of saving at all costs a now-endangered transcendental idealism.[46] This last tendency of attenuation is accentuated in *Krisis* to the extent that it is applied to the risks internal to phenomenology. Husserl traces its origin back to "the modern opposition between physicalist objectivism and transcendental subjectivism," dismissing both these two attitudes with reference to the naive dualism to which they both subscribe. Objectivism and transcendentalism are the two sides of the same coin (*Krisis*, §14). In this regard, Descartes is presented as the inaugural figure who casts his stamp upon the dual and oppositional regime in which all of later philosophy is balanced—between objectivism and subjectivism (§§18, 19, 21). With this fourth tendency a threshold is crossed. The naïveté in question does not arise simply from a unilateral direction of attention toward the object rather than toward conscious acts, but from the duality of the attitude itself, a duality that integrates both poles (object/act) in a common unilaterality.

CHAPTER EIGHTEEN

Sense and Continuum in Husserl

JEAN-MICHEL SALANSKIS

I would like to begin with a few words concerning the context of this attempt at a return to Husserl for a new understanding of his so singular undertaking.

On the one hand, recent developments in cognitive modeling point, so it would seem, to the possibility of grounding in psychoneurological nature the canonical functions described by Husserl as regulative of perception and thought: the perspective of a naturalization of Husserlian phenomenology seems sufficiently open for the question of its legitimacy to become pertinent.

On the other hand—the stakes here are from my vantage no less important—the dominant reading and understanding of Husserlian philosophy seems susceptible at the present time to a profound reworking, owing to a favorable conjunction placing us, at least in France, between two closures: that of Heidegger's interpretation of Husserl, which is still dominant even though it may be judged to be declining, and that of its logico-analytical interpretation, no doubt young and ambitious, but as yet still uncertain of its triumph.

I shall in fact attempt to propose a relationship to Husserl that avoids these two interpretative paradigms and, on this basis, to determine my own way of handling the question of naturalization. I thus expect to be able to reveal the resistance of Husserlian phenomenology to naturalization as something other than a purely formal resistance, or a strict question of principle and position of discourse.

The general key to my treatment of these subjects is given in the title of this essay: I shall attempt, in a reconstruction of the Husserlian message, to emphasize the two themes or motifs of *sense* and *continuum*. Husserlian transcendentalism should be understood as the philosophy describing how sense relates itself to a given continuum, and the confrontation with its putative "naturalization" should take place within this precise figure.

I would also like to indicate briefly the method I will be following: it is an interpretative one. I let the texts speak for themselves, and then attempt to extract the concepts I need. Whence the repeated use of quotations, which allow the reader to share, as it were, my intellectual situation (and on occasion to criticize it).

I come now to the first stage of these analyses, to the theme of the continuum.

1. THE PRIMORDIAL MONADIC FLUX

Husserl actually states, quite often and in a variety of ways, that the field that he is interested in, that he invents and opens up for us, can first of all be described as a *continuous multiplicity*.

He says as much in his canonical expositions of phenomenology. Thus we have in the second meditation of the *Cartesian Meditations* (from which the following passage is taken) Husserl's description of "the transcendental field of experience and its general structures":

> At first, to be sure, the possibility of a pure phenomenology of consciousness seems highly questionable, since the realm of phenomena of consciousness is so truly the realm of a *Heraclitean flux*. It would in fact be hopeless to attempt to proceed here with such methods of concept and judgment formation as are standard in the Objective sciences. The attempt to determine a process of consciousness as an identical object, on the basis of experience, in the same fashion as a natural object—ultimately then with the ideal presumption of a possible explication into identical elements, which might be apprehended by means of fixed concepts—would indeed be folly. Processes of consciousness—not merely owing to our imperfect ability to know objects of that kind, but a priori—have no ultimate elements or relationships, fit for subsumption under the idea of objects determinable by fixed concepts and therefore such that, in their case, it would be rational to set ourselves the task of an approximative determination guided by fixed concepts. In spite of that, however, the idea of an intentional analysis is legitimate, since, in the flux of intentional synthesis (which creates unity in all consciousness and which, noetically and noematically, constitutes unity of objective sense), *an essentially necessary conformity to type* prevails and *can be apprehended in strict concepts*. (CM, §20, trans. D. Cairns, p. 49)

This text in fact tells us that the field of consciousness is the Heraclitean flux and expresses in its own terms its nondiscrete nature ("Processes of consciousness ... have no ultimate elements or relationships, fit for subsumption under the idea of objects determinable by fixed concepts"). The text poses as the problem of phenomenology the success of an *intentional analysis* capable of extracting from this flux a noematically describable element, itself the result of an intentional integration of the flux.

One can also refer to the manner these matters are expressed in *Ideen* I. From §27 to §34, Husserl expounds the *épochè*, the bracketing of natural validations, and ends up isolating the "essence of consciousness" as his theme of research. The field of investigation is clearly the flux of mental processes considered in its proper closure, and the essence aimed for must be attained from within the continuum of this flux:

> We consider mental processes of consciousness *in the entire fullness of the concreteness* within which they present themselves in their concrete context—*the stream of mental processes*—and which, by virtue of their own essence, they combine to make up. It then becomes evident that every mental process belonging to the stream which can be reached by our reflective regard has *an essence of its own* which can be seized upon intuitively, a "content" which allows of being considered *by itself in its ownness*. (Ideen I, §34, trans. F. Kersten, pp. 68–69)

But, as we know, the conquest of this essence is destined to be the work of the method of eidetic variation. Now Husserl, having defined it at §70—in a definition referring notably to the geometer's access to essences imputed by him to the spatial continuum[1]—sets out the problem of principle concerning the possibility of such a conquest of descriptions in the flux of mental processes in §§71–73. We know that his conclusion is that such a description is not only possible but necessary. But despite his propensity to use the geometrical analogy, Husserl affirms that phenomenology cannot be a geometry of mental processes, that it cannot assure in the mathematical mode its relationship to flowing (*fluence*) from which all its givens are originally taken. This flowing is nonetheless again brought to the fore, and vigorously:

> It is peculiar to consciousness of whatever sort that it fluctuates in flowing away in various dimensions in such a manner that there can be no speaking of a conceptually exact fixing of any eidetic concreta or of any of their immediately constitutive moments. (*Ideen* I, §75, Kersten trans., p. 168)

This flowing affects in particular—and this is of the utmost importance for the descriptions undertaken by Husserl—the type of singularity which is phenomenology's affair, that is, the type of *singularity in the continuum*:

> Then the phenomenologically single example (the eidetic singularity) is that physical thing—phantasy in the entire fulness of its concretion precisely as it flows smoothly in the flux of mental processes, precisely the determinateness and indeterminateness with which it makes its physical thing appear now from one side and now from another, precisely in the distinctness or blurriness, in the vacillating clarity and intermittent obscurity, etc., which are indeed proper to it. (Ibid.)

But the clearest text on the subject of the function and status of the originary continuum of the flux is perhaps a passage from *Ideen* II, from which we may glean precious information on the nature of this *datum* and its relation to reduction.

At §20 Husserl in effect introduces the fundamental concept of the *monadic flux of mental processes* as an unsurpassable primitive:

> As the image, *stream of lived experience* (or stream of consciousness), already indicates, the lived experiences, that is, the sensations, perceptions, rememberings, feelings, affects, etc. *are not given to us in experience as annexes, lacking internal connection, of material Bodies*, as if they were unified with one another only through the common phenomenal link to the Body. Instead, *they are one by means of their very essence*; they are bound and interwoven together, they flow into one another in layers that are possible only in this unity of a stream. (*Ideen* II, §20, trans. R. Rojcewicz and A. Schuwer, p. 98)

The context of this passage is that of an effort to isolate the region of the psychic: we are, then, as it were, right in the middle of the debate with psychology and the naturalistic approach to the psyche and to the human in general. On the one hand, Husserl defines psychology as the science taking into account human "states of consciousness" in their overlapping with a body; it seems that for Husserl there can be no speaking of a dualistic/separate theory of the soul.[2] But on the other hand, and this is what the above quotation says, Husserl clearly discerns an internal coherence of the mental process independent of the corporeal substrate. This is the coherence of the flux. In light of everything preceding this, it is therefore the internal coherence of the monadic flux which bestows to phenomenology, at one and the same time, its authorizing principle and its element. All seizing upon essences or the foundation of objects is effected in terms of the experiential-evidential given of the flux and its coherence; the continuum of the flux is what allows one mental process to relate to another, what legitimates and facilitates the autonomous investigation into the secondary structurations of the flux.

My view is that what these texts all say is simply that the monadic flux of mental processes survives phenomenological reduction, is indeed the residue par excellence of what is called reduction, *epochē*, the break with the natural attitude. It is more frequently said that this residue is consciousness, the mental process as such, the pure Ego, the *cogito* or the transcendental *Ego*, to name several familiar terms. But actually we touch here on the *leitmotiv* of the Heideggerian reading of Husserl (which we mentioned above): a reading which doggedly points to the fact that Husserlian phenomenology is an "egology," following the term used by Husserl himself in the *Cartesian Meditations*. The major merit of Heidegger's thought would be to have proceeded to the destruction of the subjective agency; the central fault of Husserl's intentional analyses would be, symmetrically with Heidegger's merit, to have grounded everything in the *ego*. Regardless of whether these judgments are founded or attestable, it is important not to be misled by terms such as *lived experience* or *Ego* while forgetting the monadic flux, which is the only unavoidable *datum* from which all else derives. The immanence from whose vantage Husserl envisages the constitution of transcendences is that of the flux. It happens that the pure Ego is presented by Husserl as a structure picked out of the flux following the method of eidetic variation.[3] *Egology* constitutes, to be sure, one level of Husserlian thought, but I wonder whether it should not be seen more radically and more essentially as a *continuum-ology*.

If this primordial continuum of the flux is stressed, then two essential points have to be explained: what is the relationship of this bestowal with, on the one hand, the theoretical construction of the mathematical continuum and, on the other, with the phenomenology of time?

Let us begin with an answer to the second question. Husserl says again and again, even when time is absent from the phenomenological analyses he presents, that all syntheses are first of all temporal ones, that indeed, they are syntheses only insofar as within them, first of all, time comes to be.[4] The little book *On the Phenomenology of the Consciousness of Internal Time*, written quite early in Husserl's career and never taken up again afterward, thus retains for the rest of Husserl's work the value of a guiding presupposition and teaching.

If one recalls what this text says, the flux is clearly time or rather, time is the self-appearance of the flux. The flux generates intentionality, which Husserl ends up considering as either longitudinal intentionality or transverse intentionality. The former is the fundamental intentional phenomenon of the passage of time: the infinitesimal renewal of the field of mental process on its edge is experienced in a constant structure, that of a diagram of time, and this constancy witnesses a dimension of temporality. As for transverse intentionality, it is, in substance, the same intentionality, but with an "extra" element, the transcendent aim necessary for the constitution of temporal objects. In a well-known passage, Husserl insists on the fact that longitudinal intentionality constitutes time in a relation of self to self of the flux, and on the fact that the complex appearance of time takes place in one and the same flux, a simultaneously constituting and constituted flux:

> The flow of the consciousness that constitutes immanent time not only *exists* but is so remarkable and yet intelligibly fashioned that a self-appearance of the flow necessarily exists in it, and therefore the flow itself must necessarily be apprehensible in the flowing. The self-appearance of the flow does not require a second flow; on the contrary, it constitutes itself as a phenomenon in itself. (*PZB*, §39, trans. J. B. Brough, p. 88)

What to my mind should be retained here is that the fundamental phenomenological fact of the flux, the self-coherence proper to the mental process and named by the word *continuum*, is also what phenomenological description gives as the constituting synthesis of time. It is as a system of mental processes having their own link in the flux—a link defining the region of consciousness—that the flux harbors the synthesis of time, longitudinal intentionality raising the monadic coherence of the flux to the dignity of the phenomenological *continuum* of time.

The other question, the first one, concerns the link of this phenomenological continuum of time with the mathematical continuum, and in fact, more precisely, with the mathematical object **R**, the Cantor-Dedekind model, whose theoretical synthesis is in part contemporaneous with Husserl's work.

It must first be said that the indexation of the *Lectures* on the mathematical continuum is evident.

This is witnessed not only by diagrammatization as such, insofar as it returns to common intuition of continuous geometrical space in order to attest processes of temporalization, but also by the fact that Husserl describes the originary spatial field as a "two-fold continuous multiplicity" (*PZB*, Brough trans., p. 5), and recapitulates the originary temporal field as prescribed by the diagram in analogous terms: "Each of these temporal modifications is a non-self-sufficient limit in a *continuum*. And this *continuum* has the character of a 'rectilinear' multiplicity limited on one side" (ibid., p. 105).

The terminology of *multiplicity*, which Husserl, in *Formal and Transcendental Logic* (§30), refers explicitly to Riemann, points toward the dawning idea of *sets*; that is, a manifold which can be structured at will, and which is tantamount to the only possible basis for the continuum and for space.

Into the bargain Husserl conceives, as it were, continuous variation or the course of the continuum as its genesis: the continuum is something that engenders itself in conformity with continuity all along its linearity. This aspect of things disappears in set-theoretical modelization, but remains a potent motivation, referring us notably to the infinitesimal relation to the continuum, which, as we know, preexists (and post-exists as well) modern theorizations. Witness the following passage:

> It is inherent in the essence of every linear continuum that, starting from any point whatsoever, we can think of every other point as continuously produced from it; and every continuous production is a production by means of continuous iteration. We can indeed divide each interval *in infinitum* and, in the case of each division, think of the later point of the division as produced mediately through the earlier points; and thus any point whatsoever is finally produced through a division of infinitely many intensifications (each of which is the same infinitely small intensification). (*PZB*, Brough trans., p. 107)

What is said here is said simultaneously of the phenomenological and mathematical continuum—they are considered from the same vantage: Husserl generally thinks the continuum, as it were, *between* the infinitesimal conception, with the paradoxical notion of infinitist addition of infinitely small segments, or the notion of "continuous iteration," and the modern set-theoretical conception called into play if we are to take the word *multiplicity* seriously. It seems to me of the utmost importance to understand that Husserl does not philosophize on the continuum in an intellectual realm alien to mathematics, but rather seeks to think time from out of an informal frequentation of the mathematical continuum.[5]

2. SENSE AND SENSE BESTOWAL

The second aspect of Husserl's thought, which seems to me essential to the new discussion we are seeking to have with one another, is the notion of sense accomplishment. This notion is normally attributed, in the writings of Husserl's maturity, to the transcendental subject supposed to be subjacent to the reality effect as a whole; better and more to the point, to the effect of opposition face to face—the effect of intentionality itself. It is in the name of this sense accomplishment that Husserl is a transcendentalist, and, by the same token, hostile to any naturalistic conception. It seems then clear that if something must in all urgency be studied with the ends of the present debate in view, it is the Husserlian notion of sense accomplishment.

I would like to begin with the scathing criticism of the Husserlian idea of *Sinngebung* by Vincent Descombes in his *Grammaire d'objects en tout genre*.[6] His criticism places us from the word go at the heart of our problem. Descombes begins by extracting from the Husserlian problematic a conception of *sense* indexed on the aim awaiting its fulfillment. Husserl would call "the sense of a mental act its object" (Descombes 1983: 61) and would envisage a relationship of *convocation* of phenomenal presence by the intention of signification, a relationship which would be the life of sense: "For Husserl the intention to signify remains empty as long as the object is not itself present, as long as it persists in its remoteness. What a strange doctrine of the name inevitably suggesting an affinity between nomination and the call or invocation!" (p. 62).

Descombes then quotes the passage from *Ideen* I in which Husserl describes the principled fixity of the transcendent object "beyond" the continuous variation of its noematic predicates; and declaring that nothing can guarantee, at the level of a noematic account of experience, this invariance and this identity, he comes up with the idea that "intentional sense" is nothing but the sense of the object as the immediate, nonproblematic counterpart of all living actuality of consciousness. Descombes thus can consider that the Husserlian refusal to take into account criteria of identification controlling the referentiality of sentences leads him to consider sense as the very singularity of experiences:

> To *ascribe sense* is ordinarily said of the assignment of a sign hitherto available for a particular use. Or again this is said of the decision to complete a fragment of language with a context given to it in order to understand it. The phenomenologist does not say that we ascribe sense in one or the other of these two ways (to ascribe sense to a sign or to interpret a fragment of discourse). He calls *sense* that which distinguishes one lived experience from another. (Ibid., p. 68)

This immediately issues in the following criticism:

> Why is the difference between one experience (for example, seeing Venice) and another (imagining Venice) that between the sense of the former and the sense of the latter, if not because it is the difference between the sense of the enunciation which will narrate one and the sense of the enunciation which will narrate the other? But in this case the actual given is not a group of lived states, but a group of ways of speaking. (Ibid.)

We have here the basic elements of the dispute on intentional sense to which we are convened by the analytical reading of the Husserlian apparatus of noetico-noematic structures. We shall return to this debate, but let us begin by taking several bearings on the Husserlian conception of sense. Fundamentally, Descombes's critical reading rests on a definition and irrevocable identification of sense with "the sense of the sentence" (later, in the space of analytical philosophy, this sense-of-the-sentence is analyzed in terms of *truth conditions* or *assertability conditions* or some other variant, but what in any case is clear is that the question is one of conditions of validity in the most general sense, and even if the multifarious effects of context are taken into account through a *pragmatic* perspective, as it has ended up becoming). Hence the problem is knowing whether or not, as Descombes would suggest, Husserl is caught, regardless of what he says or wants, in the sentential referential of sense.

The first text of import on this subject is a passage from *Formal and Transcendental Logic* in which Husserl explicitly speaks of *objectivities of sense*. The context is a discussion of the function of the logical moment in scientific activity, a function defined as that of a *critical mediation*. The exposition of the logical forms of scientific discourse allows that which is intended in them to be seized upon, therefore allowing the verification of this discourse through a confrontation with what can be attested with evidence:

> In this connexion the following is to be noted. Scientific judging indeed forsakes the naïvely straightforward cognitional directedness to objective actualities that come from the naïve having of them themselves in straightforward evidence, and *continually makes the judgments thematic*, the supposed objectivities as supposed. Consequently it always terminates in propositions for which the attached predicate "correct" or "true" has been originally acquired and established—even though, as present throughout all the theoretical results, it may usually remain unexpressed. But it is obvious, on the other hand, that this procedure is subservient to determining the province itself, and that therefore *the judged propositions are only intermediary themes*. (FTL, §46, trans. D. Cairns, p. 129)

But this also means that the logical criticism of scientific discourse is the resumption of the latter under the horizon of sense, or its submission to the perspective of sense. The region of sense is in fact defined by Husserl, in sum, as that of the *reflection of intentionality*:

> It is precisely for this reason that we speak of different regions within the formal all-embracing region, "any objectivity whatever." All upper-level suppositions surely belong themselves to the region of suppositions, of "*opinions*" or "*meanings*." Instead of saying meaning, we may say *sense*; and, taking statements as our starting point, we may speak of their *significations*. To ask about the signification or sense of a statement and make its sense distinct to ourselves is manifestly to go over, from the straightforward stating-and-judging attitude in which we "have" only the pertinent objects, into the reflective attitude, the attitude in which the corresponding object-meanings and predicatively formed affair-complex-meanings become seized upon or posited. Hence we may *designate this region also as the region of senses*. (FTL, §48, Cairns trans., pp. 132–33)

From here, Husserl comes to name *sense* all intentional objectities as such. There is in fact a tension underlying this definition, between its side of sense objectivation (the intentional entities are entities of sense) and the side of the subjectivation or pragmatization of sense, the side on which sense is defined by the "asking oneself the question of sense" which is immediately the same thing as a reflection, hence a referral back to the egological agency.

On the other hand, it must be conceded that in this passage as well as in the book as a whole, the problematic is one of a fundamental distinction between predication and object or the distinction between enunciation and fulfilling intuition; in other words a problematic in fact extremely close to that of analytical thought: on this point Descombes's commentary, along with others, is on the mark.

However in this same passage, sense is not purely and simply that which points from the enunciation to its possible fulfillment, as Descombes would have it and as he says. Sense is also in radical solidarity with the reflexive redoubling of intention and something different again, which is the *question of sense*, the question of the *clarification* and *verification* motivating this redoubling.

Leaping now to the other end of Husserl's path of thought, let us see how the problem of the restitution of the sense of science is posed in *The Origin of Geometry*.

The most striking passage is certainly the following: "History is from the start nothing other than the vital movement of the co-existence and the interweaving [*des Miteinander und Ineinander*] of original formations of sense (*Sinnbildung*) and its sedimentations" (*Origin of Geometry*, trans. D. Carr, p. 174; trans. slightly modified). The passage seems in effect to relate sense to the collective action of history by humanity. But in fact the duality of the formulations *Sinnbildung* and sense sedimentation creates a problem. Sense sedimentation, following the context, is the historical play of its propositional reinscription, issuing in its written recording, which justifies the loss of contact with the originary evidence. Is it the same sense that is sedimented-betrayed from the moment of origin and which is seen formed (*gebildet*) in the intersubjective current of humanity? Originary sense undergoing sedimentation is still, it would seem, the intentioned as such, reported to a moment at once lived and reflected in which the adequation between aim and fulfillment should have prevailed. On the other hand, it seems that *Sinnbildung* must designate the active side of sense, not only sense as recorded meaning, but sense as acted upon and formed: it is this sense whose production "should" coincide with the movement of human history, and hence reside in the human "in-between" rather than stem from a singular intentional consciousness and its reflection.

This text actually sets up two dimensions in signification and its transmission, whose status raises a problem with regard to this alternative. Logical inference is, it seems, at once the way of sedimentation and the archaeological path of the restitution of sense. On the one hand, logical form is the form par excellence of sedimentation, and logical inference hence presupposes sedimentation—is borne by it. On the other hand, logical inference ensures the presence of sedimented sense in what it draws out of that sense by way of consequence, and through this dynamic function participates in sense as *Sinnbildung*:

> Through this activity, now, further activities become possible—self-evident constructions [*Bildungen*] of new judgments on the basis of those already valid for us. This is the peculiar feature of logical thinking and of its purely logical self-evidences. . . .

> Accordingly it appears that, beginning with the primal self-evidences, the original genuineness must propagate itself through the chain of logical inference, no matter how long it is. However, if we consider the obvious finitude of the individual and even the social capacity to transform the logical chains of centuries, truly in the unity of one accomplishment, into originally genuine chains of self-evidence, we notice that the [above] law contains within itself an idealization: namely, the removal of limits from our capacity, in a certain sense its infinitization. (*Origin of Geometry*, Carr trans., pp. 167–68, 168)

Logical complexity is therefore the path of a complexification-sedimentation of sense that is at one and the same time its loss and dissemination. Sense in the strong acceptation of the term can only maintain itself under the hypothesis of an infinitization of our capacity of reconstruction (after *analysis*). But from another angle, Husserl also presupposes a reception of sense as logical concatenation which is *passive comprehension*: "Passivity in general is the realm of things that are bound together and melt into one another associatively, when all meaning that arises is put together [*Zusammenbildung*] passively" (ibid., p. 165).

But this passive comprehension is not reactivation of sense: for Husserl sense is present only when the accomplishment of the aim of the logical formation and the fulfillment of constituting intentions are presently lived, adding up in a phenomenological evidence.

Hence this theory as such of sense in history, of the traditionalization of sense, curiously does not necessarily contradict the intentional theory of sense (sense as the egological internalization of the aim's adequation). This theory acknowledges a traditional (*traditionale*) *Sinnbildung* only to report it to the operations of logic, and the possibility of the appropriation of sedimented sense to a capacity of infinite logical analysis and synthesis on the one hand, and to a insufficient nonconscious pre-treatment of the logical complexity on the other.

But let us try to take this a step further and to get over the difficulties we will meet by considering at this point what is most essential: sense accomplishment in the constitution of noematic structures. Thus shall we begin to articulate our section on the continuum with the section on sense.

In §85 of *Ideen* I Husserl introduces the key conception, the one commanding the whole exposition of noetico-noematic structures, that of the oppositive distinction between sensuous *hylē* and intentional *morphē*.

The sensuous *hylē* is the ensemble of the flux of mental processes considered as primary contents, divested of sense and aim, reduced to their participation in the coherence (temporal coherence in the final analysis) of the flux. The intentional *morphē* is the adjoining of form that erects the unitary object from out of this sensuous *hylē*. Noeses bring on form. It is owing to them that new entities arise in addition to hyletic reality: noemas, non-real components of consciousness, simple intentional correlates (*Ideen* I, §85, Kersten trans., p. 203 and pp. 213–14).

If the dispersion of the *hylē* is taken seriously, as the fundamental continuous dispersion of consciousness, of the flux, it will then be asked what this noetic function can indeed be, which produces along this dispersion and within it stable units. It is described by Husserl as follows:

1. As form-bestowing (intentional *morphē*).
2. As animation: "Whether everywhere and necessarily such sensuous mental processes in the stream of mental processes bear some 'animating construing' or other (with all the characteristics which this, in turn, demands and makes possible), whether, as we also say, they always have *intentive functions*, is not to be decided here" (ibid., p. 204).
3. As the establishment of a *functional* coherence (cf. again the preceding quotation).
4. As *predelineation* [*prescription*]: "Of essential necessity the consideration turns to the multiplicities of consciousness [*Bewußtseinsmannigfaltigkeiten*], predelineated, so to speak, in or, as it were, extracted from, the mental processes themselves, their noeses of whatever sort" (p. 208).

   The French translation gives "prescription" instead of the English "predelineated" for the original German "vorgezeichneten." The German original reads as follows: "Die Betrachtung wendet sich den wesenmäßig in den Erlebnissen selbst, in ihren Sinngebungen, in ihren Noesen überhaupt gleichsam vorgezeichneten, gleichsam aus ihren herauszuholenden Bewußtseinsmannigfaltigkeiten zu" (*Ideen* I, §86, p. 213). The idea is that phenomenological insight looks at the Erlebnisse as predelineated, by what is simultaneously called "Noesen" and "Sinngebungen" (which has been purely and simply omitted in the English translation): it is clear in this context that this predelineation has nothing to do with passive prediction, but is giving the rule, thereby justifying the French translation.
5. As sense bestowal (cf. the preceding quotation, and the original German).

   But this character of sense bestowal of the noeses is at one and the same time recapitulation, the complete expression of what noetic apprehensions of the *hylē* are: the acquisition of sense is the acquisition of the noema, and all the aspects or terms which I have selected describe this very thing. Now, in justifying his recourse to the Greek *nous* to name the noetic function, Husserl is sufficiently clear on the fact that for him the *nous* is the locus of sense, inseparable from the idea of norm:

These noeses make up what is specific to *nous in the broadest sense of the word*; it refers us back, according to all its actional life-forms, to cogitationes [*sic*] and then to any intentive mental processes whatever, and as a result comprises everything (and essentially only that) which is the *eidetic presupposition of the idea of the norm*. At the same time, it is not unwelcome that the word, *noûs*, recalls one of its distinctive significations, namely precisely "*sense*" [*Sinn*]. (*Ideen* I, §85, Kersten trans., p. 205)

From out of this partial evocation of the texts, I would like to isolate three levels or three aspects of the philosophical comprehension of sense offered by Husserl:

1. Sense is for Husserl the intentional aim. But this said, sense as aim is caught up in a sort of resonance to such an extent that sense is first of all the aim of noemas, then, second, these noemas themselves as "objective" guidelines for the modalization of intention (this is what justifies the comparison with Frege), and third, the arrow pointing to the transcendent thing beyond all noema ("The noema in itself has an objective relation and, more particularly, by virtue of its own "sense"; ibid., p. 308).

2. Sense bestowal occurs in the continuous element and consists in its *functional integration* of animation, bestowal of form, and elaboration internal to the flux of a stability relentlessly updated according to the temporal variable. What is in question here and which Husserl describes countless times can only be understood and thought in relation to the mathematical concept of integration, which is, moreover (on this point I am pleased to recall that Jean Petitot says the same thing), already the crux of the theory of the constitution of time. Sense is bestowed whenever a temporally distributed system of dependencies between mental processes or clusters comes to an equilibrium in a form that, if it will haunt a linear continuum, must nevertheless be conceived as an actual morphological form, analogous to, for example, a disk or a planar surface.

3. From another point of view, however, Husserl remains within the ethico-idealist tradition for which sense is that which makes sense and is valid, that is to say, for which sense cannot be envisaged correctly outside the normative sphere or the prescriptive register. Sense bestowal is also that which manifests itself in the executory character of prescriptions relating to an organization of mental processes, that which establishes a norm or witnesses to it.

Such would be the syncretistic concept of sense bestowal for Husserl: the erection of an aim, the information-integration of the continuum, the repercussion of a prescription, the issuing of a norm.

Let us note too that phenomenology is transcendental because its concept of sense is pregnant with all this. The forms it delineates are delineated as the forms of sense bestowal, which is prescription on a backdrop of a horizon totalizing the possible (the flux). Husserl moreover quite clearly says as much:

> In its purely eidetic attitude "excluding" every sort of transcendence, on its own peculiar basis of pure consciousness, phenomenology necessarily arrives

at this entire complex of *transcendental problems in the specific sense*, and *on that account* deserves the name of *transcendental phenomenology*. On its own peculiar basis phenomenology must come to consider mental processes not as any sort of dead fact such as "content-complexes" which merely exist without signifying anything, without meaning anything; nor should it consider them only with respect to elements, complexes of constructions. (*Ideen* I, §86, Kersten trans., p. 209)

Not to consider mental processes as "any sort of dead fact" is to welcome, hear, and understand sense bestowal. And this is the very thing that *transcendental* phenomenology does.

Perhaps now we can reflect on the naturalization of Husserlian descriptions.

3. IS THERE A NATURALISTIC INTERPRETATION OF SENSE BESTOWAL?

The cognitive sciences are usually defined as an undertaking in the naturalization of the mind. This said, the mind is not something perfectly constituted as a scientific object or even as an object of experience. This is why the naturalization project presents itself more willingly and more easily, at the outset, as an attempt to naturalize such and such a type of behavior, the passage to the concept of *behavior* allowing precisely the recuperation of fragments of nature at the points of mental input and output, in order to render accessible and apprehensible what is to be naturalized. Furthermore, as we know, this naturalization project cannot be separated from the intention of *simulation*, which is sometimes altogether different, and which could ultimately be taken as *alien* to the enterprise of a scientific explanation of thought. It is in fact at the same time a project of *artificialization* as much as one of *naturalization*, without this duality ever posing a problem—which in itself can be judged bizarre.

That said, if the expression *naturalization of the mind*, or any other analogous expressions, such as the naturalization of perception, deduction, intelligence, or generally of one or another type of behavior, can be understood at all, the concept of a naturalization of epistemology or phenomenology, to consider only what Quine and Petitot have bequeathed to us on the subject, creates more unavoidable problems. What can the ushering back to nature of a historically attested activity of the mind possibly mean? Are we implicitly required to consider the "life of science" as a type of behavior, to take it for a black box whose inputs and outputs will have to be theorized?

As concerns epistemology, Quine has proposed an answer: naturalized epistemology is a discourse of cognitive psychology aiming at scientificity and replacing philosophical discourse, which establishes the norms of form and truth. It is then perfectly clear, in this case, that naturalized epistemology renders classical foundational epistemology null and void. The whole problem for Quine is how to explain how the naturalistic description of knowledge-oriented behavior can still be an epistemology in any acceptable sense of the term.

Concerning naturalized phenomenology, Jean Petitot's position is of a different nature: for him, it is never a question of negating the non-naturalistic character of the phenomenological attitude; the question is one of proposing a scientific counterpart to the descriptions given by Husserl of psychic life. A counterpart which on principle would in no respect be an implicit criticism of the phenomenological project, but which would occupy, unequivocally, another place.

My question is, then, simply put, the following: up to what point is it possible to recover the aforementioned Husserlian analyses, which are analyses showing how sense accomplishment founds such and such a type of givens, in order to present them as the matrixes of the scientific description of the *fact* of psychic functioning subjacent to such and such a type of behavior?

My thesis is that this recuperation, if it succeeds in that which cannot fail to be sought after, is necessarily a naturalization of the bestowal of sense. And this new agency of naturalization opens up a new kind of philosophical questioning.

In what case, in effect, is the scientific counterpart the right one? In the case in which it manifests not only a contingent concordance with the Husserlian description, when it does not limit itself to a simple arrangement of components in analogical relation to those of the Husserlian description. This is to say that it must be supposed that the form imposed by the counterpart on the elements it calls into play is the very form described by Husserl. But in Husserl, as we have seen, the synthesis of this form is, in one of its aspects, sense bestowal itself.

Naturalization thus necessarily relies on what was above named *functional integration*, one of the aspects of sense for Husserl. Naturalization obligatorily refers to a continuous *hylē*, as the residue of phenomenological reduction, having therefore a value of fact, and it attempts to specify the geometrical type of intentional *morphē*, given that the animation accomplishing this *morphē* is also the advent of sense.

Yves-Marie Visetti has often insisted that in order to carry out naturalization, this geometrical identification of the intentional *morphē* must be extended by imputing the obtained geometrical entities or configurations to some biological real and, simultaneously, knowing how to illustrate what is said to be the process of sense bestowal by means of an apparatus which behaves in a *totally effective* way: this is certainly true in the simulationist perspective, but even purely cognitive attestation—hence, here, neuro-scientific attestation—of the intentional *morphē* demands that the descriptive discourse be convertible into a system of verification enclosing the theoretical contents of the science called up, a system which must be radically effective. Science is a description inseparable from a totally public *praxis*, from a transparent *technē*.

The philosophical heart of the problem seems to me to lie in geometrization itself. It is undeniable that if Husserl were truly to theorize intentionality as a property of sentences, as Descombes and other readers of Husserl claim, then the geometrization of his descriptions would not be possible, sense bestowal would remain outside the range of all naturalization for reasons Hilary Putnam has finally explained. But there is in Husserl this other side to his theory of sense which relates the event to the synthesis of a form in the continuum, to the functional aggregation of a manifold stemming from the Heraclitean flux. And this is what justifies and, to a large extent, makes the proposed naturalization a pertinent undertaking.

It seems to me possible, nonetheless, to indicate what, in the Husserlian apparatus, "collapses" in such a resumption.

On the one hand, the continuous *hylē* undergoes a change in value. This is simply the result of parameterization by real numbers (or by complex entities derived from **R**): the Heraclitean flux is the residue of reductions insofar as the flux is the coherence proper to the mental processes, their endogenous way of referring to each other. **R**, as the a priori framing of all possible flowing away, of all attribution of possible properties to the flux, projects into exteriority this intimate-temporal coherence that can only be experienced, it makes it into an object of contemplation and submits it to a controlling structure. This was already Kant's problem in the *Anfangsgründe*, the transposition into internal sense of the fundamental approach of externalist science: all such transposition seems to belie the interiority of time, of the soul; it seems especially to forget the constantly and constitutively destroyed and lost character of temporal cohesion. Husserl's diagram of time is a partly metaphorical description of the infinitesimal play of this loss, and it is noteworthy that in the *Lectures on the Phenomenology of the Consciousness of Internal Time* he avoids the task of thinking a *global* model of primordial time constituted in and by the self-appearance of the flux.

On the other hand, the link between sense bestowal and the rule disappears. With Husserl, the configurations of the intentional *morphē* are always at the same time modes of noetic action reflected by the Ego as prescriptions, and in this sense they are described as controlling access to such and such a type of given. In naturalization, but even in geometrization already, the forms are communicated in standard, third-person form, and protected from all redundancy with the intimate experience of the rule. In completely opposite fashion, in the Husserlian transcendental apparatus, I am supposed to be able to "know" the law governing my intentional formations only in reflexive repetition of sense bestowal, a repetition within which the exemplary value of the form is lived.

This last remark says exactly to what extent a naturalization of sense bestowal is possible: it is possible, but only insofar as sense bestowal as the affecting of the Ego by the rule is obliterated. Another way of presenting the problem is by questioning the *fact* value of noesis: can the noema be "non-real" without the noesis becoming non-real in turn? The naturalization project would seize upon the noesis in a legitimate structure in adequation with reality. There is already an ancient ontological difficulty with classifying the geometrical form as real. But the noesis is always this form as the advent-of-the-rule, a form invested with the jurisprudential weight that is the heart of the Husserlian transcendental aim: how then, despite the fact of its being an attested activity, will it be made real?

The foregoing discussion proves that the force, originality, and grandeur of the Husserlian conception of sense lies in its three-fold character. We may not be able to think and correctly understand how sense bestowal can be simultaneously fulfillment of representational expectation (no doubt obligatorily sentential in the final analysis), synthesis of the intentional *morphē* in the continuum, and reflective repercussion of the norm. But by setting us the task of thinking this three-fold character, Husserl sets us more radically down a path of a philosophy of sense than the other philosophers of this century, who have generally glorified themselves by eliminating two of these aspects in favor of the third.

Analytical philosophy registers the first and third aspects, but proceeds to a thoroughgoing and systematic omission of the second: from the very beginning of analytical philosophy, sense—starting with Frege—is referred to the intentionality of sentences, problematized in its relation to the institution of a norm with Wittgenstein, for example, and these two aspects are relentlessly taken up again by the various masters of this school of thought. The idea of a synthesis of the *morphē* remains on the other hand inaccessible to the analytical option, for this would first require the recognition of the continuum, which is precisely what analytical philosophy wished to dispense with by means of an installation in the world of sentences (and in this respect, its rejection of Kantian epistemology proceeds from a similar gesture, one that eliminates the "metaphysics of the continuum" that the transcendental aesthetic is).

Heidegger's philosophy is fundamentally caught up in the same type of discretization. Sense, in *Sein und Zeit*, is described as the investment of a structure (that of *significance*) by a directionality which is that of transcendence, of the constituting project of *being-in the-world*. Significance is a discrete structure of relays which sets up the opening of a world. There is indeed a relationship between the effectuation of this structure and the advent of sense, but this relation is rather such that sense is first, and the articulation in the structure (at the level of what Heidegger calls *discourse* [*Rede*]), analogous to the synthesis of the *morphē* in Husserl, is second, responding to the name *signification*.[7] With Husserl, the synthesis of the *morphē* and the advent of sense seem absolutely one and the same occurrence. The third aspect of the Husserlian theory, the relation to the institution of the norm and its reflexive experience, seems to me totally forgotten by Heidegger. Because he would think only *necessity* and never obligation, or the rule, or jurisprudence. Here too, Heidegger's reading of Kant yields the same result: it will be recalled that in the *Kantbuch* Heidegger is intent on rejecting Kant's juridical language in the transcendental deduction of categories, and replaces the Kantian question ("By what right do the categories take up and connect sensible manifolds?") with an ontological question bearing on necessity ("What is the necessity of the respective being of the category and of intuition governing their speculative collaboration in experience?" Heidegger 1929, §18, trans. J. S. Churchill).

If the debate to which cognitive research has given rise could simply bring light onto this point, onto the precious and irreplaceable nature of Husserl's philosophy of sense, this would be reason enough for us to feel a good deal of gratitude toward it.

Translated by George Collins

CHAPTER NINETEEN

Cognitive Psychology and the Transcendental Theory of Knowledge

MARIA VILLELA-PETIT

Early in his philosophical life Husserl came to grips with psychology, both in the battle he led against psychologism and in his pursuit—following in Franz Brentano's wake—of a phenomenological investigation that did not at first succeed in escaping the framework of descriptive psychology. In the transcendental form it soon acquired, Husserl's phenomenology was to remain inwardly exercised by the problem of its difference from psychology, including the phenomenological psychology he himself had helped to fashion. Thus transcendental phenomenology underlines its difference from phenomenological psychology by what Husserl refers to as a *nuance*; a difference within the closest resemblance. Besides, this nuance is so critical for Husserl that he sees philosophers who have not mastered it as condemned to fail in their proper task. In this connection he speaks of "a twinning of difference and identity" (*Krisis*, §58, p. 209 [205]),[1] suggesting that the "transcendental reduction" plays the role of the law that, in view of their intimate kinship, prohibits the incest of philosophy and psychology—any psychology whatever.

We shall begin by attempting briefly to indicate why descriptive psychology, and still more every other kind of psychology, failed to satisfy Husserl, and how this dissatisfaction prompted him to undertake the transcendental reduction. Once we have clarified the meaning of that "reduction," we shall ask what relations are possible between a transcendental phenomenology and the current form of experimental psychology, which has abandoned behaviorism and put cognitive processes at the forefront of its inquiries. Our focus on cognitive psychology along with related disciplines, especially the neurosciences, which also claim the epithet "cognitive," will lead us (1) to ask about the possible meaning for phenomenology of a project of "naturalization"; and (2) to sketch the limits to the legitimacy of such a project from the standpoint of transcendental phenomenology.

1. THE FAILURE OF PSYCHOLOGY BEFORE THE ENIGMA OF COGNITION

In the antipsychologist argumentation of the first volume of *Logical Investigations* Husserl was concerned with the ideal character of logical formations and relations and rejected the idea that they could be simply derived from an empirical psychology. But despite his fight against psychologism, the phenomenology of the *Logical Investigations*, developed as a description of logical essences, ultimately failed to get beyond the sphere of a descriptive psychology. The unsatisfactory character of this situation soon became clear to him. A phenomenology that remained enclosed within the sphere of inner experience could never succeed in resolving *the enigma of cognition*[2] and by the same token it would fail to reach the *telos* of philosophy, that is, it would not become a rigorous and aprioristic science, capable of providing scientific knowledge with its "foundation." For though the motif of the correlational a priori between the object of experience and the modalities of its givenness first emerged in the *Logical Investigations*,[3] the phenomenology developed in that work was still too close to its roots in Brentano's thought to include in its realm, which Husserl defined as that of the internal, psychological experience, the transcendent object, namely, the object of the world in its reality, its objective exteriority. But it is this very objectivity which must be clarified. Still unequipped to do so, phenomenology implicitly confirmed the dualistic dissociation between a "real" object, on the one hand, and an intentional object, on the other, that is, between an object posited as really existing in the world known to physical science and the object as envisaged and grasped by natural conciousness through its perception, its imagination, and its memory. Thus stalled, the phenomenology of the *Investigations* was ultimately incapable of overcoming skepticism, in particular the Humeian type, and could not resolve what Husserl call in the *Krisis* the "enigma of enigmas" (*Rätsel aller Rätseln*), that of the connection between the knower and the known. Alluding to the limit of Kant's vision (and hence of his transcendentalism) that led him to postulate a noumenal thing-in-itself, Husserl refers to the enigma of "the deepest intrinsic link between reason and being in general" (*Krisis*, §5, p. 12 [13]).

Indeed Husserl frequently tells us, in *The Idea of Phenomenology*, as in the *Ideas* or in the *Cartesian Meditations*, that it was the problem of the transcendent object (the object posited in an exteriority to conciousness) and the connected problem of the objectivity of knowledge that prompted his transition (*Überleitung*) to a transcendental philosophy, though of a new type because truly phenomenological. In §40 of *Cartesian Meditations*, in a succinct comparative recapitulation of what distinguishes transcendental phenomenology from the Anglo-Saxon empiricist theory of knowledge, which had cast itself as a pendant to physical science in order to constitute a science of the psyche, a psychology, Husserl presents phenomenology as a *transcendental theory of knowledge* (CM, §40, p. 115 [Cairns trans., p. 81]). The upshot here is that, contrary to what traditional theories of knowledge allowed one to conceive, the philosophizing subject, once it has attained the attitude of transcendental reduction, now understands that it is the transcendent objects themselves, in the first place the objects of external perception, which demand to be understood as constituted by consciousness, as correlates of acts of consciousness which present them in both their primary qualities and their secondary ones (Villela-Petit 1996). In other words, the physical object is itself dependent on consciousness,[4] on its proper acts of constitution, which range from the grasp of the object in sensible experience on the basis of its passive pregivenness to the determination of the object in acts of theoretical objectification such as those of science.

I should now like to offer some insights about Husserl's understanding of psychology. In many of his references to psychology, what he has in mind above all is philosophical psychology, whether taking the form of a naturalist theory such as that of Locke or Mill or whether already acknowledging the intentional character of conciousness, as in Brentano's descriptive psychology. It was in relation to this philosophical psychology that Husserl sought to affirm the imperative necessity of the transcendental step, ignored by Descartes. This transcendental step allows us to differentiate effectively between the transcendental ego as subject for the world, the one for whom the world is the universal *phenomenon* on which its theoretic interest bears, and the empirical ego as a natural object of this same world (*Ideen* III, §3, p. 146 [*Nachwort*]).

However, his intellectual entourage, for instance his friendship with his Halle colleague Carl Stumpf, ensured that Husserl also took into consideration from early on the new experimental psychology and its claim to scientific status. As a matter of fact it is this experimental psychology that is the principal target of his criticism in a work closely preceding *Ideen* I, namely "Philosophy as a Rigorous Science" (hereafter cited as PsW). The phenomenological tradition has often neglected this work, not only because of its peremptory tone and maximalist claim, but more, perhaps, because besides its critique of scientism in it Husserl expressed a decisive refusal to dissociate philosophy from the general striving of reason for scientific knowledge.

Husserl's chief objection to experimental psychology as it presented itself around 1911 is at first sight a surprising one. He accuses it of remaining "pre-Galilean" (PsW, p. 31 [100]), despite its attempts to secure a solid foundation by drawing precisely on the scientific method on the model of the natural sciences, those sciences which emerged from the Galilean revolution. Husserl's point is that experimental psychology remains prescientific because of its incapacity to find a method adapted to the knowledge of psychic phenomena *as such*, and its consequent inability to form rigorous concepts: "Experimental psychology is a method of determining psycho-physical facts and norms, which may be valuable but which without a systematic inquiry of consciousness that explores the psychic in respect of what is immanent in it lack every possibility of becoming understood more deeply or utilized in an ultimately valid scientific manner" (p. 24 [93]).

Here Husserl highlights the difference in essence between psychical phenomena in their pure phenomenality precisely as lived, experienced phenomena and the natural domain of psychological or physiological fact; and at the same time, he ascribes to the phenomenological analysis of conciousness the task of elucidating the correlations established by experimental psychology. But he readily acknowledges that it is not easy to keep in view the difference at issue here, for "we do not easily overcome the inborn habit of living and thinking according to the naturalistic attitude, and thus of naturalistically adulterating the psychical" (PsW, p. 38 [109]).

That this question, which had already haunted William James, has lost none of its weight is amply demonstrated by the current psychological literature on the mind/brain problem.[5] The difficulties continually encountered in connection with this "problem" are due in large part to our persistence, not merely in the natural attitude common to all, but in the naturalistic attitude, which has been compelling since the advent of modern physical science. Here, the psychism is first envisaged, in dualistic perspective, as something *Reales*, in the sense of a "mental" substance or reality conceived on the model of the reality of the body. To surmount this dualism some philosophers attempt to reduce the mental to the cerebral, but this attempt betrays a naive scientism that ignores the ineluctable subjectivity of experience[6] and the fact the science itself is constructed "from a progressive architecture of activities" (*Krisis*, §34, p. 143 [131]) taking place in the intersubjective community of savants (not in some purely physical interaction of brains).

When Husserl deplores "the tragic failure of modern psychology" ["*das tragische Versagen der neuzeitlichen Psychologie*"] (ibid., §7, p. 17 [18]), he is referring to this triumph of physicalism in psychology, with the grave perils he senses it to entail on the ethical plane in that it implicitly reduces human beings to physical objects subject to manipulation. The failure is due to the incapacity of this psychology to acknowledge fully the field of consciousness, or in other words, the field of subjective experience. Is it not indeed this physicalism that is the principal manifestation of what in his last texts he designates and analyzes as "the crisis of the European sciences"?

In the period of "Philosophy as a Rigorous Science" he had already seen as closely connected the two issues that occupy us here, that of naturalization and that of the phenomenological status of psychophysiology. But before discussing this, we need to clarify what Husserl means by the transcendental reduction (*epochē*), in order to better understand his position as well as the decisive nuance which makes phenomenology a phenomenological philosophy and not simply a descriptive psychology of intentional experience. To bring out the significance of the reduction as a experience of thought, we turn, not to the early texts in which the necessity of effecting the transcendental reduction emerged, but to the later formulation of the sense of that reduction, especially as found in the texts of the *Krisis*, which give pride of place to the notion of subjective life.

2. THE MEANING OF THE *ĒPOCHĒ*

As an act of thought of the meditating subject, the reduction entails a change of attitude in the theoretic way of seeing. Habitually directed to the objective pole, and in the first place to that which is given on the soil and in the horizon of the life-world, in the transcendental attitude the philosopher's eye is required to attend to the cognitive operations or, in other words, to "go back to knowing subjectivity as the primal locus of all objective formations of sense and ontic validities" (*Krisis*, §27, p. 102 [99]).

In comparison with the natural attitude, which makes the world something absolute, as something independent of conciousness, the attitude that is also at the basis of scientific objectivism, "transcendentalism, to the contrary, says: The sense of being of the world given in advance in life is a subjective formation, it is the product of life in its experience, of pre-scientific life." This cognitive subjectivity—in the final analysis the transcendental intersubjectivity—"as the field where whatever has sense of being for us is constituted," is, according to Husserl, "the universal accomplishing life in which the world comes to be as existing for us constantly in flowing particularity, constantly *pregiven* to us" (*Krisis*, §38, p. 148 [145]). In summary, it is thanks to the operations or accomplishments of consciousness, of subjective life, and life within a community, that the world is constituted for each of us as the world valid for all. Transcendental consciousness thus ultimately demands to be understood as universal accomplishing life constituting the sense of all that is. That also includes the life of animals and is why

Husserl can declare about the transcendental problems that they "finally encompasses all living beings insofar as they have even indirectly but still verifiably, something like 'life,' and even communal life in the mental [*geistige*] sense" (*Krisis*, §55, p. 191 [187–88]). What this amounts to is that phenomenological philosophy is concerned with all living beings, not in the way the natural sciences are, but insofar as it envisages them as beings who can experience, though the meaning of "experience" in the case of living beings other than humans is only very indirectly accessible to us, and via a modification of the meaning we can give to experience in our own case.

These passages of the *Krisis* on the sense of the transcendental reduction highlight the specific status of life as both *locus* and *source* of all possible experience and, by the same token, of every world, beginning with the most elementary surrounding world (*Umwelt*). In short, it is only for a being capable of having experience that a world opens up, that *there is* world. At the same time, and without paradox, this world has for such a subject the sense of a world always already pregiven in advance, as the soil and horizon of the experience of which the subject is capable. A stone or a galaxy does not open any world. It is not for a stone that there is another stone; it is only for a living being that there can be stones or any such objects, in the horizon however narrow, of its surrounding world. One might also phrase it thus: it is because the living being is a "totality" connected but distinct from what is characterized as its "milieu" that it can grasp, apprehend, and in some cases transform what is given to it in its "milieu." This gap, which opens up in varying degrees the polarity of "consciousness / surrounding world," is necessarily presupposed by every orientation of the subject, indeed by all intentional life. In sum, life is here understood as the possibility for all that is physical *to appear*, to *appear to itself* (through life) and to *acquire sense*, a sense which is not or even *prima facie* of a linguistic order.

Let us confine our attention to humans as the only living beings for whom such transcendental questions can be reflexively posed, though they ultimately concern all animate beings, human or animal. With the change of attitude caused by the *épochē*, which discloses to analysis and philosophical clarification the field of subjectivity in its hidden accomplishing life, constitutive of the sense of all that is, the meditating ego ceases to have "theoretic validity as a human self," that is, it ceases theoretically to consider itself such. Husserl continues:

> I am no longer a real object within a world valid for me as existing, but I "am" only as I am posited as subject for that world, which itself is posited *as* that of which I am conscious in such or such a way, *as* appearing to me, believed, predicatively judged, valued by me in such or such a way; thus in such fashion that the certitude of its existence [*Seinsgewissheit*] itself belongs to the "phe-

nomenon," in the same way as other modes of my taking cognizance [*Bewußthabens*] and its "contents." (*Ideen* III, p. 146 [*Nachwort*])

Such is, for Husserl, the essential philosophical demarche which allows subjectivity, in its capacity for reflexive life, to know itself in the depth of its constituting and sense-granting life, and thereby to become co-responsible, with the other subjectivities whose lives are apprehended in its own, for the sense of the world, a sense forever open and by that very token forever threatened.

Without lingering on the axiological aspect of the transcendental demarche, let us now turn to what Husserl himself calls the parallelism of the psychological and the transcendental (not to be confused with the parallelism of the mind and the brain). We note first of all that in the discussion following the foregoing quotation on the loss of theoretical validity of the self as empirical self, a human self *in* the world, Husserl notices a to-and-fro between the psychological and the transcendental: "It is evident that despite the modification affecting the entire phenomenologico-psychological content of the psyche, it is precisely this content which becomes the phenomenologico-transcendental one, just as conversely the latter, by the return to the natural psychological attitude, becomes a psychological content once more" (*Ideen* III, p. 146 [*Nachwort*]).

This can only mean that the difference of attitude and the modification of sense effected by the *epochē* allow the identity of the content of consciousness to subsist nevertheless, this content being susceptible to analysis by a phenomenological psychology and by a transcendental phenomenology. But the content is now understood differently, receiving thereby a new sense. Thus, after *Krisis*, a pure psychology, which is what an authentically phenomenological psychology intent on describing the formations of consciousness ought to be, can only issue in a transcendental phenomenology, under pain of "a fatal separation" (*Krisis*, §57, p. 201 [198]). Why then maintain the distinction and, along with it, the parallelism? The answer, it seems to me, lies in the fact that conquest of the transcendental attitude, as a higher way of taking cognizance of the sense of life, does not exclude an ongoing possibility and duty of returning to the natural attitude, for every modification of sense and every cognitive attainment won in the transcendental attitude is bound to have an effect on the self-understanding of humans in the life-world.

3. TRANSCENDENTAL PHENOMENOLOGY AND NATURALIZATION

Whatever we make of certain passages in Husserl's final writings, which hint at a self-abolition of pure psychology within transcendental phenomenology, it remains necessary to deal with the issue of experimental psychology and along with it the question of a "naturalization" that would take account of the psychophysiological nature of humans. Note that Husserl not only acknowledges "the perfectly legitimate and quite indispensable psychophysical Empirie" (*Krisis*, §64, p. 255 [222]), but himself introduces the question of naturalization (and not merely to condemn it as a tragic deviation). In §8 of *Erfahrung und Urteil* we read:

> Everything that is of the world participates in nature. The naturalization of the mind is not a "trouvaille" of the philosophers—it is a fundamental error if it is wrongly interpreted and twisted from its significance, but only then. In fact it has its raison d'être and is justified in that, mediately or immediately, all that is real inasmuch as it is worldly has its place in the spatio-temporal sphere. (*EU*, §8, p. 29)

In other words, "all that is real inasmuch as it is worldly" belongs to nature. Similarly, but this time moving from the psychological to the transcendental, he says in *Krisis*: "As a human or a human soul I am first a theme for psychophysics and psychology; but then, in a higher, new dimension, I am a transcendental theme" (§58, p. 209 [205]). One gathers from this that though Husserl sees the naturalization of humans as a basic philosophical error and even a grave threat, it is nonetheless legitimate in the horizon of scientific knowledge insofar as the scientific study of human beings is methodologically obliged to objectify what phenomenology discloses as transcendental subjects and to consider them as actually belonging to nature. This need not at all entail a physicalist attitude (which is philosophical and not scientific), not to speak of a frankly eliminativist one, in the understanding of human-being.

Current psychology constructed according to the cognitivist paradigm entails an often explicit critique of the experimental psychology of the past, with its model of sense data imprinting themselves on a tabula rasa; such was the basis of behaviorism. This comes close to the phenomenological critique of that former model of psychic life, which was bound to miss the specific character of life once it approached the psyche in terms of the mechanistic schema of classical physical science. As the epithet "cognitive" suggests, the new experimental psychology, in a fair number of its representatives, not only rejects the reductionism of a causal explanation from the bottom up, stressing to the contrary the emergent properties of the brain, but it also seeks to acknowledge the causal role of the higher mental factors, as Roger Walcott Sperry asserts, after a significant turnabout, in his 1987 article "Consciousness and Causality" in *The Oxford Companion to the Mind*. William Hirst, likewise, refuses to consider consciousness as a reflection of the world or as a simple relay between stimuli and motor reactions (Hirst 1995).

While Sperry and other psychologists speak of a causal influence of the subjective or of the mind, Husserl reserves the term "causality" exclusively for strictly natural causality and prefers, for fundamental reasons, to speak of an efficacy of the mind, or even an "acting" (*wirken*), which is motivated and produces effects in the sphere of nature. But despite the difference of extension that each ascribes to the notion of "causality," both the psychologist (Sperry) and the philosopher (Husserl) fully acknowledge the efficacy of mind, whose status is no longer epiphenomenal.

Thus despite the inevitable conflict of a philosophical order that always divides its representatives, some of whom are still attached to reductionist positions, cognitive psychology aims at least to study the cognitive capacities and processes that animals and particularly humans are disposed to bring into play in order to treat the information incessantly furnished by the surrounding world and which is inherent and indispensable to life. It approaches in these terms visual, auditory, and even olfactory perception as well as the movements connected with them and which are at the basis of our actions. There is some affinity here with Husserl's focus on the "practice of life" (*Praxis des Lebens*) in the context of his reflections on the life-world (*Lebenswelt*). What should be stressed is that this environmental knowledge is inherent to human and animal living and not a secondary activity, as if knowledge came only subsequently to the subject of a world already there, already constituted, as was presupposed in classical empiricist theory. On the contrary, this knowledge concerns the very manner in which the objects are given, that is, the way they come to be and to be present for the perceiving subject, animal or human.

However, whereas Husserl deals with the "constitution" of the world by egological consciousness, a constitution by layers or strata which are to be analyzed and described, it can happen that naturalized psychology in its eagerness to explain cognitive processes, relying on the neurosciences, talks about the "construction" of reality and the world by the brain. The neuropsychologist Semir Zeki provocatively declares that reality is created by the brain. Ray Jackendoff, who interprets psychophysical functioning in terms of a computational model, uses the more holistic expression "the organism's construal of the world" (Jackendoff 1987: 139). In both phenomenology and cognitive psychology, it appears, the intrinsic interconnection of knower and known is recognized, despite all that separates phenomenological description from empirical research and the quest for explanatory models of mind.

Let us examine all this more closely, with a view to confronting certain findings of phenomenology with those of the cognitive sciences. Husserl tries to explicate the constitution of the world as a *phenomenon* for transcendental consciousness by a descriptive analytic of the transcendental field of subjective experience (such is the method of phenomenology). His resolve to be radical prompts him to start from the most originary layers of strata of this constitution, beginning with those involved in sense-experience and pointing even to the passive synthesis beneath them. Now all sense-experience refers as a matter of intrinsic necessity to an incarnate egological consciousness, an *Ich-Leib*. Thus, in perception, the "I," understood here exclusively as the perceiving pole, is intrinsically linked to the *Leib*, the organic body which as such is essentially kinesthetic (*Krisis*, §28, p. 109 [106]). But as Husserl observes in *Ideen* III, referring to sensations: "Consciousness is then given as what belongs to an animated body [*als einem Leib Zugehöriges*], whether by self-perception or by an interpreting perception" (*Ideen* III, §3, p. 14 [12]); the latter perception being that which allows us to perceive the other's body (*Körper*) as his *Leib*. This primary subjectification of the body is not proper to humans but can equally be attributed to animals, at least to the animals who have already reached the first stages of consciousness—something that can be decided only by research using empirical criteria, which are by definition hypothetical but which do not in any way undermine the a priori validity of phenomenological analysis.

What here matters is that the above-mentioned correlation between knower and known is seen as resting on the corporeal structure.[7] The very recognition of an *Ich-Leib*, that is, an incarnate egological consciousness, along with its identity with the *Körper*, the body in the world,[8] can only serve to legitimate naturalization, that is, the objective scientific examination of that which in the body as physical entity (*Körper*) functions as the "base" and the physical condition of perception as consciousness's act. In the forefront here is, of course, the brain, which reveals an extraordinary complexity in its activities even in simple vision or audition or the least volitional gesture. I shall return to this.

But first, a caution. The coincidence of *Leib* and *Körper* which allows us to identify my *Leib* with this *Körper* here, which can be objectified as a natural thing—inclusive of its hidden side, as when for example I submit to an examination by medical imagery—does not abolish the difference between the body as it is lived subjectively and the objectified body as it can be viewed by the neurosciences. The *Leib* itself, as Husserl notes, is already itself a "two-sided reality," one side turned to nature and having as physical base the corporeal in the sense of the *Körper*, the other expressive, significative, turned to the mind and to the world of interpersonal communication. All therapeutics should take account of this double aspect of the *Leib*, the subjectified body, when it deals with human beings, something that would no longer be the case if medical practice were to become entirely physicalist.

In the light of this "double face" (*Ideen* II, §62, p. 284) of the *Leib* and its formal distinction from the *Körper*, it becomes incongruous to say that it is the brain which constructs or creates the world (without of course violating physical laws). With the eyes of phenomenology one can detect a slippage of sense (and a vague use of metaphor) when the neurological researcher investigating a natural object, the brain, according to a certain logos or rationality—and whose work entails a high degree of objectification—elevates the object of his research into the subject for a world. Who is the subject who seeks to know the brain, and who has attained "a vision of the brain"? Is it a human subject, a savant to boot, or is it his brain? Is it accurate to say that a brain sees the brain, or would it not be truer and thus more rigorous to say that to be a subject who sees and who eventually investigates the functioning of the brain, one must be a knowing subject whose cognitive life is conditioned by a certain kind of brain, but also by subjective and intersubjective factors belonging to the human world (*geistige Welt*)?

When Kant praised Newton as "a great brain," using a banal metonym to designate Newton's exceptional intellectual ability, he could hardly have thought that it was the brain of Newton that wrote the *Principia*. If a "brain" as powerful as Newton's had been born in pre-Galilean society, missing the benefits of a pre-given culture and a given intentional and affective involvement with other subjects and their works, he could not have accomplished what he did in the *Principia*. Few will disagree on this, which in fact seems to justify Husserl's claim in *Ideen* II that in the constitution of the human world the sphere of culture enjoys an ontological precedence. Thus, the many philosophers who speak of the brain as the "thinking subject" are building on the ambiguities and imprecisions of scientific discourse, without fully grasping the shortcomings of the language-game in which they are involved. We can avoid such category mistakes by recalling the title given by the neuropsychiatrist Erwin Straus to the third part of his great work *Vom Sinn der Sinne*: "Man thinks, not the brain" ["Der Mensch denkt, nicht das Gehirn"]. This rectification does not eliminate the need to see the brain as a defining part of the thinking human being, without which he could not think as he does.

Neurobiologists themselves—again I think of Semir Zeki—admit, in different language, that "the great conquests of humanity have their origin in subjective mental states." But who has ever seen a mental state, a problem, or a theorem in the brain? With the help of measuring instruments one can detect physicochemical reactions, or anatomical lesions, in the brain, and one can see that when the subject under investigation has a given experience certain cerebral regions are particularly exploited or activated (cf. the measurement of rCBF, regional cerebral blood flow). But even supposing that one day some iconic engram can be observed in the brain, this would still not permit observation of the subjective experience of a person recalling the face of a friend. Here already is found the irreducible difference between the intentional and the cerebral, between the object envisaged intentionally and the brain processes which support and make possible the intentional orientation in its different modalities, perceptual, imaginative, rememorative, volitional, and so on.

Consider for a moment the regional treatment of information by the brain. It is a fact, confirmed by pathology, that when one writes, the parts of the brain involved in the activity of analysis needed for writing (especially alphabetical writing) are not the same as those activated when one speaks. This is one illustration of a matter of capital importance: cerebral functioning is at once multiple and unified, diversified and centralized. Studying monkey vision from a neurophysiological point of view, Zeki noticed that "cells in the region MT (V5) preferred visual stimuli in movement" whereas "cells in the V4 region were selective for colour" (Zeki 1995). This provides an indirect but very interesting physiological illumination of what Husserl, on the basis of subjective experience alone, the prescientific experience of things in the life-world, described as the multiplicity of the rays of the look (gaze), a look capable of analyzing the object it sees in its different determinations.

For Husserl, what constitutes the experiential foundation of an empirical judgment of the form "S is p" is just this ability to hold the perceived thing in one's grasp as the same and, at the same time, as a substrate (or an invariant) of multiple determinations of properties; this is effected already at the level of perceptual experience. "The kite I see in the sky is red." Such a predication is tacitly implied in the dissociation or dieresis (*Aussonderung*) accomplished already at the level of sense-experience ("red" dissociated from "kite" against "sky" as a ground or a horizon), visual perception in this case. What neurophysiology brings to light is the cerebral conditioning or the neuronal substructure of some of these kinds of analysis effected at the level of perception, showing that selective cellular groups are in charge of the reception of different visual stimuli, and in such a way that they grant reception its articulation.

The results gathered by Mishkin, Ungerleider, and Macko on the differing cortical routes of object vision and spatial vision—the fact that the "what" and the "where" are treated differently (as S. M. Kosslyn puts it [1995, no. 7, p. 603])—show that the inferior temporal cortex takes part primarily in acts of noticing the qualities of objects while the parietal posterior cortex is more concerned with the spatial relations between objects. This difference of cerebral circuits reinforces the difference noted by Husserl in *Erfahrung und Urteil* between the grasp of the internal determinations of an object and the grasp of its spatial relations with other objects of the same perceptual field; in other words, using Husserl's language, the difference between consideration of the internal horizon and that of the external horizon of the object.

Another convergence between Husserl and neuroscience may be seen in the way the study of the whole and the parts, begun in the third *Logical Investigation*, finds an echo in current studies of visual perception. When David Marr, for example, observes that a gaggle of geese is seen as a whole or as a single entity (Marr and Nishihara 1995: 167), he confirms what Husserl showed in his descriptions of the grasp of an object composed of independent parts. What perception apprehends is the gaggle of geese or the line of trees as a whole, so that each goose or tree taken individually emerges as an independent part of that whole. Thus a phenomenological response might be given to Marr's question: "Is a head an object?" (170). Yes, insofar as it is an independent part of a body, capable of existing by itself as a fragment.

These topics point to an essential question: what are we to understand by "object" in the perspective of phenomenology? Phenomenology has broken with the substantialist ontology on which the natural attitude converges with all its might. For it, an object is whatever can be the intentional correlate of consciousness, whatever it can direct itself to, or to which it can orient its gaze. This definition of the object includes *qualia*, although these, colors for example, can only be given as moments in dependence on something possessing extension.

To make another step in this inquiry, let us turn to pathology. One is constantly astonished at the lessons it obliges us to draw about what we call the normal. Take the female patient of Geschwind, Quadfesel, and Segarra who could not comprehend what was said to her or sustain propositional speech, though she could repeat without difficulty songs that were sung to her. In their effort to explain the intellectual deficiency of the patient, these researchers put forward the following hypothesis: "The patient's failure to comprehend presumably resulted from the fact that language inputs could arouse no associations elsewhere in the brain, and since information from other portions of the brain could not reach the speech areas, there was no propositional speech. On the other hand the intactness of the speech region and its internal connections insured correct repetition" (Geschwind 1995).

This hypothesis could profitably have been compared with others, for the experience of a divorce between words and things, which provides the theme of Hofmannsthal's *Letter of Lord Chandos*, can occur in the absence of a cerebral lesion, as one sees in depressive states. It merits, however, a phenomenological response, for it rejoins, albeit indirectly, the teaching of Husserl on the transcendental genesis of judgment. Judgment cannot be grasped adequately if we confine ourselves to the plane of understanding or language. Husserl often reproaches the tradition, especially Kant, his great predecessor as a transcendental philosopher, with a failure to clarify the presuppositions of judgment, as he will attempt to do in his project of a genealogy of logic. Such a genealogy, as decisive a moment in phenomenology as the transcendental theory of knowledge, seeks to consider predicative judgment starting from sense-experience, which in turn cannot be taken for granted but demands to be analyzed in the *constitutive activity* proper to it.

In this sense Husserl's project in the studies at the origin of *Erfahrung und Urteil* was nothing less than a rewriting of the transcendental aesthetic in a phenomenological key. As he emphasizes, if judgment is to play its cognitive role it must be founded in an a priori way on the articulation and on a typology of sense-experience, which is itself the originary layer of all knowledge. All judgment refers back to this, including the nonempirical judgments issuing from objectifications of a higher level. So, from the point of view of knowledge, a complete dissociation between experience and judgment would be fatal, so to speak. The case of the patient who had become incapable of linking language and experience, probably because of a deficiency in the brain circuits assuring that link, would thus corroborate empirically what phenomenological analysis uncovers on an a priori basis.

Many other convergences could doubtless be invoked (given the inevitable randomness of our choice of materials). We have ignored the theoretical differences between computational models and those which are more strictly neurophysiological, for we believe that the cognitivist paradigm can serve as a bridge between all who use it, despite the difference of theoretical models guiding their efforts.

Now we must ask about the philosophical import of these convergences, both for phenomenology and for the cognitive sciences.

To move toward a conclusion that can only be provisional, allow me to express my conviction that phenomenology, as Merleau-Ponty grasped, can remain alive only if it is able to renew itself under the prompting of scientific knowledge and artistic experience. Husserl, who died in 1938, did not witness the cognitivist turn of psychology and neuropsychology, which were to break to some extent with the very paradigm he had so often criticized. He would no doubt have greeted these developments as a real advance for these sciences. But it would be naive to think that scientific breakthroughs, which are never unattended by scientistic interpretations, could replace the theoretical achievements of phenomenology (*Krisis*, §58, p. 207 [204]). Phenomenology presents itself as a philosophical science dedicated to disengaging the essential structures of subjective experience considered in its transcendental dimension, in other words, the knowledge which each one has of the world viewed as correlative of one's subjective and intersubjective life. This definition makes clear that the method of phenomenological philosophy cannot be confused or amalgamated with the experimental methods of the positive sciences, since these necessarily objectify their research topic, in this case human and animal life.

Yet phenomenology cannot remain unconcerned by the lot of these sciences. First, because one misunderstands the phenomenological discovery of essences and essential structures if one leaves out of account the fact-essence relationship. Husserl teaches that to correctly isolate the sense of a fact in performing the eidetic reduction a certain degree of realization, a certain clarity of its apparition, is necessary.[9] Science in general, including technology, contributes to the empirical knowledge of the facts offered for the phenomenologist's consideration. Thus the phenomenologist does not reject scientific insights, but seeks to reveal the prescientific intelligibility that they leave unclarified. It is in this horizon that we can pose the more general question of the naturalization of phenomenology and the possible corrections to be made to some of Husserl's affirmations or descriptions, the necessity of which bears witness to the fact that, like every thinker, he was marked by the limits of his time. Should we envisage a naturalistic reorientation of phenomenology[10]—which would run the risk of forgetting that the phenomenon as such, taken in its mere phenomenality, though it has an essence, an analyzable structure of sense, has no nature? Moreover, this naturalization, by fading the decisive "nuance," I mentioned from the start, would abolish the desire which from its earliest beginnings inheres to a true philosophical attitude: not to be only a "fact-being" submitted to the natural forces and their regulations, but to live a rational and ethical life.[11] A life that Husserl thought should be put at the service of humanity.

We should aim rather at reactivating and reactualizing the to-and-fro, mutually illuminating, between the sciences, especially cognitive psychology, and transcendental phenomenology. The to-and-fro with psychology is all the more legitimate in that the transcendental ego, by the mediation of its body, is objectified as a natural being "inserted in universal spatio-temporal nature"; and as Husserl also says, as "a naturalized, localized ego, it enters into the inductive texture of the whole of nature and becomes the object of questions on the inductive rules that, beyond the physical laws of nature, regulate the psychophysical totality and in consequence the appearance and disappearance of psychical facts" (*Krisis*, suppl. 24, p. 486). This declaration on its own shows that a reading of phenomenology that issues in the elaboration of naturalistic programs of investigation of the human psyche does not clash with Husserlian phenomenology. But the transcendental status proper to phenomenology is unalienable, as is its method of describing experience.

Second, phenomenology, as a philosophy, cannot be indifferent to the way in which the positive sciences interpret their findings, or to their self-understanding, or to the way in which they attempt, de facto and sometimes in spite of themselves, to impose a view of human-being.

To give more concreteness to this remark, let us first examine how some researchers formulate their questions and their programs, for instance David Marr's formulation of the question that underlies his fine work: "For human vision to be explained by a computational theory, the first question is plain: What are the problems the brain solves when we see?" (Marr and Nishihara 1995: 165). Note the metaphor in "the problems the brain solves"—in fact, unlike the thinker, the brain doesn't "rack its brains" to solve problems, but has a complex life as the place of integration of multiple processes whereby the psychophysical subject relates to its natural and human environment. It is starting from certain stimuli touching our retina and on the basis of some of those neuro-electrochemical processes taking place in several interconnected regions and arranging themselves in a series of many hierarchical and centralized levels—as Marr himself has shown—that we see. But it is precisely because we see that the question of what the brain "does," "the problems it solves," when we see, can be the object of a desire for knowledge.

Faced with this situation, the phenomenologist could say to Marr: while you busy yourself with the brain processes using a computational model, I shall try to clarify the experience we have, which you take for granted when you use the words "when we see." We need to be clear about what that experience is, remember that when we visually perceive anything whatever, it is never given alone, but rather in a perceptual field which is defined for each of us beginning from his lived body and which arises on the basis of a horizon of anticipations predetermined by his previous experiences. Phenomenology claims to be the science of this originary, prescientific evidence which underlies all the higher objectifications of science. It seeks a rigorous elucidation of what is meant by consciousness, a notion at the center of intense debates and which some claim to have "explained"—a deplorable misunderstanding, for consciousness cannot be seen as a "phenomenon" to be explained, since there are phenomena only for consciousness. Such explanation invites an infinite regress. And contrary to the implication of Daniel Dennett's title *Consciousness Explained*, it could not really explain consciousness; what Dennett shows is our increasing knowledge of the psychophysical processes that are the condition of consciousness. Is consciousness ultimately something that requires explanation? Rather it gives itself to be known in the immanence of its productive life and knows itself in self-reflection.

This phrasing could lead to another misunderstanding, if one took self-reflection to mean an introspective reflection by personal subjects on themselves and their personal mental states. It is rather a question of a reflection bearing on the essential structures of a transcendental consciousness, ultimately intersubjective, in whose field is constituted every objecthood that has sense or existential standing, or lack thereof, for the subject, including the objectifications of science. Only thus can this self-reflection—which subjects experience to an eidetic reduction—truly be given as a transcendental theory of knowledge, never completed.

I return to my opening remarks: transcendental phenomenology harbors within itself its difference from psychology. This does not prevent it from becoming in turn a reservoir of questions for psychology, while at the same time enlightening scientific work on its own nature, on the sense it should give its findings as well as on the limits of their provisional validity. The function it can exert on behalf of the sciences is not that of some higher normative science, for phenomenology is not and cannot be such a science; scientists "have the right not to listen to philosophers," said Husserl. Rather, phenomenology provides a new *critique of reason*; new in that it takes into account the concrete operations of sense-formation and the conquests of scientific knowledge, as well as their many inevitable crises, which threaten the very destiny of reason. Thus it sets itself at the service of what Husserl calls "the noetic perfecting of all the sciences" (*Ideen* III, §19, p. 100 [86]), and especially of psychology, the science over against which it conquered and continues to conquer the transcendental dimension proper to it.

CHAPTER TWENTY

The Movement of the Living as the Originary Foundation of Perceptual Intentionality

RENAUD BARBARAS

A philosophy of perception is faced with two seemingly contradictory requirements. On the one hand, perception is openness toward reality: its object is given as residing in itself, as preceding the act that makes it appear without owing anything to this act. Nevertheless, on the other hand, the access to this reality is dependent on its appearance; that which gives itself as being is nothing *other* than that which appears. This is how we translate the fact that it is someone who perceives, that the being of the world is measured by my power to make it appear. Thus phenomenality enfolds Being, inasmuch as there is no being which is not perceived; but Being in turn embraces phenomenality, since what is proper to the perceived is that it gives itself as something that always exceeds its manifestations.

Husserl was doubtless the first to attempt to account for this situation fully, instead of merely preserving one of its aspects while condemning the other as something illusory, a gesture characteristic of the entire prior tradition. Indeed, by describing perception, as early as the *Logische Untersuchungen*, in terms of givenness through sketches, Husserl confronts the difficulty head on. On the one hand, the sketch is ostensive of the object; far from being a sign indicating another reality, it is already the object, it makes the object itself appear. But on the other hand, the sketch only makes the object appear as an appearing object, which means that even as the object is sketched, it is also evaded. The sketch only presents the object from a particular standpoint, which is necessarily partial: it withdraws in favor of the object, but it erases the object in favor of the aspect from which it is presented. In the sketch, the object is presented as something other than that which presents it, so that the sketch only reveals the object as that which has a hold on it. We must be able to grasp this situation if we are to provide an account of perception. I wish to show in what follows that a radical shift in terrain is required for this to be possible. Indeed, it is by taking as a starting point the living being's way of existing and the kind of relatedness it establishes with the environment that we will be in a position to account for perception. Through the problem of perception, defined as givenness through sketches, the question of the *nature* of intentionality is called into play. Our claim is that we cannot account for the nature of intentionality without grounding it in a living being, that is to say a natural being in the sense that it lives in the midst of a Nature. As a result, the question of the essence (nature) of intentionality calls into play the problem of the *nature of intentionality*, that is to say of the meaning of the Nature *in which* intentionality as a living movement is situated.

1. PERCEPTION: KNOWLEDGE OR MOVEMENT?

1.1. THE INADEQUACY OF HUSSERL'S APPROACH

Husserl may demonstrate an unmatched lucidity when it comes to posing the problem of perception, but his way of conceptualizing it appears strongly dependent on uncriticized presuppositions, and ultimately appears to be a step backward from his own intuition. It is obvious that even though the idea of givenness through sketches puts the idea of the subject/object duality into question—for the sketch refers to the problematic unity of the appearing and the apparent—Husserl's thematization remains dominated by a conception of this relation which ultimately stems from the rationalist tradition. Indeed, particularly in *Ideen* I, we witness what might be called a mutual *autonomization* of subject and object. The analysis of the perceived object is governed by the rational horizon of an adequate givenness of the thing, that is, of a final intuitive filling of interpretive aims. Instead of appearing as data that veil the object insofar as they present it, by thus preserving its transcendence, the sketches tend to become imperfect manifestations, which hence outline the horizon of an adequate givenness and are ultimately governed by it. The sketches appear as moments of a march toward a determination of the object in conformity with the requirements of reason. Now, this displacement appears to be inevitable once Husserl fails to question the fact that perception is the perception of an *object*, that is, of a determinate unity, which in essence is able to receive an adequate givenness. The counterpart of this objectivism is an autonomization of the subjective, resulting in a subjectivism, which in the final analysis, is itself only a more refined form of this objectivism. Indeed, as Jan Patočka showed quite well, the phenomenal field brought to light by reduction is not acknowledged in its autonomy, that is, its function of showing the object, of self-erasure in its favor, but in some sense finds itself resting on a real entity, transcendental consciousness. The task then is to *reconstitute* perceptual intentionality, starting from lived experience, as governed by the duality of the hyletic and the noetic. There again, the intuitionist requirement is that perception must be rooted in the immanence of lived experience. Insofar as subjectivity must be able to be given to itself, in an internal positing, the certainty of the "I am" is translated in terms of the positing of an egological reality. We are indeed faced with a higher form of objectivism or positivism, insofar as the phenomenal order is explicated from an entity, that is, a positive being, which this time takes on the shape of the egologically subjective. Now, this withdrawal toward lived experience obviously compromises the givenness of a transcendence, which is entirely dependent on *noesis*. As Patočka puts it bluntly: "How does lived experience, originarily given to oneself in reflection, manage to make a transcendence appear on the objective side? This is incomprehensible" (Patočka 1970: 208).

The source of this difficulty is undeniably the fact that Husserl's analysis of perception remains bound by the perspective of a theory of rational knowledge. The presupposition according to which perceiving ultimately means *knowing* is never put into question. Husserl's merit is thus, above all, that he conceived of perceptual knowledge as a base for all rational knowledge, and not as a lower-level knowledge, an obscure intellection. But Husserl's analyses remain inadequate to the intuition of givenness through sketches, because they are governed by the postulate so admirably revealed by Henri Bergson: "The interest of perception is wholly speculative . . . , it is pure knowledge" (Bergson 1896: 24). Henceforth, the condition for being able to conceive of perception in its seemingly contradictory dimensions will be that we give up this presupposition.

1.2. PERCEPTION AND MOTILITY

The path to follow would therefore consist in apprehending the subject of perception in its concrete plenitude, as a motional and practical relation to the world. Bergson chose this perspective and sought to generate perception from the brain alone, understood as a center of indeterminacy, that is, as something which does not have to transmit the impulses of the external world mechanically and can choose its reaction. To perceive would then mean to cut out the dimension of the universe in which the body has a vital interest. The crucial merit of this analysis is that it bypasses the problem of the relation of the representation to the object; for Bergson, perception takes place co-extensively with the object itself, and rigorously speaking, there is no reason to distinguish between the object itself and the object insofar as it is perceived. The representation is not added onto the presence but instead draws something from it; the perceived object is the object separated from its surroundings by its vital interest. The fact remains that the path followed by Bergson does reestablish dualism in a modified form. Pure perception appears as an objective process of selection within a universe of "images" (namely, reality itself); it is hence only an abstract moment of effective perception, which demands the intervention of a dimension of recognition, that is, of experience. The latter refers to a subjectivity that is pure mind, and whose essence excludes the dimension of incarnation. In Bergson, the price to pay for the recognition of a movement at work in perception is the loss of the effectuation of a sense, namely, the loss of intentionality. Now, if perception includes the act of a motor body, the latter must be thought in such a way that the phenomenalizing initiative of a subjectivity is not excluded.

Of course, Husserl did not fail to notice this motor dimension, and following Merleau-Ponty or Patočka, we could show that intentionality ultimately refers to an *Ich kann*, that it is the kinesthesias which ensure the insertion of perception into a space and ultimately are the bearers of the movement of intentional openness. As Merleau-Ponty says: "Our bodily experience of movement is not a particular case of knowledge; it provides us with a way of access to the world and the object, with a 'praktognosia,' which has to be recognized as original and perhaps as primary. My body has its world, or understands its world, without having to make use of my 'symbolic' or objectifying function'" (Merleau-Ponty 1962: 740). Nevertheless, it appears difficult to reconcile this direction with the specific horizon of Husserl's analysis of lived experience, for we still have to understand how the kinesthetic is connected to the hyletic. As Merleau-Ponty showed well, following Von Weiszäcker, I for instance impress on my hand the speed which is exactly necessary to perceive a wrinkle, as if touch preceded itself in movement. Likewise, my eyes take the exact position required by the richest vision of the object, as though there were in the eye's movement a vision before the vision as such. The Husserlian perspective cannot fully account for the reciprocal overlapping of sensibility and movement, which is for us the central phenomenon we have to take into account if we want to understand intentionality.

Our problem is thus becoming clearer. The understanding of perception as the givenness of a transcendence prevents us from defining it as a knowledge and demands that we place ourselves at the vital level of *motility*. But taking account of motility should not imply the return of a conception that inscribes the body in an objective totality, and thus cuts it off from intentionality. Motility is not an objective movement, a succession of positions in a geometric space: it is rather from this motility that geometrical space comes into being. Thus, as a movement, intentionality implies a situatedness that, on the other hand, cannot be understood as a localization in an objective nature and, consequently, leads us to define the sense of this nature. The aim, therefore, is to "think" the *essential* relation between sensibility and motility, a unity which the philosophy of biology, from Kurt Goldstein to Francisco Varela, has clearly brought into view. In other words, rather, since the terms "sensibility" and "motility" refer to the distinction between the *res cogitans* and the *res extensa*, the aim is to emphasize the *originary and unitary dimension* in which this relation or articulation is grounded. If this condition is fulfilled, the subjectivity of perception and its openness to a transcendence will no longer be presented as mutually exclusive alternatives.

2. LIVING AND TOTALITY

2.1. THE "FUNDAMENTAL BIOLOGICAL LAW"

Now, in a 1968 article Patočka asks if we should not be entitled to view the subjective movements described above all by Husserl, as "the modalities of a fundamental, global movement, which would coincide with living itself inasmuch as it unfolds itself toward the outside. The answer to be given to this question will be a function of another question, namely, can life itself be conceived of as self-realization, on the model of movement" (Patočka 1968: 137). In order to account for the subjective movement, we must therefore turn toward the most radical attempts to think life in its specificity and see if they do not lead us to revise the ontological presuppositions that undermine the philosophy of perception. These attempts, situated at the intersection between phenomenology and biology, all attempt to bring the category of *totality* into the foreground. There is no need to go over Goldstein's analyses, which establish that behavior cannot be understood locally, as a reaction to an action of the environment, but must be understood as a function of organic totality, that is, of a biological a priori which must be conquered or restored, faced with the constraints of the environment. The "fundamental biological law" states that all behavior refers to a "debate" between the organism and the world, a debate in which the organism maintains and fulfills an individual norm. What is important here is that the living qua totality is an ultimate category, which alone is endowed with a biological meaning. The living being may include parts which can, besides, function autonomously in pathological or catastrophic situations, but these parts are only real for an analytic attitude or for a physicochemical approach. Strictly speaking, the being of the parts of the living being resides only in totality; the segments of the organism do not make up this totality, but each of them expresses the whole of the organism. To be sure, this whole is nothing *other* than the segments themselves, for if this whole were construed as a reality, substantialism would be ushered back in, in the guise of a vital entity. If each part is indeed only the expression of the whole, the being of the whole resides in the parts, and this is why, according to Goldstein, there cannot be any struggle between the parts of the organism. This leads Goldstein to assert that the organism must be thought in and according to the relation it has with the environment. At root, this organic totality is only a particular norm or a particular style preserved in the relations which each part of the organism has with the environment. This norm cannot be thought in itself, prior to the relation to the environment. It is true that this norm structures this relation, by reestablishing an equilibrium when the organism is threatened, but it is also true that it is conquered and determined within the relations to the world themselves. It does not maintain this equilibrium *despite* the fluctuations of the environment, but *within* them, *thanks* to them; it is not a style existing prior to the history of a living being and governing it, but a style *of* this history. Therefore, if we wish, the organic whole is a theme, but one that is never played for its own sake, but rather one that only appears in its own variations, namely, specific behaviors.

This irreducibility of biological totality must be correctly assessed. As Goldstein showed, this means that biological totality runs deeper than the distinction between the somatic and the psychic, and thus cannot be reconstituted starting from this distinction. The psychic and the somatic are nothing other than modalities of the living; both express the predominance of a way of relating to the world, of a modality of the whole organism. Henceforth, as Erwin Straus shows in turn, sensing, in particular, must be understood as a mode of the living being conceived of as a totality, which means from the outset that perception cannot be reconstituted from punctual sensations, or from a conjunction of sensation and movement. The diversity must be thought from unity, not the reverse; sensations are specifications of sensing, perception is a dimension of the living being. As we can see, in this perspective the problem lies in the diversity rather than in unity.

2.2. THE ORIGINARY TOTALITY

Now, a rigorous attempt to think the living being cannot remain at this individual unity, unless by means of this organic totality it aims to establish a refined version of substantialism. We must hence take a further step. What is characteristic of a thinking of totality is that it rejects any limits, that is, it cannot stop at a level that still contains a degree of abstraction. Goldstein says that for such a thinking, "the imperfect becomes intelligible as a particular variation of the perfect, without the converse ever being possible" (Goldstein 1934: 401).

Indeed, as my initial description of the living being intimated, the totality of the organism itself can only be thought if we begin with a *higher-order totality*. Let me quote Goldstein here:

> Every creature, in some sense, simultaneously expresses a perfection and an imperfection. Considered in isolation, it is perfect, structured, and living in itself; with regard to totality, it is imperfect in varying degrees. The particular creature, in relation to the totality of being, presents the same species of being as is presented by a phenomenon isolated from the organism, in relation to the totality of the organism: it displays imperfection and rigidity, and its only being lies in totality, in being borne by totality.

Further on, Goldstein adds that "this imperfection is expressed by individuality, and stems from the artificial separation of the individual from the whole" (Goldstein 1934: 402–43). The living being is thus a being which, in its very being, brings us to a higher totality, an originary unity, of which it is only a moment. We cannot think about the organism as the subject of its relation to the world without also thinking about it as something that is part of, as something that emerges from, this relation. Indeed, as Goldstein comments, just as the being of an organic part resides in the whole of the organism, similarly, the being of the organism itself, insofar as it is individualized and hence separated from the world, resides in a more originary totality. Straus is quite consistent and also takes this fundamental step: the living being can only be thought about as a being communicating with the world, that is, a being connected in its very being to the totality of the world, totality understood initially in an ontological rather than a spatial sense. It follows from this that a given behavior, a particular sensation, must be understood as a specification of this being-connected. It becomes apparent that *biology* leads us to what might be termed, following von Weiszäcker, *metabiology*.

We still need to elucidate the strange relation existing between the living being and this originary totality, which is prior to the difference between the living being and the world, and is thus also prior to the constitution of an environment. The being of a living being implies individuality, and as such encompasses a perfection. But this perfection is just as much an imperfection, inasmuch as its individuality separates it from the totality that ultimately constitutes its being. However, the realization of this ultimate totality, which would correspond to the fulfillment of the perfection of the living being, would also mean the disappearance of the living being as something individual. In other words, the living being is a being whose being lies outside itself, and this is not accidental, but belongs to its essence, since the fulfillment of the perfection of this being would mean its end: the essence of the living being is that it is always one step short of its essence, it always misses or lacks its essence. Correlatively, if the individual essence of the living being implies the negation of the totality that ultimately constitutes its being, we must conclude that this totality only exists as its own negation, or its own absence, that is, its specification in living individualities. Insofar as the living being is separate, which implies an imperfection, it calls for this totality, but insofar as this separation is the condition of individuality, which is also a perfection, the living being denies this totality. In Goldstein's formulation, the relation of the creature to the whole of Being is indeed comparable to the relation of a part or a behavior of the organism to the organism. The life of the individual living being, that is, the particular behavior in which a style is revealed, does not have any reality in itself; its being only resides in a more originary Whole of which it is the expression. The whole of Being can therefore not be reconstituted from the relation between the living being and the world; on the contrary, this relation, that is, the unity made up of the living being and its environment, must be understood as the limitation or specification of this originary Whole. However, this originary Whole cannot be thought for itself, in a positive manner: its reality only resides in the moments that constitute it, and rigorously speaking, it is nothing other than these moments. Indeed, it is only on this condition that it can preserve a sense as totality, for if it were fulfilled, it would lose its totalizing power and would require a higher kind of totality, just as the living being can only totalize its segments because it does not distinguish itself from them as a positive reality. What we might call "pre-being" (that is, that which is not, strictly speaking, but is the condition, the source of everything which is, of every entity) only has meaning if it is not realized, if its only unity lies in, is accomplished through, the multiplicity of the moments that constitute it. Just as the essence of the organism expresses an originary totality that it specifies and limits, the essence of the Whole implies its own division in the shape of organic individualities that constitute a specific environment.

2.3. BEHAVIOR AS AN EXPRESSION OF THE TOTALITY

The fruitfulness of such an approach should be patent. Earlier, I had said that the living being must be addressed from the unity it forms with the world, and that it is ultimately the manifold, the manifold of its experiences and behavior, which poses a problem. But, as I said, the being and perfection of living beings lies only in their totality, yet this totality is nothing other than the moments that divide it up. Consequently, totality requires its *own de-totalization*, and the principle of unity is *ipso facto* the principle of diversity.

Thus living behavior can no longer be grasped as an encounter between a living being and an already constituted world, but as an expression, that is, a limitation of the initial totality. Straus saw this quite clearly. To say that the manifold of sensations must be re-apprehended from the unity of sensing, means that sensation is understood as a limitation of this sensing insofar as it is a relation of totality: "Individual sensations are limitations of the relation of totality and, as limits, they are implicitly connected to totality.... The relation of totality is a potential relation which actualizes itself in individual sensations and limits itself specifically" (Straus 1935: 397–98). Naturally, we must make the meaning of this limitation clear: it cannot be conceived of as the negation of a unity which would be given, at least de jure. On the contrary, totality constitutes itself within and through the limitation that divides and specifies it. Indeed, since the essence of totality implies its negation, every negation of totality in a living experience *will also posit it*. Hence it is within each finite experience, which limits it, that totality constitutes itself: it emerges within each negation as that which exceeds it. Here, the negation *posits* that of which it is the negation. In other words, by separating, sensation connects; by sketching out a space of interiority, an environment, experience equally opens up a depth which exceeds it and which sketches out what lies beyond the limit, as the totality of Being. Thus, just as biology leads to a metabiology, the latter in turn leads us to a *cosmology*, which could be termed *negative*. If the Whole, which constitutes the being of the living, is only posited as it is negated, this means that it must be negated to be posited. Because the essence of the whole is to remain in a position of retreat or withdrawal in relation to itself, it will not only be attained by the acts which negate it, but *constituted* by them.

We are now in a position to understand how the living being is an essentially *historical* being, something which had already been hinted at, at the level of the individual organism. This does not only mean that the living being exists in time, which is self-evident and does not singularize it in any way. More radically, we must understand this as meaning that the being of a living subject cannot be thought about independently of a history, that its essence implies a becoming: the living being is historical in the sense that its substance is made up of time. Indeed, this play of actualization and limitation of the originary Whole by the living being can only be understood within temporality, or rather as temporality. To say that totality only has meaning and unity in and through its finite actualizations amounts to saying that it exists as history. This totality would have to be conceived of as an *institution* lying at the origin of the becoming of living being. Indeed, what is characteristic of the institution, as Merleau-Ponty noticed, is that it makes a repetition possible, but also that it *requires* this repetition, inasmuch as it only derives its being from the incessant reiterations it gives rise to.[1] Every living behavior must be understood as the inseparably limiting and actualizing reiteration of an originary relation or openness: totality is historical because it only makes itself by unmaking itself.

The previous remarks should undoubtedly lead to a renewal of the terms in which the problem of perception are posed. The classical perspective, according to which perception could only be knowledge, began with the positing of a subject that, by means of sensations, had to relate to a world that was foreign to it. From now on, we must begin with totality, with what Goldstein calls the "most perfect." The essence of this totality is that it is specified in experiences, modalities of a relation to the world, and it is from these experiences, inasmuch as they are finite (inasmuch as they outline a limit), that the distinction between the perceiver and the perceived emerges.

3. INTENTIONALITY AS DESIRE

3.1. THE DESIRE

We must then draw the consequences of this analysis by inquiring into the idea of perceptual intentionality that results from this perspective on the living. The being of the living resides in a totality, an originary unity with the environment it actualizes in each experience and falls short of inasmuch as it actualizes this unity. The essence of the living does indeed consist in falling short of its essence, and in each behavioral act, it perpetuates this lack by filling it in. We could then say that the essence of intentionality is *desire*, as long as we understand what this formulation means, of course. It does not mean that the living being is capable of desiring objects, that it lacks a determinate reality, whether realizable or accessible. This would mean that desire is subordinated to cognition, and that its negativity refers to a finality. Desire is not the lack of something aimed at or given; on the contrary, it is in desire that something like an aim or a given can be constituted. The giving of something does not ground desire, but rather stems from it: desire is the core of intentionality. Indeed, if it is the case that through the object that the subject desires, it is indeed this subject which, within the object, aims at realizing itself, then living being is indeed desire, for as I said, its essence consists in lacking its own being. Correlatively, if the totality characteristic of living being can only be actualized by being negated, that which fulfills desire is also that which frustrates it; satisfaction is also dissatisfaction. Living being is desire, not insofar as a reality which could be present to it is absent—which would confuse desire and knowledge—but because that which it relates to, namely, itself in its own being, is only present as its own absence. If desire exists as that which the desired entity frustrates insofar as the desired satisfies desire, only attaining its object as something falling short of the goal, then living being *is* desire, namely, the givenness of something on the mode of lack itself rather than the lack of something. As Merleau-Ponty writes, in a somewhat different context: "The aesthesiological structure of the human body is a libidinal structure, perception is a mode of desire, a relation of being and not of knowledge" (Merleau-Ponty 1995: 272).

3.2. PERCEPTION AND MOTILITY

Thus it becomes possible to return to the problem of perception, that is, of the originary relation between sensibility and motility. Both indeed appear as abstract moments of this originary desire, so that perception must henceforth be reapprehended from the standpoint of becoming, as the history of the actualization-negation of the ultimate totality. Each experience is a limitation of totality, a limitation which actualizes it in the very moment of negation. The totality that a given experience is the negation of, is posited in the very gesture of this experience. Thus, sketching out that which exceeds it, experience always remains withdrawn into itself, as if it were already overtaken by the totality of which it is the negation. Thus one does not have a positive experience, the giving of something, of which the negative dimension would just be the reverse side of its determination. This would mean granting a positivity to totality which it lacks. On the contrary, if the negation of totality, namely, the actual moment of experience, is at the same time its positing, this moment immediately overcomes itself in favor of the totality it posits, it exceeds itself; stated differently, it is its own excess, or its own withdrawal. Insofar as it is desire, the perceptual intention only attains its object as that which disappoints it, it is only filled on the mode of deception. Here we can see the grounding of an originary interrelation between the intuitive and the interpretive, which runs deeper than Husserl's distinction. All of experience, as an act of aiming at totality, is, so to speak, larger than itself, and thus can only reach its object as the already-overcome, as that which cannot satisfy the intention. Since perception is desire, each perception brings with it a surplus of presence and it appears as the provisional determination of this presence. Von Weiszäcker saw this clearly: "Perception is an historical encounter between myself and the world, each time, and combined with movement, it is but a stage in the active evolution of this encounter towards an unknown goal" (Von Weiszäcker 1939: 156). Straus echoes this when he asserts that "sensations are only particular or transitory limits of sensing itself, they are realizations which the sensing subject always disengages itself from, by virtue of its fundamental becoming" (Straus 1935: 554). Sensation is a limit from which the subject disengages itself *at the out-*

set: it is not posited in order to be negated, but it is only posited by being negated, and this is why it is apprehended as a limit. As Von Weiszäcker writes so well, "To perceive, at root, is always to pass on to something else" (Von Weiszäcker 1939: 143). This does not mean that we first perceive, and then pass on to something else, but that perception constitutes itself as such in this movement of overcoming. Indeed, if desire is indeed at the core of perceptual intentionality, then that which it attains is its own deficiency: the perceived *is* the overcome.

The relation between sensibility and movement, then, is no longer a problem. Their unity ultimately refers to the originary unity of an experience and its own negation as the limitation of a totality which it reveals. Since all sensible experience is limitation, that is, a withdrawal in favor of totality, all sensation is movement; but since this totality, whose negation is the sensible, needs this negation in order to come forth, movement is sensibility. Perception only takes place in the movement that overcomes it; movement only takes place in the perception which disappoints it. To be sure, we can say that phenomenal movement refers to how desire tends toward totality, and perception refers to the finite shape taken by the realization of this desire, but these are two abstract moments, which are both rooted in the originary unity of an actualization and a negation.

4. CONCLUSION: THE NATURE OF INTENTIONALITY

As I said at the outset, perceptual experience is characterized by a mutual enfolding or interdependence of phenomenality and transcendence. As Husserl's theory shows, the sketch gives itself as the manifestation of an object that, while it exceeds it, is nothing other than the act of appearing in which it gives itself. It appears to me that if the living being is taken into consideration, it enables us to make some headway in understanding this phenomenological situation. Indeed, if the living being, in its effective realization, comes to negate a totality which only actualizes itself in this negation, perceptual appearing is no longer contradictory with the unveiling of an irreducible transcendence. Furthermore, perceptual appearing, insofar as it only emerges in the movement of its overcoming, ends up outlining a depth, against the background of which it stands out. On the one hand, experience is the limitation of the relation that is originary [*to*] the world, it is the absence of totality. Here, perceived being is nothing other than that which appears. But on the other hand, this absence of totality is also presence, the perceived is the overcome. Here, the perceived can clearly be made out against a horizon of transcendence, it comes forth against the background of a depth. Perception, as the relation between sensing and moving-oneself, thus expresses the mutual enfolding of the living being and the originary totality, which itself, in the final analysis, refers to the unity of the cosmological dimension and the biological one.

This standpoint is opposed to an idealist or transcendental approach which characterizes nature as dependent on mind or constituted by a transcendental subjectivity. There is no doubt that intentionality can be understood as the givenness of a transcendent world as long as it is characterized as rooted in living movement. Accordingly, intentionality can give or disclose the world insofar as its subject is originally related to an originary Totality. In other words, the essence of intentionality implies its belongingness to a Nature: as work of a living being, perceptual intentionality is an event or a mode of Nature. But, in the other hand, this conclusion does not mean a rehabilitation of any form of naturalism. On the contrary, the Nature in which intentionality takes place is the very negation of all the dimensions of the classical idea of Nature. It is not an objective Nature, lying in itself and indifferent to the living or human way of relating with it: it is a Nature *for* intentionality, that is, to a certain extent, an *anti-Nature*.

As a matter of fact, the idealist or transcendental standpoint and the naturalistic one are not two mutually exclusive alternatives. On the contrary, both are governed by the same idea of Nature as a "great object," in which all the physical laws already lie, existing in itself and owing nothing to our living or human contact with it. As Merleau-Ponty writes:

> There is a truth in naturalism. But that truth is not naturalism itself. For to acknowledge naturalism and the envelopment of consciousness in the universe of *blosse Sachen* as an occurrence, is precisely to posit the theoretical world to which they belong as primary, which is an extreme form of idealism. It is in fact to refuse to decipher the intentional references which run from the universe of *blosse Sachen*, or extended objects, to "pretheoretical object," to the life of consciousness before science. (Merleau-Ponty 1968: 148)

Thus, naturalism and idealism both take the point of view of the impartial spectator and disregard our vital link with the world.

By approaching intentionality from the living being, we are led to give up the idealist and transcendental position and, *therefore*, to overcome the naturalistic point of view. To go back to the concrete and living relationship of the subject with the world is to go beyond the standpoint of the impartial spectator and, consequently, to go back beneath the opposition between theoretical consciousness and objective Nature. Moreover, by taking into account the life of the living being, we are in a position to provide a new characterization of Nature. The living being is no longer a physical body, a fragment of a "great object," governed by physical or chemical laws; it is an active limitation of a Totality which only exists as its own negation by the living being. Accordingly, Nature, which is synonymous with the Totality, is not any longer something positive from which the living being could emerge: it is a "reality" which exists as its own absence or its own imminence, which emerges from the living movements as that which they are short of. To some extent, the living being emerges from a nature to which it gives rise. Such a Nature is indeed at the opposite of the traditional idea: it is not positive or objective but the effective and dynamic negation of any positivity or entity. It is by remaining potential and, to some extent, unfinished, that it can be a Nature, that is, that which involves everything and gives rise to everything. In other words, however paradoxical it may seem, it is by being sketched out by the living movement, as that which exceeds every finite perception, that Nature can contain the living being. It follows that, just as the living being cannot be understood without its situatedness within Nature, the latter cannot be understood without its dependence on the living being: indeed, its infinity is the exact counterpart of the unfinishedness of the living movement, that is, of the desire. Therefore, this Nature is essentially related with Life, or, more precisely, provides us a sense of Being that overcomes the difference between physical world and Life. Such a Nature—both Nature in which intentionality comes into being and Nature constituted by intentionality—as an infinite and living source of every experience and every event, would probably require a confrontation with the pre-Socratic idea of Nature. Anyhow, the naturalization of intentionality makes sense on the condition that Nature be "de-objectivized," that is, conceived as its own lack, as the unity of itself and Life.

Translated by Charles Wolfe

CHAPTER TWENTY-ONE

Philosophy and Cognition: Historical Roots

JEAN-PIERRE DUPUY

> Cybernetics is the metaphysics of the atomic age.
> —*Martin Heidegger, 1976*

What gives coherence to the many different research programs that go under the name of "cognitive science" today is the philosophical work being done in connection with them. Without "cognitive" philosophy there would be work in psychology, in linguistics, in neurobiology, in artificial intelligence—but no science of cognition. Philosophers (not psychologists, or linguists, or neurobiologists, or computer scientists) are the ones who have reflected upon and systematized the basic attitude shared by workers in the various disciplines that make up the field. The fact that there is a shared attitude—the only thing that holds these disciplines together, in fact—in no way implies the existence of a single paradigm. There are currently at least two paradigms: classical (or "orthodox") cognitivism and connectionism. But the conflict between the two is itself the source of common ground. In the end, those who find themselves on opposing sides in the controversies that have punctuated the history of the field see themselves less as adversaries than as members of the same extended, quarrelsome family. And the umpire who lays down and enforces the rules governing these family arguments, and ultimately decides their outcome, is philosophy.

In this story, there is no shortage of irony. Cognitive science likes to represent itself as having reclaimed for science all the most ancient questions posed by philosophy about the human mind, its nature and organization, its relations with the body (which is to say the brain), with other minds, and with the world. But the identity of this self-proclaimed science of mind remains profoundly philosophical. The science that speaks on behalf of the sciences and associated techniques that together make up the field (mainly the fields of neuroscience, artificial intelligence, the branch of psychology that calls itself "cognitive," and linguistics), the science that provides these sciences with the spirit (or mind) which would otherwise be missing from them, is in reality none other than philosophy. But it is a peculiar kind of philosophy—a philosophy that crept into the Trojan horse of these sciences, as it were, in order to claim dominion over the realm of the mind and to chase out from it the intruders still to be found there: rival philosophies (especially the philosophies of consciousness, namely, phenomenology and existentialism), rival psychologies (chief among them behaviorism and psychoanalysis), and rival sciences (the social sciences, particularly structuralist anthropology).

1. NATURALIZING EPISTEMOLOGY

What, then, is "cognitive" philosophy? Better known as "philosophy of mind," it stands today as the most active and flourishing branch of analytical philosophy. But to say this is to state a paradox, which rests in large part on what must seem an enigma to analytic philosophers themselves when they look back over the history of their own field.

It is, in fact, generally agreed that the decisive achievement of the various "founding fathers" or schools of thought honored as progenitors by analytical philosophy was the break with "psychologism." Let us note first off that it was by virtue of the same break that another great tradition of contemporary philosophy, phenomenology, came into existence. This parallel development was not accidental, for as we shall see, philosophy of mind shares a fundamental concept with phenomenology. Whether one thinks of the formalism of Hilbert or the logicism of Frege, Russell, and Carnap, for whom the essential thing was to cut all ties between logic and psychology, the objectivity of the former needing to be founded on something other than the contingency or facticity of the latter; or of the logical positivism of the Vienna Circle, which conceived of philosophy as an activity aimed at purifying the language of science in order to banish from it all "metaphysics"; or of Wittgenstein and the Oxford school of ordinary language philosophy, for whom there was no such thing as a "private language," which meant that the sole access to thought is through the analysis of language, so far as this is a public activity subject to norms recognized by an intersubjective community—in all these cases there was a determined refusal to base philosophy on psychology and, at the same time, an insistence on assigning priority to the study of language. From the first, analytic philosophy was a philosophy of language through and through.

This "linguistic turn" at the beginning of the century was, however, to be followed by a "cognitive" turn. Paradoxically, the rejection of psychologism would wind up eventually giving birth to a cognitive philosophy that purported to be philosophical psychology. While it is true that analytic philosophy is not much given to reviewing its past (something its counterpart—"continental" philosophy—does endlessly), it cannot help but wonder about this singular reversal. The types of reasons it gives, when it does think about it, are varied. The first type relates to the internal evolution of philosophy of language. Both the Chomskyan program of generative grammar and the pragmatic current stemming from the work of Paul Grice imply that as speakers and interlocutors we "get inside the heads" of others: without appeal to certain cognitive capacities that subjects must be assumed to possess (combinatory in the one case, inferential in the other), there would be no way on either view to account for the nature and properties of language and of verbal communication. A second set of reasons draws upon the development and progress of cognitive science itself. Thanks to this research, it is maintained, it is now possible to successfully carry out the program that Quine hoped and prayed for—"the naturalization of epistemology." Henceforth the questions traditionally posed by philosophy concerning the objective foundations of our knowledge can be given answers based on research in the empirical sciences. These answers involve causal processes, in principle reducible to the laws of physics, that explain how we obtain knowledge (in the sense of justified belief) and, more generally, why our "mental states" are adapted to the external world.

A moment's reflection suffices to show that these reasons explain nothing. The reasons philosophy had for cutting itself off from psychology, as from the natural sciences as a whole, in order to conduct its own inquiry into the objective validity of knowledge and the very *legitimacy* of a science of nature—an inquiry first opened up by Kant, which he christened "transcendental"—were reasons of principle, and perfectly independent of the progress of the empirical sciences. A transcendental inquiry into the truth content of knowledge is not to be imagined as the limit of a factual inquiry into the actual genesis of knowledge as the precision and reliability of this inquiry approaches the infinite. In other words: the *quid juris* is not the limit of a *quid facti*, since a question of right can never be given the same type of answer as a question of fact—that is, the "ought-to-be" is not reducible to the "it is."

These Kantian distinctions were the very source of Frege's antipsychologism, just as they were of Husserl's. To attempt to justify the cognitive turn of analytical philosophy by the progress made recently by the sciences of cognition is therefore utterly futile. It would be truer to say that the change brought about by the emergence of a cognitive branch within analytical philosophy is much less radical than it seems, and this for two reasons: the first is that, even if it is not as conscious of the fact as it should be, cognitive philosophy preserves still today something of its Kantian heritage, and therefore continues to keep its distance from "psychologism"; the second is that it has not wholly managed to free itself from the priority initially given to language.

The first point has been defended in an important article by Joëlle Proust, above all with regard to what she calls the "implicit philosophy" of artificial intelligence (see Proust 1987). Proust urges us not to be misled by the way in which its leading practitioners, particularly Allen Newell and Herbert Simon, conceived of their work, and especially the way in which they presented it to the public and to their sponsors when it became necessary to defend and illustrate the ambitions of the new discipline. For them it was a matter of showing that artificial intelligence was a respectable science that, although a science of the "artificial," contributed to the empirical understanding of nature: to construct a machine that embodies a hypothesis about reality or constitutes a model of it, and to test this hypothesis or model by running the machine, was to be faithful to the predominant experimental method of the natural sciences.

The truth of the matter, Proust shows, is very different. The very concern for universality exhibited by artificial intelligence makes it possible to regard this enterprise in an entirely new light: artificial intelligence as a philosophy, and a philosophy of a transcendental type at that. It was intended as a search for the formal conditions of cognitive activity common to all systems that are capable of such activity, whether they may be human subjects, animals, or machines. It set itself the task of exploring all the possible modes of intelligence, beyond those particular ones that human beings are capable of displaying. The purpose of this inquiry was ultimately to discover the a priori, necessary, and sufficient conditions that both made knowledge possible and grounded the objectivity, which is to say the universality, of this knowledge.

Of course the solution proposed by artificial intelligence to this problem was not the same as the Kantian solution. The transcendental subject was replaced by the "physical symbol system" and the universality of the synthetic a priori by the universality of the Turing machine. But in both cases the distinction between psychology and the critique of knowledge, between the contingent laws of cognition and necessary rules, was carefully made. It might be said that, in naturalizing and mechanizing its transcendental inquiry, artificial intelligence deprived it of all meaning. But let us not forget that what guarantees the universality of the Turing machine is only a thesis, a metaphysical thesis—metaphysical in the same sense that Popper speaks of a "metaphysical program of research." Kantian metaphysics, as the science of the a priori powers of the knowing subject, is not so very far removed from this.

The object of my own inquiry is the cybernetic phase of the genesis of cognitive science. This detour through the history of philosophy of mind is not, however, without a point. What Joëlle Proust says about artificial intelligence applies equally to its predecessor, and in particular to the undertaking advocated by Warren McCulloch. One notices in McCulloch the same tension between the desire to bring natural science to the point where it can purport to include in its scope the empirical study of mind, on the one hand, and a concern for philosophical inquiry. On the one hand, there is his ambition to build an "experimental epistemology," of which the idealized neuron model was to constitute the finest flower; on the other, there is the insistent reference to Kant, for it was McCulloch's intention to take up the challenge of providing a physical basis for synthetic a priori judgments. He was the first to stress that the *material* mechanisms represented by the neuronal model were sufficient but hardly necessary conditions for giving an account of the faculties of mind. This does not mean that it was not a matter, *at the formal level*, of searching for necessary *and* sufficient conditions. Seymour Papert, a former student of McCulloch and himself a pioneer of artificial intelligence, makes this point clear in his preface to *Embodiments of Mind* (see McCulloch 1965). As Jean Mosconi has commented with reference to this preface,

> There is more to [McCulloch's way of thinking] than [simply] a certain attitude that can be observed in anyone who constructs "models" of nervous activity. As against those who contented themselves with ensuring the adequacy of "pragmatic tests," McCulloch proposed (according to Papert) "a rational quest for necessity and comprehension," which was revealed especially by his interest in constructing a theoretical structure indifferent to the various contingent choices that can be made regarding the characterization of formal neurons. That this study sometimes limited itself to particular cases did not detract from the generality of the project, according to Papert: it was rather a question of style, or of a lack of [suitable] mathematical tools. (See Mosconi 1989.)

To which it might be added that McCulloch, emboldened by his equivalence theorem,[1] was imbued with the universalist spirit of the Turing machine — which is to say, therefore, of his own machine.

2. THE OBSTACLE OF INTENTIONALITY

Let us come back to analytical philosophy. It will be recalled that the second reason which led us to strongly qualify the importance of its "cognitive turn" was that the philosophy of mind that has resulted from it remains profoundly marked by the philosophy of language. The issue at hand, here, is that of representation.

In one of the rare studies that compares what today has become known as connectionism with the McCulloch-Pitts model, Daniel Andler takes McCulloch and Pitts to task for having utterly ignored the problem of representation (see Andler 1992). Andler defends the thesis according to which the decisive move of contemporary connectionism has been to link itself up with the cognitivist mainstream (even if only to be in a better position to devour it) by borrowing from the orthodox tradition virtually the whole of its notion of representation. Nothing in principle prevents present-day neural networks of the parallel distributed processing type (see Rumelhart, McClelland, and the PDP Research Group 1986), for example, from exhibiting those higher cognitive properties which until now have been the privileged possession of classical artificial intelligence—thus avoiding the ghetto of perception in which research of the Perceptron variety seemed to have gotten stuck. It may be particularly hoped that connectionism will soon be able to account for the capacity of a network to "produce" logic, taking this capacity to be an *emergent* property of the network as a whole—which means that it cannot be localized at some lower level, and in particular not at the level of its elements. "But," it may be protested, "how can that be? Did not McCulloch long ago provide a demonstration that each neuron can be interpreted as a logical calculator, embodying, for example, one of the set of logical connectives; and that the network in its entirety can be treated as a universal symbolic calculator?" No, Andler forcefully replies, nothing of the sort can be said to have been demonstrated. That logic may serve to model the network does not imply that the network can be regarded as a model of logical thought. What McCulloch's argument fails to do, but must do if it is to be philosophically sound, is to show how the signal transmitted by a given neuron is able to represent a proposition about the world; to show how the coding that allows an equivalence to be established between some thought content and a calculation effected by the network can be assigned a meaning in terms of representation.

Andler's argument is powerful and convincing. Note, however, that it takes for granted that knowing subjects *have* representations; and that a representation's mode of being corresponds to the idea of representation found in cognitive philosophy. With regard to the latter point, a "mental state" represents something to the extent that it has a content and that this content concerns the world. Cognitive philosophy resorts to a technical term to designate this representative capacity of mental states: they are called "intentional." The intentionality of mental states is bound up with their "aboutness"—the fact that they are *about* certain objects. These objects are heterogeneous with respect to mental states, being things-in-themselves (or properties of such things, or otherwise relations among several such things). One might immediately object that this shows cognitive philosophy is out of step with the general movement to which cognitive science belongs, a movement that can be summed up with the phrase: "to think is to simulate." Then, as Proust points out, pushing her Kantian reading of artificial intelligence à la Newell and Simon a step further,

> To refer, for a physical symbol system, is necessarily to *simulate* symbolically the structure and the properties of an object. The main presupposition of simulation is that it preserves the structure of reality. However the notion of "reality" must in its turn be contained/apprehended in the terms of the system.... The idea of a fact [that is] radically heterogenous with the "knowing" system has ... simply no meaning. (Proust 1987)

In Kantian terms: the object of representation is not the thing-in-itself; it is the appearance of this thing within the representation itself in the form of the phenomenon, which thereby acquires an objective validity.

If, by contrast, one posits that the object of representation is the thing-in-itself, as cognitive philosophy does, then this thing certainly cannot be said to constitute its *content*. When I think that I may have forgotten to lock my bicycle, for example, the actual object made out of metal and leather and rubber is not found contained in my mind. The thing-in-itself does not exist in the representation: it is constitutively absent from it. What, then, is the nature of the content of a representation? The answer that philosophy of mind provides to this question is what continues to make it a philosophy of language, however much it may wish it were not. The answer it gives is a linguistic one, on two levels. Take the mental states which have long occupied the attention of cognitive science, and which since Bertrand Russell gave them their name have been known as "propositional attitudes." As the name indicates, they are supposed to connect a (psychological) attitude of the type "to believe that," "to desire that," "to fear that," "to have the intention of," and so on, with a proposition about the world. In the functionalist, computational, and representational version of philosophy of mind defended today by Jerry Fodor or Zenon Pylyshyn, this proposition is expressed in a sentence of the "language of thought"—a private language whose symbols are inscribed in the material substrate of the brain.

To be sure, this hypothesis of a language of thought is not shared by all philosophers of mind—far from it; but all of them, or almost all, accept that the criterion of the "intentionality" of the mental is linguistic at a second level: the sentences of the public language we use to attribute mental states endowed with content to others possess the property of being intensional. By that it is meant that they violate the rules of logical extensionality, the first of which has to do with existential generalization. From the truth of the statement "Maurice's cow grazes in the meadow" it may be inferred that there necessarily exists a meadow in which Maurice's cow grazes; by contrast, neither the truth nor falsity of the statement "Maurice believes that the boozoos are fatter in Savoy than in the Dolomites" permits us to conclude the existence or nonexistence of boozoos.

The second rule violated by an intensional expression concerns the substitutability of terms having the same reference. My son, who just turned twelve years old, does not know that Tegucigalpa is the capital of Honduras; on the other hand, despite his lack of interest in logic, he knows that "the capital of Honduras is the capital of Honduras." It is this property that Quine made famous as the quality of "referential opacity." But it was in fact Roderick Chisholm who, in a book published in 1957, first proposed this linguistic interpretation of intentionality (see Chisholm 1957 and 1956). There he gave the following example: "Most of us knew in 1944 that Eisenhower was the one in command; but although he was identical with the man who was to succeed Truman, it is not true that we knew in 1944 that the man who was to succeed Truman was the one in command" (Chisholm 1957).

The difficulties that philosophy of mind meets with today arise in large part from its early commitment to language. Many of its practitioners accept the linguistic characterization of intentionality while at the same time trying to "naturalize" it—that is to say, to supply an analysis of it founded ultimately on the laws of physics. The problem is that they want this "physicalist" enterprise to preserve something that ordinary psychology takes for granted, namely, that the contents of mental states have causal relevance in the explanation of our behavior. If Maurice went to Savoy rather than to the Dolomites to hunt boozoos, it is *because* he believed that he would find plumper animals there. For a long time the obstacle seemed insurmountable, because philosophy of mind had convinced itself that the semantic content of a mental state, as described by its conditions of truth and of reference, depends on the entire physical and social environment of the subject; but if this content is supposed to have causal power in the physicist's sense, it can only be conceived in terms of the intrinsic properties of the mental state. It therefore appeared that the theory of knowledge could be naturalized only at the cost of depriving mental properties and states of all causal efficacy insofar as they are mental—thus making them pure "epiphenomena."

One of the most original theoretical proposals for overcoming this obstacle is the "anomalous monism" advocated by Donald Davidson in a famous 1970 article called "Mental Events." Davidson postulated that every mental *event* is identical to a physical event; nonetheless, there is no identity relation between classes or types of mental events and classes or types of physical events. In holding that properties, whether mental or physical, are just such classes of singular events, this philosophical position combined an ontological monism (namely, the view that ultimately "there are" only physical events) with a dualism of concepts and properties (namely, the view that mental concepts cannot be reduced to physical ones). Such a nonreductionist monism is "anomalous" in the following sense: while mental events cause other mental events as well as physical events, the *relation* of causality connects events with one another only insofar as they are events of the world, independently of whatever description, mental or physical, that we may give of them. The causal relation is therefore extensional, and underlying it is a law of physics. By contrast, an *explanation* that involves properties or mental concepts, after the fashion of the explanations furnished by ordinary psychology, can only be intensional, for which very reason it instantiates no strictly deterministic law in the physicist's sense—whence its nonnomological, or "anomalous," character. In short, while mental or psychological concepts enjoy an explanatory autonomy, ontologically the relation of causality does not involve the mental insofar as it is mental. This remains an epiphenomenon (one hardly dares say "superstructure").

Reviewing the various attempts that have been made to give substance to a naturalistic materialism, notably functionalism and anomalous monism, Pascal Engel (1994) comments,

> This dual concern with the reduction of mental concepts to concepts acceptable from the point of view of a scientific psychology and with support for the autonomy of such concepts well illustrates the permanent dilemma of a materialist theory of mind. Indeed, the more successful the reduction (which is to say, the more one manages to "explain" mental concepts in "physicalist" or "naturalist" terms), the less our usual mental concepts (those of commonsense psychology and of our pretheoretical conception of the mind) seem correct—and the more one is tempted to "eliminate" [mental concepts] in favor of [physical concepts], to hold that there simply are no such things as beliefs, desires, sensations, and so on. In other words, materialism ceaselessly oscillates between its "eliminativist" and "non-reductionist" versions. The project of a "naturalized" philosophy of mind similarly oscillates between these two tendencies.

To this one might add that the instability emphasized by Engel is still stronger than he claims if one takes account of the fact that nonreductionist versions flirt rather often with disguised forms of dualism.

Once again we encounter an irony of history. Looking back, one may say that the naturalization of transcendental philosophy was paradoxically perhaps easier to carry through to a successful conclusion than the naturalization of a psycholinguistic philosophy of mind—and that while this task was within the power of cybernetics to accomplish, cybernetics had no idea how to go about doing it.

3. BRENTANO BETRAYED

To illustrate these two claims, it is necessary to make a brief foray into that other great current of twentieth-century philosophy, phenomenology. The decisive role played in its development by the concept of intentionality is well recognized, of course, and one suspects that its relation with what the same term stands for in cognitive philosophy is distant at best, since in Husserl it is mental *activity* that enjoys the property of being intentional, this property constituting the "essence of the concept of consciousness." What is less generally realized is that the intentionality that figures in philosophy of mind shares a common ancestor with Husserlian intentionality in the philosophical psychology of Franz Brentano. Husserl studied with Brentano in Vienna from 1884 to 1886, an experience that would prove decisive in shaping his later work, as the *Logical Investigations* (1900–1901) attest. The great Austrian philosopher's legacy to philosophy of mind was to be conveyed through the efforts of Roderick Chisholm, whom we have already mentioned in connection with his invention of the linguistic version of intentionality: earlier he had been responsible for introducing Brentano's thought to the United States, publishing translations as well as commentaries of several of his works, on the strength of which he came to be regarded as a leading authority on Brentano. One of the two, however, must have betrayed his master. Was it Husserl, or was it Chisholm?

"All consciousness is consciousness of something": Husserl found the inspiration for this formula (famous in France for the use that was later made of it by Sartre in that variant of phenomenology known as existentialism) in Brentano's thought; more precisely, in the following passage that he cites from his teacher's *Psychology from an Empirical Standpoint* (1874): "Every mental phenomenon is characterized by what the Scholastics of the Middle Ages called the intentional (or mental) inexistence of an object, and what we might call, though not wholly unambiguously, reference to a content, direction toward an object (which is not to be understood here as meaning a thing) or immanent objectivity."[2]

Every word here is potentially a trap. "Intentional," Brentano reminds us, is a scholastic term used by Thomas Aquinas, for example, in the sense of "mental" (as opposed to "real"). Form is united with matter in the real object, which is to say outside the mind; the "intentional" object is present only in its form. *Inexistenz* ("inexistence") comes from the Latin *in-esse*, meaning "to be inside of": here, quite obviously, taking "inexistent" to mean "nonexistent" would be a serious mistranslation. The object *toward* which the mind *tends* (i.e., its *intention*) is located *inside* the mind: hence the reason why its presence is said to be "immanent."

Mental life, according to Brentano, is above all an activity, a dynamic process. This activity is "presentation." Brentano adds, "By presentation, I do not mean that which is presented but rather the act of presentation." This activity has a content, or more precisely an "object." The object is that very thing which is presented to the mind: the sound that we hear, the color that we see, the cold that we feel. Further confusing matters is the fact that Brentano calls these objects of presentation "physical phenomena"—by contrast with the previously defined mental activity. But he goes on to say, in order to dispel any possible ambiguity, that these "physical" phenomena are part of "the data of our consciousness."

Mental activity is intrinsically conscious of itself. When we think, we have an immediate perception of the fact that we are thinking, and this perception of the thinking activity is simultaneously a perception of the object of thought. This internal perception cannot be an observation, Brentano notes, for that would imply an infinite regression of mental activities, each one pointing to a further one. It is by means of a global and unique act of apprehension that thought as activity is related both to itself and to its intentional object:

> Do we *perceive* the mental phenomena which exist within us? The question must be answered with an emphatic "yes" for where would we have got the concepts of presentation and thought without such perception? On the other hand, it is obvious that we are not able to *observe* our present mental phenomena. . . . This suggests that there is a special connection between the object of inner presentation and the presentation itself and that both belong to one and the same mental act. The presentation of a sound and the presentation of the presentation of a sound belong to one and the same mental phenomenon; it is only by considering it in its relation to two different objects, one of which is a physical phenomenon and the other a mental phenomenon that we divide it conceptually into two presentations. . . . In the same mental phenomenon in which the sound is present to our mind we simultaneously apprehend the mental phenomenon itself. (Brentano 1874, trans. D. B. Terrell and L. L. McAlister, pp. 127–28)

We know what Husserl was to make of this idea. He used it to derive the classic phenomenological gesture, the *épochè* or "reduction," which amounts to deciding to see in the object of representation only the correlate (*noema*) of mental activity (*noesis*)—putting to one side the problem of the relation between the object of representation (the intentional object) and the thing-in-itself. Construed in this way, intentionality was to become Husserl's principal weapon in his critique of psychologism, as Alain Renaut has shown:

> To say that, for there to be consciousness, the object and the subject must link up in such a way that the object comes to "intentionally in-exist" for the subject (that is, to assume the form of the object of representation, as distinct from what it is outside of consciousness), was in effect also to designate a relation between object and subject that was no longer a question for psychology. . . . There exists, with regard to our representations, a level of questioning more radical than that of psychology: where the latter now and always presupposes the fact that we have representations, in order to limit itself to showing the role played by perception, memory, attention, and feelings, [phenomenology] is interested in posing the pre-psychological question of whether *in fact* there are representations and, if so, what is the *mode of being* of the object of representation—an *ontological* question, if you like, in the sense that the existence and the essence of representations are at stake; or, if you prefer, a *transcendental* question, in the sense that it is a matter of determining under what conditions representation is possible. (Renaut 1993: 97–98)

Let us now imagine an ungifted first-year philosophy student who, having been asked to read the passages of Brentano cited here, systematically gets the meaning of the key terms wrong. On this misreading of Brentano, the object toward which representation tends is a *nonexistent physical object*. Accordingly, it must be the thing-in-itself. When I think of a cow or a boozoo, what in fact is absent from my representation? In the case of the boozoo, the physical flesh-and-bones beast is missing, for the reason that boozoos do not exist; in the case of the cow, the physical cow with its udders and milk and the rest is likewise missing, but for the reason that, although cows do exist (unlike boozoos), they exist only outside of my mind. Intentionality is therefore no longer the mental *activity* that goes beyond itself while remaining within itself, in the direction of an object that also remains internal to it—that "transcendence in immanence" that Husserl sought to detect; it now becomes a mental *state* endowed with a content, which in turn is related to an object whose existence is not guaranteed by the fact that the mental state itself exists. Therefore the content can only be intensional, and hence linguistic.

As enormous and as obvious as this trap may seem to us, it is the interpretative trap that ("consciously" or "unconsciously") Roderick Chisholm fell into—and, in any event, the trap into which he caused his readers, an entire generation of analytic philosophers, to fall. Unquestionably the foremost and most celebrated of these was Quine.[3] In a famous passage in *Word and Object* (1960: 45), a work that strongly influenced many younger philosophers, some of whom were later to become influential in their own right, Quine relies on Chisholm's "illuminating" reading to attribute to Brentano a "thesis" with which he pronounces himself in agreement—since, as he says, it is identical with his own thesis of the radical indeterminacy of translation between languages, or of the mental states that a listener attributes to a speaker. The so-called "Brentano thesis" is in fact none other than Chisholm's thesis. It asserts that mental states (and mental states alone) are endowed with the property of intentionality, understood as a linguistic relation to objects or states of affairs of the external world—external to the mind. Intentional expressions are irreducible to the terms that we use to describe "physical" phenomena. "One may accept the Brentano thesis either as showing the indispensability of intentional idioms and the importance of an autonomous science of intention," Quine concludes, "or as showing the baselessness of intentional idioms and emptiness of a science of intention. My attitude, unlike Brentano's, is the second" (ibid., p. 221). That was all the encouragement that his followers needed. Some, less "eliminatively" inclined than Quine, more conscious of the limits to any attempt to "naturalize epistemology," were to go on to propose "nonreductionist monisms" capable of reconciling "Brentano's thesis" with a relative physicalism. The rest of the story is in any case well known.

One may be tempted to deplore this misreading. That would be a mistake. The history of philosophy well justifies the charge that philosophers are their own worst readers—but it is equally true that their blunders and misinterpretations do from time to time occasion rich works of great originality whose arguments come to gain wide acceptance. This is the sole thing that should matter to the historian of ideas.

4. THE MISSED ENCOUNTER WITH PHENOMENOLOGY

Daniel Andler is right to emphasize that it would be hard to find a notion of representation in cybernetics that prefigures in the least the psycholinguistic theory which today constitutes the hard core of cognitive science. Is this to say that the transcendental question "whether *in fact* there are representations and, if so, what is the *mode of being* of the object of representation" therefore slipped out of the cyberneticians' grasp as well?

In hindsight it seems fair to say that if there existed a possibility of scientifically modeling—and therefore, if you will, of "naturalizing"—intentionality as it was first conceived by Brentano, and then developed by Husserl, this lay in the study of networks as conceived and developed by Warren McCulloch. For cybernetics to have been able to come up with a feasible plan for research, however, it would have had to regard an idealized neural network from an entirely different point of view than McCulloch's.

McCulloch and Pitts saw their networks as logic machines. Inspired by the revolutionary spirit of Turing's thesis, and armed with the equivalence theorem identifying their machine with his, they set themselves the pedagogical task of showing that one could conceive of a network capable of reproducing each of the principal faculties of mind. Now in Turing's scheme, a mental function was interpreted as a function in the mathematical sense: as an operator transforming inputs (stimuli) into outputs (responses). For many years this perspective (a behaviorist perspective, when you get right down to it) constituted an obstacle to the Gestalt switch that would have permitted researchers to see the network as an "autonomous" dynamic system, informationally and organizationally closed, with neither input nor output. The alternative approach came to command attention only much later with the confluence of several new movements or schools of research. One of these, an offspring of the second cybernetics, was identified with the various attempts made during the 1970s and 1980s to formalize the self-organization of biological systems using Boolean automata networks: in France this work was conducted chiefly by a team directed by Henri Atlan and including Françoise Fogelman-Soulié, Gérard Weisbuch, and Maurice Milgram;[4] in the United States, by Stuart Kauffman (see Kauffman 1993), a former student of Warren McCulloch, and others at the Santa Fe Institute for the Study of Complex Systems. Another, also springing from the second cybernetics, was the Chilean school of autopoiesis, which went so far in its conception of informational closure as to deny the existence of representations altogether: this tradition of research was founded by Humberto Maturana and Francisco Varela, with the blessing of Gregory Bateson. Varela exploited various formalisms familiar from the theory of automata networks (see Varela 1979). A third movement, which grew up in the very heart of neoconnectionism (though it is to be distinguished from the "PDP" school mentioned previously, whose interest is in extending and enriching "Perceptron"-style research), was the Attractor Neural Network (ANN) school led by physicists studying the emergent properties of (almost) completely connected networks in which information is propagated in all directions: founded by John Hopfield at Caltech, this movement has enjoyed remarkable development due to the work of Daniel Amit in Israel, as well as the related research being done in France by Jean Petitot applying dynamical systems theory to the study of automata networks (see Hopfield 1982, Amit 1989, and Petitot 1995b).

All of this work, despite its profusion and variety, has one thing in common. All of it treats a complex network of interacting elementary calculators as an "autonomous" being, as it were—autonomous in the sense that, being endowed with a spontaneity of its own, it is itself the source of its own determining characteristics and not a simple transducer converting input messages into output messages. From the McCulloch-Pitts model to that of Daniel Amit, the model as a mathematical creature has not changed: it remains, at bottom, a threshold automaton. What has completely changed is the way one looks at it: one is no longer interested in its computational capacities, only in its "self-behaviors" (or *eigenbehaviors*, to use the hybrid English-German phrase of quantum mechanics, from which systems theory borrowed this concept). What does it imply? Like every automaton with an internal state, a network calculates its state in the next period as a function of its state during the current period. Now, a very general property characteristic of such networks is that, after a transition period (often quite a short one), its collective behavior stabilizes to a "limit cycle"—that is, a periodic spatiotemporal configuration—of weak periodicity: where the period is equal to one, as it may be the case, the state is said to be "stationary," or "fixed-point." Everything occurs as though this stable collective behavior were *self*-reproducing, as though it were produced by itself—hence the term "self-behavior"—when in fact it is produced by the network. Let us take, for example, the case of an elementary automaton, or neuron, which happens never to be fired in the course of the limit cycle. It would thus appear to have no causal effect upon the outcome of the cycle. But this is an illusion: one needs only to remove the neuron, along with its synapses, from the structure of the network to realize that the collective behavior of the latter is affected by the absence of the former.

A given network usually possesses a multiplicity of self-behaviors, or as they are sometimes called, "attractors" (a term borrowed from dynamical systems theory), and converges toward one or another depending on the initial conditions of the network. The "life" of a network can thus be conceived as a trajectory through a "landscape" of attractors, passing from one to another as a result of perturbations or shocks from the external world. Note that these external events come to acquire meaning in the context of the network as a result of the network's own activity: the *content*— the meaning—which the network attributes to them is precisely the self-behavior, or attractor, that results from them. Obviously, then, this content is purely endogenous, and not the reflection of some external "transcendent" objectivity.

It should be clear as well that this line of argument will take us where we want to go. For does it not provide us with at least the germ of a very satisfactory model of what Brentano called "immanent objectivity"? Some philosophers have already set to work on the problem. The attractor is a being that both fully participates in the activity of the network and yet in some sense, by virtue of the fact that it results from a higher level of logical complexity, transcends the activity of the network. The dynamics of the network may therefore be said to *tend toward* an attractor, although the latter is only a product of these dynamics. The network is thus an *intentional* creature in Brentano's and Husserl's sense. Systems theory was to coin another term to describe this paradoxical relationship between the dynamics of a system and its attractor, referring to it as "autotranscendence." This is not very different really from Husserl's notion of "transcendence within immanence." It is not surprising, then, that certain cognitive scientists who rely upon automata networks in their research (and who are considered "marginal" by their peers) should more or less explicitly invoke the authority of some kind of transcendental phenomenology: in France, one thinks of Atlan, Petitot, and Varela (see Atlan 1994: 67–87; Petitot 1992b,1993; and Varela et al. 1991).

Was there any chance, at the time of the Macy Conferences, that cybernetics might have taken this road? I have already called attention to the ideological obstacle constituted by the Turing paradigm. But other circumstances intervened as well, particularly as a consequence of the training and philosophical interests of the conference participants. The sole professional philosopher to take part in the Macy Conferences was Filmer Northrop, a Yale professor who enjoyed a certain reputation during the period. However, his influence upon the group of cyberneticians was negligible. The philosophical training of the latter was restricted for the most part to philosophical logics: Wiener had studied with Russell at Cambridge, von Neumann with Hilbert at Göttingen, and Pitts with Carnap at Chicago. McCulloch, for his part, was a great admirer of Russell, G. E. Moore, Peirce, and the Wittgenstein of the *Tractatus*.

An encounter with Husserlian phenomenology, or rather with one of its offshoots, did nonetheless take place, though in the form of a confrontation—and a failed one at that—with Gestalt psychology. This school, a product of the intellectual life of Weimar Germany, had come to the United States as part of the wave of immigration accompanying the rise of Nazism. Wolfgang Köhler had been one of the founders of the movement in the 1920s, at the Psychological Institute of Berlin, where he had taken over the directorship from his teacher Carl Stumpf, who himself had been a student of Brentano and close to Husserl. The project of his research team at the Institute, which included Kurt Koffka, Max Wertheimer, and Kurt Lewin, was to resolve the problems posed by Husserlian phenomenology by means of an experimental type of scientific psychology that drew upon the concepts of quantum mechanics (Köhler had studied physics with Planck as well), particularly that of a field. Their ambition was to discover the laws (in the sense in which the term is understood in the natural sciences) governing perception and the immediate experience that we have of things, with the aim, above all, of preserving their "holistic" character as organized wholes.

In the early 1920s Köhler had postulated a "psychophysical isomorphism" between the physical events occurring in the brain and the facts of psychological experience. The isomorphism he sought to detect experimentally was topological in character: the content of an internal perception of a figure, for example, ought to have, he believed, a corresponding geometric pattern in the brain. Once settled in the United States, Köhler was to undertake neurophysiological experiments in the hope of discovering a physical correlate to the phenomena of perception in the form of continuous electric fields in cerebral tissue. When the cyberneticians invited him to the fourth Macy Conference, in October 1947, they expected (as their experience with other advocates of a continualist model of cerebral function had led them to anticipate) that the discussion would concern the relative merits of this model over the idealized neural model. In the event, Köhler delivered a speech that his listeners judged to be purely ideological, devoid of any reference to "concrete neurophysiological data," and the discussion abruptly came to a halt.[5] This missed opportunity was partially made up for the following year, at the Hixon Symposium, though there the confrontation between McCulloch's mechanism and Köhler's holism took on something of the quality of a religious war.

When all is said and done, the one who came closest to naturalizing the transcendental inquiry was not, paradoxically, the phenomenologist Köhler but the logical atomist McCulloch. Köhler believed in a geometrical parallelism obtaining between perception and its material substrate; McCulloch inquired into the formal and material conditions under which knowledge was possible at all. One of his most remarkable successes in this regard was the experimental work he carried out much later on the frog with Pitts, Jerome Lettvin, and Humberto Maturana (out of which came the Chilean school of "autopoietic systems"). This research, published under the memorable title "What the Frog's Eye Tells the Frog's Brain,"[6] drew attention to the existence of receptors in the visual system responding selectively to certain features of the stimulus, such as convexity, and interpreted them as the material equivalents of the categories of a priori synthetic judgment. Shortly thereafter, Hubel and Wiesel were to confirm these results in the cat, which won them the Nobel Prize in medicine.

5. A PHILOSOPHY OF MIND WITHOUT ANY SUBJECT

Kantianism, yes, but without the transcendental subject—as Paul Ricoeur said about the structuralism of Claude Lévi-Strauss (Ricoeur 1963: 618). This formula applies wonderfully well to cybernetics. The neural network of McCulloch and Pitts neither was, nor pretended to be, a model of the subject—any more than Newell and Simon's "physical symbol system" did. A model of the mind, yes; of the subject, no. Whence perhaps the most significant contribution of cybernetics to philosophy: mind minus the subject. The connection with Lévi-Strauss is all the more irresistible considering that the great anthropologist explicitly referred to cybernetics in his introduction to the work of Marcel Mauss, widely regarded as the first manifesto of French structuralism. The task of social anthropology, he asserted, was to reveal the "unconscious mental structures" at work behind such practices as the exchange of gifts in "archaic" societies. These structures, which play the role of a synthetic a priori, are manifested in the phenomena of communication, with "symbolic thought" being structured in the way that language is structured (see Lévi-Strauss 1950). The year was 1950: Lévi-Strauss had just turned toward semiotics, under the influence of Roman Jakobson; he was also influenced by the recent publication of Wiener's *Cybernetics* (1948) and Shannon and Weaver's *Theory of Communication* (1949). Lévi-Strauss quickly came around to the view that a mathematical theory of communication introduced into anthropology by linguistics was the way of the future for the social sciences.

By inventing a type of transcendental inquiry that did away with the subject, cybernetics was to greatly assist the deconstruction of the metaphysics of the subject. This is a crucial point, one that is too rarely recognized. In a well-known interview, published in 1976 in *Der Spiegel*, Heidegger pronounced the anathema quoted at the head of this chapter: "Cybernetics is the metaphysics of the atomic age." For most of his followers, but for many other philosophers as well, cybernetics seemed to raise the "philosophy of the *cogito*" to its greatest height, the final outcome of a misguided metaphysics that assigned to man the task of making himself master and possessor of all things. Cybernetics, as the *summum* of the will to power and of the will to will, would be responsible for our missing "the essence of technology"—which, for Heidegger, lies outside technology, in this mode of revelation and unveiling of Being that goes by the name of *Gestell*. "So long as we represent technology as an instrument," Heidegger declared in his famous paper on the essence of technique, first presented in 1949, "we remain transfixed in the will to master it" (Heidegger 1977: 314). This instrumental and anthropological definition of technology was to receive its fullest expression, on the Heideggerian view, with the advent of cybernetics.

Those who go on repeating this condemnation appear never to have pondered over the following troubling point. When, at the beginning of the 1950s, French practitioners of the "sciences of man" (whose intellectual debt to Heidegger's thought, in both their structuralist and post-structuralist versions, is indisputable) were looking for a way to say something about the mystery of Being, its unveiling, and so forth, they turned in their search for metaphors (poetic language not being their strong suit) to cybernetics. In the interest of showing that humanity is *not* its own master, that, far from mastering language, it is language that masters humanity, and that "symbolic order" is irreducible to human experience, it was the vocabulary of cybernetics and information theory that they systematically drew upon. The most typical case was that of Jacques Lacan. Cybernetics was the main topic of his seminar during the academic year 1954–55, the culmination of which was the reading of Edgar Allan Poe's *The Purloined Letter* in terms of automata theory.[7] Lacan was later to begin his *Ecrits* by revisiting his seminar on Poe's story, the key to which he claimed to furnish in an "Introduction" that took the form of cybernetic variations on the game of odd or even intended to illustrate "how a formal language determines the subject." Even if this part of his teaching seems to have passed over the head of more than one student, one cannot conclude from this that Lacan did not take cybernetics seriously. His lecture on psychoanalysis and cybernetics ("Psychanalyse et cybernétique, ou de la nature du langage"), given in June 1955, testifies further to his interest in the subject. Later the new literary criticism, caught up in its turn by the excitement of detecting the autonomy of signifiers and their infinite drift, was to display great dexterity in operating various types of "textual machines," desiring or other. Even the vogue of *mise en abyme*—schemes of infinite repetition and other forms of literary self-reference—found it interesting to resort to cybernetic concepts.[8]

What one discovers in the cybernetic project, in reality, is exactly the ambiguity that Heidegger spoke of in connection with the essence of the technological (see Heidegger 1977: 314–15). Technology reveals truth (the Heideggerian truth) about Being—a truth that involves the deconstruction of the metaphysical view of the subject; but, at the same time, its particular way of unveiling truth forces both humanity and the world to run the risk of being swallowed up in a frenetic quest after power and mastery.

There is no question that the ambiguity of the cybernetic project appears most clearly in the interpretation given to research on automata. On the one hand, this research can be seen as the height of the anthropomorphization of technique. This was certainly the aspect to which the public was most sensitive. One can, however, just as easily regard the cybernetic automaton as the mechanization of the human, as the unveiling of what is not human in man—thus Lacan's remark: "The question of knowing whether [the machine] is human or not is obviously completely settled—it is not. But there is the question too of knowing whether the human, in the sense in which you understand it, is as human as [you suppose]" (Lacan 1978: 367).

Marc Jeannerod perfectly captures the spirit of cybernetics (even if he does so negatively, and in a reproving sort of way) when he alludes to the demonstrated existence of nerve cells that, like biochemical clocks, exhibit spontaneous rhythmic activity: these spontaneous oscillation generators, he says, "allow the functioning of the nervous system to be reduced to that of a machine which 'works by itself' once it is started up, or which can almost be said even to start itself up. Such a physiology of spontaneity remains, however, a singularly limited explanation of behavior. While it accounts well enough for the automatic aspects of [the] behavior [of the nervous system], it cannot be generalized to account for its other aspects without turning it into *behavior without a subject*" (Jeannerod 1983: 156). But this was precisely the objective of the cyberneticians. In their own way, they too contributed to the critique of the metaphysics of subjectivity.

As for the French Heideggerians, it is precisely because they were sensitive (and quite rightly so) to this side of cybernetics that they appealed to it to say what they had to say; and what they had to say, they said in a coherent way. When Vincent Descombes, in his otherwise excellent study of French postwar philosophy, reproaches structuralism for incoherence in claiming to struggle against the "philosophy of consciousness" while drawing its concepts from "an engineering style of thought," he only betrays an ignorance of cybernetics that is widely shared—and which the unfortunate choice of the very name "cybernetics" (from the Greek, meaning "steersman," and implying a theory of command, governance, and mastery) cannot excuse (see Descombes 1979: 123–24).

REFERENCE MATTER

NOTES

FOREWORD

1. See Gardner 1985.
2. This expression will hereafter designate not only the phenomenology of Husserl himself, but all phenomenology of Husserlian kind or origin, in order to distinguish it from other theories vindicating phenomenological titles but making no connection with the Husserlian tradition.

CHAPTER 1

1. For an introductory account of this episode of the history of the sciences of cognition, see Dupuy 1994, Gardner 1985, and Osherson and Smith 1990.
2. Accordingly, in this chapter we reserve the capitalized form of the expression for this specific hypothesis, and we use the lowercase form for the general notion of a theory of cognition.
3. Among the most prominent contributors to this debate, one should certainly mention (without any pretension to being exhaustive) Block 1978, Shoemaker 1984, Levine 1983, Jackson 1986, Lycan 1990, and McGinn 1983.
4. For a recent sample, see Hameroff, Kaszniak, and Scott 1996.
5. These distinct levels of investigation are not necessarily disconnected: some Cognitive Scientists working at the upper levels are quite interested into how functional processes are implemented in an organism or an artificial device, whereas others claim that purely functional characterizations of cognitive processes are totally autonomous. It is in any case important that an explicit link between the functional level and its realization be provided.
6. Cf. Block 1978: "You ask: What is it that philosophers have called qualitative states? I answer, only half in jest: As Louis Armstrong said when asked what jazz is: "If you got to ask, you ain't never gonna get to know."
7. In *Consciousness Reconsidered* (Flanagan 1992), Flanagan has for instance recommended such an extended use of the term.
8. Perceptual phenomena such as illusory contours, which reveal a great deal about what is happening in the visual system, provide a good example in favor of this approach.

9. Cf. Lakoff 1987 and Salanskis 1993.
10. The phrase is Owen Flanagan's.
11. Nagel 1970: 163, as reprinted in Block 1980.
12. Ibid., p. 166.
13. For a recent introduction to Husserl's theory, see Smith and Smith 1995.
14. This terminology, borrowed from traditional psychology and philosophy of mind, is used in the *Logische Untersuchungen*; but it is rejected by Husserl in §38 of *Ideen* I, where an opposition between immanent and transcendent intuitions is substituted for it. However, since the immanent/transcendent opposition is also used for a distinction more crucial to the definition of the domain of phenomenology, we will retain that early terminology here for the sake of simplicity and clarity.
15. Unless otherwise specified, the translations of Husserl are ours, and the page numbers refer to the Husserliana edition. When a translation is mentioned, the page numbers refer to the translation.
16. See the studies collected in the first section of the volume for more details.
17. *Ideen* I, §76: "On the other hand, as having the modification effected by parenthesizing, the whole world with all its psychical individuals and their psychical processes, belongs in phenomenology: all of it as a correlate of absolute consciousness. Consciousness therefore makes its appearance here in different modes of apprehension and different contexts, and different ones moreover within phenomenology itself: namely, within the latter itself first as absolute consciousness and secondly, in the correlate, as psychological consciousness which occurs in the natural world—as in a certain manner revalued yet without loosing the content peculiar to it as consciousness. Those are difficult and extraordinarily important relationships" (Kersten trans., p. 172).
18. First developed in a 1905 course and later further analyzed in a series of manuscripts, these texts are collected in *Zur Phänomenologie des inneren Zeitbewußtseins (1893–1917)* (hereafter cited as *PZB*).
19. Husserl speaks to this problem in numerous other texts. See all three parts of his *Zur Phänomenologie der Intersubjektivität* (hereafter cited as *ZPI* I, II, and III).
20. See Depraz 1995b.
21. Husserl, *Analysen zur passiven Synthesis (1918–1926)* (hereafter cited as *Analysen*).
22. *ZPI* I, II, and III.
23. It is also worth mentioning here some recent interpretations of William James in the light of genetic phenomenology. James's notion of experience as flow is prepersonal and in *Radical Empiricism* represents a transcendental turn only partially accomplished in his *Principles*. This reading of James is close to the generative dimensions developed by the later Husserl and some more immediate followers such as Eugen Fink.
24. The history and analysis of this movement has been the subject of many studies, in particular K. Otto Appel 1979.
25. As a matter of fact, this is how such a project is explicitly presented by the Vienna Circle reductionism, a recent antecedent of contemporary naturalism: cf., for instance, Hempel 1980.

26. For the phenomenology of Daubert, see Schuhmann and Smith 1985 and Schuhmann 1985 and 1989.

27. "This phenomenon [of the phantom limb] distorted equally by physiological and psychological explanations is, however, understood in the perspective of being-in-the-world. . . . What rejects in ourselves mutilation and deficiency is an 'I' committed to a certain physical and inter-human world who continues to tend toward this world despite perhaps handicaps and amputations" (Merleau-Ponty 1945: 96, our translation).

28. For an introduction to and a detailed bibliography on these theories, see Petitot 1992b.

29. Cf., for example, Thom 1980.

30. See also Rigal 1991 and Roy 1992 and 1995b.

31. For further details on the "Fregean reading of Husserl," developed on the basis of Føllesdal's article, see Fisette 1994.

32. For further details, see Roy 1998b and 1995a.

33. For a good discussion of this issue, see Langsdorf 1985.

34. For just a few examples of representative orientations in this renewal, see Barbaras 1992; Jonas 1966; Bermúdez, Marcel, and Eilan 1995; and Depraz 1995a.

35. On robotics and artificial intelligence, see Winnograd and Flores 1987, Agree 1995, and Beer 1991. On linguistics, see Johnson 1991 and Marbach 1993. On neuroscience, see Varela, Thompson, and Rosch 1991 and Clark 1997. On developmental cognition, see Thelen and Smith 1995. On medicine, see Leder 1991 and Toobs 1994.

36. Cf. Holenstein's studies of the Husserlian origin of R. Jakobson's structuralism.

37. See B. Smith 1982 and 1988.

38. See, in particular, Hempel 1980.

39. See, in particular, Borst 1970.

40. For a recent discussion of these issues, see Gallagher (in press).

41. "Zurück zu den Sachen selbst" (Husserl, *LU* II/1, p. 6).

42. Run under the auspices of CNRS and the ENS by Pierre Vermersch, with the collaboration of Natalie Depraz and Francisco Varela.

43. As well as in some sessions of the interdisciplinary seminar "Philosophie de l'action et de la perception" organized at the University of Strasbourg II by the Centre d'Analyse des Savoirs Contemporains, under the direction of Jean-Luc Petit.

CHAPTER 2

Epigraph: Rilke, Eighth Elegy from the *Duino Elegies* (trans. Stephen Mitchell). I thank the editors of this volume—Jean Petitot, Francisco Varela, Bernard Pachoud, and Jean-Michel Roy—for valuable comments on the penultimate draft of this essay, as well as for their vision in organizing the conference "Actualité cognitive de la phénoménologie" in Bordeaux. Various participants offered helpful responses to my presentation of these ideas there. I would also like to thank Jeffrey Barrett and

Charles Dement for comments on the penultimate draft of the essay, and Andrew Cross, Charles Dement, Dagfinn Føllesdal, Ronald McIntyre, Martin Schwab, and Peter Simons for our discussion of certain issues raised here.

1. N.B.: the term "material" will be used always to contrast with "formal," not to mean physical, or composed of matter-energy.

2. In 1993 the inaugural Jean Nicod lectures on philosophy of mind and cognitive science were given by Jerry Fodor in Paris, published in 1994 as *The Elm and the Expert*. In 1994 the Jean Nicod lectures were given by Fred Dretske in Paris, published in 1995 as *Naturalizing the Mind*. The aim of the conference in Bordeaux in October 1995, for which this paper was written, was to assess the challenges of naturalization for principles of Husserlian phenomenology. I have used these books by Fodor and Dretske to set the stage for my project by articulating, in the most up-to-date terms, key issues in naturalizing mind.

3. The following remarks about Husserl's ontology rest on my reconstruction thereof in D. W. Smith 1995b.

4. Again, see D. W. Smith 1995b.

5. Compare McIntyre 1986.

6. Quine's mature view of reification is found in Quine 1992.

7. Compare Quine and Ullian 1978.

8. In biology, systematics is the discipline of classifying living beings: distinguishing individuals, populations, species or taxa, and categories (Taxon, Family, etc.) from one another in terms of phena (observable qualities), synapomorphs (shared derived traits), and so on. Here I borrow the term "systematics" for the ontological discipline of classification of entities. The distinction between formal and material categories defines one type of ontological systematics. I focus on the formal/material distinction as a device that increases "systematic" complexity in fruitful ways, but ultimately the goal is to use ontological complexity to account for important distinctions concerning intentionality and other features of ontological structure. My conception of ontological systematics derives from discussions with Charles W. Dement and Peter Simons, in connection with the PACIS project at Ontek Corporation.

9. Wittgenstein's *Tractatus* posited such a structure in the world, at least the world as we find it, the world as represented in our logical systems. David Armstrong has argued recently for such an ontology of states of affairs, in Armstrong 1997. See also Armstrong 1989. Husserl's conception of states of affairs as a "formal" ontological category, however, can be found in both *Logische Untersuchungen* and *Ideen zu einer reinen Phänomenologie*, which predate Wittgenstein's work.

10. The ontology of dependence is launched in *LU* I, Third Investigation. Husserl's basic notion is reconstructed and elaborated in B. Smith 1982 and in Simons 1987. A detailed model of dependence is developed in Thomasson 1995.

11. States of affairs are "formal" structures in the ontology in *Logische Untersuchungen*. They play a similar role in Wittgenstein's *Tractatus*.

12. These formal categories are transformed, for example, in Whitehead's categorial ontology, where "actual occasions" are tied *in nexū* to "forms" as well as to other actual occasions. See Whitehead 1978. Whitehead's actual occasions replace Aristotle's substances, and his demi-Platonic forms tied to actual occasions do not

reside in a Platonic heaven. Still, actual occasions would count as individuals in the present formal/material categories (though Whitehead posits his own system of categories with many differences from the simpler scheme sketched here). Thus, in the categorial ontology we have so far sketched, it remains to specify the status of species, qualities, relations, and so on. They might be treated as Platonic forms that can be exemplified by particular natural objects, or as Aristotelian universals that gain reality only insofar as they are instantiated, or as "tropes" or Husserlian "moments" (particularized universals) falling under the categories Species, Quality, etc., or as Whiteheadian forms concretely tied into actual occasions. Alternatively, Platonized naturalism might posit Platonic forms as falling under the formal categories of Species, Quality, Relation, etc., in an ontology of natural objects. Compare Linsky and Zalta 1995, with a specific formulation of a Mallian ontology that mixes abstract and concrete objects in a systematic ontology.

13. See the account of the world of common sense in B. Smith 1995.

14. On my reconstruction of Husserl's ontology, the same concrete individuals or events—in the world of "facts"—may instantiate the very different ideal "essences" of Nature, Culture, and Consciousness. See D. W. Smith 1995b.

15. See Kim 1993.

16. See *Logische Untersuchungen* and *Ideen* I and II, and Searle 1983, 1992. My approach in D. W. Smith 1989 defines a contextualist variant of internalism, which I now see as a third way, neither internalist nor externalist, emphasizing dependence or "grounding" of intentionality in context.

17. See Fodor 1994 and Dretske 1995.

18. The relations between the intentionality of consciousness and the intensionality of sentences about intentional states are detailed in Smith and McIntyre 1982.

19. These structures are analyzed in detail in D. W. Smith 1989, chap. 2.

20. The reasoning in Quine's position is expressed in Quine 1992. See D. W. Smith 1994. Quine's thesis of the indeterminacy of translation was a further reason, given in Quine 1960, for renouncing a science of intention, and thus phenomenology. I shall not treat that problem here, though Quine's modified views in Quine 1992 lead, I would argue, to a different take on indeterminacy, notably where empathy plays a role in understanding others.

21. See the bibliography for relevant works of the authors cited. Compare Fodor 1994: 14–15, which summarizes some current attitudes.

22. See Quine 1969.

23. On the controversies surrounding connectionism, see Horgan and Tienson 1991.

24. Philosophy of mind in cognitive science has centered on the issue of how the mental might be reduced to the physical, focusing on what might be the structure of causal or computational process that defines mind. The structure of intentionality might then be *preserved* either as a language of thought ("sentences in the head," on Fodor's earlier view) or as a flow of physical "information" outside the head (Dretske's view, partly adopted recently by Fodor). Or intentionality might be *eliminated* (as the Churchlands have sometimes urged, assuming, mistakenly, that intentionality must have the structure of sentences in the head). But there is a wide range of options

between these extremes, preserving some intentional structures and eliminating others. Moreover, the ontological issues are joined by questions about the relations among our different levels of *theory* about mind and brain. The complexity of these issues is brought out in Bickle 1992a, 1992b, and 1998.

25. See Searle 1983 and 1992.

26. See Quine and Ullian 1978, for the basic principles of framing knowledge in general and scientific theory in particular. In Quine 1992, Quine begins to make room for the intentional: see D. W. Smith 1994.

27. See D. W. Smith 1989.

28. The new attitude is evident, for instance, in Crick 1994 and Churchland 1995.

29. See Flanagan 1992. The proclamation is a reviewer's remark printed on the back of the book. Flanagan's discussion is indeed sensitive to a wide variety of phenomenological issues about consciousness, and he explicitly says that "it is incredible to think that we could do without phenomenology altogether" (p. 12), proceeding to argue for how phenomenological claims should be combined with empirical results of neuroscience. However, many issues of phemenological analysis of structures of consciousness are explored in great depth and detail in the writings of Husserl, Heidegger, Sartre, Merleau-Ponty, and many others in the phenomenological tradition. Good science cannot pass over these results, any more than it can pass over significant empirical experiments such as those of split-brain patients, blindsight, and so on.

30. See Chalmers 1995 and 1996.

31. See D. W. Smith 1995b.

32. Even if there are many metaphysically possible worlds, each is a unified system: that is the point of unionism. And even if the "many-worlds" version of quantum mechanics is true, the different parallel worlds are related in an ordered way, and the "world" we find ourselves in has its unity: that is the point here stressed by unionism. Unionism is thus orthogonal to the issue of other possible worlds in modal ontology (actualism denies that view), and to the issue of other parallel worlds of quantum mechanics. I would also argue that unionism is orthogonal to the issue of nominalism, often construed as ruling out abstract entities because they belong in a Platonic heaven apart from the natural world. Even a Platonist says particulars exemplify universals, thus tying the concrete and abstract realms together into a unified system; the nominalist would object to the efficacy of this claim, but the Platonist can be construed as aiming at a unionist position.

33. See Searle 1992.

34. As a skeptic might have it: see Rey 1988.

35. The intentionality of a thought depends on a background of not only personal beliefs and skills, but also attitudes and ideas extant in one's culture. This conception of background is explored in D. W. Smith's (1995a) "The Background of Intentionality." Somewhat different notions of background are found in Husserl and Searle. See Husserl's notion of horizon in *Ideen* I and II, reconstructed in Smith and McIntyre 1982; Husserl stresses implicit "meaning" in an act of consciousness. And

see Searle's notion of background in Searle 1983 and Searle 1992; Searle stresses practical capacities that enable intentional states to represent.

36. The term "meme" was coined by Richard Dawkins and championed in Dennett 1991.

37. A cognate ontology is expressed in the PACIS computer system under development by Ontek Corporation. That ontology is the collective work of Charles W. Dement, Peter Simons, and myself. Parts of the ontology are previewed in Simons and Smith (with Dement) 1993. Simons 1994/95 reflects on a more recent version of our PACIS categories.

CHAPTER 3

This article is a short version of a much longer unpublished study covering the same ground with more argumentative details, especially in its criticism of Fodorian representationalism. Hopefully this simplified presentation will nevertheless succeed in establishing the main point with sufficient strength.

1. The problem has nevertheless been addressed by a few philosophers. See, for instance, Bouveresse 1995 and Pacherie 1995a; see also E. Pacherie's contribution to this volume.

2. As it has been denied by a number of people: see, for example, F. Varela's enactive approach (cf. Chapter 1, sec. 1.1).

3. This by no means implies that the second stage of Fodor's strategy is considered acceptable. I personally share among other things the belief that the Fodorian theory does not succeed in making mental properties causally efficacious (cf. Roy 1998a, 1998c, 1999).

4. Cf. Fodor 1987b, chap. 1. According to Fodor the properties to be saved also include those which were firmly established in the course of previous attempts at turning folk intentional realism into science. Cf. Fodor 1981a.

5. There is no Greek term directly corresponding to the adjective "intentional." *Stochastikos* is said of a person who goes straight to the point. I owe this mischievous translation to the erudition of my colleague Jean-François Courtine.

6. It could be argued in particular that in "How Direct Is Visual Perception?" (Fodor and Pylyshyn 1981), Fodor and Pylyshyn have tried to demonstrate that a direct theory of perception such as Gibson's does not contradict a symbolic conception of cognition. The truth is that the notion of directness at stake in this debate is different from the one under discussion here. In the first case it refers to a noninferential cognitive process, in the second one to an unmediated intentional relation.

7. Cf. quotation in sec. 2.2.2.

8. In "Propositional Attitudes" (Fodor 1981a), Fodor actually makes the following revealing remark: "If we do say this, then we can make sense of the notion that propositional attitudes are relations to propositions—viz., they are *mediated* relations to propositions, with internal representations doing the mediating. This is, quite generally, the way that representational theories of the mind work. So, in clas-

sical versions, thinking of John (construed opaquely) is a relation to an 'idea'—viz., to an internal representation of John. But this is quite compatible with its also being (transparently) construable as a relation to John. In particular, when Smith is thinking of John, he (normally) stands in relation to John and does so in virtue of his standing in relation to an idea of John" (p. 201).

9. See Roy forthcoming.

10. I will deliberately leave aside, in this essay, the implications of such a difference. However important it is, I do not think it creates insurmountable difficulties for what I call here a naturalist appropriation of Husserlian intentionalism.

11. *LU* II/1, Fifth Investigation, §26, p. 454, my translation. Unless otherwise specified, all quotations of the *Logische Untersuchungen* are from the Findlay translation and the page numbers refer to it; when they are not from Findlay, all page numbers refer to the German edition.

12. I will adopt this translation here. The English term "experience," commonly used by translators, is to my mind too ambiguous.

13. Husserl, *Philosophie der Arithmetik*, p. 237. On the indirectness of symbolic intentionality, see also the Sixth Investigation, §20; the First Investigation, §23; and the Sixth Investigation, §27.

14. Fifth Investigation, §20, p. 589 (translation modified); cf. also the Sixth Investigation, §26.

15. The same is true for Husserl, within the intuitive kind, of the opposition between imaginative and perceptive intentionality.

16. Cf. in particular the Sixth Investigation.

17. Sixth Investigation, §25, p. 739; cf. also §§26 and 22.

18. Cf. Fifth Investigation, §26.

19. Cf. Sixth Investigation, §23, p. 734.

20. Cf. Sixth Investigation, §26, p. 741.

21. Cf. ibid.

22. Cf., e.g., Fifth Investigation, where he writes: "[Presentative sensory contents] constitute the act, provide necessary *points d'appui* which render possible an intention, but are not themselves intended, not the objects presented in the act. I do not see colour-sensations but coloured things, I do not hear tone-sensations but the singer's song" (§11, p. 559; cf. also §14).

23. See Roy 1996 for additional developments.

CHAPTER 4

1. As opposed to intentional realism, interpretativism claims that the existence of states with intrinsic intentionality is a myth. According to the interpretativist approach, intentionality is not a fact but a norm that guides our interpretation of interpersonal behaviors. Intentionality would then be constitutively linked with interpretation.

2. Among the main promoters of this approach are Fodor 1981b and Pylyshyn 1984.

3. A solipsist may claim that the problem of intentionality concerns mind/mind relations rather than mind/world relations. But besides the fact that solipsism may not be the most satisfactory philosophical option, solipsistic approaches to intentionality meet with serious difficulties. For a discussion of these difficulties, see, for instance, Fodor 1987b and 1990 and Pacherie 1993.

4. For a defense of such an approach, see, for instance, Dretske 1981 and 1988 and Fodor 1987b and 1990.

5. Following Dretske, we may distinguish between three forms of intensionality that correspond to the capacity to signify *F* without signifying *G*, even though, respectively, *F* and *G* are extensionally equivalent, all *F*s are *G*s in virtue of a law of nature, and it is analytically necessary that all *F*s are *G*s.

6. For a more detailed examination of those difficulties, see McGinn 1989.

7. In blindsight, patients who sincerely deny having any conscious visual experience are nevertheless capable, under certain conditions, of behaving in ways that show that they have processed part of the visual information presented to them. However, these subjects are seriously handicapped in their daily life, since, being unaware that they have access to visual information, they do not spontaneously produce behaviors based on the exploitation of this information. For more details, see Weizkrantz 1986.

8. My translation; the German original says: "Der Gegenstand steht in der Wahrnehmung als leibhafter da, er steht, genauer noch gesprochen, als aktuell gegenwärtiger, als selbstgegebener im aktuellen Jetzt da. In der Phantasie steht der Gegenstand nicht in der Weise der Leibhaftigkeit, Wirklichkeit, aktuellen Gegenwart da. Es steht uns zwar vor Augen, aber als kein aktuell jetzt Gegebenes; eventuell mag er als ein Jetzt oder mit dem aktuellen Jetzt Gleichzeitiges gedacht sein, aber dieses Jetzt ist ein gedachtes und nicht dasjenige Jetzt, das zur Leibhaftigkeit, zur Wahrnehmungsgegenwart, gehört" (*Ding und Raum*, §4, pp. 14–15; hereafter cited as *DR*).

9. My translation. The German says: "Das essentielle Charakter der Wahrnehmung ist es, 'Bewußtsein' von leibhaftiger Gegenwart des Objektes zu sein, d. i. Phänomen davon zu sein" (*DR*, §4, p. 15).

Although §4 of *Ding und Raum* and many other passages suggest that Husserl held a conjunctivist account of perceptual content, his view may not be as straightforwardly conjunctivist as it seems. For a discussion of this question, see Mulligan 1995: 210ff.

10. The question of the nature of those figural representations has given rise to intense debates, one illustration being the heated debate concerning the status of mental imagery. For a presentation of the imagery debate, see Tye 1991. In order to account for the specific character of perceptual representations, the British philosopher Christopher Peacocke (1992) has recently introduced the notions of "scenario content" and "protopropositional content."

11. The work of J. J. Gibson (see Gibson 1966 and 1979) has been very influential in bringing to the fore the importance of this dynamic dimension of perception. This idea also plays an important role in the work of certain continuators of Marr's computational approach to vision; see Petitot 1990 for more detail.

12. For a much more complete and detailed presentation of Husserl's theory of perception, see Mulligan 1995.

13. The German says: "Zum Wesen jeder Wahrnehmung eine Art Wahrnehmungszusammenhang gehört; nämlich zu ihrem Wesen gehört eine gewisse Extension" (*DR*, §19, p. 61).

14. "Nur wenn in der Einheit der Erfahrung der stetige Übergang von der einen Wahrnehmung in die andere gewährleistet ist, dürfen wir von der Evidenz sprechen, daß die Identität gegeben sei. Die Einheit des Gegenstandes weist sich nur aus in der Einheit der die mannigfaltigen Wahrnehmungen kontinuierlich verknüpfenden Synthesis" (*DR*, §44, p. 155).

15. "All diese kontinuierlichen Reihen stehen zueinander in gesetzmäßiger Wesenbeziehung, sie sind selbst miteinander kontinuierlich vermittelt, und erst in der allumfassenden Einheit dieser Reihen kommt das Quadrat wirklich 'allseitig' vollständig zur Gegebenheit. Es ist, was es ist, nur als das Identische in der systematischen Einheit dieser Abschattungen oder Abschattungsmöglichkeitens" (*DR*, §30, p. 104).

16. "Alle Räumlichkeit konstituiert sich, kommt zur Gegebenheit, in der Bewegung, in der Bewegung des Objektes selbst und in der Bewegung des 'Ich,' mit dem dadurch gegebenen Wechsel der Orientierung" (*DR*, §44, p. 155).

17. The original reads: "in einer kinästhetisch motivierten Erscheinungsmannigfaltigkeit."

18. "Eine neue Dimension, die aus dem Bild das Ding schafft und aus dem okulomotorischen Feld den Raum" (*DR*, §67, p. 236).

19. By "perceptual-motor activity," I mean motor activity the purpose of which is to obtain perceptual information from the world by modifying the flow of incoming sensory input. The effects of this activity on perception can be of greater or lesser strength. For instance, moving one's head usually has a marked effect on the flow of visual information, which is not the case with straightening one's back or moving one's toes. Besides, a change in the informational flow can be a side effect of some motor activity aiming at different goal, or it can be the intended effect of motor activity. In the latter case we have an instance of perceptual-motor exploration activity.

20. The first proponent of the hypothesis seems to have been von Helmholtz. The hypothesis was then developed by von Holst and Mittelstaedt (1950) with the concept of *efference copy* and Sperry (1950) with the concept of a *corollary discharge* in order to explain psychophysiological data in the domain of oculomotricity. This hypothesis has also played an important role in research on sensations of innervation and their physiological correlates. For surveys of more recent work, see, for instance, Scheerer 1987, Jeannerod 1994, and Gandevia and Burke 1993.

CHAPTER 5

1. In *Consciousness Explained* Dennett writes: "Like other attempts to strip away interpretation and reveal the basic facts of consciousness to rigorous observa-

tion, such as the Impressionistic [sic] movements in the arts and the Introspectionist psychologies of Wundt, Titchener, and others, Phenomenology has failed to find a single, settled method that everyone could agree upon" (1991: 44). This statement is misinformed in several respects. First, Dennett wrongly lumps together Impressionism and Introspectionism: whereas the Impressionists looked to the world and tried to present the true play of light and color there, the Introspectionists tried to scrutinize experience to discern within themselves those elementary units of which they thought experience had to consist. Second, Dennett confuses Introspectionism with Phenomenology, when in fact both the Gestalt and the phenomenological psychologists completely rejected Introspectionism. The Gestalt psychologists rejected it for assuming that experience had elementary, atomic units; they advocated what they thought of as natural or spontaneous observation, rather than atomistically minded introspection (see Kanizsa 1995). The phenomenologists continued in this vein, but also developed a method of phenomenological *reflection* that is fundamentally different in its procedures and aims from *introspection*, and that *is* generally recognized and agreed upon by phenomenologists (see Spiegelberg 1994: 677–719 and Ihde 1977). Of course, not "everyone" accepts this method, but then many visual scientists do not accept the computational method of explanation as advocated by Marr or the ecological method of explanation as advocated by Gibson, many biologists do not accept adaptationist methods of explanation in evolutionary biology, and so on.

2. The suppression of the response to uniform regions is much clearer for luminance than for color. For example, Wiesel and Hubel (1966) described the most frequent LGN cells as not showing spatial low-frequency attenuation for color contrast (see also Livingstone and Hubel 1984 and De Valois and De Valois 1993).

3. In visual science the term "filling-in" often has the sense of providing a roughly continuous spatial representation of a visual region. But the difference between Dennett's two stories enables one to see how there could be a purely symbolic-inferential version of the filling-in debate (compare Nakayama and Shimojo 1990). Here the issue would be: how many of the premises need to be "filled in" in inferential processing? How often can one simply "jump to the conclusion" without bothering to fill in the premises? Cf. Dennett 1993: 208: "The difference I am after is the difference between jumping to a conclusion and stepping to a conclusion by making some bogus steps on which to rest the conclusion (e.g., paint in the region, and then use that painted-in region as one's 'evidence' for the conclusion subsequently drawn)." Notice how this runs together the elements we are trying to disentangle.

4. Dennett's position on filling-in has provoked a critical response from Churchland and Ramachandran (1993). They disagree with Dennett because they think that the brain isn't merely "finding out" in the perceptual completion of the blind spot and artificial scotomata. They also disagree with Dennett's claim that there are no neural responses devoted to the lind spot, citing recent work from the laboratory of Ricardo Gattass (Fiorani et al. 1992) as showing the contrary. As far as we can see, however, Churchland and Ramachandran do not think that the brain fills in, in the sense of providing a roughly continuous spatial representation. In fact, on the basis of Ramachandran's other writings (1992a, 1992b, 1993; Ramachandran and

Gregory 1991), it seems to us that they might be prepared to accept some variant of the second story we attribute to Dennett—the one where the brain attaches a label. In any case, we think the debate would be better conducted in relation to issues about isomorphism and linking propositions. We go on to discuss this.

5. In view of the importance we place on careful conceptual and phenomenological descriptions of perceptual experience, we would like to note here that calling such contours and figures "illusory" is problematic and reflects certain methodological and theoretical assumptions (Spillman and Dresp 1995: 1341). We prefer the terms "apparent contours" and "anomalous contours" as being less theoretically biased by causal-explanatory assumptions. Nevertheless, "illusory contours" is widespread in the literature and used in the studies we cite. We therefore follow this usage.

6. In a recent study, Grosof, Shapley, and Hawken (1993) suggested the existence of neurons in V1 of the macaque that respond to line-end stimuli similar to offset gratings. The results remain controversial, however, and await further controls to establish the role these neurons play in illusory contour perception (see Lesher 1996).

7. The spatial (topographic) organization of the cell responses, as well as their gradual increase in firing rate as a function of the number of lines in grating stimuli, point to an analogic, spatially continuous form of representation. This issue could be probed further if data on the temporal nature of the cell responses could be compared to temporal perceptual data, further weakening the likelihood of a label code (see the discussion at the conclusion of 4.2).

8. In discussing the neon color spreading effect, Dennett (1991: 353) acknowledges neural filling-in as an "empirical possibility," and he gestures toward the sort of experiments he thinks would favor neural filling-in, ones that would probe the temporal dynamics of the effect: "It would be impressive, for instance, if the color could be shown under some conditions to spread slowly in time—bleeding out from the central red lines and gradually reaching out to the subjective contour boundaries. I don't want to prejudge the question."

9. Nevertheless, Todorović goes on to say that "given the lack of relevant data, the single-cell type of bridge locus is a heuristically useful assumption." We disagree (see Pessoa, Thompson, and Noë, in press).

10. The same sort of reasoning lies behind Dennett's discussion of the blind spot. After asserting that the brain does not fill in the blind spot, but rather jumps to a conclusion by ignoring the absence of signals from that region of the retina, he writes: "Once the brain has made a particular discrimination (e.g., of motion or of the uniformity of color in an area), the task of interpretation is done.... Applying the thrifty producer principle, it is clear that any further representations with special representational properties would be gratuitous. But it certainly does not seem that way from the 'first-person point of view'" (1992: 47). Again the implication is that you do not really see a uniformly colored region, that your seeing such a region is an illusion, and again the reason seems to be that it does not seem to you from your first-person point of view that your brain jumps to a conclusion. This is true, but then neither does it seem from your first-person point of view that there is *neural* filling-in.

11. Dennett (1991: 401) has rightly called attention to the "philosopher's syndrome" of mistaking a failure of imagination for a conceptual or metaphysical im-

possibility (i.e., an insight into necessity). It is therefore worth pointing out that phenomenological claims about essences and "eidetic" necessities are not grounded on the (typically underdescribed) "intuition pumps" of current philosophy of mind. On the contrary, ideation through imaginative variation requires sustained attention to and careful description of the phenomena in all their ramifications. Furthermore, the phenomena must be attended to not simply as particularities, but as fields of possibilities defined by certain forms or structural invariants. Finally, success in this endeavor depends on unprejudiced reflection, that is, on suspending or refraining from making use of any judgments about how things might be apart from our experience of them. This is the famous phenomenological *epoché*, which, as Husserl (in *Ideen* I, §§31–32) describes it, consists in "bracketing" the "general positing" of the "natural attitude."

12. This point is very reminiscent of Wittgenstein's remarks about phenomenology in his "middle period." See Noë 1994 for discussion.

13. Merleau-Ponty calls this assumption "the prejudice of the world." Suspending this prejudice is part of the bracketing performed in the phenomenological *epoché* mentioned in note 11, although here the bracketing concerns not so much the general positing of the natural attitude, but rather the naturalistic attitude of causal-explanatory theorizing.

14. Sedivy (1995: 475) makes the same point when she says that one of Dennett's unstated "substantive theses" is that "personal and subpersonal contents must be of the same *type*."

15. From a phenomenological standpoint, this is a result of the essentially directed or intentional character of all experience. See Wilshire 1968 for an important study of how William James grappled with this point in his discussions of the stream of consciousness in *The Principles of Psychology*.

CHAPTER 6

I am grateful to Jean Petitot, Jean-Michel Roy, and Francisco Varela for their helpful comments on earlier versions of this essay, and to Dr. Christopher Macann, research fellow at the University of London, for translating it into English.

1. The naturalist conception of intentionality developed by R. Millikan is sometimes presented in a teleological light but in an evolutionary sense of the term that is completely different.

2. *DR*, §7, p. 20. In general, quotations from Husserl have been retranslated into English.

CHAPTER 7

1. Husserl, *Manuscript C 16, IV* (Mar. 1932) (hereafter cited as *C 16*). This quotation, like many of the quotations from Husserl in this paper, is our translation.

2. Husserl, *Manuscript D 12, I* (5 Sept. 1931), p. 3 (hereafter cited as *D 12*):

"From a genetic point of view, kinesthetic circuits are originally involuntary, while the I is inactive and yet 'on the move.'" C 16, vol. 4: "As an active and conscious I, I am constantly 'moving myself'; the primordiality of the kinesthetic sphere."

3. DR, §46, p. 161:

> However, I should note straight away that, from a terminological point of view, the term sensation of movement [*Bewegungsempfindung*] is useless for us. For it would be wrong to think that we feel the movement of the thing any more than that the movement of the thing is apparent in such sensations. Obviously, the term relates only to what moves itself [*der sich Bewegende*], and must be understood in a psychological sense. While ruling out this psychological meaning, we will make use of the term *kinesthetic sensation* which, as a foreign term, turns out to be less misleading. With "movements of the eyes, of the head, of the hand," etc., we are of course dealing with continuous sensational circuits [*Empfindungsverläufen*] which can be terminated at will and each phase of which can be extended in time without change of content. These unchanging sensations yield simple kinesthetic sensations [*schlichte*] in contrast to kinesthetic changes or circuits.
>
> Obviously, we do not specify the concept of this group of sensations in a psychological or psycho-physical way but phenomenologically.

DR, §49, p. 171: "It is not relevant for us to determine whether the term 'kinesthetic sensations' designates an essentially new kind of simple sensation [*einfache*], but simply to point out that here phenomenological sensations and circuits of sensations can be found which form pluridimensional continuous multiplicities and which, across the apprehension of the thing, possess a constitutive function with regard to visual sensations and circuits and, in this connection, with the spatial thing."

4. ZPI III, p. 604: "The originary horizon made up of hereditary factors is, in its originary sense, an empty horizon."

5. Ibid., p. 609: "The whole process corresponding to the phylogenetic development is sedimented in each monadically germinal cell that is engendered."

6. D 12, 1: 28: "In the conscious child, the still uncontrolled circuit of kinesthetic reflexes is, before being visual, based on a 'doing' which is instinctively enforced with 'more or less energy': the kinestheses associated with wriggling, with the position of the head, etc., impact upon each other; in the absence of tension the normal position of the organs first forms the kinesthetic zero, on the basis of which a position of normal rest manifests itself, a position where all the kinestheses are at rest: I am standing up with my feet, my head, my hand, my arm in the normal position; sitting down constitutes another position at rest. From each position at rest, transition to activity, return to rest."

7. Kant 1974: I, I, 1, §2: "Man kann sich niemals eine Vorstellung davon machen, daß kein Raum sei."

8. DR, §54, p. 187: "Diese Bilderkontinuität ist eine lineare Mannigfaltigkeit, herausgegriffen aus einer mehrdimensionalen Mannigfaltigkeit möglicher Bilder." Cf. ibid., §80, p. 269.

9. Ibid., §54, p. 187: "Diese Bilderkontinuität ... ist von gleicher Mächtigkeit mit stetigen Mannigfaltigkeit der möglichen K."

10. Ibid., §54, p. 187: "If intentions only ran through this system (of images), if this systematic type (of disclosive sensation) could not be brought under a systematic

type which included it, to which elements of appearance (elements of apprehension) could be referred, the thing would be completely constituted in this multiplicity (of images); the thing would stand in no relation to movement and change. But in that case the thing certainly would not be a thing."

11. Ibid., §57, p. 202: "Every rearrangement of the posture of the body [*Körperhaltung*] introduces into the oculomotor system of kinesthetic images a modification which was not prefigured precisely because it is not motivated by oculomotor kinestheses alone. Thus we arrive at, so to speak, new dimensions for the constitution of thinghood."

12. Husserl, *Manuscript D 11*, p. 5: "I move the eyes and I say: the same appearance from close up and far away." This remark is in line with the Lectures. But in what follows, something else emerges. Cf. *D 12*, 2: 7: "New moment of constitution: we reach out for things, grasp them in our hands, hold them and turn them around and then we lay them down and know what they look like from every angle, including those parts of their surface on which they rest." Also cf. ibid., p. 32:

> Even if haptic touching is still not practical, like pure vision, it can, by means of forceful tension, be changed into placing, striking, sliding, etc., but also into a placing together of the fingers which touch a thing on different sides, thanks to which it can become a gripping of the object, grasping it and then, by bringing into play other kinestheses, a lifting, carrying, etc. From pure touching in which a shadow of the *res extensa* is haptically constituted, there arises a world in which we can intervene by acting, by moving what is at rest, bringing about in ourselves changes which take place of themselves and, in this way, we subjectify what is simply there of itself in external things, by including it within our organism.

13. *D 12*, 1: 25: "In experience, in lived experience, the complex comes first."

14. *DR*, §47, p. 163: "The result of all this is, in the end, the introjection of all sensations and of all appearances, of all phenomenological events in the I and the body of the I, as well as the possibility of incorporating introjectively, into other physical things, 'psychic events,' 'sensational and perceptual lived experiences,' and so of apprehending them as 'animate bodies.' But this already escapes from our line of thinking."

15. *C 16*, 7: 11: "Human beings are linked together through their practical intentions, they are socialized by their actions; they produce works in common, they act together; the unity of an action in which two partners interact with each other; all this presupposes a level of understanding appropriate for the action in question ... 'understanding the other': at the very least I understand the other at the most basic level of his own physical activity, as having an experience and exerting a physical action on other bodies (striking, pushing)." Ibid., p. 12: "Even actions subjected to elementary instincts are understood, at least in accordance with some crude typology."

16. *ZPI* III, Texte 23, p. 394: "In the human context, all activity, every action figures in the world at the same time that it is represented as intelligible for humans under the spiritual head of 'action,' and the same holds of what results from action, whether anticipated or not (its secondary results, its residual effects still bear witness to a human doing)."

17. Cf. the description of methods and results in Goodwin et al. 1972: 709–29, fig. 2, p. 712.

18. Cf. Lackner and Taublieb 1984: 104–5: "The position sense of the body is often thought to be determined by the multiple topographic maps of somatosensation that have been identified in the thalamus and cortex using single-unit recording techniques (cf. Mountcastle et al. 1959, 1968).... It seems unlikely however on the basis of the findings reported here, that the position sense of the body can be coded solely in the activity patterns of these somato-sensory maps; instead, reference and correlation with other afferent domains also seems to be involved. Our observations show for example complex influences of vision and muscle spindle signals on position sense, influences that are bidirectional with each afferent channel also affecting the spatial localizations mediated by the other."

19. Cf. Petit 1996, lectures 7 to 9, where I show the advantages of Husserl's theory of *Einfühlung* over those of Lipps and Scheler.

CHAPTER 8

A preliminary version of this paper appeared in the *Electronic Journal of Analytic Philosophy*, no. 4 (Spring 1996). Where differences exist, this version takes precedence. This paper benefited greatly from conversations with, or suggestions from Robert Port, William Blattner, and Francisco Varela.

1. Notable collections of Husserl's writings on time consciousness are found in *PZB*. Varela (this volume, Appendix 1) provides a succinct and useful overview.

2. See Blattner, Brough 1989, and Miller 1984. There is a remarkable level of agreement among these commentators, and so we can be confident that the basic outlines of Husserl's position on time consciousness have been correctly explicated.

3. Brough's treatment is especially useful for the nonspecialist: comprehensive yet succinct, and very accessible. The presentation here relies particularly heavily on Brough's work, though of course he must not be held accountable for its deficiencies.

4. *PZB*, p. 226; quoted by Brough 1989: 266.

5. *PZB*, p. 227; quoted by Brough 1989: 267.

6. *PZB*, p. 415; quoted by Brough 1989: 273.

7. This sidestepping is really just a manifestation of a wider neglect of temporal issues in mainstream computational cognitive science. Time is notoriously hard to think about, and so is Mind. Philosophy in the Western tradition has, rather prudently, attempted to keep these topics apart as much as possible. Mind has been studied as if it were only an incidental fact that it happens to be in time. For example, one of the greatest philosophical attempts to link Mind and Time was that of Immanuel Kant. He held that time was a "form of intuition," or in other words a structural feature of the way we perceive the world. Thus, for Kant, time is "in the mind" rather than mind being in time. Mainstream cognitive science inherited, via the theory of digital computation, philosophy's tendency to bracket temporal issues. Turing machines and equivalent formal models of computation abstract away from the richness of time, reducing it to a mere order among digital states (t_1, t_2, etc.). Theories of cog-

nition based on these kinds of formal models treat time as little more than a sequence of discrete moments at which the system can instantaneously occupy one computational state or another. What matters is not when the system occupies these states, or for how long, or how the direction of change might depend on such details; rather, all that matters is how many operations take place and in what order, and whether the goal state is reached. However, just as philosophers such as Husserl, Heidegger, and Merleau-Ponty came to recognize that temporality is essential to mind, so cognitive scientists are increasingly coming to see that real time is essential to cognition. The growth of dynamical cognitive science is part and parcel of a shift to a scientific perspective which sees how cognitive processes unfold in time as just as important as which cognitive states a system happens to pass through. For more discussion, see van Gelder and Port 1995.

8. See Pylyshyn 1984.

9. Newell 1991.

10. For an overview of the dynamical approach, see Port and van Gelder 1995.

11. See Anderson 1994 and Port, McAuley, and Anderson 1996.

12. Caution: the rolling marble picture is just an analogy and should not be relied on too heavily. For example, an important difference between the path of the marble and the trajectory of a dynamical system is that the path of the marble is affected by its current momentum, whereas the state of the system depends only on its current position.

13. It must be admitted that the term "neurophenomenology" probably holds the aesthetic advantage over "cognophenomenology."

CHAPTER 9

This paper is the result of many months of gestation in the productive atmosphere provided by several colleagues in Paris in the form of two working groups, on Phenomenology and Cognitive Science and on Phenomenological Psychology, who have generously provided instruction, suggestions, and encouragement. My special thanks go to Natalie Depraz, Bernard Pachoud, Jean Petitot, Jean-Michel Roy, and Pierre Vermersch. The work carried on with my research group on neurodynamics has provided me much of the empirical substrate for this discussion; I am specially grateful to Jacques Martinerie and Michel Le Van Quyen. The joint work with Evan Thompson has continued to provide insights and resources at every stage. Finally, the incisive commentaries to the text by Amy Cohen-Varela and Shaun Gallagher were very helpful. To all of these friends my heartfelt thanks; I am fully responsible for the remaining errors and shortcomings.

1. A forewarning: I will not provide a naturalized account in the sense of "explaining away" or "giving substance" to the phenomenological description. My aim is just as much to naturalize phenomenology as it is to phenomenalize cognitive science. For reasons of historical tradition and brevity, the label "naturalized" is used. For more on the history of this issue and various interpretations of naturalization, see Chapter 1 of this volume.

2. The text reads: "We know so little of the intimate nature of the brain's activity that even where a sensation monotonously endures, we cannot say that the earlier moments of it do not leave fading processes behind which coexist with those of the present moment. *Duration and events together form our intuition of the specious present with its content. Why* such an intuition should result from such a combination of brain-processes I do not pretend to say. All I aim at is to state the *elemental* form of the psycho-physical conjunction" (James 1950, 1: 633–34; James's emphasis).

3. "Négliger cette maxime essentielle de la phénoménologie, à savoir qu'elle procéde par description . . . d'une expérience que l'on doit donc refaire" (Besnier 1993: 322; emphasis added).

4. For the overall discussion about reduction there are, of course, numerous published and unpublished texts, including Fink 1988. But concerning an explicit, step-by-step pragmatics phenomenologists (including Husserl) have been notoriously circumspect. For a recent discussion about the varieties of reduction, see Bernet 1994b: 5–36. The methodological precisions for the practice of reduction require extensive developments; our point of view is presented in Depraz, Varela, and Vermersch (forthcoming).

5. The expression is James's. In fact, Husserl carefully underscored in his copy of *Principles* the term "specious present" and suggested, in Gabel shorthand, a German translation that remains undeciphered! I am grateful to Shaun Gallagher for bringing this to my attention.

6. In this paper I prefer to use the compound expression "object-event" to render *Zeitobjekte*. Although the terminology used by Granel (1968), "tempo-object," would be better, it is ungrammatical.

7. The section or page numbers correspond to *PZB* (see Appendix A). The English translation used here comes from the texts by J. Brough, J. Churchill, or R. Bruzina when available, or else I have modified them or provided my own (as indicated).

8. See note 5. Here is another example. Husserl insists that although every act of intentional consciousness is temporal, the content of some object-events is not. The judgment "2 + 3 = 5" is atemporal since ideal (*PZB*, pp. 133–34). This is not convincing: "2 + 3 = 5" expresses an invariant aspect of a very transient and temporal object which is the mental content of adding numbers. According to what we know about such cognitive phenomena, the very content of this object-event, the sum of two numbers, is quite specific. Only in a Platonic view of mathematics can one claim that both the sense and content of this kind has no location in time, e.g., my perception of Pythagoras's theorem today is not the same as the one I had when I was in high school. The question whether there are such things as atemporal objects is not settled, but here is not the place to examine this further. This criticism merely highlights the fact that it is quite essential to have in mind a particular experiential grounding to advance any analysis.

9. See, for example, Ihde 1977, chap. 6.

10. This is usually attributed to M. Merleau-Ponty's work, but it is very explicitly articulated by Husserl in materials available only recently. See Zahavi 1994.

11. Some classics are von Holst, Piaget, and Gibson. For recent discussion, see Varela, Thompson, and Rosch 1991 and Kelso 1995.

12. See Varela 1979; Varela, Thompson, and Rosch 1991; and Thompson and Varela, forthcoming.

13. Port and van Gelder (1995) provide an excellent survey of contemporary issues, including an accessible discussion of dynamical tools for the cognitive scientist.

14. See Varela et al. 1981, Dennett and Kinsbourne 1992, Pöppel 1988, and Pöppel and Schill 1995.

15. In chap. 15 of *Principles*, James provides an elegant description of these data, which were extensively explored in the nineteenth century.

16. This section draws substantially from a previous publication (Varela 1995), which discusses more extensively the literature and history of these ideas.

17. The precise timing is necessarily flexible (30–100 msec; 0.5–1.3 secs), since such events can naturally vary in their detailed timing depending on a number of factors: context, fatigue, type of sensorial mode utilized, age, and so on. This is why I speak of an order of magnitude, not of absolute value.

18. This unusual term translates well: *Vergegenwärtigung*, a rich mixture of waiting (*Warten*), present (*Gegen-wart*), and moving-from-present (*Ver-gegen-wärtigung*). This translation marks also the contrast with presentation (*Gegenwärtigung*). A nonliteral translation in a psychological context could be that of evocative memory (including remembrance and imagination), in contrast to short-term or iconic memory.

19. Thus the usual association between St. Augustine's and Husserl's views on time are misleading, since Augustine's examination does not distinguish between the presence of the past as an evocative memory of a person's entire life and the past as living present.

20. Besnier 1993: 339. For the relations with the term *Ent-gegenwärtigung* as "de-presentation," see note 18 on presentation and presentification.

21. For a more detailed discussion, see Larrabee 1994 and Miskiewicz 1985.

22. T. van Gelder called my attention to this telling remark; it is the source for the title to his contribution in this volume. Van Gelder also introduces a cognitive-dynamical reading of Husserl's temporal analysis. Our respective ideas were presented simultaneously (yet developed independently) at the conference "Contemporary Issues in Phenomenology and Cognitive Science," Bordeaux, October 1995. For some significant differences in our respective analyses, see below.

23. These difficulties have been discussed eloquently by Besnier (1993). In fact this section owes a lot to him: I have liberally let myself be guided by some of his arguments and textual indications. Unfortunately, I have been unable to take into consideration the material from Fink's unpublished manuscripts (Bruzina 1993, 1994). The analysis of flow seemed to have arisen in close parallel to Husserl's efforts to study intersubjectivity, the question of common time, and the phenomenological basis of historicity. This is surely one of the most fascinating and still largely unexplored areas in phenomenological research. The paucity of published sources does not make things easier (see Depraz 1991, 1994).

24. This is also a statement about the relative poverty of the continued cultiva-

tion of reductive capacities. In the Buddhist corpus of the Abhidharma, long-term cultivation of a variant of phenomenological reduction is reported to give access to very detailed descriptions of the rapid successions of immediate reflection (see Varela, Thompson, and Rosch 1991 for more on the Abhidharma corpus). I do not pursue the issue of levels of reductive expertise, but its central importance is highlighted in Depraz, Varela, and Vermersch, forthcoming.

25. Merleau-Ponty 1964: 244–45, 296–98, as discussed by Besnier 1993: 356 n. 9.

26. Merleau-Ponty 1945: 488.

27. *PZB*, §39 and p. 368.

28. In the Madhaymika tradition this resurfaces as the key link between appearance and emptiness (*sunya*), the basis of the cultivation of human capacities beyond their natural attitude (see Varela, Thompson, and Rosch 1991).

29. Gallagher (1979) discusses this asymmetry as well and points out that Husserl speaks of the differences in "style" between protention and retention (in *Analysen*, pp. 323–24).

30. Merleau-Ponty 1945: 487. "Die Zeit ist ihrem Wesen nach reine Affektion ihrer selbst" (Heidegger 1929: 180–81).

31. The chosen translation for *Umsicht* is "circumspection," which I find exact but cumbersome. I prefer here *transparent*, which is also literally used in the text (*Durchsichtig*). The danger is to suggest invisibility, but I justify the choice on the basis that it is closer to common speech and given the many ways in which *Umsicht* is used by Heidegger.

32. Heidegger 1927: 76, my translation. The passage is difficult, and the standard (Macquarrie and Robinson's) translation (p. 107) is more literal, but less readable.

33. I am grateful to Fernando Flores for sharing his insights on these topics with me; they are described in documents for internal use in his consulting firm Business Design Associates, Emeryville, California.

34. Cf. "In its factical Being, any Dasein is as it already was, and it is 'what' it already was. It is its past, whether explicit or not" (Heidegger 1927, trans. J. Macquarrie and E. Robinson, p. 41).

35. For the basic studies of instinct and emotion in animals, the foundational studies of Konrad Lorenz (1972) are still useful. For a more recent and provocative survey, see de Waals 1995.

36. See Ekman and Davidson 1994 for a recent survey of psychological studies, and Rorty 1980 for cognitive views.

37. The original description is by Deecke, Scheid, and Kornhuber (1969). A vast literature on these preconscious electrical correlates has been produced since.

38. This is referred to as evolution by natural drift in Varela, Thompson, and Rosch 1991.

39. I cannot resist pointing out that the overall shape of this new figure recalls a conformal mapping of a complex fractional function, for example, the field around an electromagnetic dipole (the present now) on a curved surface.

40. Incidentally: in his introduction, Heidegger barely acknowledges the work

of Stein, a woman and a Jew, a gesture that does little to enhance his academic credibility.

41. I am grateful to Wioletta Miskiewicz's work (1985) for first calling to my attention the importance of the *Bernauermanuskripten*.

42. This appendix is based on Le Van Quyen, Schuster, and Varela 1996. The reader should refer to that article for details, including references not included herein.

CHAPTER 11

Thanks to Christopher Macann for the English version of this text. All quotations from Husserl are my translation. Unless otherwise specified, references are to the German editions of Husserl's works.

1. For a general epistemological reflection concerning the naturalization problem, see Chapter 1 of this volume.

2. See Chapter 1 of this volume and Petitot 1993 and 1994a.

3. To be lexically rigorous we would need three different items for indicating the different dimensions of phenomenological appearance: *appearance*, *appearing*, and *apparition*. We will use the term "appearance," with its strong sense of "what appears." The connotation of "illusory" is, therefore, completely ruled out.

4. In transcendentalist traditions, and especially in Husserl's phenomenology, there exists a strong opposition between *presentation* (*Darstellung*, the appearance of what is given) and *representation* (*Vorstellung*). To avoid any ambiguity, we will use, therefore, the rather unusual adjective "presentational" when necessary. When "presentation" no longer refers to an abstract concept, but to concrete appearances presenting external objects in perception, we will use the term "display." In this text, "display" is therefore always implicitly linked with "presentation."

5. See, e.g., Smith and Mulligan 1982.

6. See, e.g., Petitot 1993 and 1994b.

7. For an introduction to the concept of *Gestalt* (in particular in Stumpf, von Ehrenfels, and Meinong), see B. Smith 1988.

8. It is a matter of type/token distinction.

9. For some precision concerning the fundamental concept of phenomenal "merging," see B. Smith 1988. Husserl uses it also for describing the "figural" moments of unity in discrete collections, such as "lines" of trees, "piles" of stones, "swarms" of bees, and so on. See also Petitot 1994d.

10. Concerning this difficult point, see Chapter 1.

11. See Petitot 1993, 1994a, and 1995a.

12. From *sunéchès* = "continuous."

13. See Riemann's philosophical works.

14. See Boi 1995 and G. Longo's contribution to this volume.

15. For an introduction to locally trivial structures (coverings, fibrations, sheaves, etc.), see Petitot 1979 and its bibliography.

16. See Petitot 1994d, 1997, and Tondut and Petitot 1998.
17. See Thom 1980.
18. Let us recall that an open set is a neighborhood of each of its points.
19. A simple way to categorize a space is to introduce a dynamic. Prototypes are then interpreted as attractors of the dynamic, categories as basins of attraction, and boundaries as basin separators. Such dynamical models can be implemented in connectionist nets.
20. We must emphasize the fact that diffusion is here relative to *scale* and not to time.
21. See Alvarez, Lions, and Morel 1992.
22. For the concept of multiscale geometry, see Koenderink 1984, Florack 1993, Petitot 1994c, and Hamy 1997.
23. See Chapter 1 of this volume.
24. Consciousness being "pure" (nonpsychological), this realization is not a material implementation. Husserl's perspective is "functionalist."
25. The figures are computed with *Mathematica*. For simplicity's sake we needed an uncomplicated image that was still sufficiently differentiated and asymmetrical. We chose a dodecahedron, and left the image pixelized intentionally.
26. See Ninio 1989.
27. It must be stressed here that the young Husserl was an excellent mathematician, whose doctoral dissertation (defended under Weierstrass's direction) was devoted to the calculus of variations.
28. See Petitot 1995c. See also Casati's paper in this volume.
29. See Petitot 1994b and 1994d.
30. See Atiya and Baldi 1989, Engel et al. 1992, Petitot 1994c, and Varela's essay in this collection.

CHAPTER 12

This paper stems from joint work with Achille Varzi on spatial representation. I am grateful to him for our inspiring discussions.

1. See, for example, Simon 1947 and 1954.
2. Absolute space exists for common sense; it might be that common sense is wrong about that, but even if it were right, it would be right for the wrong reasons (because it generalizes from its wrong belief that the Earth is motionless).
3. Along with some others, these principles are part of pre-Newtonian conceptions of space (in spite of Newton's declarations of distance from common sense). We shall quote occasionally some Newtonian axioms for rest and motion from his "Scholium on Absolute Space and Time," in the *Principia*, pagination in brackets from Earman 1989. See the last section below for more remarks on Newton's notions.
4. It would of course be interesting to have some formal characterization of s. As things stand here, *identity* with s is a model for S—an interpretation that is much too

weak. Characterizing *s* as the sum of all absolutely resting bodies would entail its uniqueness.

5. See Varzi 1996. "O" stands for "overlap."

6. See Casati and Varzi 1997. The region functor maps any object onto the region of space at which it is localized.

7. Our theory is extensional in the sense that its statements are true even at instants.

CHAPTER 13

I am grateful to Charles Parsons, Solomon Feferman, Cheryl Dawson, John Dawson, Richard Tieszen, Dag Prawitz, Per Martin-Löf, Dick Haglund, Christian Beyer, and Herman Ruge Jervell for their valuable comments on drafts that are in part included in the present paper. I also thank the Axel o Margaret Ax:son Johnson Foundation for support of this and other work.

1. "The Modern Development of the Foundations of Mathematics in the Light of Philosophy," pp. 9–10. unpublished manuscript, probably for a lecture that Gödel was invited to give as a newly elected member of the American Philosophical Society, but never did. In Feferman et al. 1995: 287.

2. Gödel owned the 1968 edition of Husserl's *Logische Untersuchungen* (Max Niemeyer Verlag, Tübingen, first edition, 1900–1901), which is unchanged from the second edition (1913: vol. 1 and vol. 2, part 1; and 1921: vol. 2, part 2). He owned the Husserliana edition of *Ideen* I, *Cartesianische Meditationen und Pariser Vorträge* (2d edition, 1963), *Die Krisis der europäischen Wissenschaften und die transzendentale Phänomenologie* (2d edition, 1962). He also owned Quentin Lauer, *Phenomenology and the Crisis of Philosophy* (New York: Harper Torchbooks, Harper and Row, 1965), which is an English translation of Husserl's two essays "Philosophy as Rigorous Science" (1911) and "Philosophy and the Crisis of European Man" (1935). Gödel also owned both volumes of the second edition (1965) of Herbert Spiegelberg, *The Phenomenological Movement*, Phenomenologica 5 (Nijhoff: The Hague). All of these books are heavily annotated by Gödel, with the exception of *Logical Investigations*. In the latter were found, however, several pages of Gödel's shorthand notes, referring to page numbers in the text, indicating that Gödel probably had based his study of that text on a borrowed copy. The work was out of print for many years before the 1968 edition was published. The notes indicate that the text Gödel had used was the second edition, which first appeared in 1913–21 and was reprinted in 1922, 1928, and 1968. References to Husserl in the following will be, as usual, to page and line in the Husserliana editions.

3. Husserl studied with Weierstrass in Berlin in 1878–81. Weierstrass advised him on his doctoral dissertation, and in 1883 Husserl was Weierstrass's assistant.

4. Letter quoted in Kern 1964: 276n.

5. See, e.g., Husserl, *Formal and Transcendental Logic* (*FTL*), §58 (Husserliana XVII, 164, 32–34, here and in the following, references to Husserl's works are to

page and line number in the Husserliana edition), and Husserl, *Krisis*, §73 (Husserliana VI, 270, 28–29).

6. For documentation of this way of interpreting Husserl, see Føllesdal 1988.

7. Husserl, *Krisis*, §36 (Husserliana VI, 143, 29–30; Carr's translation, slightly amended, p. 140).

8. Husserl, *Krisis*, §34e (Husserliana VI, 134, 35–37; Carr, p. 132).

9. Husserl, *FTL*, §96b (Husserliana XVII, 249, 18–20; Cairn's translation, p. 242).

10. There is one apparent exception to this: in a lecture delivered to the Mathematical Association of America in Cambridge, Mass., 29–30 December 1933, Gödel talked about "a kind of Platonism, which cannot satisfy any critical mind" (Feferman et al. 1995: 50). However, read in context, this remark need not apply to Platonism per se, but may just reflect Gödel's dissatisfaction with the axioms he discusses in this lecture and the kind of Platonism they would presuppose, if interpreted as meaningful statements.

11. Gödel's letter to Schilpp, in Gödel's *Nachlaß*, my emphasis. Here quoted from Parsons 1995.

CHAPTER 14

I would like to warmly thank Jean Petitot for his many detailed comments on an earlier version of this paper, in particular on Husserl's philosophy, as well as for his constant and critical encouragement. Thierry Coquand, Françoise Longy, and Valeria DePaiva made further helpful comments.

1. It is interesting to note how we usually talk, in mathematics and in logic, about the "reduction" (à la Cantor-Dedekind) of the real numbers to the integers, as if the reals were already "there," as if the "informal practice" of the mathematical continuum (see Cauchy's demonstration of 1821) made reference to an external objectivity, that we must understand by reduction (the same way we reduce some chemical realities to physics). This is comprehensible in the naive Platonic practice of mathematics, but it is less so for the formalist/definitionist vision of mathematics still prevailing in logic.

2. In set theory, in writing $\forall y$ for "for all y," a set b is defined impredicatively if, typically, it is given in the form $b = [x|\forall y \in A\ P(x, y)]$ where b can be an element of A (the same set or collection A of sets which appears in the definition of b). Briefly, in an impredicative theory there is no stratification of the mathematical universe, and it is acceptable to define one element b using a predicate or set A which can contain b. Informally we cannot comprehend the parts, the elements, without comprehending at the same time the whole, or a big part of the whole.

3. In the sequence of his fundamental reflections Weyl first joined the ranks of intuitionism, then he embraced a more open view of mathematical knowledge. But the mathematics of Brouwer and the logical systems of Heyting are compatible with the impredicative notions: in fact even the definition of an intuitionist proof is impredicative (see Longo 1987 for more: yet the interplay is between theory and metatheory,

so it is acceptable for many). After that, in his logical-philosophical writings (see the French version of Weyl 1918a for many references), Weyl was never to return to his predicative analysis. On the contrary, he was to develop a very rich vision of the connections between mathematics and physics, which would culminate in *Symmetry* (Weyl 1953), his last book, a Husserlian masterpiece, clearly antiformalist: mathematics emerges from the effort to know the world (physically, chemically, artistically . . .) as a "transcendental objectivity." See also Weyl 1985 for a very balanced and "secular" view of the instruments of demonstration in mathematics.

4. In intuitionistic mathematics we distinguish between "lawlike" sequences and "lawless" ones. Here the "law" is an algorithmic (or effective) rule. For example, π is the limit of a lawlike sequence (the algorithm for constructing it), whereas a real whose decimals are given by successively rolling a die is the limit of a lawless sequence. But even a convergent lawless sequence obeys a rule and follows a convergence criterion: in the lawless sequence above, one rolls the die and add its results as decimal numbers. The limit is unique and well-defined: the criterion of convergence is given by the fact that "we add as decimals" the results of the throw. It is the existence (of the limit) that is weak and noneffective.

5. Leibnizian infinitesimals became the new real numbers, smaller than any other standard real number. Then $x \approx y$ if $x - y$ is infinitesimal and hence a function is continuous if $f(x) \approx f(x + h)$ for all infinitesimal h.

6. Axiom of choice (AC): "For all non-empty collections of non-empty sets, we can construct a set which contains exactly one element from each set of the family." The axiom of choice is essential in many demonstrations, including some that concern the continuum: without AC the definitions of limit based on neighborhoods and the one based on sequences are not equivalent (it is necessary to *construct* a sequence, by *choosing* a point for each successive environment).

7. The few technical notions in this section will not be used in the sequel: they are just examples of elementary connections between principles of proof and principles of construction. For more details on intuitionistic systems of types and category theory, see Lambek and Scott 1986 and Asperti and Longo 1991.

8. We could say the same about Girard's linear logic, since its nature makes even classical linear logic "constructive." See Girard 1991.

9. See the note "D'Anaxagore à Dedekind," 1926, in the French version of Weyl 1918a.

10. We can continue with $\epsilon_1, \epsilon_2, \ldots, \epsilon_\omega$ and having understood the mechanism, which after ϵ_0 is not that simple, we can continue with $\epsilon_{\epsilon_0}, \ldots$

11. But this method of proof was not considered very convincing by many, for the heart of the problem of consistency for arithmetic is the *consistency of induction*, the key principle of Peano's arithmetic: one should not use an even more powerful induction to show it. There are other ways of proving it, using formally equivalent, yet more convincing, methods.

12. This means reiterate the constructions formalized by the axiom of power of a set, the replacement, for example, of the image of a set by a function, etc.—so long as these constructions are definable in the language of set theory.

13. The theorems of cut-elimination and normalization for the higher-order sys-

tems give extremely solid bases to the impredicative definitions. The consequence is that every proof in the system can be simplified to a "minimal form" (a normal form or without cuts), or that there are no "incontrollable propositions" that can introduce themselves into proofs. We must note that the second principle of proof mentioned here is sufficient to prove the theorem of normalization, but the proof of Girard, which uses both principles, displays very clearly, for its elegance, the issues of the construction. See also Fruchart and Longo 1998 for an application of a recent theorem to the justification of impredicative definitions.

14. In particular the formalized proposition, which says "this proposition is not provable."

15. We could mention that beyond products and coproducts, which correspond so well to the intuitionist conjunction and disjunction, the effective topos, which is the basis of the sketched second-order constructions, is itself constructed using principles that go beyond the other "pure" intuitionist rules (the principles of uniformity and of Markov, among others): hence the effective topos shows the truth of non-demonstrable propositions of the systems of intuitionistic logic, of which it is a model. The genericity theorem (see Longo 1995 and Fruchart and Longo 1998) gives another mismatch between the topos and intuitionistic logic.

16. See also Petitot 1992b, §2.1.

17. For a philosophical introduction to the "geometry of perception," and also for the numerous applications to which it refers, see Petitot 1995b. About the role of the continuum in linguistics, see Fuchs and Victorri 1994.

CHAPTER 15

This paper is derived from an earlier version called "Naturalizing Phenomenology: The Very Idea," presented at the international conference of philosophy "Actualité cognitive de la phénoménologie: Les Défis de la naturalisation," Bordeaux, France, October 19–21, 1995.

1. Dretske 1995. Page numbers in the text will refer to this work.

2. I oversimplify Husserl's version of "internalism" here. The intentionality of a particular act is also affected by its relation to background beliefs and other items internal to the experiencing subject. See Smith and McIntyre 1982: 246–56.

CHAPTER 16

Preparation of this paper was supported by the Universidad Nacional de Colombia (Bogotá) and the Instituto Colombiano para el Desarrollo de la Ciencia y la Tecnología "Francisco José de Caldas"—COLCIENCIAS. I benefited also from the friendly hospitality of the Centre de Recherches en Epistémologie Appliquée—CREA, in Paris. I thank Jean-Michel Roy, Jean Petitot, and Bernard Pachoud for helpful comments on an earlier version.

1. This book is a collection of five lectures given by Husserl in 1907 as an introduction to his course *The Fundamental Points of Phenomenology and the Critique of Reason*. This is a quite ambiguous work in that it has an avowed epistemological purpose (the "critique of knowledge") that is both carried out in a Cartesian way and couched in Kantian language, yet it goes beyond pure epistemology to criticize the thought of both Descartes and Kant.

2. It is a *special* sense because the "as" in "perception-of-as" functions as "as" only from the point of view of this external description. But this is an analysis we perform on the act and not an internal distinction within itself.

3. There is a great deal of phenomenological terminology involved here that I want to avoid for the present

4. This point is made by J. N. Mohanty in Mohanty 1978.

5. Cf. Hoyos 1986, *Los intereses de la vida cotidiana y las ciencias*, from which I have borrowed concerning transcendental logic (cf. especially chap. 2).

6. In this context, where there are no risks of confusion with the linguistic level, I employ "meaning" and "sense" as identical to render the Husserlian expression *Sinn*.

7. It is worth saying also that the deep reasons that led Wittgenstein to raise this problem are linked to the Tractarian pictorial theory of language. Language ("picture theory") is only applicable when things can be, or can be imagined to be, otherwise. Propositions have the possibility of being false. This is what connects language and the world. And it is this connection that gives the proposition its sense. Propositions that rule out the possibility of being false (or true) belong to logic, and they say nothing about the world. (Cf. Wittgenstein 1964, §83, and 1953: 251–52). Thus, Husserlian *apodictic propositions* would not describe anything at all. Cf. Stern 1995.

8. Cf. Husserl, *Krisis*, §35, where Husserl compares the attitude involved in making *epochē* to attain the life-world to a "religious conversion."

9. This view would also cast doubt on an account of intersubjectivity based primarily on empathy, or *Einfühlung*. Practical social relationships seem to be the most original way to constitute both myself and the others as persons.

10. From now on, see Wittgenstein 1969.

11. See Varela 1979, for the sense in which I understand this "coupling."

12. I mean to use this expression in the sense of F. Varela, though I'm not sure about the results. See Varela, Thompson, and Rosch 1991.

CHAPTER 17

These reflections owe much to long, demanding, intense, and at times unfathomable though always engaging discussions which I have had the pleasure of exchanging for more than three years with Pierre Vermersch and Francisco Varela. At the very outset of this inquiry they therefore both deserve my warmest thanks.

1. See the Appendix at the end of the chapter.

2. *LU* II/1, Second Investigation, p. 112: "Of course, the term 'idealism' does not refer here to a metaphysical doctrine but to that form of the theory of knowledge which recognizes in the ideal the condition of the possibility of any objective knowledge in general, rather than one that seeks to get rid of it through a psychological interpretation." (Most of the quotations from Husserl in this paper are the translator's own.)

3. *LU* II/1, *Einleitung*, §3, p. 14: "The source of all these difficulties lies in the antinatural orientation of intuition and of the thinking that phenomenological analysis requires."

4. *LU* II/1, *Einleitung*, §3, p. 14: "This intellectual orientation runs counter to our most deeply rooted habits, and so gets ceaselessly confirmed from the very beginning of our psychic development. Hence the almost ineradicable tendency to fall back constantly from the phenomenological into the objective attitude."

5. See the already mentioned Appendix.

6. With a view to illustrating this risk, cf. Richir 1992 and Henry 1996; cf. also the preface by Bernet to Depraz 1995b.

7. Fink 1988, §1: "Our situation is now that of having surmounted the naïveté of the world only to find ourselves in a new naïveté, a transcendental naïveté. The latter consists in this, that we only explicate and deploy transcendental life by presenting it just as it is given to us through the reduction, without engaging in a detailed analysis regarding the 'internal horizons' of this life, in its efforts at constitution" (my translation). Cf. Husserl, *Erste Philosophie* (hereafter cited as *EPh*), part 2, lesson 53: "So there can be a transcendental naïveté—running parallel to the natural naïveté—to which a particular meaning cannot be accorded.... In this second sense not only is a natural knowledge which is untouched by the transcendental *epochē* naive but also any knowledge which arises on the basis of transcendental subjectivity in as much as the latter (this knowledge) fails precisely to be subjected to any apodictic critique and in as much as no attempt is made to call in question the absolute justification of transcendental knowledge."

8. *ZPI* II, n. 6, suppl. 21, p. 195: "Wir neigen zum Naturalismus"; Husserl, "Philosophie als strenge Wissenschaft," p. 12: "Was alle Formen des extremen und konsequenten Naturalismus, angefangen vom populären Materialismus bis zum neuesten Empfindungsmonismus und Energetismus, charakterisiert, ist einerseits die Naturalisierung des Bewußtseins, einschließlich aller intentional-immanenten Bewußtseinsgegebenheiten; anderseits die Naturalisierung der Ideen und damit aller absoluten Ideale und Normen"; *ZPI* II, suppl. 1, p. 34: "Doch dürfen wir hier nicht mit naturalistischen Begriffen herankommen." Cf. also Husserl, *Krisis*, §18, with reference to the "psychologizing falsification of the ego."

9. *ZPI* III, n. 36, p. 639: "Die Monadisierung, die monadische Konstitution ist wesensmässig so, daß sie impliziert die Naturalisierung jeder Monade, die Verzeitlichung derselben in die Raumzeitlichkeit." Cf. also *ZPI* III, suppl. 41, p. 589.

10. *Ideen* I, §117, p. 290, and *Krisis*, §58.

11. Cf. Jacob 1970, Heisenberg 1990, and Bachelard 1934.

12. Cf. Chapter 1 of this volume, sections 2.2.2. and 3.5.

13. G. W. Leibniz returns regularly in his works to the existence of *petites perceptions* or *perceptions insensibles*, which require from us an unusual effort of attention.

14. Henceforward, when we talk about consciousness, we should be taken to mean something for which the predicates "subjective" and "human" are not essential features.

15. Cf. Merleau-Ponty 1945 and 1995 and Heidegger 1951: 63.

16. Lectures of 1919–1920 and 1927 (MS F I 32 for this last, which is cited and commented on in Kern 1964: 414–20).

17. For the human spirit itself moves in this direction, however, conscious it might be of its de-humanization, as Descartes already acknowledged at the end of his through-the-looking-glass exercise of methodical doubt: "This programme is painful and laborious and a certain laziness unconsciously [*me reducit*] carries me along the train of ordinary life. . . . I fall back unconsciously [*sponte relabor*] into my former opinions." In Descartes 1967: 412.

18. The mathematical and psychological translations of phenomenology cannot be taken in isolation. As a specifically new approach, they are valuable only if they are pursued conjointly. Their isolated employment tends to lead to a new reductionism.

19. This view of the cognitive sciences from a phenomenological standpoint as so many more or less naturalizing attitudes is based on the following appraisals: Varela 1996; Andler 1992; Varela, Thompson, and Rosch 1991; and Dupuy 1994.

20. We are taking "emergence" in the broad sense, thereby including the second and the third attitudes. The level at which the confrontation has to be situated is, moreover, that of a theory of knowledge, a level lying between the formal mathematical level (practicing the nonlinear hypothesis or deploying a *mathesis universalis* alias formal ontology) and a strictly experimental/experiential level.

21. *Ideen* I, §86. In a remark (p. 215), Husserl himself points out the origin of the term *Funktion* in Stumpf, even while distancing himself from its essentially psychological meaning, which thereby integrates Stumpf's phenomenology in the context of an eidetic psychology of a hyletic kind. With reference to this notion of function, cf. also Cassirer 1910, chap. 8.

22. *Ideen* I, §86. Cf. also the third *Cartesian Meditation*, which undertakes a parallel analysis.

23. Ibid.: "The term 'consciousness' does not apply to 'psychic complexes,' to 'contents' which are founded together in 'bundles' [*Bündel*] or to a flux of 'sensations' which by virtue of not possessing a meaning in themselves could undergo any kind of mixture which ever engendering a 'meaning.'"

24. Cf. *Analysen*, pp. 336–46; ZPI II, suppl. 1, pp. 34–42. Cf. also Kern 1989 and Welton 1977. Depraz, in Bégout et al. 1995: 479–82, presents a sketch of an understanding of the relation between these two methods.

25. *Analysen* adopts this genetic approach in an exemplary fashion. *Erfahrung und Urteil* adopts also this approach by extending the problematic announced in *Krisis*. In utilizing the decisive notion of the *Rückfrage*, the latter also adopts this

regressive approach but confers upon it a new communitarian dimension. Cf. also Depraz 1996a.

26. Cf. *Analysen*, especially suppl. 18, for the notion of *Resonanz*.

27. Cf. "Conversations: Sentient Beings," in Hayward and Varela 1992. Cf., in the same volume, R. B. Livingston, "Development of the Human Brain."

28. *Phénoménologie hyper-esthésique* is an expression for which we bear the entire responsibility. Depraz, *Lucidité du corps: Pour un empirisme transcendantal en phenomenologie* (forthcoming). A precursor in this domain is G. W. Leibniz, with his notion of "unconscious perceptions." On the basis of the Buddhist tradition of attentive presence, Varela has opened up a possibility with regard to such a phenomenology (cf. Varela, Thompson, and Rosch 1991). By the same token, it is at this limiting point of the investigation of a *new scientific phenomenology* that the technique of explicating lived experience by an intersubjectively mediated evocative act takes on its full significance. This approach has been explored by Vermersch (1994, 1993): there could well turn out to be a resource which is indispensable for the acute and differentiated apprehension of these micro-perspective levels, commonly regarded as inapprehensible.

29. Kant could also without difficulty lay claim to just such a characterization of the living organism (cf. *Critique of Judgment*, part 1, which deals with the teleology of living organisms), at least to this extent, that finality appears to dominate the Kantian project. It remains residual with Husserl, with regard to an open teleology. As for evolution, it presupposes a coherent structuring of the living but contains within itself the possibility of mutation. Cf. the notion of autopoiesis developed by Varela 1979. Cf. also Dumouchel and Dupuy 1983.

30. The idea of a "generative phenomenology" is from Steinbock 1995, which opens up this theme so essential to Husserlian phenomenology and so gives meaning and coherence to the problematic of the life-world.

31. Cf. Depraz 1991. Cf. also Varela 1996: 35, which links "to enact" with Heidegger's *Geschehen* (in Heidegger 1927, §72), the double origin of birth as being-for-life and as historicality.

32. MS F I 32, p. 110/b, quoted by Kern 1989: 414.

33. Cf. the final and prophetic sentence of *Wiener Vortrag*: "Out of the ashes of great weariness will rise up the phoenix of a new life-inwardness and spiritualization, the pledge of a great and distant future for man: for the spirit alone is immortal."

34. On the basis of such a practical, nondualist metaphysics there arises the possibility of constituting a new scientific phenomenology whose exemplary topics would evidently be time, space, imagination, and intersubjectivity. Such fields of investigation should be undertaken on their own account and will be the object of further work, work that will require the specific competences of scientists (neurobiologists and psychologists), of philosophers (phenomenologists), and of practitioners. Cf. Varela (in this volume). Regarding the complete methodology of such a departure, cf. Depraz, Varela, and Vermersch (forthcoming).

35. Throughout the length and breadth of his work Husserl never ceases to employ the adjective "naive" to define the absence of phenomenological rigor.

36. *LU* I, §17, which cites J. S. Mill's *System of Logic* (1843) and Theodor Lipps's *Grundzüge der Logik* (1896) in defense of this position.

37. Husserl speaks of *Psychologismus* and of *Psychologisten* as the contemporary Anglo-Saxon world speaks of phenomenologists.

38. *LU* I, §19. In the end, antipsychologism owes more to Kant, regulated as it is by the constitutive opposition of the natural and the moral.

39. Murphy 1980 and Donnici 1989.

40. After having, in *Philosophy of Arithmetic*, himself adopted a "psychologistic" position by studying the empirical genesis of the concept of number. Cf. Duquesne 1984.

41. Cf. the fifth logical investigation, which employs a descriptive psychology of lived experience, then, in the 1920s, *Phenomenological Psychology*, the title of volume 9 of *Husserliana*, which situates the positivist study of psychic data with reference to the transcendental claim. We will avoid attempting to cut the Gordian knot that binds phenomenological psychology and transcendental phenomenology. The literature on this question is abundant if not always illuminating: see Paci 1963, Gurwitsch 1965, Kockelmans 1967, Landgrebe 1968, Yee 1969, Ströker 1983, and Arlt 1984.

42. In this passage, and at this time, Husserl does not distinguish among specific, general, and ideal.

43. Cf. in the following French translations of Husserl: A. Lowit, "Avertissement du traducteur," in E. Husserl, *L'Idée de la phénoménologie* (Paris: Presses Universitaires de France, 1985), pp. 5–34; J. F. Lavigne, "Introduction," in E. Husserl, *Chose et espace: Leçons de 1907* (Paris: Presses Universitaires de France, 1989), pp. 5–19; and J. English, "Indications générales," in *E. Husserl: Problèmes fondamentaux de la phénoménologie* (Paris: Presses Universitaires de France, 1991), pp. 7–84.

44. Cf. Ingarden 1918, where the realism-idealism problem is broached for the first time. From 1913, H. Conrad-Martius expressed his disagreement with Husserl in Conrad-Martius 1916. Cf. also Ingarden 1929 and 1964–65.

45. *EPh* I, 12th Lesson, "The Naive Dogmatism of Objectivism" (Locke); 24th Lesson, "Empirico-inductive Objectivism in Hume"; 26th Lesson, "Fundamental Features Characterizing the Positive and Constructive Current in Modern Rationalism and Its Dogmatism."

46. Ibid., appendix: "Kant and the Idea of Transcendental Philosophy," where idealism is justified as "scientific system."

CHAPTER 18

1. Husserl, *Ideen* I, §70, trans. F. Kersten, p. 159: "In his investigative thinking the geometer operates on the figure or model incomparably more in phantasy than in perception.... In phantasy, to be sure, he must make an effort to attain clear intuitions from which he is exempted by a sketch or model. But in actually sketching and constructing a model he is restricted; in phantasy he has incomparably more

freedom reshaping at will the figures feigned, and in running through continuously modified possible shapings, thus in generating an immense number of new formations; a freedom opens up to him for the very first time an access to the expanses of essential possibilities with their infinite horizons of eidetic cognitions."

2. We read, at the beginning of *Ideen* II, §19, trans. R. Rojcewicz. p. 96: "Let us now proceed to investigate the essence of the soul, the human or animal soul, as it is, in its connection with the material Body, an Object of natural-scientific research."

And now this, at the beginning of §20, Rojcewicz trans., p. 97: "It is in connection with what is material that the psychic is given to us. Among material things there are certain ones, or from an eidetic standpoint there are certain ones a priori possible, which are soulless, 'merely' material. On the other hand, there are also certain ones which have the rank of 'Bodies' and as such display a connection with a new stratum of being, the psychic stratum, as it is called here."

3. May the issue be judged by the following passage from *Ideen* I, §57, Kersten trans., p. 132: "The Ego seems to be there continually, indeed, necessarily, and this continualness is obviously not that of a stupidly persistant mental process, a 'fixed idea.' Instead, the Ego belongs to each coming and going mental process; its 'regard' is directed 'through' [*durch*] each actional cogito to the objective something. This ray of regard [*Blickstrahl*] changes from one cogito to the next, shooting forth anew with each new cogito and vanishing with it. The Ego, however, is something identical. At least, considered eidetically, any cogito *can* change, come and go, even though one may doubt that every cogito is *necessarily* something transitory and not simply, as we find it, something *in fact* transitory. In contradistinction, the pure Ego would, however, seem to be something essentially necessary; and, as something absolutely identical throughout every actual or possible change in mental processes, it *cannot in any sense be a really inherent part or moment* of the mental processes themselves."

4. Let us thus read the following from the introduction to §85 of *Ideen* I, which will expose the "noetico-noematic structures," that is, the synthesis of the noema: "At the level of consideration to which we are confined until further notice, a level which abstains from descending into the obscure depths of the ultimate consciousness which constitutes all such temporality as belong to mental processes, and instead takes mental processes as they offer themselves as unitary temporal processes in reflection on what is immanent" (Kersten trans., p. 203).

5. This of course in no way means that Husserl's proposal for a phenomenology of time is *ipso facto* a phenomenology of the mathematical continuum or vice versa. Between the phenomenological problems created by real numbers and those posed by time, there is, in accordance with the maxim of respect for regionalities proper to the phenomenological undertaking, no communication. This said, it can be remarked that in the *Philosophie der Arithmetik* the "continuous combination" (Husserl means, as he explains it here, the linkage of parts in a continuum) is identified as a primary rather than psychical relation, that is to say, in substance, following the vocabulary in use later, non-intentional. Whereas everything on the order of number is conceived by early Husserlian phenomenology as intentional correlates: it is moreover well known to what extent this Husserlian position has influenced the philoso-

phy of mathematics in France. As far as my knowledge of the corpus permits, it would appear that Husserl never correlated the failure of any intentional construction to synthesize the continuum (the one the mathematician wants) and the primitiveness of a certain modality of the continuum, which the concept of "combination" evoked here points up in passing. But this does not prevent Husserl, in the establishment of the phenomenological blueprint of time, to have in mind, as a sort of authorized guide, the theoretical image associating itself with the construction of the linear continuum in mathematics.

6. [All translations of this work are my own. Trans.]

7. Concerning everything which has just been said, cf. §§32–34 in Heidegger 1927.

CHAPTER 19

1. In this citation "205" is a reference to a page number in the translation listed in the Bibliography. I will use this format throughout this essay.

2. Let us notice that the use by Husserl of expressions such *enigma* or *sphinx* ("the sphinx of knowledge") or the above allusions to *kinship*, all of them associated with Oedipus, as hero of the desire for truth or knowledge, echo, most certainly, his reading of Hugo von Hoffmansthal. The Austrian poet and writer, whom Husserl admired, not only had translated Sophocles' *Oedipus Rex*, but had himself written a tragedy titled *Oedipus und die Sphinx*. On the use of the expression "sphinx of knowledge" by Husserl, cf. Wioleta Miskiewicz 1994.

3. Husserl, *Krisis*, §48, p. 170 [166].

4. Such a position recalls the one adopted by William James in his "radical empiricism," but with this not negligible difference that James opposed any sort of transcendentalism, probably because he could not see it in other than Kantian terms. It is in this same sense, but also in a clear opposition to the positivistic attitude, that James, in his essay "Does 'Consciousness' Exist?" (1976), refused existence to consciousness. But this was his path to avoid dualism, what as matter of fact Husserl could do precisely through his transcendental idealism, so badly understood, in so far it is interpreted in terms of the metaphysical opposition between realism and idealism, whereas Husserlian transcendental idealism is absolutely compatible with commonsense realism.

5. See, for instance, Von Wright's critical remark on "scientism" (1995): "The most vulgar examples of these tendencies we find, it seems to me, in contemporary philosophy of mind, be it in the form of the physicalists' 'identification' of so-called mental states with brain processes or the eliminative materialists' rejection of our common sense psychological concepts—what they call 'folk-psychology'—as a 'radically false theory' eventually to be replaced by a perfect neuroscience."

6. That philosophy could not stop entering this fray bears witness today in, among others, Thomas Nagel's work. As he writes in his introduction to *The View From Nowhere* (1986): "For many philosophers the exemplary case of reality is the

world described by physics, the science in which we have achieved our greatest detachment from a specifically human perspective on the world. But for precisely that reason physics is bound to leave undescribed the irreducibly subjective character of conscious mental processes, whatever may be their intimate relation to the physical operation of the brain. The subjectivity of consciousness is an irreducible feature of reality—without which we couldn't do physics or anything else—and it must occupy as fundamental a place in any credible world view as matter, energy, space, time, and numbers." However, this acknowledgment of the irreducible character of subjectivity differs from the one inherent in Husserlian phenomenology. To a *constitutive* phenomenology it would not be appropriate to bring consciousness into line with physical realities as matter or energy or with ideal entities as numbers, for these realities only get meaning by and for consciousness.

7. Without relying on phenomenology, Simone Weil (1974) had a clear insight of this role of the body for the correlation between the knower and the known and put it in a very suggestive way: "The world's order which is perceptible by us is like the pattern we find on the slice of a stump when it has been sawed. Cut it at another place and we would find a pattern, another one, but still a pattern. Our universe is like a slice of the universe opened up at a place corresponding to the dimensions and the structure of our living body. The world is known to us only subjectively; as is our organism; but the match between the two is a fact."

8. Consciousness of this identity presupposes the tearing away from the solipsistic sphere of one's own (*Mir-Eigenes*) thanks to the constitution of an intersubjectivity. Hence Husserl's question (in *Krisis*, §28, p. 109 [107, translation modified]): "How consciousness arises in such a way that through it my living body acquires the ontic validity of one physical body (*Körper*) among others, and how, on the other hand, certain physical bodies in my perceptual field come to count as living bodies, living bodies of 'alien' ego subjects—these are now necessary questions." In other words, how may my living body be set as a physical body and as such become, in our world, an object of research by a natural science?

9. See Mohanty 1964, and de Muralt 1958, §6.

10. On naturalization, see Petitot's important essay, "La Réorientation naturaliste de la phénoménologie" (Petitot 1995a).

11. See de Boer's (1978) "Conclusion."

CHAPTER 20

1. Merleau-Ponty 1968: 108: "Thus what we understand by the concept of institution are those events in experience which endow it with durable dimensions, in relation to which a whole series of other experiences will acquire meaning, will form an intelligible series or an history—or again those events which sediment in me a meaning, not just as survivals or residues, but as the invitation to a sequel, the necessity of a future."

CHAPTER 21

Adapted from Dupuy 1994, chap. 4.
1. Equivalence between the computational capabilities of his machine and Turing's.
2. Brentano 1874. The McAlister edition is based on Oskar Kraus's third edition of 1925. On Husserl's relation to Brentano, particularly insofar as the former represents the point of common origin from which Heidegger split off in one direction and Sartre in another, see Renaut 1993: 88–102.
3. See McAlister 1974: 328–38. In truth the affair is still more complicated than this, for Brentano himself was later, first in 1905, and then in the second edition of the *Psychologie*, published in 1911, to reject the thesis that "physical phenomena" are contained within mental phenomena (that strange "Kehre" led Brentano to adopt a doctrine that he himself called "reism"). The problem is that Chisholm never referred to any other edition than that of 1874. Certain analytical philosophers specializing in Brentano's thought maintain that no reversal ever took place and that Brentano was a "reist" from the start. On this view, then, it was the Husserlian tradition that was gravely mistaken! See Aquila 1977.
4. An accessible introduction to this work can be found in Fogelman-Soulié 1991.
5. Steve Heims has succeeded in reconstructing the essential details of this encounter, of which, it will be recalled, no written record was made. See Heims 1991, chap. 10, in particular pp. 236–39.
6. Originally published in 1959 and reprinted in McCulloch 1965: 230–55.
7. See Lacan 1978, chaps. 15 and 16 ("Séminaire sur 'La Lettre volée'").
8. For an assessment of this work one may consult my own article: Dupuy 1989: 491–515.

BIBLIOGRAPHY

RECENT RESEARCH IN PHENOMENOLOGY AND COGNITIVE SCIENCE

This section lists conferences, books, and special issues of journals that over the last few years have dealt explicitly with the interface between Husserlian or Merleau-Pontian phenomenology and cognitive science from the perspective of the naturalization problem. Entries are listed in chronological order. This section does *not* pretend to be exhaustive, but we have made every effort to include the most relevant items that have come to our attention. Individual articles are not included, and we apologize in advance for missing items. Needless to say, numerous other works have been devoted to phenomenology during this period but from a perspective other than the one on naturalization explored here.

CONFERENCES

"Phenomenology and Gestalt Theory, History, and Actuality of Formal Ontology." Conference at the Institut des Hautes Etudes Scientifiques, Bures-sur-Yvette, and the Ecole des Hautes Etudes en Sciences Sociales, Paris, France, 1985.
  Organizer: J. Petitot.
  Participants (selection): K. Fine, E. Holenstein, K. Mulligan, P. Simons, B. Smith, and R. Thom.

"Phenomenological and Existential Issues in Modern Cognitive Science." Conference at the Center for Cognitive Science, University of San Marino, May 31–June 2, 1991.
  Organizers: Francisco J. Varela and Gordon Globus.
  Theme: This seems to have been the first international meeting dealing explicitly with this topic. It was an informal, exploratory gathering, and no publication was intended.
  Participants: H. Dreyfus, T. van Gelder, D. Dennett, J. Haugeland, E. Pöppel, Paul Churchland, M. Johnson, M. Sullivan, E. Thompson, and J. Petitot.

"L'Intentionalité en question entre les sciences cognitives et le renouveau phénoménologique." Conference at the Centre de Recherches d'Histoire des Idées, CNRS URA 1256, Nice, France, June 11–13, 1992.
  Organizer: Dominique Janicaud.
  Theme: As announced in its title, the conference focused on intentionality, which was

broached from a very wide variety of angles, including not only Husserlian but also existential phenomenology.

Participants: H. Atlan, F. Cayla, R. Celis, J. F. Courtine, D. Davidson, P. Engel, G. Granel, M. Haar, K. Held, M. Henry, S. Ijsseling, R. Legros, A. Lingis, P. Livet, P. Loraux, J. Proust, M. Richir, E. Rigal, S. Robert, and J. Sallis.

Publication: *L'Intentionalité en question: Entre phénoménologie et recherches cognitives*, edited by D. Janicaud. Paris: J. Vrin, 1995.

"Phenomenology and Cognitive Science." Development Project. The Tempus Programme of the European Union Project 4310, including England, Germany, Italy, Austria, and Slovenia, 1992–1994.

Coordinator: Wolfgang L. Gombocz, University of Graz, Austria.

Theme: The project intended a wide number of exchanges, including two courses in Ljubljana (1993) and London (1994), which resulted in a publication that presents both phenomenology and some of its interfaces with cognitive science in a clear and informative manner.

Publication: *Handbook: Phenomenology and Cognitive Science*, edited by E. Baumgartner, W. Baumgartner, B. Borstner, M. Potrc, J. Shawe-Taylor, and E. Valentine. Dettelbach, Germany: Verlag Josef Röll, 1996.

"Formal Ontology in Conceptual Analysis and Knowledge Representation." International workshop at Padua, Italy, March 17–19, 1993.

Organizers: Nicola Guarino and Roberto Poli.

Participants (selection): N. Guarino, B. Smith, J. F. Sowa, R. Poli, N. B. Cocchiarella, C. Eschenbach, J. Petitot, G. Link, J. Dölling, K. Dahlgren, J. R. Hobbs, A. Cohn, P. Terenziani, P. Gerstl, F. Bonfatti, T. R. Gruber, J. A. Bateman, and T. Pirlein.

Publication: *The Role of Formal Ontology in the Information Technology*. Special issue of the *International Journal of Human and Computer Studies* 43, no. 5/6 (1995).

"Back to the Things Themselves." Conference at Southern Illinois University at Carbondale, March 21–23, 1996.

Organizers: Anthony Steinbock, Helen Fielding, and Glen Mazis.

Theme: A wide array of topics examined from the Husserlian and existentialist perspectives, to include gender, movement, vision, dialogue, touch, ecology, and others relating to science.

Publication: Forthcoming in *Human World*.

"Philosophie de l'action et neurosciences." Conference series at the Centre d'Analyse des Savoirs Contemporains, Université des Sciences Humaines de Strasbourg, France, 1993–96.

Organizer: Jean-Luc Petit.

Theme: A wide range of contributions linking current work in neuroscience to issues of motion, voluntary action, and phenomenological analysis.

Participants (selection): D. Andler, A. Berthoz, B. Bioulac, F. Dastur, C. Debru, N. Depraz, P. Engel, V. Gurfinkel, P. Jacob, M. Jeannerod, P. Livet, C. Macann, W. Miskiewicz, J. N. Missa, R. Misslin, R. Ogien, E. Pacherie, B. Pachoud, J.-L. Petit, J. Petitot, J. Proust, G. Rizzolatti, J. P. Roll, J.-M. Roy, A. Soulez, F. Varela, and D. Widlocher.

Publication: *Les Neurosciences et la philosophie de l'action*, edited by J.-L. Petit. Paris: Vrin, 1997.

SPECIAL PUBLICATIONS

Bermúdez, José, Anthony Marcel, and Naomi Eilan, eds. 1995. *The Body and the Self*. Cambridge: MIT Press. A collection dealing mostly with body and self-image, drawing from neuroscientific and developmental perspectives and strongly influenced by Merleau-Ponty's phenomenology.

Casati, R., B. Smith, and G. White, eds. 1994. *Philosophy and the Cognitive Sciences*. Vienna: Hölder-Pichler-Tempsky.

Eschenbach, C., C. Habel, and B. Smith, eds. 1994. *Topological Foundations of Cognitive Science*. Hamburg: Graduiertenkolleg Kognitionswissenschaft.

Guarino, N., and R. Poli, eds. 1993. *Proceedings of the International Workshop on Formal Ontology in Conceptual Analysis and Knowledge Representation*. Padua: Institute for Systems Theory and Biomedical Engineering of the Italian National Research Council.

Guarino, N., L. Vieu, and S. Pribbenow, eds. 1994. *Parts and Wholes: Conceptual Part-Whole Relations and Formal Mereology*. Eleventh European Conference on Artificial Intelligence, Amsterdam, 8 August. Amsterdam: European Coordinating Committee for Artificial Intelligence.

Haaparanta, Leila, and Sara Heinämaa, eds. 1995. *Mind and Cognition: Philosophical Perspectives on Cognitive Science and Artificial Intelligence*. Acta Philosophica Fennica, vol. 58. Helsinki: University of Finland.

Marbach, Eduard. 1993. *Mental Representation and Consciousness: Towards a Phenomenological Theory of Representation and Reference*. Dordrecht: Kluwer Academic Publishers. Marbach contrasts the positions of the two sciences on the subject of representation, which carries well the distinction between those neuroscientific hypotheses involving some kind of physical mechanism (symbolic or connectionist) and the phenomenological approach based on methodologically controlled reflective introspection.

Petitot, J., ed. 1990. *Sciences cognitives: Quelques aspects problématiques*. Special issue of *Revue de synthèse* 4, no. 1/2. Contributions by J. Proust, J.-P. Desclés, M. Piatelli-Palmarini, D. Andler, F. Varela, and J. Petitot.

———, ed. 1995. *Sciences cognitives et phénoménologie*. Special issue of *Archives de philosophie* 58, no. 4: 529–631. Contributions by J.-M. Roy, B. Pachoud, J. Proust, E. Pacherie, J.-L. Petit, M. Villela-Petit, W. Miskiewicz, and J. Petitot.

"Phénoménologie et psychologie cognitive." 1991. *Les Etudes philosophiques* 1.

Poli, R., and P. M. Simons, eds. 1996. *Formal Ontology*. Dordrecht: Kluwer Academic Publishers.

Salanskis, J.-M., ed. 1993. *Philosophie et sciences cognitives*. Special issue of *Intellectica* 17, no. 2. Contributions by D. Andler, B. Bachimont, H. L. Dreyfus, Y. Gueniffey, J. Lassègue, J. Petitot, J.-M. Salanskis, B. Smith, R. Casati, and T. Winograd.

Smith, B., ed. 1982. *Parts and Moments: Studies in Logic and Formal Ontology*. Munich: Philosophia.

———, ed. 1988. *Foundations of Gestalt Theory*. Munich: Philosophia.

Smith, B., and D. W. Smith, eds. 1995. *Cambridge Companion to Husserl*. Cambridge: Cambridge University Press.
Willard, Dallas. 1984. *Logic and the Objectivity of Knowledge*. Athens: Ohio University Press.
Wrathhall, M., ed. 1996. *Existential Phenomenology and Cognitive Science*. Special issue of the *Electronic Journal of Analytic Philosophy*, no. 4 (Spring). Contributions by M. Wrathhall and S. Kelly, M. Okrent, H. Dreyfus, J. Sanders, and T. van Gelder.

WORKS CITED IN THIS VOLUME

THE WORKS OF HUSSERL

Analysen zur passiven Synthesis. 1918–26. Husserliana 11. Edited by M. Fleischer. The Hague: M. Nijhoff, 1966. (Cited as *Analysen*.)
Cartesianische Meditationen und Pariser Vorträge. 1931. Husserliana 1. Edited by S. Strasser. The Hague: M. Nijhoff, 1950. Originally published in French under the title *Méditations cartésiennes: Introduction à la phénoménologie*, trans. G. Peiffer and E. Levinas (Paris: Armand Colin, 1931). Translated into English by D. Cairns under the title *Cartesian Meditations: An Introduction to Phenomenology* (Dordrecht: Kluwer Academic Publishers, 1988). *Pariser Vorträge* was translated into English by P. Koestenbaum under the title *The Paris Lectures* (The Hague: M. Nijhoff, 1975). (Cited as *CM*.)
Ding und Raum: Vorlesungen. 1907. Husserliana 16. Edited by U. Claesges. The Hague: M. Nijhoff, 1973. (Cited as *DR*.)
Erfahrung und Urteil: Untersuchungen zur Genealogie der Logik. Edited by L. Landgrebe. Prague: Academia Verlagsbuchhandlung, 1939. Reprint. Hamburg: Claassen & Goverts, 1954. Translated by J. S. Churchill & K. Ameriks under the title *Experience and Judgement* (London: Routledge & Kegan Paul, 1973). (Cited as *EU*.)
Erste Philosophie (1923/1924). Part 1: *Kritische Ideengeschichte*. Husserliana 7. Edited by R. Boehm. The Hague: M. Nijhoff, 1956. (Cited as *EPh* I.)
Erste Philosophie (1923/1924). Part 2: *Theorie der phänomenologischen Reduktion*. Husserliana 8. Edited by R. Boehm. The Hague: M. Nijhoff, 1959. (Cited as *EPh* II.)
Formale und Transzendentale Logik: Versuch einer Kritik der logischen Vernunft. 1929. Husserliana 17. Edited by P. Janssen. The Hague: M. Nijhoff, 1974. Translated by D. Cairns under the title *Formal and Transcendental Logic* (The Hague: M. Nijhoff, 1969). (Cited as *FTL*.)
Die Idee der Phänomenologie. 1907. Husserliana 2. Edited by W. Biemel. The Hague: M. Nijhoff, 1950. Translated by W. Alston and G. Nakhnikian under the title *The Idea of Phenomenology* (The Hague: M. Nijhoff, 1964).
Ideen zu einer reinen Phänomenologie und phänomenologischen Philosophie.

Book 1: *Allgemeine Einführung in die reine Phänomenologie.* 1913. Husserliana 3. Edited by W. Biemel. The Hague: M. Nijhoff, 1950. Translated into English under the title *Ideas Pertaining to a Pure Phenomenology and to a Phenomenological Philosophy. First Book: General Introduction to Pure Phenomenology*, by W. R. Boyce Gibson (New York: Collier Books, 1972), and by F. Kersten (The Hague: M. Nijhoff, 1982). (Cited as *Ideen* I.)
Ideen zu einer reinen Phänomenologie und phänomenologischen Philosophie. Book 2: *Phänomenologische Untersuchungen zur Konstitution.* 1912–28. Husserliana 4. Edited by M. Biemel. The Hague: M. Nijhoff, 1952. Translated by R. Rojcewicz and A. Schuwer under the title *Ideas Pertaining to a Pure Phenomenology and to a Phenomenological Philosophy, Second Book: Studies in the Phenomenology of Constitution* (Dordrecht: Kluwer Academic Publishers, 1989). (Cited as *Ideen* II.)
Ideen zu einer reinen Phänomenologie und phänomenologischen Philosophie. Book 3: *Die Phänomenologie und die Fundamente der Wissenschaften.* Husserliana 5. Edited by M. Biemel. The Hague: M. Nijhoff, 1952. Translated by T. E. Klein and W. E. Pohl under the title *Ideas Pertaining to a Pure Phenomenology and to a Phenomenological Philosophy: Third Book: Phenomenology and the Foundations of the Sciences* (Dordrecht: Kluwer Academic Publishers, 1980). (Cited as *Ideen* III.)
Die Krisis der europäischen Wissenschaften und die transzendentale Phänomenologie. Eine Einleitung in die phänomenologische Philosophie. 1936. Husserliana 6. Edited by W. Biemel. The Hague: M. Nijhoff, 1954. Translated by D. Carr under the title *The Crisis of European Sciences and Transcendental Phenomenology: An Introduction to Phenomenological Philosophy* (Evanston, Ill.: Northwestern University Press, 1970). (Cited as *Krisis.*)
Logische Untersuchungen. 1st ed. Halle: M. Niemeyer, 1900–1901. 2d ed. Halle: M. Niemeyer, 1913–21. Husserliana 18. *Logische Untersuchungen.* Vol. 1, *Prolegomena zur reinen Logik.* Edited by E. Holenstein. The Hague: M. Nijhoff, 1975. Husserliana 19/1, 19/2. *Logische Untersuchungen.* Vol. 2, parts 1 and 2: *Untersuchungen zur Phänomenologie und Theorie der Erkenntnis.* Edited by U. Panzer. 1984. Translated by J. N. Findlay under the title *Logical Investigations* (London: Routledge and Kegan Paul, 1973). (Cited as *LU*, by volume and part, and by investigation number, paragraph, and page.)
The Origin of Geometry. Translation of Annex 3 of *Die Krisis der europäischen Wissenschaften und die transzendentale Phänomenologie* by D. Carr. In J. Derrida, *Edmund Husserl's Origin of Geometry.* Translated by J. P. Leavey. Stony Brook, N.Y.: N. Hays, 1978.
Phänomenologische Psychologie. Vorlesungen Sommersemester 1925. Husserliana 9. Edited by W. Biemel. The Hague: M. Nijhoff, 1962. Translated by J. Scanlon under the title *Phenomenological Psychology. Lectures, Summer Semester 1925* (The Hague: M. Nijhoff, 1977). (Cited as *PP.*)
"Philosophie als strenge Wissenschaft." 1911. In *Logos* 1: 289–314. Reprint. Frank-

furt am Main: Klostermann, 1981. Published in English under the title "Philosophy as Rigorous Science," in Lauer 1965: 69–147. (Cited as PsW.)

Philosophie der Arithmetik: Psychologische und logische Untersuchungen. Vol. 1. Halle a. S.: Pfeffer, 1891. Husserliana 12. Edited by L. Eley. The Hague: M. Nijhoff, 1970.

Studien zur Arithmetik und Geometrie. Texte aus dem Nachlaß (1886–1901). Husserliana 21. Edited by I. Strohmeyer. The Hague: M. Nijhoff, 1983.

Zur Phänomenologie des inneren Zeitbewußtseins (1893–1917). Husserliana 10. Edited by R. Boehm. The Hague: M. Nijhoff, 1966. Translated in part by J. S. Churchill under the title *The Phenomenology of Internal Time Consciousness* (Bloomington: Indiana University Press, 1964), and by J. Barrett Brough under the title *On the Phenomenology of the Consciousness of Internal Time* (Dordrecht: Kluwer Academic Publishers, 1991). (Cited as PZB.)

Zur Phänomenologie der Intersubjektivität. Texte aus dem Nachlaß. Part 1, 1905–1920. Husserliana 13. Edited by I. Kern. The Hague: M. Nijhoff, 1973. (Cited as ZPI I.)

Zur Phänomenologie der Intersubjektivität. Texte aus dem Nachlaß. Part 2: 1921–1928. Husserliana 14. Edited by I. Kern. The Hague: M. Nijhoff, 1973. (Cited as ZPI II.)

Zur Phänomenologie der Intersubjektivität. Texte aus dem Nachlaß. Part 3: 1929–1935. Husserliana 15. Edited by I. Kern. The Hague: M. Nijhoff, 1973. (Cited as ZPI III.)

Manuscripts D 11; D 12 I, II (1931). Husserl's archives.
Manuscripts C 16 IV (1932), C 16 VII (1933). Husserl's archives.

OTHER SOURCES

Agree, Ph. 1995. "Introduction." *Artificial Intelligence* 36.

Alvarez, L., P. L. Lions, and J. M. Morel. 1992. "Image Selective Smoothing and Edge Detection by Non Linear Diffusion." *SIAM Journal of Numerical Analysis* 29: 845–66.

Amit, D. J. 1989. *Modeling Brain Function: The World of Attractor Neural Networks.* Cambridge: Cambridge University Press.

Anderson, S. E. 1994. "A Computational Model of Auditory Pattern Recognition." Technical Report 112. Bloomington: Indiana University Cognitive Science Program.

Andler, D. 1987. "Progrès en situation d'incertitude." *Le Débat* 47: 5–25.

———. 1992. "From Paleo to Neo-Connectionism." In G. Van der Vijver, ed., *New Perspectives on Cybernetics*, 125–46. Dordrecht: Kluwer Academic Publishers.

———, ed. 1992. *Introduction aux sciences cognitives.* Paris: Gallimard.

Appel, K. O. 1979. *Die Erklären-Verstehen-Kontroverse in Transzendental-Pragmatischer Sicht.* Frankfurt am Main: Suhrkamp Verlag. Translated by G. Warnke under the title *Understanding and Explanation* (Cambridge: MIT Press, 1984).

Aquila, R. 1977. *Intentionality: A Study of Mental Acts*. University Park: Pennsylvania State University Press.
Arbib, M. A. 1995. *Handbook of Brain Theory and Neural Networks*. Cambridge: MIT Press.
Aristotle. 1963. *Categories* and *De Interpretation*. Translated by J. L. Akrill. Oxford: Oxford University Press.
Arlt, G. 1984. "Transzendental Philosophie und Psychologie. Zum Begriff der 'Phänomenologische Psychologie' bei Husserl." *Perspektiven der Philosophie* 10: 161–79.
Armstrong, D. M. 1989. *Universals: An Opinionated Introduction*. Boulder, Colo.: Westview Press.
———. 1997. *A World of States of Affairs*. Cambridge: Cambridge University Press.
Armstrong, D. M., and M. Norman. 1984. *Consciousness and Causality*. Oxford: Basil Blackwell.
Arrington, K. 1994. "The Temporal Dynamics of Brightness Filling-In." *Vision Research* 34: 3371–87.
———. 1996. "Directional Filling-In." *Neural Computation* 8: 300–318.
Artuso, R., E. Aurell, and P. Cvitanovic. 1990. "Recycling of Strange Sets. I. Cycle Expansions." *Nonlinearity* 3: 325–59.
Asperti, A., and G. Longo. 1991. *Categories, Types, and Structures*. Cambridge: MIT Press.
Atiya, A., and P. Baldi. 1989. "Oscillations and Synchronisation in Neural Networks: An Exploration of the Labeling Hypothesis." *International Journal of Neural Systems* 1, no. 2: 103–24.
Atlan, H. 1994. "Intentionality in Nature." *Journal for the Theory of Social Behavior* 24, no. 1: 67–87.
Auerbach, D., P. Cvitanovic, J. P. Eckmann, G. Gunaratne, and I. Procaccia. 1987. "Exploring Chaotic Motion Through Periodic Orbits." *Phys. Rev. Lett.* 58: 1377–80.
Avenarius, R. 1912. *Der menschliche Weltbegriff*. Leipzig: O. R. Reisland.
Bachelard, G. 1934. *Le Nouvel Esprit scientifique*. Paris: Presses Universitaires de France.
Ballard, D. H. 1991. "Animate Vision." *Artificial Intelligence* 48: 57–86.
Barbaras, R. 1992. "Motricité et phénoménalité chez le dernier Merleau-Ponty." In M. Richir and E. Tassin, eds., *Merleau-Ponty: Phénoménologie et expériences*, 27–43. Grenoble: Millon.
———. 1996. "L'Espace et le mouvement vivant." *Alter* 4: 11–31.
Barlow, H., and R. Hill. 1963. "Evidence for a Physiological Explanation of the Waterfall Phenomenon and Figural Aftereffects." *Nature* 200: 1345–47.
Barreau, H., and J. Hartong, eds. 1989. *La Mathématique non standard*. Paris: Editions du CNRS.
Beer, R. 1991. *Intelligence as Adaptive Behavior*. New York: Academic Press.
Bégout, B., N. Depraz, M. Mavridis, and S. Nagaï. 1995. "Passivité et phénoménologie génétique (L. Landgrebe, E. Holenstein, I. Yamaguchi, N.-I. Lee)." *Alter* 3: 409–502.

Benacerraf, P., and H. Putnam, eds. 1964. *Philosophy of Mathematics: Selected Readings*. Englewood Cliffs, N.J.: Prentice-Hall.

Bergson, H. 1896. *Matière et mémoire*. Paris: PUF.

Berkeley, M., B. Debruyn, and G. Orban. 1994. "Illusory, Motion, and Luminance-Defined Contours Interact in the Human Visual System." *Vision Research* 34: 209–16.

Bermúdez, J., A. Marcel, and N. Eilan, eds. 1995. *The Body and the Self*. Cambridge: MIT Press / Bradford Books.

Bernet, R. 1985. *Texte zur Phänomenologie des inneren Zeitbewußtseins: Texte nach Husserliana X*. Hamburg: Felix Meiner.

———. 1991. "Le Concept husserlien de noème." *Les Etudes philosophiques* 1: 79–100.

———. 1994a. "Finitude et téléologie de le perception." In Bernet 1994b.

———. 1994b. *La Vie du sujet*. Paris: Presses Universitaires de France.

Berthoz, A. 1991. "Reference Frames for the Perception and Control of Movement." In J. Paillard, ed., *Brain and Space*. Oxford: Oxford University Press.

———. 1997. *Le Sens du mouvement*. Paris: O. Jacob.

Besnier, B. 1993. "Remarques sur les leçons sur la conscience intime du temps de Husserl." *Alter* 1: 319–56.

Bickle, J. 1992a. "Mental Anomaly and the New Mind-Brain Reductionism." *Philosophy of Science* 59: 217–30.

———. 1992b. "Revisionary Physicalism." *Biology and Philosophy* 7: 411–30.

———. 1998. *Psychoneural Reduction*. Cambridge: MIT Press.

Blackmore, S. J., G. Brelstaff, K. Nelson, and T. Trosianko. 1995. "Is the Richness of Our Visual World an Illusion? Transsaccadic Memory for Complex Scenes." *Perception* 24: 1075–81.

Blattner, W. 1999. *Heidegger's Temporal Idealism*. Cambridge: Cambridge University Press.

Block, N. 1978. "Troubles with Functionalism." In *Perception and Cognition: Issues in the Foundations of Psychology*, 261–325. Minnesota Studies in the Philosophy of Science, 9. Minneapolis: University of Minnesota Press.

———. 1980. *Readings in the Philosophy of Psychology*. Cambridge: Harvard University Press.

Boi, L. 1995. *Le Problème mathématique de l'espace*. Berlin: Springer Verlag.

Borst, C. V., ed. 1970. *The Mind-Brain Theory*. London: Macmillan, St. Martin's Press.

Bortoft, H. 1997. *The Wholeness of Nature: Goethe's Way Toward a Science of Conscious Participation in Nature*. Hudson, N.Y.: The Lindisfarne Press.

Bosio, F. 1962. "La lotta contro lo psicologismo e l'idea della logica pura in Husserl." *Ataut* 71: 373–82.

Bouveresse, J. 1992. "Weyl, Wittgenstein et le problème du continu." In Salanskis and Sinaceur 1992.

———. 1995. *Langage, perception et réalité*. Vol. 1. Nîmes: Ed. Jacqueline Chambon.

Boynton, R. 1983. "Mechanisms of Chromatic Discrimination." In J. Mollon and L. Sharpe, eds., *Colour Vision: Physiology and Psychophysics*, 409–23. New York: Academic Press.

Brand, G. 1955. *Welt, Ich und Zeit*. The Hague: M. Nijhoff.

Brentano, F. 1874. *Psychologie vom empirischen Standpunkt*. 1st ed. (Reprinted as vol. 1 of the 2d ed.) Leipzig: Duncker & Humblot. Translated by A. C. Rancurello, D. B. Terrell, and L. L. McAlister under the title *Psychology from an Empirical Standpoint*. London: Routledge & Kegan Paul, 1974.

Bridgeman, B. 1983. "Isomorphism Is Where You Find It." *Behavioral and Brain Sciences* 6: 658–59.

Brough, J. 1989. "Husserl's Phenomenology of Time-Consciousness." In J. N. Mohanty and W. R. McKenna, eds., *Husserl's Phenomenology: A Textbook*. Lanham, Md.: University Press of America.

Brouwer, L. E. 1927. "Intuitionistic Reflections on Formalism." In J. Van Heijenoort, *From Frege to Gödel: A Source Book on Mathematical Logic, 1879–1931*. Cambridge: Harvard University Press, 1967.

Bruzina, R. 1993. "The Revision of the Bernau Time-Consciousness Manuscripts: Status Questionis—Freiburg 1928–1930." *Alter* 1: 357–83.

———. 1994. "The Revision of the Bernau Time-Consciousness Manuscripts: New Questions—1930–1933." *Alter* 2: 367–95.

Carnap, R. 1969. *The Logical Structure of the World*. Berkeley: University of California Press.

Casati, R., and A. C. Varzi. 1994. *Holes and Other Superficialities*. Cambridge: MIT Press / Bradford Books.

———. 1995. "Basic Issues in Spatial Representation." In M. De Glas and Z. Pawlak, eds., *Proceedings of the 2nd World Conference on the Fundamentals of Artificial Intelligence*, 63–72. Paris: Angkor.

———. 1996a. "The Structure of Spatial Localization." *Philosophical Studies* 82: 205–39.

———, eds. 1996b. *Events*. Aldershot, Eng., and Brookfield, Vt.: Dartmouth University Press.

———. 1997. "Spatial Entities." In O. Stock, ed., *Reasoning About Space and Time*, 73–96. Dordrecht: Kluwer Academic Publishers.

Cassirer, E. 1910. *Substanz und Funktion*. Berlin: Wissenschaftliche Buchgesellschaft, 1969.

Chalmers, D. 1995. "The Puzzle of Conscious Experience." *Scientific American*, December 1995: 80–86.

———. 1996. *The Conscious Mind: In Search of a Fundamental Theory*. Oxford: Oxford University Press.

Chambon, R. 1974. *Le Monde comme perception et realité*. Paris: Vrin.

Chandarasekharan, K. 1986. *Hermann Weyl*. Berlin: Springer Verlag.

Changeux, J.-P. 1982. *L'Homme neuronal*. Paris: Fayard.

Chatelet, G. 1993. *Les Enjeux du mobile*. Paris: Seuil.

Chisholm, R. M. 1956. "Sentences About Believing." *Proceedings of the Aristotelian Society*, no. 56.

———. 1957. *Perceiving: A Philosophical Study*. Ithaca, N.Y.: Cornell University Press.

Church, R. M., and H. Broadbent. 1990. "Alternative Representation of Time, Number and Rate." *Cognition* 37: 55–81.

Churchland, P. M. 1984. *Matter and Consciousness*. Cambridge: MIT Press.

———. 1995. *The Engine of Reason, the Seat of the Soul*. Cambridge: MIT Press.

Churchland, P. S. 1986. *Neurophilosophy: Toward a Unified Science of the Mind-Brain*. Cambridge: MIT Press.

Churchland, P. S., and V. S. Ramachandran. 1993. "Filling In: Why Dennett Is Wrong." In B. Dahlbom, ed., *Dennett and His Critics*. Oxford: Basil Blackwell.

Clark, A. 1997. *Being There: Putting Brain, Body, and World Together Again*. Cambridge: MIT Press / Bradford Books.

Clarke B. L. 1981. "A Calculus of Individuals Based on 'Connection.'" *Notre Dame Journal of Formal Logic* 22: 204–18.

Cobb, R. 1982. "A Fresh Look at James' Radical Empiricism." In R. Bruzina and B. Willshire, eds., *Phenomenology: Developments and Bridges*. Albany, New York: SUNY Press.

Cohn, A. G., and N. M. Gotts. 1994. "A Theory of Spatial Relations with Indeterminate Boundaries." In Eschenbach, Habel, and Smith 1994: 131–50.

Conrad-Martius, H. 1916. "Zur Ontologie und Erscheinungslehre der Außenwelt." *Jahrbuch für Philosophie und phänomenologische Forschung*.

Cornsweet, T. N. 1970. *Visual Perception*. New York: Academic Press.

Craik, K. J. W. 1940. "Visual Adaptation." Ph.D. diss., Cambridge University.

Creutzfeldt, O. D. 1990. "Brain, Perception, and Mind." In L. Spillman and J. S. Werneer, eds., *Visual Perception: The Neurophysiological Foundations*. San Diego: Academic Press.

Crick, F. 1994. *The Astonishing Hypothesis: The Scientific Search for the Soul*. New York: Scribner.

Cutland, N., ed. 1988. *Non-Standard Analysis and Its Applications*. Cambridge: Cambridge University Press.

Damasio, A. 1994. *Descartes' Error*. New York: Grossman-Putnam.

Davidson, D. 1970. "Mental Events." Reprinted in *Essays on Actions and Events*. New York: Oxford University Press, 1980.

De Boer, T. 1978. *The Development of Husserl's Thought*. Translated by T. Plantinga. Phaenomenologica 76. The Hague: M. Nijhoff.

Deecke, L., P. Scheid, and H. Kornhuber. 1969. "Distribution of Readiness Potentials Preceding Voluntary Finger Movements." *Exp. Brain Res.* 7: 158–68.

De Muralt, A. 1958. *L'Idée de la phénoménologie: L'Exemplarisme husserlien*. Paris: PUF.

Dennett, D. 1981. *Brainstorms*. Cambridge: MIT Press.

———. 1987. *The Intentional Stance*. Cambridge: MIT Press.

———. 1988. "Quining Qualia." In A. Marcel and E. Bisiach, eds., *Consciousness in Contemporary Science*. Oxford: Oxford University Press.

———. 1991. *Consciousness Explained*. Boston: Little, Brown.

---. 1992. "Filling In Versus Finding Out: A Ubiquitous Confusion in Cognitive Science." In H. L. Pick Jr., P. van den Broek, and D. C. Knill, eds., *Cognition: Conceptual and Methodological Issues*. Washington, D.C.: American Psychological Association.

---. 1993. "Back from the Drawing Board." In B. Dahlbom, ed., *Dennett and His Critics*. Oxford: Basil Blackwell.

---. 1996. "Seeing Is Believing—or Is It?" In K. Akins, ed., *Perception*. New York: Oxford University Press.

---. Forthcoming. *Consciousness: More like Fame than Television*.

Dennett, D., and M. Kinsbourne. 1992. "Time and the Observer: The Where and When of Time in the Brain." *Behavioral and Brain Sciences* 15: 183–247.

Depraz, N. 1991. "La Vie m'est-elle donnée?" *Etudes philosophiques* 4.

---. 1994. "Temporalité et affection dans les manuscrits tardifs sur la temporalité (1929–1935) de Husserl." *Alter* 2: 63–86.

---. 1995a. *Transcendance et incarnation: Le Statut de l'intersubjectivité comme altérité à soi chez Husserl*. Paris: Vrin.

---. 1995b. "Y a-t-il une animalité transcendantale?" *Alter* 3: 81–114.

---. 1996a. "La Logique génétique husserlienne, quelle logo-phanie?" In. J.-F. Courtine, ed., *Phénoménologie et logique*. Paris: P.E.N.S.

---. 1996b. "Qu'est-ce que la hylè transcendentale?" *Analecta Husserliana* 50: 115–23.

---. 1998. "Can I Anticipate Myself?" In D. Zahavi, ed., *Temporality, Alterity, and Self-awareness*. Dordrecht: Kluwer Academic Publishers.

---. Forthcoming. *Lucidité du corps: Pour un empirisme transcendantal en phénoménologie*.

Depraz, N., F. Varela, and P. Vermersch. Forthcoming. *On Becoming Aware: Steps to a Phenomenological Pragmatics*.

Descartes, R. 1967. *Méditations métaphysiques*. 1641. In *Œuvres philosophiques*, vol. 2. Paris: Garnier. translated by J. Cottingham, R. Stoothoff, and D. Murdoch in *The Philosophical Writings of Descartes* (Cambridge: Cambridge University Press, 1984).

Descombes, V. 1979. *Le Même et l'autre*. Paris: Minuit.

---. 1983. *Grammaire d'objets en tout genre*. Paris: Minuit.

De Valois, R., M. Webster, and K. De Valois. 1986. "Temporal Properties of Brightness and Color Induction." *Vision Research* 26: 887–97.

De Valois, R. L., and K. K. De Valois. 1993. "A Multi-Stage Color Model." *Vision Research* 33: 1053–65.

Devlin, K. J. 1973. *Aspects of Constructibility*. Lecture Notes in Mathematics. Berlin: Springer Verlag.

De Waals, F. 1995. *Good Natured*. Cambridge: Harvard University Press.

DeYoe, E. A., and D. C. Van Essen. 1995. "Concurrent Processing in the Primate Visual Cortex." In Gazzaniga 1995.

Donnici, R. 1989. *Husserl e Hume: Per una fenomenologia della natura umana*. Milan: Collana di filosofia, Franco Angeli.

Dretske, F. 1981. *Knowledge and the Flow of Information*. Cambridge: MIT Press.
———. 1988. *Explaining Behavior*. Cambridge: MIT Press.
———. 1995. *Naturalizing the Mind*. Cambridge: MIT Press.
Dreyfus, H. 1982. "Husserl's Perceptual Noema." In Dreyfus and Hall 1982.
———. 1988. "Husserl's Epiphenomenology." In H. R. Otto and J. A. Tuedio, eds., *Perspectives on Mind*. Dordrecht: D. Reidel.
———. 1991. *Being in the World*. Cambridge: MIT Press.
Dreyfus, H., and H. Hall, eds. 1982. *Husserl, Intentionality, and Cognitive Science*. Cambridge: MIT Press.
Duhem, P. 1985. *To Save the Phenomena: An Essay on the Idea of Physical Theory from Plato to Galileo*. Reprint. Chicago: University of Chicago Press, Midway.
Dumouchel, P., and J.-P. Dupuy, eds. 1983. *L'Auto-organisation: De la physique au politique*. Actes du Colloque de Cerisy. Paris: Seuil.
Dupuy, J.-P. 1989. "Self-Reference in Literature." *Poetics*, no. 18: 491–515.
———. 1994. *Aux origines des sciences cognitives*. Paris: La Découverte. Translated into English by M. DeBevoise (Princeton: Princeton University Press, forthcoming).
Duquesne, B. 1984. "Les Calculs dans le psychologisme du jeune Husserl (vers les sciences pures)." *Revue philosophique de Louvain* 82: 80–98.
Earman, J. 1989. *World Enough and Space-Time*. Cambridge: MIT Press.
Ekman, P., and R. Davidson, eds. 1994. *The Structure of Emotions*. New York: Oxford University Press.
Engel, A., P. König, C. Gray, and W. Singer. 1992. "Temporal Coding by Coherent Oscillations as a Potential Solution to the Binding Problem: Physiological Evidence." In H. Schuster, ed., *Nonlinear Dynamics and Neural Networks*. Berlin: Springer Verlag.
Engel, P. 1994. *Introduction à la philosophie de l'esprit*. Paris: La Découverte.
Eschenbach, C., C. Habel, and B. Smith, eds. 1994. *Topological Foundations of Cognitive Science*. Hamburg: Graduiertenkolleg Kognitionswissenschaft.
Feferman, S. 1988. "Weyl Vindicated: *Das Kontinuum* 70 Years Later." In Carlo Cellucci and Giovanni Sambin, eds., *Atti del congresso: Temi e prospettive della logica e della filosofia della scienza contemporanee*, vol. 1, *Logica*. Bologna: CLUEB.
———. Forthcoming. "The Developement of Programs for the Foundations of Mathematics: Logicism, Predicativism, Set-Theoretical Platonism, Intuitionism and Formalism." In *Enciclopedia italiana della scienza*.
Feferman, S., J. W. Dawson, W. Goldfarb, C. Parsons, and R. Soloway, editors. 1995. *Collected Works of Kurt Gödel*. Volume 3. Oxford: Oxford University Press.
Feferman, S., J. W. Dawson Jr., S. C. Kleene, G. H. Moore, and R. M. Soloway, eds. 1990. *Collected Works of Kurt Gödel*. Vol. 2: *Publications, 1938–1974*. Oxford: Oxford University Press.
Fink, E. 1988. *VI. Cartesianische Meditation*. Part 1, *Die Idee einer transzendentalen Methodenlehre*. Dordrecht: Kluwer Academic Publishers. Translated by R. Bruzina under the title *Sixth Cartesian Meditation* (Bloomington: Indiana University Press, 1995).

Fiorani, M., M. G. P. Rosa, R. Gattass, and C. E. Rocha-Miranda. 1992. "Dynamic Surrounds of Receptive Fields in Primate Striate Cortex: A Physiological Basis for Perceptual Completion." *Proceedings of the National Academy of Sciences* 89: 8547–51.

Fisette, D. 1994. *Lecture frégéenne de la phénoménologie*. Combas: L'Eclat.

Fisher, G. H. 1967. "Measuring Ambiguity." *Am. J. Psychol.* 80: 541–47.

Flanagan, O. 1992. *Consciousness Reconsidered*. Cambridge: MIT Press / Bradford Books.

Florack, L. 1993. "The Syntactical Structure of Scalar Images." Ph.D. diss., University of Utrecht.

Fodor, J. 1975. *The Language of Thought*. New York: Thomas Y. Crowell.

———. 1981a. "Propositional Attitudes." In Fodor 1981b.

———. 1981b. *Representations*. Cambridge: MIT Press.

———. 1984. *The Modularity of Mind*. Cambridge: MIT Press.

———. 1987a. "Mental Representation: An Introduction." In N. Rescher, ed., *Scientific Inquiry in Philosophical Perspective*. Lanham, Md.: University Press of America.

———. 1987b. *Psychosemantics*. Cambridge: MIT Press.

———. 1990. *A Theory of Content*. Cambridge: MIT Press / Bradford Books.

———. 1994. *The Elm and the Expert: Mentalese and Its Semantics*. Cambridge: MIT Press.

Fodor, J., and Z. Pylyshyn. 1981. "How Direct Is Visual Perception? Some Reflections on Gibson's 'Ecological Approach.'" *Cognition* 9: 139–96.

Fogelman-Soulié, F., ed. 1991. *Les Théories de la complexité: Autour de l'oeuvre d'Henri Atlan*. Paris: Seuil.

Føllesdal, D. 1969. "Husserl's Notion of Noema." *Journal of Philosophy* 66: 680–87. Reprinted in Dreyfus and Hall 1982.

———. 1979. "Husserl and Heidegger on Actions in the World." In E. Saarinnen, R. Hilpinen, I. Niiniluoto, and M. Provence Hintikka, eds., *Essays in Honour of Jaakko Hintikka*, 365–78. Dordrecht: D. Reidel.

———. 1988. "Husserl on Evidence and Justification." In R. Sokolowski, ed., *Edmund Husserl and the Phenomenological Tradition: Essays in Phenomenology*. Washington, D.C.: The Catholic University of America Press.

Frith, C. D. 1992. *The Cognitive Neuropsychology of Schizophrenia*. Hove, U.K.: Lawrence Erlbaum.

Fruchart, T., and G. Longo. 1998. "Carnap's Remarks on Impredicative Definitions and the Genericity Theorem." In Cantini et al., eds., *Logic, Methodology, and Philosophy of Science: Logic in Florence*. Dordrecht: Kluwer Academic Publishers.

Fuchs, C., and B. Victorri. 1994. *Continuity in Linguistic Semantics*. Amsterdam: Benjamins.

Gallagher, S. 1979. "Suggestions Towards a Revision of Husserl's Phenomenology of Time-Consciousness." *Man and World* 12: 445–64.

———. In press. "Mutual Enlightenment: Phenomenology in Cognitive Science." *J. Consc. Studies*.

Gandevia, S. C., and D. Burke. 1993. "Does the Nervous System Depend on Kinesthetic Information to Control Natural Limb Movements?" *Behavioral and Brain Sciences* 15: 614–32.

Gandevia, S. C., and J. C. Rothwell. 1987. "Knowledge of Motor Commands and the Recruitment of Human Motoneurons." *Brain* 110: 1117–30.

Gaos, J. 1931. "La critica del psychologismo en Husserl." *Universidad* 8: 3–26; 9: 625–45, 877–904.

Gardner, H. 1985. *The Mind's New Science: A History of the Cognitive Revolution.* New York: Basic Books.

Gazzaniga, M. S., ed. 1995. *The Cognitive Neurosciences.* Cambridge: MIT Press / Bradford Books.

Geschwind, N. 1995. "The Organization of Language and the Brain." 1965. In S. M. Kosslyn and R. T. Andersen, eds., *Frontiers in Cognitive Science.* Cambridge: MIT Press.

Gibson, J. J. 1966. *The Senses Considered as Perceptual Systems.* Boston: Houghton-Mifflin.

———. 1972. "A Theory of Direct Visual Perception." In J. R. Royce and W. W. Rozeboom, eds., *The Psychology of Knowing.* New York: Gordon & Breach.

———. 1979. *The Ecological Approach to Visual Perception.* Boston: Houghton-Mifflin. Reprint. Hillsdale, N.J.: Lawrence Erlbaum Associates, 1986.

Girard, J.-Y. 1991. "A New Constructive Logic: Classical Logic." *Mathematical Structures in Computer Science* 1, no. 3: 255–96.

Girard, J.-Y., Y. Lafont, and P. Taylor. 1989. *Proof and Types.* Cambridge: Cambridge University Press.

Glass, L., and M. C. Mackey. 1988. *From Clocks to Chaos.* Princeton: Princeton University Press.

Gödel, K. 1944. "Russell's Mathematical Logic." In Schilpp 1944. Reprinted in Benacerraf and Putnam 1964 and in Feferman et al. 1990.

———. 1947. "What Is Cantor's Continuum Problem?" *American Mathematical Monthly* 54: 515–25; errata, 55: 151. Reprinted, with added appendix, in Benacerraf and Putnam 1964 (see Gödel 1964) and in Feferman et al. 1990.

———. 1951. "Some Basic Theorems on the Foundations of Mathematics and Their Implications." Gibbs lecture. In Feferman et al. 1995.

———. 1953. "Is Mathematics Syntax of Language?" (Unfinished contribution to Schilpp 1963.) In Feferman et al. 1995.

———. 1961. "The Modern Development of the Foundations of Mathematics in the Light of Philosophy." In Feferman et al. 1995.

———. 1964. "What Is Cantor's Continuum Problem?" Expanded version of Gödel 1947 in Benacerraf and Putnam 1964, reprinted in Feferman et al. 1990.

Goldstein K. 1934. *Der Aufbau des Organismus.* The Hague: M. Nijhoff.

Goodwin, G. M., D. I. McCloskey, and P. B. C. Matthews. 1972. "The Contribution of Muscle Afferents to Kinæsthesia Shown by Vibration Induced Illusions of Movement and by the Effects of Paralysing Joint Afferents." *Brain* 95: 705–48.

Granel, G. 1968. *Le Sens du temps et de la perception chez E. Husserl.* Paris: Gallimard.

Gregory, R. 1972. "Cognitive Contours." *Nature* 238: 51–52.
Gregory, R. L., ed. 1987. *The Oxford Companion to Mind*. Oxford: Oxford University Press.
Grosof, D., R. Shapley, and M. Hawken. 1993. "Macaque V1 Neurons Can Signal 'Illusory' Contours." *Nature* 365: 550–52.
Grossberg, S. 1983. "The Quantized Geometry of Visual Space: The Coherent Computation of Depth, Form, and Lightness." *Behavioral and Brain Sciences* 6: 625–92.
Grossberg, S., and D. Todorović. 1988. "Neural Dynamics of 1-D and 2-D Brightness Perception: A Unified Model of Classical and Recent Phenomena." *Perception and Psychophysics* 43: 241–77.
Gurfinkel, V. S., and Y. S. Levick. 1991. "Perceptual and Automatic Aspects of the Postural Body Scheme." In J. Paillard, ed., *Brain and Space*. Oxford: Oxford University Press.
Gurwitsch, A. 1964. *The Field of Consciousness*. Pittsburgh: Duquesne University Press.
———. 1965. "Edmund Husserl's Conception of Phenomenological Psychology." *Review of Metaphysics* 19: 689–727.
———. 1966. *Studies in Phenomenology and Psychology*. Evanston, Ill.: Northwestern University Press.
Habel, C. 1994. "Discreteness, Finiteness and the Structure of Topological Spaces." In Eschenbach, Habel, and Smith 1994: 81–90.
Hameroff, S., A. W. Kaszniak, and A. C. Scott, eds. 1996. *Toward a Science of Consciousness*. Cambridge: MIT Press.
Hamy, H. 1997. "Méthodes géométriques multi-échelles en vision computationnelle." Ph.D. diss., Ecole Polytechnique, Paris.
Harney, M. 1984. *Intentionality, Sense and the Mind*. Phaenomenologica 94. The Hague: M. Nijhoff.
Hauser, M. D., et al. 1996. "Numerical Representations in Primates." *Proc. Natl. Acad. Sci.* 93.
Hayward, J. W., and F. Varela, eds. 1992. *Gentle Bridges: Conversations with the Dalai Lama on the Sciences of Mind*. Boston: Shambhala Publications.
Heidegger, M. 1927. *Sein und Zeit*. Tübingen: M. Niemeyer. Translated by J. Macquarrie and E. Robinson under the title *Being and Time* (New York: Harper & Row, 1968).
———. 1929. *Kant und das Problem der Metaphysik*. Frankfurt am Main: Klostermann. Translated by J. S. Churchill under the title *Kant and the Problem of Metaphysics* (Bloomington: Indiana University Press, 1962).
———. 1951. *Über den Humanismus*. Frankfurt am Main: V. Klostermann.
———. 1954. *Vortrage und Aufsätze*. Pfullingen: G. Neske. Translated by William Lovett under the title *Basic Writings* (New York: Harper & Row, 1977).
———. 1977. "The Question Concerning Technology." In Martin Heidegger, *Basic Writings*, trans. William Lovett. New York: Harper & Row, 1977.
Heims, S. 1991. *The Cybernetics Group*. Cambridge: MIT Press.
Heinemann, E. 1972. "Simultaneous Brightness Induction." In D. Jameson and

L. Hurvich, eds., *Handbook of Sensory Physiology*, 7-4: 146–49. Berlin: Springer Verlag.

Heisenberg, W. 1990. *La Partie et le tout*. Paris: Flammarion.

Held, K. 1966. *Lebendige Gegenwart: Die Frage nach der Seinsweise des transzendentalen Ich bei Edmund Husserl, entwickelt am Leitfaden der Zeitproblematik*. The Hague: M. Nijhoff.

Hempel, C. 1980. "The Logical Analysis of Psychology." In N. Block, ed., *Readings in the Philosophy of Psychology*. Cambridge: Harvard University Press.

Henry, M. 1990. *Phenomenologie matérielle*. Paris: Presses Universitaires de France.

———. 1996. *C'est moi, la vérité: Pour une philosophie du christianisme*. Paris: Seuil.

Hering, E. 1964. *Outlines of a Theory of the Light Sense*. 1878. Translated by L. Hurvich and D. Jameson. Cambridge: Harvard University Press.

Hintikka, J. 1995a. *From Dedekind to Gödel: Essays on the Development of the Foundations of Mathematics*. Synthese Library, vol. 251. Dordrecht: Kluwer Academic Publishers.

———. 1995b. "The Phenomenological Dimension." In B. Smith and D. Woodruff Smith, eds., *The Cambridge Companion to Husserl*. Cambridge: Cambridge University Press.

Hirst, W. 1995. "Cognitive Aspects of Consciousness." In Gazzaniga 1995.

Hodges, A. 1995. "Alain Turing and the Turing Machine." In J. Herken, ed., *The Universal Turing Machine*. Rev. ed. Berlin: Springer Verlag.

Hofmannsthal, H. v. 1978. "Ödipus und die Sphinx." In *Gesammelte Werke. Dramen II*. Berlin: S. Fischer Verlag.

Holenstein, E. 1992. "Phenomenological Structuralism and Cognitive Semiotics." In R. Benatti, ed., *Scripta Semiotica*, 1: 133–58. Frankfurt am Main: Peter Lang.

Hopfield, J. J. 1982. "Neural Networks and Physical Systems with Emergent Collective Computational Abilities." Reprinted in J. Anderson and E. Rosenfeld, eds., *Neurocomputing*. Cambridge: MIT Press, 1988.

Horgan, T., and J. Tienson, eds. 1991. *Connectionism and the Philosophy of Mind*. Dordrecht: Kluwer Academic Publishers.

Horwich P. 1977. "On the Existence of Times, Spaces, and Space-Times." *Noûs* 12: 396–419.

Hoyos, G. 1986. *Los intereses de la vida cotidiana y las ciencias*. Bogotá: Ed. U. Nacional.

Hubel, D., and T. Wiesel. 1962. "Receptive Fields, Binocular Interaction, and Functional Architecture in the Cat's Visual Cortex." *Journal of Physiology* 160: 106–54.

———. 1968. "Receptive Fields and Functional Architecture of Monkey Striate Cortex." *Journal of Physiology* 195: 215–43.

Hyland M., 1988. "A Small Complete Category." *Annals of Pure and Applied Logic* 40.

Ihde, D. 1977. *Experimental Phenomenology: An Introduction*. New York: Putnam & Sons.

Ingarden, R. 1918. "Letter to Husserl of 24 June 1918." Partial English translation by T. Tymieniecka in *Analecta Husserliana* 4. Dordrecht: D. Reidel, 1976.
———. 1929. "Bemerkungen zum Problem Idealismus-Realismus." In *Festschrift Edmund Husserl zum 70. Geburtstag gewidmet. Jahrbuch für Philosophie und phänomenologische Forschung*, 159–90. Halle: Max Niemeyer.
———. 1964–65. *Der Streit um die Existenz der Welt*. Tübingen: Niemeyer.
Jackendoff, R. 1983. *Semantics and Cognition*. Cambridge: MIT Press.
———. 1987. *Consciousness and the Computational Mind*. Cambridge: MIT Press / Bradford Books.
Jackson, F. 1986. "What Mary Didn't Know." *The Journal of Philosophy* 83, no. 5: 291–95. Reprinted in D. M. Rosenthal, ed., *The Nature of Mind* (Oxford: Oxford University Press, 1991), pp. 392–94.
Jacob, F. 1970. *La Logique du vivant*. Paris: Gallimard.
James, W. 1950. *The Principles of Psychology*. 1890. 2 vols. Reprint. New York: Dover.
———. 1961. *Psychology: The Briefer Course*. 1892. Reprint. Notre Dame: University of Notre Dame Press.
———. 1976. *Essays in Radical Empiricism*. Cambridge: Harvard University Press.
Jeannerod, M. 1983. *Le Cerveau machine: physiologie de la volonté*. Paris: Fayard.
———. 1994. "A Theory of Representation-Driven Actions." In U. Neisser, ed., *The Perceived Self: Ecological and Interpersonal Sources of Self-Knowledge*. Cambridge: Cambridge University Press.
Jech, T., 1973. *The Axiom of Choice*. Amsterdam: North-Holland.
Johnson, M. 1991. *The Body in the Mind. The Bodily Basis of Meaning, Imagination, and Reason*. Chicago: University of Chicago Press.
Jonas, H. 1966. *The Phenomenon of Life: Toward a Philosophical Biology*. Chicago: University of Chicago Press.
Kalinowski, G. 1992. *Expérience et phénoménologie: Husserl, Ingarden, Scheler*. Paris: Editions Universitaires.
Kanizsa, G. 1955. "Margini quasi-percettivi in campi con stimulazione omogenea." *Rivista di psicologia* 49: 7–30.
———. 1979. *Organization in Vision: Essays in Gestalt Perception*. New York: Praeger Press.
———. 1995. "Gestalt Theory Has Been Misinterpreted, but Also Has Some Real Conceptual Difficulties." *Philosophical Psychology* 7: 149–62.
Kant, E. 1974. *Kritik der reinen Vernunft*. 1781. In *Werke*, vol. 3, edited by Wilhelm Weischedel. Frankfurt am Main: Suhrkamp. Translated by N. K. Smith under the title *Critique of Pure Reason* (London: Macmillan, 1929).
———. 1980. *Critique of Judgment*. 1790. Translated by J. C. Merdith. Oxford: Clarendon Press.
Katz, S. 1987. "Is Gibson a Relativist?" In A. Costalland and A. Still, eds., *Cognitive Psychology in Question*, 115–27. Brighton: Harvester.
Kauffman, S. A. 1993. *The Origins of Order: Self-Organization and Selection in Evolution*. New York: Oxford University Press.

Kelso, J. A. S. 1995. *Dynamic Patterns: The Self-Organization of Brain and Behavior.* Cambridge: MIT Press.

Kelso, J. A. S., P. Case, T. Holroyd, E. Horvath, E. Raczaszek, B. Tuller, and M. Ding. 1994. "Multistability and Metastability in Perceptual and Brain Dynamics." In M. Staedler and P. Kruse, eds., *Multistability in Cognition.* Berlin: Springer Series on Synergetics.

Kerby, A. P. 1991. *Narrative and the Self.* Bloomington: Indiana University Press.

Kern, I. 1964. *Husserl und Kant. Eine Untersuchung über Husserls Verhältnis zu Kant und zum Neukantianismus.* Phenomenologica 16. The Hague: Martinus Nijhoff.

———. 1989. "Statische und genetische Konstitution." In R. Bernet, I. Kern, and E. Marbach, eds., *E. Husserl. Darstellung seines Denkens.* Hamburg: F. Meiner.

Khoury, A. G. 1970. "Edmund Husserl's Auseinandersetzung mit dem Psychologismus." Ph.D. diss., University of Hannover.

Kim, J. 1993. *Supervenience and Mind.* Cambridge: Cambridge University Press.

Kingdom, F., and B. Moulden. 1989. "Border Effects on Brightness: A Review of Findings, Models and Issues." *Spatial Vision* 3: 225–62.

Kinney, J. 1967. "Color Induction Using Asynchronous Flashes." *Vision Research* 7: 299–318.

Kockelmans, J. J. 1967. *Edmund Husserl's Phenomenological Psychology.* Pittsburgh: Dusquesne University Press.

Koenderink, J. J. 1984. "The Stucture of Images." *Biological Cybernetics* 50: 363–70.

Köhler, W. 1920. *Die physischen Gestalten in Ruhe und im stationären Zustand.* Braunschweig: Veiweg.

———. 1929. "An Old Pseudoproblem." In *The Selected Papers of Wolfgang Köhler*, ed. Mary Henle. New York: Liveright, 1971.

———. 1930. "The New Psychology and Physics." In *The Selected Papers of Wolfgang Köhler*, ed. Mary Henle. New York: Liveright, 1971.

———. 1940. *Dynamics in Psychology.* New York: Liveright.

———. 1947. *Gestalt Psychology: An Introduction to New Concepts in Modern Psychology.* New York: Liveright.

———. 1960. "The Mind-Body Problem." In *The Selected Papers of Wolfgang Köhler*, ed. Mary Henle. New York: Liveright, 1971.

———. 1969. *The Task of Gestalt Psychology.* Princeton: Princeton University Press.

Kosslyn, S. M. 1995. "Aspects of a Cognitive Neuroscience of Mental Imagery." In S. M. Kosslyn and R. T. Andersen, eds., *Frontiers in Cognitive Neuroscience.* Cambridge: MIT Press / Bradford Books.

Krauskopf, J. 1963. "Effect of Retinal Image Stabilization on the Appearance of Heterochromatic Targets." *Journal of the Optical Society of America* 53: 741–44.

Kreisel, G. 1980. "Kurt Gödel, 28 April 1906–14 January 1978." *Biographical Memoirs of Fellows of the Royal Society* 26: 148–224.

Kubovy, M., and J. Pomerantz. 1981. "Perceptual Organization: An Overview." In Kubovy and Pomerantz, eds., *Perceptual Organization.* Hillsdale, N.J.: Lawrence Erlbaum Associates.

Lacan, J. 1978. *Le Séminaire*. Book 2, *Le Moi dans la théorie de Freud et dans la technique de la psychanalyse*. Edited by Jacques-Alain Miller. Paris: Seuil. Translated into English by S. Tomaselli, with notes by J. Forrester, under the title *The Seminar of Jacques Lacan*, book 2, *The Ego in Freud's Theory and in the Technique of Psychoanalysis, 1954–55* (New York: Cambridge University Press, 1988).

Lackner, J. R., and M. S. Levine. 1979. "Changes in Apparent Body Orientation and Sensory Localization Induced by Vibration of Postural Muscles: Vibratory Myesthetic Illusions." *Aviation, Space, and Environmental Medicine* 50, no. 4.

Lackner, J. R., and A. B. Taublieb. 1984. "Influence of Vision on Vibratio-Induced Illusions of Limb Movement." *Exp. Neuro.* 85.

Lakoff, G. 1987. *Women, Fire, and Dangerous Things*. Chicago: University of Chicago Press.

Lakoff, G., and M. Johnson. 1980. *Metaphors We Live By*. Chicago: University of Chicago Press.

Lambek, J., and P. J. Scott. 1986. *Introduction to Higher Order Categorical Logic*. Cambridge: Cambridge University Press.

Land, E. 1977. "The Retinex Theory of Color Vision." *Scientific American* 237: 108–28.

Landgrebe, L. 1968. "Das Problem der phänomenologischen Psychologie bei Husserl." In *Akten der 14. Internationalen Kongresses für Philosophie*, 2: 151–63. Vienna.

Langacker, R. 1987/1991. *Foundations of Cognitive Grammar*. 2 vols. Stanford, Calif.: Stanford University Press.

Langsdorf, L. 1985. "Review of Dreyfus 1982." *Husserl Studies* 3: 303–11.

Larrabee, M. 1994. "Inside Time-Consciousness: Diagramming the Flux." *Husserl Studies* 10: 181–210.

Lassègue, J. 1994. "L'Intelligence artificielle et la question du continu: Remarques sur le modèle de Turing." Ph.D. diss., University of Paris.

Lauer, Q. 1965. *Phenomenology and the Crisis of Philosophy*. New York: Harper & Row, Harper Torchbooks.

Leder, D. 1991. *The Absent Body*. Chicago: University of Chicago Press.

Leibniz, G. W. 1965. *Monadologie*. In *Philosophischen Schriften I*. Darmstadt: Wissenschaftliche Buchgesellschaft.

Leonardi, P., and M. Santambrogio, eds. 1995. *On Quine*. Cambridge: Cambridge University Press.

Leopold, D., and N. Logothetis. 1996. "Activity Changes in Early Visual Cortex Reflect Monkey's Percepts During Binocular Rivalry." *Nature* 379: 549–53.

Lesher, G. W. 1996. "Illusory Contours: Toward a Neurally Based Perceptual Theory." *Psychonomic Bulletin and Review* 2: 279–321.

Le Van Quyen, M., J. Martinerie, C. Adam, J.-Ph. La chaux, M. Baulac, B. Renault, and F. Varela. 1997a. "Temporal Patterns in Human Epileptic Activity Are Modulated by Perceptual Discriminations." *Neuroreport* 8: 1703–10.

Le Van Quyen, M., J. Martinerie, C. Adam, H. Schuster, and F. Varela. 1997b. "Unstable Periodic Orbits in Human Epileptic Activity." *Physica E.* 56: 3401–11.

Le Van Quyen, M., H. Schuster, and F. Varela. 1996. "Fast Rhythms Can Emerge from Slow Neuronal Oscillators." *Int. J. Bifurcation Chaos* 6: 1807–16.

Levinas, E. 1988. *En découvrant l'existence avec Husserl et Heidegger*. Paris: J. Vrin.

Lévi-Strauss, C. 1950. "Introduction à l'oeuvre de Marcel Mauss." In Marcel Mauss, *Sociologie et Anthropologie*. Paris: Presses Universitaires de France.

Levine, J. 1983. "Materialism and Qualia: The Explanatory Gap." *Pacific Philosophical Quarterly* 64: 354–61.

Linsky, B., and E. N. Zalta. 1995. "Naturalized Platonism and Platonized Naturalism." *Journal of Philosophy* 92, no. 10: 525–55.

Lipps, T. 1903a. "Einfühlung, innere Nachahmung, und Organenempfindung." In *Archiv f. die Ges. Psy.*, vol. 1, part 2. Leipzig: W. Engelmann.

———. 1903b. *Grundlegung der Ästhetik*. Bamburg and Leipzig: Leopold Voss.

Livingstone, M. S., and D. H. Hubel. 1984. "Anatomy and Physiology of a Color System in the Primate Visual Cortex." *Journal of Neuroscience* 7: 3416–68.

Llinás, R. 1988. "The Intrinsic Electrophysiological Properties of Mammalian Neurons." *Science* 242: 1654–64.

Longo, G. 1987. "Some Aspects of Impredicativity: Notes on Weyl's Philosophy of Mathematics and on Today's Type Theory." *Logic Colloquium* 87, Studies in Logic, ed. Ebbinghaus et al. Amsterdam: North-Holland. (Reprints of Longo's papers listed here, including Asperti and Longo 1991, can be downloaded from http://www.dmi.ens.fr/Longo.)

———. 1995. "Parametric and Type-Dependent Polymorphism." *Fundamenta Informaticae* 22, nos. 1–2: 69–92.

———. 1997. "The Difference Between Clocks and Turing Machines." Conference on Models of Cognition and Complexity Theory, Rome, 1994. Reprinted in *La Nuova Critica* 29.

Longo, G., and E. Moggi. 1991. "Constructive Natural Deduction and Its 'Omega-Set' Interpretation." *Mathematical Structures in Computer Science* 1, no. 2: 113–54.

Lorenz, K. 1972. *Gesammelte Abhandlungen*. 2 vols. Munich: Piper Verlag.

Lycan, W. 1990. "What Is the Subjectivity of the Mental?" In J. Tomberlin, ed., *Philosophical Perspectives*, vol. 4. Northridge, Calif.: Ridgeview.

Mach, E. 1886. *Beiträge zur Analyse der Empfindungen*. Jena: G. Fischer.

———. 1959. *The Analysis of Sensations and the Relation of the Physical to the Psychical*. 1906. Translated by C. M. Williams. New York: Dover.

———. 1965. "Über die Wirkung der räumlichen Verteilung des Lichterizes auf die Netzhaut." Reprinted in F. Ratliff, *Mach Bands: Quantitative Studies on Neural Networks in the Retina*. San Francisco: Holden-Day. Originally published in *Sitzungsberichte der mathematisch-naturwissenschaftlichen Classe der kaiserlichen Akademie der Wissenschaften* 52 (1865): 303–22.

———. 1967. *Grundlinien der Lehre von den Bewegungsempfindungen*. 1875. Amsterdam: E. J. Bonset.

Marbach, E. 1993. *Mental Representation and Consciousness: Towards a Phenomenological Theory of Representation and Reference*. Dordrecht: Kluwer Academic Publishers.

Marr, D. 1982. *Vision.* New York: W. H. Freeman.
Marr, D., and H. K. Nishihara. 1995. "Visual Information Processing: Artificial Intelligence and the Sensorium of Sight." 1978. In S. M. Kosslyn and R. T. Andersen, eds., *Frontiers in Cognitive Science.* Cambridge: MIT Press / Bradford Books.
Martin, K. A. C. 1988. "From Enzymes to Visual Perception: A Bridge Too Far?" *Trends in Neurosciences* 9: 380–84.
McAlister, L. L. 1974. "Chisholm and Brentano on Intentionality." *Review of Metaphysics* 28, no. 2: 328–38.
McClamrock, R. 1995. *Existential Cognition: Computational Minds in the World.* Chicago: University of Chicago Press.
McCulloch, W. 1965. *Embodiments of Mind.* Cambridge: MIT Press.
McDowell, J. 1994. "The Content of Perceptual Experience." *Philosophical Quarterly* 44: 190–205.
McGinn, C. 1983. *The Subjective View.* Oxford: Clarendon Press.
———. 1989. *Mental Content.* Oxford: Basil Blackwell.
McInerney, P. 1991. *Time and Experience.* Philadelphia: Temple University Press.
McIntyre, R. 1986. "Husserl and the Representational Theory of Mind." *Topoi* 5: 101–13.
McIntyre, R., and D. W. Smith. 1982. "Husserl's Identification of Meaning and Noema." In Dreyfus and Hall 1982.
Meiland, J. W. 1976. "Psychologism Is Logic: Husserl's Critique." *Inquiry* 19: 325–40.
Merleau-Ponty, M. 1962. *Phenomenology of Perception.* Translated by C. Smith. London: Routledge & Kegan Paul. Originally published as *Phénoménologie de la perception* (Paris: Gallimard, 1945).
———. 1963. *The Structure of Behavior.* Translated by A. L. Fisher. Boston: Beacon Press. Originally published as *La Structure du comportment* (Paris: Presses Universitaires de France, 1942).
———. 1964. *Le Visible et l'invisible.* Paris: Gallimard.
———. 1968. *Résumés de cours. Collège de France, 1952–1960.* Paris: Gallimard. Translated by J. O'Neill in *In Praise of Philosophy and Other Essays* (Evanston, Ill.: Northwestern University Press, 1970).
———. 1995. *La Nature.* Paris: Seuil.
———. 1996. *Notes de cours, 1959–1961.* Paris: Gallimard.
Michotte, A., G. Thines, and G. Crabbe. 1984. *Les Compléments amodaux des structures perceptives.* Louvain: Publications Universitaires de Louvain.
Miller, I. 1984. *Husserl, Perception and Temporal Awareness.* Cambridge: MIT Press.
Mirollo, R., and S. Strogartz. 1990. "Synchronisation of Pulse-Coupled Biological Oscillators." *SIAM J. Appl. Math.* 50: 1645–62.
Mishkin, M., L. G. Ungerleider, and K. A. Macko. 1995. "Object Vision and Spatial Vision: Two Cortical Pathways." 1983. In S. M. Kosslyn and R. T. Andersen, eds., *Frontiers in Cognitive Science.* Cambridge: MIT Press / Bradford Books.
Miskiewicz, W. 1985. "La Phénoménologie du temps chez Husserl." Ph.D. diss., University of Paris, Sorbonne.

———. 1994. "Le Sphinx de la connaissance: Husserl et l'énigme de l'a priori corrélationnel." *Revue de métaphysique et de morale*, no. 3 (1994).
Mohanty, J. N. 1954. "The 'Object' in Edmund Husserl's Phenomenology." *Philosophy and Phenomenological Research* 14: 343–53.
———. 1964. *Edmund Husserl's Theory of Meaning.* The Hague: M. Nijhoff.
———. 1978. "Husserl's Transcendental Phenomenology and Essentialism." *Review of Metaphysics* 32.
Morel, J.-M., and S. Solimini. 1995. *Variational Methods in Image Segmentation.* Berlin: Birkhäuser.
Moschovakis, Y. 1980. *Descriptive Set Theory.* Amsterdam: North-Holland.
Mosconi, J. 1989. "La Constitution de la théorie des automates." Ph.D. diss., Université Paris-I.
Movshon, J., B. Chambers, and C. Blakemore. 1972. "Interocular Transfer in Normal Humans, and Those Who Lack Stereopsis." *Perception* 1: 483–90.
Muirhead, R. F. 1887. "The Laws of Motion." *The Philosophical Magazine* 5, no. 23: 473–89.
Müller, G. E. 1896. "Zur Psychophysik der Gesichtsempfindungen" (Concerning the psychophysics of visual sensations) I. *Zeitschrift für Psychologie* 10: 1–82.
Mulligan, K. 1995. "Perception." In B. Smith and D. W. Smith, eds., *The Cambridge Companion to Husserl*, 168–238. Cambridge: Cambridge University Press.
Mulligan, K., P. Simons, and B. Smith. 1984. "Truth-Makers." *Philosophy and Phenomenological Research* 44, no. 3: 287–321.
Mumford, D. 1994. "Bayesian Rationale for the Variational Formulation." In Romeny 1994: 141–53.
Mumford, D., and J. Shah. 1988. "Boundary Detection by Minimizing Functionals." *Proceedings IEEE Computer Vision and Pattern Recognition Conference.* Ann Arbor, Michigan.
———. 1989. "Optimal Approximations by Piecewise Smooth Functions and Associated Variational Problems." *Communications on Pure and Applied Mathematics* 42, no. 4.
Murakami, I. 1995. "Motion Aftereffect After Monocular Adaptation to Filled-In Motion at the Blind Spot." *Vision Research* 35: 1041–45.
Murphy, R. T. 1980. *Hume and Husserl: Towards Radical Subjectivism.* The Hague: M. Nijhoff.
Nagel, T. 1970. "What Is It Like to Be a Bat?" *Philosophical Review* 79: 394–403. Reprinted in N. Block, ed., *Readings in the Philosophy of Psychology* (Cambridge: Harvard University Press, 1980).
———. 1986. *The View from Nowhere.* New York: Oxford University Press.
Nakayama, K., and S. Shimojo. 1990. "Toward a Neural Understanding of Surface Representation." *Cold Spring Harbor Symposia on Quantitative Biology* 55: 911–24.
Newell, A. 1991. *Unified Theories of Cognition.* Cambridge: Harvard University Press.
Newton, I. 1962. *Mathematical Principles of Natural Philosophy.* 1729. Berkeley: University of California Press.

Ninio, J. 1989. *L'Empreinte des sens*. Paris: Odile Jacob.
Noë, A. In press. "Perception and Content: Continuing Commentary on Ned Block, On a Confusion About a Function of Consciousness." *Behavioral and Brain Sciences* 18: 227–87.
Noë, R. A. 1994. "Wittgenstein, Phenomenology, and What It Makes Sense to Say." *Philosophy and Phenomenological Research* 54: 1–42.
———. 1995. "Experience and the Mind: An Essay on the Metaphysics of Perception." Ph.D. diss., Harvard University.
———. 1997. "Perception and Content." *Behavioral and Brain Sciences* 20: 154–55.
Nuñez, A., F. Amzica, and M. Steriade. 1993. "Electrophysiology of Cat Association Cortical Cells in Vivo: Intrinsic Properties and Synaptic Responses." *J. Neurophysiol.* 70: 418–30.
O'Brien, V. 1958. "Contour Perception, Illusion, and Reality." *Journal of the Optical Society of America* 48: 112–19.
Ojeda, A. 1993. *Linguistic Individuals*. Stanford, Calif.: CSLI.
O'Regan, K. 1992. "Solving the 'Real' Mysteries of Visual Perception: The World as an Outside Memory." *Canadian Journal of Psychology* 46: 461–88.
Osherson, D. N., and E. E. Smith, eds. 1990. *An Invitation to Cognitive Science*. Cambridge: MIT Press.
Ott, E., T. Sauer, and J. Yorke, eds. 1993. *Coping with Chaos*. New York: Wiley.
Pacherie, E. 1992. "Perspectives physicalistes sur l'intentionnalité." Ph.D. diss., EHESS, Paris.
———. 1993. *Naturaliser l'intentionnalité*. Paris: PUF.
———. 1995a. "Théories représentationnelles de l'intentionnalité perceptive et *Leibhaftigkeit* de l'objet dans la perception." In J. Petitot, ed., *Phénoménologie et sciences cognitives*. Special issue of *Archives de philosophie*.
———, ed. 1995b. *Fonctionnalismes*. Intellectica 2, no. 21 (1995).
Pachoud, B. 1995. "Conceptions de l'intentionnalité selon Husserl et selon J. Searle et leurs implications temporelles." *Archives de philosophie* 58, no. 4: 549–62.
Paci, E. 1963. "La psicologia fenomenologica e la fondazione della psicologia come scienzia." *Aut aut* 74: 7–19.
Paillard, J., "Motor and Representational Framing of Space." In J. Paillard, ed., *Brain and Space*. Oxford: Oxford University Press.
Panza, M. 1989. *La statua di fidia*. Milan: Unicopoli.
———. 1992. "De la continuité comme concept au continu comme objet." In Salanskis and Sinaceur 1992.
Paradiso, M., S. Shimojo, and K. Nakayama. 1989. "Subjective Contours, Tilt-Aftereffects, and Visual Cortical Organization." *Vision Research* 29: 1205–13.
Paradiso, M. A., and K. Nakayama. 1991. "Brightness Perception and Filling-In." *Vision Research* 31: 1221–36.
Parker, S., and K. Gibson. 1990. *Language and Intelligence in Monkeys and Apes*. Cambridge: Cambridge University Press.
Parsons, C. 1980. "Mathematical Intuition." *Proceedings of the Aristotelian Society*, n.s., 80 (1979–80): 146.
———. 1983. *Mathematics in Philosophy*. Ithaca, N.Y.: Cornell University Press.

———. 1995. "Quine and Gödel on Analyticity." In Leonardi and Santambrogio 1995.

Patočka, J. 1968. "Phänomenologie und Metaphysik der Bewegung." Translated by E. Abrams in *Papiers phénoménologiques* (Grenoble: Jérôme Millon, 1995).

———. 1970. "Le Subjectivisme de la phénoménologie husserlienne et la possibilité d'une phénoménologie 'asubjective.'" Translated by E. Abrams in *Qu'est-ce que la phénoménologie?* (Grenoble: Jérôme Millon, 1988).

———. 1988. *Qu'est-ce que la phénoménologie?* Translated by E. Abrams. Grenoble: Jérôme Millon.

———. 1995. *Papiers phénoménologiques.* Translated by E. Abrams. Grenoble: Jérôme Millon.

Peacocke, Christopher. 1992. *A Study of Concepts.* Cambridge: MIT Press.

Pessoa, L., E. Thompson, and A. H. Noë. In press. "Finding Out About Filling In: A Guide to Perceptual Completion for Visual Science and the Philosophy of Perception." *Behavioral and Brain Sciences.*

Peterhans, E., and R. von der Heydt. 1989. "Mechanisms of Contour Perception in Monkey Visual Cortex. II. Contours Bridging Gaps." *Journal of Neuroscience* 9: 1749–63.

Petit, J.-L. 1996. *Solipsisme et intersubjectivité: Quinze leçons sur Husserl et Wittgenstein.* Paris: Eds. du Cerf.

———, ed. 1997. *Les Neurosciences et la philosophie de l'action.* Paris: J. Vrin.

Petitot, J. 1979. "Locale/Globale." *Enciclopedia Einaudi* 8: 429–90. Turin: Einaudi.

———. 1990. "Le Physique, le morphologique, le symbolique, remarques sur la vision." *Revue de synthèse* 4, no. 1/2: 139–83.

———. 1992a. "Continu et objectivité: La Bimodalité objective du continu et le platonisme transcendantal." In Salanskis and Sinaceur 1992.

———. 1992b. *Physique du sens.* Paris: Editions du CNRS.

———. 1993. "Phénoménologie naturalisée et morphodynamique: La Fonction cognitive du synthétique 'a priori.'" In J.-M. Salanskis, ed., *Philosophie et sciences cognitives.* Special issue of *Intellectica,* no. 17 (1992/93): 79–126.

———. 1994a. "Phénoménologie computationnelle et objectivité morphologique." In J. Proust and E. Schwartz, eds., *La Connaissance philosophique: Essais sur l'œuvre de Gilles-Gaston Granger,* 213–48. Paris: Presses Universitaires de France.

———. 1994b. "Phenomenology of Perception, Qualitative Physics and Sheaf Mereology." In R. Casati, B. Smith, and G. White, eds., *Philosophy and the Cognitive Sciences: Proceedings of the 16th International Wittgenstein Symposium,* 307–408. Vienna: Verlag Hölder-Pichler-Tempsky.

———. 1994c. "La Sémiophysique: De la physique qualitative aux sciences cognitives." In M. Porte, ed., *Passion des formes,* 499–545. Fontenay-St-Cloud: ENS Editions.

———. 1994d. "Sheaf Mereology and Space Cognition." In Eschenbach, Habel, and Smith 1994: 41–62.

———. 1995a. "La Réorientation naturaliste de la phénoménologie." In *Sciences cognitives et phénoménologie.* Special issue of *Archives de philosophie,* 631–58.

———. 1995b. "Morphodynamics and Attractor Syntax. Dynamical and Morphological Models for Constituency in Visual Perception and Cognitive Grammar." In T. van Gelder and R. Port, eds., *Mind as Motion: Explorations in the Dynamics of Cognition*, 227–81. Cambridge: MIT Press.

———. 1995c. "Sheaf Mereology and Husserl's Morphological Ontology." *International Journal of Human-Computer Studies* 43: 741–63.

———. 1997. "Sheaf Mereology and Space Cognition." *Modelli della cognizione e teoria della complessità, La nuova critica* 29, no. 1: 49–74.

Petitot, J., and B. Smith. 1991. "New Foundations for Qualitative Physics." In J. E. Tiles, G. J. McKee, and G. C. Dean, eds., *Evolving Knowledge in Natural Science and Artificial Intelligence*, 231–49. London: Pitman.

———. 1996. "Physics and the Phenomenal World." In R. Poli and P. Simons, eds., *Formal Ontology*, 233–53. Nijhoff International Philosophy Series, vol. 53. Dordrecht: Kluwer Academic Publishers.

Pitts, A. 1987. "Polymorphism Is Set Theoretic, Constructively." In A. Pitts et al., eds., *Symposium on Category Theory and Computer Science*. Springle Lecture Notes in Computer Sciences 283. Edinburgh.

Pöppel, E. 1988. *Mindworks: Time and Conscious Experience*. Boston: Harcourt Brace Jovanovich.

Pöppel, E., and K. Schill. 1995. "Time Perception: Problems of Representation and Processing." In Arbib 1995: 987–90.

Port, R., and T. van Gelder, eds. 1995. *Mind as Motion: Explorations in the Dynamics of Cognition*. Cambridge: MIT Press.

Port, R. F., J. D. McAuley, and S. E. Anderson. 1996. "Toward Simulated Audition in an Open Environment." In E. Covey, H. Hawkins, T. McMullen, and R. Port, eds., *Neural Representation of Temporal Patterns*. New York: Plenum Publishing.

Prescott, J. R. V. 1978. *Boundaries and Frontiers*. London: Croom Helm; Totowa, N.J.: Rowman & Littlefield.

Proust, J. 1987. "L'Intelligence artificielle comme philosophie." *Le Débat* 47.

———. 1990. "De la difficulté d'être naturaliste en matière d'intentionnalité." In J. Petitot, ed., *Sciences cognitives: Quelques aspects problématiques*. Special issue of *Revue de synthèse* 4, no. 1/2: 13–32.

Pylyshyn, Z. W. 1984. *Computation and Cognition: Toward a Foundation for Cognitive Science*. Cambridge: MIT Press / Bradford Books.

Quine, W. V. 1960. *Word and Object*. Cambridge: MIT Press.

———. 1969. *Ontological Relativity and Other Essays*. New York: Columbia University Press.

———. 1990. "From Stimulus to Science." Unpublished lecture given at Lehigh University, October 15, 1990, and at Franklin and Marshall College, April 17, 1992.

———. 1992. *Pursuit of Truth*. Cambridge: Harvard University Press.

———. 1995. "Reactions." In Leonardi and Santambrogio 1995.

Quine, W. V., and J. S. Ullian. 1978. *The Web of Belief*. New York: Random House.

Ramachandran, V. S. 1992a. "Blind Spots." *Scientific American* 266: 86–91.

———. 1992b. "Filling in Gaps in Perception: Part 1." *Current Directions in Psychological Science* 1: 199–205.

———. 1993. "Filling In Gaps in Perception: Part 2." *Current Directions in Psychological Science* 2: 56–65.
Ramachandran, V. S., and R. Gregory. 1991. "Perceptual Filling In of Artificially Induced Scotomas in Human Vision." *Nature* 350: 699–702.
Ratliff, F., and L. Sirovich. 1978. "Equivalence Classes of Visual Stimuli." *Vision Research* 18: 845–51.
Redies, C., J. Crook, and O. Creuzfeldt. 1986. "Neuronal Responses to Borders with and Without Luminance Gradients in Cat Visual Cortex and Dorsal Lateral Geniculate Nucleus." *Exp. Brain Res.* 61: 469–81.
Renaut, A. 1993. *Sartre: Le Dernier Philosophe*. Paris: Grasset.
Rey, G. 1988. "A Question About Consciousness." In R. H. Otto and J. A. Tuedio, eds., *Perspectives on Mind*, 5–24. Dordrecht: D. Reidel.
Reynolds, J. 1984. "Polymorphism Is Not Set-Theoretic." In G. Kahn, S. MacQueen, and G. Plotkin, eds., *Symposium on Semantics of Data Types*. Lecture Notes in Computer Science 173. Berlin: Springer Verlag.
Richir, M. 1992. *Méditations phénoménologiques: phénoménologie et phénoménologie du langage*. Grenoble: J. Millon.
Ricoeur, P. 1963. "Structure et herméneutique." *Esprit*, no. 11: 596–627.
Rigal, E., ed. 1991. "Phénoménologie et psychologie cognitive." *Les Etudes philosophiques* 1.
Rizzolatti, G. 1994. "Nonconscious Motor Images" (commentary on M. Jeannerod's "Motor Imagery"). *Behavioral and Brain Sciences* 17.
Rizzolatti, G., et al. 1992. "Understanding Motor Events: A Neurophysiological Study." *Exp. Brain Res.* 91: 176–80.
———. "Premotor Cortex and the Recognition of Motor Actions." *Cogn. Brain Res.* 3: 131–41.
Rock, I., and R. Anson. 1979. "Illusory Contours as a Solution to a Problem." *Perception* 8: 665–81.
Roll, J.-P. 1993. "'Le Sentiment d'incarnation': Arguments neurobiologiques." *Rev. de méd. psychosom.* 35.
Romeny, B., ed. 1994. *Geometry-Driven Diffusion in Computer Vision*. Dordrecht: Kluwer Academic Publishers.
Rorty, E., ed. 1980. *Explaining Emotions*. Berkeley: University of California Press.
Rosolini, G. 1986. "Continuity and Effectiveness in Topoi." Ph.D. diss., Oxford University.
Rossi, A., and M. Paradiso. 1996. "Temporal Limits of Brightness Induction and Mechanisms of Brightness Perception." *Vision Research* 36: 1391–98.
Roy, J.-M. 1995a. "Le Dreyfus bridge: Fodorisme et husserlianisme." In J. Petitot, ed., *Phénoménologie et sciences cognitives*. Special issue of *Archives de philosophie*.
———. 1996. "La Dissociation husserlienne du *Sinn* et de la *Bedeutung*." In J. F. Courtine, ed., *Phénoménologie et logique*, 149–69. Paris: Presses de l'Ecole Normale Superieure.

———. 1998a. "Causalité intentionnelle et système symbolique." In J.-L. Petit, ed., *Les Neurosciences et la philosophie de l'action*. Paris: Vrin.

———. 1998b. "L'Intentionnalité ou carrefour de la phénoménologie et de la tradition sémantique." In Elizabeth Rigal, ed., *Jaakko Hintikka: Questions de logique et de phénoménologie*, 246–58. Paris: Vrin.

———. 1998c. "Mouvement volontaire et préemption de la causalité physique." In Jean Lorenceau, Arlette Steri, Bernard Victorri, and Yves-Marie Visetti, eds., *Le Mouvement*. Actes de la VI Ecole d'été de l'Association pour la Recherche Cognitive. ARC, Paris, France.

———. 1999. "Conception émergentiste du mental et explication causale." In Marie-José Durand-Richard, ed., *Des lois de la pensée au constructionisme: Conceptions et modélisations de l'acte de connaître*. Paris: Editions de la Maison des Sciences de l'Homme.

———. Forthcoming. "Linguistic Turn and Cognitive Turn." The Proceedings of the 20th World Congress of Philosophy. Philosophy Documentation Center.

———, ed. 1992. *La Théorie computationnelle de l'esprit*. Special issue of *Les Etudes philosophiques*.

———, ed. 1995b. "Signification, phénoménologie et philosophie analytique." *Les Etudes philosophiques* 1.

Rugg, M. 1995. "Event-Related Potential Studies of Human Memory." In Gazzaniga 1995.

Rumelhart, D. E., J. L. McClelland, and the PDP Research Group. 1986. *Parallel Distributed Processing: Explorations in the Microstructure of Cognition*. Vol. 1, *Foundations*. Cambridge: MIT Press.

Rynasiewicz, R. 1995. "Absolute Versus Relational Theories of Space and Time: A Review of John Earman's 'World Enough and Space-Time.'" *Philosophy and Phenomenological Research* 55: 675–687.

Salanskis, J.-M. 1991. *L'Herméneutique formelle*. Paris: Editions du CNRS.

———. 1993. "Philosophie et sciences cognitives." In *Philosophie et sciences cognitives*. Special issue of *Intellectica* 17: 9–25.

Salanskis, J.-M., and H. Sinaceur. 1992. *Le Labyrinthe du continu*. Berlin: Springer Verlag.

Scheerer, E. 1987. "Muscle Sense and Innervation Feelings: A Chapter in the History of Perception and Action." In H. Heuer and A. F. Sanders, eds., *Perspectives on Perception and Action*. Hillsdale, N.J.: Lawrence Erlbaum.

———. 1994. "Psychoneural Isomorphism: Historical Background and Current Relevance." *Philosophical Psychology* 7: 183–210.

Schiller, P. 1995. "Effects of Lesions in Visual Cortical Area V4 on the Recognition of Transformed Objects." *Nature* 376: 342–44.

Schilpp, P. A. 1944. *The Philosophy of Bertrand Russell*. La Salle, Ill.: Open Court.

———. 1963. *The Philosophy of Rudolf Carnap*. La Salle, Ill.: Open Court.

Scholtz, E. 1992. "Riemann's Vision of a New Approach to Geometry." In L. Boi, D. Flament, and J.-M. Salanskis, eds., *1830–1930: A Century of Geometry*, 22–34. Berlin: Springer Verlag.

Schuhmann K. 1985. "Structuring the Phenomenological Field: Reflections on a Daubert Manuscript." In W. S. Hamrick, ed., *Phenomenology in Theory and Practice*. The Hague: M. Nijhoff.

———. 1989. "Husserl's Concept of the Noema: A Daubertian Critique." *Topoi* 8: 53–61.

Schuhmann, K., and B. Smith. 1985. "Against Idealism: Johannes Daubert vs Husserl's Ideas I." *Review of Metaphysics* 39: 763–93.

———. 1987. "Questions: An Essay in Daubertian Phenomenology." *Philosophy and Phenomenological Research* 47: 353–84.

Schütz, A. 1959. "Type and Eidos in Husserl's Late Philosophy." *Philosophy and Phenomenological Research* 20, no. 2: 147–65.

Searle, J. R. 1983. *Intentionality*. Cambridge: Cambridge University Press.

———. 1992. *The Rediscovery of the Mind*. Cambridge: MIT Press.

Sedivy, S. 1995. "Consciousness Explained: Ignoring Ryle and Co." *Canadian Journal of Philosophy* 25: 455–83.

Sekuler, R., and R. Blake 1985. *Perception*. New York: Alfred A. Knopf.

Shanker, S. 1988. "Wittgenstein's Remarks on the Meaning of Gödel's Theorem." In Shanker, ed., *Gödel's Theorem on Focus*. London: Croom Helm.

Shepard, G. M. 1994. *Neurobiology*. New York: Oxford University Press.

Shoemaker, S. 1984. "Functionalism and Qualia: Absent Qualia Are Impossible—a Reply to Block." In *Identity, Cause, and Mind: Philosophical Essays*. Cambridge: Cambridge University Press.

Simon, H. 1947. "The Axioms of Newtonian Mechanics." *The Philosophical Magazine* 7, no. 38: 888–905. Reprinted in H. Simon, *Models of Discovery* (Dordrecht: D. Reidel, 1977), 349–69.

———. 1954. "Discussion: The Axiomatization of Classical Mechanics." *Philosophy of Science* 21: 340–43. Reprinted in H. Simon, *Models of Discovery* (Dordrecht: D. Reidel, 1977), 370–375.

———. 1959. "Definable Terms and Primitives in Axiom Systems." In L. Henkin, P. Suppes, and A. Tarski, eds., *The Axiomatic Method*, 443–53. Amsterdam: North-Holland. Reprinted in H. Simon, *Models of Discovery* (Dordrecht: D. Reidel, 1977), 376–86.

Simons, P. 1987. *Parts*. Oxford, Oxford University Press.

———. 1994/95. "New Categories for Formal Ontology." *Grazer Philosophische Studien* 49: 77–99.

Simons, P., and D. W. Smith. 1993. "The Philosophical Foundations of PACIS." Paper prepared for presentation at the International Ludwig Wittgenstein Symposium, Kirchberg am Wechsel, Austria, August 19, 1993.

Singer, W. 1993. "Synchronization of Cortical Activity and Its Putative Role in Information Processing and Learning." *Ann. Rev. Physiol.* 55: 349–74.

———. 1995. "Time as Coding Space in Neocortical Processing: A Hypothesis." In Gazzaniga 1995.

Smith, A., and R. Over. 1975. "Tilt Aftereffects with Subjective Contours." *Nature* 257: 581–82.

———. 1976. "Color-Selective Tilt Aftereffects with Subjective Contours." *Perception and Psychophysics* 20: 305–8.
———. 1977. "Orientation Masking and the Tilt Illusion with Subjective Contours." *Perception* 6: 441–47.
———. 1979. "Motion Aftereffect with Subjective Contours." *Perception and Psychophysics* 25: 95–98.
Smith, B. 1993. "Putting the World Back into Semantics." *Grazer Philosophische Studien* 43: 91–109.
———. 1994. "Fiat Objects." In N. Guarino, L. Vieu, and S. Pribbenow, eds., *Parts and Wholes: Conceptual Part-Whole Relations and Formal Mereology*, 15–23. Eleventh European Conference on Artificial Intelligence, Amsterdam, 8 August 1994. Amsterdam: European Coordinating Committee for Artificial Intelligence.
———. 1995. "Common Sense." In Smith and Smith 1995: 394–437.
———. 1996. "Mereology: A Theory of Parts and Boundaries." *Data and Knowledge Engineering* 20: 281–303.
———. Forthcoming. "Objects and Their Environments: From Aristotle to Ecological Psychology."
———, ed. 1982. *Parts and Moments. Studies in Logic and Formal Ontology.* Munich: Philosophia.
———, ed. 1988. *Foundations of Gestalt Theory.* Munich: Philosophia Verlag.
Smith, B., and K. Mulligan. 1982. "Parts and Moments: Pieces of a Theory." In B. Smith 1982: 15–109.
Smith, B., and D. W. Smith, eds. 1995. *The Cambridge Companion to Husserl.* Cambridge: Cambridge University Press.
Smith, B., and A. C. Varzi. In press (a). "The Niche." *Noûs.*
———. In press (b). "Fiat and Bona Fide Boundaries." *Philosophy and Phenomenological Research.*
Smith, D. W. 1989. *The Circle of Acquaintance.* Dordrecht: Kluwer Academic Publishers.
———. 1994. "How to Husserl a Quine—and a Heidegger Too." *Synthese* 98, no. 1 (January): 153–73.
———. 1995a. "The Background of Intentionality." Manuscript.
———. 1995b. "Mind and Body." In Smith and Smith 1995: 323–73.
Smith, D. W., and R. McIntyre. 1982. *Husserl and Intentionality: A Study of Mind, Meaning, and Language.* Dordrecht: D. Reidel.
Sperry, R. W. 1950. "Neural Basis of the Spontaneous Optokinetic Response Produced by Visual Inversion." *J. Comp. Physiol. Psychol.* 43: 482–89.
———. 1987. "Conscience et causalité." In Gregory 1987.
Spiegelberg, H. 1965. *The Phenomenological Movement.* Vols. 1 and 2. Phenomenologica 5. 2d ed. The Hague: M. Nijhoff.
———. 1972. *Phenomenology in Psychology and Psychiatry.* Evanston, Ill.: Northwestern University Press.
———. 1994. *The Phenomenological Movement.* Dordrecht: Kluwer Academic Publishers.

Spillman, L., and B. Dresp. 1995. "Phenomena of Illusory Form: Can We Bridge the Gap Between Levels of Explanation?" *Perception* 24: 1333–64.

Steels, L., and R. Brooks, eds. 1995. *The Artificial Life Route to Artificial Intelligence: Building Embodied, Situated Agents.* Hillsdale, N.J.: Lawrence Erlbaum Associates.

Steinbock, A. 1995. *Home and Beyond: Generative Phenomenology After Husserl.* Evanston, Ill.: Northwestern University Press.

Stern, D. G. 1995. *Wittgenstein on Mind and Language.* Oxford: Oxford University Press.

Stoper, A. E., and J. G. Mansfield. 1978. "Metacontrast and Paracontrast Suppression of a Contourless Area." *Vision Research* 18: 1669–74.

Straus, E. 1935. *Vom Sinn der Sinne (Ein Beitrag zur Grundlegung der Psychologie).* Berlin: Springer Verlag. Translated into English by J. Needleman under the title *The Primary World of Senses* (Toronto: The Free Press of Glencoe, 1963).

Ströker, E. 1983. "Phänomenologie und Psychologie: Die Frage ihrer Beziehung bei Husserl." *Zeitschrift für philosophische Forschung* 37: 3–19.

Takeuti, J. 1987. *Proof Theory.* 2d ed. Amsterdam: North-Holland.

Talmy, L. 1996. "The Windowing of Attention in Language." In M. Shibatani and S. Thompson, eds., *Essays in Semantics*, 235–87. Oxford: Oxford University Press.

Teller, D. Y. 1980. "Locus Questions in Visual Science." In C. Harris, ed., *Visual Coding and Adaptability.* Hillsdale, N.J.: Erlbaum Associates.

———. 1984. "Linking Propositions." *Vision Research* 24: 1233–46.

———. 1990. "The Domain of Visual Science." In L. Spillman and J. S. Werneer, eds., *Visual Perception: The Neurophysiological Foundations.* San Diego: Academic Press.

Teller, D. Y., and E. N. Pugh. 1983. "Linking Propositions in Color Vision." In J. D. Mollon and L. T. Sharpe, eds., *Colour Vision: Physiology and Psychophysics.* London: Academic Press.

Thelen, E., and A. Smith. 1995. *A Dynamical Approach to Development.* Cambridge: MIT Press.

Thom, R. 1980. *Modèles mathématiques de la morphogenèse.* Paris: Christian Bourgois.

———. 1990. *L'Apologie du logos.* Paris: Hachette.

———. 1992. "L'Antériorité ontologique du continu sur le discret." In Salanskis and Sinaceur 1992.

Thomasson, A. L. 1995. "The Ontology of Fiction: A Study of Dependent Objects." Ph.D. diss., University of California, Irvine.

Thompson, E. 1995. *Colour Vision: A Study in Cognitive Science and the Philosophy of Perception.* London: Routledge.

Thompson, E., and F. Varela. Forthcoming. *Why the Mind Isn't in the Head.* Cambridge: Harvard University Press.

Thompson, E., A. Palacios, and F. Varela. 1992. "Ways of Coloring: Comparative Color Vision as a Case Study for Cognitive Science." *Behavioral and Brain Sciences* 15: 1–74.

Tieszen, R. 1989. *Mathematical Intuition*. Boston: Kluwer Academic Publishers.
———. Forthcoming. "Kurt Gödel and Phenomenology." *Philosophy of Science*.
Todorović, D. 1987. "The Craik-O'Brien-Cornsweet Effect: New Varieties and Theoretical Implications." *Perception and Psychophysics* 42: 545–600.
Tondut, Y., and J. Petitot. 1998. "Géométrie de contact et champ d'association dans le cortex visuel." Research report no. 9725. Paris: CREA, Ecole Polytechnique.
Toobs, K. 1994. *The Meaning of Illness*. Dordrecht: Kluwer Academic Publishers.
Traub, R. D., M. Whittington, I. Stanford, and J. Jeffreys. 1996. "A Mechanism for Generation of Long-Range Synchronous Fast Oscillations in the Cortex." *Nature* 383: 621–24.
Troelstra, A. S. 1973. *Metamathematical Investigation of Intuitionistic Logic and Mathematics*. Lecture Notes in Mathematics 344. Berlin: Springer Verlag.
Tye, M. 1991. *The Imagery Debate*. Cambridge: MIT Press.
Vaadia, E., I. Haalman, M. Abeles, H. Bergman, Y. Prut, H. Slovin, and A. Aertsen. 1995. "Dynamics of Neuronal Interactions in Monkey Cortex in Relation to Behavioural Events." *Nature* 373: 515–18.
Van Gelder, T., and R. Port. 1995. "It's About Time: An Overview of the Dynamical Approach to Cognition." In Port and van Gelder 1995.
Van Tuijl, H. F. J. M. 1975. "A New Visual Illusion: Neonlike Color Spreading and Complementary Color Induction Between Subjective Contours." *Acta Psychologica* 39: 441–45.
Varela, F. 1979. *Principles of Biological Autonomy*. Amsterdam: North Holland.
———. 1989. *Connaître: Les Sciences cognitives, tendances et perspectives*. Paris: Seuil. Reprinted as *Invitation aux sciences cognitives* (Paris: Seuil, 1996).
———. 1995. "Resonant Cell Assemblies: A New Approach to Cognitive Functioning and Neuronal Synchrony." *Biol. Research* 28: 81–95.
———. 1996. "Neurophenomenology: A Methodological Remedy for the Hard Problem." *J. Consc. Studies* 3: 330–50.
———. 1997. "The Naturalization of Phenomenology as the Transcendence of Nature: Searching for Generative Mutual Constraints." *Alter* 5: 365–81.
Varela, F., E. Thompson, and E. Rosch. 1991. *The Embodied Mind: Cognitive Science and Human Experience*. Cambridge: MIT Press.
Varela, F., A. Toro, E. R. John, and E. Schwartz. 1981. "Perceptual Framing and Cortical Alpha Rhythms." *Neuropsychologia* 19: 675–86.
Varzi A. C. 1993. "Spatial Reasoning in a Holey World: A Sketch." In F. Anger, H. Guesgen, and J. van Benthem, eds., *Proceedings of the Workshop on Spatial and Temporal Reasoning. Thirteenth International Joint Conference on Artificial Intelligence*, 47–59. Chambéry: IJCAI.
———. 1994. "On the Boundary Between Mereology and Topology." In R. Casati, B. Smith, and G. White, eds., *Philosophy and the Cognitive Sciences. Proceedings of the 16th International Wittgenstein Symposium*, 423–42. Vienna: Hölder-Pichler-Tempsky.
———. 1996. "Parts, Wholes, and Part-Whole Relations: The Prospects of Mereotopology." *Data and Knowledge Engineering* 20: 259–86.

Vermersch, P. 1993. "Pensée privée et représentation dans l'action." In A. Weill-Fassina, P. Rabardel, and D. Dubois, eds., *Représentations pour l'action*. Paris: Octares.

———. 1994. *L'Entretien d'explication*. Paris: ESF.

Villela-Petit, M. 1995. "Réceptivité anté-prédicative et familiarité typique." *Archives de philosophie* 58, no. 4. Paris: Beauchesne.

———. 1996. "L'Expérience anté-prédicative." In J.-F. Courtine, ed., *Phénoménologie et logique*. Paris: Presses de l'Ecole Normale Supérieure.

Von der Heydt, R., and E. Peterhans. 1989. "Mechanisms of Contour Perception in Monkey Visual Cortex. I. Lines of Pattern Discontinuity." *Journal of Neuroscience* 9: 1731–48.

Von der Heydt, R., E. Peterhans, and G. Baumgartner. 1984. "Illusory Contours and Cortical Neuron Responses." *Science* 224: 1260–62.

Von Helmholtz, H. 1866. *Handbuch der physiologishen Optik*. Leipzig: Vos.

Von Holst, E., and H. Mittelstaedt. 1950. "Das Reafferenzprinzip. Wechselwirkungen zwischen Zentralnervensystem und Peripherie." *Naturwissenschaften* 37: 464–76.

Von Weizsäcker, V. 1950. *Der Gestaltkreis*. 1939. 4th ed. Stuttgart: G. Thieme.

Von Wright, G. H. 1995. "Wittgenstein and the Twentieth Century." In R. Egidi, ed., *Wittgenstein: Mind and Language*. Dordrecht: Kluwer Academic Publishers.

Waldenfels, B. 1980. "Intentionalität und Kausalität." In *Der Spielraum des Verhaltens*. Frankfurt am Main: Suhrkamp.

Wang, H. 1974. *From Mathematics to Philosophy*. London: Routledge & Kegan Paul.

———. 1978. "Kurt Gödel's Intellectual Development." *The Mathematical Intelligencer* 1: 182–84.

———. 1981. "Some Facts About Kurt Gödel." *The Journal of Symbolic Logic* 46: 653–59.

———. 1987. *Reflections on Kurt Gödel*. Cambridge: MIT Press.

Weil, S. 1974. *Cahiers III*. Paris: Plon. Translated by A. F. Wills under the title *The Notebooks of S. Weil*, 2 vols. (New York: Putnam's Sons, 1956).

Weizkrantz, L. 1986. *Blindsight: A Case Study and Implications*. Oxford: Oxford University Press.

Welton, D. 1977. "Structure and Genesis in Husserl's Phenomenology." In F. A. Elliston and P. McCormick, eds., *Husserl: Expositions and Appraisals*. Notre Dame: University of Notre Dame Press.

Wertheimer, M. 1912. "Experimentelle Studien über das Sehen von Bewegung." *Zeitschrift für Psychologie* 61: 161–265.

Weyl, H. 1918a. *Das Kontinuum*. Berlin: Walter de Gruyter. Translated into French by J. Largeault (Paris: Vrin, 1994).

———. 1918b. *Raum-Zeit-Materie*. Berlin and Leipzig: Springer Verlag.

———. 1923. *Mathematische Analyse des Raumproblem*. Berlin: Springer Verlag.

———. 1934. *Mind and Nature*. Philadelphia: University of Pennsylvania Press.

———. 1953. *Symmetry*. Princeton: Princeton University Press.

———. 1985. "Axiomatic Versus Constructive Procedures in Mathematics." Ed-

ited by T. Tonietti. *The Mathematical Intelligencer* 7, no. 4. New York: Springer Verlag.
Whitehead, A. N. 1978. *Process and Reality*. 1929. Corrected edition, edited by D. R. Griffin and D. W. Sherburne. New York: The Free Press.
Wiesel, T., and D. Hubel. 1966. "Spatial and Chromatic Interactions in the Lateral Geniculate Body of the Rhesus Monkey." *Journal of Neurophysiology* 29: 1029–40.
Wild, J. 1940. "Husserl's Critique of Psychologism: Its Historic and Contemporary Relevance." In M. Farber, ed., *Philosophical Essays in Memories of Edmund Husserl*. Cambridge: Harvard University Press.
Willard, D. 1977. "The Paradox of Logical Psychologism: Husserl's Way Out." In F. A. Elliston and P. McCormick, eds., *Husserl: Expositions and Appraisals*. Notre Dame: University of Notre Dame Press.
Wilshire, B. 1968. *William James and Phenomenology: A Study of the "Principles of Psychology."* Bloomington: Indiana University Press.
Winfree, A. 1980. *The Geometry of Biological Time*. New York: Springer Verlag.
Winnograd, T., and F. Flores. 1987. *Understanding Cognition and Computers*. Reading, Mass.: Addison-Wesley.
Wittgenstein, L. 1953. *Philosophical Investigations*. Oxford: Basil Blackwell.
———. 1956. *Remarks on the Foundation of Mathematics*. Edited by G. H. von Wright, R. Rhees, and G. E. Anscombe. Oxford: Basil Blackwell.
———. 1964. *Philosophische Bermerkungen / Philosophical Remarks*. Oxford: Basil Blackwell.
———. 1969. *On Certainty*. Oxford: Basil Blackwell.
———. 1974. *Tractatus Logico-Philosophicus*. 1921. Translated by D. F. Pears and B. F. McGuiness. London and New York: Routledge.
———. 1975. *Philosophical Remarks*. Chicago: University of Chicago Press; Oxford: Basil Blackwell.
———. 1980. *Remarks on the Philosophy of Psychology*. Edited by T. I. G. H. von Wright and E. Anscombe. Oxford: Basil Blackwell.
Yarbus, A. L. 1967. *Eye Movements and Vision*. New York: Plenum Press.
Yee, S. S. T. 1969. *Edmund Husserl's Idea of Phenomenological Psychology and the Problem of Its Relation to Transcendental Philosophy*. Ann Arbor: University of Michigan Press.
Zahavi, D. 1994. "Husserl's Phenomenology of the Body." *Etudes phénoménologiques* 19: 63–84.
Zeki, S. M. 1995. "The Functional Organization of Projections from Striate to Prestriate Visual Cortex in the Rhesus Monkey." 1976. In S. M. Kosslyn and R. T. Andersen, eds., *Frontiers in Cognitive Science*. Cambridge: MIT Press.
Zeki, S., and S. Shipp. 1988. "The Functional Logic of Cortical Connections." *Nature* 335: 311–17.

INDEX OF PERSONS

In this and the following index an "f" after a number indicates a separate reference on the next page, and an "ff" indicates separate references on the next two pages. A continuous discussion over two or more pages is indicated by a span of page numbers, e.g., "57–59." *Passim* is used for a cluster of references in close but not consecutive sequence.

Adjukiewicz, K., 62
Albertazzi, L., 63
Anderson, S., 252
Aristotle, 85f, 91, 102, 401, 406
Armstrong, D. M., 101
Arnold, V., 367
Atlan, H., 552
Augustine, Saint, 266
Avenarius, R., 229f

Bergson, H., 402, 527
Berkeley, Bishop, 86
Bernet, R., 200, 331
Bernstein, A., 312
Bernstein, N., 234
Besnier, B., 267
Blattner, W., 246
Bohr, N., 17
Bolzano, B., 89, 390, 392
Bouveresse, J., 151–53, 402
Brentano, F., 2, 27, 78, 86, 99, 197, 386, 442, 543ff, 508ff
Brough, J., 246

Cantor, G., 392, 401, 412, 418
Cantor-Dedekind (model), 403–10 *passim*, 415, 495
Carnap, R., 65, 397, 540
Casati, R., 63
Cauchy, A., 404, 408ff
Chalmers, D., 4, 20, 105
Chambon, R., 54, 69

Châtelet, G., 402, 418
Chisolm, R., 548
Churchland, P., 101, 108
Clark, A., 6
Cohen, P., 412, 420
Craik-O'Brien-Cornsweet (effect), 165, 183
Crick, F., 102

Daubert, J., 52, 326ff
Davidson, D., 101, 546
Dennett, D., 4, 11, 13, 21–23, 167f, 173f, 180, 184–95, 258, 277, 523
De Saussure, F., 242
Descartes, R., 29, 87f, 102, 243, 251, 510
Descombes, V., 496f, 505, 558
De Valois, K., 178, 180
Dilthey, W., 44, 471
Dirac, P., 18
Dretske, F., 80, 84f, 97f, 101–4, 108, 429–39
Dreyfus, H., 13, 57–60, 72, 252, 442
Duchêne de Boulogne, 234

Espagnat, B., 16

Fink, E., 467
Flannagan, O., 4, 7, 23, 104
Fodor, J., 58, 69f, 84f, 88, 97–99, 101–3, 107f, 251, 435, 545
Føllesdal, D., 57–60, 402, 440
Fraassen, B. van, 16
Freeman, W., 312

Frege, G., 25, 57f, 103, 392, 412, 422, 506, 540
Frith, C. D., 215

Galileo, G., 3, 40, 46, 418
Gandevia, S. C., 222
Gauss, C. F., 393
Gentzen, G., 418, 422
Geschwind, N., 520
Gibson, J. J., 6, 61, 69f
Girard, G., 419f, 422, 425
Gödel, K., 79, 385, 390, 392, 395–400, 402, 412, 420, 435
Goldstein, K., 53, 531
Goodman, N., 394
Goodwin, G. M., 235
Gregory, R., 176
Grothendieck, A., 416
Gurfinkel, V., 236
Gurwitch, A., 54

Hall (effect), 57
Harney, M., 440
Hartong, J., 410
Heidegger, M., 59, 105, 230, 243, 252, 298, 319, 493, 507, 556
Heisenberg, W., 17
Herbart, J.-F., 338
Hering, E., 170, 324
Heydt, R. Van der, 176
Hilbert, D., 422, 425
Hill, C., 63
Hintikka, J., 57f, 60, 440, 442, 446
Hirst, W., 515
Hofmannsthal, H., 521
Hofstadter, D., 242
Hopefield, J., 18, 552
Hume, D., 2, 230, 509

Jackendoff, R., 4, 8, 20, 23, 73, 515
James, W., 190, 222
Jastrow, J., 386
Jeannerod, M., 21, 214
Johnson, M., 21

Kanizsa, G., 175
Kant, E., 2, 16, 65, 224f, 251, 331, 392, 394, 446f, 464, 505–9 *passim*, 518, 521, 541
Kelso, J. S., 285
Kim, J., 102
Koffka, W. F., 53, 312, 554
Köhler, W., 53, 171, 173, 233, 242, 312

König (lemma), 419
Kosslyn, S. M., 519
Krauskopf, J., 164
Kreisel, G., 410

Lacan, J., 557
Lackner, J., 235f
Lakoff, G., 13, 21
Langacker, R., 326f
Lawvere, W., 415f, 425
Lebesgue, H., 406
Leibniz, W. G., 2, 86f, 251, 401, 405, 409
Lesniewski, S., 62
Lettvin, J., 555
Levi-Strauss, C., 556
Lewin, K., 554
Lipps, T., 230, 241, 243
Lobry, C., 410
Locke, J., 510
Lotze, H., 350
Lukasiewicz, J., 62
Lutz, R., 410

Mach, E., 170, 194, 212, 229, 324
Macko, K. A., 519
Mahler, G., 249
Maine de Biran, J., 214
Malik, J., 348
Marr, D., 20, 520, 523
Matthew, P. B. C., 235
Maturana, H., 552
Mauss, M., 556
McCloskey, D. I., 235
McCulloch, W., 312, 542
McGinn, C., 150
McIntyre, R., 59f
Meinong, A., 78, 247, 258
Merleau-Ponty, J., 53, 59, 61, 103, 188, 190, 218, 234, 251, 281, 319, 528, 538
Mill, J. S., 44, 510
Miller, I., 246
Mishkin, M., 519
Mittelstaedt, H., 214
Morel, J.-M., 346
Mosconi, J., 543
Müller, G. E., 171
Mulligan, K., 63, 334
Mumford, D., 346

Nagel, T., 2, 9, 15f, 19, 23, 100
Nakayama, K., 178
Navier-Stokes (equations), 18
Newell, A., 251, 542

Newman, J. von, 5
Newton, I., 2, 18, 46, 254, 374, 384, 418
Nortrop, F., 554

Ockham, G., 86
Over, R., 177

Papert, S., 543
Paradiso, M., 178, 180
Parsons, C., 398
Patočka, J., 218, 529
Peano, G., 422
Peano-Dedekind (axioms), see Peano, G.
Peirce, C. S., 339
Perona, P., 348
Petitot, J., 402, 420, 425, 502, 504, 552
Piaget, J., 61
Plato, 85, 251
Poincaré, H., 47, 406
Poli, R., 63
Port, R., 252
Proust, J., 545
Pugh, E. N., 181
Putnam, H., 71, 505
Pylyshyn, Z., 69f, 545

Quine, W. O., 89, 101, 244, 386, 391, 394, 448, 503, 551

Ratliff, F., 173
Rawls, J., 394
Reeb, G., 410
Riemann, B., 226, 339, 495
Rizzolatti, G., 238, 240
Rock, J., 176
Rossi, A. F., 180
Rothwell, J. C., 222
Russell, B., 25, 29, 540, 545
Ryle, G., 252

Salanskis, J.-M., 410
Sartre, J.-P., 100, 103f, 108
Scheler, M., 319
Schereiber, T., 311
Schilpp, P. A., 396
Scholtz, E., 339
Schrödinger, E., 18

Schumann, C., 52
Scott, D., 409, 412, 425
Searle, J., 13, 97, 103, 105, 197
Sherrington, C., 235
Shoemaker, S., 11
Simon, H., 542
Simons, P., 63, 334
Sirovich, L., 173
Smale, S., 367
Smart, J. J. C., 64
Smith, A., 177
Smith, B., 63, 334
Sperry, R. W., 214, 515f
Steinbock, A., 73
Straus, E., 54, 518
Stumpf, C., 334, 336, 510, 554

Tait-Girard (normalisation theorem), see Girard, G.
Talmy, L., 325ff
Teller, D., 67, 172, 181
Thom, R., 342, 351, 367, 402ff, 408
Todorović, D., 182, 183
Turing, A., 5, 251

Ungerleider, L. G., 519

Van Gelder, T., 287
Varela, F., 252, 263–65, 552
Visetti, Y. M., 504
Von Foerster, H., 312
Von Helmholtz, H., 213f
Von Holst, E., 214, 312
Von Weiszäcker, E., 535

Webster, M., 178, 180
Weierstrass, V., 390, 409
Wertheimer, M., 171, 554
Weyl, H., 401f, 406, 410
Whitney, H., 351, 367
Wiles, A., 390
Wittgenstein, L., 88f, 91, 188, 237, 242, 386, 402, 404, 453f, 506
Wundt, W., 222

Zeki, S., 516, 518f

INDEX OF TOPICS

Abhebung, see Saliency
Aboutness, 114, 117, 123–26
Abschattung, see Adumbration; Profile
Abstraction, 40, 56
Acquaintance, 104, 124, 449
Act, 30, 33, 60, 97, 99, 130–48 *passim*, 319, 441–46
Action, 108, 159f, 215, 228, 231, 237ff, 456–59 *passim*
Activity spreading, 178
Adaptation, 69
Adequacy, 27, 30
Adjunction, 416
Adumbration, 27, 50, 155, 331, 333f, 362–70 *passim*, 443, 453. *See also* Profile
Affect, 289, 295–302 *passim*
Affection, 221
Aftereffect, 174, 177
Algorithm, 47f
Analogy, 172
Analytic/synthetic distinction, 89
Analytics, 57, 60, 146, 540
Animation, 448
Anschauung, see Intuition
Anticipation, 77f, 199ff, 214, 219, 364f, 386, 393
Antinaturalism, 38f, 42, 75, 105, 469
Antipsychologism, 509
Appearance, 9, 123, 155–59 *passim*, 225, 444, 446, 525
Apprehension, 135, 140, 333, 448
Artificial intelligence, 62, 544
Aspect graph, 370
Attention, 133, 145, 352
Attitude: natural, 26, 39, 50f, 354, 443, 445, 455, 460, 463, 511f, 514; propositional, 22, 127, 154, 332, 545
Attractor, 256, 287, 366, 553
Auffassung, see Apprehension

Automata, 72
Autopoiesis, 555
Awareness, 10, 96, 151, 154, 156, 247
Axiom, 374
Axiomatic(s), 31, 37, 40, 42f, 49, 64
Axiomatization, 40, 52

Background, perceptual, 109, 440, 454–62 *passim*
Behaviorism, 4, 64, 71, 101
Bifurcation, *see* Phase transition
Biology, 260, 531
Black box, 4, 12
Blindsight, 12, 151, 160
Blind spot, 162, 169
Body, 27, 39, 45, 83, 87, 204f, 234, 236; and *Leib/Körper* distinction, 35f, 61f, 66, 78, 105, 204f, 234, 243, 449, 470, 477, 517f
Boundary, 164, 178, 320f, 324, 327, 351
Bracket, 33f, 445, 455
Brain, 67, 78
Bridge locus, 165, 181

Calculability, 149
Cartesian theater, 167
Categories, 83–87 *passim*, 95, 367, 413, 507, 456; formal, 29, 83, 87–94 *passim*, 95–100 *passim*, 109f; material, 83, 87–100 *passim*, 109f
Categorization, 46, 56, 343, 358, 370
Cauchy sequence, 415
Causalism, 102–7 *passim*
Causality, 26, 72, 83, 87, 95, 98ff, 107–10, 114f, 117, 150
Causes, causation, 76, 85, 91, 107, 116, 150
Cellular rhythms, 273
Center-periphery model, 304ff
Certitude, 457

635

Chaos, 310
Choice, axiom of, 412, 418, 421
Choice operator, 370
Code, 154
Cogito, 444f, 493
Cognition, 93, 95, 100, 113, 116, 147
Cognitive Revolution, xiii, 4, 13, 64
Cognitive Science, 3–15 *passim*, 18, 48, 58, 60, 62, 66, 74; as science, 83, 99, 102, 104, 110, 250, 474, 539f
Cognitivism, 56–60 *passim*, 120, 146, 149, 154, 539
Coincidence, 442
Common sense, 318f, 373
Communication, 233, 241
Community, 232, 458f
Completion, perceptual, 162, 195
Complexity, 48, 83, 97
Compositionality, of the continuum, 403
Computation, 8, 13, 48, 83ff, 95, 98, 101ff, 106, 108, 119f, 251, 258f
Computationalism, 72f, 102–7 *passim*, 149
Computational process, 59, 83, 87, 95, 108–10, 129
Connectionism, 4ff, 61, 84, 103, 120, 475, 539, 544
Consciousness, 7–14 *passim*, 20ff, 31f, 36, 52f, 58, 69, 83–85, 108f, 168, 247, 470, 476, 511f, 523f; as a material category, 87f, 92, 99ff, 102f, 106; intentional, 440–45 *passim*, 449; of time, 246–50 *passim*, 258, 260. *See also* Stream of consciousness
Consistency, 421
Constitution, 35ff, 50, 59, 69f, 155f, 221–24, 319, 332, 354, 392, 447–50, 456, 468, 476, 480, 510, 517; of space, 207, 215, 225; of the human world, 518; intersubjective, 229, 233, 241; kinaesthetic, 228, 237; static/dynamic, 224. *See also* Passive synthesis
Construction principles, 407, 412, 421
Content, 57, 94f, 98, 104, 156f, 446; intentional, 57f, 84, 98, 103, 114, 123, 126, 148, 150, 442, 445, 450; representative/presentative, 131, 135f, 139, 140–47 *passim*, 156
Context, 97, 209
Continuum, 32, 79, 155, 262, 326, 353, 446, 490, 495. *See also* Compositionality
Continuum hypothesis, 413, 418, 420
Contour, 67, 175f, 367
Control, 214ff, 354f

Convention, 89
Convergence criterion, 408
Coping, 298
Corollary discharge, 214, 222
Correlation, 13, 149f, 157, 159, 319, 333, 402, 447
Critical point, 366
Culture, 83, 87f, 93, 105ff
Cybernetics, 543, 552, 556

Darstellung, *see* Display; Presentation
Dasein, 298
Deckung, 442 *see* Coincidence
Deduction, transcendental, 507
Denaturalization, 39
Dependence, 62f, 83, 88–91, 96ff, 100, 337
Description, 24, 43, 48ff, 52, 63, 67f, 73f, 88, 132, 146, 453f, 459ff
Descriptives, 31, 37, 41, 49, 55f, 130, 267
Desire, 534
Determinable X, *see* Object = X
Differentiable, manifold, 338
Dimension, 20f, 50, 151, 154–59 *passim*, 351, 453
Directedness, 94, 99
Directness, 112f, 124f, 128, 134, 138, 142ff, 146, 154
Discontinuity, 155, 163, 336
Discourse, 233
Display, 331f, 365
Disposition, 297
Doubt, 29f, 441, 444
Dualism, 84, 96, 108
Duration, 34, 273
Dynamic(al), dynamics, 5f, 53, 55, 61, 68, 71f, 77f, 148, 155, 157f, 251f, 255, 258, 272, 283, 301, 310, 474, 552

Earth, 372
Ecologism, 69f
Efferent copy, *see* Corollary discharge
Ego, 33, 36f, 88, 445, 493, 510, 522
Egology, 493
Eidetic(s), 25, 28–31 *passim*, 41, 51, 56, 79, 338, 371, 388, 390, 492
Eidos, *see* Essence
Eigen behaviors, 553
Einfühlung, *see* Empathy
Eliminativism, 4, 45, 101, 462
Embodiment, 1, 39, 53, 61, 66
Emergence, 6, 67, 279, 474
Emotion, 95, 296, 300

Empathy, 229–33 *passim*, 241, 243
Empiricism, and transcendentalism, 388, 480
Enactive approach, 5f, 62f, 272, 298, 474–81 *passim*
Epistemology, 450, 543
Épochē, 26, 30, 53, 65, 108, 157, 452, 460–62, 465, 491, 512, 514. See also Reduction
Erfüllung, see Filling-in
Erlebniss, see Experience, lived
Erscheinung, see Appearance
Essence, 28, 31, 37, 55, 105, 198ff, 387–89, 451, 460f, 492
Event, 93
Evidence, 442, 448f
Exactness, 31f, 40
Expectation, 393
Experience, 9, 11, 94–105 *passim*, 151–54 *passim*, 160, 203, 209, 431, 440–48 *passim*, 450–54 *passim*, 457, 461, 465; lived (*Erlebniss*), 25–30 *passim*, 33, 39, 49ff, 65, 477, 527; as faculty of some living beings, 513. See also *Empathy*
Explanation, 111, 172
Exponential object, 415
Expression, 132f, 142, 145
Expressive intentionality, 132, 134–36, 143–47 *passim*
Extension, 26, 334f
Externalism, 97f, 103–7 *passim*, 434, 439
Externality, 20, 26f, 134

Fiber product, 415
Fibration, 339, 415
Field, 50, 79, 156f
Figures of time, 281
Filling-in, 77, 162, 168, 334
Filtering, 352
First-person, 22, 68
Fitzhugh-Nagumo equations, 313
Flow, 32, 84, 101, 104, 108, 278, 289, 333
Flux (of experiences) 37, 50, 53, 78, 154, 288ff, 491, 493, 505
Focalization, 352
Folk theory, 459
Form, 40, 53, 59, 85–89 *passim*, 103, 140, 447f, 454
Formality, *see* Category; Ontology
Foundations, 23–26, 75, 79, 151, 334, 441, 443, 448, 451, 457, 477
Frame, 380

Fringe, 190
Fulfillment, 442
Fullness, 139, 141, 365, 367, 442
Functionalism, 72, 97, 102–4 *passim*, 149
Functionality, 5, 71f, 97, 447, 502, 504
Fusion, 198

Gamma band, 275
Ganglionary cell, 351
Gap, 3–11 *passim*, 18
Gegenständlichkeit, see Objectity
Geisteswissenschaften, 44
Genealogy, of logic, 521
Generativity, 37, 68, 482, 541
Genetic(s), 37, 73, 78, 450f, 289, 301
Geography, 321f
Geometrization, 505
Geometry, 40–42, 55, 64, 79, 318
Germ, 344
Gestalt, 62f, 189, 334
Given, 27, 75, 80, 148, 152, 154, 158, 440–58 *passim*
Givenness, 157, 159, 199, 202, 227, 332f, 441–44, 447, 449, 456
Glaubhaftigkeit, see Attitude
Gravitation, 47
Ground, 440f, 448, 451, 455, 457, 461
Grouping, 171

Hemilateral, 12
Heterophenomenology, 22
Historicism, 84
Homunculus fallacy, 153
Horizon, 199, 324, 417, 452, 461, 520, 523
Hylē, 33, 333, 447f, 500, 504, 506. See also *Materie*

Idea, 446ff
Ideal, 38, 40
Idealism, 29, 30, 52, 84, 101, 105, 392
Ideality, 331
Identity, 29, 64, 68, 71, 198ff, 332, 353, 360, 370, 443, 446
Illusion, perceptual, 162, 207f, 210
Imagination, 154
Immanence, 25f, 29, 444f, 479
Immediacy, 153f
Implementation, 83
Implication, 415
Impredicativity, 406, 416, 419
Impression, 249, 261
Inadequacy, 30, 155

Incompleteness, 155, 421f
Indexicality, 104
Indicating function, 430–34 passim
Indication, 104
Indirectness, 112f, 124ff, 133, 135, 138, 142–46
Individual, 83, 86f, 89–92, 106
Individuation, 31, 391, 398
Inexactness, 40, 56
Information, 4, 6, 20, 48, 70, 84f, 104f, 108, 149f, 159
Instability, 292ff, 298
Integers, 406
Intensionality, 150, 357, 370, 430
Intention, 94, 133–37, 144, 442
Intentional, 12, 58, 60, 98, 115, 130, 150f, 441f, 444; correlate, 124, 132f, 137, 140, 145f; experience, 83, 89, 95, 447
Intentionalism, 111f, 120, 123, 128f, 131, 146
Intentionality, 1, 27, 30f, 35, 57, 76f, 83f, 92, 97–99, 104f, 107–31 passim, 120, 144, 147–51, 155, 199, 218, 221, 290, 294ff, 440, 448, 451, 526, 534ff, 543f; as a formal category, 84, 86–99 passim, 101; naturalized, 83, 85, 101, 526, 536, 546; symbolic, 132, 134, 138, 142–44
Interest, 352
Internal(ism), 10, 26f, 97
Interpretation, 136, 139, 146, 333
Intersubjectivity, 17, 23, 36, 78, 230–33, 243, 392, 481, 512
Intrinsic rhythms, 282, 313
Introspection, 12, 85, 100, 104
Introspectionism, 15
Intuition, 124f, 132f, 134, 140, 388, 397, 402, 408, 411; and Husserlian phenomenology, 25–29, 31, 79, 445
Intuitionism, 25
Intuitionist logic, see Logic
Intuitive, 30, 131–43 passim, 319, 442, 477
Invariant, 69f, 73f
Inverse problem, 355, 368
Isomorphism, 167, 183
Iteration, 408

Judgment, 38, 521

Kind, 8, 86
Kinesthesis, 35, 156f, 159, 207–16 passim, 222f, 227–30 passim, 234ff, 241, 353f, 361f, 449

Knowledge, 25, 30, 441–49 passim, 455–60 passim, 510
Körper, see under Body
Korsakoff syndrome, 277

Language, 20, 56, 89, 318, 325, 453f, 460; of thought, 84, 101, 119–21
Laws, 28, 38, 91, 404
Lebenswelt, see Life-world
Leib, see under Body
Leibhaftigkeit, 148, 152ff, 157–60, 332. See also Givenness
Level, 5, 13, 20, 23, 45, 47, 51f, 55, 59, 73, 111, 149
Lexin model, 255, 262, 287
Life, 454f, 514
Life-world, 61, 92, 228, 241, 318, 394, 450–52, 460f, 463, 471, 516
Limit, 40ff, 76, 15, 17f, 471ff
Linear dynamics, 310
Linguistic(s), 59, 61f, 116–18, 132f, 154
Living/lived present, 272, 280, 470
Localization, 344
Local sign, 350
Location, 86
Logic, 38, 64, 88, 407, 413f, 419, 450, 452, 474

Manifold, 55, 226, 249, 262, 350
Mannigfaltigkeit, see Manifold
Materialism, 5, 84, 102, 108, 167, 192
Materie, 130–47 passim
Mathematics, 31f, 40, 42, 48f, 78f, 122, 388, 413
Mathematization, 42, 47f, 56
Mathesis universalis, 87
Matter, 85, 87, 447. See also Materie
Meaning, 116, 121, 146f, 149f, 221, 239, 243, 440, 443, 449, 451f, 462f
Mean value theorem, 404, 410
Mechanics, 16f, 43f, 46–48, 90ff, 108
Mechanism, 65
Memory, 154
Mental, 22, 48, 86f, 93, 95f, 100, 114, 118f, 148, 151
Mentalism, 114
Mereology, 79, 371, 379
Mereotopology, see Topology
Merging, 334, 346–48
Methodology, 73
Mind, 2, 5, 13, 21, 83f, 86f, 92–94, 99; philosophy of, 88, 97f, 151, 157, 540

Mind/Body problem, 5f, 8f, 15, 149
Modalities, 159
Mode, 87, 446
Model, 251, 262
Monism, 107
Mood, 300
Morphē, 500, 504, 506
Morphodynamics, 70, 79
Morphology, 19, 40, 53, 55, 69, 331, 348, 451
Motion, 79, 372
Motivation, 72, 75
Motor, 158f, 287
Movement, 35, 43, 47, 157, 222, 373, 403, 525–36; perception of, 205ff, 209, 211f, 218, 220
Multiplicity, 495
Multistability, 285, 291
Myth, 74f, 454

Natural, Naturalism, 8, 23, 26, 28, 38f, 44, 50, 57, 80, 83–85 *passim*, 94, 96, 101–8 *passim*, 115, 128, 148, 466ff
Naturalization, xiii, 42–56 *passim*, 63, 72f, 76, 85, 101f, 115f, 122, 127, 129, 146, 148, 151, 214, 243, 317, 330, 338, 461f, 503, 512–15 *passim*, 522, 541
Nature, 28, 54, 83, 87–89, 96, 105ff, 537
Naturwissenschaften, 44
Necker cube, 270, 285, 292
Network, neural, 6, 84, 252, 479
Neural assembly/ensemble, 267, 273
Neurodynamics, 78, 154, 158, 301, 309ff, 470
Neuron, 78, 238, 240
Neurophenomenology, 67, 267–302 *passim*, 305
Neurophysiology, 159
Neuroscience, 23f, 62, 77, 94, 98, 104, 107f, 469
Newtonian space, *see* Space
Niche, ecological, 317f
Noema, 33, 52, 57–60, 147, 331, 440, 443–48 *passim*, 456
Noematic, 33, 40f, 60, 147, 199, 331, 360f, 370, 500f
Noesis, 130, 446ff, 500, 527
Noetic, 33, 41, 447, 476
Nominalism, 86, 89
Nonlinear dynamics, 6, 55, 283, 295, 309–12 *passim*
Nonstandard analysis, 405, 409

Normalization theorem, 416, 419, 420
Nucleus, 446, 450

Object, 25f, 29f, 33–37 *passim*, 50, 78, 93f, 134f, 140–44, 152, 155f, 269f, 319, 321, 443–48 *passim*, 520; intentional, 130, 140–44, 509
Object = X, 370, 390, 446
Objectity, 25f
Objectivism, 468
Objectivity, 16f, 41, 198, 226, 396, 441, 509
Ontogeny, 274
Ontology, 28, 31, 44ff, 83f, 85, 89–99 *passim*, 104f, 107–10, 112, 299, 361f, 461; formal/material, 29, 62, 78, 86ff, 401, 446; transformation, 362
Order parameter, 284
Organism, 88

Parallelism, 52, 117, 119, 123, 165, 171, 456, 462, 514
Particular, 85f
Part/Whole, 171, 520
Passive synthesis, 332, 478ff, 500, 517
Path, 354, 358
Pattern, 375
Perception, 12, 20, 26, 34f, 40, 52, 69, 79, 95, 108, 131, 145, 148–62 *passim*, 200–203 *passim*, 388, 441ff, 448f, 525
Person, 88, 92
Phase locking, 275ff
Phase space, 291f, 309
Phase transition, 255, 284, 311
Phenomenality, 1, 9f, 20–23
Phenomenalization, 11, 54f, 68
Phenomenological data, 3, 7ff, 11f, 15f, 18, 23, 33, 42, 48, 50, 64, 454
Phenomenology, 18–23 *passim*, 29–32 *passim*, 34, 37, 41, 210, 232, 551ff; genetic/static, 227, 289, 294, 473–77 *passim*; Husserlian, xiii, 2, 24, 43, 48f, 56, 63, 72, 74, 146; naturalized, 1, 19f, 23, 464–83 *passim*; transcendental, 464, 508–14 *passim*, 524
Phenomenon, 7, 9f, 16, 112, 122f, 125–29, 146, 152
Philosophy, 25, 57, 75, 460. *See also under* Mind
Phusis, 54
Physicalism, 102f, 107
Physics, 28, 40, 55, 64, 90f, 132

Platonism, 392, 420
Point/line, 404
Point tracking, 358
Practice, 454
Predicate, 59, 374, 446
Predication, 371
Prediction, 65
Presence, 140
Present, 35, 62, 141. *See also* Living present; Specious present
Presentation, 150, 459. *See also* Display
Pre-Socratics, 538
Process, 15, 20, 111, 114, 121
Profile, 21, 155–57, 453. *See also* Adumbration
Profiling, 326
Proof principles, 412, 421
Property, 12, 26, 44–48 *passim*, 65, 71f, 76f, 93, 105, 115, 122, 148, 159, 433, 435f; semantic, 112, 117, 121, 147
Proprioception, 212
Protention, 35, 78, 247, 250, 260, 280, 295–302 *passim*, 358, 365
Prototype, 343, 366f
Psychologism, 38, 451, 467, 508
Psychology, 23, 24, 27ff, 34, 38, 51, 49–52 *passim*, 73, 77, 115, 130, 508–12; folk, 65, 101f, 114ff, 122f
Purity, 25, 51

Qualia, 9, 11, 21ff, 79f, 85, 99f, 104, 434–39 *passim*
Qualitative, 11, 40, 55, 69, 151
Quality, 29, 40, 83, 90f, 98, 100, 130
Quantity, 86

Rationality, 447
Ray, intentional, 358
Realism, 52, 79, 114ff, 119, 121, 127f, 148f, 395
Reality, 26, 202f
Recategorization, 46, 48, 71
Receptive field, 351
Recognition, 256
Reduction, 26–30, 33, 36, 39, 51, 58, 64, 72ff, 117–27 *passim*, 155, 445, 449, 452, 460, 512; phenomenological, 267, 469, 475, 493; transcendental, 508, 512f
Reductionism, 63, 65, 119, 473
Reference, 150, 391, 446
Reflection, 498
Reflexivity, 100, 290

Region, 15, 25f, 30, 37, 51, 87, 105f, 333, 383
Relation, 29, 62, 86, 90f, 98f, 114, 121, 150; intentional, 112, 123ff, 130–35 *passim*, 140–47 *passim*
Relativity, 17
Relaxation time, 274, 313
Reorientation, xiii, 57
Representation, 20, 430; mental, 84f, 111f, 118–21, 146, 148f, 153–58 *passim*, 429; as *Vorstellung*, 130f, 135; as *Repräsentation*, 131ff, 137f, 140–43, 146f, 149, 139–42 *passim*
Representational, 77, 112, 116, 121, 127f, 146–54 *passim*, 157–60 *passim*, 433, 442, 459, 433
Representationalism, 3, 6, 11, 113, 119ff, 128–31, 153, 434f
Resonance, 275, 479
Rest, 373
Retention, 35, 68, 78, 247, 250, 260, 280ff, 352, 358
Reversal, 50, 52
Revolution, scientific, 48
Riemannian geometry, 369
Rigidity, 380
Robustness, 150
Rotation, 382
Rule, 59, 455

Sachverhalt, *see* State-of-affairs
Saliency, 334, 336
Scale, 352, 404, 410
Schema, 333, 367
Schematization, 330, 338
Science, 3, 26–31 *passim*, 37, 44f, 47, 54f, 102, 112, 115, 450
Section, of a fibration, 341
Sedimentation, 499. *See also* Strata
Segmentation, 79, 334, 346–48
Selbstellung, *see* Self-position
Selbstgegebenheit, *see also* Givenness
Self-affectedness, 297
Self-organization, 6, 18, 48, 55, 311
Self-position, 155, 332
Self-report, 12
Self-similarity, 351
Semantics, 88, 121, 149, 414
Sensation, 145, 156
Sense, 139f, 431ff, 447ff, 456, 490, 496–502 *passim*, 505
Sinnbildung, *see* Sense

Index of Topics 641

Sinngebung, see Sense
Sensible, 131, 40f
Series, 156–59
Set theory, 404, 422
Sheaf, 371
Signification, 133–37 *passim*, 144
Signitive, 134f, 442
Singularity, 55, 368, 492
Sinn, 57f, 60, 139, 147, 442–48 *passim*
Skepticism 15f, 76
Sketch, 525
SOAR, 251
Solipsism, 36, 58
Sonderung, see Segmentation
Soul, 102
Space, 26, 86, 154–56, 159, 528, 384
Spatial order, 335
Spatio-temporality, 26
Species, 29, 86ff, 92
Specious present, 266 ff
Spirit, 105
Stance, 22, 66, 149, 462
State-of-affairs, 29, 83, 87–90 *passim*, 114, 120, 328; intentional, 112–16 *passim*, 123–35 *passim*, 138, 142, 146
Static, 37, 68, 78, 148, 154, 157f, 447, 475
Stereopsis, 361
Strata, 202, 208, 222, 517
Stratification, 343, 408
Stream of consciousness, 269
Structural stability, 367
Subject, 15, 53, 94, 537, 557
Subjective, 5, 17, 19
Subjectivity, 9f, 445, 447, 451f, 455
Substance, 87, 98
Supervenience, 96, 102, 106
Surface, 324
Symbol, 57ff, 88, 102, 108, 112f, 116–28 *passim*, 133–36, 140–47, 149
Symbolic, 4f, 59f, 84, 112, 119, 121, 125f, 129, 149, 154
Synchrony, 275ff, 313
Synechology, 339
Syntactic, 59, 88, 102f, 108, 123f, 149
Syntax, 108
Synthesis, 155, 157, 332f, 353f, 442
Synthetic *a priori*, 353
System, 6, 55, 61, 69, 88, 90, 96, 111f, 119f, 128, 141, 146, 149, 252

Teleology, 218, 238, 447
Temporal coding, 371

Temporal(ity), 34, 62, 78, 154–58, 268, 278, 302
Thing, 26f, 96, 131, 156f, 452
Thought, 95
Time, 26, 34, 68, 78, 86, 266–301 *passim*, 307ff, 402
Topological grammar, 326
Topology, 54, 79, 326, 171, 318, 326
Topos theory, 371, 416
Totality, 529
Trajectory, 252, 283, 310, 358
Transcendence, 27, 36, 155, 444ff, 479
Transcendent, 25–27, 33f, 52, 198ff, 319, 389, 509f
Transcendental, 30–32 *passim*, 50, 58–61, 72, 106, 331f, 362, 443–45 *passim*, 452, 476, 503, 512–17 *passim*
Transcendentalism, 36, 69, 106, 129, 451, 466, 512
Transduction, 70
Transparency, 298ff
Truth, 328
Turn, linguistic, 58, 540
Type theory, 114, 120f, 367, 407
Typicality, 452, 461

Unconscious, 96
Unionism, 69, 83, 85, 94, 97, 107
Unity, 156f

Vagueness, 31f, 188
Variability, 415
Vection, 212
Vector field, 358
Verschmelzung, see Merging
Vestibular information, 212
Vienna Circle, 16, 562
Vision, 62, 185, 287, 324f
Visual atom, 351
Visual field, 324, 349, 362
Vitalism, 45, 65
Volition, 95

Wesensschau, see Essence
What-it-is-like, 9f, 100
Windowing, 326
Wooden iron, 262, 291
World, 36, 46, 53, 85, 88, 229, 231f, 513; unity of, 83f, 90, 96, 99, 107, 110

Library of Congress Cataloging-in-Publication Data

Naturalizing phenomenology : issues in contemporary
  phenomenology and cognitive science / edited by Jean
  Petitot . . . [et al.].
     p.   cm. — (Writing science)
  Includes bibliographical references and index.
  ISBN 0-8047-3322-8 (cloth : alk. paper). —
  ISBN 0-8047-3610-3 (pbk. : alk. paper)
    1. Phenomenology. 2. Cognitive science. I. Petitot,
  Jean, 1944– . II. Series
  B829.5.N38 1999
  142′.7—dc21   99-28716

⊗ This book is printed on acid-free, recycled paper.
Original printing 1999
Last figure below indicates year of this printing:
08 07 06 05 04 03 02 01 00 99